VERMONT VOICES,

1609 THROUGH THE 1990s:

A Documentary History
of the Green Mountain State

Designed by Ray Denney

Library of Congress Cataloging-in-Publication Data

Vermont voices, 1609 through the 1990s: A documentary history of the Green Mountain State / J. Kevin Graffagnino, Samuel B. Hand, and Gene Sessions, editors.
p. cm.
Includes bibliographical references (p.) and index.
ISBN 0-934720-42-8 (alk. paper)
1. Vermont—History—Sources. I. Graffagnino, J. Kevin. II Hand, Samuel B., 1931-.
III. Sessions, Gene.

F49 .V59 1999
974.3 21—dc21
99-043537

Printed in the United States of America

04 03 02 01 00 99 2 3 4 5 6

First Printing, August 1999
Second Printing, June 2004

VERMONT VOICES,

1609 THROUGH THE 1990s:

A Documentary History
of the Green Mountain State

J. KEVIN GRAFFAGNINO, SAMUEL B. HAND,
AND GENE SESSIONS, EDITORS

VERMONT HISTORICAL SOCIETY

VERMONT VOICES

Contents

SECTION ONE
1609-1760
Early Settlement

SECTION TWO
1760-1777
Struggle for the Grants

SECTION THREE
1777-1791
Independent Vermont

SECTION FOUR
1791-1820
Early Statehood

SECTION FIVE
1820-1850
An Era of Social Ferment

SECTION SIX
1850-1870
Emergence of a Mature Society

SECTION SEVEN
1870-1896
Old Ideals and New Ideas

SECTION EIGHT
1896-1917
Pastoral Politics

SECTION NINE
1917-1941
Serpents in the Garden

SECTION TEN
1941-1966
The Emergence of Modern Vermont

SECTION ELEVEN
Since 1965
Microchips and Maple Syrup

VERMONT VOICES

Foreword

Pick up any American history college textbook and look for coverage of Vermont's history and you will be disappointed. Most general accounts mention Ethan Allen and his brief role in the American Revolution, they note that the Vermont Constitution of 1777 was the first to abolish slavery, and they have a sentence stating that Vermont was the fourteenth state to join the Union in 1791, and little else. *The Encyclopedia of American History* has only three references to Vermont, and one of the most popular college history texts fails to have even one listing for Vermont in the index. Some texts and general accounts mention in passing that Vermont (with Utah) had the distinction of being one of two states to vote for the Republican candidate, William Howard Taft, in 1912, and (with Maine) one of two states to vote for Republican Alfred Landon in 1936. "As Maine goes, so goes Vermont," was the ironic cry. A few writers noted in the 1990s that Vermont, once the most conservative state, at least in politics, had become one of the most liberal, as it had reelected Democratic governors by large margins and had sent an independent socialist to Congress.

If Vermont plays an insignificant role in most general accounts of American history, it does get into the footnotes as the birthplace of many who went on to fame and fortune, and sometimes notoriety, in other states. Two of the least distinguished presidents, Calvin Coolidge and Chester A. Arthur, were born in Vermont (and their birthplaces are proudly maintained as tourist attractions), but Coolidge rose to power in Massachusetts and Arthur in New York. Also born in Vermont were Stephen A. Douglas, the "Little Giant" of the Illinois Democratic Party who debated Lincoln in the famous "Lincoln-Douglas Debates" of 1858; Thaddeus Stevens, the fiery leader of the Radical Republicans during Reconstruction; George Jones, cofounder of the *New York Times*; Joseph Smith and Brigham Young, pioneer founders of the Church of Christ of Latter-day Saints; and John Humphrey Noyes, who organized the Oneida Community and experimented with socialism, complex marriage, and human breeding. The list goes on and on: John Dewey, the

philosopher, Frederick Billings, the railroad builder, and James Fisk, the notorious railroad and Wall Street manipulator, were born in the state, as were the inventor of the elevator, the founders of Alcoholics Anonymous, and many others. But Vermont rarely gets credit or blame for their achievements.

Even for many Vermonters the only important history associated with the state is the romantic story of Ethan Allen and the Green Mountain Boys and the fight for Vermont independence against Great Britain, New York, and the United States government. I must say that was my conception of Vermont history when I was growing up in the declining granite town of Hardwick, Vermont, in the 1930s and 1940s. Some people find a personal connection to history by visiting a Civil War battlefield or a historic-house museum; for me it was a family visit to the Bennington Battle Monument and Fort Ticonderoga the summer I was ten. The Bennington Battle Monument was impressive, and I still have a photograph of my tired family taken in front of the obelisk that commemorates the most important Vermont Revolutionary War battle (which unfortunately took place in New York State). But it is the reconstructed fort that I especially remember, although I did not know it was reconstructed at the time. I had read Daniel P. Thompson's *The Green Mountain Boys* and a story about Rogers' Rangers. It suddenly struck me that the stories I had been reading about Ethan Allen, Seth Warner, Remember Baker, and the rest had really happened. I was hooked on history, and I went on to read the novels of Kenneth Roberts, books by Francis Parkman, and any account I could find in the Judevine Memorial Library in Hardwick on Vermont history, the history of New England, or the story of the French and Indian War and the American Revolution.

My interest in Vermont history began to fade as I studied for a Ph.D. and eventually wrote and taught history. I became fascinated with urban history, the Progressive period, and with social and cultural history. It was ten years before I realized that my experiences while growing up in Vermont—the granite industry, my grandfather's general store, my uncle's farm before electricity, the prejudice against French-Canadian Catholics, even my grandmother's quilts—were history too. In fact, research and writing about Vermont has been relatively slow to respond to the changes in historiography and has lagged behind that of other states—Massachusetts, Wisconsin, and Illinois, for example. Perhaps this is because there is no university in the state that awards the Ph.D. in history, or possibly it is related to the popular belief that all history worth studying is about great men and ends when Vermont becomes a state, or at least with the end of the War of 1812.

There are many signs, however, that things are changing. In the last decade a number of innovative and interesting books and articles have been published on all aspects of Vermont history, including social, economic, and cultural history, the history of women, reform, and religion. A few detailed community studies have been written and young scholars have explored the rise of the market economy, the beginning of the tourist industry, reading habits, material culture, furniture, and folk art. New books have even traced a more complex and nuanced account of the Allen clan, and they have related political history to the social order. At the same time there has been a resurgence of interest in local history and a revitalization of local historical societies. Unfortunately, most of the new town histories have been written without reference to the new social and cultural history.

This book should further stimulate writing and teaching about Vermont history. It is a rich collection of primary materials together with carefully crafted introductions. You will find contemporary articles, and excerpts from books, memoirs, speeches, government documents, and court cases. There are also cartoons, poems, and other material. Together they tell the story of Vermont history, from the observations of Samuel de Champlain in 1609 as he described the view of the virgin wilderness that would eventually become Vermont, to a poster from 1991 opposing the land-use regulation that would preserve Vermont's dwindling wilderness. The documents also range from a pre-1600 Abenaki oral account of the creation of the Champlain Valley to a 1993 Supreme Court decision overturning a lower court ruling that the Abenaki held "aboriginal title" to the land, and thus were immune from the state's hunting and fishing regulations.

The documents describe in detail the fascinating story of the settling of Vermont, the controversy over the New Hampshire Grants, the battles against the British, Indians, and New York, even the negotiations that could have made Vermont a part of Canada and the British Empire. However, these documents and the introductions make the stories about Ethan Allen and the Green Mountain Boys more complex and complicated, and more believable than the version I learned while growing up in Hardwick. Several selections from captivity narratives describe the ordeal of the early settlers and their capture and torture by Indians, but the Indian side of the story is told as well. Native Americans play an important role in this collection of documents, as do women and occasionally African-Americans, and ethnic minorities. Vermont is perhaps the least ethnically and racially diverse state in the Union, and the least affected by multicultural influences, but as this book points out, it has not been immune to the forces of immigration, racism, and nativism.

It is easy to view Vermont and its history as a "special world," different from (and to some, superior to) the rest of the country; to see it as a place untouched by the forces of urbanism, industrialism, commercialism, even modernism, that have transformed the rest of America. It is tempting to look back nostalgically to a nineteenth-century, rural world of a Currier and Ives print, or even to a twentieth-century vision of small-town harmony as depicted by Norman Rockwell. It is easy to view Vermont's history through the lens of the tourist bureau and the advertisers who try to picture the state as a rural paradise untroubled and untouched by the problems that beset the rest of the country.

One of the great strengths of this collection is that the editors make the history of the state complex and they select documents that display the ambivalent and contradictory nature of much of Vermont's past. They do not shy away from discussing poverty and racial, ethnic, and class conflict. One of the underlying themes of the book is that Vermont was influenced by the larger forces that shaped American history. Even though the state is often left out of the textbooks, it is very much a part of the American story.

Vermont's very existence was directly related to the course of early American history, part of the struggle between Britain and France for North America, and an accidental by-product of the American Revolution. The state's history was dictated by economic forces. The early settlers were not so much motivated by a struggle for freedom and democracy as they were driven by a search for wealth and cheap land, just as many Vermonters over the years left the state to search elsewhere for economic opportunity.

Vermont history has been influenced and changed by wars. The Revolution, the War of 1812, even the Civil War, if one counts the St. Albans' raid, were fought in part along the state's borders. The Civil War, the two World Wars, Korea, and Vietnam took many Vermont young people away from the state and sometimes encouraged their migration elsewhere. Vermont contributed a great many soldiers to the Union army. The monuments to that war, and to those who served in it, dot town squares around the state, and the gravestones in almost all the cemeteries scattered around the state pay tribute to the cost of human lives. Vermont attics and historical societies are filled with the letters, diaries, and tintypes from that war, and the rarely told stories of the women and children who stayed behind are also documented in various collections.

Vermont was touched by the various reform and religious revivals that seem to come in cycles in American history. In fact, one can argue that, along with the "burned-over" district of New York State, Vermont played a crucial role in leading religious revivalism and the temperance, women's rights, and anti-slavery movements of the 1830s and 1840s. Mormonism, founded by Joseph Smith, and Perfectionism, begun by John Humphrey Noyes, both had their roots in Vermont, as did the Adventist Church, which was formed when the prediction of Vermonter William Miller that the world would come to an end in 1843 failed to come true. Of all the states, Vermont was probably the one most influenced by the Anti-Masonic movement. Vermont was the only state to cast its electoral votes in 1832 for William Wirt, the Anti-Masonic Party candidate for president. The party dominated the Vermont General Assembly from 1831 to 1835 and elected the governor from 1831 to 1834. Most of the supporters of the Anti-Masonic Party in Vermont viewed Freemasonry as aristocratic, elitist, and opposed to the Vermont tradition of democracy. The turmoil created by the Anti-Masonic movement revealed tensions created by a time of great change.

Vermont, like most of the nation, was transformed by the transportation revolution created by canals and railroads. The market revolution altered even the smallest towns and the most remote farms. The international economy led to the end of the sheep boom in the state and influenced the price of milk and butter. One doesn't think of Vermont as part of the industrial revolution, but Burlington, Springfield, Rutland, Bellows Falls, and Barre — even Island Pond and Hardwick — became industrial centers, with all the problems that beset the larger urban centers. Vermont produced its own industrial capitalists and robber barons, and the clash between labor and capital led to bitter strikes in Barre and Rutland. The Knights of Labor won a foothold in Rutland and the Industrial Workers of the World in Barre.

Vermont was not very much influenced by Populism, and it did not produce a William Jennings Bryan or a Mary Lease (who told the farmers of Kansas to raise less corn and more hell), but almost every small town had its Grange Hall, and the Patrons of Husbandry tried to regulate railway rates. More important probably were the farmers' attempts to organize in practical and pragmatic ways. However, no amount of organizing could prevent farms from being abandoned at the end of the nineteenth century as Vermonters sought opportunities elsewhere. The migration out of Vermont and the fear that those moving in, whether tourists or French Canadians, would alter the special nature of the state, make up one of the subthemes of the book. One famous Vermont author decried the out-migration and feared that the population of Vermont was being "diluted by the increasing foreign elements." Vermont did not escape the ethnic and racial prejudice that troubled the nation.

Vermont was relatively untouched by the Progressive movement, though Theodore Roosevelt campaigned in the state in 1912 and there were efforts to pass "progressive" measures such as a direct primary law. The New Deal had a greater impact on the state even though the majority of Vermonters refused to vote for Franklin Roosevelt at the ballot box. Many unemployed Vermonters were put to work by the Works Progress Administration, while many young men cut ski trails, or built roads and picnic areas for the Civilian Conservation Corps. The Rural Electrification Administration, at the end of the 1930s, brought electric lines to many remote Vermont farms and connected them to the twentieth century.

World War II and the prosperity it created helped to modernize the state. Thirty-eight thousand men and women from the state served in the armed forces, and about twelve hundred of those were killed or declared missing in action (a far smaller percentage than in the Civil War). No bombs were dropped on Vermont and there was never any threat of invasion. Still, Vermonters joined Civilian Defense Organizations, planted Victory Gardens, collected scrap metal, and endured rationing. In the end it was the prosperity and the mobility that the war created that left its mark on the state. The war meant jobs, and men and women moved to where the jobs were. Towns like Springfield boomed because of its machine-tool industry, but for many the war meant moving out of the state to the industrial cities of New England and the Northeast. Vermonters, like the rest of the nation, barely had time to celebrate VJ Day before the tensions and the disruptions of the Cold War settled across the land, and Vermont did not escape those tensions nor the abridgment of freedom and the hysteria of the McCarthy era. Alex Novikoff, a distinguished biochemistry professor at the University of Vermont, was fired from his job because he took the Fifth Amendment and refused to testify before a U.S. Senate committee about his communist associations prior to moving to Vermont.

At the end of the twentieth century, Vermont remained influenced by all the same forces that were transforming the rest of the United States. Cable television, fax machines, e-mail, and the Internet connected even the most remote farmhouse to an international world. Pollution from the coal-fired plants in the Ohio Valley caused acid rain that stunted the growth of trees on Camel's Hump, and taught Vermonters that the politics of a clean environment could not stop at the borders of the state. McDonald's, Burger King, Midas Muffler, shopping malls, and auto salerooms created an urban sprawl on the Barre-Montpelier Road, on Route 7 south of Burlington, and at other places in the state, creating a landscape that could be "Anywhere, U.S.A." At the same time, tourists flocked to the state in order to eat at restaurants in restored Georgian mansions or take part in a simple life in the Vermont hill towns that had missed the industrial revolution. These tourists rarely noticed the poor families living in "mobile homes," or the rundown farmhouses on land that could no longer support a dairy herd. This Vermont underclass, which the tourist brochures denied, was becoming further marginalized by the technological and communication revolution that was transforming the rest of the state.

Vermont at the end of the twentieth century was filled with paradox and contradiction, but so has been its entire history. That is one of the principal messages of this book. It makes Vermont history more interesting and more complex than the romantic retelling of the legends of the Green Mountain Boys, or the standard narratives of corruption and modernism. It underscores the fact that although on occasion Vermont has been out of step with the nation, its history has been marked by the same influences that make the story of American history both fascinating and disturbing.

Allen F. Davis

VERMONT VOICES

Introduction

The items selected as reading for this volume range from seventeenth-century royal charters to twentieth-century bumper stickers. All serve to illuminate Vermont's past. Such contemporary records are the essential ingredients used by historians in the writing of history. Examining them brings the reader face to face with past events—as they were seen at the time—and imparts the eyewitness's sense of urgency and energy. Understanding a primary source, however, can be complicated. It may be interpreted in multiple ways. The careful reader, consequently, will also ask questions: about the authenticity of the item; about the attitudes and circumstances that underlay and influenced its creation; about the credibility of its details, the biases that may distort the reporting, and the existence of corroborating evidence. By engaging these questions, the reader enters into the historian's enterprise.

A few particular issues involving the selections included in this volume merit elaboration. The first and most obvious is that with one exception all are printed or written sources that have survived in their original form. The one exception is the very first entry, Section 1, Document 1, an Abenaki Indian account of the creation of the Champlain Valley. Although it has apparently been told in other versions and was not fixed in print until the second half of the twentieth century, the editors assume, based on a large body of circumstantial evidence, that it circulated in Abenaki oral tradition long before the first Europeans penetrated the region.

The Abenaki inhabiting Vermont prior to the first European settlers, lacking a written alphabet, not to mention the technological skills and archival practices essential to the systematic preservation of records, have not provided posterity with personal judgments or recordings of specific events. Recent ethnographic and archaeological research have uncovered significant evidence of the patterns of life that they and their predecessors experienced, but not in the form of evidence reproducible in a reader of primary sources such as this. As a result, while more recent Abenaki activities—their 1992 petition for federal tribal recognition is one

such example— are reproduced here in their original printed form, surviving accounts of exchanges between Indians and white settlers come to us from the journals of Indian fighters such as Major Robert Rogers or the captivity narratives of abducted colonists. These journals and memoirs, preserved in print in the absence of concurrent Abenaki sources, supplied the European perspective of Native Americans that for generations went unchallenged.

Each of these readings should also be viewed in terms of its relationship, as a contemporary record, to the event being examined. A government document such as the 1764 King in Council order fixing the Connecticut River as the boundary between New York and New Hampshire constitutes an action in itself. It was this ruling that precipitated the struggle that culminated in an independent Vermont. Memoirs such as Susanna Johnson's narrative of her ordeals as an Indian captive reveal much about her experiences, yet because memoirs are often written long after the events described (this was true in the instance of Susanna Johnson), the extent to which intervening events may have colored the narrator's perspective is an open question. Ethan Allen's account of the 1775 capture of Fort Ticonderoga included in his memoir, *A Narrative of Colonel Ethan Allen's Captivity*, and written only after thirty-two months of British captivity, is so obviously self-serving that it should put readers on their guard. Nonetheless, as the fullest account of the storming of Fort Ticonderoga by its most exalted participant, it is of immense value as a primary source.

Before completing this volume, the reader will likely conclude that oral histories can suffer many of the same liabilities as written memoirs. The editors would concur with this assessment. They would also note that oral histories are elicited not only from celebrated personalities but also from individuals unlikely to otherwise leave memoirs or retain a personal archive. Historians have lately moved beyond the once-standard view that history is the story of "great men" and political and business elites, and have widened their research focus to include the experiences of working people, immigrants, minorities, and other "ordinary people" traditionally silent in history. As the interviews in this volume testify, the tape recorder has facilitated the retention of human memories that might otherwise perish along with the narrator.

Most historians rate journals and diaries as more reliable than written memoirs and oral histories. The reasons are quite simple. They are almost always written close to the event and, if not subsequently tampered with, are more likely to accurately record impressions at the time of the event. Journals and diaries, of course, are also subject to critical assessment. The trustworthiness of these materials, as with other sources written or oral, depends on such standard considerations as the author's nearness to events discussed, competence to observe, general reliability and disinterestedness, and the apparent purpose for the diary- or journal-keeping. The late historian-ethnologist Gordon Day discovered Abenaki stories confirming Rogers' attack on their Odinak village but differing in important details from the journal account. Day argues persuasively that these stories were passed along to their descendants by Abenaki survivors of Rogers' Raid.

Cartoons, ephemera, and maps have been included in this collection. Visual sources have the capacity to communicate information with immediacy and vividness that is not always apparent in traditional written records. Thoughtful use of material of this kind yields information not only about its specific subject matter and intended audience, but also about the circumstances, character, "local color," and aesthetic judgments of the times in which it was created. One type of visual source, photographs, has not been included in the collection because in the judgment of the editors, single photographs (despite their immense historic value) are generally less self-sufficient in carrying the narrative than are other documents that have been included.

Although this is a collaborative effort with all three editors contributing to all sections, Sections 1 through 4 were the primary responsibility of J. Kevin Graffagnino, Sections 5 through 7 were prepared by Gene Sessions, and Sections 8 through 11 were handled by Sam Hand. The introductions that precede each section are intended to provide context to help readers assess and interpret the documents, encourage consideration of their meaning, and facilitate an understanding of the contours of Vermont history. The editors' approach in preparing the documents has been to minimize editorial interference, preserving original spelling, grammar, puntuation, and capitalization. Ellipsis points have been used to indicate that a portion of a lengthy document's text has been omitted, and brackets within a document serve to set off editors' notes intended to clarify unfamiliar words, phrases, or names.

The idea for the book came from J. Kevin Graffagnino while serving as curator of Special Collections at the University of Vermont's Bailey/Howe Library. He recruited Sam Hand, then a University of Vermont history professor and former president of the Vermont Historical Society, and together they enlisted the collaboration of Gene Sessions, a Norwich University history professor and former editor of *Vermont History*. The collaboration persisted despite professional relocations and a retirement, and in due course acquired debts and obligations too numerous to acknowledge individually on this page. Specific thanks, nevertheless, must be expressed to the Vermont Historical Society for generously funding the transcription of the manuscript; Tom Bassett, whose work in the field of Vermont history has made easier the task of those who have followed after; and staff members of University of Vermont Special Collections for their professionalism and very special efforts to assist this project.

The project's greatest debt, however, is to Karen Stites Campbell, who typed virtually every word of every document at least once and then worked and reworked them at the whim of the editors, and who did so with her characteristic good humor and professionalism.

VERMONT VOICES

SECTION ONE

1609-1760
Early Settlement

Vᴇʀᴍᴏɴᴛ Vᴏɪᴄᴇs

Sᴇᴄᴛɪᴏɴ Oɴᴇ

1609-1760
Early Settlement

Introduction

The focus of these readings is on the initial period of interaction among Europeans and Native American peoples in the area that would become Vermont, an era marked by European conflict and confusion over jurisdiction and geography. **Document 1**, "Big Moon," an Abenaki account of the creation of the Champlain Valley, has circulated in Abenaki oral tradition since before the first Europeans penetrated the North American continent; it was hundreds of years old in 1609, when Samuel de Champlain made his celebrated voyage along the lake he named for himself and claimed for France. Reputed to have been the first European to view what is now Vermont, Champlain observed in **Document 2**, an excerpt from his *Voyages*, that the lake shores were unpopulated because the Indians had withdrawn "as deep into the land as possible to avoid surprise attacks." Until quite recently, Champlain's statement has lent credence to the theory that Vermont was a no-man's land, a passage for Indian war parties and without permanent settlements until 1665 when the French established a military outpost, Fort St. Anne, at Isle La Motte. The first English settlement was Fort Dummer, built along the Connecticut River in 1724. Although modern scholars Gordon Day, William Haviland, Marjory Power, and Colin Calloway have refuted the contention that Vermont was without Indian settlements, the lack of a written Abenaki language and the corresponding absence of written Indian documents inevitably skews a collection such as this toward a European perspective of the encounter period. Document 2 also includes reference to an encounter between the Iroquois and their sworn enemy the Algonquins in which Champlain sided with the latter; some historians attribute the subsequent alliance of the Iroquois with the British against the French to that event. And finally, believers in Champ, the "monster" occasionally sighted in Lake Champlain, often cite the Chaosarou as proof that such creatures have long inhabited the lake.

Document 3 is an excerpt from a grant from King Charles II of England to his brother James, then Duke of York. The grant, which encompassed tens of thousands of square miles, including much of present-day Vermont, followed the British conquest of New Amsterdam in 1664, which removed the Dutch from North America. It was not until the eighteenth century, however, that the full significance of the grant became apparent, and by then an entirely new set of circumstances prevailed. Upon the death of King Charles in 1685, the Duke of York ascended to the throne as James II, and all lands assigned to him under the grant fell under the direct authority of the Crown. Another factor belying its ultimate significance was that most of the lands originally granted to the duke, including all but the southernmost regions of modern Vermont, were effectively under French control until 1759.

The area encompassed in **Document 4**, a 1688 New York grant of the Hossick/Hoosac patent, lies approximately two hundred miles south of Isle La Motte and includes the southwesternmost tip of Vermont. Granted by the governor of New York Province by authority of King James II, the former Duke of York, it marks the earliest claims by individuals under British authority to land in Vermont. It is also significant to note that the recipients established a claim to the patent through purchase from the local Indians.

The frontier separating British and French settlements in western Vermont was somewhere between Albany and Isle La Motte. By 1755, when the French built Fort Carillon (later renamed Fort Ticonderoga), they controlled the entire lake, with troops and Indian allies poised within striking distance of Albany. **Document 5**, an excerpt from the Reverend John Williams' *The Redeemed Captive Returning to Zion*, makes explicit how vulnerable British Connecticut River settlements were to Indian attack during the periodic wars between the French and British. In the 1704 raid on Deerfield, Massachusetts, part of the conflict known in the colonies as Queen Anne's War, the French and their Algonquin allies killed forty settlers and carried off one hundred. Some of the Deerfield prisoners, including the Reverend Mr. Williams, were eventually ransomed or "redeemed" and returned from captivity in Canada. To defend against future raids, in 1724 the Massachusetts colony built and maintained Fort Dummer as a northern frontier outpost on the Connecticut River. It was located on the western bank of the river, a few miles north of present-day Brattleboro. As

Document 6 makes clear, the fort also served as a trading post and a site for negotiations between British colonists and local Indians.

In 1741 the British government in London settled a boundary dispute between Massachusetts and New Hampshire much to the territorial advantage of New Hampshire. The Crown decision almost doubled the size of the colony and placed Fort Dummer within its jurisdiction. New Hampshire neglected to maintain the fort until a royal order threatened to restore the fort to Massachusetts, along with other territory acquired by New Hampshire from the recent boundary settlement.

Neither the conflict over Fort Dummer's jurisdiction nor the threat from hostile Indians completely discouraged British settlers from moving north along the Connecticut prior to 1763. **Document 7**, an excerpt from *A Narrative of the Captivity of Nehemiah How*, describes the capture of How from a settlement fourteen miles north of Fort Dummer. How's account furnishes a prototype for captivity narratives, a popular early American literary genre, that typically related the white captive's gruesome ordeals at the hands of merciless "savages." New Englanders relied heavily upon these narratives to justify their own depredations against Native Americans, while subsequent generations of historians have mined them for their depictions of Indian customs, values, and actions.

Readers today, freed from the hunger for Indian lands and the fear of Indian retaliations, may gain from these narratives a more complex and less definitive message. The absence of any Native American perspective leaves the impression that Indians acted solely from savage impulses, omits explicit references to rivalries and inconstant loyalties within and among Indian bands, and obscures the fact that European encroachments posed a genuine threat to their civilization. Yet there are portions of the How narrative describing cordial encounters with Indian friends from before his capture and mentioning Eunice Williams, the daughter of Rev. John Williams (Document 5) who married an Indian and refused repatriation to Deerfield. Unquestionably, Indian-European-settler interaction in eighteenth-century Vermont encompassed far more than the simple dichotomy between civilization and barbarism that most early European accounts emphasized.

Document 8, a map showing French grants in the Champlain Valley in 1748, brings us back to the western half of Vermont. The map depicts grants rather than settlements and in so doing overstates the French presence in the valley. Nonetheless, though the French were less successful than the British in promoting settlement in what became Vermont, by 1748 French forces controlled Lake Champlain and both its shores. British settlers meanwhile had inched their way north of the Hossick/Hoosac patent (**Document 4**). For students of Vermont history the most significant of these settlements was Bennington, chartered in 1749 in the name of King George II by New Hampshire Governor Benning Wentworth. The charter, excerpted as **Document 9**, precipitated a chain of events that culminated in Vermont's separation from New York and New Hampshire, its emergence as an independent republic, and ultimately its designation as the fourteenth state. Independence and statehood were hardly inevitable consequences of colonial New Hampshire grants, but without the Bennington and subsequent New Hampshire charters, Vermont might today exist as counties in northeastern New York.

Although historians have generally agreed that financial gain was Benning Wentworth's principal motivation for issuing the Vermont grants, the legitimacy of his actions continues to be debated. In all likelihood, Wentworth assumed his grants would be validated, for his contention that Bennington lay within New Hampshire's borders was plausible, particularly in light of the dispute over responsibility for maintaining Fort Dummer (Document 6). Nonetheless, Governor Wentworth, recognizing he would provoke resistance from New York, wrote New York Governor George Clinton defending New Hampshire's authority to issue such grants (**Document 10**).

Though settlers with New Hampshire titles proceeded to populate the region, New York resisted Wentworth's claims. **Document 11** is from a report by the New York Council repudiating all New Hampshire (and incidentally all Massachusetts Bay Colony) claims west of the Connecticut River. New York maintained that Charles II's grant to the Duke of York (Document 3) had fixed New York's eastern boundary at the Connecticut River. The boundary controversy persisted, with both New York and New Hampshire granting patents between the Connecticut and Hudson rivers, until 1754, when the outbreak of the French and Indian War, the final conflict between France and England over control of North America, halted settlement in the Vermont area.

What most distinguished this war, referred to in Europe as the Seven Years' War, from previous colonial conflicts was that, rather than being a sideshow, the North American continent was the grand prize. As **Document 12**, passages from *A Narrative of the Captivity of Mrs. Johnson,* relates, however, British settlers along the Connecticut River initially saw little hope of victory. Susanna Johnson's account, among the most popular and influential New England captivity narratives, retells the story of her family's capture and eventual release by Abenakis allied with the French. As in the captivities of Reverend John Williams (Document 5) and Nehemiah How (Document 7), Abenaki bands crossed to the Connecticut from Lake Champlain, raided English settlements, and then withdrew with their captives back to the safety of the Champlain-Richelieu valley. From there the captives traveled to the Abenkai village of St. Francis, where Mrs. Johnson and her baby remained while most other prisoners were sold to French families in Montreal. After four years the Johnson family was reunited and released.

Though the first years of the war favored French interests, by 1759 the British reversed their fortunes. That year, an *annum mirabilus* for British arms, they captured Fort Carillon, Montreal, and Quebec City in North America while also enjoying successes in Europe and Asia.

Securing Carillon, which the British renamed Ticonderoga, was of immediate consequence for the New Hampshire Grants. Immediately after its capture, General Jeffrey Amherst ordered Major Robert Rogers, commander of a battalion of colonial irregulars attached to the British army, to neutralize the Abenakis by slipping north along the lake with his Rangers and raiding St. Francis, the principal Abenaki village. **Document 13** is from Rogers' account of that raid, excerpted from his *Journals,* as published in London in 1765. The *Journals* brought Rogers considerable fame, in part because of a colorful description of the Rangers' attack on the Abenaki village and the tribulations they endured in their retreat to British lines. Since celebrated in novels, motion pictures, and television, the folklore of Rogers' Raid usually depicts it as a heroic episode in the European conquest of their savage neighbors. More recently, Abenaki accounts of the raid have surfaced from translations of oral accounts preserved over generations that challenge details of Rogers' version of the story.

The Treaty of Paris, in 1763, concluded 150 years of Anglo-French conflict for control of North America, with the French ceding their territorial claims on the continent to the British. The Abenakis, now without access to the resources and protection of a powerful ally, also accepted the British peace, although without benefit of a formal compact. With French and Indian impediments to settlement eliminated, New York and New Hampshire resumed disbursing grants in the disputed region and thus set the stage for the next chapter in the Vermont story.

DOCUMENT 1

"Big Moon"

AN ABENAKI ACCOUNT OF THE CREATION OF THE CHAMPLAIN VALLEY (PRE-1600)

The elders say our land
was shaped by Oh-zee-ho-so,
The Changer, who formed himself
out of the dust which fell
from Creator's hands
after making the world.
He pushed against
the earth to rise
and great mountains rose up
on either side.
Then the waters flowed into
the place where he stood
and made Lake Champlain,
the lake we call Peh-ton-ba-gok,
the waters between.

When Oh-zee-ho-so's travels
on this earth were done,
he came back to rest
by this lake once again,
making the circle complete.

So it is that our own
People of the Dawn
place one final moon
at the end of each cycle.
We call it Kit-chee Kee-sos, Big Moon.
Its name is the last
in our circle of seasons,
thirteen moons
on Old Turtle's back.

Source: Joseph Bruchac and Jonathan London, *Thirteen Moons on Turtle's Back: A Native American Year of Moons* (New York: Philomel Books, 1992), p. 30.

DOCUMENT 2

Voyages (1609)

SAMUEL DE CHAMPLAIN

We left the next day, continuing on the Richelieu river to the foot of the lake. It had a number of beautiful islands, low, covered with fine woods and meadows where fowl and game animals, such as stags, fallow deer, fawns, roebucks, bears and other species, come from the mainland. We took a great many of them. There are also many beavers, both on the river and on many small streams that fall into it. No savages live there since their wars, although it is pleasant. They withdraw as deep into the land as possible, to avoid surprise attacks.

The next day we entered the lake, a long one, perhaps 50 or 60 leagues, where I saw 4 beautiful islands, 10, 12, and 15 leagues long, formerly occupied by the savages, like the River of the Iroquois. But they have been abandoned since the war. Several rivers empty into the lake, bordered by fine trees of the same species we have in France. The vines are finer than I have seen anywhere else. Many chestnuts — and I had seen none before — grow only on the lakeshore. Many kinds of fish are in great abundance; among others, one the local savages call *chaosarou*. I saw one 5 feet long, thigh-thick, its head as big as two fists, a beak two and a half feet long, with a double row of sharp, dangerous teeth. Its body is like a pike's, but its scales are so tough a poignard cannot pierce them. It is silver-gray. The savages gave me the head of one, saying that when they have a headache, they bleed themselves by scratching the spot that hurts with this fish's teeth, and the pain immediately leaves them.

Pursuing our course along the west shore and viewing the landscape, I saw very high mountains to the east, with snow on their summits. I asked the savages if any one lived there. They answered, "Yes, the Iroquois," and claimed there were beautiful valleys and fertile fields of maize, and numberless other fruits.

On July 29, as we paddled on without making a sound, we met the Iroquois about ten o'clock at night, at the end of a point on the west shore. They were on the warpath. Both sides began yelling at each other and preparing their arms. We retreated farther from shore, and the Iroquois landed, beaching their canoes close together. They began to fell trees with poor axes, which they sometimes capture in war, and with others of stone, barricading themselves very well.

We spent the night in our canoes, fastened together with poles, so that none could drift off, and we would be ready to fight if necessary. We were on the water an arrow's shot from their barricade. When they were armed and ready, they detached two canoes and sent to know if their enemy wanted to fight. The Algonquins and Hurons answered that they wanted nothing else, but there was not much light, and it would be necessary to wait for dawn, to be able to recognize each other. As soon as the sun rose, the Iroquois would offer us battle. We agreed. While we waited, on both sides the whole night was spent dancing and singing, with endless taunts and other talk, such as what little courage we had, what weak resistance to their arms; when day came we should realize it to our ruin. We replied in kind, telling them they would see such weapon-handling as they had never seen before — the kind of jibing common at a siege.

After all this song, dance and palaver, day came. My French companions and I stayed out of sight, preparing our arms as best we could. We were separated, each in one of the canoes of the savage Montagnais. After we had put on light armor, we each took an arquebus and went ashore.

I saw the enemy leave their barricade — almost 200 of them strong and vigorous — and advance slowly toward us with admirable dignity and confidence, three chiefs at their head. Our men also advanced in the same order, telling me that those with three long eagle feathers were their only chiefs, and that I should try my best to kill them. I promised to do what I could. I said I was very sorry our warriors could not understand me, because if I could improve the order of attack, we would utterly defeat them. But since nothing could be done about that, I was most willing to encourage them and show my goodwill when we were in battle.

As soon as we were ashore they began to run about 200 paces toward their enemies, who held their ground. They had not yet noticed my companions, who went into the woods with some savages. Our side began to call loudly for me, and divided ranks to let me through to the front. I marched some 20 paces ahead, until I was 30 paces from the enemy. As soon as they saw me

they stopped and stared, and I at them. As I saw them aim at us, I leveled my musket and aimed at one of the chiefs. With one shot two fell to the ground, and another was wounded, who later died. I had loaded 4 balls in my musket. Our men began to yell like thunder, while the arrows flew on both sides. The Iroquois were amazed, and alarmed that two men had been killed at once, despite their armor of woven cotton and wood, proof against their arrows. As I was reloading, one of my companions fired a shot from the woods, which so redoubled their astonishment, seeing their chiefs dead, that they lost courage and fled into the woods, abandoning the field and their breastworks. I pursued them and killed some others. Our savages also killed several and took ten or twelve prisoners. The rest escaped with the wounded. Fifteen or sixteen of our men had arrow wounds, which soon healed.

After our victory our men took a large amount of Indian corn and meal and arms left behind by the enemy in order to run faster. We spent three hours feasting, dancing and singing; then we started back with the prisoners.

This attack occurred at latitude 43 [degrees] and some minutes. I called the lake Champlain.

After going eight leagues, toward evening they took one of the prisoners, charged him and his tribe with merciless cruelties toward them, and told him to prepare for the like. They ordered him to sing, if he had the courage; and he did, but the song was very sad to hear.

Meanwhile our men lighted a fire, and when it was burning well, each took a brand and burned this poor unfortunate, little by little, to increase his torture. Sometimes they stopped and threw water on his back. Then they tore out his nails, and put flame to his fingertips and genitals. After that they scalped him and poured hot gum on his head. Then they pierced his arms near the wrists, and pulling out the tendons with sticks, tried to tear them out; but failing, cut them.

This miserable wretch uttered extraordinary cries, arousing my pity to see him treated so. All the while he was so steady that one would have said that he sometimes felt no pain. They kept urging me to take a brand and do like them. I protested that we Europeans use no torture, but execute with one blow. If they would, I should gladly fire the *coup de grace*. They said no, because then he would feel no pain. I went away in revulsion at such cruelties. When they saw that I was disgusted, they called me and told me to shoot him; and I did without his seeing.

After he was dead they were still not satisfied. They opened his belly and threw his guts into the lake; then cut off his head, arms and legs and scattered them about, keeping the scalp with those of all the other enemies killed in the battle.

They committed still another atrocity, cutting his heart into several pieces and giving it to his brother and other prisoners to eat. They put it in their mouths but would not swallow it. Some Algonquin savages guarding them made some of them spit it out, and threw it into the water. That is how these people treat their prisoners. It would be better for them to die fighting, or kill themselves suddenly, as many do, than to fall into the hands of their enemies. After the execution we moved on with the rest of the prisoners, who kept up a chant, with no hope of being better treated.

Reaching the falls of the Iroquois, the Algonquins returned to their country. The Hurons left too, with a share of the prisoners, well satisfied with the outcome of the war and with my ready participation. We parted with great show of friendship, and they invited me to their country, to be with them always like a brother and I promised to come.

Source: Samuel de Champlain, *Voyages*, B.K.3 (Paris: 1632), pp. 146-154. Translated by T. D. Seymour Bassett.

DOCUMENT 3

Grant to James, Duke of York (1664)
CHARLES II

GRANT OF NEW NETHERLAND, &C., TO THE DUKE OF YORK

Charles the Second by the Grace of God King of England, Scotland, France and Ireland Defender of the Faith, &c. To all whom these presents shall come Greeting. Know ye that we for divers good Causes and Considerations us thereunto moving Have of our especial Grace, Certain knowledge and mere motion Given and Granted and by these presents for us Our heirs and Successors Do Give and Grant unto our Dearest Brother James Duke of York his Heirs and Assigns All that part of the maine Land of New England beginning at a certain place called or known by the name of St Croix next adjoining to New Scotland in America and from thence extending along the Sea Coast unto a certain place called Petuaquine or Pemaquid and so up the River thereof to the furthest head of the same as it tendeth Northwards and extending from thence to the River Kinebequi and so Upwards by the Shortest course to the River Canada Northward. And also all that Island or Islands commonly called by the several names of Matowacks or Long Island situate lying and being towards the West of Cape Cod and the Narrow Higansetts [Narragansett] abutting upon the main land between the two Rivers there called or known by the several names of Connecticut and Hudsons River together also with the said River called Hudsons River and all the Land from the West side of Connecticut to the East side of Delaware Bay and also all those several Islands called or known by the Names of Martin's Vinyard and Nantukes otherwise Nantuckett. . . . And the said James Duke of York doth for himself his Heirs and Assigns convenant and promise to yield and render unto us our Heirs and Successors of and for the same yearly and every year forty Beaver skins when they shall be demanded or within Ninety days after. And We do further of our special Grace certain knowledge and mere motion of us our Heirs and Successors Give and Grant unto our said Dearest Brother James Duke of York his Heirs, Deputies, Agents, Commissioners and Assigns by these presents full and absolute power and authority to correct, punish, pardon, govern and rule all such the subjects of us Our Heirs and Successors who may from time to time adventure themselves into any the parts or places aforesaid or that shall or do at any time hereafter inhabit within the same according to such Laws, Orders, Ordinances, Directions and Instruments as by our said Dearest Brother or his Assigns shall be established. . . .

Source: E. B. O'Callaghan, ed., *Documents Relative to the Colonial History of the State of New-York*, Vol. 2 (Albany: Weed, Parsons, and Co., 1858), pp. 295-297.

DOCUMENT 4

New York Patent of Hossick/Hoosac (1688)

Recorded for Maria Van Ransler
Hendrick Van Ness &c the 28th July 1688.

THOMAS DONGAN Capt. Genl. & Governor, in Cheife in and over the Province of New Yorke and Territoryes Depending thereon in America under his most Sacred Majesty JAMES the Second by the Grace of God King of England Scottland France & Ireland Defendor of the faith &c: To all to whom these Presents shall come Sendeth Greeting Whereas Maria Van Ranslear of Renslerwick in the County of Albany Widdow, Hendrick Van Nesse of the same Place Yeoman, Gerritt Tunissen of Kattskill in the same County Yeoman and Jacobus Van Cortland of the Citty of New Yorke Marchant by Virtue of my Lycence Consent and Approbacon have Purchased of & from the Indyans Naturall owners and Possessors of the same all that Tract of Land with itts Appurtennces Scituate Lyeing & being above Albany on both sides of a Certaine Creek Called Hossick beginnin att the Bounds of Schackoock and from thence Extending to the said Creeke to a Certaine Fall Called Quequick and from the said Fall upwards along the Creek to a Certaine Place Called Nachawickquaak being in Breadth on each side of the said Creek two English that is to say two English Miles on the one side of said Creek & two English Miles on the other side of the said Creek the whole Breadth being fouer English Miles & is in Length from the Bounds off Schackoock aforesaid to the said Place Called Nachawickquaack. . . . By Virtue of [my] Commission & Authority. . . I hereby Give Grant & Confirme to the said Maria Van Ranslaer, Hendrick Van Nesse, Gerritt Tunissen & Jacobus Van Cortlandt their Heirs and Assignes for ever All that the before Recited Tract of Land. . . in Free and Common Soccage According to the Tenure of East Greenwick in the County of Kent in his Matis. Kingdom of England Yeilding Rendring & Paying therefor unto his said Matie: his Heirs and Successors Yearly & every Yeare the Quantity of ten Bushells of Good Sweett Marchantable Winter Wheat to be Delivered att the Citty of Albany unto such Officer or Officers as shall from time to time be Empowred to Receive the same as a Quitt Rent. . . . Affixed this Second Day of June in the fourth Yeare of his Matis Reigne and in the Yeare of our Lord 1688.

Tho: Dongan

May it Please your Excelly
The Attourney Genl: has Perused this Grant & finds nothing therein Prejudiciall to his Majestys Intrest— Examd May 31: 1688   W. Nicolls

Source: Mary Greene Nye, ed., *State Papers of Vermont*, Vol. 7, New York Land Patents, 1688-1786 (Montpelier: Secretary of State, 1947), pp. 19-20.

DOCUMENT 5

The Redeemed Captive Returning to Zion (1704)
REV. JOHN WILLIAMS

. . . On Tuesday, the 29th of February, 1703-4, not long before break of day, the enemy came in like a flood upon us; our watch being unfaithful; — an evil, the awful effects of which, in the surprisal of our fort, should bespeak all watchmen to avoid, as they would not bring the charge of blood upon themselves. They came to my house in the beginning of the onset, and by their violent endeavors to break open doors and windows, with axes and hatchets, awaked me out of sleep; on which I leaped out of bed, and, running towards the door, perceived the enemy making their entrance into the house. I called to awaken two soldiers in the chamber, and returning toward my bedside for my arms, the enemy immediately broke into the room, I judge to the number of twenty, with painted faces, and hideous acclamations. I reached up my hands to the bed-tester for my pistol, uttering a short petition to God, for everlasting mercies for me and mine, on account of the merits of our glorified Redeemer; expecting a present passage through the valley of the shadow of death; saying in myself, as Isa. xxxviii. 10, 11, "I said, in the cutting off of my days, I shall go to the gates of the grave: I am deprived of the residue of my years. I said, I shall not see the Lord, even the Lord, in the land of the living: I shall behold man no more with the inhabitants of the world." Taking down my pistol, I cocked it, and put it to the breast of the first Indian that came up; but my pistol missing fire, I was seized by three Indians who disarmed me, and bound me naked, as I was in my shirt, and so I stood for near the space of an hour. Binding me, they told me they would carry me to Quebeck. My pistol missing fire was an occasion of my life's being preserved; since which I have also found it profitable to be crossed in my own will. The judgement of God did not long slumber against one of the three which took me, who was a captain, for by sunrising he received a mortal shot from my next neighbor's house; who opposed so great a number of French and Indians as three hundred, and yet were no more than seven men in an ungarrisoned house. . .

After this, we went up the mountain, and saw the smoke of the fires in the town, and beheld the awful desolations of Deerfield. And before we marched any farther, they killed a sucking child belonging to one of the English. There were slain by the enemy of the inhabitants of Deerfield, to the number of thirty-eight, besides nine of the neighboring towns. We travelled not far the first day; God made the heathen so to pity our children, that though they had several wounded persons of their own to carry upon their shoulders, for thirty miles, before they came to the river, yet they carried our children, incapable of travelling, in their arms, and upon their shoulders. When we came to our lodging place, the first night, they dug away the snow, and made some wigwams, cut down some small branches of the spruce-tree to lie down on, and gave the prisoners somewhat to eat; but we had but little appetite. I was pinioned and bound down that night, and so I was every night whilst I was with the army. Some of the enemy who brought drink with them from the town fell to drinking, and in their drunken fit they killed my negro man, the only dead person I either saw at the town, or in the way.

In the night an Englishman made his escape; in the morning (March 1), I was called for, and ordered by the general to tell the English, that if any more made their escape, they would burn the rest of the prisoners. He that took me was unwilling to let me speak with any of the prisoners, as we marched; but on the morning of the second day, he being appointed to guard the rear, I was put into the hands of my other master, who permitted me to speak to my wife, when I overtook her, and to walk with her to help her in her journey. On the way, we discoursed of the happiness of those who had a right to an house not made with hands, eternal in the heavens; and God for a father and friend; as also, that it was our reasonable duty quietly to submit to the will of God, and to say, "The will of the Lord be done." My wife told me her strength of body began to fail, and that I must expect to part with her; saying, she hoped God would preserve my life, and the life of some, if not of all our children with us; and commended to me, under God, the care of them. She never spake any discontented word as to what had befallen us, but with suitable expressions justified God in what had happened. We soon made a halt, in which time my chief surviving master came up, upon which I was put upon marching with the foremost, and so made my last farewell of my dear wife, the desire of my eyes, and companion in many mercies and afflictions. Upon our separation from each other, we asked for each other grace sufficient for what God should call us to. After our being parted from one another, she spent the few remaining minutes of her stay in reading the Holy Scriptures; which she was wont personally every day to delight her soul in reading, praying, meditating on, by herself, in her closet, over and above what she heard out of them in our family worship. I was made to wade over a small river, and so were all the English, the water above knee deep, the stream very swift; and after that to travel up a small mountain; my strength was almost spent, before I came to the top of it. No sooner had I overcome the difficulty of that ascent, but I was permitted to sit down, and be unburdened of my pack. I sat pitying those who were behind, and entreated my master to let me go down and help my wife; but he refused, and would not let me stir from him. I asked each of the prisoners (as they passed by me) after her, and heard that, passing through the above-said river, she fell down, and was plunged over head and ears in the water; after which she travelled not far, for at the foot of that mountain, the cruel and bloodthirsty savage who took her slew her with his hatchet at one stroke, the tidings of which were very awful. And yet such was the hard-heartedness of the adversary, that my tears were reckoned to me as a reproach. My loss and the loss of my children was great; our hearts were so filled with sorrow, that nothing but the comfortable hopes of her being taken away, in mercy to herself, from the evils we were to see, feel, and suffer under, (and joined to the assembly of the spirits of just men made perfect, to rest in peace, and joy unspeakable and full of glory, and the good pleasure of God thus to exercise us,) could have kept us from sinking under, at that time. That Scripture, Job i. 21, "Naked came I out of my mother's womb, and naked shall I return thither: the Lord gave, and the Lord hath taken away; blessed be the name of the Lord," — was brought to my mind, and from it, that an afflicting God was to be glorified; with some other places of Scripture, to persuade to a patient bearing my afflictions.

We were again called upon to march, with a far heavier burden on my spirits than on my back. I begged of God to overrule, in his providence, that the corpse of one so dear to me, and of one whose spirit he had taken to dwell with him in glory, might meet with a Christian burial, and not be left for meat to the fowls of the air and beasts of the earth; a mercy that God graciously vouchsafed to grant. For God put it into the hearts of my neighbors, to come out as far as she lay, to take up her corpse, carry it to the town, and decently to bury it soon after. In our march they killed a sucking infant of one of my neighbors; and before night a girl of about eleven years of age. I was made to mourn, at the consideration of my flock being, so far, a flock of slaughter, many being slain in the town, and so many murdered in so few miles from the town; and from fears what we must yet expect, from such who delightfully imbrued their hands in the blood of so many of His people. When we came to our lodging place, an Indian captain from the eastward spake to my master about killing me, and taking off my scalp. I lifted up my heart to God, to implore his grace and mercy in such a time of need; and afterwards I told my master, if he intended to kill me, I desired he would let me know of it; assuring him that my death, after a promise of quarter, would bring the guilt of blood upon him. He told me he would not kill me. We laid down and slept, for God sustained and kept us. . .

Source: John Williams, *The Redeemed Captive Returning to Zion: or, A Faithful History of Remarkable Occurrences in the Captivity and Deliverance of Mr. John Williams* (Northampton, Mass. : Hopkins, Bridgman, and Co., 1853), pp. 10-11, 14-17.

DOCUMENT 6

English-Indian Treaty, Fort Dummer (1737)

Province of the Massachusetts Bay — Fort Dummer, 1737.

Pursuant to an order from his Excellency the Governor to us the subscribers directed, appointing us to confer with Ontaussoogoe and other delegates of the Cagnawaga tribe of Indians, we came to Fort Dummer aforesaid, where we arrived on the 5th of October Anno Domini 1737.

We acquainted the said delegates that his Excellency the Governor having been informed that they were to come to Fort Dummer to treat about some publick affairs, he had thereupon ordered and appointed us on behalf of the Government of the said Province to confer with them of such matters as were given them in charge, and that we should be ready to hear what they had to say when they were prepared to speak. The usual ceremonies being over, they withdrew.

October 6. Being met in the morning, Ontaussoogoe said to us as follows vizt. "Brother the Broadway, two years past I was at Deerfield; the matter then delivered to us by you was, that the old covenant of peace and unity between our brother the Broadway and us might be continued.

We now return in answer for our three tribes, that our desire is that it might remain firm and unshaken, and do from our heart promise that the covenant shall not be broken on our part, but if ever there should be any breach, it shall begin on yours, and the God of Heaven who now sees us and knows what we are doing, be witness of our sincerity." Then laid down a belt of Wampum.

Ontaussoogoe then said again, "We your brethren of the three tribes have learned by hear say, that our Brother the Broadway has lost his wife. Such losses ought to be made up. We did not know whether the Govr would be capable of a Treaty under his affliction, but find that he is, and are thankful for it." Then gave a belt of Wampum to quiet the Govr mind and remove his grief for the loss of his wife, and added, "I rowl myself in the dust for the loss of our great men."

Ontaussoogoe said again, "We do in the name of our three tribes salute the Govr and all the Gentlemen belonging to him Tho' at a great distance and strangers, yet something acquainted. This was their desire and our design when we came from home thus to salute you with this belt, wishing you happiness and prosperity;" laid it down, and said they had done speaking.

We then said to them, we would take what they had delivered into consideration, and return answer thereto in the afternoon. We then drank King George's health to them. They also drinked King George's health and the Governor's and to us.

In the afternoon being met, We said to them, "You have in strong terms assured us that the covenant of friendship renewed two years ago at Deerfield between this Government and the Cagnawaga tribe shall always remain firm and unshaken, and we do in the name and behalf of the Government, assure you that they will cultivate the friendship they have contracted with your tribe, and that nothing in our own hearts, nor the instigation of others, shall ever prevail upon us to break our solemn engagements to you, but we shall always hold ourselves under the strongest obligations to a punctual observance of what we have promised." We then gave a Belt of Wampum.

"You have in your speech to us this day condoled the death of the Governour's Lady. Her death was the cause of much grief to him. We doubt not but your sympathizing with him, will tend to abate and lighten his sorrow. We take this occasion to express our concern for the death of your firends and to comfort your hearts under your afflictions." We then gave three black Blankets instead of a Belt.

"We kindly accept the salutation of your people, and esteem it a token of their respect and friendship to us, and we do in the name of the Government return the like salutation to your old men and young, both to your counsellors and to your men of war, to all of them we wish prosperity and happiness for ever." Then we gave a Belt of Wampum.

Ontaussoogoe said, "Gentn, I return thanks, you have rehearsed all that has been said this day — are glad your hearts are disposed as we find they are to friendship and desire that they always may, and declare that ours ever will, and thank God for it — and wishes to all."

We then drinked the Govrs health.

The speeches being ended, we then in the name of the Govt Gave a present to them of the value of seventy pounds ten shillings.

John Stoddard, Eleazr Porter, Thos Wallis,
Joseph Kellogg, Isr. Williams, Comrs.

Source: Benjamin H. Hall, *History of Eastern Vermont* (New York: D. Appleton & Co., 1858), pp. 736-738.

DOCUMENT 7

A Narrative of the Captivity of Nehemiah How (1745)
NEHEMIAH HOW

At the Great-Meadow-Fort fourteen Miles above Fort-Dummer, October 11th 1745, where I was an Inhabitant, I went out from the Fort about 50 Rods to cut Wood; and when I had done, I walk'd towards the Fort, but in my Way heard the crackling of Fences behind me, & turning about, saw 12 or 13 Indians, with red painted Heads, running after me: On which I cry'd to God for Help, and ran, and hollow'd as I ran, to alarm the Fort; but by that I had ran ten Rods, the Indians came up with me and took hold of me: At the same Time the Men at the Fort shot at the Indians, and kill'd one on the Spot, wounded another, who died fourteen Days after he got Home, and likewise shot a Bullet thro' the Powder-Horn of one that had hold of me. They then led me into the Swamp and pinion'd me. I then committed my Case to God, and Pray'd, that since it was his Will to deliver me into the Hands of these cruel Men, I might find Favour in their Eyes: Which Request, God of his infinite Mercy was pleased to grant; for they were generally kind to me while I was with 'em: Some of the Indians, at that Time, took the Charge of me, others ran into the Field to kill Cattle. They led me about half a Mile; where we staid in open Sight of the Fort, 'till the Indians who were killing Cattle came to us laden with Beef: Then they went a little further to a House, where they stay'd to cut the Meat from the Bones, and cut the Helve off my Ax, and stuck it into the Ground, pointing the Way we went.

Then we travel'd along by the River Side; and when we got about three Miles, I espied a Canoe coming down on the further Side the River, with David Rugg and Robert Baker belonging to our Fort. I made as much Noise as I could, by Hamming &c. that they might see us before the Indians saw them, and get ashore, and happily escape; but the Indians saw them, and shot a-cross the River twenty or thirty Guns at them, and kill'd the first mention'd Person, viz. David Rugg, but Robert Baker the other Person got ashore, and escaped. Then some of the Indians swam over the River, and bro't the Canoe over the River, scalp'd and stript the dead Man, and then went about a Mile further, when we came to another House, where we stop'd; while there, we heard Men running by the Bank of the River, whom I knew to be Jonathan Thayer, Samuel Nutting, & my Son Caleb How: Five of the Indians ran to head them. My Heart ak'd for them, & pray'd to God to save them from the Hands of the Enemy. I suppose they hid under the Bank of the River; for the Indians were gone some Time, but came back without them, blessed be God.

We went about a Mile further, where we lodg'd that Night, and roasted the Meat they had got: The next Day we travel'd very slow, by Reason of the Indian who was wounded, which was a great Favour to me. We lodg'd the second Night against Number Four; the third Day we likewise travel'd slowly, and stop'd often to rest, & to get along the wounded Man; we lodg'd that Night by the second small River that runs into the great River against Numb. Four.

The fourth Day Morning, the Indians . . . bid me write my Name, & how many Days we had travel'd; for, said they, *May be English-Men will come here.* That was a hard Day to me; for it was a wet Day, and we went over prodigious Mountains, so that I became weak & faint; for I had not eaten the value of one Meal from the Time I was taken. . . . When I came first to the Foot of those Hills, I tho't it was impossible for me to ascend them, without immediate Help from God; therefore my constant Recourse was to him for Strength; which he was graciously pleased to grant me; and for which I desire to Praise him. We got that Day a little before Night to a Place where they had a hunting House, a Kettle, some Beef, Indian Corn, and Salt: They boil'd a good Mess of it; I drank of the Broth, eat of the Meat & Corn, and was wonderfully refreshed, so that I felt like another Man.

The next Morning we got up early, and after we had eaten, my Master said to me, *You must quick walk to Day, or I will kill you.* I told him I would go as fast as I could, and no faster, if he did kill me: At which, an old Indian who was the best Friend I had, took Care of me. We travel'd that Day very hard, and over steep Hills, but it being a cool windy Day, I perform'd it with more Ease than before; yet I was much tired before Night, but dare not complain.

The next Day the Indians gave me a Pair of their Shoes, so that I travel'd with abundant more Ease than when I wore my own Shoes; tho' I eat but very little, our Victuals being almost spent; when the Sun was about two Hours high, the Indians scattered to hunt, and they soon kill'd a Fawn, & three small Bears; so that we had again Meat enough, some of which we boil'd, and eat heartily of, by which I felt strong.

The next Day we travel'd very hard, and perform'd it with Ease; insomuch that one of the Indians told me, I was a very strong Man: About three of the Clock we came to the Lake, where they had five Canoes, and Pork, Indian Corn, & Tobacco. We got into the Canoes, when the Indians stuck up a Pole about eight Feet long with the Scalp of David Rugg on the Top of it, painted red, with the Likeness of Eyes and Mouth on it: We sail'd about ten Miles, and then went on Shore; and after we had made a Fire, we boil'd a good Supper, and eat heartily.

The next Day we set sail for Crown-Point, but when we were within a Mile of the Place, they went on Shore, where were eight or ten French & Indians, but before I got on Shore two of them came running into the Water Knee deep, and pull'd me out of the Canoe; there they sang and danced round me, after which one of them bid me set down, which I did; and then they pull'd off my Shoes and Buckles, and took them from me. Soon after we went along to Crown-Point . . . two of the Indians took me out of the Canoe, and leading me, bid me run, which we did; it was about twenty Rods from the Fort; the Fort is large, built with Stone & Lime; they led me up to the third Loft, where was the Captain's Chamber; a Chair was bro't that I might set by the Fire and warm me. Soon after the Indians that I belong'd to, and others that were there, came into the Chamber, among whom was one I knew, named Pealtomy; he came and spake to me, and shook Hands with me; and I was glad to see him: He went out, but soon return'd and brought to me another Indian named Amrufus,

Husband to Mrs. Eunice Willams, Daughter of the late Rev. Mr. Williams of Deerfield; he was glad to see me, and I to see him. He asked me after his Wife's Relations, and shew'd a great deal of Respect to me. A while after this, the Indians sat in a Ring in the Chamber, and Pealtomy came to me, and told me, I must go sing and dance before the Indians; I told him, I could not: He told me over some Indian Words, and bid me sing them: I told him, I could not. With that the rest of the Fort who could speak some English came to me, & bid me sing it in English, which was, *I don't know where I go*; which I did, dancing round that Ring three Times; and then I sat down by the Fire: The Priest came to me, and gave me a Dram of Rum; after that the Captain brought me Part of a Loaf of Bread and a Plate of Butter, and ask'd me to eat, which I did heartily; for I had not eaten any Bread from the Time I was taken till then. The French Priest and all the Officers shew'd me a great deal of Respect: The Captain gave me a Pair of good Buckskin Shoes, the Priest fix'd them on my Feet; and we stay'd there that Night; where I slept with the Priest, Captain & Lieut. . . .

The next Morning, which was the tenth Day from the Time of my being taken, we went off in a Canoe, and the Night after we arriv'd at the wide Lake, and there we stay'd that Night; some of the Indians went a hunting, and kill'd a fat Buck-Deer, so that we had Victuals plenty, for we had a full Supply of Bread given us at the Fort at Crown-Point.

The next Morning the Wind being calm, we set out about two Hours before Day; soon after came to a Schooner lying at Anchor, went on Board, the French treated us very civilly: They gave each of us a Dram of Rum, and Victuals to eat. As soon as it was Day we left the schooner, & two Hours before Sun-set got over the Lake, & next Day came to Shamballee, where we met 300 French and 200 Indians. . . . I was taken out of the Canoe by two Frenchmen, and fled to a House about ten Rods off as fast as I could run, the Indians flinging Snow-Balls at me. As soon as I got to the House, the Indians stood round me very thick, and bid me sing & dance; which I did with them, in their Way, then they gave a Shout, and left off. Two of them came to me, one of whom smote me on one Cheek, to'ther on the other, which made the Blood run plentifully. Then they bid me sing and dance again, which I did with them, and they with me, shouting as before. Then two French Men took me under each Arm, and run so fast that the Indians could not keep up with us to hurt me: We ran about 40 Rods to another House; where a Chair was bro't for me to set down: The House was soon full of French & Indians, and round the House they were looking in at the Windows. A French Gentleman came to me, took me by the Hand, and led me into a small Room, where none came in but such as he admitted: He gave me Victuals and Drink: Several French Gentlemen and Indians came in, and were civil to me. . . . A while after this, the Indians whom I belong'd to, came to me, and told me we must go; which we did; and after going down the River about two Miles, we came to the thickest of the Town, where was a large Fort built with Stone and Lime, & very large and fine Houses in it; where was the General of the Army. . . . He asked me, what News from London and Boston; I told him such as I tho't convenient, and omitted the rest; and then went down to the Canoes, when some of the Indians went and got a plenty of Bread & Beef, which they put into the Canoes, and then we went into a French House, where we had a good Supper: There came in several French Gentlemen to see me, who were civil to me; one of them gave me a Crown Sterl. We lodg'd there 'till about two Hours before Day, when we arose, and went down the River; I suppose we went a Hundred Miles that Day, which bro't us into the great River call'd Quebec-River; we lodg'd that Night in a French House, and were civilly treated. . . .

Source: Victor Hugo Paltsits, *A Narrative of the Captivity of Nehemiah How in 1745-1747* (Cleveland: Burrows Brothers Co., 1904), pp. 27-37.

DOCUMENT 8

Carte du Lac Champlain (1748)
ANGIER/DE LERY

(depicted on facing page)

Source: Special Collections, Bailey/Howe Library, University of Vermont. Reprinted courtesy of Special Collections, UVM Libraries.

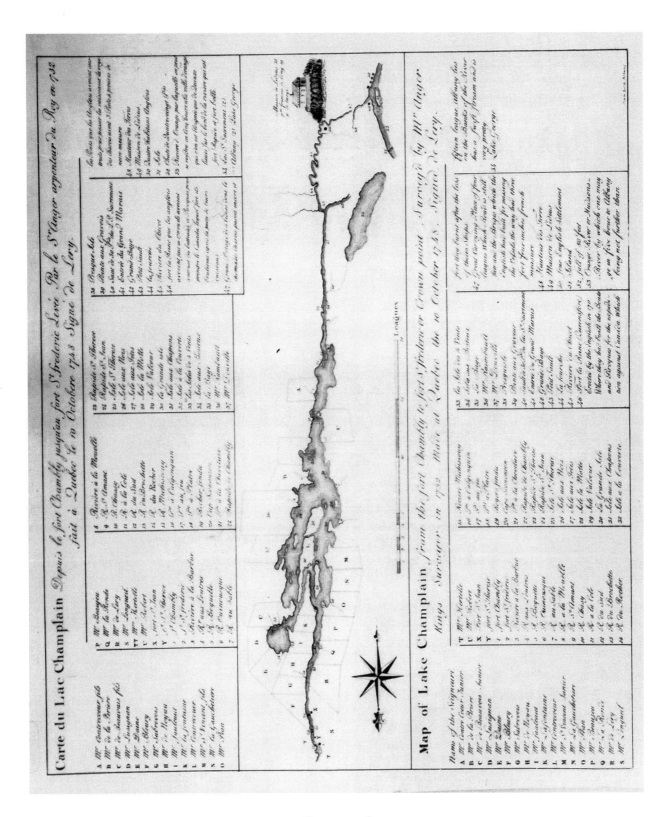

Document 8

DOCUMENT 9

New Hampshire Charter for the Town of Bennington (1749)

BENNING WENTWORTH

Province of New Hampshire

George the Second by the Grace of God of Great Brittain France And Ireland King Defender of the faith &c—

To All Persons to whom these Presents Shall come, Greeting

Know ye that We of our Especial Grace, Certain Knowledge & Mere Motion for the Due Encouragement of Settling A New Plantation within Our Sd Province By and with the Advise of Our Trusty & well beloved Benning Wentworth Esq our Governour & Com'ander in Chieff of our Said Province of New Hampshire in America And Of Our Council of the Said Province Have upon the Conditions & reservations herein after made Given & Granted — And by these Presents for us our heirs & Successors Do give And Grant in Equal Shares unto our Loveing Subjects Inhabitants of our Said Province of New Hampshire And his Majesties Other Govermts And To thier heirs and Assignes for ever whose names Are Entred on this Grant to be Divided to and Amonst them into Sixty four Equal Shares All that Tract or Parcell of Land Scituate Lying & being within our Said Province of New Hampshire Containing by Admeasurement Twenty three thousend & forty Acres which Tract is to Contain Six Miles Square & no more Out of which An Allowence is to be made for high ways & unimproveable Lands, by Rock, Ponds Mountains & Rivers One thousand And forty Acres free According to A Plan & Survey thereof made by our Said Governour's order by Mathew Clesson Surveyer returnd into the Secretarys office And hereunto Annexed Butted and Bounded as follows Vix — Beginning at A Crotched Hemlock Tree Marked W : W : Six miles Due North of A White Oak Tree Standing in the Northern Boundary Line of the Province of the Massachusetts Bay Twenty four Miles East of Hudsons River Marked M: C : J : T : and from Said Hemlock Tree West Ten degrees North four Miles to A Stake & Stones which is the South West Corner and from Said Stake & Stones North Ten degrees East Six miles to A Stake & Stones which is the North West Corner and from Said Stake & Stones East Ten Degrees South Six Miles to A Stake & Stones which is the North East Corner And from thence South Ten degrees West Six Miles to a Stake & Stones which is the South East Corner & from thence West Ten degrees North two Miles to the Crotched Hemlock First mentioned — And that the Same be & hereby is Incorporated into a Township By the Name of BENNINGTON and the Inhabitants that do or Shall hereafter Inhabit the Said Township Are hereby Declared to be Enfranchized with and Intituled to All & Every the Previledges & Imunities that Other Towns within Our Province by Law Exercize & Enjoy and further that the Said Town as Soon as there Shall be fifty families resident And Settled thereon Shall have the Liberty of Holding two Fairs One of which Shall be held On the first Monday in the Month of March and the Other on the first Monday in the Month of September Annually which fairs Are not to Continue And be held Longer than the respective Saturdays following the Said Mondays And that As Soon as the Said Town Shall Consist of fifty Families A market Shall be Opened & kept one or more Days in Each Week as may be tho't most Advantagious to the Inhabitants Also that the first Meeting for the Choice of Town officers Agreeable to the Laws of Our Said Province Shall be held on the Last Wednesday of March next which Said Meeting Shall be notified by Coll William Williams who is hereby also Appointed the Moderator of the Said first Meeting which he is to Notify & Govern Agreeable to the Laws & Custom of our Said Province And that the Annual Meeting forever hereafter for the Choice of Such officers for the Sd Town Shall be on the Last Wednesday of March Annually — TO HAVE & TO HOLD the said Tract of Land as above Expressed togeather with All Previledges And Appurtenances to them & thier respective Heirs And Assignes for ever upon the following Conditions Viz —

Imprimis That every Grantee his heirs or Assignes Shall Plant And Cultivate Five Acres of Land within the Term of five years for Every fifty Acres Contained in his or thier Share or Proportion of Land in Said Township And Continue to Improve & Setttle the Same by Aditionall Cultivations on Penalty of the forfieture of his Grant or Share in the Said Township and of its reverting to his Majesty his hiers & Successors to be by him or them regranted to Such of his Subjects as Shall Effectually Settle & Cultivate the Same

Secundo That All white & other Pine Trees within the said Township fit for masting our Royal Navy be carefully Preserved for that Use And None to be Cut or felld without his Majtys Especial Lycence for So doing first had & Obtained upon the Penalty of the forfeiture of the right of Such Grantee his hiers or Assignes to us our hiers or Successors as well as being Subject to the Penalty of Any Act or Acts of Parliament that now are or hereafter Shall be Enacted

Tertio That before Any Division of the Said Land be made to and Amoung the Grantees a Tract of Land as near the Center of the Said Township as the Land will admit of, Shall be reserved & Marked Out for Town Lotts one of which Shall be Allotted to Each Grantee of the Contents of One Acre —

Quarto Yielding & Paying therefor to us our Hiers & Successors for the Space of Ten Years to be Computed from the Date hereof the rent of one Ear of Indian Corn only on the Twenty fifth Day of December Annually if Lawfully Demanded the first Payment to be made on the Twenty fifth Day of December next Ensueing the Date hereof —

Quinto Every Proprietor Settler or Inhabitant Shall Yield & Pay unto us our hiers & Successors Yearly & every Year for ever from & after the Expiration of Ten years from the Date hereof Namly on the Twenty fifth Day of December which will be in the year of Our Lord 1760 — One Shilling Proclamation Money for every Hundred Acres he So Owns Settles or Possesses and so in Proportion for a greater or A Lesser Tract of the Said Land which money Shall be paid by the Respective Persons above Sd thier hiers or Assignes in our Council Chamber in Portsmouth or to Such officer or officers as Shall be Appointed to receive the Same and this to be in Lieu of all other rents or Services whatsoever

In Testamony whereof We have Caused the Seal of our Said Province to be hereunto Affixed Wittness Benning Wentworth Esq our Governour & Com'ander in Chieff of our Said Province the Third Day of January in the Year of Our Lord Christ One thousand Seven hundred & forty Nine and in the Twenty third Year of Our Reign —

B Wentworth

By his Excelencys Comand
with Advice of the Council
Theodr Atkinson Secry.
Record the 11th of Janry 1749

Source: Albert Stillman Batchellor, ed., *The New Hampshire Grants: The Charters of Townships*, Vol. 26 (Concord, N.H. : Edward N. Pearson, 1895), pp. 29-31.

DOCUMENT 10

Letter to George Clinton on Granting Lands West of the Connecticut River (1749)

BENNING WENTWORTH

Portsmouth, November 17th 1749

Sir

I have it in command from His Majesty to make Grants of the unimproved Lands within my Government, to Such of the Inhabitants and others, as shall apply for Grants for the Same, as will oblige themselves to Settle and improve, agreeable to his Majesty's Instructions.

The War hitherto has prevented me from making So great a progress as I hoped for, on my first appointment; but as there is a prospect of a lasting peace with the Indians, in which Your Excellency has had a great Share, people are daily applying for Grants of Land in All Quarters of this Government, And particularly Some for Townships to be laid out in the Western part thereof, which will fall in the Neighbourhood of your Government.

I think it my duty to apprize You thereof, and to Transmit to your Excellency the description of New Hampshire, as the King has determined it in the words of my Commission, which after you have Considered, I shall be glad you will be pleased to give me your Sentiments in that manner it will affect the Grants made by you or preceeding Governours, it being my intention to avoid as much as I can, Consistant with his Majesty's Instructions, Interferring with Your Government.

In Consequence of his Majesty's Determination of the boundary's between New Hampshire and the Massachusets, A Surveyor and proper Chainmen were appointed to Run the Western Line, from three Miles North of Pautucket Falls, And the Surveyor upon Oath has declared, that it Strikes Hudsons River about eighty poles between, where Mowhawks River comes into Hudson's River, which I presume is North of the City of Albany, for which Reason it will be necessary for me to be informed how far North of Albany the Government of New York Extends by his Majesty's Commission to your Excellency, and how many Miles to the Eastward of Hudson's River, to the Northward of the Massachusets Line, that I may Govern myself accordingly. And if in the Execution of the King's Commands. With respect to the Lands, I can oblige any of your Excellency's Friends I am allways at your Service.

I am with the greatest respect
Sir Your Excellencys
most Obedient humble Servant
B. Wentworth.

Source: E. B. O'Callaghan, ed., *The Documentary History of the State of New-York*, Vol. 4 (Albany: Charles Van Benthuysen, 1851), pp. 531-532.

Document 11

New York Council Report on Jurisdiction over the Vermont Area (1753)

To the Honorable James Delancey Esqr his majesty's Lieutenant Governor and Commander in Chief in an over the Province of New York and the Territories depending thereon in America.

The Presentation of the Committee of his Majesty's Council of the Province of New York and the Commissioners appointed to examine into the Eastern Boundaries of the said province.

May it please your Honour. . . .

1st Tho' the Eastern Boundarys of this province and the Western Boundarys of New Hampshire so far as they Bound on one another (Being Both under his Majesty's immediate government) intirely depend on his Majesty's pleasure, Yet as the Eastern Boundary of this Province, was by the Grant of King Charles the Second to the Duke of York, 1663-4, fixed at Connecticut river, now near ninety year ago, where it has ever since remained So far as Concerns New Hampshire, we humbly Conceive that his Majesty will make no alteration of the Bounds thereof without sufficient Reasons, and we know not of any, nor has Governour Wentworth pointed out any, But sundry Reasons appear against any alteration, which are particularly Set forth in the Surveyor Generalls Letter Entered in the minutes of Councill of Octr 18, 1751.

2dly Governour Wentworth is pleased To Say that, "the Massachusetts Bay have allowed the Government of New York To extend their Claim also Twenty miles East of Hudson's River." On which we observe that this is a Very new kind of Title that Governour Wentworth says his Majesty has to a great part of this his province *the allowance of his Subjects of the Massachusetts Bay*, We apprehend that no good Title can be within his Majestys Dominions But under valid Grants of the Crown, and know of no valid Grant that *Massachusetts Bay* have to any Soil or Jurisdiction west of Connecticut River, and that they have none appears in a Strong Light by a Report approved in the Councill of this province on the 20th of february Last (which contains the substance of and more than the Attorney Generals Representation before mentioned) which has been Communicated to the Government of the Massachusetts Bay, and To which no direct answer has as yet Been given, tho again and again requested. . . .

4thly Governour Wentworth is pleased to express himself thus, "presuming it will Be his Majesty's pleasure that a North and South line should divide both the Massachusetts and New Hampshire from the Government of New-York" On which we Observe that had Governour Wentworth been Informed, as We Believe the Truth is, that a North and South Line from the Northwest Corner of Connecticut Colony would have Crossed Hudson's River, some miles Southward or Below the City of Albany, and would Leave that City, and a great part of Hudson's River, To the Eastward of that Line, he could have had no reason for advancing that Presumption, and the rather, had he Been informed, as the fact Is, that the Dutch Settled Albany by the name of fort Orange and had a fort and Garrison there about 140 years agoe, many years before the Grant to the Councill of Plymouth under which the Massachusetts Bay had their first Claim.

5thly Governour Wentworth is pleased to Say. "I have extended the Western Boundary of New Hampshire as far West as the Massachusetts Bay have done theirs, that is within Twenty miles of Hudson's River" On which we Beg Leave to observe that his having done so, after Being informed of the Boundarys of this province by the Minite of Councill of the 3d of April 1750 before mentioned, and by the Minute of June 5th 1750 that the Massachusetts Settlements Westward of those Boundarys, were made By Intrusion, is very Extraordinary: and we are further of Opinion that the Intrusions of the Massachusetts Bay within this province, Could be no good reason for Governour Wentworth to Committ the Like.

6thly We apprehend that New Hampshire has no concern with the Northern Boundarys of New York Because we Conceive that the North Two degrees West line, the Eastern Boundary of New Hampshire will (if Mr. Pople's Large map be right) Intersect Connecticut River, the Eastern Boundary of this province; and if so, then New Hampshire is bounded to the West and North By Connecticut River.

7thly Governour Wentworth has been greatly misinformed, Concerning the patents made by the Crown, To the Duke of York. Viz. of March 12th 1663/4 and June 29th 1674 Both which do grant to him in fee, "All that Island or Islands Commonly called by the several name or names of Matowacks or Long Island, Situate and being towards the West of Cape Codd, and the Narrow Higgansettes abutting upon the Main Land Between the Two rivers there called or known By the several names of Connecticut and Hudson's River Together also with the said River Called Hudson's river and all the Land from the West side of Connecticut *River* to the East Side of Delaware Bay," and there is nothing in either of those patents (which are all we ever heard of) that Could give the Least Colour or Ground, for Governour Wentworth's suggestion that the Dukes Grant Commences at the Sea, and runs only sixty miles North into the Country: and was that Grant such as Mr. Wentworth imagines it to be the North Bounds of it would Cross Hudson's River above 100 miles South of or Below Albany instead of Twenty, as he supposes;

for Albany is 150 miles distant from the City of New York, and New York about 20 miles from the Sea.

Upon the whole Sir, We humbly Conceive it is highly necessary that this Representation and Copies of the necessary Papers referred to therein should be laid before the Lords Commissioners for Trade and Plantations that their Lordships may be informed of the objections which we conceive may with good Reason be made to the Line Gouvernour Wentworth points out to be fixed as the Division Line between this and the province of New Hampshire Which Papers together with this Representation we present to your Honour and humbly pray you will be pleased to transmit the Same to their Lordships.

By Order of the Committee John Chambers
Chairman
By Order of the Commissioners Paul Richard
Chairman
City of New York 14th: November 1753
6th June. Read in Council and approved of and the Council advised his Honour to transmit the same to the Board of Trade as desired.

Source: E. B. O'Callaghan, ed., *The Documentary History of the State of New-York*, Vol. 4 (Albany: Charles van Benthuysen, 1851), pp. 550, 552-556.

DOCUMENT 12

A Narrative of the Captivity of Mrs. Johnson (1754)
SUSANNA JOHNSON

. . . In the morning we were roused before sunrise: the Indians struck up a fire, hung on their stolen kettles, and made us some water gruel for breakfast. After a few sips of this meagre fare I was again put on the horse, with my husband by my side to hold me on. My two fellow prisoners took the little girls, and we marched sorrowfully on for an hour or two, when a keener distress was added to my multiplied afflictions. I was taken with the pangs of childbirth. The Indians signified to us that we must go on to a brook. When we got there they showed some humanity by making a booth for me. Here the compassionate reader will drop a fresh tear for my inexpressible distress; fifteen or twenty miles from the abode of any civilized being, in the open wilderness, rendered cold by a rainy day, in one of the most perilous hours, and unsupplied with the least necessary that could yield convenience in the hazardous moment. My children were crying at a distance, where they were held by their masters, and only my husband and sister to attend me. None but mothers can figure to themselves my unhappy fortune. The Indians kept aloof the whole time. About ten o'clock a daughter was born. They then brought me some articles of clothing for the child which they had taken from the house. My master looked into the booth and clapped his hands with joy, crying, "Two moneys for me! two moneys for me!" I was permitted to rest the remainder of the day. The Indians were employed in making a bier for the prisoners to carry me on, and another booth for my lodging during night. They brought a needle, and two pins, and some bark to tie the child's clothes, which they gave my sister, and a large wooden spoon to feed it with. At dusk they made some porridge, and brought a cup to steep some roots in, which Mr. Labaree had provided. . . . For supper they made more porridge and some johnny cakes. My portion was brought me in a little bark. I slept that night far beyond expectation.

In the morning we were summoned for the journey, after the usual breakfast of meal and water. I, with my infant in my arms, was laid on the litter, which was supported alternately by Mr. Johnson, Labarree, and Farnsworth. My sister and son were put upon Scoggin, and the two little girls rode on their masters' backs. Thus we proceeded two miles, when my carriers grew too faint to proceed any farther. This being observed by our masters, a general halt was called, and they imbodied themselves for council. My master soon made signs to Mr. Johnson that if I could ride on the horse I might proceed, otherwise I must be left behind. Here I observed marks of pity in his countenance; but this might arise from the fear of losing his two moneys. I preferred an attempt to ride on the horse rather than to perish miserably alone. Mr. Labarree took the infant, and every step of the horse almost deprived me of life. My weak and helpless condition rendered me, in a degree, insensible to every thing. My poor child could have no sustenance from my breast, and was supported entirely by water gruel. My other little children, ren-

dered peevish by an uneasy mode of riding, often burst into cries; but a surly check from their masters soon silenced them. We proceeded on with a slow, mournful pace. My weakness was too severe to allow me to sit on the horse long at a time. Every hour I was taken off and laid on the ground to rest. This preserved my life during the third day. At night we found ourselves at the head of Black River Pond. . . . Here we prepared to spend the night.

In the morning, half chilled with a cold fog, we were ordered from our places of rest, were offered the lean fare of meal and water, and then prepared for the journey. Every thing resembled a funeral procession. The savages preserved their gloomy sadness. The prisoners, bowed down with grief and fatigue, felt little disposition to talk; and the unevenness of the country, sometimes lying in miry plains, or others rising into steep and broken hills, rendered our passage hazardous and painful. Mr. Labarree kept the infant in his arms and preserved its life. The fifth day's journey was an unvaried scene of fatigue. The Indians sent out two or three hunting parties, who returned without game. As we had in the morning consumed the last morsel of our meal, every one now began to be seriously alarmed; and hunger, with all its horrors, looked us earnestly in the face. At night we found the waters that run into Lake Champlain. . . . Before dark we halted; and the Indians . . . made a fire. They soon adopted a plan to relieve their hunger. The horse was shot, and his flesh was in a few moments broiling on embers; and they, with native gluttony, satiated their craving appetites. To use the term politeness, in the management of this repast, may be thought a burlesque; yet their offering the prisoners the best parts of the horse certainly bordered on civility. An epicure could not have catered nicer slices, nor in that situation served them up with more neatness. Appetite is said to be the best sauce; yet our abudance of it did not render savory this novel steak. My children, however, ate too much, which made them very unwell for a number of days. Broth was made for me and my child, which was rendered almost a luxury by the seasoning of roots. After supper countenances began to brighten. . . .

Our Arrival at East Bay, in Lake Champlain

In the morning of the sixth day the Indians exerted themselves to prepare one of their greatest dainties. The marrow bones of old Scoggin [the horse] were pounded for a soup; and every root, both sweet and bitter, that the woods afforded, was thrown in to give it a flavor. Each one partook of as much as his feelings would allow. The war whoop then resounded, with an infernal yell, and we began to fix for a march. My fate was unknown, till my master brought some bark and tied my petticoats as high as he supposed would be convenient for walking, and ordered me to "munch." With scarce strength to stand alone, I went on half a mile with my little son and three Indians. The rest were advanced. My power to move then failed; the world grew dark, and I dropped down. I had sight enough to see an Indian lift his hatchet over my head; while my little son screamed, "Ma'am, do go; for they will kill you." As I fainted, my last thought was, that I should presently be in the world of spirits. When I awoke my master was talking angrily with the savage who had threatened my life. By his gestures I could learn that he charged him with not acting the honorable part of a warrior, by an attempt to destroy the prize of a brother. A whoop was given for a halt. My master helped me to the rest of the company, where a council was held, the result of which was, that my husband should walk by my side and help me along. This he did for some hours; but faintness then overpowered me, and Mr. Johnson's tenderness and solicitude were unequal to the task of aiding me farther. Another council was held: while in debate, as I lay on the ground gasping for breath, my master sprang towards me with his hatchet. My husband and fellow-prisoners grew pale at the sight, suspecting that he by a single blow would rid themselves of so great a burden as myself. But he had yet too much esteem for his "two moneys." His object was to get bark from a tree, to make a pack saddle for my conveyance on the back of my husband. He took me up, and we marched in that form the rest of the day. Mr. Labarree still kept my infant. Farnsworth carried one of the little girls, and the other rode with her master. They were extremely sick and weak, owing to the large portion of the horse which they ate; but if they uttered a murmuring word, a menacing frown from the savages soon imposed silence. None of the Indians were disposed to show insults of any nature except the youngest. . . . He often delighted himself by tormenting my sister, by pulling her hair, treading on her gown, and numerous other boyish pranks, which were provoking and troublesome. We moved on, faint and wearily, till

night. The Indians then yelled their war whoop, built a fire, and hung over their horse broth. After supper my booth was built as usual, and I reposed much better than I had the preceding nights.

In the morning I found myself greatly restored. Without the aid of physicians, or physic, Nature had begun to cure of that weakness to which she had reduced me but a few days before. The reader will be tired of the repetition of the same materials for our meals; but if my feelings can be realized, no one will turn with disgust from a breakfast of steaks which were cut from the thigh of a horse. After which Mr. Johnson was ordered to take the infant and go forward with part of the company. I "munched" in the rear till we came to a beaver pond, which was formed in a branch of Otter Creek. Here I was obliged to wade. When half way over, up to the middle in cold water, my little strength failed, and my power to speak or see left me. While motionless and stiffened, in the middle of the pond, I was perceived from the other side by Mr. Johnson, who laid down the infant and came to my assistance. He took me in his arms; and when the opposite side was gained, life itself had apparently forsaken me. The whole company stopped; and the Indians, with more humanity that I supposed them possessed of, busied themselves in making a fire to warm me into life. The warm influence of the fire restored my exhausted strength by degrees; and in two hours I was told to munch. The rest of the day I was carried by my husband. In the middle of the afternoon we arrived on the banks of one of the great branches of Otter Creek. Here we halted; and two savages, who had been on a hunting scout, returned with a duck. A fire was made, which was thrice grateful to my cold, shivering limbs. Six days had now almost elapsed since the fatal morn in which we were taken; and by the blessing of that Providence whose smiles give life to creation we were still in existence. . . .

Source: Colin G. Calloway, comp., *North Country Captives: Selected Narratives of Indian Captivity from Vermont and New Hampshire* (Hanover, N.H.: University Press of New England, 1992), pp. 45, 59-63.

DOCUMENT 13

Account of the Raid on St. Francis and Retreat through Vermont (1759)

ROBERT ROGERS

Camp at Crown Point
Sept. 13, 1759
Orders to Major Robert Rogers

You are this night to set out with the detachment as ordered yesterday, viz. of 200 men, which you will take under your command, and proceed to Missisquey Bay, from whence you will march and attack the enemy's settlements on the south-side of the river St. Lawrence, in such a manner as you shall judge most effectual to disgrace the enemy, and for the success and honour of his Majesty's arms.

Remember the barbarities that have been committed by the enemy's Indian scoundrels on every occasion, where they had an opportunity of shewing their infamous cruelties on the King's subjects, which they have done without mercy. Take your revenge, but don't forget that tho' those villains have dastardly and promiscuously murdered the women and children of all ages, it is my orders that no women or children are killed or hurt.

When you have executed your intended service, you will return with your detachment to camp, or to join me wherever the army may be.

Your's, &c.

Jeff. Amherst

In pursuance of the above orders, I set out the same evening with a detachment; and as to the particulars of my proceedings, and the great difficulties we met with in effecting our design, the reader is referred to the letter I wrote to General Amherst upon my return, and the remarks following it.

Copy of my Letter to the General upon my return from St. Francis:

No. 4
Nov. 5, 1759
Sir,

The twenty-second day after my departure from Crown Point, I came in sight of the Indian town St. Francis in the evening, which I discovered from a tree that I climbed, at about three miles distance. . . . I left the detachment, and took with me Lieut. Turner and Ensign Avery, and went to reconnoitre the town, which I did to my satisfaction, and found the Indians in a high frolic or dance. I returned to my party . . . and marched it to within five hundred yards of the town. . . .

At half an hour before sun-rise I surprised the town when they were all fast asleep, on the right, left, and center, which was done with so much alacrity by both the officers and men, that the enemy had not time to recover themselves, or take arms for their own defence, till they were chiefly destroyed, except some few of them who took to the water. About forty of my people pursued them, who destroyed such as attempted to make their escape that way, and sunk both them and their boats. A little after sun-rise I set fire to all their houses, except three, in which there was corn, that I reserved for the use of the party.

The fire consumed many of the Indians who had concealed themsleves in the cellars and lofts of their houses. About seven o'clock in the morning the affair was completely over, in which time we had killid at least two hundred Indians, and taken twenty of their women and children prisoners, fifteen of whom I let go their own way, and five I brought with me. . . . I likewise retook five English captives, which I also took under my care. . . .

I cannot forbear here making some remarks on the difficulties and distresses which attended us, in effecting this enterprize upon St. Francis, which is situated within three miles of the river St. Lawrence, in the middle of Canada, about half way between Montreal and Quebec. . . . Our party was reduced by accident and still farther by numbers tiring and falling sick afterwards. It was extremely difficult while we kept the water (and which retarded our progress very much) to pass undiscovered by the enemy, who were then cruizing in great numbers upon the lake; and had prepared certain vessels, on purpose to decoy any party of ours, that might come that way, armed with all manner of machines and implements for their destruction; but we happily escaped their snares of this kind, and landed . . . the tenth day at Missisquey Bay. Here, that I might with more certainty know whether my boats (with which I left provision sufficient to carry us back to Crown Point) were discovered by the enemy, I left two trusty Indians to lie at a distance in sight of the boats, and there to stay till I came back, except the enemy found them; in which latter case they were with all possible speed to follow in my track, and give me intelligence. It happended the second day after I left them, that these two Indians came up to me in the evening, and informed me that about 400 French had discovered and taken my boats, and that about one half of them were hotly pursuing on my track. This unlucky circumstance (it may well be supposed) put us into some consternation. Should the enemy overtake us, and we get the better of them in an encounter; yet being so far advanced into their country, where no reinforcement could possibly relieve us, and where they could be supported by any numbers they pleased, afforded us little hopes of escaping their hands. Our boats being taken, cut off all hope of a retreat by them; besides, the loss of our provisions left with them, of which we knew we should have great need at any rate, in case we survived, was a melancholy consideration. It was, however, resolved to prosecute our design at all adventures, and, when we had accomplished it, to attempt a retreat (the only possible way we could think of) by way of [Fort] No. 4; and that we might not be destroyed by famine in our return, I dispatched Lieut. M'Mullen by land to Crown Point, to desire of the General to relieve me with provision at Amonsook River, at the end of Cohase Intervales on Connecticut River [near present-day Wells River, Vermont], that being the way I should return, if at all, and the place appointed being about sixty miles from No. 4, then the most northerly English settlement.

This being done we determined if possible to outmarch our pursuers, and effect our design upon St. Francis before they could overtake us. We marched nine days through wet sunken ground; the water most of the way near a foot deep, it being a spruce bog. When we encamped at night, we had no way to secure ourselves from the water, but by cutting the bows of trees, and with them erecting a kind of hammocks. We commonly began our march a little before day, and continued it till dark at night.

The tenth day after leaving Missisquey Bay, we came to a river about fifteen miles above the town of St. Francis to the south of it; and the town being on the opposite or east side of it, we were obliged to ford it, which was attended with no small difficulty, the water being five feet deep, and the current swift. I put the tallest men up stream, and then holding by each other, we got over with the loss of several of our guns, some of which we recovered by diving to the bottom for them. We had now good dry ground to march upon, and discovered and destroyed the town, which in all probability would have been effected with the loss of no man but the Indian who was killed in the action, had not my boats been discovered, and our retreat that way cut off.

This nation of Indians was notoriously attached to the French, and had for near a century past harassed the frontiers of New England, killing people of all ages and sexes in a most barbarous manner, at a time when they did not in the least suspect them; and to my own knowledge, in six years' time carried into captivity 400 persons. We found in the town hanging on poles over their doors, &c. about 600 scalps, mostly English. . . .

[After the battle] I examined the prisoners who gave the following intelligence: "That a party of 300 French and some Indians were about four miles down the river below us; and that our boats were waylaid. . . . Whereupon I called the officers together to consult the safety of our return who were of opinion there was no other way for us to return with safety, but by No. 4 on Connecticut River. I marched the detachment eight days in a body that way; and when provisions grew scarce . . . I divided the detachment into small companies . . . who were to assemble at the mouth of Amonsook River, about sixty miles above No. 4, as I expected provisions would be brought there for our relief, not knowing which way I should return. . . .

It is hardly possible to describe the grief and consternation of those of us who came to Cohase Intervales. Upon our arrival there (after so many days tedious march over steep rocky mountains, or thro' wet dirty swamps, with the terrible attendants of fatigue and hunger) to find that here was no relief for us, where we had encouraged ourselves that we should find it, and have our distresses alleviated; for the officer I dispatched to the General discharged his trust with great expedition, and in nine days arrived at Crown Point, which was an hundred miles thro' the woods. The General, without delay, sent Lieut. Stephans to No. 4 with orders to take provisions up the river to the place I had appointed, and there wait as long as there was any hopes of my returning; yet the officer that was sent being an indolent fellow, tarried at the place but two days, when he returned, taking all the provisions back with him, about two hours before our arrival. Finding a fresh fire burning in his camp, I fired guns to bring him back, which guns he heard, but would not return, supposing we were an enemy.

Our distress upon this occasion was truly inexpressible; our spirits, greatly depressed by the hunger and fatigues we had already suffered, now almost entirely sunk within us, seeing no resource left, nor any reasonable ground to hope that we should escape a most miserable death by famine. At length I came to a resolution to push as fast as possible towards No. 4 leaving the remains of my party, now unable to march further, to get such wretched subsistence as the barren wilderness could afford (this was ground-nuts and lilly roots), till I could get relief to them, which I engaged to do within ten days.

I, with Capt. Ogden, one Ranger, and a captive Indian boy, embarked upon a raft we had made of dry pine trees. . . . The second day we reached White River Falls, and very narrowly escaped being carried over them by the current. . . .

At the bottom of these falls . . . I attempted the forming a new raft for our further conveyance. Being not able to cut down trees, I burnt them down, and then burnt them off at proper lengths. This was our third day's work after leaving our companions. The next day we got our materials together, and completed our raft, and floated . . . down the stream to within a small distance of No. 4 where we found some men cutting of timber, who gave us the first relief, and assisted us to the fort, from whence I dispatched a canoe with provisions, which reached the men at Cohase four days after, which (agreeable to my engagement) was the tenth after I left them. . . .

Source: Robert Rogers, *Journals of Major Robert Rogers . . .* (London: n.p., 1765), pp. 144-158.

SECTION TWO

1760-1777
Struggle for the Grants

VERMONT VOICES

SECTION TWO

1760-1777
Struggle for the Grants

Introduction

The Treaty of Paris, formally concluding the French and Indian War, opened all of modern Vermont to English settlement, while the appearance of thousands of new settlers exacerbated the conflict between New York and New Hampshire titleholders. The continuing uncertainty over title and jurisdiction is highlighted in the first five documents of this section. Responding to New Hampshire's claims to jurisdiction (between 1749 and 1764, Governor Wentworth granted 129 townships in the disputed region), New York Lieutenant Governor Cadwallader Colden attempted to implement his province's jurisdiction by ordering all New York civil officers to exercise their functions as far east as the banks of the Connecticut River and to report any individuals living in the region under New Hampshire title so that "they may be preceded against according to law" (**Document 1**).

Unfazed, Governor Wentworth countered with his own proclamation, **Document 2**. Alleging the patent to the Duke of York upon which New York staked much of its claim to be "obsolete," Wentworth commanded New Hampshire civil officers to maintain their jurisdiction "as far westward as to include the grants made."

Document 3, a 1764 King's Order in Council declaring the west bank of the Connecticut River "to be" the boundary between the New York and New Hampshire provinces, illustrates both the growing interest of the London government in directing colonial affairs and the ineffectiveness of long-distance implementation. Issued in consequence of spiraling settlement fifteen years after the onset of the Grants dispute, the decision in favor of New York rested more on Cadwallader Colden's enumeration of benefits that would accrue to the Crown under New York jurisdiction than on affirmations of historic claims.

The Order in Council extinguished New Hampshire's claim to jurisdiction, but failed to resolve the issue of land titles. New Hampshire titleholders maintained that the King's Order established the boundary in July 1764, and therefore New Hampshire grants issued before that date were as valid as New York grants. New York refused to accept that interpretation, although it was not until 1770 that an Albany court ruled all New Hampshire titles invalid.

As is evident from **Document 4**, an Abenaki lease of Swanton Falls to James Robertson, the uncertainty over land titles was compounded by the presence of Indians who claimed and occupied significant acreage, particularly in the Missisquoi Bay-Swanton region. James Robertson chose to rely on neither a New Hampshire nor a New York title but rather a ninety-one-year lease from these Native Americans.

Most eighteenth-century Grants settlers held New Hampshire titles. **Document 5**, a petition to the king asking that New Hampshire administer the Grants, reveals their cost and quit-rent obligations were lower than those New York charged. Furthermore, New York fees to confirm New Hampshire titles were substantial enough to deter settlers and potential settlers from purchasing New York confirmation of their town charters. Document 5 was from settlers and potential settlers reluctant to proceed with settlement because of the continuing land-title uncertainty. Other settlers, most prominently the Allen family, were attracted by the opportunities uncertainty supplied.

Ethan Allen, the oldest of five Allen brothers and leader of the clan, arrived in the Grants from Massachusetts in 1770. He began speculating in Wentworth titles by purchasing grant rights in Poultney and Castleton. An imposing figure of blustering eloquence, he was chosen that same year by New Hampshire titleholders centered in Bennington as General Agent to organize their defense in the Albany court. New York had instituted ejectment suits against Hampshire titleholders whose legal defense was based on the principle that the New York-New Hampshire boundary had been established by the 1764 King's Order in Council (Document 3) and that pre-1764 New Hampshire charters were valid. The Albany court, however, dominated by personnel with competing New York claims, rejected that defense. Unwilling to accept the court ruling, Ethan returned to Bennington and in the summer of 1770 helped form and was elected Colonel Commandant of the Green Mountain Boys, a quasi-military organization dedicated to frustrating New York efforts to evict Wentworth titleholders and populate the Grants with Yorkers.

Document 6, "The Vision of Junus, the Benningtonite," was published anonymously but is generally attributed to Ethan Allen. Cast in the biblical cadence of a New Testament prophet, it serves as an indictment of the Yorkers most prominently associated with the Albany court decision and exults in such Green Mountain Boy exploits as thwarting Yorker efforts at forcible ejection of New Hampshire titleholders, the rescue of Green Mountain Boy leader Remember Baker from an Albany sheriff's posse, and the harassment New York officials.

Document 7 provides excerpts from the fragmentary autobiography of Ira Allen, Ethan's youngest brother, suggesting how the Green Mountain Boys operated to defend settlers against Yorker interests while at the same time acquiring a considerable financial stake in discredited New Hampshire titles. It was Ira who organized the Onion River Land Company, which for a considerable time made the Allens the largest Yankee land speculators on the Grants.

One of the ways in which New York attempted to assert its authority over the Grants was by integrating it into the province's county system. New York divided the region east of the Green Mountains into Cumberland and Gloucester counties and incorporated the region west of the mountains into Albany and Charlotte counties. Both western counties provided the setting for violent confrontations between the Green Mountain Boys and New York authorities. The incident described by Ira Allen in Document 7 occurred in Charlotte County, and this and similar incidents so frustrated the New York authorities that in 1774 Governor William Tryon pushed the "Bloody Act" through the New York legislature (**Document 8**). Tryon had arrived in New York after repressing the North Carolina Regulator movement. The Regulators, in common with the Green Mountain Boys and backcountry settler movements in Pennsylvania, Maine, and other frontier regions, resisted what they saw as a corrupt legal system designed to deprive them of their property. Tryon crushed the North Carolina movement through a military expedition that won a pitched battle against the Regulators. Proposed to resolve the New Hampshire Grants dispute by a less extreme method, the "Bloody Act," by restricting the customary right of assembly and imposing a death penalty without trial, was nonetheless dripping with "the crimson of North Carolina" in the eyes of Ethan Allen and his allies.

Document 9, excerpts from "Yankee Response to the 'Bloody Act,'" is an early example of how the New Hampshire titleholders linked their land claims to natural law and the preservation of revered New England institutions. Rhetorical association of the New York legislation with repressive laws that Draco imposed on Athens in the seventh century B.C. inspired the Yankee propagandists to label it the "Bloody Act."

Document 10, Ethan Allen's "Warning to the East-Side Yorkers," illustrates the existence of opposition to Green Mountain Boy leadership among settlers in the eastern region of the Grants, many of whom had either purchased confirmation of their New Hampshire titles or otherwise acquired an interest in New York titles. Crean Brush and Samuel Wells, representatives for Cumberland County in the New York legislature, were vocal supporters of the "Bloody Act" and publicly denounced the Green Mountain Boys as lawless rioters. This warning, made public shortly after the details of the "Bloody Act" became known, was Allen's way of intimidating Yorker supporters and advertising the power of the Green Mountain Boys.

Though the matter of New Hampshire titles was never as divisive a concern in the east as in the west, by March 1775 other issues precipitated a breakdown of New York authority in Cumberland and Gloucester counties. Chief among these was the operation of the New York court system, both the symbol and instrument of economic oppression. The incident that effectively ended that authority was a court riot, the celebrated Westminster Massacre. As depicted in **Document 11** by participant Reuben Jones, the "massacre" originated in distrust of Cumberland County officials who failed to disclose to town officials communications from New York City's Committee of Correspondence. Others have described the Westminster Massacre as different from scores of other court riots only in its consequences. As Reuben Jones makes clear, its immediate cause was an effort by impoverished settlers to postpone debt proceedings. Their demand was that no court be held until after harvest, when they could pay debts more easily. Whatever the reasons for the incident, the two protesters killed in the courthouse became martyrs to the cause of liberty, irrespective of a larger justice.

Jones properly notes the rioters received immediate support from the New Hampshire and Massachusetts patriot associations. The support of a delegation of Green

Mountain Boys from the west came later but proved more important, for the lasting significance of the Westminster riot was that it united rebellious factions from both sides of the Grants in opposition to New York.

The larger conflict over governance of Great Britain's North American colonies through the British Parliament added a new dimension to the struggle over the New York-New Hampshire Grants. Colonial resistance to constricting British control shaded events even before Westminster, but it was in April 1775 that the Revolutionary movement came to full boil. Although there are Vermonters who insist that the first blood spilt in the American Revolution was at Westminster, historians date the war from April 19 and the military engagements at Lexington and Concord. **Document 12**, "The Bennington Declaration for Freedom," affirmed Grants support for resistance against England, but its authors, perhaps seeking colonial unity, failed to associate their New York opponents with the Tory cause.

Ethan Allen quickly remedied this omission. As Michael Bellesiles has noted, "Allen's greatest political accomplishment proved his carefully wrought linkage of the American cause and republican ideology with the Grants settlers' claims to their own land and institutions.[1] The capture of Fort Ticonderoga was part of this strategy. Ethan was not the only observer to appreciate the fort's strategic value, but seizing it propelled him into the front ranks of national heroes. Allen's *Narrative*, excerpted in **Document 13**, describes how acting under "directions" received from Connecticut, he and his Green Mountain Boys won a great military victory by capturing a fort located in New York. Published four years after the deed that demonstrated the caliber of the Green Mountain Boys, the *Narrative* enjoyed a popularity that publicized the virtue of their cause and led Congress to commission them as a regiment.

Document 14, a letter from Ethan Allen to the Continental Congress, was his hasty reaction to learning that Congress anticipated abandoning Fort Ticonderoga and relocating troops and captured artillery to the southern end of Lake George. Allen was outraged. Not only would this strategy leave settlers on the western shores of the Grants vulnerable to attacks, it also repudiated Allen's grand plan for an immediate invasion of

Canada. When Congress sent an army into Canada several months later, Ethan went along, and on September 25, 1775, he was captured by the British while leading a poorly conceived assault of Montreal. He remained a British prisoner until May 31, 1778.

Ethan's departure had no influence over military operations on Lake Champlain. Control of the Lake Champlain corridor, constituting the largest segment of a principal military and commercial highway connecting New York City and Quebec, remained a major military and political objective of the combatants. Early in the war the Champlain Valley served as a route for an American invasion of Canada. By October 1776, however, the rebel forces had retreated and the British mounted a drive south with the recapture of Fort Ticonderoga as their immediate objective.

As revealed in **Document 15**, a British account of the Battle of Valcour, a major obstacle to the British advance was a rebel fleet built by and under the command of the American general Benedict Arnold. Arnold had accompanied the Green Mountain Boys in the capture of Fort Ticonderoga and fashioned much of the Champlain corridor's defense strategy. His decision to build a Lake Champlain fleet forced the British to build one as well and delayed their offensive for several months. Arnold's tactics in engaging the vastly superior British fleet provide testimony to his courage and seamanship, but creating an American fleet was the greater achievement. Some historians question Arnold's decision to engage the British at Valcour Island, since shortly after the battle and faced with a long siege and the onset of winter, Carleton abandoned the campaign and returned to Canada. These historians suggest Arnold should have saved his fleet to oppose the British the following summer.

Document 16 is the Grants' formal declaration of independence and a petition to Congress for representation in that body as a state, adopted January 1777, after a series of earlier westside conventions. Styling itself New Connecticut and reciting grievances against New York while enunciating natural law principles embodied in the American Declaration of Independence, its framers set forth their right "to form themselves into a separate state or government," and set the date for a convention the following June in Windsor, where they would promulgate a constitution for the new state that would take the name Vermont.

---

[1]Michael Bellesiles, *Revolutionary Outlaws: Ethan Allen and the Struggle for Independence on the Early American Frontier* (Charlottesville: University of Virginia Press, 1993), p. 105.

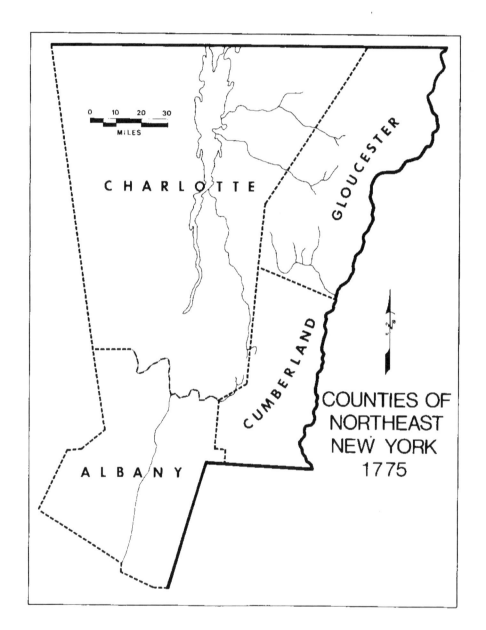

Source: H.N. Muller, III and Samuel B. Hand, eds., *In A State of Nature: Readings in Vermont History* (Montpelier, Vt.: Vermont Historical Society, 1982), p. 44.

Proclamation Reasserting New York Control of the Vermont Area (1763)

CADWALLADER COLDEN

Whereas King Charles the Second, by his several Letters Patent . . . did give and grant in Fee, unto his Brother, James Duke of York, certain Lands of which the Province of New York is a Part; containing among other Tracts, "All that Island or Islands, commonly called by the several Name or Names of Matowacks, or Long Island, situate and being towards the West of Cape Cod, and the Narrow Higgansetts, abutting upon the main Land between the two Rivers there called or known by the several names of Connecticut and Hudson's River. Together also with the said River, called Hudson's River, and all the land from the West Side of Connecticut River, to the East Side of Delaware Bay. . . ."

And whereas it manifestly appears by the several Grants or Letters Patent above recited, that the Province of New York is bounded to the Eastward by the River Connecticut: That the Province of New-Hampshire, being expressly limited in its Extent Westward and Northward by His Majesty's other Government, is confined to the same River as to its Western Boundary; and that the said Government of New-Hampshire is not intituled to Jurisdiction Westward, beyond the Limits of that River.

And whereas the said Government of New-Hampshire, tho' fully apprized of the Right of this Government . . . hath granted Lands Westward of Connecticut River, within the Limits and Jurisdiction of the Government of New-York; in Virtue whereof, sundry Persons, ignorant that they could not derive a legal Title under such Grants, have attempted the Settlement of the Lands included therein, and have actually possessed themselves of Soil before granted within this Province; while others claiming under the said Government of New-Hampshire, have endeavored to impose on the Inhabitants here, by offering to Sale, at a low Rate, whole Townships of Six Miles Square, lately granted by the said Government Westward of Connecticut River.

To prevent therefore the Incautious from becoming Purchasers of the Lands so granted; to assert the Rights, and fully to maintain the Jurisdiction of the Government of this His Majesty's Province of New-York; I have thought fit, with the Advice of His Majesty's Council, to issue this Proclamation, hereby commanding and requiring all Judges, Justices, and other Civil Officers within the same, to continue to exercise Jurisdiction in their respective Functions, as far as to the Banks of Connecticut River, the undoubted Eastern Limits of that Part of the Province of New-York, notwithstanding any Contrariety of Jurisdiction claimed by the Government of New-Hampshire, or any Grants of Land Westward of that River, made by the said Government. AND I DO hereby enjoin the High Sheriff of the County of Albany, to return to me or the Commander in chief, the Names of all and every Person and Persons, who under the Grants of the Government of New-Hampshire, do or shall hold the Possession of any Lands Westward of Connecticut River, that they may be proceeded against according to Law.

Given under my Hand and Seal at Arms, at Fort-George, in the City of New-York, the Twenty-eighth Day of December, 1763, in the Fourth Year of the Reign of our Sovereign Lord George the Third, by the Grace of God, of Great Britain, France, and Ireland, King, Defender of the Faith, and so forth.

Cadwallader Colden

God Save the King

Source: E.P. Walton, ed., *Records of the Governor and Council of the State of Vermont*, Vol. 8 (Montpelier: Steam Press, 1880), pp. 366-368.

DOCUMENT 2

Proclamation Reasserting New Hampshire Control of the Vermont Area (1764)

BENNING WENTWORTH

Whereas his Honor, Cadwallader Colden, Esq. Lieutenant Governor and Commander in Chief of his Majesty's Province of New-York, hath lately issued a Proclamation, of a very extraordinary nature, setting forth, that King Charles the Second, on the 12 day of March, 1663-4, and the 29th June, 1764, did, by his several letters patent, of those dates, grant, in Fee, to his brother, the Duke of York, among other things, all the land from the west side of Connecticut River to the east side of Delaware Bay; and therein also set forth, and describes the bounds of New-Hampshire; in which description there is a very material mistake; besides, there is omitted the fact, on which the description of New-Hampshire depended, viz. His Majesty's determination of the north and western boundaries of the Province of the Massachusetts Bay, in 1739. And nothing can be more evident, than that New-Hampshire may legally extend her western boundary as far as the Massachusetts claim reaches; and she claims no more; but New-York pretends to claim even to the banks of Connecticut River, although she never laid out and settled one town in that part of his Majesty's lands, since she existed as a government. . . .

At present, the boundaries of New-York, to the northward, are unknown; and as soon as it shall be his Majesty's pleasure to determine them, New-Hampshire will pay ready and cheerful obedience thereunto, not doubting but that all grants made by New-Hampshire, that are fulfilled by the grantees, will be confirmed to them, if it should be his Majesty's pleasure to alter the jurisdiction.

For political reasons, the claims to jurisdiction by New-York, might have been deferred, as well as the strict injunction on the civil power, to exercise jurisdiction in their respective functions, as far as the eastern banks of Connecticut River.

The said Proclamation, carrying an air of government in it, may possibly affect and retard the settlement of his Majesty's lands, granted by this government. For preventing an injury to the crown, of this kind, and to remove all doubts that may arise to persons holding the king's grants, they may be assured, that the patent to the Duke of York is obsolete, and cannot convey any certain boundary to New-York, that can be claimed as a boundary, as plainly appears by the several boundary lines of the Jersies on the west, and the Colony of Connecticut on the east, which are set forth in the Proclamation, as part, only, of the land included in the said patent to the Duke of York.

To the end therefore, that the grantees now settled and settling on those lands, under his late and present Majesty's charters, may not be intimidated, or any way hindered or obstructed in the improvement of the lands so granted, as well as to ascertain the right, and maintain the jurisdiction of his Majesty's government of New-Hampshire, as far westward as to include the grants made:

I have thought fit, by and with the advice of his Majesty's council, to issue this Proclamation, hereby encouraging the several grantees, claiming under this government, to be industrious in clearing and cultivating their lands, agreeable to their respective grants.

And I do hereby require and command all civil officers, within this Province, of what quality soever, as well those that are not, as those that are inhabitants on the said lands, to continue and be diligent in exercising jurisdiction in their respective offices, as far westward as grants of land have been made by this government; and to deal with any person or persons, that may presume to interrupt the inhabitants or settlers on said lands, as to law and justice do appertain; the pretended right of jurisdiction mentioned in the aforesaid Proclamation, notwithstanding.

Given at the Council-Chamber, in Portsmouth, the 13th day of March, 1764, and in the fourth year of his Majesty's Reign.

B. Wentworth

God Save the King

Source: William Slade, comp., *Vermont State Papers* (Middlebury, Vt: J.W. Copeland, 1823), pp. 17-18.

DOCUMENT 3

Order in Council Fixing the Connecticut River as the Boundary between New York and New Hampshire (1764)

At the Court of St. James the 20th Day of July 1764
Present
The Kings most Excellent Majesty

Lord Steward	Earl of Hilsborough
Earl of Sandwich	Mr. Vice Chamberlain
Earl of Halifax	Gilbert Elliot Esqr.
Earl of Powis	James Oswald Esqr.
Earl of Harcourt	

Whereas there was this Day read at the Board, a Report made by the Right Honourable the Lords of the Committee of Council for Plantation affairs dated the 17th of this Instant, upon Considering a Representation from the Lords Commissioners for Trade and Plantations, relative to the Disputes that have some years Subsisted between the Provinces of New Hampshire and New York concerning the Boundary Line between those Provinces. His Majesty taking the same into consideration was pleased with the advice of his privy Council to approve of what is therein proposed, and doth accordingly hereby Order and Declare the Western Banks of the River Connecticut, from where it enters the Province of the Massachusets Bay, as far North as the forty fifth Degree of Northern Latitude, to be the Boundary Line between the said two Provinces of New Hampshire and New York. Whereof the respective Governors and Commanders in Chief of his Majesty's said Provinces of New Hampshire and New York for the time being and all others whom it may Concern are to take notice of his Majesty's Pleasure hereby signified and Govern themselves accordingly.

Source: William Slade, comp., *Vermont State Papers* (Middlebury, Vt.: J.W. Copeland, 1823), p. 19.

DOCUMENT 4

Abenaki Lease of Swanton Falls to James Robertson (1765)

Know all men by these presents, that we, Daniel Poorneuf, Francois Abernard, Francois Joseph, Jean Baptiste, Jeanoses, Charlotte, widow of the late chief of the Abenackque nation at Missique, Mariane Poorneuf, Theresa, daughter of Joseph Michel, Magdalene Abernard, and Joseph Abomsawin, for themselves, heirs, assigns, etc., do sell, let, and concede unto Mr. James Robertson, merchant of St. Jean, his heirs, etc., for the space of ninety one years from the 28th day of May, 1765, a certain tract of land lying and being situated as follows, viz: being in the bay of Missisque on a certain point of land, which runs out into the said bay and the river of Missisque, running from the mouth up said river near east, one league and a half, and in depth north and south running from each side of the river sixty arpents, bounded on the bank of the aforesaid bay and etc., and at the end of the said league and a half to lands belonging to Indians joining to a tree marked on the south side of the river, said lands belonging to old Abernard; and on the north side of said river to lands belonging to old Whitehead; retaining and reserving to the proprietors hereafter mentioned, to wit; on the north side of said river five farms belonging to Pierre Peckenowax, Francois Nichowizet, Annus Jean, Baptiste Momtock, Joseph Comprent, and on the south side of said river seven farms belonging to Towgisheat, Cecile, Annome Quisse, Jemonganz, Willsomquax, Jean Baptiste the Whitehead, and old Etienne, for them and their heirs, said farms contain two arpents* in front nearly, and sixty in depth.

Now the condition of this lease is, that if the aforesaid James Robertson, himself, his heirs, and assigns or administrators, do pay and accomplish unto the aforesaid Daniel Poorneuf et als, their heirs, etc., a yearly rent of fourteen Spanish dollars, two bushels of Indian corn, and one gallon of rum, and to plow as much land for each of the above persons as shall be sufficient for them to plant their Indian corn every year, not exceeding more than will serve to plant one quarter of a bushel for each family, to them and their heirs and assigns; for which and every said article well and truly accomplished the said James Robertson is said to have and to hold for the aforesaid space of time, for himself, his heirs, etc., the aforesaid tract of land as mentioned aforesaid, to build thereon and establish the same for his use, and to concede to inhabitants make plantations, cut timber of what sort or kind he shall think proper for his use or the use of his heirs, etc., and for the performance of all and every article of the said convenant and agreement either of the said parties bindeth himself unto the other firmly be these presents.

* Arpent: French measure of approximately one acre

Source: Colin G. Calloway, ed., *Dawnland Encounters: Indians and Europeans in Northern New England* (Hanover, N.H.: University Press of New England, 1991), pp. 206-207.

DOCUMENT 5

Petition to the King by New Hampshire Grants Settlers Asking That Grants Be Put under New Hampshire Jurisdiction (1766)

Sheweth to Your Majesty;

That we obtained at considerable Expence of Your Majesty's Governor of the Province of *New-Hampshire*, Grants and patents for more than One Hundred Townships in the Western Parts of the said supposed Province; and being about to settle the same, many of Us, and others of us, having actually planted Ourselves on the same, were disagreeably surprized and prevented from going on with the further intended Settlements, by the News of its having been determined by your Majesty in Council, That those Lands were within the Province of *New-York*; and by a Proclamation issued by Lieutenant Governor Colden, in Consequence thereof forbidding any further Settlement until Patents of Confirmation should be obtained from the Governor of *New-York*. Whereupon We applied to the Governor of said Province of *New-York*, to have the same Lands confirmed to Us in the same Manner as they had been at first granted to Us by the Governor of the said Province of *New-Hampshire*; when, to our utter Astonishment, We found the same could not be done,

without our paying as Fees of Office for the same, at the Rate of *Twenty Five Pounds*, *New-York* Money, equal to about *Fourteen Pounds* Sterling, for every Thousand Acres of said Lands, amounting to about *Three Hundred and Thirty Pounds* Sterling at a Medium, for each of said Townships, and which will amount in the Whole to about £33,000 Sterling, besides a Quit-rent of *Two Shillings and Six Pence* Sterling, for every Hundred Acres of said Lands; and which being utterly unable to do and perform, We find Ourselves reduced to the sad Necessity of losing all our past Expence and Advancements; and many of Us of being reduced to absolute Poverty and Want, having expended Our All in making said Settlements.

Whereupon Your Petitioners beg Leave most Humbly to observe,

1. That when We applied for and obtained said Grants of said Lands, the same were and had been at all Times fully understood and reputed to lie and be within the said Province of *New-Hampshire*, and well within the Power of the Governor of that Province to grant: So that Your Petitioners humbly hope they are equitably entitled to a Confirmation of the said Grants to them.

2. The said Grants were made and received on the moderate Terms of Your Petitioners paying as a Quit-rent *One Shilling* only, Proclamation Money, equal to *Nine Pence* Sterling per Hundred Acres; and which induced Us to undertake to settle said Townships throughout, and thereby to form a full and compacted Country of People, whereas the imposing the said *Two Shillings* and *Six Pence* Sterling per Hundred Acres, will occasion all the more rough and unprofitable Parts of said Lands not to be taken up; but Pitches, and the more valuable Parcels only to be laid out, to the utter preventing the full and proper Settlement of said Country, and in the Whole to the lessening Your Majesty's Revenue.

3. Your humble Petitioners conceive, that the insisting to have large and very exorbitant Fees of Office to arise and be computed upon every Thousand Acres in every Township of Six or perhaps more Miles square, and that when one Patent, one Seal, and one Step only of every Kind, toward the completing such Patents of

Confirmation respectively, is necessary, is without all reasonable and equitable Foundation, and must and will necessarily terminate in the totally preventing Your Petitioners obtaining the said Lands, and so the same will fall into Hands of the Rich, to be taken up, the more valuable Parts only as aforesaid, and those perhaps not entered upon and settled for many Years to come; while Your Petitioners with their numerous and helpless Families, will be obliged to wander far and wide to find where to plant themselves down, so as to be able to live.

Whereupon Your Petitioners most humbly and earnestly pray, that Your Majesty will be graciously pleased to take their distressed State and Condition into Your Royal Consideration, and order that We have Our said Lands confirmed and quitted to Us, on such reasonable Terms, and in such Way and Manner, as Your Majesty shall think fit. Further, We beg Leave to say, that if it might be consistent with Your Majesty's Royal Pleasure, We shall esteem it a very great Favour and Happiness, to have said Townships put and continued under the Jurisdiction of the Government of the said Province of *New-Hampshire*, as at the first, as every Emolument and Convenience both publick and private, are in Your Petitioners' humble Opinion, clearly and strongly on the Side of such Connection with said *New-Hampshire* Province. All which Favours or such and so many of them as to Your Majesty shall seem meet to grant, We humbly ask; or that Your Majesty will in some other Way grant Relief to Your Petitioners; and they, as in Duty bound, shall ever pray.

Dated in New-England, November 1766. *And in the* Seventh *Year of His Majesty's Reign.*

Source: *Collections of the Vermont Historical Society*, Vol. 1 (Montpelier: Vermont Historical Society, 1870), pp. 279-281.

DOCUMENT 6

"The Vision of Junus, the Benningtonite" (1772)
[ETHAN ALLEN?]

The word of the L—d, which came unto Junus, the servant of the L—d, when Dunmore,

Duane, Colden and Kemp, with all their confederates, found against Bennington, and the adjacent country. Thus saith the L—d: "Son of man, set thy face towards the bloody city, and I will show thee what thou must reveal on the house tops, even the great abomination of the Yorkites, and their outrages committed on my chosen people in the North."

So I turned my face towards the abominable city, and the spirit of the L—d rested upon me, and I saw, and behold an evil spirit from the devil seated on the heads of Duane amd Kemp, and they conspired together against the L—d's inheritance, striving to set the Lord's anointed against his people, falsely accusing them before the Court of Great Britain, purposing, by fallacy, craft and hostility, to lay waste the holy hill of Bennington, and drive the pople from the goodly land of which the L—d said unto them: "Go in and possess it, thou and thy seed, forever, and drive out the heathen before thee."

And he said unto me: "Son of man, hast thou seen all of this? Turn thee towards Albany, and I will show thee greater abominations than these."

So the spirit lifted me up, and turned my face thither, and, behold, the Albanians, Schanachidyans, Kocksochkeens, and the Kinderhookites, Claverichites and the Saintcoichites, and sundry other tribes of the Yorkites, who know not the L—d, has assembled themselves together in great numbers against the chosen people of the L—d. For a lying spirit had gone forth from New York, and had commanded and inveigled the Yorkites, saying, "Go up to Bennington and smite, and ravage the Holy Mount."

They likewise compelled many of the servants of the L—d, who wished well to the Mount Bennington, to go with them. But the L—d disconcerted the Yorkites at that time, putting his hook in their nose, and turning them back by the way that they came, not suffering them to afflict his Elect.

And he said unto me: "Son of man, turn thee yet again towards New York, and I will show you greater abominations."

So the spirit lifted me up, and brought me to the door of the Court House at New York, which looketh towards the east, and said, "Go in." So I went in, and, behold, suborned men stood before the elders, with censers in their hands, and thick cloud of perjury went up, while they falsely accused the People of the L—d, the inhabitants of Bennington and the adjacent country, before George, the L—d's anointed.

But their device shall not prosper, neither shall it take effect, for the heart of my anointed is right before me, saith the L—d, and he shall administer justice to my people, and defend my holy hill of Bennington from the ravages of the Yorkites.

And the hand of the L—d was upon me, and brought me to the house of his servant [Remember] Baker, the Arlingtonite, and, behold, the house was polluted with blood, Baker severely wounded and taken prisoner by the enemies of the L—d, and his wife and eldest son lamenting in their gore, not so much on account of their own wounds as the loss of tender husband and father.

And I was amazed and sore troubled, and said, L—d how is it that thou sufferest thy chosen ones to be trodden down by the heathen, who do not regard thy great name? And he said unto me, "Son of man, fear not, for in the fullness of time I will appear for my people, and confound the Yorkites."

And the L—d stirred up the spirit of the valiant Green Mountain Boys, and they pursued, and retook Baker.

He also enraged the spirit of his servants Sagacious and Foresight, and wrought powerfully upon his old servant Substantial, and moved the hearts of the distressed people, as the hearts of the trees are moved with the winds, and they discomfited the perfidious Yorkites that dwelt among them, and they fled to New York with great wrath, hoping to excite the power of government to destroy the inhabitants of the L—d, and make Bennington a heap of stones. . . .

And the word of the L—d came yet again unto me, saying, Son of man, prophecy against the oppressive city, and say unto it, behold, I have given you a goodly sea-port situation, near *Hell-gate*, and also a navigable river; and thou hast greatly extended thy trade, and art grown very rich: wherefore, then, covetest thou the lands and labors of my servants in the North? Why will ye grind the face of new settlers, and distress the needy? Let your own portion suffice you; for if you again your posse, and go forth to fight against Bennington, the Green Mountain Boys will not be frightened, and they shall ambush you, saith the L—d, for they well understand the narrow passes of the mountains, and are lusty and strong, and are well skilled in the use of the bow; and in very deed, for this purpose have I raised them up, that they should defend my holy

hill of Bennington, and the adjacent country, from the oppression of the Yorkites.

And the word of the L—d came again unto me, saying, Speak unto the Yorkites, and say unto them: Why are ye so greedy after dominion as to annex that part of the Bay province west of the Connecticut River to the Province of New York and County of Albany? Know ye not that unbounded desires are unfailing sources of unbounded troubles? For the Massachusetts inhabitants will not be imposed upon by your tricks, but they will make you tremble at their vengeance.

And the word of the L—d came yet again unto me, saying, Son of man, speak unto Duane and Kemp, and their associates, and say unto them: You have been the principal cause of troubling my people, and except ye do now speedily repent and turn from your hateful abominations, and cease troubling my people, and leave them to the quiet and peaceable possession of their inheritance, it shall happen unto you as it did unto Pharaoh, King of Egypt. I will send my plagues upon you, and on each of your houses and families, and ye shall be afflicted day and night, and languish out your lives by severe pangs of conscious guilt and repeated disappointments, and die in excruciating pain and horror. For I will never withdraw my hand until I have fully avenged the cause of my people.

And lastly, the word of the L—d came unto me, saying, Son of man, prophecy against Munro and Willoughby, and cry against them, saying: Wo! Wo! Wo! unto them, for thus saith the L—d, because ye have laid waste the house of my servant Baker, and polluted yourselves in blood, as also in that of his innocent family, of which their maimed limbs are a witness, even to this day, and because ye mocked him, crying aha! at his groans, when in thy hands, and because ye have clapped your hands against my people in despite of them, I will, for these things, stretch out my hands upon each of you, and your malicious accomplices, and ye shall become a spoil to your enemies, and I will cut you off from among my people, and cause you to perish from off that good land that I gave the New Hampshire settlers for an inheritance, so I will surely destroy thee, that others may hear and fear, and do no more so wickedly.

Junus.

Source: "The Vision of Junus, the Benningtonite," in *Collections of the Vermont Historical Society*, Vol. 1 (Montpelier: Vermont Historical Society, 1870), pp. 106-108.

DOCUMENT 7

"Autobiography" (1772-1773)
IRA ALLEN

[September 1772] We proceeded to Shelburn and stopped at Acres Point, being wind-bound, when [Remember] Baker and I. Vanornom set out through the woods to see and lands and find New Huntington corner, which Baker had seen when in pursuit of Cockburn; and to see if they could discover any sign of N. York surveyors in the woods. We were to meet at the falls of Onion river as soon as the wind would admit. The other men with me went on with the boat to said falls. On landing, I found a camp with some provisions &c. that induced me to suppose that a New York surveyor was in the woods. I carefully left the camp, leaving no signs of our having been there, and went down the river about two miles to a large intervale, and there formed a camp. I left a sentinel to look out for Baker at the falls, and to see who might come to the camp. My sentinels not being old soldiers, were inattentive, and Baker passed them; and, not finding me, or any signs of my being there, was very hungry and ate some of said stores. After we met, we continued a sentinel and waited some days for the party to come in. When they arrived, Capt. Stevens the Surveyor discovered that somebody had been there, and before we could attack the camp, made his escape with most of his party, leaving two men in the camp, which we made prisoners of. Not being able to learn certainly where Stevens was gone, we waited till near dark; when we took Stevens' boat, stores, and prisoners, and set out for our camp. In the twilight, two boats were discovered coming towards us, who turned and made off faster than we could persue; nor could we discover their numbers &c. We hurried them by our stores &c., which we had taken the precaution in some measure to secrete. It was then agreed to remain there for the night and keep a lookout. In the morning before sun rise we discovered two boats coming up the river towards us, which proved to be two bark canoes, four of his men and ten Indians, all well armed with guns &c. and our whole party was seven men. Capt. Baker had a cutlass, I. Vanornam a gun and I a case of pistols. These were all the arms we had; nevertheless, we determined to defend the ground. I prepared our men with axes, clubs, &c., and arranged ourselves on the bank about two rods from the water, tying our prisoners to a pole behind. Stevens was the first man out of the canoes, and while the rest were getting out, he came up the bank with a hatchet in his hand, with large pistols pocket, and made towards Baker, brandishing his hatchet. Baker opened his brest, inviting to strike, if he dared. Stevens demanded why his men were tied. Baker answered it was his pleasure. Stevens drew a scalping knife from his bosom, and turned towards them, (not daring to attempt to strike Baker, as Vanornam's gun was pointed on him.) When about 30 feet of me, I presented a pistol at him, with a solemn word that death was his portion instantly if he stepped one step farther, or attempted to touch the pistols in his pocket. At this, he stopped with a pale countenance, & by this time, his party appeared prepared to come up the bank; when I spoke to Vanornam, who had been a prisoner with the Indians to tell the redmen in their own language, that they and we were brothers, that they were welcome to hunt &c., on our lands when they pleased, that this was a land quarrel, that did not concern them. Vanornam spoke to them in their own language to that effect, and they instantly leaped to their canoes, leaving Stevens and his men prisoners. Stevens then asked me whether I should have fired if he had not stopped. I told him I should for I [had] no notion of being a prisoner & tryed by the Supreme Court of New York by the acts of outlawry &c. Then pointing the same pistol to a small mark, less than a dollar, in a pole, about the same distance as Stevens was from me, observing that I would suppose that pole to be his body and the mark his heart, I fired. The ball (by chance) struck the pole about half an inch under the mark. There being a truce between Govr. Tryon and the people of the district of the New Hampshire Grants, we thought it would not be politic to inflict corporial punishment on Stevens. He and his men were dismissed, on pain of death never to come within the district of the New Hampshire Grants again. Their boat, stores &c. were also returned to them and we parted.

While waiting for the surveying party to come out of the woods, I explored the intervales below the falls of said Onion river, and pitched my tent by a large pitch pine tree nearly opposite to an island, about one and a half miles below the falls, where I had observed large intervales on both sides of the river, when I first went up, and landed for the first time I ever set my foot on the fertile soil of Onion river, at the lower end of the meadow now known by the name of the old fields, where I discovered from my boat an opening like cleared lands. In consequence, I directed my men to refresh themselves with spirits and water, while I went to view the lands. I went up the open meadow where the blue joint grass &c., was thick till in sight of a large and lonely elm. Computing the open field about fifty acres, I was much pleased with this excursion, promising myself one day to be the owner of that beautiful meadow. . . .

[Summer 1773] In the course of this Summer, to prevent settlements under N. York, Col. Ethan Allen with near one hundred Green Mountain Boys came to New Haven falls, and erected a block fort, disconcerting a party of Scotchmen brought out from Scotland by the influence of Col. Reed to settle there.

For personal safety, &c. Capt. Baker and I though proper to erect a block fort near the falls of Onion river, twenty by thirty two feet, every stick of timber was at least eight inches thick. In the second story, were 32 port holes for small arms. The roof was so constructed, in case of fire, we could throw it off—the second story jutted four inches over the other, so that we could fire down, or throw water to put out fire; and the fort was built over a boiling spring for certainty of water. We made double doors, blocks, for the windows, and every part proof against small arms. We never walked out without at least a case of pistols. In this situation, we were a terror to the New York claimants &c. . . .

[Summer 1773] Then ambition, vigor of youth, with a firm constitution united to acquire a character and fortune; but I had many difficulties to surmount. I had very little learning, what property I had acquired was principally in lands in Poultney, Castleton, and Hubbardton, which I had left in the agency of my Brother Zimry Allen, to sell to the best advantage. After these discoveries, I wrote to him pressingly to sell the whole, or any part that would command ready pay, or that could be realized early the next winter, to apply to the purchase of lands contiguous to Onion river, and lake Champlain; for that was the country my soul delighted in, and where, at all events, I was determined to make settlement. Zimry was an enterprising young man, very attentive and active in business, but of slender constitution, and could not therefore accompany

me to the woods, but could ride about and attend to business. But the disputes with New York, the great quantities of land for sale, the towns aforesaid, especially Hubbardton, not being of the best, put it out of his power in the course of this year to make any sales of consequence.

When the partnership of the Onion river Co. was agreed on in the preceeding winter, my brother Heman engaged me to look out for him the best place for trade, at or near lake Champlain. He then contemplated Skeensborough, as in his opinion, from the knowledge of the country he had acquired, to be the place; but wishes me to have a view to this object when exploring the country; which I faithfully attended to, and gave Burlington Bay the preference of any part of the country, from the discoveries I had made in the preceeding expeditions. Skeensborough I considered as an unhealthy place, therefore illy applied to Hemans weakly constitution. Besides, although the head of navigation in the lake, it was too near the river Hudson to be of consequence. From different considerations, Burlington would, from its situation, become a place of consequence; and that the fertile intervals, &c., adjacent, being in large proportions owned by the Allen family, might induce them to move to that part of the country, and by their influence and friends, make it of consequence in their day, both for commerce and society in the neighborhood. With these views, I went and pitched a number of hundred acre lots contiguous to Burlington Bay. The land in itself, was the greater part poor looking pine plain. This move of mine astonished my friends, who had observed me to be very enterprising in pitching good lands, and that much good lands remained untouched in Burlington, I gave no reasons for my conduct, which raised many questions and disputes. Indeed I did not but in part explain myself to my worthy friend and partner Baker, for I found he had little opinion of that place; but looked for good lands more than situations, observing; that good lands would certainly be of consequence, but it was hard to determine where places of consequence would arise in a country so extensive and new. . . .

Source: Ira Allen, "Autobiography," in James B. Wilbur, *Ira Allen: Founder of Vermont, 1751-1814*, Vol. 1 (Boston: Houghton Mifflin Co., 1925), pp. 16-18, 44, 53-55.

DOCUMENT 8

New York's "Bloody Act" (1774)

WHEREAS a spirit of riot and licentiousness has, of late, prevailed in some parts of the counties of Charlotte *and* Albany, *and many acts of outrage and cruelty have been perpetrated by a number of turbulent men, who, assembling from time to time, in arms, have seized, insulted and menaced, several magistrates,—rescued prisoners for debt—assumed to themselves military commends, and judicial powers—burned and demolished houses and property, and beat and abused the persons of many of his Majesty's subjects—expelled others from their possessions—and finally, have put a period to the administration of justice within, and spread terror and destruction throughout, that part of the country which is exposed to their oppression: Therefore, for the preventing and suppressing such riots and tumults, and for the more speedy and effectual punishing the offenders therein.*

1. *Be it enacted*, by his Excellency the Governor, the Council, and the General Assembly, and it is hereby enacted, by the authority of the same, That, if any persons, to the number of three, or more, being unlawfully, riotously, and tumultuously assembled, within either of the said counties, to the disturbance of the public peace, at any time after the passing of this act, and being required or commanded, by any one or more justice or justices of the peace, or by the high sheriff, or his under sheriff, or by any one of the coroners of the county where such assembly shall be, by proclamation to be made in the King's name . . .

   to disperse themselves, and peaceably to depart to their habitations, or to their lawful business, shall, to the number of three, or more, notwithstanding such proclamation made, unlawfully, riotously, and tumultuously remain or continue together, to the number of three, or more, after such command or request made by proclamation, shall for every such offence, upon conviction thereof, in due form of law . . . suffer twelve months imprisonment, without bail . . . and such further corporal punishment as the respective

   courts before which he, she, or they, shall be convicted, shall judge fit, not extending to life and limb. . . .

3. *And be it further enacted* by the authority aforesaid, That if any person or persons do, or shall, with force and arms, wilfully and knowingly oppose, obstruct, or in any manner, wilfully and knowingly let, hinder or hurt any person or persons, who shall begin to proclaim, or go to proclaim, according to the proclamation hereby directed to be made, whereby such proclamation shall not be made; . . . such person or persons . . . shall be adjudged felony, without benefit of clergy; and that the offenders therein, shall be adjudged felons, and shall suffer death, as in cases of felony without benefit of clergy. . . .

4. *And be it further enacted* by the authority aforesaid, That if such persons so unlawfully, riotously and tumultuously assembled, or any three or more of them, after proclamation made in manner aforesaid, shall continue together, and not forthwith disperse themselves, it shall and may be lawful to and for every such justice of the peace, sheriff, under sheriff, coroner, or constable, of any country or township where such assembly shall be: . . . to seize and apprehend . . . such persons so unlawfully, riotously, and tumultuously assembled together . . . in order to their being proceeded against for such their offences according to law.

   And that, if the persons so unlawfully, riotously and tumultuously assembled, or any of them, shall happen to be killed, maimed, or hurt, in the dispersing, seizing or apprehending them, by reason of their resisting the persons so dispersing, seizing, or apprehending, or endeavouring to disperse, seize, or apprehend them; that then, every such justice of the peace, sheriff, under sheriff, coroner or constable, and all and singular persons aiding and assisting to them, or any of them, shall be freed, discharged, and indemnified, as well against the King's Majesty, his heirs and successors, as against all and every other person or persons, of, for, or concerning the killing, maiming, or hurting of any such person or persons, so unlawfully, riotously, and tumultuously assembled, that shall happen to be so killed, maimed, or hurt as aforesaid.

5. *And be it further enacted* . . . That, if any person or persons, within the said counties, or either of them, not being lawfully authorized a judge, justice, or magistrate, shall assume judicial power . . . or if any person or persons shall aid or assist in such illegal proceedings, or shall enforce, execute or carry the same into effect; or if any person or persons shall, unlawfully, seize, detain, or confine, or assault and beat any magistrate or civil officer . . . in order to compel him to resign, renounce, or surcease his commission or authority, or to terrify, hinder, or prevent him from performing and discharging the duties thereof; or if any person or persons, either secretly or openly, shall, unlawfully, wilfully and maliciously, burn or destroy the grain, corn or hay, of any other person, being in any inclosure; or if any persons, unlawfully, riotously, and tumultuously assembled together, to the disturbance of the public peace, shall, unlawfully, and with force, demolish or pull down, or begin to demolish or pull down, any dwelling-house, barn, stable, grist-mill, saw-mill, or out-house, within either of the said counties; that then, each of the said offences, respectively, shall be adjudged felony, without benefit of clergy; and the offenders therein shall be adjudged felons, and shall suffer death, as in cases of felony without benefit of clergy.

6. And whereas complaint and proofs have been made, as well before his Excellency the Governor in Council, as before the General Assembly, That *Ethan Allen*, some time of *Salisbury*, in the colony of *Connecticut*, late of *Bennington*, in the county of *Albany*, yeoman; *Seth Warner*, late of *Bennington*, in the said county, yeoman; *Remember Baker*, late of *Arlington*, in the said county, yeoman; *Robert Cochran*, late of *Ruport*, in the county of *Charlotte*, yeoman; *Peleg Sunderland* and *Silvanus Brown*, late of Socialborough, in the same county, yeoman; *James Brackenridge*, late of *Wallumschack*, in the county of *Albany*, yeoman; and *John Smith*, late of *Socialborough*, yeoman; have been principal ring-leaders of, and actors in, the riots and disturbances aforesaid; and the general assembly have, thereupon, ad-

dressed his Excellency the Governor, to issue a proclamation offering certain rewards for apprehending and securing the said offenders, and for bringing them and the other perpetrators and authors of the riots to justice: And forasmuch as such disorderly practices are highly criminal and destructive to the peace and settlement of the country, and it is indispensably necessary for want of process to outlawry (which is not used in this colony) that special provision be made for bringing such offenders, in future, to trial and punishment. . . .

Be it further enacted . . . by the authority aforesaid, That it shall and may be lawful to, and for, his Excellency the Governor, or the Governor and Commander in Chief, for the time being, by, and with, the advice of the council, . . . to make his order in council, thereby requiring and commanding such offender or offenders to surrender themselves, respectively, within the space of seventy days next after the first publication thereof, in the *New-York* Gazette, and Weekly Mercury, to one of his Majesty's justices of the peace, for either of the said counties respectively. . . . And in case the said offenders shall not respectively surrender themselves . . . [they] shall, from the day to be appointed for his or their surrendry as aforesaid, be adjudged, deemed, and (if indicted for a capital offence hereafter to be perpetrated) to be convicted and attainted of felony, and shall suffer death, as in cases of persons convicted and attainted of felony, be verdict and judgment, without benefit of clergy. . . .

Source: William Slade, comp.,*Vermont State Papers* (Middlebury, Vt.: J.W. Copeland, 1823), pp. 42-46.

DOCUMENT 9

"Yankee Response to the 'Bloody Act'" (1774)

ETHAN ALLEN ET AL.

His Excellency, Governor *Tryon*, in conformity to the addresses of the general assembly of the colony of *New-*

York, having, on the 9th day of March, 1774, with the advice of his Council, issued his proclamation, offering, therein, large sums of money for the purpose of apprehending and imprisoning the following persons, viz. *Ethan Allen, Seth Warner, Remember Baker, Robert Cochran, Peleg Sunderland, Silvanus Brown, James Brackenridge,* and *James Smith.*

And whereas his Excellency the Governor, by the same proclamation, hath, strictly, enjoined and commanded all magistrates, justices of the peace, sheriffs, and other civil officers of the counties of *Albany* and *Charlotte*, to be active and vigilant in apprehending and imprisoning the persons above-named; and we, the aforesaid persons, who have hereunto subscribed, being conscious that our cause is good and equitable in the sight of GOD, and all unprejudiced and honest men, are determined, at all events, to maintain and defend the same, till his Majesty's pleasure shall be known concerning the validity of the *New-Hampshire* grants. —And we now proclaim to the public, not only for ourselves but for the *New-Hampshire* grantees, and occupants in general, that the spring, and moving cause, of our opposition to the government of *New-York*, was self-preservation, *viz.* Firstly, the preservation and maintaining of our property: and secondly, since that government is so incensed against us, therefore it stands us in hand to defend our lives; for, it appears, by a late set of laws passed by the legislature thereof, that the lives and property of the *New-Hampshire* settlers are manifestly struck at . . . [and] that their pretended zeal for good order and government, is fallacious, and that they aim at the lands and labours of the grantees and settlers aforesaid; and that they subvert the good and wholesome laws of the realm, to corroborate with, and bring about their vile and mercenary purposes.

And, inasmuch as the malignity of their disposition towards us, hath flamed to an immeasurable and murderous degree, they have, in their new-fangled laws, calculated for the meridian of the *New-Hampshire* grants, passed the 9th of March, 1774, so calculated them, as to correspond with the depravedness of their minds and morals. . . . The emblems of their insatiable, avaricious, overbearing, inhuman, barbarous, and blood-guiltiness of disposition and intention is therein portraited in that transparent image of themselves, which cannot fail to be a blot, and an infamous reproach to them, to posterity.—We cannot suppose that every

of his Majesty's Council, or that all the members of the general assembly were active in passing so bloody and unconstitutional a set of laws. Undoubtedly, some of them disapproved thereof; and it is altogether possible, that many that were active in making the law, were imposed upon by false representations, and acted under mistaken views of doing honor to government; but be this as it will, it appears that there was a majority. And it has been too much the case with that government, for a number of designing schemers, and land-jockeys, to rule the same. Let us take a view of their former narrow and circumscribed boundaries, and how, that by legerdemain, bribery and deceptions of one sort or other, they have extended their domain far and wide. They have wrangled with, and encroached on their neighbouring governments, and have used all manner of deceit and fraud to accomplish their designs: their tenants groan under their usury and oppression; and they have gained, as well as merited, the disapprobation and abhorence of their neighbours; and the innocent blood they have already shed, calls for heaven's vengeance on their guilty heads; and if they should come forth in arms against us, thousands of their injured and dissatisfied neighbours in the several governments, will join with us, to cut off, and extirpated such an execrable race from the face of the earth! . . .

To quote the laws, and make remarks thereon, would be matter sufficient for a volume: however, we will yet make some short observations.

1st. Negatively, it is not a law for the Province of *New-York* in general, but,

2nd. Positively, it is a law but for part of the counties of *Charlotte* and *Albany*, viz. such parts thereof as are covered with the *New-Hampshire* charters; and it is well known those grants compose but a minor part of the inhabitants of the said Province; and we have no representative in that assembly. The first knowledge we had of said laws, was the completion of them; which informed us, that if we assembled, three or more of us together, to oppose (that which they call legal) authority, we shall be adjudged felons, and suffer the pains of death. . . . If we oppose civil officers, in taking possession of our farms, we are, by these laws, denominated felons; or if we defend our neighbours who have been indicted rioters, only for defending our property; we are likewise adjudged felons. In fine, every opposition to their monarchical government is deemed felony, and at the end of every such sentence, there is the word DEATH! And the same laws further impowered the respective judges, provided any persons, to the number of three, or more, that shall oppose any Magistrate, or other civil officer, and be not taken, that after a legal warning of seventy days, if they do not come and yield themselves up to certain officers appointed for the purpose of securing them; then it shall be lawful for the judges aforesaid, to award execution of DEATH, the same as though he or they had been convicted or attainted before a proper court of judicature, &c. . . .

Those bloody law-givers know we are necessitated to oppose their execution of law, where it points directly at our property, or give up the same: but there is one thing is matter of consolation to us, viz. that printed sentences of death will not kill us when we are at a distance; and if the executioners approach us, they will be as likely to fall victims to death as we: and that person, or country of persons, are cowards indeed, if they cannot, as manfully, fight for their liberty, property and life, as villains can do to deprive them thereof.

The *New-York* schemers accuse us with many things; part of which are true, and part not. —With respect to rescuing prisoners for debt, it is *false*. As to assuming judicial powers, we *have not*, except a well-regulated combination of the people to defend their just rights, may be called so. As to forming ourselves into military order, and assuming military commands, the *New-York* possies, and military preparations, oppressions, &c. *obliged us to it*. Probably Messieurs *Duane, Kemp,* and *Banyar,* of *New York*, will not discommend us for so expedient a preparation; more especially since the decrees of the 9th of *March*, are yet to be put in execution: and we flatter ourselves, upon occasion, we can muster as good a regiment of mark's-men and scalpers, as *America* can afford; and we now give the gentlemen above-named, together with Mr. *Brush*, and Col. *Ten Broeck*, and in fine, all the land-jobbers of *New-York*, and invitation to come and view the dexterity of our regiment; and we cannot think of a better time for that purpose, than when the executioners come to kill us, by virtue of the authority their judges have lately received to award and sentence us to death in our absence. There is still one more notable complaint against us, viz. That we have insulted and menaced several magistrates, and other civil officers, so that they dare not execute their respective functions. This is *true*, so far as it relates to the magistrates. But the public should be informed, what the functions of those magistrates are:—they are commissioned for the sole purpose of doing us all the harm and mischief they possibly can, through their administration and influence; and that they might be subservient to the wicked designs of the *New-York* schemers. These are their functions; and the public need no further proof than the consideration that they are the tools of those extravagant law-makers; and it must be owned, they acted with great judgement, in choosing the most infernal instruments for their purpose.

Draco, the *Athenian* law-giver, caused a number of laws (in many respects analogous to those we have been speaking of,) to be *written* in blood. They well know we shall, more than *three*, nay, more than *three times three hundred*, assemble together, if need be, to maintain our common cause, till his Majesty determines who shall be and remain the owners of the land in contest. *"Wilt not thou possess that which Chemoth, thy God, giveth thee to possess?"* So will we possess that which the Lord our God (and King) giveth us to possess. . . .

Signed by   Ethan Allen,
                                 Seth Warner,
                                 Remember Baker,
                                 Robert Cockran,
                                 Peleg Sunderland,
                                 John Smith,
                                 Silvanus Brown.

Bennington, April 26, 1774.

The following lines, composed by Thomas Rowley, distinguished, in *those days*, for wit and poetry, appear to have been annexed to the foregoing.

> When *Caesar* reigned King at *Rome*
> St. *Paul* was sent to hear his doom;
> But *Roman* laws, in a criminal case,
> Must have the accuser face to face,
> Or *Caesar* gives a flat denial. —
> But here's a law made now of late,
> Which destines men to awful fate,
> And hangs and damns without a trial.

Which made me view all nature through,
To find a law where men were ti'd,
By legal act which doth exact
Men's lives before they're try'd.
Then down I took the sacred book,
And turn'd the pages o'er,
But could not find one of this kind,
By God or man before.

Source: William Slade, comp., *Vermont State Papers* (Middlebury, Vt.: J.W. Copeland Printers, 1823), pp. 49-54.

DOCUMENT 10

"Warning to the East-Side Yorkers" (1774)

ETHAN ALLEN

Mess'rs Crean Brush and Saml. Wells
Representatives for the County of Cumberland
Brattleborough

Bennington 19th of May 1774

Sr   I have sundry ways recd Intelligence of Your hatred and Malice Towards the N. Hampshire settlers on the west side the Range of Green Mountains and particularly Towards me the Repourt you made in behalf of Mr. Clinton is Noticed by the Green M Boys they have also Took a retrospective View of a Number of Learned Attorneys and Gentlemen (by Birth) Interested in the Lands (by N. York Title) on which they Dwell Deludeing the Assembly Part of the Members of which Undoubtedly are Honestly Disposed and Beguileing them Into a false Opinion that Those People You Call the Bennington Mob are Notorious Rioters &ce. You Know better and are sensible that they Onely Contend for their Property and that they have No Design Against the Government any further than to Protect the same I know it was the Land Schemers Influenced the Assembly to Pass the 12 Bloody Acts the 9th of March Ult. (Mr. Samuel Wells was very officious bringing it about) they then Laid a Trap for the Lives of those persons Proclamated for and Wells and you are but busie

Understrappers to a Number of More Overgrown Villains which Can Murther by Law without remorse, but I Have to Inform that the Green Mountain Boys will Not Tamely resign their Necks to the Halter to be Hang'd by your Curst Fraternity of Land Jockeys who Would Better Adorn a Halter than we, therefore as Your regard Your Own Lives be Carefull Not to Invade ours for what Measure You Meat it shall be Measured to You again.

Given Under my hand   Ethan Allen
the Day and Date afforesaid

P.S. Mr. Brush Sir/as a Testimony of Gratitude for the many unmerited kindnesses, and services, you have Done us the last sessions at New York &c. &c. we Intend Shortly visiting your Abode, where we hope to have the Honour of Presenting you with the BEECH SEAL: —which we Beg your kind Acceptance Off, as a mark of the high Esteem we have of your Person and as a Token of our Approbation for the Eminent Exertions you Displayed of your Abilitys in Bringing about the Salutary act of the 9th of March Last.

We Have the Honor Sir
To be yours sincearly
The Green Mountain Boys

Source: Allen Family Papers, Box 3, Folder 67; Special Collections, Bailey/Howe Library, University of Vermont.

DOCUMENT 11

The Westminster Massacre (1775)

A relation of the proceedings of the people of the County of Cumberland, and Province of New-York

In June, 1774, there were some letters came to the supervisors of said county, from the committee of correspondence at New-York, signed by their chairman, Mr. Low; which letters said supervisors, through ignorance or intention, kept until September, when they had another meeting; and it is supposed that they intended always to have kept them, and the good people would have remained in ignorance about them until this time, had it not been by accident that it was whispered abroad, so that Dr. Reuben Jones of Rockingham, and Capt. Azariah Wright of Westminster heard of it, and took proper care to notify those towns. A meeting was called in the two towns aforesaid, and a committee was chosen by each town, to wait on the supervisors, at their meeting in September, to see if there were any papers that should be laid before the several towns in the county; and they found that there were papers come from the committee of correspondence, that should have been laid before the towns in June. The supervisors made many excuses for their conduct: some plead ignorance, and some one thing, and some another: but the most of them did seem to think, that they could send a return to the committee at New-York, without ever laying them before their constituents; which principle, at this day, so much prevails, that it is the undoing of the people. Men, at this day, are so tainted with the principles of tyranny, that they would fain believe, that as they are chosen by the people to any kind of office, for any particular thing, that they have the sole power of that people by whom they are chosen, and can act in the name of that people in any matter or thing, though it is not in any connection with what they were chosen for. But the committees would not consent to have a return made, until every town in the county, had Mr. Low's letters laid before them; which was done, and a county congress was called; return was made, a committee was chosen to see that it was put in print; but, through interest, or otherwise, it never was published in any of the papers.

Immediately after, the people of the county aforesaid received the resolves of the continental congress. They called a county congress, and did adopt all the resolves of the continental congress as their resolves, promising religiously to adhere to that agreement or association. There was a committee of inspection moved for, to be chosen by the county, according to the second resolve of the association aforesaid: but being much spoken against by a justice and an attorney, and looked upon by them as a childish, impertient thing, the delegates dared not choose one. At this time there were tory parties forming, although they were under disguise; and had laid a plan to bring the lower sort of the people into a state of bondage and slavery. They saw that there was no cash stirring, and they took that opportunity to collect debts, knowing that men had no other way to pay them, than by having their estates taken by execution and sold at vendue. There were but very few men among us that were able to buy; and those men were so disposed, that they would take all the world into their own hands, without paying any thing for it, if they could, by law; which would soon bring the whole country into slavery. Most, or all of our men in authority, and all that wanted court favours, seemed much enraged, and stirred up many vexatious law-suits, and imprisoned many, contrary to the laws of this province, and the statutes of the crown. One man they put into close prison for high treason; and all that they proved against him, was, that he said if the King had signed the Quebec bill, it was his opinion that he had broke his coronation-oath. But the good people went and opened the prison door and let him go, and did no violence to any man's person or property.

Our men in office would say that they did like the resolutions of the contintental congress. . . . Then they said, that this would do for the Bay-Province, but it was childish for us to pay any regard to them. Some of our court would boldly say, that the King had a just right to make the revenue-acts, for he had a supreme power; and he that said otherwise was guilty of high treason, and they did hope that they would be executed accordingly. . . . When the good people considered that the [N.Y.] general assembly were for bringing them into a state of slavery, (which did appear plain by their not acceding to the best method to procure their liberties, and the executive power so strongly acquiescing in all that they did, whether it was right or wrong;) the good people of said county thought it time to look to themselves. And they thought that it was dangerous to trust their lives and fortunes in the hands of such enemies to American liberty; but more particulary unreasonable that there should be any court held; since, thereby, we must accede to what our general assembly had done, in not acceding to what the whole continent had recommended; and that all America would break off all dealings and commerce with us, and bring us into a state of slavery at once. Therefore in duty to God, ourselves, and posterity, we thought ourselves under the strongest obligations to resist and to oppose all authority that would not accede to the resolves of the continental congress. But knowing that many of our court were men that neither feared or regarded men, we thought it was most prudent to go and persuade the judges to stay at home. Accordingly there were about forty good true men sent from Rockingham to Chester, to dissuade Col. Chandler, the chief judge, from attending court. He said he believed it would be for the good of the county not to have any court, as things were: but there was one case of murder that they must see to, and if it was not agreeable to the people, they would not have any other case. One of the committee told him that the sheriff would raise a number with arms, and that there would be bloodshed. The Colonel said that he would give his word and honour that there should not be any arms brought against us; and he would go down to court on Monday the 13th of March inst., which was the day that the court was to be opened. We told him that we would wait on him, if it was his will. He said, that our company would be very agreeable; likewise he returned us his hearty thanks for our civility, and so we parted with him.

We heard from the southern part of the state, that Judge Sabin was very earnest to have the law go on, as well as many petty officers. There were but two judges in the county at that time, Col. Wells being gone to New-York. There was a great deal of talk in what manner to stop the court; and at length it was agreed on to let the court come together, and lay the reasons we had against their proceeding, before them, thinking they were men of such sense that they would hear them. But on Friday, we heard that the court was going to take the possession of the house on the 13th inst., and to keep a strong guard at the doors of said house, that we could not come in. We being justly alarmed by the deceit of our court, though it was not strange, therefore we thought proper to get to court before the armed guards were placed; for, we were determined that our grievances should be laid before the court, before it was opened. On Monday, the 13th of March inst., there were about 100 of us entered the court-house, about four o'clock in the afternoon. But we had but just entered, before we were alarmed by a large number of men, armed with guns, swords, and pistols. But we, in the house, had not any weapons of war among us, and were determined that they should not come in with their weapons of war, except by the force of them.

Esq. [Sheriff William] Patterson came up at the head of his armed company, within about five yards of the door, and commanded us to disperse; to which he got no answer. He then caused the King's Proclamation to be read, and told us, that if we did not disperse in fifteen minutes, by G—d he would blow a lane through us. We told him that we would not disperse. We told them that they might come in, if they would unarm themselves, but not without. One of our men went out at the door, and asked them if they were come for war; told them that we were come for peace, and that we should be glad to hold a parley with them. At that, Mr. Gale, the clerk of the court, drew a pistol, held it up, and said, d—n the parley with such d—d rascals as you are; I will hold no parley with such d—d rascals, but by this,—holding up his pistol. They gave us very harsh language, told us we should be in hell before morning; but, after a while, they drew a little off from the house, and seemed to be in a consultation. Three of us went out to treat with them; but the most, or all that we could get from them, was, that they would not talk with such d—d rascals as we were; and we soon returned to the house, and they soon went off.

Col. Chandler came in, and we laid the case before him, and told him that we had his word that there should not be any arms brought against us. He said that the arms were brought without his consent, but he would go and take them away from them, and we should enjoy the house undisturbed until morning; and that the court should come in the morning without arms, and should hear what we had to lay before them; and then he went away. We then went out of the house and chose a committee, which drew up articles to stand for, and read them to the company. . . .

About midnight, or a little before, the sentry, at the door, espyed some men with guns, and he gave the word to man the doors, and the walk was crowded. Immediately, the sheriff and his company marched up fast, within about ten rods of the door, and then the word was given, take care, and then, fire. Three fired immediately. The word fire was repeated; G—d d—n you fire, send them to hell, was most or all the words that were to be heard for some time: on which, there were several men wounded; one was shot with four bullets, one of which went through his brain, of which wound he died next day. Then they rushed in with their guns, swords, and clubs, and did most cruelly mammoc [mangle] several more; and took some that were not wounded, and those that were, and crowded them all into close prison together, and told them that they should all be in hell before the next night, and that they did wish that there were forty more in the same case with that dying man. When they put him into prison, they took and dragged him as one would a dog; and would mock him as he lay gasping, and make sport for themselves, at this dying motions. The people that escaped took prudent care to notify the people in the county, and also in the government of New-Hampshire, and the Bay; which being justly alarmed at such an unheard of an aggravated piece of murder, did kindly interpose in our favour.

One Tuesday the 14th inst. about 12 o'clock, nearly 200 men, well armed, came from New-Hampshire government; and before night there were several of the people of Cumberland county returned, and took up all they know of, [the Sheriff's force] that were in the horrid massacre, and confined them under a strong guard; and afterwards they confined as many as they could get evidence against, except several that did escape for their lives. On the 15th inst. the body formed, chose a moderator and clerk, and chose a committee to see that the coroner's jury of inquest were just, impartial men; which jury on their oath did bring in, that W. Patterson, &c. &c. did, on the 13th March inst., by force and arms, make an assault on the body of William French, then and there lying dead, and shot him through the head with a bullet, of which wound he died, and not otherwise. Then, the criminals were confined in close prison, and, on the evening of the same day, and early the next morning, a large number came from the southern part of the county of Cumberland, and the Bay Province. It is computed, that in the whole, there were 500 good martial soldiers, well equipped for war, that had gathered. On the 26th inst. the body assembled; but being so numerous that they could not do business, there was a vote passed, to choose a large committee to represent the whole, and that this committee should consist of men who did not belong to the county of Cumberland, as well as of those that did belong thereto; which was done. After the most critical and impartial examination of evidence, voted, that the heads of them should be confined in Northampton jail, till they could have a fair trial; and those that did not appear so guilty, should be under bonds, holden to answer at the next court of oyer and terminer in the county aforesaid; which was agreed to. On the 17th inst. bonds were taken for those that were to be bound, and the rest set out under a strong guard for Northampton.

We, the committee aforesaid, embrace this opportunity to return our most grateful acknowledgments and sincere thanks to our truly wise and patriotic friends in the government of New-Hampshire and the Massachusetts-Bay, for their kind and benevolent interposition in our favour, at such time of distress and confusion aforesaid; strongly assuring them, that we shall be always ready for their aid and assistance, if by the dispensations of divine providence, we are called thereto.

Signed by order of the Committee.

REUBEN JONES, *Clerk.*
Cumberland County, March 23d, 1775.

Source: William Slade, comp., *Vermont State Papers* (Middlebury, Vt. : J.W. Copeland, 1823), pp. 55-59.

DOCUMENT 12

The Bennington Declaration for Freedom (1775)

Persuaded that the Salvation of the rights and liberties of America depend under God on the firm union of its inhabitants, in a vigorous prosecution of the measures necessary for its safety and convinced of the necessity of preventing the Anarchy and Confusion which attend a dissolution of the Powers of Government; we the freeholders and inhabitants of the town of Bennington, on the New Hampshire grants in the County of Albany and province of N. York being greatly alarmed at the avowed design of the Ministry to raise a revenue in America and shocked by the bloody scene now acting in the Massachusetts bay, do in the most solemn manner resolve never to bee Slaves; and do associate under all the ties of religion, honour and love to our Country, do adopt and endeavor to Carry into execution what ever Measures may be recommended by the Continental Congress or resolved upon by our Provincial Convention for the purpose of preserving our Constitution and opposing the execution of Several arbitrary and oppressive acts of the British Parliament until a reconciliation between Great Britain and

America on Constitutional principles (which we most ardently desire) can be obtained and that we Will in all things follow the advice of our general Committee Respecting the Purpose aforesaid, the preservation of Peace and Good Order and the Safety of Individuals and Private Property.

[39 ms. signatures]

Source: *Proceedings of the Vermont Historical Society* (Montpelier: Vermont Historical Society, 1911-1912), pp. 109-110.

DOCUMENT 13

The Capture of Fort Ticonderoga (1775)

ETHAN ALLEN

Ever since I arrived to a state of manhood, and acquainted myself with the general history of mankind, I have felt a sincere passion for liberty. The history of nations doomed to perpetual slavery, in consequence of yielding up to tyrants their natural born liberties, I read with a sort of philosophical horror; so that the first systematical and bloody attempt at Lexington, to enslave America, thoroughly electrified my mind, and fully determined me to take part with my country: And while I was wishing for an opportunity to signalize myself in its behalf, directions were privately sent to me from the then colony (now state) of Connecticut, to raise the Green Mountain Boys; (and if possible) with them to surprise and take the fortress Ticonderoga. This enterprise I cheerfully undertook; and, after first guarding all the several passes that led thither, to cut off all intelligence between the garrison and the country, made a forced march from Bennington, and arrived at the lake opposite to Ticonderoga, on the evening of the ninth day of May, 1775, with two hundred and thirty valiant Green Mountain Boys; and it was with the utmost difficulty that I procured boats to cross the lake: However, I landed eighty-three men near the garrison, and sent the boats back for the rear guard commanded by col. Seth Warner; but the day began to dawn, and I found myself under a necessity to attack the fort, before the rear could cross the lake; and, as it was viewed hazardous, I harangued the officers and soldiers in the manner following; "Friends and fellow soldiers, you have, for a number of years past, been a scourge and terror to arbitrary power. Your valour has been famed abroad, and acknowledged, as appears by the advice and orders to me (from the general assembly of Connecticut) to surprise and take the garrison now before us. I now propose to advance before you, and in person conduct you through the wicket-gate; for we must this morning either quit our pretensions to valour, or possess ourselves of this fortress in a few minutes; and, in as much as it is a desperate attempt, (which none but the bravest of men dare undertake) I do not urge it on any contrary to his will. You that will undertake voluntarily, poise your firelocks."

The men being (at this time) drawn up in three ranks, each poised his firelock. I ordered them to face to the right; and, at the head of the centre-file, marched them immediately to the wicket gate aforesaid, where I found a centry posted, who instantly snapped his fusee at me; I ran immediately toward him, and he retreated through the covered way into the parade within the garrison, gave a halloo, and ran under a bomb-proof. My party who followed me into the fort, I formed on the parade in such a manner as to face the two barracks which faced each other. The garrison being asleep, (except the centries) we gave three huzzas which greatly surprised them. One of the centries made a pass at one of my officers with a charged bayonet, and slightly wounded him: My first thought was to kill him with my sword; but, in an instant, altered the design and fury of the blow to a slight cut on the side of the head; upon which he dropped his gun, and asked quarter, which I readily granted him, and demanded of him the place where the commanding officer kept; he shewed me a pair of stairs in the front of a barrack, on the west part of the garrison, which led up to a second story in said barrack, to which I immediately repaired, and ordered the commander (capt. Delaplace) to come forth instantly, or I would sacrifice the whole garrison; at which the capt. came immediately to the door with his breeches in his hand, when I ordered him to deliver to me the fort instantly, who asked me by what authority I demanded it; I answered, "In the name of the great Jehovah, and the Continental Congress." (The authority of the Congress being very little known at that time) he began to speak again; but I interrupted him, and with my drawn sword over his head, again demanded an immediate surrender of the garrison; to which he then complied, and ordered his men to be forthwith paraded without arms, as he had given up the garrison; in the mean time some of my officers had given orders, and in consequence thereof, sundry of the barrack doors were beat down, and about one third of the garrison imprisoned, which consisted of the said commander, a lieut. Feltham, a conductor of artillery, a gunner, two serjeants, and forty four rank and file; about one hundred pieces of cannon, one 13 inch mortar, and a number of swivels. This surprise was carried into execution in the gray of the morning of the 10th day of May, 1775. The sun seemed to rise that morning with a superior lustre; and Ticonderoga and its dependencies smiled on its conquerors, who tossed about the flowing bowl, and wished success to Congress, and the liberty and freedom of America. . . .

Source: Ethan Allen, *A Narrative of Colonel Ethan Allen's Captivity* (New York: The Georgian Press, 1930), pp. 5-9.

Document 14

Letter to the Continental Congress (1775)

Ethan Allen

Crownpoint 29th of May, 1775

Worthy Gentlemen

An abstract of the minutes of Council from the Continental Congress signed pr Mr Charles Thomson Secretiary has Just Came to Hand and Tho, it Approves of the Takeing the Fortresses on Lake Champlain and the Artillery &c. I am Nevertheless much Surprised that Your Honours Should recommend it to us to remove the Artillery to the South End of Lake George and to [*sic*] there to make a Stand, the Consequence of which must ruin the Frontier Settlements which are Extended at Least one Hundred miles to the Northward from that Place[.] Probable Your Honours were Not Informed of those Settlements which Consist of Several Thousand families who are Seated on that Tract of Country Called the New Hampshire Grants[.] the Misfortune and real Injury to Those Inhabitants by makeing the

South End of Lake George the Northermost front of Protection will more fully appear from the following Consideration[:] Namely It was at the Special request and Solicitation of the Governments of the Province of Massachusetts Bay & Connecticut that Those Very Inhabitants Put their Life into the hand of them Governments and made those Valuable Acquisitions for the Colonies, by Doing it they have Insensed Governor Carlton and all the ministerial Party in Canada against them and provided they should after all their Good Service in behalf of their Country be Neglected and Left Exposed they will be of all men the most Consummately miserable. The South Promuntary of Lake Champlain and Lake George as to a Southern Direction are Near the Same and if we Should Give up the Soveranity of Lake Champlain we may May [*sic*] as well Give up the whole[.] if the Kings Troops Should be again in Possession of Ticondaroga and Crown-point and Command the Lake the Indians and Canadians will be much more Inclined to Join with them and make Incursions into the Heart of our Country[,] but as the Colonies are Nown in the Possession and Actual Command of the Lake[,] having Taken the Armed Sloop from George the Third which was Cruising in the Lake and Also Seized a Schooner belonging to Major Sceene at South Bay and have armed and named them both for the Protection of Our Country and the Constitution and Civil Priviledges and Liberties thereof. by a Council of war held on board the Sloop the 27th Instant it was agreed to advance to the Point of fare with the Sloop and Schooner and a Number of armed Boates well maned and there make a Stand and Act on the Defencive and by all means Command the Lake and Defend the frontiers and wait for the Special Directions of the Honble Contintental Congress and Govern our selves accordingly[.] we are Now almost ready to sail to that station which is about Six miles this side Latitude forty five Degrees North, a small force with the armed Vessels will at Present Command the Lake and Secure the frontiers[.] the Canadians[,] all Except the Nobliss[,] and also the Indians appear at Present to be Very friendly to us, and it is my Humble Opinion that the more Vigurous the Colonies Push the war against the Kings Troops in Canada the more friends we shall find in that Country[.] Provided I had but five hundred men with me at saint Johns when we Took the Kings Sloop I would have advanced to Montreal[.] Nothing Strengthens our friends in Canada Equal to our Prosperity in Takeing the Severanity of Lake Champlain[,] and Should the Colonies forthwith send an army of Two or Three Thousand men and attack Montreal[,] we Should have but Little to fear from the Canadians or Indians and would Easily make a Conquest of that Place and Set up the Standard of American Liberty in the Extensive province of Quebec whose Limit was Enlar[g]ed purely to Subvert the Liberties of America[.] Strikeing Such a Blow would Intimidate the Torie party in Canada the same as the Commensment of the war at Boston Intimidated the Tories in the Colonies[.] they are a Set of Gentlemen that will Not be Converted by reason but are easily wrought upon by fear. advancing an Army into Canada will be agreeable to our friends and it is bad policy to fear the resentment of an Enemy[.] if we Lie Easie and in a supine State and Governor Carlton Exerts himself agains[t] us Vigurously[,] as we know he will[,] and who by a Legal Constitution Can Oblige our Friends to assist him[,] he will by slow Degrees Discourage our friend[s] and Incourage our Enemies and form Those that are at Present Indifferent into Combination against us. Therefore the Possible way to Circumvent him and the Scheme of the Ministry is to Nervously Push an army into Canada. but if the wisdom of the Continent in Congress Should View the Proposed Invasion of the Kings Troops in Canada as premature or Impolitick[,] Nevertheless I Humbly Conceive when Your Honours Come to the Knowledge of the the [sic] before mentioned facts You will at Least Establish some Advantageous Situation Twards the Northerly Part Part [sic] of Lake Champlain as a Frontier in Stead of the South Promontary of Lake George[.] there are many advantages in forming the frontier Near the County of the Enemy[.] as first[,] it will be in our Power to ravage and make Inroads into the Heart of the enemies Country the same as they might Easily Do were they in Possession and Command of Lake Champlain[.] this advantage will be of the Utmost Consequence[,] be it in the hands of which Party it will[.] Tho, it is Now in our hands[,] to Give it up to them would be fatal [to] the Interest

of the Colonies but more Particularly to Those who were Instrumental in the achievement of the Supremacy of that Lake[.] but secondly[,] Commanding the Northerly Part of the Lake Puts it in our Power to work our Policy with the Canadians and Indians[.] we have mad[e] Considerable proficiency this way already[.] Sundry Indians have been to Visit us and have returned to their Tribes to use their Influence in our favour[.] we have sent Capt. Abraham Nimham[,] a Stockbridge Indian[,] as our Imbassador of Peace to the Several Tribes of Indians in Canada[.] he was Accompanied with Mr Winthrop Hoit[,] who has been a Prisoner with the Indians and Understands their Tongue. I Do Not Imagine[,] Provided we Command Lake Champlain[,] there will be any Need of a war with the Canadians or Indians[.] Pray Pardon me on Account of any Impertinency or Inaccuracy in this Composition[,] as it is but a rought Draught wrote in Great Haste from Your Honours Ever faithfull Most Obedient and Humble Servant

Ethan Allen

DOCUMENT 15

Battle of Valcour (1776)
(depicted on following page)

An Account of the Expedition of the British Fleet on Lake Champlain, under the Command of Captain Thomas Pringle, and of the Defeat of the Rebel Fleet, commanded by Benedict Arnold, on the 11th and 13th of October, 1776

Taken from the Letters of Sir Guy Carleton, Captains Douglas and Pringle, dated off Crown Point, 15th October 1776

After attending, for the space of six weeks, the naval equipment for the important expedition on Lake Champlain, was seen, with unspeakable joy, the reconstructed ship, now called the Inflexible, commanded

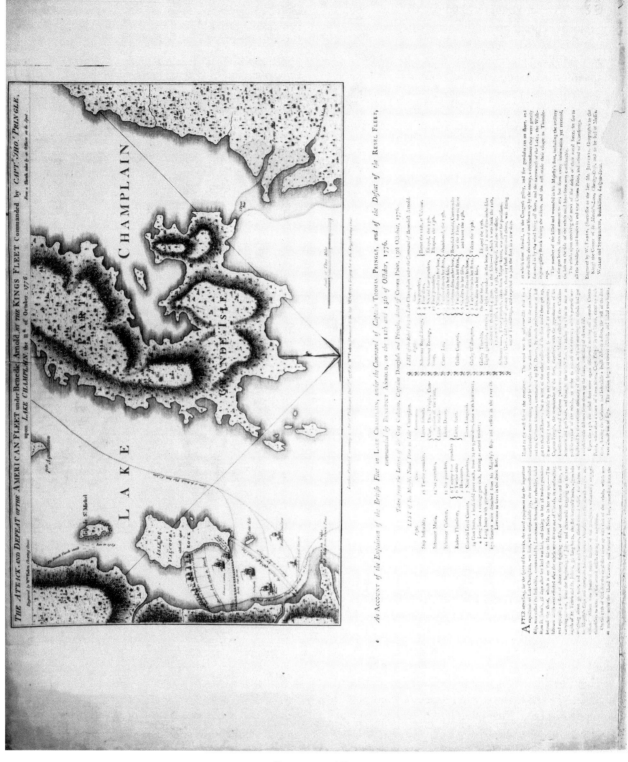

Document 15

by Lieutenant Schank, her rebuilder, sailed from St. John's, 28 days after her keel was laid, and taking in her 18 twelve pounders beyond the shoal, which is on this side the Isle aux Noix, in her way up.—The labours which were effected after the rebels were driven out of Canada, in constructing and equipping a fleet of above thirty fighting vessels, of different sorts and sizes, all carrying cannon, since the beginning of July; and afterwards dragging up the two rapids of St. Teresa and St. John's, 30 long boats, the flat-bottom'd boats, a gondola weighing about 30 tons, and above 400 battoes, almost exceed belief, the sailors of her Majesty's ships and transports having exerted themselves to the utmost on this occasion: Above two hundred prime seamen of the transports voluntarily engaged themselves to serve in the armed vessels during the expedition.

On the 11th of October the royal fleet came up with that of the rebels, which was at anchor under the Island Valcour, and formed a strong line, extending from the Island to the west side of the continent. The wind was so unfavourable that for a considerable time nothing could be brought into action with them, but the gun boats, and the Carleton schooner, commanded by Mr. Dacres, by much perservance at last got to their assistance: but as none of the other vessels of the fleet could then get up, it was thought not advisable by any means to continue so unequal an engagement; Captain Pringle, the commander of the fleet, therefore, with the approbation of his Excellency General Carleton (who was on board the Maria) called off the Carelton Schooner and gun boats, and brought the whole fleet to anchor in a line as near as possible to that of the rebels, in order to cut off their retreat; which purpose was frustrated by the extreme obscurity of the night, as by the morning the rebels had got a considerable distance from them up the Lake, consisting of eleven sail.

Upon the 13th the rebel fleet were again discovered making off towards Crown Point, when after a chace of seven hours, Capt. Pringle in the Maria, came up with them, having Carleton and Inflexible a small distance a-stern, the rest of the fleet were almost out of sight. The action began at twelve o'clock, and lasted two hours, at which time Arnold, in the Congress galley, and five gondolas ran on shore, and were directly abandoned and blown up by the enemy, a circumstance they were greatly favoured in by the wind being off shore, and the narrowness of the Lake; the Washing-ton-galley struck during the action, and the rest made their escape to Ticonderoga.

The number of the killed and wounded in his Majesty's fleet, including the artillery in the gun boats, does not amount to 40; but from every information yet received, the loss on the side of the rebels must have been very considerable.

The rebels upon receiving the news of the defeat of their naval force, set fire to all the buildings and houses in and near Crown Point, and retired to Ticonderoga.

Source: William Faden map, Special Collections, Bailey/Howe Library, University of Vermont. Reprinted courtesy of Special Collections, UVM Libraries.

DOCUMENT 16

New Connecticut's Declaration of Independence (1777)

To the honorable convention of representatives from the several towns on the west and east side of the range of Green Mountains, within the New-Hampshire grants, in convention assembled.

Your committee to whom was referred the form of a declaration, setting forth the right the inhabitants of said New-Hampshire grants have, to form themselves into a separate and independent state, or government, beg leave to report, viz.

Right 1. That whenever protection is withheld, no allegiance is due, or can of right be demanded.

2d. That whenever the lives and properties of a part of a community, have been manifestly aimed at by either the legislative or executive authority of such community, necessity requires a separation. Your committee are of opinion that the foregoing has, for many years past, been the conduct of the monopolizing land claimers of the colony of New-York; and that they have been not only countenanced, but encouraged, by both the legislative and executive authorities of the said state or colony. Many overt acts in evidence of this truth, are so fresh in the minds of the members, that it would be needless to name them.

And whereas the Congress of the several states, did, in said Congress, on the fifteenth day of May, A.D.

1776, in a similiar case, pass the following resolution, viz. "*Resolved*, That it be recommended to the respective assemblies and conventions of the United Colonies, where no government, sufficient to the exigencies of their affairs, has been, heretofore, established, to adopt such government as shall, in the opinion of the representatives of the people, best conduce to the happiness and safety of their constituents in particular, and of America in general."—Your committee, having duly deliberated on the continued conduct of the authority of New-York, before recited, and on the equitableness on which the aforesaid resolution of Congress was founded, and considering that a just right exists in this people to adopt measures for their own security, not only to enable them to secure their rights against the usurpations of Great-Britain, but also against that of New-York, and the several other governments claiming jurisdiction in this territory, do offer the following declaration, viz.

"This convention, whose members are duly chosen by the free voice of their constituents in the several towns, on the New-Hampshire grants, in public meeting assembled, in our own names, and in behalf of our constituents, do hereby proclaim and publicly declare, that the district of territory comprehending and usually known by the name and description of the New-Hampshire grants, of right ought to be, and is hereby declared forever hereafter to be considered, as a free and independent jurisdiction, or state; by the name, and forever hereafter to be called, known, and distinguished by the name of New-Connecticut, alias Vermont: And that the inhabitants that at present are, or that may hereafter become residents either by procreation or emigration, within said territory, shall be entitled to the same privileges, immunities, and enfranchisements, as are allowed; and on such condition, and in the same manner, as the present inhabitants, in future, shall or may enjoy; which are, and forever shall be considered to be such privileges and immunities to the free citizens and denizens, as are, or at any time hereafter, may be allowed, to any such inhabitants of any of the free and independent states of America: And that such privileges and immunities shall be regulated in a bill of rights, and by a form of government, to be established at the next adjourned session of this convention. . . ."

Your committee [recommends] . . . that proper information be given to the honorable Continental Congress of the United States of America, of the reasons, why the New-Hampshire grants have been declared a free state, and pray the said Congress to grant said state a representation in Congress; and that agents be appointed to transfer the same to Congress, or the committee be filled up that are already appointed, and that a committee be appointed to draw the draught: That a committee of war be appointed on the east side of the mountains, to be in conjuction with the committee of war on the west side of the mountains, to act on all proper occasions: That some suitable measures be taken to govern our internal police for the time being, until more suitable measures can be taken: that some suitable way be taken to raise a sum of money, to defray the expenses of the agents that are to go to Congress; and for printing the proceedings of the convention, which, we are of opinion, ought to be printed. All which is humbly submitted to the convention, by your committee.

By order of Committee,
THOMAS CHANDLER, *Chairman*

The Declaration and Petition of the Inhabitants of the New-Hampshire Grants, to Congress, announcing the District to be a Free and Independent State

To THE HONORABLE THE CONTINENTAL CONGRESS.

The declaration and petition of that part of North America, situate south of Canada line, west of Connecticut river, north of the Massachusetts Bay, and east of a twenty mile line from Hudson's river, containing about one hundred and forty four townships, of the contents of six miles square each, granted your petitioners by the authority of New-Hampshire, besides several grants made by the authority of New-York, and a quantity of vacant land, humbly sheweth,

That your petitioners, by virtue of several grants made them by the authority aforesaid, have, many years since, with their families become actual settlers and inhabitants of the said described premises; by which it is now become a respectable frontier to three neighboring states, and is of great importance to our common barrier Tyconderoga; at it has furnished the army there with much provisions, and can muster more than five thousand hardy soldiers, capable of bearing arms in defense of American liberty:

That shortly after your petitioners began their settlements, a party of land-jobbers in the city and state of New-York, began to claim the lands, and took measures to have them declared to be within that jurisdiction:

That on the fourth day of July, 1764, the king of Great-Britain did pass an order in council, extending the jurisdiction of New-York government to Connecticut river, in consequence of a representation made by the late lieutenant governor Colden, that for the convenience of trade, and administration of justice, the inhabitants were desirous of being annexed to that state:

That on this alteration of jurisdiction, the said lieutenant governor Colden did grant several tracts of land in the above described limits, to certain persons living in the state of New-York, which were, at that time, in the actual possession of your petitioners; and under color of the lawful authority of said state, did proceed against your petitioners, as lawless intruders upon the crown lands in their province. This produced an application to the king of Great-Britain from your petitioners, setting forth their claims under the government of New-Hampshire, and the disturbance and interruption they had suffered from said post claimants, under New-York. And on the 24th day of July, 1767, an order was passed at St. James's, prohibiting the governors of New-York, for the time being, from granting any part of the described premises, on pain of incurring his Majesty's highest displeasure. Nevertheless the same lieutenant governor Colden, governors Dunmore and Tryon, have, each and every of them, in their respective turns of administration, presumed to violate the said royal order, by making several grants of the prohibited premises, and countenancing an actual invasion of your petitioners, by force of arms, to drive them off from their possessions.

The violent proceedings, (with the solemn declaration of the supreme court of New-York, that the charters, conveyances, &c. of your petitioners' lands, were utterly null and void) on which they were founded, reduced your petitioners to the disagreeable necessity of taking up arms, as the only means left for the security of their possessions. The consequence of this step was the passing twelve acts of outlawry, by the legislature of New-York, on the ninth day of March, 1774; which were not intended for the state in general, but only for part of the counties of Albany and Charlotte, viz. such

parts thereof as are covered by the New-Hampshire charters.

Your petitioners having had no representative in that assembly, when these acts were passed, they first came to the knowledge of them by public papers, in which they were inserted. . . . These laws were evidently calculated to intimidate your petitioners into a tame surrender of their rights, and such a state of vassalage, as would entail misery on their latest posterity. . . .

By a submission to the claims of New-York your petitioners would be subjected to the payment of two shillings and six pence sterling on every hundred acres annually; which, compared with the quit-rents of Livingston's Phillip's, and Ransalear's manors, and many other enormous tracts in the best situations in the state, would lay the most disporportionate share of the public expense on your petitioners, in all respects the least able to bear it. . . . When the declaration of the honorable the Continental Congress, of the fourth of July last past, reached your petitioners they communicated it throughout the whole of their district; and being properly apprized of the proposed meeting, delegates from the several counties and towns in the district, described in the preamble to this petition, did meet at Westminster in said district, and after several adjournments for the purpose of forming themselves as a free and independent state, capable of regulating their own internal police, in all and every respect whatsoever; and that the people, in the said described district, have the sole, exclusive right of governing themselves in such a manner and form, as they, in their wisdom, should choose; not repugnant to any resolves of the honorable the Continental Congress. And for the mutual support of each other in the maintenance of the freedom and independence of said district or separate state, the said delegates did jointly and severally pledge themselves to each other, by all the ties that are held sacred among men, and resolve and declare that they were at all times ready, in conjuction with their brethren of the United States, to contribute their full proportion towards maintaining the present war against the fleets and armies of Great-Britain.

To convey this declaration and resolution to your honorable body, the grand representative of the United States, were we (your most immediate petitioners) delegated by the united and unanimous voices of the representatives of the whole body of the settlers on the described premises, in whose name and behalf, we humbly pray, that the said declaration may be received, and the district described therein be ranked by your honors, among the free and independent American states, and delegates therefrom admitted to seats in the grand Continental Congress; and your petitioners as in duty bound shall ever pray.

New-Hampshire Grants, Westminster, Jan. 15th, 1777.

Signed by order, and in behalf of said inhabitants,
JONAS FAY,
THOMAS CHITTENDEN,
HEMAN ALLEN,
REUBEN JONES.

Source: William Slade, comp., *Vermont State Papers* (Middlebury, Vt.: J.W. Copeland, 1823), pp. 69-73.

SECTION THREE

1777-1791
Independent Vermont

VERMONT VOICES

SECTION THREE

1777-1791
Independent Vermont

Introduction

In 1777, Dr. Thomas Young, friend and mentor to the young Ethan Allen, resided in Pennsylvania. Meeting in Philadelphia with a four-man delegation from the New Hampshire Grants after it failed to gain congressional recognition, he counseled a new strategy for seeking statehood. In **Document 1**, a letter "To the Inhabitants of Vermont," Young recommended that representatives "meet at an early date to choose Delegates for the General Congress, a Committee of Safety, and to form a Constitution." As justification for this action he enclosed with his letter a May 1776 congressional resolution calling upon the rebellious British colonies to adopt new governments. Young believed that until the New Hampshire Grants formed itself into a "body politic" Congress could not recognize it as a free state. His final contributions were to provide the Grants delegates with a copy of the recently adopted Pennsylvania constitution he hoped would serve as a model, and the suggestion that since New Connecticut, the name the Grants accepted for its Declaration of Independence, had been designated as a region of northwestern Pennsylvania, they refer to their state as Vermont.

The delegates, among whom was future Governor Thomas Chittenden, returned to the Grants, where by early July they succeeded in implementing Young's suggestions at a convention in Windsor. **Document 2** includes the Preamble and Chapter 1 of Vermont's 1777 Constitution. The substance of the Constitution, Chapter 1 (a bill of rights) and Chapter 2 (the frame of government), borrow heavily from the Pennsylvania model, but there are some significant differences. Chapter 1, Article 1, which prohibits slavery, for example, was not included in any previous state constitution. The 1777 Vermont bill of rights remains basically unaltered to this day.

The Preamble, also a Vermont contribution, provides the rationale for establishing a government separate from both Great Britain and New York. Its authors, as had Thomas Young in Document 1, followed the lead of Ethan Allen and the Green Mountain Boys by linking the legitimacy of the New Hampshire land grants to the natural-rights-of-man philosophy that served as the intellectual centerpiece of the Revolutionary struggle against British tyranny.

Document 3, Bernard Romans' "Chorographical Map of the Northern Department of North-America," provided the most unique and impressive single piece of Vermont propaganda. Romans, an able military engineer and surveyor, served in the Connecticut contingent that helped Ethan Allen seize Fort Ticonderoga and thereafter continued active in the Revolutionary cause. His map, first issued in 1778, is the first cartographic depiction of Vermont as an independent state and includes textual denunciations of Yorkers as "Princes of Land Jobbers" and "Harpy land jobbers," dismissing New York land claims as not being "thought worth while to note them." An Ira Allen biographer has written that Romans' map "probably spoke as persuasively as any pamphlet or broadside from [Ira's] pen."[1]

In early July 1777, British General John Burgoyne and his army advanced southward along the shores of Lake Champlain. News of the July 6 fall of Ticonderoga and the defeat of Seth Warner's Green Mountain Boys regiment at Hubbardton (the only Revolutionary War battle fought in Vermont) the following day had reached the Windsor delegates on July 8. With the security of all western Vermont threatened, the delegates concluded work on the Constitution, appointed a Council of Safety, and adjourned. Reinforcements in the form of militia units requested from nearby states contributed to an important victory over the British on August 16 in what is known to history as the Battle of Bennington (although it was fought just west of Bennington in New York State). Under the command of New Hampshire General John Stark, militia volunteers from New Hampshire and Massachusetts along with Seth Warner's Green Mountain Boys and a company of Stockbridge Indians routed Lieutenant Colonel Friedrich Baum and the German mercenaries Burgoyne had sent to plunder the military depot in Bennington for horses and provisions to augment his dwindling supplies. That failure along with the heavy

---

[1] J. Kevin Graffagnino, *The Shaping of Vermont* (Rutland, Vt.: Vermont Heritage Press, 1983), p. 55.

casualties the Germans suffered contributed to Burgoyne's subsequent defeat and the surrender of his army at Saratoga in October. The failure of the invasion conceded to Vermont, at least temporarily, control of its own borders. **Document 4** is General Stark's account of the battle.

The British military threat and congressional disapproval of Vermont's pretensions to independence were not the new state's only problems in the summer of 1777. There was considerable internal opposition as well, which persisted almost until Vermont's admission into the Union as the fourteenth state in 1791. East of the Green Mountains a strong Yorker faction was adamant in its refusal to accept the new state, but equally unsettling were rivalries among competing factions to determine Vermont's destiny as a new state. With the election of Thomas Chittenden as governor in 1778, the Chittenden-Allen faction held the formal levers of power. Based primarily west of the Green Mountains, they opposed recurring efforts by the Dresden faction (so-called because Dartmouth College, center of the movement, was located in the district of Hanover, New Hampshire, known as Dresden) to annex New Hampshire towns along the Connecticut River. The so-called East Union (incorporation of New Hampshire townships into Vermont), temporarily executed in 1778-79 and again in 1780-81, threatened the supremacy of the Chittenden-Allen faction by shifting the balance of political power in Vermont east of the Green Mountains, while simultaneously infuriating New Hampshire.

Document 5, *A Public Defence of the Right of the New Hampshire Grants (so called) on Both Sides of the Connecticut River, to Associate Together, and Form Themselves into an Independent State*, excerpted, provides the rationale for such consolidation. Signed by Vermonters Jacob Bayley and Elisha Payne and Dartmouth College administrator Bezaleel Woodward, the *Public Defence* showed that the idea of a state centered on the Connecticut River had considerable appeal on both sides of the river. After much work by the Arlington Junto, the Chittenden-Allen faction, Vermont's legislature repudiated this first East Union when General George Washington assured Ethan Allen that if Vermont retired to its former borders, Congress would acknowledge its "independence and sovereignty."

Document 6 illustrates Congress' ineffectiveness in dealing with the Vermont disputes along with its displeasure at Vermont's functioning as an independent state. Rather than intimidate, however, it incited Vermont to more extreme defiance. The following year, lured by the Dresden party enticements, thirty-four New Hampshire towns joined with Vermont to establish the second East Union. This time, rather than directly subvert the process, the Arlington Junto annexed fifteen New York towns as a counterweight to the Dresden party.

The protection of Vermont's borders has been suggested as a primary motive for its expansionist impulses. As **Document 7** makes clear, the state was also secretly negotiating with Frederick Haldimand, governor-general of Canada, for readmission into the British Empire. Apparently the Arlington Junto reasoned that if the Haldimand negotiations succeeded in reuniting Vermont with the English, the additional New York and New Hampshire territory would provide buffer zones that the U.S. military would have to cross before reaching the original Vermont borders in any invasion of Vermont. **Document 8**, Haldimand's terms under which Vermont would be welcomed back into the empire, stipulates the state's borders as encompassing the East and West Union towns. Despite Haldimand's generous terms, reunion was never consummated, largely because in the months after the Battle of Yorktown (October 1781) the British reconciled themselves to American independence and abandoned their designs on Vermont.

Historians remain divided over the motives of the Vermont negotiators. Some praise the scheme as a diplomatic ploy through which the Arlington Junto deterred a British invasion through the Champlain Valley and thus advanced the Revolutionary cause. After details of the negotiations were leaked, however, U.S. observers were sufficiently suspicious of the Allen-Chittenden flirtation with the British to prepare to invade Vermont, as is evident from **Document 9**, a plan for a U.S. expedition against Vermont. Although Vermont's leaders likely considered the British overture as one of several options they might pursue to preserve state interests, it was an option that most of the state's inhabitants opposed. As hostilities with Great Britain wound down, Vermonters refocused their efforts on admission to the American union as a state, and in February 1782 the legislature dissolved the East and West Unions.

Documents 10 and **11** treat with the molding of domestic institutions. Unlike the original thirteen states, which were territorial communities inherited from the colonial period, Vermont created a government and identity where none had previously existed; thus Vermont formed "the only true republic because it alone had created itself."[2] **Document 10**, "An Act for Setting Disputes Respecting Landed Property," is one in a series of legislative measures known as the Betterment or Improvement Acts. Controversies over land titles, originating in the New York/New Hampshire disputes, were a problem throughout Vermont's early history that were compounded by confiscations during the Revolution, shoddy surveying, and primitive record keeping. At ejectment proceedings, Vermont courts, following the dictates of common law, evicted without compensation occupants who improved the land while unknowingly possessing faulty titles. Believing this unjust, the legislature acted to provide compensation for any improvements an evicted occupant might have made upon the land.

Document 11, Thomas Rowley's poem calling for a legal-tender act, alludes to a second crisis faced by Vermont, the dearth of specie and the lack of an accepted currency. As Rowley indicates, this shortage of money was particularly burdensome to debtors who were continuously hounded by creditors through the courts. While Rowley's poem provides a humorous commentary on the creditor dilemma, he clearly supports alleviating the debtor predicament.

Doubtless the most important of all debtor riots occurred with Shays's Rebellion in the neighboring state of Massachusetts. Daniel Shays, a debt-ridden farmer and former captain in the Revolutionary army, led a small army against the state government after it had ignored petitions to reform its monetary policy. Routed by the state militia in their attempts to seize the federal arsenal in Springfield, Shays along with some of his followers escaped to Vermont. Given Vermont's own history of resistance to similar oppression, the Westminster Massacre (Section 2, Document 11) being a prime example, Shays may well have anticipated a warm welcome. Instead, Vermont's formal reaction

was the proclamation by Governor Chittenden reproduced as **Document 12**.

Chittenden's proclamation illustrates how Vermont was evolving from the era of Ethan Allen, the Green Mountain Boys, and frontier justice toward a more settled, peaceful society. The proclamation struck the right "law and order" note for outside observers wondering whether Vermont should be admitted as the fourteenth state, while the excerpt from the *Vermont Gazette* that forms the second half of Document 12 affirmed to neighboring states Vermont's newly acquired civility. Despite the rhetoric, however, Vermont never actually apprehended Shays, but allowed him to remain in Arlington for several years of quiet, anonymous poverty.

Document 13, an exchange of letters between Nathaniel Chipman and Alexander Hamilton on how they might cooperate in bringing Vermont into the federal union under the new United States Constitution, is important from a number of perspectives. At one level it initiated negotiations that resulted in Vermont's becoming the fourteenth state. At another it confirmed, Chittenden excepted, the passing of the pioneer leadership that had secured Vermont's independence to a younger, smoother, better-educated generation.

A former officer in the Continental army, Chipman arrived in Vermont in 1779 with a degree from Yale College and quickly gained admission to the Vermont bar. More conservative than the Allens in social and economic matters, Chipman and similarly inclined associates used their mastery of the legal details demanded by the growing and increasingly complex Vermont society to move to the front ranks of Vermont's leadership, replacing the Allens and their fellow frontiersmen.

Though this new political elite would soon dominate Vermont politics, subsistence farmers continued to dominate the ranks of Vermont's new settlers. **Document 14**, Seth Hubbell's account of his and his family's sufferings on the northern frontier, provides a firsthand description of the rigors these pioneers faced in establishing their Vermont farms. Hubbell's concluding benediction to the "benign Benefactor" gives testimony to a persistent religious faith despite the dearth of traditional Christian congregations. The Reverend Nathan Perkins, a Connecticut Congregationalist and ardent missionary, hoped to help remedy this deficiency with

---

[2]Peter Onuf, *The Origins of the Federal Republic* (Philadelphia: University of Pennsylvania Press, 1983), p. 145.

a tour of Vermont in 1789 to chronicle the state's particular need for religious instruction. Yet contemporary readers of **Document 15**, excerpts from *A Narrative of a Tour through the State of Vermont*, may be more impressed by the harsh living conditions Vermonters faced than the absence of "sensible preaching."

Document 16, the Vermont-New York agreement on their jurisdiction dispute, emerged from the initial exchange of letters between Nathaniel Chipman and Alexander Hamilton (Document 13) that paved the way for Vermont's admission to the Union. It provided that in consideration for thirty thousand dollars, New York would renounce its jurisdiction over Vermont and assume responsibility for outstanding New York land titles. Vermont accepted the New York terms, and with New York opposition eliminated, statehood was assured.

Document 17, the last in Section 3, is an excerpt from the proceedings of the January 1791 convention in Bennington convened to ratify the United States Constitution. With Thomas Chittenden presiding and Nathaniel Chipman the principal speaker, the convention voted 105 to 4 in favor of ratification. The convention vote was transmitted to Congress, and on March 4, 1791, the state of Vermont was "received and admitted into the Union as a new and entire member of the United States of America."

Document 1

"To the Inhabitants of Vermont" (1777)

DR. THOMAS YOUNG

IN CONGRESS, MAY 15, 1776.

WHEREAS his Britannic Majesty, in conjunction with the Lords and Commons of Great-Britain, has by a late Act of Parliament excluded the inhabitants of these United Colonies from the protection of his Crown: AND WHEREAS no answer whatever to the humble Petitions of the Colonies for redress of grievances and reconciliation with Great-Britain, has been or is likely to be given; but the whole force of that kingdom, aided by foreign mercenaries, is to be exerted for the destruction of the good people of these Colonies: AND WHEREAS it appears absolutely irreconcilable to reason and good conscience, for the people of these Colonies now to take the oaths and affirmations necessary for the support of any government under the Crown of Great Britain, and it is necessary that the exercise of every kind of authority under the said Crown should be totally suppressed, and all the powers of government exerted under the people of the Colonies, for the preservation of internal peace, virtue and good order, as well as for the defence of their lives, liberties and properties against the hostile invasions and cruel depredations of their enemies:

RESOLVED therefore, That it be recommended to the respective Assemblies and Conventions of the United Colonies, where no government sufficient to the exigencies of their affairs has been hitherto established, to adopt such government as shall in the opinion of the Representatives of the people best conduce to the happiness and safety of their constituents in particular and America in general. Extract from the Minutes,

CHARLES THOMPSON, *Secretary.*

To the Inhabitants of Vermont, a Free and Independent State, bounding on the River Connecticut and Lake Champlain
                    Philadelphia, April 11, 1777.
GENTLEMEN,—Numbers of you are knowing to the zeal with which I have exerted myself in your behalf from the beginning of your struggle with the New York Monopolizers. As the Supreme Arbiter of right has smiled on the just cause of North America at large, you in a peculiar manner have been highly favored. God has done by you the best thing commonly done for our species. He has put it fairly in your power to help yourselves.

I have taken the minds of several leading Members in the Honorable the Continental Congress, and can assure you that you have nothing to do but send attested copies of the Recommendation to take up government to every township in your district, and invite all your freeholders and inhabitants to meet in their respective townships and choose members for a General Convention, to meet at an early day, to choose Delegates for the General Congress, a Committee of Safety, and to form a Constitution for your State.

Your friends here tell me that some are in doubt whether Delegates from your district would be admitted into Congress. I tell you to organize fairly, and make the experiment, and I will ensure your success at the risk of my reputation as a man of honor or common sense. Indeed they can by no means refuse you! You have as good a right to choose how you will be governed, and by whom, as they had.

I have recommended to your Committee the Constitution of Pennsylvania for a model, which, with a very little alteration, will, in my opinion, come as near perfection as any thing yet concerted by mankind. This Constitution has been sifted with all the criticism that a band of despots were masters of and has bid defiance to their united powers.

The alteration I would recommend is, that all the Bills intended to be passed into Laws should be laid before the Executive Board for their perusal and proposals of amendment. All the difference then between such a Constitution and those of Connecticut and Rhode-Island, in the grand outlines is, that in one case the Executive power can advise and in the other compel. For my own part, I esteem the people at large the true proprietors of governmental power. They are the supreme constituent power, and of course their immediate Representatives are the supreme Delegate power; and as soon as the delegate power gets too far out of the hands of the constituent power, a tyranny is in some degree established.

Happy are you that in laying the foundation of a new government, you have a digest drawn from the purest fountain of antiquity, and improved by the readings and observations of the great Doctor Franklin, David Rittenhouse, Esq., and others. I am certain you may build on such a basis a system which will transmit liberty and happiness to posterity.

Let the scandalous practice of bribing men by places, commissions, &c. be held in abhorrence among you. By entrusting only men of capacity and integrity in public affairs, and by obliging even the best men to fall into the common mass of the people every year, and be sensible of their need of the popular good will to sustain their political importance, are your liberties well secured. These plans effectually promise this security.

May Almighty God smile upon your arduous and important undertaking, and inspire you with that wisdom, virtue, public spirit and unanimity, which insures success in the most hazardous enterprizes!

THOMAS YOUNG

April 12, 1777.

Your committee have obtained for you a copy of the Recommendation of Congress to all such bodies of men as looked upon themselves returned to a state of nature, to adopt such government as should in the opinion of the Representatives of the people best conduce to the happiness and safety of their constituents in particular and America in general.

You may perhaps think strange that nothing further is done for you at this time than to send you this extract. But if you consider that till you incorporate and actually announce to Congress your having become a body politic, they cannot treat with you as a free State. While New-York claims you as subjects of that government, my humble opinion is, your own good sense will suggest to you, that no time is to be lost in availing yourselves of the same opportunity your assuming mistress is improving to establish a dominion for herself and you too.

A WORD TO THE WISE IS SUFFICIENT.

Source: E. P. Walton, ed., *Records of the Council of Safety and Governor and Council of the State of Vermont*, Vol. 1 (Montpelier: Steam Press, 1873), pp. 394-396.

Document 2

Constitution of the State of Vermont: Preamble and Chapter 1 (1777)

As Established by Convention,
July 2, 1777.
[Preamble]

WHEREAS, all government ought to be instituted and supported, for the security and protection of the community, as such, and to enable the individuals who compose it, to enjoy their natural rights, and the other blessings which the Author of existence has bestowed upon man; and whenever those great ends of government are not obtained, the people have a right, by common consent, to change it, and take such measures as to them may appear necessary to promote their safety and happiness.

And whereas, the inhabitants of this State have, (in consideration of protection only) heretofore acknowledged allegiance to the King of Great Britain, and the said King has not only withdrawn that protection, but commenced, and still continues to carry on, with unabated vengeance, a most cruel and unjust war against them; employing therein, not only the troops of Great Britain, but foreign mercenaries, savages and slaves, for the avowed purpose of reducing them to a total and abject submission to the despotic dominion of the British parliament, with many other acts of tyranny, (more fully set forth in the declaration of Congress,) whereby all allegiance and fealty to the said King and his successors, are dissolved and at an end; and all power and authority derived from him, ceased in the American Colonies.

And whereas, the territory which now comprehends the State of *Vermont*, did antecedently, of right, belong to the government of *New-Hampshire*; and the former Governor thereof, viz. his Excellency *Benning Wentworth*, Esq., granted many charters of lands and corporations, within this State, to the present inhabitants and others. And whereas, the late Lieutenant Governor *Colden*, of *New-York*, with others, did, in violation of the tenth command, covet those very lands; and by a false representation made to the court of Great Britain, (in the year 1764, that for the convenience of trade and administration of justice, the inhabitants were desirous of being annexed to that government,) obtained jurisdiction of those very identical lands, *ex-parte*; which ever was, and is, disagreeable to the inhabitants. And whereas, the legislature of *New-York*, ever have, and still continue to disown the good people of this State, in their landed property, which will appear in the complaints hereafter inserted, and in the 36th section of their present constitution, in which is established the grants of land made by that government.

They have refused to make re-grants of our lands to the original proprietors and occupants, unless at the exorbitant rate of 2300 dollars fees for each township; and did enhance the quitrent, three fold, and demanded an immediate delivery of the title derived before, from *New-Hampshire*.

The judges of their supreme court have made a solemn declaration, that the charters, conveyances, &c., of the lands included in the before described premises, were utterly null and void, on which said title was founded; in consequence of which declaration, writs of possession have been by them issued, and the sheriff of the county of Albany sent, at the head of six or seven hundred men, to enforce the execution thereof.

They have passed an act, annexing a penalty thereto, of thirty pounds fine and six months imprisionment, on any person who should refuse assisting the sheriff, after being requested, for the purpose of executing writs of possession.

The Governors, *Dunmore, Tryon,* and *Colden,* have made re-grants of several tracts of land, included in the premises, to certain favorite land jobbers in the government of *New-York,* in direct violation of his Britannic majesty's express prohibition, in the year 1767.

They have issued proclamations, wherein they have offered large sums of money, for the purpose of apprehending those very persons who have dared boldly, and publicly, to appear in defence of their just rights.

They did pass twelve acts of outlawry, on the 9th day of March, A.D. 1774, impowering the respective judges of their supreme court, to award execution of death against those inhabitants in said district that they should judge to be offenders, without trial.

They have, and still continue, an unjust claim to those lands, which greatly retards emigration into, and the settlement of, this State.

They have hired foreign troops, emigrants from *Scotland,* at two different times, and armed them, to drive us out of possession.

They have sent the savages on our frontiers, to distress us.

They have proceeded to erect the counties of Cumberland and Gloucester, and establish courts of justice there, after they were discountenanced by the authority of Great Britain.

The free Convention of the State of *New-York,* at *Harlem,* in the year 1776, unanimously voted, "That all quit-rents formerly due to the King of Great Britain, are now due and owing to this Convention, or such future government as shall be hereafter established in this State."

In the several stages of the aforesaid oppressions, we have petitioned his Britannic majesty, in the most humble manner, for redress, and have, at very great expense, received several reports in our favor; and in other instances, wherein we have petitioned the late legislative authority of *New-York,* those petitions have been treated with neglect.

And whereas, the local situation of this State, from *New-York,* at the extream part, is upwards of four hundred and fifty miles from the seat of that government, which renders it extream difficult to continue under the jurisdiction of said State,

Therefore, it is absolutely necessary, for the welfare and safety of the inhabitants of this State, that it should be, henceforth, a free and independent State; and that a just, permanent and proper form of government, should exist in it, derived from, and founded on, the authority of the people only, agreeable to the direction of the honorable American Congress.

We the representatives of the freemen of *Vermont,* in General Convention met, for the express purpose of forming such a government,—confessing the goodness of the Great Governor of the Universe, (who alone, knows to what degree of earthly happiness, mankind may attain, by perfecting the arts of government,) in permitting the people of this State, by common consent, and without violence, deliberately to form for themselves, such just rules as they shall think best for governing their future society; and being fully convinced that it is our indispensable duty, to establish such original principles of government, as will best promote the general happiness of the people of this State, and their posterity, and provide for future improvement, without partiality for, or prejudice against, any particular class, sect, or denomination of men whatever,—do, by virtue of authority vested in us, by our constituents, ordain, declare, and establish, the following declaration of rights, and frame of government, to be the CONSTITUTION of this COMMONWEALTH, and to remain in force therein, forever, unaltered, except in such articles, as shall, hereafter, on experience, be found to require improvement, and which shall, by the same authority of the people, fairly delegated, as this frame of government directs, be amended or improved, for the more effectual obtaining and securing the great end and design of all government, herein before mentioned.

CHAPTER I.

A Declaration of the Rights of the Inhabitants of the

State of Vermont

I. That all men are born equally free and independent, and have certain natural, inherent and unalienable rights, amongst which are the enjoying and defending life and liberty; acquiring, possessing and protecting property, and pursuing and obtaining happiness and safety. *Therefore, no male person, born in this country, or brought from over sea, ought to be holden by law, to serve any person, as a servant, slave or apprentice, after he arrives to the age of twenty-one years, nor female, in like manner, after she arrives to the age of eighteen years, unless they are bound by their own consent, after they arrive at such age, or bound by law, for the payment of debts, damages, fines, costs, or the like.*

II. *That private property ought to be subservient to public uses, when necessity requires it; nevertheless, whenever any particular man's property is taken for the use of the public, the owner ought to receive an equivalent in money.*

III. That all men have a natural and unalienable right to worship ALMIGHTY GOD, according to the dictates of their own consciences and understanding, regulated by the word of GOD; and that no man ought, or, of right, can be compelled to attend any religious worship, or erect, or support any place of worship, or maintain any minister, contrary to the dictates of his conscience; nor *can any man who professes the protestant religion* be justly deprived or abridged of any civil right as a citizen, on account of his religious sentiment, or peculiar mode of religious worship, and that no authority can, or ought to be vested in, or assumed by, any power whatsoever, that shall in any case, interfere with, or in any manner controul, the rights of conscience, in the free exercise of religious worship; *nevertheless, every sect or denomination of people ought to observe the Sabbath, or the Lord's day, and keep up, and support, some sort of religious worship, which to them shall seem most agreeable to the revealed will of God.*

IV. *That the people of this State have the sole, exclusive and inherent right of governing and regulating the internal police of the same.*

V. That all power being originally inherent in, and consequently, derived from the people; therefore, all officers of government, whether legislative or executive, are their trustees and servants, and at all times accountable to them.

VI. That government is, or ought to be, instituted for the common benefit, protection, and security of the people, nation or community; and not for the particular emolument or advantage of any single man, family or set of men, who are a part only of that community; and that the community hath an indubitable, unalienable and indefeasible right to reform, alter, or abolish government, in such manner as shall be, by that community, judged most conducive to the public weal.

VII. That those who are employed in the legislative and executive business of the State, may be restrained from oppression, the people have a right, at such periods as they may think proper, to reduce their public officers to a private station, and supply the vacancies by certain and regular elections.

VIII. That all elections ought to be free; and that all freemen, having a sufficient, evident common interest with, and attachment to, the community, have a right to elect officers, or be elected into office.

IX. That every member of society hath a right to be protected in the enjoyment of life, liberty and property, and therefore, is bound to contribute his proportion towards the expense of that protection, and yield his personal service, when necessary, or an equivalent thereto; but no part of a man's property can be justly taken from him or applied to public uses, without his own consent, or that of his legal representatives; nor can any man who is conscientiously scrupulous of bearing arms, be justly compelled thereto, if he will pay such equivalent; nor are the people bound by any law, but such as they have in like manner, assented to, for their common good.

X. That, in all prosecutions for criminal offences, a man hath a right to be heard, by himself and his counsel—to demand the cause and nature of his accusation—to be confronted with the witnesses—to call for evidence in his favor, and a speedy public trial, by an impartial jury of the country; without the unanimous consent of which jury he cannot be found guilty; nor can he be compelled to give evidence against himself; nor can any man be justly deprived of his liberty, except by the laws of the land or the judgment of his peers.

XI. That the people have a right to hold themselves, their houses, papers and possessions free from search or seizure; and therefore warrants, without oaths or affirmations first made, affording a sufficient foundation for them, and whereby any officer or messenger may be commended or required to search suspected places, or to seize any person or persons, his, her or their property, not particularly described, are contrary to that right, and ought not to be granted.

XII. *That no warrant or writ to attach the person or estate of any free-holder within this state, shall be issued in civil action, without the person or persons, who may request such warrant or attachment, first make oath, or affirm, before the authority who may be requested to issue the same, that he, or they, are in danger of losing his, her or their debts.*

XIII. That, in controversies respecting property, and in suits between man and man, the parties have a right to a trial by jury; which ought to be held sacred.

XIV. That the people have a right to freedom of speech, and of writing and publishing their sentiments; therefore, the freedom of the press ought not to be restrained.

XV. That the people have a right to bear arms for the defence of themselves and the State; and, as standing armies, in the time of peace, are dangerous to liberty, they ought not to be kept up; and that the military should be kept under strict subordination to, and governed by, the civil power.

XVI. That frequent recurrence to fundamental principles, and a firm adherence to justice, moderation, temperance, industry and frugality, are absolutely necessary to preserve the blessings of liberty, and keep government free. The people ought, therefore, to pay particular attention to these points, in the choice of officers and representatives, and have a right to exact a due and constant regard to them, from their legislators and magistrates, in the making and executing such laws as are necessary for the good government of the State.

XVII. That all people have a natural and inherent right to emigrate from one State to another, that will receive them; or to form a new State in vacant countries, or in such countries as they can purchase, whenever they think that thereby they can promote their own happiness.

XVIII. That the people have a right to assemble together, to consult for their common good—to instruct their representatives, and to apply to the legislature for redress of grievances, by address, petition or remonstrances.

XIX. *That no person shall be liable to be transported out of this State, for trial, for any offence committed within this State. . . .*

Source: E. P. Walton, ed., *Records of the Council of Safety and Governor and Council of the State of Vermont*, Vol. 1 (Montpelier: Steam Press, 1873), pp. 90-95.

Document 3

"A Chorographical Map of the Northern Department of North-America" (1778/80)

BERNARD ROMANS

(depicted on following page)

Source: Special Collections, Bailey/Howe Library, University of Vermont. Reprinted courtesy of Special Collections, UVM Libraries.

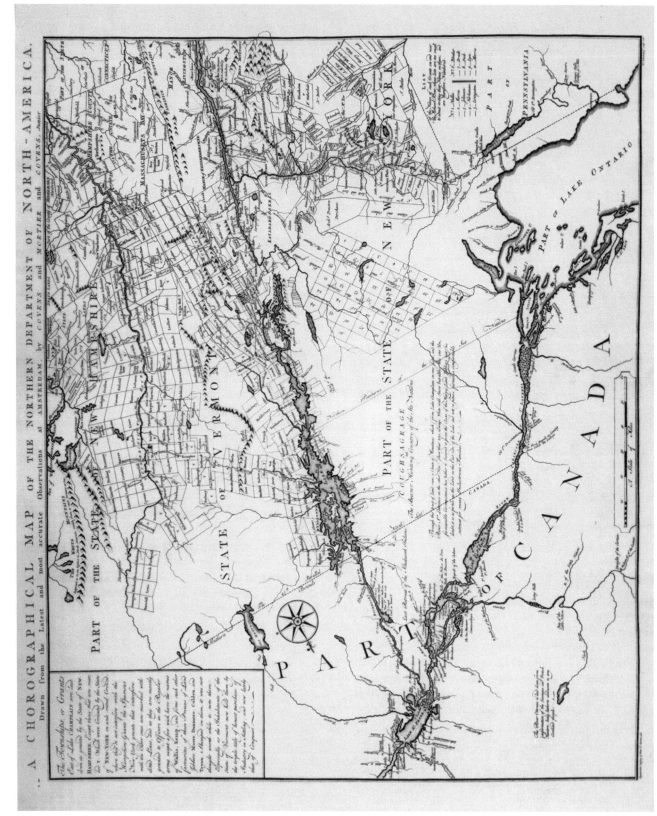

Document 3

DOCUMENT 4

Account of the Battle of Bennington (1777)

GENERAL JOHN STARK

Bennington, August 18th, 1777

GENTLEMEN—I congratulate you on the late success of your Troops under my command; by express I purpose to give you a brief account of my proceedings since I wrote to you last.

I left Manchester on Sunday the 8th Inst. And arrived here the 9th. The 13th I was inform'd that a party of Indians were at Cambridge which is 12 miles distant from this place on their march thither. I detached Col [William] Gregg with 200 men under his command to stop their march. In the evening I had information by express that there was a large body of the enemy on their way with their field pieces, in order to march through the country, commanded by Govern[o]r Skene. The 14th I marched with my Brigade & a few of this States' Militia, to oppose them, and to cover Gregg's retreat, who found himself unable to withstand their superior numbers: About four miles from the Town. I accordingly met him on his return, and the Enemy in close pursuit of him, within half a mile of his rear; but when they discovered me they presently halted on a very advantageous piece of ground. I drew up my little army on an eminince in open view of their encampments, but could not bring them to an engagement. I marched back about a mile, and there encamp'd. I sent out a few men to skirmish with them, kill'd thirty of them with two Indian Chiefs. The 15th it rain'd all day; I sent out parties to harass them.

The 16th I was join'd by this States' Militia and those of Berkshire County; I divided my army into three Divisions, and sent Col. [Moses] Nichols with 250 men on their rear of their left wing; Col Hendrick in the Rear of their right, with 300 men, order'd when join'd to attack the same.

In the mean time I sent 300 men to oppose the Enemy's front, to draw their attention that way; Soon, after I detach'd the Colonels [David] Hubbart

[Hobart] & [Thomas] Stickney on their right wing with 200 men to attack that part, all which plans had their desired effect. Col Nichols sent me word that he stood in need of a reinforcement, which I readily granted, consisting of 100 men, at which time he commenced the attack precisely at 3 o'clock in the afternoon, which was followed by all the rest. I pushed forward the remained with all speed; *our people behaved with the greatest spirit & bravery imaginable: Had they been Alexanders or Charleses of Sweden, they could not have behaved better.* The action lasted two hours, at the expiration of which time, we forced their Breastworks at the muzzles of their guns, took two pieces of Brass cannon, with a number of prisoners;—but before I could get them into proper form again, I recd intelligence that there was a large reinforcement within two miles of us on their march, with occasion'd us to renew our attack. But luckily for us Col [Seth] Warner's Regiment came up, which put a stop to their career. We soon rallied, & in a few minutes the action became very warm & desperate, which lasted till night; we used their own cannon against them, which prov'd of great service to us. At Sunset we obliged them to retreat a second time; we pursued them till dark, when I was obliged to halt for fear of killing my own men. We recovered two pieces more of their cannon, together will all their Baggage, a number of horses, carriages &c. kill'd upwards of two hundred of the enemy in the field of Battle, the number of the wounded is not yet known as they are scattered about in many places.

I have 1 Lieut. Col since dead, 1 major, 7 Captains, 14 Lieuts, 4 Ensigns, 2 Cornets, 1 Judge advocate, 1 Barron, 2 Cannadian officers, 6 Sergeants, 1 Aid-de-camp & seven hundred prisoners;—I almost forgot 1 Hessian Chaplain. I enclose you a copy of General Burgoyne's Instructions to Col [Freidrich] Baum, who commanded the detachment that engaged us. Our wounded are 42; ten private & four officers belonging to my Brigade is dead. The dead & wounded in the other Corps I do not know, as they have not brought in the returns as yet.

I am Gentlemen, with the greatest regard & respect,

Your most obedient, Hum[b]le ser[an]t
[John Stark]

I almost forgot 3 Hessian surgeons.

N.B. I have sent you by the Post, Josiah Crosby, one hundred seventy four Dollars & two thirds, of Hampshire currency, which I had to give Contin[enta]l for to my men, as there is scarce any other will pass here.

Gentlemen—I think we have return'd the enemy a proper Complim't in the above action, for the Hubbart-town engagement.

Source: *State Papers, Documents and Records of New-Hampshire . . . from 1776 to 1783*, Vol. 8 (Concord, N.H.: Edward A. Jenks, 1874), pp. 670-71.

DOCUMENT 5

A Public Defence of the Right of the New-Hampshire Grants (so called) on both Sides of the Connecticut-River, to Associate Together, and Form Themselves into an Independent State (1779)

Dresden: Printed by Alden Spooner, 1779

. . . We shall now offer some reasons of the propriety of the Grants being a distinct State, upon principles of prudence and equity.

And, 1st. As to *their local situation*—the lands near Connecticut-River, between the mountains heights on each side, that are suitable for cultivation, in a general way are about thirty-six or forty miles wide, and about one hundred and fifty miles in length from Massachusetts North line (as they now exercise jurisdiction) to Canada South line, as settled in 1764; through which Connecticut-River runs so as about equally divides it lengthwise, and therefore the River's being made a dividing line between two States, divides a country that Providence has wisely calculated to belong together, and so situated that the inhabitants living thereon may, by being united, manage their political affairs with convenience; and so calculated by proper intervales

through the western mountains or heights, that the passes to and from the inhabitants on the Grants west of the Green Mountains (so called) are convenient.

2. The *connections and commerce of the people* on each side of the river, are, and always will be, so *interwoven and connected* with each other, that it would be very disadvantageous to be in two different jurisdictions.

3. The inhabitants (almost to a man) emigrated from the Massachusetts-Bay and Connecticut, but chiefly from Connecticut; whereby their *manners, customs and habits are conformable to each other*, and their principles and sentiments the same in regard to religion and civil government; but very different from the people of the States of New-York and New-Hampshire: which different principles by education and custom are become so habitual and hereditary, that it is beyond the power of man to eradicate them, and therefore will cause a jarring discord between them so long as they are continued together.

4. The Grants (exclusive of those in the northeast part which lie more contiguous to the center of *New-Hampshire*) will make a respectable State by themselves, and the other two States not be injured thereby, especially New-York; and as to New-Hampshire, it will be much larger than it ever was until since the last war, and more than twice as large in extent of territory as the State of Rhode-Island.

5. The people inhabiting these lands, having undergone the hardships and fatigues of settling this once howling wilderness, and the sufferings and losses occasioned by the war; and having exerted themselves to their utmost (in the grand American cause) with their brethren of the United States, ought not after all to be divided and apportioned to and between New-York and New-Hampshire, merely to serve themselves of us, for their political and interested purposes— and all because they will establish that arbitrary line of 1764.

6. *These Grants* are so situated that they *will always be an important frontier to the United States* (so long as Canada continues under the control of Great-Britain) and by being a distinct

State, will be in a much better capacity to act their part as such, than by being the outskirts of other States.

7. In the early settlement of this country, the Reverend Doctor Wheelock's charity school, [Dartmouth College] founded on the most noble and benevolent basis, and incorporated with a University by a grant or patent from the King of Great-Britain, was introduced and settled in this part of the country; which we esteem an inestimable benefit and advantage to this new State, as well as to the Continent; and which the inhabitants of this State are disposed to patronize to their utmost—but on the contrary, if it falls into the State of New-Hampshire, it will be in a State which has heretofore (as such) shewn a very cool disposition towards it, and probably will continue the same neglect of it, and principally (perhaps) on account of its situation.

8. The people on the Grants are well agreed and united in their plan of government already adopted, whereas New-Hampshire have not as yet agreed on any, and there is very little prospect (by accounts) that they will soon. And as to New-York constitution or plan of government, if there was no other objection, that alone would be a sufficient bar in the way of connecting them.

9. The great distance most of the towns would be at from their several seats of government, in case they were connected with New-York and New-Hampshire, is a powerful reason why they should not belong to them, if there was nothing else to be offered on the head.

10. Therefore, on the whole of the foregoing facts and observations, we are fully persuaded (and believe every impartial judge will be also) that the people on the Grants, considered in every point of view, have a natural, legal and equitable right to unite together and form themselves into a distinct State or Government, in the manner they have done, and that they are all on both sides of the river, upon the same political foundation, and have an equal right to act in the affair: for certainly if the line settled in 1764 is established for New-Hampshire, it is also for New-York: and if it is void to New-York, it is also void as to New-Hampshire: but sufficient has been already offered to shew that it is void as to both.

And as we are determined to be and remain together, and not be split up and divided merely to serve the interested and designing purposes of New-York and New-Hampshire, or any others; and to convince all that our motives do not arise (as has been represented) from ambitious and schismatical principles: but on the contrary, that they are only to obtain the privileges and benefits of civil government in common with our American brethren, and to put an end to all disputes on account of our being a distinct State, &c. We would recommend that the following terms and proposals be made to the Assembly of New Hampshire, viz.

1. To agree upon and settle a dividing line between New Hampshire and the Grants, by committees from each party, or otherwise, as they may mutally agree.

Or, 2. That the parties mutually agree in a Court of Commissioners of disinterested, judicious men, of the three other New-England States, to hear and determining the disputes.

Or, 3. That the whole dispute with New-Hampshire be submitted to the decison of Congress, in such way and manner as Congress in their wisdom shall prescribe.

Provided always, That the Grants be allowed equal privilege with the other party, in espousing and conducting their cause.

Or, 4. If the controversy cannot be settled on either of the foregoing articles, and in case we can agree with New-Hampshire upon a plan of government, inclusive of extent of territory, that we unite with them, and become with them one entire State, rejecting the arbitrary line drawn on the western bank of Connecticut river, by the King of Great Britain in 1764. . . .

JACOB BAYLEY,
    ELISHA PAYNE,
        BEZA WOODWARD, Committee

New-Hampshire Grants, Dec. 1, 1778.

Source: E. P. Walton, ed., *Records of the Governor and Council of the State of Vermont*, Vol. 5 (Montpelier: Steam Press, 1877), pp. 536-539.

DOCUMENT 6

Congress Attempting to Settle Vermont Disputes (1780)

WHEREAS it is represented to Congress, and by authentic evidence laid before them it appears, that the people inhabiting the district of country commonly known by the name of the New-Hampshire Grants, and claiming to be an independant state, have, notwithstanding the resolutions of Congress of the 24th of September and 2d of October, proceeded, as a separate government, to make grants of lands and sales of estates by them declared forfeited and confiscated; and have also, in divers instances, exercised civil and military authority over the persons and effects of sundry inhabitants within the said district who profess themselves to be citizens of and to owe allegiance to the state of New-York:

RESOLVED, That the acts and proceedings of the people inhabiting the said district, and claiming to be an independant state as aforesaid, in contravening the good intentions of the said resolutions of the 24th of September and 2d of October last, are highly unwarrantable and subversive of the peace and welfare of the United States.

That the people inhabiting the said district and claiming to be an independant state as aforesaid be and they hereby are strictly required to forbear and obtain from all acts of authority, civil or military, over the inhabitants of any town or district who hold themselves to be subjects of, and to owe allegiance to, any of the states claiming the jurisdiction of the said territory, in whole or in part, until the decisions and determinations in the resolutions afore mentioned shall be made.

And whereas the states of New-Hampshire and New-York have complied with the said resolutions of the 24th of September and 2d of October last, and by their Agents and Delegates in Congress declared themselves ready to proceed in supporting their respective rights to the jurisdiction of the district aforesaid, in whole or in part, according to their several claims, and in the mode prescribed in the said resolutions: And whereas Congress, by their order of the 21st of March last, did postpone the consideration of the said resolutions, nine states, exclusive of those who were parties to the question, not being represented; and by their order of the 17th of May last have directed that letters be written to the states not represented, requesting them immediately to send forward a representation:

RESOLVED, That Congress will, as soon as nine states, exclusive of those who are parties to the controversy, shall be represented, proceed to hear and examine into and finally determine the disputes and differences relative to jurisdiction between the three states of New-Hampshire, Massachusetts-Bay and New-York, respectively, or such of them as shall have passed such laws as are mentioned in the said resolutions of the 24th day of September and 2d of October last, on the one part, and the people of the district aforesaid, who claim to be a separate jurisdiction, on the other, in the mode prescribed in and by the said resolutions.

Extract from the minutes,
In Congress, June 2d, 1780.

Source: "Congress Attempting to Settle Vermont Disputes," June 1780, Broadside, Special Collections, Bailey/Howe Library, University of Vermont.

DOCUMENT 7

Vermont Participants Justify the Haldimand Negotiations (1781)

Certificate for the Protection of Colonel Ira Allen
Whereas this state is not in union with the United States, although [it] often requested [to be]. This the British power are acquainted with and are endeavoring to take advantage of these disputes thereby to court a connexion with this state on the principle of establishing it a British province. From various accounts we are well assured that the British have a force in Canada larger than this state can at present raise and support in the field, and this state have no assurance of any assistance from any or either of the United States however hard the British forces may crowd on this state from the province of Quebec by the advantage of the waters of lake Champlain, etc. Although several expresses

have been sent by the governor of this state to several of the respective governors of the United States with the most urgent requests to know whether any assistance would be afforded in such case, yet no official answer has been made to either of them.

Wherefore we the subscribers do fully approbate Col. Ira Allen sending a letter dated Sunderland, July 10, 1781, and directed to Gen. Haldimand, and another letter to Capt. Justice Sherwood, purporting an intention of this state's becoming a British province, etc. This we consider a political proceeding to prevent the British forces from invading this state, and being a necessary step to preserve this state from ruin, when we have too much reason to apprehend that this has been the wishes of some of our assuming neighbors, in the mean time to strengthen the state against any insult until this state receives better treatment from the United States or obtain a seat in Congress.

THOMAS CHITTENDEN JONAS FAY
JOHN FASSETT [Jr.]   SAMUEL ROBINSON
TIMOTHY BROWNSON JOSEPH FAY

Source: E. P. Walton, ed., *Records of the Governor and Council of the State of Vermont*, Vol. 2 (Montpelier: Steam Press, 1874), p. 431.

DOCUMENT 8

Proclamation Welcoming Vermont into the British Empire (1781)

FREDERICK HALDIMAND

Whereas, his Majesty, persevering in his humane endeavours to prevent the Calamities of War, Hath been Graciously pleased to grant unto me, in general Terms, permission to treat with, and to propose to His Subjects in the District of Country called Vermont such Terms for accommodation as might appear to me best calculated to recall them to their Allegiance, and to rescue them from the oppression of their interested deluders, by re-uniting them upon a respectable and permanent footing, with the Mother Country—Happy in the prospect of being Instrumental to so desirable an event, I embrace this mode, as the most public, of declaring to the people of Vermont, that upon their cor-

dially and effectually re-uniting themselves, as a Government under the Crown of Great Britain, they shall be considered by the same a separate province, independent of, and unconnected with every Government in America, and will be entitled to and shall enjoy every prerogative and immunity promised to the other provinces in the Proclamation of the King's Commissioners, comprehending Charter rights, as formerly enjoyed by the province of Connecticut, the right of appointing a governor excepted, which must rest in the Crown.

In order the more effectually to remove every jealousy on the part of the people of Vermont (industriously infused by designing Men into the minds of the Ignorant) of Great Britain's wishing to deprive them of their liberty, and to curtail their Interest by limitting their possessions—and in order to remove the injuries said to have been exercised against them by the New York Government, in obtaining Grants of Land which had, in consequence of Grants from New Hampshire, been cultivated by the labour and industry of the Inhabitants of the Green Mountains—I hereby further promise, that, until such time as His Majesty's pleasure shall be signified to me, or that I shall have authority from one of the King's Commissioners (for which I have already made application) to confirm to the said people of Vermont their late acquisition of Territory, together with their Landed Property, as granted under New Hampshire, Viz—From the North Line of Massachusetts, North, to the South Line of Canada, and from the Hudson's River, East, to the Mason Line, I shall consider the same, to all intents and purposes, belonging to the Province of Vermont, and I shall to them the same protection, privileges and Immunities herein promised to the Inhabitants of the original District.

A free Trade with Canada will likewise be granted and encouraged, and the more effectually to protect the said people of Vermont in their possessions, a co-operative Force sufficient for that purpose will, at all times, be provided by the Crown, and the Vermont Troops shall have every present and future Advantage in common with the provincials now serving with the King's Army.

Thus, it is hoped, Terms so eminently humane and generous will not leave a doubt remaining with the people of Vermont of the sincere and friendly intentions of Great Britain, and dispose them, tho' late, to give a virtuous Example to their Countrymen by acknowledging, tho' late, their Error, and putting a stop to a ruinous and unnatural War, destructive to the harmony and mutual affection, which, until its fatal Commencement, constituted the happiness and Strength of both Countries, and successfully defended their religion and Laws against the baneful Influence of Despotism.

Given, &c.,   [Signed]   F. H.

Source: E. P. Walton, ed., *Records of the Governor and Council of the State of Vermont*, Vol. 2 (Montpelier: Steam Press, 1874), pp. 447-448.

DOCUMENT 9

U.S. Plan to Invade Vermont (1782)

October 7, 1782

In case the expedition should be serious, let the whole of New Hampshire and the eastern parts of Mass. march suddenly up to [Fort] No. 4 and enter the Vermont Country on the East side of it, and seize every horse and horn cattle of whatever age or size and hogs and sheep, takeing an account of the persons names & residence from whom they are taken, and to whom they are to be delivered regular in Townships if possible, such horses and horn cattle as are most fit for the [team?], should be retained awhile to draw together in four or five convenient deposits wide of the lakes all the grain & corn they can find, leaving the families two months provisions. The cattle fit for beef should be driven down to our army. The inhabitants of the country should be informed, that in case of their good and faithfull behaviour to the United States &c. they should have their property restored to them, but in case of a contrary behaviour, their country should be laid desolate. Thus the Brittish General instead of obtaining any assistance from the Vermonteers would find himself incumbered with some thousands of useless mouths, whom he in honor would be obliged to maintain.

When from good evidence it should be reduced to a certainty that the enemy are approaching, and that the Vermonteers are about to join them or furnishing them with provision, teams or any other assistance, the above plan ought to be instantly carried into execution in the most rapid manner, and therefore it may be worthy consideration how far it will be necessary or prudent to trust the secret with those States which are to execute it.

The Governors of New York and New Hampshire should at the same time issue their proclamations giveing their promises of full pardon of all past offences to all such as do immediately come to proper persons to be appointed for that purpose, and their take the oaths of allegiance to the respective State they of right should belong to and title to the land they possess from the proprietors of the soil in such States and binding themselves with their neighbours as securities for the payment of the rent and consideration money as to be agreed on and also engageing to assist in detecting and takeing prisoners and delivering up the Gov. and the leading men who are active opposeing the government of the said two States; and when they have thus shown themselves faithfull to the said two States and the enemy haveing retired to Canada, they shall have their cattle and other property restored to them, but that all others shall have no property restored to them untill they have paid up their arrears of taxes from the time of their revolt and all other damages they have done the said States and proprietors of the land they have withheld from them.

It might perhaps be going far enough to seize and drive of all the cattle and swine and sheep, for if they are deprived of those they can neither eat meat, nor remove their grain or any other bulky property, and consequently out of their power to give the enemy any usefull assistance, but while the business is begun they had best go thro' with it for their future good behaviour. + another body might enter of the SW side from Berkshire & Charlote Counties to cut off their immediate communication with the enemy.

Source: "Memorandum," October 7, 1782, manuscript document, Special Collections, Bailey/Howe Library, University of Vermont. Reprinted courtesy of Special Collections, UVM Libraries.

"An Act for Settling Disputes Respecting Landed Property" (1785)

October 27, 1785

Whereas many persons have purchased supposed titles to land within this State, and have taken possession of such lands under such titles, and made large improvements on the same; and who having no legal title to such Lands, must, if the strict rules of the common law be attended to, be turned off from their possessions made at great expense.

Be it enacted and it is hereby enacted by the Representatives of the freemen of the State of Vermont in General Assembly met, and by the authority of the same, that when any person or persons in the actual possession and improvement of lands to which he or she or they so in possession, or those under whom they hold, had purchased a title supposing at the time of purchase, such title to be good in fee, and having in consequence of such purchase, entered and made improvements upon such lands shall be prosecuted before any Court by action of ejectment, or any other real or possessory action to final judgment, and judgment shall be given against such person or persons in possession as aforesaid, such person or persons as aforesaid against whom judgment shall be finally given as aforesaid, shall have right by action to recover of the person or persons in whom the legal right shall be found by such judgment, the value of the improvements and betterments made on such lands by such possessor or possessors, or those under whom they hold: And the manner of process shall be that the recoveree or recoverees in such action as aforesaid shall within forty eight hours after judgment or during the sitting of said Court file a declaration in an action of the case against the recoveror or recoverors for so much money as the Estate is made better as aforesaid in the Clerks office of the Court where such judgment was obtained, which shall be deemed as sufficient notice to the adverse party to appear and defend in such action on the case, at the next session of said Court . . . and if on trial it shall be found necessary that a view be had of the premises, to ascertain how much the Estate is made better as aforesaid, the Court on motion made by either party may grant such view, and all the reasonable charges arising by such view shall be paid by the party moving the same.

And be it further enacted by the authority aforesaid, that the Jury in estimating the value of the improvements shall assess the value of the lands as they were when the settlement was begun by the possessor or possessors, and shall also assess the value of such Lands at the time of such assessment, as if the same were then uncultivated, and shall allow to the possessor or possessors the one half of what such lands have risen in value and shall in addition thereto assess to the possessor or possessors the just value of making the improvements, with the buildings and other betterments made on such lands by the possessor or possessors, or those under whom they hold; and if any doubt shall arise respecting the quantity of such land to be estimated by the Jury, it is hereby declared to be the duty of such Jury to appraise the improvements and betterments on all the Land described in such action.

And be it further enacted by the authority aforesaid that when any person or persons, who have entered and made improvements on lands to which he, she, or they, had no such supposed title as aforesaid, shall be prosecuted before any Court by action of ejectment, or other real or possessory action, and judgment shall be finally given against such possessor or possessors, he, she, or they, shall have right to recover of the legal owner thereof the value of his, her or their, improvements, to be estimated in manner as aforesaid. . . .

Source: John A. Williams, ed., *Laws of Vermont*, Vol. 14 (Montpelier: Secretary of State, 1966), pp. 64-65.

Document 11

Poem Calling for a Legal-Tender Act (1786)

THOMAS ROWLEY

By hardy creditors oppressed,
Who of our ruin make a jest,
While to assist them in their plans,
The law has furnished numerous clans

Of judges, justices and lawyers,
Relentless as their vile employers;
Sheriffs and deputies by scores,
That still are thundering at our doors;
And if we dare not given them battle,
Seize on our hogs, sheep, and cattle,
And to our creditors transfer them,
Who, with themselves and lawyers, share them.
Is not the Scripture full of phrases,
That speak aloud all poor men's praises?
Declaring *them* God's chosen ones,
To whom the earth of right belongs?
Forbidding all t'oppress their debtors,
Whom God esteems so much their betters?
Is't not declared damnation waits
All creditors of great estates?
That they'll be saved less easily
Than camel pierces needle's eye?
Their good, far more than *ours*, we seek,
To make them humble, poor and meek,
That they may share those heavenly mansions,
To which they now have no pretensions.

Source:*Vermont Gazette* (Bennington), 21 August 1786.

DOCUMENT 12

Vermont's Reaction to Shays's Rebellion (1787)

By his Excellency
THOMAS CHITTENDEN,
*Esq; Captain-General, Governor, and Commander in
Chief, in and over
the STATE OF VERMONT,*
A PROCLAMATION

WHEREAS the General Court of the Commonwealth of Massachusetts, by their act of the fourth of February instant, declared, that a horrid and wicked rebellion did exist in said Commonwealth, and that DANIEL SHAYS of Pelham, and LUKE DAY of West Springfield, in the county of Hampshire, ADAM WHEELER of Hubbardston, in the county of Worcester, and ELI PARSONS, of Adams, in the county of

Berkshire, were the principal aiders and abettors of said Rebellion, and there being great reason to fear that some of the citizens of this State who dwell near to and adjoining the said Commonwealth may incautiously and unadvisedly give aid to the promoters and abettors of the said rebellion, and thereby violate the duty they owe to law and good government:

I have therefore thought fit, by and with the advice of the Council, and at the request of the General Assembly, to issue this proclamation, strictly commanding and enjoining it upon all the citizens of this State, not to harbour, entertain, or conceal the said DANIEL SHAYS, LUKE DAY, ADAM WHEELER, and ELI PARSONS. And I do hereby require all and every the Justices of the Peace within this State, to issue their warrants when required, to apprehend and convey the aforesaid persons, or either of them, to the Commonwealth of Massachusetts, there to be delivered to some civil or military officer, authorised to receive them:

And all the citizens of this State are absolutely and most solemnly forbidden to take arms in support of, or to engage in the service, or contribute to the relief of the abettors and promoters of the said rebellion, by furnishing them with arms, ammunition, or otherwise, as they will answer it at their peril.

*Given under my Hand, in Council, Bennington, this
27th Day of February, A.D. 1787, and the eleventh Year
of the Independence of this State.*

THOMAS CHITTENDEN
By His Excellency's command,
JOSEPH FAY, *Secretary.*

Source: E. P. Walton, ed., *Records of the Governor and Council for the State of Vermont*, Vol. 2 (Montpelier: Steam Press, 1874), pp. 377-378.

* * *

Messrs. Printers,—As many unfavorable allegations have been spread abroad, to injure the good people of Vermont, relative to their harboring the insurgents from Massachusetts, the following transaction may serve to shew our disposition not to encourage factious and rebellious fugitives who have fled from justice.

On Monday se'nnight [April 30] about one hundred of the rebels from Massachusetts, who fled from justice, met at Captain Galusha's in Shaftsbury, in convention, to agree on measures for continuing their opposition to that government. The authority of Shaftsbury, being alarmed at such an illegal collection, immediately met, and demanded of the insurgents the occasion of their meeting. A committee, consisting of a Col. Smith (who was appointed their president) and four others, were chosen to make answer to this demand, which was, "That they were driven from their country, and had convened with a view of concerting measures whereby they might return and enjoy their properties," and on being duly questioned they produced two letters, one from Shays and one from another of their principals, encouraging them to hold out and be spirited in their opposition for a few weeks longer and they might be assured of relief. Judge [Gideon] Olin, who acted as principal on the part of the authority, conducted with a spirit truly patriotic and noble. He informed them, that if they were met for the purpose of petitioning the legal authority of Massachusetts for pardon and leave to return, that their proceedings would be deemed highly commendable, but if their views were hostile, and their business was to concert plans for committing depredations and continuing their opposition to that government, they must disperse immediately, for no such unlawful assembling would be allowed in Vermont. Col. Smith answered, that the hope of any advantage by petitioning was at an end.

The sheriff of the county [Jonas Galusha], who had been previously notified, was present for the purpose of dispersing them in case they refused to withdraw. The rebels plead for leave to be by themselves for a few minutes which was granted, after which they dispersed, and proceeded immediately to White-Creek, in the State of New York, where we have understood there was a considerable body collected, who sat in convention from day to day, without opposition.

The Governor and Council of this State have given the strongest assurances to his Excellency Governor Bowdoin, that in case the insurgents residing in this State pursue any measures that are hostile, the most effectual measures shall be taken by the force of this State, for apprehending and delivering them up to his authority for punishment.

Source: *Vermont Gazette* (Bennington), 7 May 1787.

DOCUMENT 13

Chipman-Hamilton Correspondence on Vermont's Joining the Union (1788)

Nathaniel Chipman to Alexander Hamilton

Tinmouth, July 15, 1788.

Sir:—Your character as a federalist, although personally unknown to you, induces me to address you on a subject of very great importance to the state of Vermont, of which I am a citizen, and from which, I think, may be derived a considerable advantage to the federal cause. Ten states having adopted the new federal plan of government [U.S. Constitution], that it will now succeed is beyond a doubt. What disputes the other states may occasion, I know not. The people of this state, I believe, might be induced almost unanimously to throw themselves into the federal scale, could certain obstacles be removed. You are not unacquainted with the situation of a very considerable part of our landed property. Many grants were formerly made by the government of New York, of lands within this territory while under that jurisdiction. On the assumption of government by the people of this state, the same lands, partly it is said for want of information respecting the true situation of these grants, and partly from an opinion prevailing with some of our then leaders, that the New York grants within this territory were of no validity, have been granted to others under the authority of this state.

It is now generally believed, that, should we be received into the union, the New York grants would, by the federal courts, be preferred to those of Vermont. The legislature of this state have in some instances made a compensation to the grantees under New York; and I am persuaded would do the same for others were it in their power, but they are in possession of no more lands for that purpose. For these reasons, and I presume for no others, the governor and several gentlemen deeply interested in these lands granted by Vermont, have expressed themselves somewhat bitterly against the new federal plan of government. Indeed, were we to be admitted into the union unconditionally, it would produce much confusion. Now, sir, permit me to ask whether you do not think it probable that the federal legislature, when formed, might, on our accession to the union, be induced on some terms, to make a compensation to the New York grantees, out of their western lands, and whether those grantees might not be induced to accept such compensation? Let me further suggest, whether it might not be favorable for Vermont to make some of those amendments, which have been proposed by several states, the basis of her admission?

Could the difficulties I have mentioned be removed, all interests in opposition would be reconciled; and the idea of procuring justice to be done to those whom we had, perhaps, injured by our too precipitate measures, and of being connected with a government which promises to be efficient, permanent and honorable, would, I am persuaded, produce the greatest unanimity on the subject. If you think these matters worthy the attention of the friends of the confederacy, be good enough to write by my brother, who will be the bearer of this. Our legislature will meet in October, when these matters will be taken up seriously. Several gentlemen of my acquaintance, who are men of influence and will be members of the legislature, have requested me to procure all the information in my power on this subject. Anything which you may suggest to me in confidence will be sacredly attended to, of which Mr. Kelley, who writes by the same opportunity, will give you the fullest assurance.

I am, with great respect,
Your obedient, humble servant,
NATHANIEL CHIPMAN

* * *

Alexander Hamilton to Nathaniel Chipman
Poughkeepsie, July 22, 1788
Sir:—Your brother delivered me your letter of the 15th inst. which I received with pleasure, as the basis of a correspondence that may be productive of the public good.

The accession of Vermont to the confederacy is doubtless an object of great importance to the whole; and it appears to me that this is the favorable mo-

ment for effecting it upon the best terms for all concerned. Besides more general reasons, there are circumstances at the moment which will forward a proper arrangement. One of the first subjects of deliberation with the new congress will be the independence of Kentucky, for which the southern states will be anxious. The northern will be glad to find a counterpoise in Vermont. These mutual interests and inclinations will facilitate a proper result.

I see nothing that can stand in your way but the interfering claims under the grants of New York. As to taxation, the natural operation of the new system will place you exactly where you might wish to be. The public debt, as far as it can prudently be provided for, will be by the western lands, and the appropriation of some general fund. There will be no distribution of it to particular parts of the community. The fund will be sought for in indirect taxation; as, for a number of years, and except in time of war, direct taxes will be an impolitic measure. Hence, as you can have no objection to your proportion of contribution as consumers, you can fear nothing for the article of taxation.

I readily conceive, that it will be scarcely practicable for you to come into the union, unless you are secured from the claims under New York grants. Upon the whole, therefore, I think it will be expedient for you, as early as possible, to ratify the constitution, upon condition that congress shall provide for the extinguishment of all existing claims to land under grants of the State of New York, which may interfere with claims under the State of Vermont.

You will do well to conform your boundary to that heretofore marked out by congress, otherwise insuperable difficulties would be likely to arise with this state. I should think it altogether unadvisable to annex any other condition to your ratification. For there is scarcely any of the amendments proposed that will not have a party opposed to it; and there are several that will meet with a very strong opposition: and it would therefore be highly inexpedient for you to embarrass your main object by any collateral difficulties. As I write in convention, I have it not in my power to enlarge.

You will perceive my general ideas on the subject. I will only add, that it will be wise to lay as little impediment as possible in the way of your reception into the union. I am, with much esteem, sir, your obedient, humble servant,

A. HAMILTON

Source: E. P. Walton, ed., *Records of the Governor and Council of the State of Vermont*, Vol. 3 (Montpelier: Steam Press, 1875), pp. 441-443.

DOCUMENT 14

A Narrative of the Sufferings of Seth Hubbell & Family (1789)

SETH HUBBELL

. . . In the latter part of February, 1789, I set out from the town of Norwalk, in Connecticut, on my journey for Wolcott, to commence a settlement and make that my residence; family consisting of my wife and five children, they all being girls, the eldest nine or ten years old. My team was a yoke of oxen and a horse. After I had proceeded on my journey to within about one hundred miles of Wolcott, one of my oxen failed, but I however kept him yoked with the other till about noon each day, then turned him before, and took his end of the yoke myself, and proceeded on in that manner with my load to about fourteen miles of my journey's end, when I could get the sick ox no further, and was forced to leave him with Thomas W. Connel, in Johnson; but had neither hay nor grain for him. I then proceeded on with some help to Esq. McDaniel's in Hydepark: this brought me to about eight miles of Wolcott, and to the end of the road. It was now about the 20th of March; the snow not far from four feet deep; no hay to be had for my team, and no way for them to subsist but by browse. As my sick ox at McConnel's could not be kept on browse, I interceded with a man in Cambridge for a little hay to keep him alive, which I backed, a bundle at a time, five miles, for about ten days, when the ox died. On the 6th of April I set out from Esq. McDaniel's, his being the last house, for my intended residence in Wolcott, with my wife and two eldest children. We had eight miles to travel on snow-shoes, by marked trees—no road being cut: my wife had to try this new mode of travelling, and she performed the journey remarkably well. The path had been so trod-

den by snow-shoes as to bare [bear] up the children. Esq. Taylor, with his wife and two small children, who moved on with me, had gone the day before. We were the first families in Wolcott: in Hydepark there had two families wintered the year before. To the east of us it was eighteen miles to inhabitants, and no road but marked trees: to the south, about twenty, where there was infant settlements, but no communication with us; and to the north, it was almost indefinite, or to the regions of Canada. . . .

I moved from Connecticut with the expectation of having fifty acres of land given me when I came on, but this I was disappointed of, and was under the necessity soon after I came on of selling a yoke of oxen and a horse to buy the land I now live on, which reduced my stock to but one cow; and this I had the misfortune to loose [lose] the next winter. That left me wholly destitute of a single hough [hoof] of a creature: of course the second summer I had to support my family without a cow. I would here notice that I spent the summer before I moved, in Wolcott, in making preparation for a settlement, which, however, was of no avail to me, and I lost the summer; and to forward my intended preparation, I brought on a yoke of oxen, and left them, when I returned in the fall, with a man in Johnson, to keep through the winter, on certain conditions; but when I came on in the spring, one of them was dead, and this yoke of oxen that I put off for my land was made of the two surviving ones. But to proceed, in the fall I had the good fortune to purchase another cow; but my misfortunes still continued, for in the June following she was killed by a singular accident. Again I was left without a cow, and here I was again frustrated in my calculations: this last cow left a fine heifer calf that in the next fall I lost by being choaked. Here I was left destitute—no money to buy, or article to traffic for one: but there was a door opened. I was informed that a merchant in Haverhill was making snakeroot and sicily. This was a new kind of traffic that I had no great faith in; but I thought to improve every means or semblance of means in my power. Accordingly, with the help of my two oldest girls, I dug and dried a horse-load, and carried this new commodity to the merchant; but this was like most hearsay reports of fine markets, always a little way ahead, for he knew nothing about this strange article, and would not even venture to make an offer; but after a long conference I importuned with the good merchant to give me a three year old heifer for my roots, on certain conditions too tedious to mention. I drove her home, and with joy she was welcomed to my habitation, and it has been my good fortune to have a cow ever since. Though my faith was weak, yet being vigilant and persevering, I obtained the object, and the wilderness produced me a cow.

When I came into Wolcott my farming tools consisted of one axe and an old hoe. The first year I cleared about two acres, wholly without any team, and being short of provision was obliged to work the chief of the time till harvest with scarce a sufficiency to support nature. My work was chiefly by the river. When too faint to labour, for want of food, I used to take a fish from the river, broil it on the coals, and eat it without bread or salt, and then to my work again. This was my common practice the first year till harvest. I could not get a single potato to plant the first season, so scarce was this article. I then thought if I could but get enough of this valuable production to eat I would never complain. I rarely see this article cooked, but the thought strikes my mind; in fact to this day I have a great veneration for this precious root. I planted that which I cleared in season with corn; and an early frost ruined the crop, so that I raised nothing the first year: had again to buy my provision. My seed corn, about eight quarts, cost me two and a half yards of whitened linen, yard wide, and this I had to go twenty miles after. Though this may be called extortion, it was a solitary instance of the kind; all were friendly and ready to assist me in my known distress, as far as they had ability. An uncommon degree of sympathy pervaded all the new settlers, and I believe this man heartily repented the act, for he was by no means indigent, and was many times reminded of it by way of reproof. . . .

I have here given but a sketch of my most important sufferings. The experienced farmer will readily discover, that under the many embarrassments I had to encounter, I must make but slow progress in clearing land; no soul to help me, no funds to go to: raw and inexperienced in this kind of labor, though future wants pressed the necessity of constant application to this business, a great portion of my time was unavoidably taken up in pursuit of sustenance for my family: however reluctant to leave my labor, the support of nature must be attended to, the calls of hunger cannot be dispensed with. I have now to remark, that at this present time, my almost three score years and ten, I feel the want of those forced exertions of bodily strength that were spent in those perils and fatigues, and have worn down my constitution, to support my decaying nature.

When I reflect on those past events, the fatigue and toil I had to encounter, the dark scenes I had to pass through, I am struck with wonder and astonishment at the fortitude and presence of mind that I then had to bear me up under them. Not once was I discouraged or disheartened: I exercised all my powers of body and mind to do the best I could, and left the effect for future events to decide, without embarrassing my mind with imaginary evils. I could lay down at night, forgetting my troubles, and sleep composed and calm as a child; I did in reality experience the just proverb of the wise man that "the sleep of the laboring man is sweet, whether he eat little or much." Nor can I close my tale of sufferings without rendering my feeble tribute of thanks and praise to my benign Benefactor, who supplies the wants of the needy and relieves the distressed, that in his wise Providence has assisted my natural strength both of body and of mind to endure those scenes of distress and toil.

Source: J. Kevin Graffagnino, ed., *A Narrative of the Sufferings of Seth Hubbell & Family*, 1824 reprint (Bennington, Vt.: Vermont Heritage Press, 1986), pp. 2-4, 5-8, 24-25.

DOCUMENT 15

A Narrative of a Tour through the State of Vermont (1789)
NATHAN PERKINS

. . . Friday came to Bennington 6 miles—Capitol at present of Vermont—a good town of land, people, proud—scornful—conceited & somewhat polished—small meeting house—considerably thick-settled, as many, as can possibly get a living;—no stone;—no fencing timber;—some elegant building;—a County town;—a tolerable Court-house & jail;—a good grammar school. The Revd Mr. Swift their Minister, ye Apostle of Vermont—well esteemed among his own people, & in ye State, at large; put up at his house:—he not at home; gone over to ye College.—his wife handsome,—serious,—weakly,—Lawyer Sedgwick's sister,—ten children one at ye breast,—two daughters grown up, homely,—unpolished,—countrified in manners, and without any elegance. Visited Judge [Moses] Robinson,—Chief justice of ye State. A man of sense & of religion, rich & uncommonly dutiful to an aged Mother, eminent for her attainments in goodness. . . . Monday 9th May,—went to Rutland on ye Otter-creek, a County town, considerably settled, called on Mr. Williams, Esq. and was introduced to Dr. Williams from Cambridge, Massachusetts, late professor of philosophy there, but was guilty of forgery & resigned,—a well looking & learned man—a good speaker, lofty & haughty in his air—& preaching there, to my surprise, elevated with ye idea of having a College there.— Lodged at Mr. Flints in Brandon,—meanest of all lodging,—dirty,—fleas without number. . . .

Thursday 20 of May set out for Williston where governor Chittenden lives.—baptised five children, rode through ye woods, 14 miles, ye riding as bad at it could be, almost half of ye trees in ye woods blown down by ye violence of ye wind last year. Came to one Deacon Talcotts and he accompanied me to his Excellency's Governor Chittenden's. A low poor house.—a plain family—low, vulgar man, clownish, excessively parsimonious,—made me welcome,—hard fare, a very great farm,—1000 acres,—hundred acres of wheat on ye onion river—200 acres of extraordinary interval land. A shrewd cunning man—skilled in human nature & in agriculture—understands extremely well ye mysteries of Vermont, apparently and professedly serious. Williston a fine township of land,— soil fertile. And all ye towns upon ye lake Champlain & for three teer back ye best sort of land. Not very heavy timbered, or stony or mountainous, well intersected with streams, & ye streams full of small fish.— Two noted streams ye Otter-Creek and ye onion river— About 200 towns in the State of Vermont—6 miles square—about 40 of ye towns upon ye green mountains—very cold—snow upon ye top of them till June; commonly—good grazing land about half way up ye green mountains—they almost end at latitude 44 1-2— I go up as far as there are any Settlements large enough to gather a Congregation—within thirty miles of Canada line—days perceiveably longer—in reality 20 minutes longer. Moose plenty on ye mountains over

against Jericho, Essex & Colchester—people hunt them—eat them in lieu of beef—& get their tallow. Bears & wolves plenty—timber, beach,—maple,— pine, hemlock, cherry,—birch & some oak and Walnut—about as many as 40 families, in a town, upon an average, about 40 towns totally unsettled—land extraordinarily good—from Rutland & Tinmouth clear to Canada line. Curiosities of ye country—ye innumerable high mountains 3 & 4 miles up them—1—1-2 perpendicular.—covered with snow now three feet in depth—Lime stone in abundance scattered every where, but no good building stone—a lime pit of two acres in Sunderland—the lower end of ye State poor compared to ye North end—narrow & rough,—No cheese any where—no beef—no butter—I pine for home—for my own table.—Words cannot describe ye hardships I undergo, or ye strength of my desire to see my family—& to be with them. How affectionately do I remember them, hundreds of times every day, & shed a tear, in ye woods—got lost twice in ye woods already—heard ye horrible howling of ye wolves. Far absent—in ye wilderness—among all strangers—all alone—among log-huts—people nasty—poor—low-lived—indelicate—and miserable cooks. All sadly parsimonious—many, profane—yet cheerful & much more contented than in Hartford—and the women more contented than ye men—turned tawny by ye smoke of ye log-huts—dress coarse, & mean, & nasty, & ragged.—Some very clever women & men—serious & sensible. Scarcely any politeness in ye State— Scarcely any sensible preaching—will soon settle Ministers in most of ye towns—and in a few years be a good Country, pleasant, & well to live in.—Some of our Ministers from Connecticut disesteemed, because injudicious—about one tenth part of ye State quakers & anabaptists—Episcopalians, and universalists; & a 1-4 deists. The body of ye people will be like Connecticut—& ye land, take it together rather preferable to ye land in our State—rather more feasible. . .

My living & situation is a paradise compared to Vermont:—far:—far happier than any I have seen.— O how happy! happy am I at home. I will study to be more contented,—more serene,—more thankful. And to make my family so. When I go from hut to hut, from town to town, in ye Wilderness, ye people nothing to eat,—to drink,—or wear,—all work, & yet ye women quiet,—serene,—peaceable,—contented, loving their husbands,—their home,—wanting never to return,—nor any dressy clothes; I think how strange!—I ask myself are these women of ye same species with our fine Ladies? tough are they, brawny their limbs,—their young girls unpolished—& will bear work as well as mules. Woods makes people love one another & kind & obliging and good natured. They set much more by one another than in ye old settlements. Leave their doors unbarred. Sleep quietly *amid flees—bedbuggs—dirt & rags.* . . .

One thing is now deeply affecting. The frowns of ye Almighty are on this State for their sins. The seasons have been for two years back very unfavorable. A famine is now felt in this land. I have heard.—I have read of famines, but never saw one before, or was in ye midst of one. the year 1789 will be remembered by Vermont as a day of calamity and famine—*dearness of truck & want of bread in all their dwellings.* It is supposed by ye most judicious & knowing that more than 1-4 part of ye people will have neither bread nor meat for 8 weeks—and that some will starve. How affecting ye idea! I have mourned with ye inhabitants. Several women I saw had lived four or five days without any food, and had eight or ten Children starving around them—crying for bread & ye poor women had wept till they looked like Ghosts. Many families have lived for weeks on what ye people call Leeks—a sort of wild onion—very offensive to me—it poisons all ye milk & Butter of ye new settlements, while ye Cows go in ye woods. . . .

Vermont will not be a grain Country after a few years. Not a wheat—or rye—or Indian corn Country, particular spots excepted. Nor a very good Country for Orchards. I suffer as much for ye want of drink as any thing. Brook-water is my chief drink. The maple cyder is horrible stuff—no malt in ye Country.—Their beer poor bran beer.—Visited about 50 new towns. preached about 6 days in seven. . . .

Burlington & Shelburn.—Arrived at *Onion-river* & passed by Ethan Allyn's grave. An awful Infidel, one of ye wickedest men yt ever walked this guilty globe. I shopped & looked at his grave with a pious horror.—Rode on to Burlington Bay—one of ye most delightful places in nature. Passed over Colchester-bridge, one of ye greatest curiosities of Vermont—ye Bridge about sixty feet from ye ground on two high rocks on each bank, where all ye waters of ye onion river are compressed into a narrow space of 40 feet.—From Burlington Bay, I set out alone unaccompanied to Shelburn through ye wilderness on ye Lake Champlain—next to no rode—mud up to my horse's belly—roots thick as they could be, no house for 4 miles.—I got lost. My horse nearly gave out, excessively worried with ye bad travelling. O how anxious was I! I expected every step to be killed.—I was hungry, dry, had been almost exhausted by labours in preaching, conversing & gathering a Church.—How much would I have given to have been at home—to have seen my dear wife & children. It seemed as if I never should have ye pleasure again to see them. Night come on—I could travel no farther—I found a little log hut & put up there. Could get no supper—my horse no feed—Slept on a Chaff-bed without covering—a man, his wife & 3 children all in ye same nasty stinking room. . . .

Source: Nathan Perkins, *A Narrative of a Tour through the State of Vermont from April 27 to June 12, 1789* (Woodstock, Vt.: The Yankee Bookshop, 1937), pp. 12-13, 15, 17-19, 20-21, 21-22, 23, 24-25.

DOCUMENT 16

Vermont-New York Agreement on the Jurisdiction Dispute (1790)

AN ACT directing the payment of thirty thousand dollars to the State of New-York, and declaring what shall be the boundary line between the State of Vermont and the State of Newyork; and declaring certain grants therein mentioned, extinguished.

Whereas, Robert Yates, John Lansing, Junr., Gulian Verplank, Simeon De Witt, Egbert Benson and Melancton Smith Esquires, Commissioners appointed by an act of the Legislature of the State of Newyork, entitled "An act appointing commissioners with power to declare the consent of the legislature of the State of Newyork, that a certain territory within the jurisdiction thereof, should be formed into a new State," passed the sixth day of March, A.D. 1790—did, by virtue of the powers to them granted for the purpose, among other things, declare the consent of the legislature of the State of Newyork, that the State of Vermont be admitted into the union of the United States of America, and that immediately from such admission, all claim of jurisdiction of the State of New York, within the State of Vermont, should cease, and, thenceforth, the perpetual boundary line between the State of New York and the State of Vermont should be as follows viz: Beginning at the northwest corner of the State of Massachusetts, thence westward along the south boundary of Pownal, to the southwest corner thereof, thence northerly, along the western boundaries of the townships of Pownal, Bennington, Shaftsbury, Arlington, Sandgate, Rupert, Pawlet, Wells and Poultney, as the said townships are now held or possessed, to the river commonly called Poultney River, thence down the same through the middle of the deepest channel therof, to East Bay, thence through the middle of the deepest channel of East Bay and the waters thereof, to where the same communicate with Lake Champlain, thence through the middle of the deepest channel of Lake Champlain, to the eastward of the islands called the Four-Brothers, and the westward of the islands called the Grand Isle and Long Isle, or the Two Heroes, and to the westward of the Isle la Mott, to the forty-fifth degree of north latitude; and the said commissioners, by virtue of the powers to them granted, did declare the will of the legislature of the State of New York, that, if the legislature of the State of Vermont should, on or before the first day of January, 1792, declare that, on or before the first day of June 1794, the said State of Vermont would pay to the State of Newyork the sum of thirty thousand dollars, that, immediately from such declaration by the legislature of the State of Vermont, all rights and titles to lands within the State of Vermont, under grants from the government of the late colony of New York or from the State of New York (except as is therein excepted) should cease; wherefore,

It is hereby enacted and declared by the General Assembly of the State of Vermont, that the State of Vermont shall, on or before the first day of June 1794, pay the State of New York thirty thousand dollars. And the Treasurer of this State, for and in behalf of this State, and for the purposed mentioned in the act of the commissioners aforesaid, shall pay to the State of New York the sum of thirty thousand dollars on or before the first day of June, 1794—And

It is hereby further Enacted, that the said line described in the said act of the said Commissioners shall, henceforth, be the perpetual boundary line between the State of Vermont and the State of New York; and all

grants, charters or patents of land, lying within the State of Vermont, made by or under the government of the late colony of New York, except such grants, charters or patents as were made in confirmation of grants, charters or patents made by, or under, the government of the late province or colony of Newhampshire, are hereby declared null and void, and incapable of being given in evidence in any court of law within this State. [Passed Oct. 28, 1790.]

Source: E. P. Walton, ed., *Records of the Governor and Council of the State of Vermont*, Vol. 3 (Montpelier: Steam Press, 1875), pp. 459-460, 462-463.

DOCUMENT 17

Proceedings of the Bennington Convention to Ratify the Constitution of the United States (1791)

Bennington, January 1791.
Mr. N. Chipman rose, and addressed the house, as follows;
Mr. President,

The subject, on which we are now called to deliberate, is a subject of great importance, and involves in it many and mighty consequences. I shall wave at present any consideration of the particular circumstances in which we may be supposed to stand with the united states, on account of the former claim of Newyork, and the late compromise between Vermont and that state—and shall first make a few observations on our local and relative situation as a state and the consequences that will attend the event, either of our continuing independent, or of our accession to the union. I will then briefly observe on the principles and tendency of the federal constitution.

In viewing our situation, the first thing that strikes the mind, is the narrow limits of our territory: wholly inadequate to support the dignity, or to defend the rights of sovereignty—nor can we but reflect on the fortune that usually pursues such limited independencies.

The division of an extensive territory into small independent sovereignties greatly retards civil improvements—this was formerly the case in Europe; and the consequence was a long continuance in savage, and almost brutal manners. But it has been observed, that where, through an extensive country, the smaller states have united under one general government, civilization has proceeded more rapidly, and the kindly affections have much sooner gained an ascendent than where they still remained under numerous neighboring governments. The reason why one state is more favorable to civil improvements than the other is founded in the constitution of human nature; among small independent states, as among independent individuals, without a common judge, the weak are jealous of the strong—and endeavor by art and cunning to supply their want of power. The strong are ever ready to decide every question by force, according to their own present interest—hence follows a total want of public faith—recriminations—animosities—and open violence—under the idea of reprisals—and the name of foreigner becomes but another name for an enemy. In this situation the minds of men are kept in a constant state of irritation—their turbulent spirits ill brook the restraints of law—the passion of revenge, which, in proportion to the weakness of government becomes necessary for the protection of the individual, is soon inflamed to a degree of enthusiasm. Common danger alone, and that imminently impending, can suspend its baneful influence even among members of the same society: a situation fit only for savages—and in this situation savages have ever existed: but in an extensive government, national prejudices are suppressed—hostilities are removed to a distance—private injuries are redressed by a common judge—the passion of revenge, now no longer necessary for the protection of the individual, is suspended—the people no longer behold an enemy in the inhabitants of each neighboring district—they view all as members of one great family, connected by all the ties of interest, of country, of affinity and blood: thus are the social feelings gratified—and the kindly affections expanded and invigorated.

Vermont, continuing independent, would not be liable to all the inconveniencies I have mentioned—but she will be liable to many and great inconveniencies. In the vicinity of, and almost encircled by, the united states, now become great and powerful through the means of an energetic system of government, our intercourse with them must be on very unequal, and frequently on very mortifying terms. Whenever our interests clash (and clash they will at some time) with those of the union, it requires very little political sagacity to foretel that every sacrifice must be made on our part. When was it ever known that a powerful nation sacrificed, or even compromised their interest in justice to a weak neighbor, who was unable to make effectual demands? and who shall be a common judge?

Nay, such is the constitution of human nature, that men in such cases, were they disposed, are in a great measure incapable of judging with candor and impartiality.

We have experienced the disposition of states whose interests were averse to our own; and well know the consequences: extravagent, and as we deemed them unjustifiable claims, on their part; animosities, factions, and even blood shed, among ourselves.

Our vicinity to an extensive province of the british empire, is worthy of consideration. There is not any prospect of an immediate war between the united states and Great-britain; but from their mutual recriminations relative to the observance of the late treaty; and from the retention of the frontier posts in the hands of the british, contrary to express stipulation; such an event is one day to be apprehended. Should that take place, Vermont would be in a situation much to be regreted.

Our local situation with the united states, and our connection with many of their inhabitants—cemented by all the ties of blood and kindred affection, would forbid an alliance with Great-britain. As allies of the united states, we should experience all the resentment of an enemy, whom, by our voluntary alliance, we had made such, and to whose depredations, from our frontier situation, we should be continually exposed. And should we experience in the united states that quick sense of the injuries we should suffer? would they fly to our defence with the same alacrity, with the same national spirit, as they would defend themselves, if attacked in one of their own members? would they attend equally to our interest as to their own, in the settlement of peace, or in finally adjusting the expenditures of the war? The supposition is highly chimerical: nor less chimerical the idea, that by observing a neutral conduct, we may enjoy the blessing of peace, while the flames of war rage on every side. Our country, from its situation, would become a rendezvous, and a thoroughfare to the spies of both nations. Our citizens would frequently be tempted by both to engage in a nefarious correspondence of that kind: every act of friendship, or even of common courtesy, to one party, would excite the jealousy of the other. Their armies, to whom we should not be in a condition to refuse a passage, would think themselves justified, on the very least pretext of necessity, in seizing our property for the use of their service. Thus we should be equally misused, equally despised, and equally insulted and plundered by both.

Again, we may view this subject as it relates to the improvement of knowledge, and liberal science. Confined to the narrow limits of Vermont, genius, for want of great occasions, and great objects, will languish in obscurity: the spirit of learning, from which nations have derived more solid glory than all heroic achievements, and individuals, beyond the common lot of humanity, have been able to contribute to the happiness of millions, in different parts of the globe—will be contracted; and busy itself in small scenes, commensurate to the exigencies of the state, and the narrow limits of our government. In proportion as the views are more confined—more local; the more firmly rivited on the mind are the shackles of local and systematic prejudices—But received into the bosom of the union, we at once become brethren and fellow-citizens with more than three millions of people: instead of being confined to the narrow limits of Vermont, we become members of an extensive empire: here is a scene opened that will expand the social feelings;—the necessity and facility of mutual intercourse, will eradicate local prejudices;—the channels of information will be opened wide, and far extended; the spirit of learning will be called forth by every motive of interest and laudable ambition;—genius, exalted by the magnitude of the objects presented, will soar to the heights of science;—our general interests will be the same with those of the union—and represented in the national councils, our local interests will have their due weight. As an inland country, from the encouragement given to arts and manufactures, we shall receive more than a proportional advantage. And in the event of a war, an attack upon us will be felt through every member of the union: national safety—national pride, and national resentment—a resentment, not the petulance of a tribe, but great as the nation offended, will all conspire in our defence—in a word, independent, we must ever remain little, and I might almost say, contemptible;—but united, we become great, from the reflected greatness of the empire with which we unite. . . .

In this age of improvement, no less in the science of government than in other sciences, [the] novelty [of the federal constitution] would not be made a serious objection: yet it is acknowledged, that however beautiful as delineated on paper, or in political theory, its efficiency in point of practice might still be considered as problematical—had we not seen it evinced by actual experiment. The idea only of the efficiency of that government, at the instant of its organization, added strength to the states governments, and put an end to those turbulent commotions, which made some of them tremble for our political existence. Nor has this state reaped an inconsiderable advantage from the suppression of that contagious spirit in the neighboring governments: two years have not yet elapsed since the commencement of that administration. They have made provision for funding the debts of the union—they have, in a great measure, restored public credit; which from the weakness of the former government, they found almost in a state of desperation—they have availed the nation of a very productive revenue—they have made many laws and regulations, the wisdom, justice, and equality of which, are fully evinced by a prompt and almost universal observance: in very few instances have their courts been called to animadvert on a breach of their laws. But this, it may be said, arises from a confidence of the people in the members of that government: this undoubtedly has its influence, but a people free, jealous and discerning, as the americans are, do not suffer measures to pass unexamined: they will not give to any man or set of men an unmerited confidence. It is probable the national council will long retain and that deservedly, the confidence of the people. The people when called to chuse rulers and legislators for an extensive empire, experience a dilation of mind; they rise above vulgar and local prejudices, and confer their suffrages only on men, whose integrity and abilities are equal to the task of empire.

One important consideration ought not to be omitted—the federal constitution is still subject to amendments—whatever shall in practice be found dangerous or impracticable, redundant or deficient, may be retrenced and corrected: that wisdom which formed it, aided and matured by experience, may carry it to a far greater degree of perfection than any thing which has been known in government.

Thus sir, I have briefly hinted the disadvantages that will accrue to us, continuing independent; upon a supposition of its practicability. I have observed some of the happy effects of an accession to the union. I have pointed out the leading principles of the constitution, and its probable and actual efficiency in strengthening the government of the several states, and in securing the tranquility, happiness and prosperity of the union. The more minute investigations I leave at present; fully persuaded at the same time, that when accurately examined with that candor and impartiality which will doubtless mark the deliberations of this convention, every material objection, either to the constitution, or to the accession of Vermont to the union, will be easily obviated or totally disappear.

Source: E. P. Walton, ed., *Records of the Governor and Council of the State of Vermont*, Vol. 3 (Montpelier: Steam Press, 1875), pp. 468-472.

SECTION FOUR

1791-1820
Early Statehood

VERMONT VOICES

SECTION FOUR

1791-1820
Early Statehood

Introduction

The focus of this section is on Vermont's social, political, and economic development from a rough frontier to an integral part of the American union. U. S. census records reflected the good times, reporting that in 1791 the state's population stood at 85,341 and by 1810 totaled 217,895. The period immediately following, however, brought embargoes and the War of 1812 along with social and economic dislocations that affected the state for several decades. Documents 1 and 2 provide glimpses of conditions in Vermont in the years immediately after statehood and demonstrate the promise the state seemed to offer to newcomers looking for opportunity and advancement.

Document 1 is an excerpt from John Lincklaen's *Travels in the Year 1791 and 1792 in Pennsylvania, New York and Vermont*. Lincklaen's report to the Holland Land Company reads in sharp contrast to Nathan Perkins' *Narrative of a Tour through the State of Vermont* (Section 3, Document 15), written just three years earlier. Where Perkins noted only godlessness and poverty, Lincklaen found settlements populated by hospitable inhabitants and described the "rich soil" particularly suited for growing grains. **Document 2** is from Samuel Williams' *Natural and Civil History of Vermont*, the first published history of the state. Williams, with Ira Allen one of Vermont's foremost eighteenth-century boosters, was a former Harvard professor and co-founder of the *Rutland Herald*. He depicted Vermont as a land of milk and honey salted with rich mineral deposits and possessing the potential for manufacturing and gin distilleries. Williams attributed the incentive for distilleries to the inability of the Vermont farmer to otherwise market his grain surplus. Much of the state's early prosperity was rooted in supplying Vermont's new settlers. Once the surge of immigrants receded, remoteness from major markets became an impasse limiting further economic growth.

Although Vermont encountered obstacles to full integration into the national economy, it plunged without pause into national politics. By 1794, Thomas Jefferson's Democratic Societies, portent of the nation's emerging political realignments, reached Vermont. **Document 3**, excerpts of the "Constitution of the Demo-cratic Society in the County of Addison," clearly defined the issues separating Jeffersonians from Alexander Hamilton's Federalist faction. The Addison County Society protested the adoption of a financial system that envisioned a permanent national debt and the establishment of a national bank, and it criticized President George Washington's neutrality policy, preferring closer ties with France. Most ominous for continued Federalist domination of the national government was Article 5 of the Jeffersonians' constitution, a provision to maintain communication with similar Democratic Societies elsewhere in the United States. The coalescing of these societies culminated eventually in the establishment of the Democratic-Republican Party.

Nathaniel Chipman, foremost advocate of Vermont's admission as the fourteenth state (See Section 3, Documents 13 and 17), was rumored to subscribe to Democratic Society sentiments, and **Document 4**, excerpts of a letter to the *New York Herald* criticizing Vermont's Democratic-Republican Societies, contains his rebuttal and rationale for opposing them. Chipman, a devout Federalist, was a former chief judge of the Vermont Supreme Court and a future U.S. senator when his letter first appeared in the *Herald*, then the most widely circulated newspaper in Vermont. Federalists and Democratic-Republicans contended closely for control of state government until almost the end of the War of 1812, with contested election results scarring the political landscape.

Document 5, letters and petitions discussing Native American land claims, provides a sobering reminder that promises of prosperity and assurances of democracy applied only to white settlers. In this exchange among the chiefs of the Seven Nations (later joined by an Abenaki representative), and the governor and Governor's Council, the Native American claims to a large area of northwestern Vermont are rejected. Reasoning in a manner strikingly similar to that of a recent Vermont Supreme Court decision (Section 11, Document 14), state officials concluded that the Native Americans' claim was "extinguished." They no longer had a real claim "in either justice or equity," if indeed any such claim "ever did exist." Governor Tichenor's confidence that the Native Americans were "fully sat-isfied" by this reasoning and "will not trouble the Leg-islature in the future," was, however, misplaced.

Document 6 relates to Matthew Lyon, son-in-law of Thomas Chittenden and fiery Democratic-Republi-can congressman representing western Vermont. It is a cartoon depicting a struggle between Lyon and Feder-alist congressman Roger Griswold on the floor of the House chamber. The humorous drawing circulated widely and symbolized the fervor with which partici-pants waged early national politics. Lyon was the most eminent of ten Jeffersonians convicted under the pro-visions of the Sedition Act. The act, passed in July 1798 by a Federalist Congress to repress political opposition, made it a high misdemeanor for anyone to "publish any false, scandalous and malicious writing" that brought the U.S. government, Congress, or the president into disrepute. Lyon's printed references to President John Adams cost him a one-thousand-dollar fine and four months in the Vergennes jail. Lyon was hailed as a martyr and reelected to Congress while still in prison.

The Sedition Act clearly compromised unfettered political competition, and Republicans attacked it, along with the Alien Act and the Alien Enemies Act, which impeded immigration and naturalization, as unneces-sary, despotic, and unconstitutional. There was not yet, however, a settled procedure to void unconstitutional legislation, and Thomas Jefferson and James Madison proposed the Kentucky and Virginia Resolutions to deal with such matters. Although the resolutions differed in detail, both invoked the compact theory of government that maintained individual states had the responsibility to identify infractions of the Constitution and "inter-pose" themselves between the national government and the citizens of their state to "arrest the progress of the evil." Copies of these resolutions went from Kentucky and Virginia to all other states, and **Document 7** con-sists of the replies of the Vermont legislature to the reso-lutions. The Vermont legislature rejected the notion that the United States was formed by state legislatures and contended that the people of the United States formed the federal Constitution. Although the furor raised by the Alien and Sedition Acts subsided with the election of Jefferson in 1800 (Vermont cast its four electoral votes for John Adams), the dispute over "who formed" the federal constitution persisted until the Civil War.

Document 8, "The Nature and Importance of True Republicanism," is excerpted from a discourse pre-sented on July 4, 1801, by Lemuel Haynes, who served for thirty years as pastor of the West Rutland Congre-gational Church. An African-American who had served in the Continental army during the Revolution, Haynes filled a pulpit in Manchester and preached in Bennington as part of his long Vermont career. In addition to shed-ding light on Green Mountain politics and religion, Haynes' discourse also suggests evidence of a greater black participation in Vermont society than is gener-ally appreciated.

Document 9 relates to illegal trade by Vermonters with Canada. In 1808, President Thomas Jefferson im-posed a land embargo against Canada in an attempt to gain Great Britain's recognition of the United States' neutral rights. Trade with Canada was, however, the economic lifeblood of western Vermont, and smuggling became so widespread with popular sentiment so sup-portive that the president felt compelled to issue a special "Proclamation to Curb Champlain Valley Smug-gling." The Collector of Customs for Vermont, Jabez Penniman (who had married the widow of Ethan Allen), attempted to implement the president's order, but his efforts met with armed resistance, as Document 9, an account of the "*Black Snake* Affair" from a Republican broadside, details. Despite the broadside's plea for sup-port of law and order through reelection of the "present patriotic governor and councillors," Vermont opposi-tion to the embargo was so great that only a few months after the *Black Snake* affair the state elected a Federal-ist governor and Federalists to three of the state's four congressional seats. Republicans nonetheless retained sufficient strength to deliver the state's six electoral votes to James Madison.

The federal government had enacted the embargoes, and other legislation curtailing U.S. commerce, in or-der to help preserve American neutrality and neutral rights throughout twenty-five years of intermittent world war in which England and France were the principal adversaries. Finally, in June 1812, despairing of resolv-ing its differences with England by peaceful means, the United States declared war. Documents 10 and 11 sug-gest that war failed to silence criticism of foreign policy or stop the illegal trade. **Document 10**, "Union, Peace, & Commerce," is a report of a meeting held in Williston shortly after the declaration of war.

Document 11 is a state law enacted in November 1812 by a newly elected Republican legislature and gov-ernor. This law was intended to deter smuggling with

Canada which had not ceased with American entry into the war against Great Britain. The statute had little effect: A historical marker on Vermont State Highway Route 108 at Smugglers Notch notes that "the Notch gained its name after Jefferson's Embargo Acts of 1809 and the War of 1812, when cattle were driven north and Canadian goods were smuggled into New England through this picturesque gap beside majestic Mt. Mansfield, remote from revenue officers."

By 1813, with the state experiencing economic disruptions from loss of trade and the war going badly for the Americans, the state also suffered a catastrophic epidemic first detected among troops stationed in Burlington. In **Document 12**, excerpts of *Sketches of Epidemic Diseases in the State of Vermont*, Dr. Joseph Gallup reports that what first appeared to be a recurrence of spotted fever was soon identified as the far more deadly peripneumony, which in 1813 was estimated to have cost five thousand Vermont lives.

Such bitter fruits of "Mr. Madison's War" facilitated Federalist victories in the 1813 elections and Federalist control of state government. Martin Chittenden, who as congressman had voted against the war, was now governor, and one of his first official acts was to order home units of the state militia stationed in Plattsburgh, New York. The Third Brigade of the Vermont militia had gone there to reinforce American defenses preparing for a British invasion moving south from Canada along Lake Champlain. Chittenden reasoned, however, that as an extensive section of the Vermont frontier had been left unprotected and as "the Military strength and resources of [Vermont] must be reserved for its own defence and protection," the militia should return to its home state. The officers of the Third Brigade responded with a broader, more national concept of American defense. **Document 13**, Chittenden's proclamation recalling troops from New York, along with the officers' refusal to obey, elaborates the arguments of both sides.

In September 1814 the joint land and sea British offensive reached Plattsburgh. The British army of eleven thousand seasoned veterans of the Napoleonic Wars greatly outnumbered the American defenders, but the American fleet of Commodore Thomas Macdonough defeated a larger British naval force commanded by Captain George Downie in the Battle of Plattsburgh Bay. With his naval support destroyed, British general Sir George Prevost chose not to challenge the entrenched Americans on land, and the invaders withdrew to Canada. In the fashion of the day, Macdonough's startling success inspired a popular ballad. **Document 14**, "Battle of Plattsburgh and Victory on Lake Champlain," is the contribution of an anonymous poet who celebrated the triumph of American arms in a war that to that point had produced few objects of national pride.

Macdonough's victory influenced England's willingness to sign the Peace of Ghent, formally ending the war on December 24, 1814; and along with Andrew Jackson's defeat of the British army at New Orleans in January 1815, it helped transform "Mr. Madison's War" into a noble cause, America's second war for independence. From a political perspective the American victory was a spectacular Republican triumph compounded by Federalist bad luck and ineptitude. During December 1814 and early January 1815 a Federalist convention, convened in Hartford, Connecticut, and conducted in secrecy by delegates from New England states, adopted resolutions to reduce the authority of the national government and condemn its conduct of the war (rumors purported that extremist Federalists proposed secession). Ironically the convention's final report echoed the states' rights doctrine of Madison's Virginia Resolutions. News of the victory at New Orleans and the peace treaty made the Hartford Convention the butt of unremitting abuse and damaged the Federalist Party beyond repair. **Document 15**, a cartoon from *The Hartford convention in an uproar! and The wise men of the East confounded!*, is an example of the ridicule unleashed on the Federalists. Josiah Dunham, who stands unhappily at the right edge of the scene, was a prominent Vermont Federalist who attended the Hartford Convention as an observer after Vermont refused to send any official delegates. Both Dunham and his political party shortly disappeared from Vermont, Dunham to obscurity in Kentucky and the Federalist Party to oblivion in the Democratic-Republican domination of state and national politics that followed America's "victory" in the war.

The restoration of peace, however, did not bring back the growth and optimism Vermonters once enjoyed. Instead, as Section 5 details, Vermont entered an era of economic and social transformation that left most Vermonters anxiously searching for ways to recapture a share of the nation's prosperity and potential.

Document 1

Travel Journal (1791)

John Lincklaen

Monday, [September] 26th. From Lansingburgh to Bennington is 30 miles, there are settlements all along the way, lands mediocre, many hills and stony ground.

At Bennington very comfortable at Duis. This place is quite a country town.

The State of Vermont is divided into townships of 6 miles square, divided among 56 proprietors, so that each has something more than 400 acres—which is called a *Grant*. The Legislature never gives more than one to an individual, to prevent undue influence, & to encourage population.

Lands in Bennington township sell at from 15 to 25 Dollars pr. acre. 20 bushels of wheat an acre is considered a good yield.

Tuesday, 27th. From Bennington to Shaftesbury 7 miles, all inhabited, from there to Arlington at Merwin's 7 miles—a good public house; from there to Manchester 8 miles at Allis', good tavern, the land good but mountainous & stony, a good harvest is 20 to 25 bushels of wheat an acre. We made the acquaintance of a Mr. Meinders who has a store & a Mr. Smith—these gentlemen told us that lands were selling in this neighborhood as high as 20 Dolls. the acre.

Wednesday, 28th. Passed through the township of Dorset 5 miles, Harwich 7 miles, Danby 6 miles, where we dined sufficiently well at a Mr. Antony's—this man has sold his farm of 60 acres at 19 Dlr. the acre, thence to Wallingford 7 miles to Mrs. Hull's, a good widow's where we were comfortable & found two good beds.

Thursday, 29th. Passed through Clarendon to Rutland, we stopped on the way at the house of a Thomas Rice, whom we met in the Genesee country, where he had bought 400 acres at 1 Dlr. pr. acre with the intention of settling there. We found there a good farm, land good & well tilled & a new house not even finished. It is astonishing to see a man 50 years old who has spent the best part of his life in clearing his land & enhancing its value, leaving it all just as he begins to enjoy the fruits of his labor, in order to bury himself anew in the forest, & expose himself to all the difficulties of forming a new settlement! But it is usually the case with Americans, beginning quite poor they buy a few acres in a new country for almost nothing; when after 8 or 10 years of rugged toil they have augmented the worth of their lands, they find themselves with a numerous family, & their little territory, however valuable it may be, does not suffice to support them. Then they sell at a very high price, & so gain a sufficient sum to buy in the Genesee, where the lands are cheaper, three times the quantity, enough to maintain & establish around them a dozen children. . . .

Sunday, [October] 2nd. . . .Burlington is very pleasantly situated on Lake Champlain which there makes a little bay. All the other settlements are new, but people begin to live at their ease. The soil is very rich, particularly for growing wheat & maize, they harvest of the former so much as 40 bushels, but more generally from 20 to 30 bushels the acre, of maize up to 70 bushels, Their greatest traffic is with Canada, they sometimes supply this province with grain, & principally with cattle, & receive in return European products but the English do not permit the importation of anything manufactured.

When a canal shall have been cut between Skeensborough & the North River, which will be only 6 miles long, & which they have offered to make for 40,000 Livres, all the exports of Vermont will come to New York, but the opinion is that Canada, in order not to lose this branch of commerce, will cut on her side a canal from St. Johns to Chamblee, which will be 12 miles long, but which is easier to build than the other, since use can be made of Little River which flows into the Sorrel River below the rapids; thus Vermont will find herself between two markets & will derive a great advantage from the activity of her neighbours.

The English still retain at Lake Champlain two posts in the territory of the United States. One commanded by a Captn. at Pointe du fer in the State of New York, the other on the Island of North Hero in Vermont, where a Sergt. is stationed with 12 men. There is besides a brig of 16 guns on the Lake.

By the last census the State of Vermont contains 85,708 souls, it is divided into 7 counties, & each county into a number of Townships of 6 miles square. There are no great land holders as in the Southern States. The legislature has always believed it was its policy to grant only a small number of acres to any one person, for the greater preservation of equality, & preventing too great individual influence. This seems to me one reason that the lands have risen to a price so high that they are sold from 10 to 20 Dlrs. an acre, and it would not even be possible to buy a large quantity at that rate. The largest landowner in the State is a Genl. [Ira] Allen in Chittenden County Colchester Township who has about 120,000 acres. Govr. Chittenden 30,000 acres.

There is in the whole State a considerable number of Mapple Trees, but the people do not seem to me to be persuaded of the advantage they might gain from this tree; in the Southern parts where the settlements are older, & the land almost all cleared, the people have cut down almost all the trees, keeping only a small quantity necessary for their own consumption. In the North, where there is more forest, the quantity is more considerable, but no more prized than towards the South. However as these parts are too distant from all markets, people could never raise more grain than they need for their own use, & will consequently be restricted to grazing & cattle, which may lead them to make sugar, since in cutting all trees except the Maple, the pasture is excellent, & much hay can be made, but experience has shown that the ground is so light here, that when the Maples stand alone the least wind uproots them, an inconvenience for which a remedy should be sought. They also say that in these mountains the depth of the snow prevents their gathering sap at the proper time, that towards the South however one man makes 250 lbs. Finally the chief reason for not making sugar is that they have no home market, & that the price of transportation by land is too dear, for the same reason the kettles & other utensils are so hard to get, but to me it does not appear improbable that in forming an establishment in the middle of that part of the State where is the most Maple, that should furnish the inhabitants with the necessary utensils, & that should buy their sugar for ready money, they might be induced to cultivate the trees & gather enough sugar & at a sufficiently reasonable price as to leave a mediocre profit, especially if navigation is opened from Skeensborough to the North River which would greatly lessen transportation charges. . . .

Thursday, 6th. We left Burlington at 11 o'clock for Jerico on the Onion River 10 miles, In the Afternoon we crossed the river, & went to pay a visit to the Governor of the State, Thomas Chittenden living in the Township of Williston. He received us without ceremony, in the country fashion. He is a man of about 60 years, destitute of all education, but possessing good sense, & a sound judgement, which at once put him at the head of affairs when the States of New York and New Hampshire disputed between themselves the territory of Vermont. It is chiefly to him that the State owes her present Government. He related to us at much length the history of the revolution & how much he had contributed to it, was not ashamed to say that when he placed himself at the head of those who wished a separation from the State of New York, he scarcely knew how to write. Born in the State of Connecticut, he still retains the inquisitive character of his compatriots, & overwhelms one with questions to which one can scarcely reply. He is one of the largest & best farmers of the State, & is believed to own 40,000 acres beside a considerable number of horned cattle. His house & way of living have nothing to distinguish them from those of any private individual but he offers heartily a glass of Grog, potatoes, & bacon to anyone who wishes to come and see him. . . .

Source: John Lincklaen, *Travels in the Years 1791 and 1792 in Pennsylvania, New York and Vermont* (New York: G.P. Putnam's Sons, 1897), pp. 81-84, 86-89, 90-91.

Document 2

Natural and Civil History of Vermont (1794)
SAMUEL WILLIAMS

MANUFACTURES—Next to agriculture, the chief source of employment is manufactures. These are chiefly of the *domestic kind*, designed to procure clothing for families. In no part of the United States, does the farmer meet with more success in raising sheep. The climate agrees well with the breed of sheep, that is spred over the territory: And the richness of the pastures, in new settlements, gives an extraordinary sweetness to the meat, and richness to the fleece. It is not uncommon for a sheep of two or three years old to weight one hundred and twenty pounds, and to afford three or four pounds of wool. And from the wool of their own raising, the bigger part of the farmers manufacture the woolens, which are used in their families. In no places does flax succeed better, than on the new lands. The common produce from one acre is from four to five hundred pounds. Every family raises a quantity of flax, and carries on a small manufacture of linen. These domestic manufactures, are of the highest importance to the people. When the country shall be well settled, wool and flax will become two of its most capital productions. At present, there is not enough of either annually produced to supply the inhabitants.

Great advantages may be derived to the state, from the *manufactures of iron*. Large quantities of iron ore are found in several of the towns, on the west side of the green mountains. Tinmouth, Rutland, Pittsford, and Shoreham, contain great quantities. The ore in these towns is of a reddish kind, mixed with earth tinctured with yellow ore. It melts easily, and produces from one seventh to one fourth of iron. The iron is mostly of the coldshire kind, works easily, and make excellent nails. The principal part of the ore that has hitherto been used in this state, has been brought from a mountain on the west side of Lake Champlain, about four miles north of Crown Point. This ore is of a black, heavy kind; mostly iron, mixed with a grey flintstone. The iron in this ore, appears in large grains, some of them nearly as large as a pea: These grains appear to be of pure iron. Some of this ore is so peculiarly rich, that when it is well managed, it will yield four sevenths of pure iron; but is exceeding hard to melt. When the ore is well worked, it produces the best iron for chains, horse shoes, nails, &c. and such matters as are drawn lengthways. When applied to uses which require plaiting widthways, it does not answer so good a purpose; though it is neither coldshire nor redshire. The same kind of ore is found in many of the mountains, on the west side of the Lake, as far south as its waters extend. —A country thus abounding with the richest kind of iron ore, naturally invites the settlers to the iron manufactures.

And they have already (1792) erected several forges and furnaces. In Bennington county they have one forge; in Rutland county fourteen; in Addison county four; and in Chittenden county two. In addition to which three furnaces are also erected, in the county of Rutland. From these works, large quantities of bar iron are annually produced. The manufacture of nails is already become common, and profitable; and every other branch of the iron manufacture, must soon be

so.—These manufactures, like every thing else in the new settlements, are as yet in their infancy. But if we may judge from the plenty, or the ease and cheapness, with which an immense quantity of the best kind of iron ore may be procured, we shall be apt to conclude that nature has designed this part of the United States, to be the seat of very flourishing manufactures of every thing that can be made of iron, or steel.

The manufacture of *pot and pearl ashes* is still more extensive, and useful. The immense quantity of wood, with which the country is every where covered, may supply any quantity of ashes for this purpose: And the greatest economy takes place in collecting the ashes, made either by culinary fires, or those which are designed to burn up the wood, where the inhabitants are clearing the lands. In almost every new settlment, one of the first attempts is to erect works for the pot and pearl ash manufacture: And there are probably as many works of this kind, as there are settled towns in the state. The business is every where well understood; and there is no better pot or pearl ashes made in any part of America, than that which is produced in Vermont. It has hitherto taken from four hundred and fifty to four hundred and eighty bushels of ashes, to make one ton of pot ash. Constant attempts are now made, to find out a way of extracting more of the salts from the ashes, than has been heretofore done by the common method of bleaching; and also to extract more salts from the ashes, which have been thrown aside as useless. Flattering prospects seem to have attended some chymical experiments of this kind; and improvements have been made in the method of constructing the works for the pot ash. But much further improvements are necessary, before these imperfect attempts, can be of any very valuable use to the manufacturer.—The quantity of pot and pearl ashes, which is annually made in Vermont, cannot be exactly stated. From the best accounts I could procure, in the year 1791, the quantity might be estimated at about one thousand tons. Probably this may be near the truth. But whatever may be the quantity produced at present, it is rapidly increasing; and probably will for several years, bear some proportion to the increase of the inhabitants. As the mountains will not fail to supply wood for this manufacture, for centuries yet to come, it seems that Vermont will be one of the states, in which this manufacture will be attended with its greatest perfection and profit.

The manufacture of *maple sugar* is also an article of great importance to the state. Perhaps two thirds of the families are engaged in this business in the spring, and they make more sugar than is used among the people. Considerable quantities are carried to the shop-keepers; which always find a ready sale, and good pay.—The business is now carried on, under the greatest disadvantages; soley by the exertions of private families, in the woods, and without any other conveniences than one or two iron kettles, the largest of which will not hold more than four or five pailfulls. Under all these disadvantages, it is common for a family to make two or three hundred pounds of maple sugar, in three or four weeks. This manufacture is capable of great improvements. The country abounds with an immense number of the sugar maple trees. The largest of these trees are five and an half or six feet in diameter; and will yield five gallons of sap in one day; and from twelve to fifteen pounds of sugar, during the season. The younger and smaller trees afford sap or juice, in a still greater proportion. Were the workmen furnished with proper apparatus and works, to collect and boil the juice, the quantity of sugar might be increased, during the time of making of it, in almost any proportion: And it might become an article of much importance, in the commerce of the country.—I have never tasted any better sugar, than what has been made from the maple, when it has been properly refined; it has a peculiarly rich, salubrious, and pleasant taste. But it is generally made under so many unfavourable circumstances, that it appears for the most part, rough, coarse, and dirty; and frequently burnt, smoaky, or greasy, when it is first made.—In one circumstance only, does nature seem to have set bounds to this manufacture, and that is with respect to time. It is only during four or five weeks in the spring, that the juice can be collected. While the trees are frozen at night, and thawed in the day, the sap runs plentifully: But as soon as the buds come on, the sap ceases to flow in such a manner, as that it can any longer be collected.—We cannot determine with much accuracy what quantity of this sugar is annually made in the state. In the town of Cavendish, in the spring of the year 1794, the quantity made by eighty three families, was fourteen thousand and eighty pounds. If the families in the other towns manufacture in the same proportion, there must be above one thousand tons annually made in Vermont.

Several *distilleries* have of late been erected in this state. The object of them is to make such spirituous liquors, as can be extracted from grain. Considering the large quantities of wheat, rye, and barley, that are raised in the country, it seems probable that these distilleries will soon be in a flourishing state. All kinds of grain are raised so easily upon our lands, and in such quantities, that the farmer can find no sale, and has no use for them. They might immediately be raised to double their present quantity, if there was any demand for them. The distilleries have met with good success in their attempts to make gin. And nothing seems wanting, but time, and experience, to produce large quantities of all those spirits, that can be produced from grain. As yet these works are in their infancy; probably they will become a lucrative branch of business to their owners, and of very considerable to the state. . . .

Source: Samuel Williams, *The Natural and Civil History of Vermont* (Walpole, N.H.: Isaiah Thomas and David Carlisle, Jr., c. 1794), pp. 315-320.

DOCUMENT 3

The Democratic Society in the County of Addison (1794)

Constitution, September 9, 1794
CONSTITUTION
of the Democratic Society in the County of Addison.

WE, the undersigned, compact and associate ourselves into a Society, on the principles, for the reasons, and to promote the political ends expressed in the following articles, which shall be considered constitutional of our Society.

ARTICLE 1st. We make no apology for thus associating ourselves (altho' an inconsiderable body of citizens of the United States) to consider, animadvert upon, and publish our sentiments, on the political interests, constitution and government of our country; this is a right, the disputation of which reflects on political freedom, and wears an appearance peculiarly absurd, proceeding from the tongue or pen of an American.

ART. 2d. We declare the following, among others, to be some of our political sentiments, and principles of government, which, whether in an individual or associated capacity, we are bound, under the laws of reason and morality, to maintain and defend.—That all men are naturally free, and possess equal rights.—That all legitimate government originates in the voluntary and social compact of the people.—That no rights of the people are surrendered to their rulers, as a price of protection and government.—That the constitution and laws of a country, are the expressions of the general will of the body of the people or nation, that all officers of government are the ministers & servants of the people, and, as such, are amenable to them, for all their conduct in office.—That it is the right, and becomes the duty of a people, as a necessary means of the security and preservation of their rights, and the future peace and political happiness of the nation, to exercise watchfullness and inspection, upon the conduct of all their public officers; to approve, if they find their conduct worthy of their high and important trusts—and to reprove and censure, if it be found otherwise. That frequent elections, directly from the body of the people, of persons, to important offices of trust, have an immediate tendency to secure the public rights, as less opportunities intervene for abuse of power; that compensations for public service ought to be reasonable (and even moderate, when the debts and exigencies of a nation require it,) and a reward only for actual service; that a public debt (and a financial funding system to continue the same) is a burthen upon a nation, and ought, by the oeconomical exertions of the nation, to be reduced and discharged; that an increase of public officers, dependant on the executive power,—a blending the distinct branches of government together, in the functions and offices of one man, or body of men;—a foolish copying of ancient corrupt and foreign governments and courts, where the equal rights of men, are trampled under the feet of kings and lords; and a standing army,—are all highly dangerous to liberty; and that the constitution, laws, and government of a country, are always of right, liable to amendment and improvement.

ART. 3d. We are convinced that the present political state of our country, calls for the rational, wise and vigilent attention of its citizens. The price which Americans have paid to obtain liberty and independence, as republicans;—the hope which wise and great men in Europe, have placed on our revolution, as eventual of a better understanding of the rights of men, and a more enlightened and equal policy and government, on which account many are emigrating from lands of tryranny and arbitrary power, to enjoy the freedom denied them in their native land; the confidence which the French nation, in their present unparalleled struggle with despotism, have reason to repose in us as their friends, from our alliance, but more from gratitude, and the goodness and greatness of their cause. The fate and happiness of the millions of the unborn posterity of America, to indeterminable ages;—our own happiness, and that of our immediate posterity; the progress of truth, reason, and humanity in the world, and that aspect on the political fate of all mankind, which a maintenance, or desertion of the principles of liberty and true republicanism at the present day, may occasion, are, with us (and we trust they are so, with our attentive American fellow-citizens in general). . . . But it is our DUTY not to conceal, that we . . . possess a degree of serious concern, at—the state of our national debt—The expences of our government, and in the causes of those debates and divisions which have agitated Congress, particularly during their last session.

ART. 4. It shall be the objects of the business and pursuit of this society—to study the Constitution, to avail ourselves of the journals, debates, and laws of Congress-reports and correspondencies of secretaries, and such other publications as may be judged necessary to give information as to the proceedings of Congress and the departments of government and also of the conduct of individual officers in the discharge of their trusts, whether in Congress, or in the departments of the executive, or judiciary. And on information, we will speak; and upon deliberation, we will write and publish our sentiments. . . . But, let no unfaithful servant of the public, or plotter of the ruin of his country's freedom, however dignified his station, hereupon, affect the contempt of independency of office, or flatter himself to escape censure with impunity.

ART. 5. We will correspond with other Societies, in this, & the United States, formed upon similar principles.

ART. 6. A Chairman, Clerk or Clerks, and Committee, or Committees, shall regulate and conduct the formal proceedings and business of this Society, from time to time, as occasion may require, under the direction of the Society.

By Order of the meeting.   Isaiah Gilbert,
Chairman
Thomas Tolman,
Clerk

Source: *Farmers' Library* (Rutland), 9 September 1794.

DOCUMENT 4

Letter Criticizing Vermont's Democratic-Republican Societies (1794)

NATHANIEL CHIPMAN

. . . If Sir, you will have the patience to read so long a letter, I will give you my reasons for believing such societies not merely useless, but mischievous and a very dangerous imposition. Simple democracies, in which the people assemble in a body, to enact laws & decide on all public measures, have, from the earliest ages, exhibited scenes of turbulence, violence and fluctuation, beyond any other kind of government. No government has ever been able to exist under the form for any length of time. Experience has evinced, that the people collected in a body are impatient of discussion; that they are fatally incapable of reasoning; but they are highly susceptible of passions. To those the more artful direct their whole attention. By these every decision in the numerous and heterogeneous assemblies of the people at large, is irresistably influenced. In a simple democracy, there can be no fixed constitution. Every thing is liable to be changed by the frenzy of the moment, or the influence of popular faction. In such a government, where all are immediate actors no accountability can exist; consequently, in no government, have there been instances of a more flagrant violation of rights, or a tyranny more cruel and remediless than that which has been exercised over a minority of the citizens, or against an unpopular individual. Many public measures, whether they regard the internal legislation of the state, or its conduct towards foreign

powers, will often be, not a little complicated. Many of the people for want of the means of information, for want of leisure, patience or abilities, will come forward wholly ignorant of the relative circumstances necessary to be known, in order to a just and proper determination; and I believe you will agree with me, that, on such occasions, presumption, passionate zeal, and obstinacy, are always in proportion to the ignorance of the actors. In such governments, the measures, will, of necessity, be frequently unjust, violent and fluctuating.

Such is not the government under which we live. Our national government and the governments of the several states, are representative democracies. This kind of government is calculated to give a permanent security to all the essential rights of man, life, liberty and property, the equal rights of acquisition and enjoyment, in a just compromise with the rights of all, which a simple democracy by no means secures. This kind of government is designed in its constitution to provide equally against the tyranny of the few and the tyranny of the many. The people have endeavored to place their delegated rulers in a constant state of accountability. This is the hinge on which American liberty turns. That the most perfect freedom of deliberation might be secured, the members of the legislature are, in their public conduct, made amenable only to the sentiments of the people, by the interest which they have in the approbation of their constituents. The executive is made accountable to the public sentiment, and is further amenable to a constitutional tribunal, for every violation of trust. The powers and duties of the several departments, are in many instances, limited by the laws of the constitution, by which the people have said to their rulers, thus far shall ye go; and no farther. Many things are left to their integrity and discretion, to act for the best good of the nation. Congress are, from their situation furnished with the necessary information relative to the present state of things, as they may affect the nation, whether internally or externally. All this is, in their debates, handed out, and circulated among the people, together will all the reasons for, and against any measure that could be suggested by the most mature deliberation. By these means, the people have in their power, sufficient information to judge calmly and rationally of the measures which have from time to time been adopted.

Proceeding in this way, I am persuaded that a representative democracy may secure to a people more civil and political happiness than any of the kinds of governments which have hitherto existed. Such is the state of things, that knowledge in the complicated affairs in civil society comes not by intuition. The means of information, and frequently, diligent investigation are necessary. The knowledge of the people will follow, but can rarely procede, a public discussion. They will generally approve or disapprove with judgment, but in dictating, are exposed to all the rashness of ignorance, passion and prejudice.

Our self created societies and clubs, as it appears to me, have a tendency, directly or indirectly, to introduce into the measures of government, all the precipitation, all the heat and ungovernable passions, of a simple democracy. Have we reason to believe that these self pronounced dictators, have a free access to the means of information, that they have been able more fully to comprehend the present circumstances, the principles and reasons which ought to direct public measures, than those to whom the people have confided that talk? Or even than their more peaceable and quiet fellow citizens? Certainly they have given us no unequivocal proof of either.

Their professed design has been to promote political knowledge; but wherever they have established themselves, they have assumed a dictorial style in their resolves. Where any man, or body of men have refused their dictates, or presumed to differ from them in opinion, no length of meritorious services, no virtue or integrity of character, has been proof against their bold proscriptions. Like the demagogues of simple democracy they have applied wholly to the passions and jealousies of the people. They have assumed to speak the sentiments of the people, though, in point of numbers they are certainly a very inconsiderable minority. . . .

If however these societies are unable directly to dictate measures to the national governments, they will still have a very pernicious effect. When once, though under the thickest clouds of ignorance, they have prejudged a measure, and assumed to dictate it, unless they have more candour than most men, their

prejudices will rarely yield to any light of conviction. This, as far as their influence extends, will, in a great degree, prevent the happy effect of the wisest and best measures. It is perhaps, of as much importance, in general, that the people should see and acknowledge the measures of government to be wise and good, as that they should be really wise and good. If there is a failure in either respect they will not secure the happiness of the people. It is of great consequence that the people, with the means of information should cultivate a disposition to judge with coolness and impartiality, and that legislators should endeavour to render the reasons of their measures plain and intelligible to the common sense of mankind.

I know that it is frequently said, that in a republic it is necessary to the maintenance of liberty, the people, should be jealous of their rulers. But I have never been able to persuade myself, that to be a good republican a man must imbibe prejudices, which is the necessary consequence of jealousy. That certainly is an unfortunate situation which renders candour dangerous, or jealously a species of virtue. In no government are rulers held more strictly and generally accountable than in our representative democracies. Their continuance in place depends constantly on a faithful discharge of their trust. . . . Notwithstanding what has been observed, I do not mean to insinuate, that such associations as our democratic societies are a crime animadverted upon *by law as and restrained* by constitution. The exercise of such a power would be more dangerous to liberty than the associations themselves. They must be left to rise or fall, solely by the good sense of the people. Nor would I insinuate that it can never be expedient for the people to assemble on occasion to petition for a redress of grievances, whether *constitution* or legislative. But it would be well if the petitions and representations of the people, unless when they come from known corporate bodies, were always to be signed individually, that it might appear how far they are expressive of the public sentiment. When they come forward from voluntary societies, there is often a deception. It is not known whether they contain ten or ten thousand individuals.

From these observation you will be convinced that I am no friend to such societies, and that my name ought not to have been brought forward as one who favored their principles.

Nathaniel Chipman

Source: *The Herald* (New York), 14 July 1794.

DOCUMENT 5

Documents on Native American Petitions and Claims for Compensation from the State of Vermont (1798-1800)

His Excellency Isaac Tichenor, Esq. Governor of the State of Vermont: *Great Brother*,—We the Chiefs and Councillors of the Seven Nations of lower Canada Indians, send our love and respect to you, and your family, by five of our agents, which we the chiefs have sent to you to treat about our *hunting lands*, that lie in your state. Beginning on the east side of Ticonderoga, from thence to the great falls on Otter Creek, and continues the same course to the height of land, that divides the streams between Lake Champlain, and the river Connecticut; from thence along the height of lands [to] opposite Missisque and then down to the Bay:— That is the land belonging to the seven nations, which we have sent to settle for with you, as we have settled with York state. So we hope you will be pleased to receive our agents, and that it will be settled, so that both sides will be contented.

Cognahwagha, the 29th of September, 1798.
[Signed by twenty chiefs of the different nations]

. . .

Report of Gov. Tichenor—1799.
IN GENERAL ASSEMBLY, Oct. 28, 1799.

A message from the Governor [and Council] by Mr. Whitney their secretary.

Mr. Speaker—I am directed to lay before the House a communication from his Excellency, the Governor, relating to claims of the seven nations of Indians of Lower Canada, which he laid on the table and then he withdrew.

The communication was then read as followeth, to wit:

Gentlemen of the House of Representatives,— Herewith I do myself the honor to lay before you the result of the enquiries I have made, relative to the claims of the seven nations of Indians, of Lower Canada, in pursuance of the act of the Legislature on this subject passed at their session in October last.

I cannot learn that the state of New York were governed so much by a principle of justice, as policy, in the compensation made by them, in their late treaty with these people. The claims of the Indians to lands in the state of New York, and for which they received a compensation from that government, I conceive to be somewhat variant from their claims to lands in this state. The greater part of our lands was granted by the King of England, without any express reservation of an Indian claim; while the lands in New York were principally vacant, and the hunting ground of the claimants.

It has not been in my power to obtain any documents that would give any accurate information of the ancient claim of these Indians to the lands in question, but from the long and settled usage [and] principles which have governed nations in similar cases, I conceive their right, whatever it may have been, extinguished.

These Indians, the Cognawagahs, are anciently of the confederacy called the five nations; which confederacy, or some nation of that confederacy, might have once had a good right to the territory now claimed.

In the former wars, between the English and French, while the English king held the governments of this country, it is believed the Cognawagahs separated from the confederacy, removed into Canada, put themselves under the French, and joined their fortunes with the French king in his wars with the English: the latter being victorious conquered the French, and all their allies in this country and in Canada; upon which the whole country was yielded to the English, in right of conquest.

The treaty which terminated that war, and which was made for all those who were united with the French, or were inhabitants or held rights in the province of Canada, reserved certain rights and privileges, to all the conquered people of that province. Their rights, so reserved, were considered to extend beyond the limits of that province; in this the Indians acquiesced, for and during all the time the English were in the possession and government of this country. It is also believed that the Indians never caused the voice of their claims to be heard, respecting these lands, during the existence of this government, or at any period since the conquest, or since the grant of these lands by his Britannic majesty.

I may also add, that in the year 1775, when the king of England, who had granted these lands, made war upon this country, these Indians were his allies in that war, and thereby subjected themselves and interest to its consequences. The people of the United States were victorious, and the king of England, by treaty, yielded to the United States all the lands to the south of Canada. Thus, in my view, the claims of the Indians have been extinguished.

Although by the act submitting the examination of the Indian claim to me, it becomes my duty to make known the result of the investigation to the Indians in the first instance, yet the importance of the subject induces me to lay my views of it before the legislature, and receive such further communications as they may direct.

The present of one hundred dollars has been received by the chiefs, and their expenses paid while at Vergennes. No expence has been incurred, in the management of this business, except a small sum, given by judge Hathaway, to influence the chiefs, on their way to attend at this place, to return back. All which, with due deference and respect, is submitted to the consideration of the Legislature.

ISAAC TICHENOR

Report of Gov. Tichenor—1800.
AT MIDDLEBURY, IN COUNCIL CHAMBER,
Oct. 27, 1800.

Mr. Speaker: In pursuance of a Resolution of the House of Representatives, passed in November last, relative to the Indian titles to lands in this state, it became my duty to make known to their people the determination of the government respecting their claims.

In January last, I had a conference with five of their nations, and furnished them a copy of the aforesaid resolution respecting their claim. They alleged, as they were on other business, they could not officially receive it. During the session of the present Legislature a new set of Chiefs, joined by a representation from the Abernaki nation, have come forward, properly authorized to make a final settlement of their claims.

In the repeated conferences I have had with them, I have endeavored to explain to them, in a clear and explicit manner, the reasons which induced the Legislature to decide against the justice of their claims. It would be too tedious, as well as in some measure unentertaining, to detail on paper to the General Assembly, everything that has passed at the different interviews I have had with the Chiefs. The secretary of Council will lay before you the official papers on this subject, and, in particular, my last address to them.

I cannot but flatter myself that they are now fully satisfied, if ever a claim existed, it is wholly extinguished; and although they will not acknowledge it, in their official capacity, yet I am well persuaded that they will not trouble the Legislature in the future. As to the hint in the close of my last address to them—that probably the legislature will give them something to help them in their way home, you will be pleased to take such order thereon as shall seem expedient.

I can not, however, forbear to remark that in my opinion such measures ought to be adopted as will be calculated to promote the highest harmony and good understanding between them and the good citizens of this State.

I have the honor to be, gentlemen, with due consideration, your humble servant,

ISAAC TICHENOR

Source: E. P. Walton, ed., *Records of the Governor and Council of the State of Vermont*, Vol. 8 (Montpelier: Steam Press, 1880), pp. 313-314, 319-322.

DOCUMENT 6

Cartoon Depicting Matthew Lyon Clubbing Roger Griswold in Congress (1798)

(depicted on following page)

Source: Geoffrey Touchstone, *The House of Wisdom in a Bustle* (Philadelphia, 1798), Special Collections, Bailey/Howe Library, University of Vermont. Reprinted courtesy of Special Collections, UVM Libraries.

DOCUMENT 7

Replies of Vermont to the Kentucky and Virginia Resolutions of 1798 (1799)

To his Excellency the Governor, the Hon. Council, and General Assembly convened in joint committee, your sub-committee to whom was referred the resolutions of the states of Kentucky and Virginia, beg leave to report the following answer to the resolutions of the State of Kentucky.

To the Legislature of the state of Kentucky.

We have maturely considered your resolutions of November 10th, 1798. As you invite our opinion, you will not blame us for giving it without disguise, and with decision. In your first resolution, you observe, in substance, "That the states constituted the general government, and that each state as party to the compact, has an equal right to judge for itself as well of infractions of the constitution, as of the mode and measure of redress." This cannot be true. The old confederation, it is true, was formed by the state Legislatures, but the present constitution of the United States was derived from an higher authority. The people of the United States formed the federal constitution, and not the states, or their Legislatures. And although each state is authorized to propose amendments, yet there is wide difference between proposing amendments to the con-

stitution, and assuming, or inviting, a power to dictate or control the general government.

In your second resolution, you certainly misconstrue and misapply an amendment to the Federal Constitution, which, if your construction be true, does not surely warrant the conclusion that as a state you have a right to declare any act of the General Government, which you shall deem unconstitutional, null and void. Indeed, you actually do declare two acts of the Congress of the United States null and void. If, as a state, you have a right to declare two acts of the Congress of the United States unconstitutional and therefore void, you have an equal right to declare all their acts unconstitutional. Suppose each Legislature possess the power you contend for, each state Legislature would have the right to cause all the acts of Congress to pass in view before them, and reject or approve at their discretion, and the consequences would be, that the government of the Union, falsely called General, might operate partially in some states, and cease to operate in others. Would not this defeat the grand design of our Union?

In the eighteenth article [sub-division] in the eighth section of the Constitution of the United States, we read, "That Congress shall have power to make all laws which shall be proper for carrying into execution the Government of the United States." If you enquire, where is our redress, should the Congress of the United States violate the Constitution, by abusing this power? We point to the right of election, [and] the Judicial courts of the Union; and, in a jury of our fellow citizens, we find the ever watchful and constitutional guard against this supposed evil.

In your third resolution you again severely reprehend the act of Congress commonly called "the Sedition bill." If we possessed the power you assumed, to censure the acts of the General Government, we could not consistently construe the Sedition bill unconstitutional; because our own constitution guards the freedom of speech and the press in terms as explicit as that of the United States, yet long before the existence of the Federal Constitution, we enacted laws which are still in force against sedition, inflicting severer penalties than this act of Congress.

And although the freedom of speech and of the press are declared unalienable in our bill of rights, yet the railer against the civil magistrate, and the blasphemer of his Maker, are exposed to grievous punish-

Document 6

ment. And no one has been heard to complain that these laws infringe our state Constitution. Our state laws also protect the citizen in his good name: and if the slanderer publish his libel, he is not in a criminal prosecution indulged, as by the act of Congress, in giving the truth of the facts as exculpatory evidence. Thus accustomed to construe our own Constitution, you will readily conceive that we acquiesce in a similar construction of the Constitution of the United States.

In your fourth resolution, you declare the Alien Act to be of no force, and not law; that Congress have, in passing that law, assumed a power not delegated by the Constitution, and have thereby deprived the alien of certain Constitutional rights. We ever considered that the Constitution of the United States was made for the benefit of our own citizens; we never conjectured that aliens were any party of the federal compact; we never knew that aliens had any rights among us, except what they derived from the law of nations, and rights of hospitality, which gives them a right to remain in any country while inoffensive—subjects them to punishment if disobedient, and to be driven away if suspected of designs injurious to the public welfare.

The construction of [that clause of] the Constitution which prohibits Congress from passing laws to prevent emigration ["migration or importation"] until the year 1808, in your fifth resolution, is certainly erroneous. This clause, we ever apprehended, had for its object *Negro Slaves*; and to give it any other construction would be to infer that Congress, after the year 1808, would have power to put a capitation tax upon every alien who should come to reside among us. The idea is too inhospitable to be admitted by a free and generous people.

In your sixth resolution, you allege that the President is vested with a dangerous power; that, by his simple order, he may remove a suspected alien. We conceive that the President of the United States, as the head of the Government, possesses the best means of knowing the emissaries of our enemies, and we have the fullest confidence in his using his power and knowledge for the public good. You say that an alien has a constitutional right to a trial by jury, to be informed of the nature and cause of the accusation, to be confronted with the witnesses against him, and to have a compulsory process for obtaining witnesses in his favor, and to have the assistance of counsel for his de-

fence. If an alien among us commit a crime he may indeed by tried by a jury of the country, to which he owes *local* allegiance; but by what law shall a man be tried by jury for suspicion? If our country were threatened with invasion, a thousand spies might be sent to spy out our weakness, and to prepare bad men to assist, and weak men to submit to the enemy. Do not the common principles of self-defence enable a government to arrest such emissaries and send them from the country, if only suspected of designs hostile to the public safety? If not, should some foreign invader approach our coasts, with a powerful fleet and army, those aliens would have a constitutional right to a trial by jury.

In your last resolution, you say, "That confidence is everywhere the parent of despotism; free government is founded in jealousy, and not in confidence." This is a sentiment palpably erroneous, and hostile to the social nature of man. The experience of ages evinces the reverse is true, and that jealousy is the meanest passion of narrow minds, and tends to despotism; and that honesty always begets confidence, while those, who are dishonest themselves, are most apt to suspect others.

Resolved, That his Excellency, the Governor, be requested to transmit a copy of the foregoing answer to the Resolutions of the state of Kentucky, to the executive of that state, to be communicated to the Legislature.

The foregoing answer to the resolutions of the state of Kentucky was read and accepted.

THE ANSWER TO THE RESOLUTIONS OF THE STATE OF VIRGINIA

To his Excellency the Governor, the Hon. Council, and General Assembly, convened in joint committee, your sub-committee, appointed to report a resolution in answer to the resolutions of the state of Virginia, beg leave to report the following resolution, to be recommended by this committee to the Legislature for adoption.

Resolved, That the General Assembly of the state of Vermont do highly disapprove of the resolutions of the state of Virginia, as being unconstitutional in their nature, and dangerous in their tendency. It belongs not to *State Legislatures* to decide on the constitutionality of laws made by the general government; this power being exclusively vested in the *Judiciary Courts of the Union*.

That his Excellency the Governor be requested to transmit a copy of this resolution to the Executive of Virginia, to be communicated to the General Assembly of that state.

Which report was accepted by the committee.

The answer to Virginia was adopted, 104 to 52; and the answer to Kentucky, 101 to 50.

Source: E. P. Walton, ed., *Records of the Governor and Council of the State of Vermont*, Vol. 4 (Montpelier: Steam Press, 1876), pp. 526-528.

DOCUMENT 8

"The Nature and Importance of True Republicanism" (1801)
LEMUEL HAYNES

A discourse delivered at Rutland, July 4, 1801,- It being the 25th Anniversary of American Independence.

. . . There cannot be a greater source of evil to mankind than to imbibe wrong sentiments about true greatness.—In a land like ours, where the people are free and view each other as brethren engaged in one common cause, virtue and philanthropy will be considered as the true criterions of distinction.—He will be esteemed great who is servant of all, who is willing to devote his talents to the public good. These are the prominent features of a free, republican government, and should attach us to our present constitution.

Again, A free, independent administration, like ours, is very friendly to knowledge and instruction; it expands the human mind, and gives it a thirst after improvement. The amazing progress that these states have made in useful arts and science, of almost every kind, during the twenty five years of our independence, will justify the present remark; perhaps no history will be read to better advantage.—When men are made to

believe that true dignity consists in outward parade and pompous titles, they forget the thing itself, and the greater part of the community view the other as unattainable, they look up to others as above them, and forget to think for themselves, nor retain their own importance in the scale of being. Hence, under a monarchal government, people are commonly ignorant; they know but little more than to bow to despots, and crouch to them for a piece of bread.

The propriety of this idea will appear strikingly evident by pointing you to the poor Africans, among us. What has reduced them to their present pitiful, abject state? Is it any distinction that the God of nature hath made in their formation? Nay—but being subjected to slavery, by the cruel hands of oppressors, they have been taught to view themselves as a rank of beings far below others, which has suppressed, in a degree, every principle of manhood, and so they become despised, ignorant, and licentious. This shews the effects of despotism, and should fill us with the utmost detestation against every attack on the rights of men: while we cherish and diffuse, with a laudable ambition, that heaven-born liberty wherewith Christ hath made us free. Should we compare those countries, where tyrants are gorged with human blood, to the far more peaceful regions of North America, the contrast would appear striking.

On the whole, does it not appear that a land of liberty is favourable to peace, happiness, virtue and religion, and should be held sacred by mankind?

In the last place—A few directions were promised, as necessary means to secure, or maintain our liberties and independence. The fate of the once noble republic of Rome, and many others: What took place in the interregnum of eleven years and four months in England, between the reigns of Charles First and Second, may shew that 'tis more than possible that such a precious diamond may lose its lustre, and undergo a total extinction. The present unhappy divisions among us, do not wear the most favourable aspects, as to this matter.

In the first place—It is quite necessary that people well understand the true *nature* of republicanism and independence; that they import something noble and excellent; nothing vain and licentious, but what is promotive of order, virtue and morality.—The state of mankind, is such, that they cannot live without law: break down this barrier, and our case at once becomes alarming. It is nothing strange, if through the perverseness of human nature, our system has been misunderstood, as falling in with the lusts of men, and favorable to a dissolute life: than which nothing can be more subversive of the scheme. That even in regenerated France, there has been something of this nature, is too evident.—We should always keep in mind that a true republican is one who wishes well to the good constitution and laws of the commonwealth, is ready to lend his heart, his sword and his property for their support; gives merit its proper place; respects magistrates, according as they appear to regard the happiness of society, and seeks the general good.—He is peaceable and quiet under an wholesome administration; but anarchy and confusion are of all things most detestable, while he grows better under the benign influence of good government. It is very common for people to expect too much from such a system, and cannot in any degree be satisfied without a perfect administration. This is not to be expected in this degenerate world; Therefore some imperfections in those who serve the public, must be dispensed with.—This is an idea of peculiar importance in a republican government like ours, where civil officers are so directly amenable to the people. Let it be remembered, that true independence has religion, regularity, and a veneration for good order for its objects. . . .

5. Might I be endulged a little, I would say, that education and the diffusion of useful knowledge, is very favorable to a free government. Oppression and usurpation hold their empires where ignorance and darkness spread their sable domain. Let people be well instructed, let them read the history of kings, and know the rights of men, and it will be difficult to make them believe that the names, King, Lord, Sovereign, Prince, Viscount, and such childish trumpery, ought to command their purse, their property, and liberty; but that goodness, virtue or benevolence, are things that demand veneration.

6. The end and design of government, which is to secure the natural rights of men, suggests another idea of importance as necessary to support our present Constitution, viz. That such men be appointed to office whose characters comport with it.—If to preserve our lives and property, and to defend the public from every encroachment, are the great objects of civil government, then men of a philanthropic spirit, who will naturally care for mankind, ought only to occupy places of public betrustment. He that would wish to become consequential in any other way, only in seeking the good of the neighbor, is dangerous to society.—"But ye shall not be so;" says my text, "but he that is greatest among you, let him be as the younger, and he that is chief, as he that doth serve."—The end of the appointment is to serve our generation by the will of God; then men of a narrow selfish, mercenary spirit should forever be excluded from posts of preferment. The fawning sycophant, who is seeking promotion only to gratify his pride and ambition, will if an opportunity presents, sell his country for less than thirty pieces of silver.

The sentiment now inculcating receives abundant energy from oracles of divine truth, and should ever be held sacred.

7. In a word, it would be an unpardonable error should I forget to mention that which after all is the great and only source of felicity, peace and prosperity among men, I mean religion. A republican government has its basis in this. Can we form a more noble idea of piety and Christianity than what is comprised in the words benevolence and true patriotism. To love God and one another, and to seek the happiness and good of the universe, involves every thing that is great, noble, virtuous and excellent. Selfishness enervates every social band and endearment, sets men at variance, and is the source of every evil. Vice debases and weakens the human mind; and is to the body politic what sickness is to the natural constitution. No sooner did Sampson trespass on the rules of religion & morality, than he became a weak, menial slave, and did grind in the prison house. Pride, dissipation and impiety, have crumbled empires in the dust, and buried their names in everlasting oblivion. A sacred regard to holy institutions is necessary to secure the divine favour and protection, and to maintain the order of society. Those words of inspiration cannot too often be repeated, and are worthy to be written in indelible characters on the fleshly tables of our hearts: "Righteousness exalteth a nation; but sin is a reproach to any people."

Source: Richard Newman, ed., *Black Preacher to White America: The Collected Writings of Lemuel Haynes, 1774-1833* (Brooklyn, N.Y.: Carlson Publishing, Inc., 1990), pp. 81-83, 84-85.

DOCUMENT 9

The *Black Snake* Affair (1808)

TO THE PEOPLE OF VERMONT

FELLOW CITIZENS,

IT IS DONE! The cup of guilt is full! Treason, rebellion and murder stalk abroad at noon-day! Our land has been stained with the blood of our citizens, acting in defence of the government and laws of our country. By whom? A foreign foe? No: but, (horrid to relate) by the bloody hands of domestic traitors.

Capt. JONATHAN ORMSBY, a respectable farmer, belonging to Burlington; Mr. ELLIS DRAKE and Mr. ASA MARSH, two respectable young men, belonging to Capt. Pratt's company of militia, stationed at Windmill Point, were all killed at Burlington, on Wednesday the 3d instant, about noon, in a most wanton and barbarous manner, by a party of insurgents, employed in smuggling potash into Canada, in violation of the laws. The Collector detached Lieut. Farrington, a sergeant and twelve men, in pursuit of a boat, which had gone up Onion river after a load of potash.—The Lieutenant found the boat and took possession of her, notwithstanding the insurgents threatened to blow out his brains if he attempted to meddle with her. The Lieutenant dropped down the river, with the cutter and the boat he had taken, about half a mile; when the insurgents fired upon him and killed Drake. The Lieutenant then ordered both boats to be rowed on shore, near the place whence the fire proceeded: he landed with his men, and ascended the bank of the river:—immediately the insurgents discharged a large gun, called a wall-piece, the barrel of which is eight feet in length, and was loaded with sixteen ounce balls, and some buck shot—which carried instant death to Captain Ormsby and Mr. Marsh, severely wounded the Lieutenant in the head, the left arm, and slightly wounded him in the right shoulder. Capt. Ormsby had been laboring in his field during the forenoon, near the fatal spot, was on his return to dinner, had just reached the place where the government troops entered the road, when the murderous discharge took place, which, at the same instant, sent two soul companions into eternity.

If any thing can add to the horror of this too horrid scene, it is the observation of certain federal characters on the vicinity, who even lay claim to the name of respectability, tending to screen the assassins, and throw the whole weight of guilt on the part of the government.—Says one, *The men were sent here by Penniman to steal an empty boat, and died like fools*—Says another, *I hope to God Penniman will be hung for it*—Says another, *I should care but little about it, if I did not fear it would influence the ensuing election*—Says another, on hearing of the melancholy event, *I am glad of it, they are republicans who are killed.*—Such was the current of expression which poured from the mouths of federalism, while the blood was still gushing from the weltering bodies of our countrymen, murdered by federal hands at mid-day, within the boundaries of that town which boasts itself of being the strong hold of federalism, and some of whose principal merchants furnished the insurgents with powder and ball, for the express purpose of performing this bloody work.

The federalists now begin to lengthen their faces, and pretend to feel regret for the transaction, but their hypocritical tears will not avail them. This horrid deed has been done by their procurement; they are partners in the guilt of the perpetrators, and they are accountable to their country and their God, for all the blood that has been shed.

When a large body of men, and more especially those in the higher walks of life, who arrogate to themselves all the virtue, all the talents, and all the religion of the country, combine together for the purpose of opposing the laws of their country; when they openly and publicly, by printing and speaking, treat the government and the officers of the government, from the President of the United States down to the lowest executive officer, with abuse, ridicule and contempt; when they trample on the laws of their country, by daily exciting, both by precept and example, the violation of those laws by force and arms; when they exult at the success of the insurgents in every act of treason they commit; when they bid defiance to government, and threaten the officers with assassination if they attempt to do their duty; when with more than savage barbarity they exult over the bleeding bodies of our murdered citizens; and when they even insult the faithful soldier while oppressed with grief at the loss of his beloved comrade:—then is the cup of guilt full; then is it time

TO ROUSE IN DEFENCE OF YOUR COUNTRY AND YOUR LIVES.

This is no ordinary contest. It is not a simple question, who shall be governor and councillors; but it is a struggle for the existence of your government; for the protection of those rights purchased with the blood of your fathers, and for the protection of your lives. Should that faction whose hands are still reeking with the blood of your brethren, come into power, what have you to expect? If they have done these things in the face of law, in the face of authority, what will they do when clothed with power? This bloody scene is but an opening wedge to the measures they would pursue. The tragedy of Roberspierre would be reacted in the United Sates; and every distinguished character, who is a friend to his country, might expect to be sacrificed to the malice of an unprincipled and vindictive faction.

Fellow citizens, on you depends the fate of your country—by your suffrages at the approching election, you will decide, whether you deserve the name of freemen; whether you are worthy of your father; whether you will defend the government of your country, and protect your wives, your children, and your own lives; or whether you will tamely give up your dear bought rights, and submit your necks to the axe of the guilotine.

By supporting our present patriotic governor and councillors, you will perpetuate the existence of our government, and transmit to posterity the blessings we now enjoy.

By neglecting to attend the poll, or by voting for the federal ticket, you will entail on your country all the horrors of slavery, oppression and murder.

MONITOR.

Source: "The *Black Snake* Affair," August 1808, Broadside Collection, Vermont Historical Society, Montpelier, Vermont.

DOCUMENT 10

"Union, Peace, & Commerce": Anti-Jeffersonian Resolutions (1812)

It is with peculiar pleasure we communicate the result of the meeting at WILLISTON, August 27, 1812. The friends of Union, Peace and Commerce, in the county of Chittenden, have conducted worthy the high character they have sustained and of the interesting cause they espouse. The meeting assembled at about one o'clock, P.M. and a most respectable and dignified assemblage, we are confident was never witnessed in the county. The greatest proportion of the assembly consisted of men past the middle age of life. It seemed as if the patriots of '76 had returned to the earth once more to snatch their country from ruin. Young men in the bloom of life, men in maturer years, and old age leaning upon its crutch, came impressed with the alarming situation of our country, and conscious of their dignity and their rights, to express their sentiments upon the measures of government.

Honorable DANIEL FARRAND, was appointed Chairman, and MILO COOK, Esquire, Secretary. . . .

RESOLVED, That the alarming situation of our country demands the solemn consideration of every friend and lover of national liberty.

Resolved, That the distresses which we seek, and the more grievous ones which we fear, are occasioned by the imprudent and impolitic measures pursued by Mr. Jefferson & Mr. Madison.

Resolved, That the protection of commerce was one of the grand objects for which our government was formed, and its destruction ruinous to the prosperity of the eastern States, and tends to dry up the life blood of the nation.

Resolved, That the late restrictive measures of our government are inefficient and partial, injurious to ourselves and unworthy [of] a great and independent neutral nation.

Resolved, That the differences which exist between this country and Great Britain, might in the opinion of this meeting, long since have been settled by honorable negotiation, and that the last dreadful appeal to arms was not demanded by the interest or honor of the United States.

Resolved, That in the defenseless situation of our country, and when such a vast amount of property and such numbers of our citizens are exposed to capture on the ocean, the declaring war, is a wanton departure from duty on the part of administration.

Resolved, That we consider any political connexion with the Tyrant of France, as the surrender of our independence, and we have reason to fear, that our rulers are improperly pledged to aid and abet his cause.

Resolved, That in the opinion of this meeting, the late orders for calling out the militia, are not warranted by the letter nor spirit of the constitution; and that the forcing them from their farms at this busy season of the year, is a cruel abuse of authority.

Resolved, That while we claim the unrestrained exercise of the right of conscience, of private opinion, of freedom of speech, of writing and publishing our sentiments concerning the transactions of government, and of assembling together to consult for the common good, we deprecate every unlawful attempt to resist the constituted authorities of our country.

Resolved, That the last violent proceedings in restraining the freedom of debate, in destroying the liberty of the press, & murdering individuals in the peaceable exercise of their most valuable rights, by an outrageous and savage mob, ought to excite the utmost alarm.

Resolved, That the present crisis demands the exertions of the lovers of peace, and that it is a duty incumbent upon every real lover of his country to exercise his elective franchise at the next election, to call to office those men, whose talents, integrity, and virtue are pledges of the faithful execution of their trust . . . .

Source: "Union, Peace, & Commerce," 1812, Broadside, Special Collections, Bailey/Howe Library, University of Vermont.

DOCUMENT 11

"An Act to Prevent Intercourse with the Enemies of This and the United States on the Northern Frontiers" (1812)

Chapter 102

AN ACT,
To prevent intercourse with the enemies of this and the United States on the Northern Frontiers.

WHEREAS the United States are now at War with the United Kingdom of Great Britain and Ireland, and their dependencies, by reason of which the peace and safety of the citizens of this State would be endangered by an intercourse between the citizens of this, or any other of the United States, and the enemy of our country on our northern frontiers;

THEREFORE,

Sect. 1. *IT is hereby enacted by the General Assembly of the state of Vermont*, That from and after the passing of this act, no person shall be allowed to pass through or from this state into the province of Lower Canada, under any shew, pretense, or pretext whatever, nor to pass through, or come into, this state from the said province, without a permit from the Governor. . . . And if any person shall so presume or attempt to pass from this State, into the said Province, or shall come from the said Province into this State . . . without a permit first had and obtained as aforesaid, shall forfeit and pay to the Treasurer of this State a sum not exceeding one thousand dollars, and shall moreover be sentenced to hard labor into the State's Prison, a term not exceeding seven years, or either, or both of said punishments, as the court in their discretion shall think proper. Provided, Nothing in this section contained shall subject to any pains and penalities any person coming from said Province into this State, and going directly to the nearest person authorised to give such permit, and going to make application for the same.

Sect. 2. *And it is hereby further enacted*, That if any person or persons shall be driving any horses, or cattle, or conveying any property towards the Province of Lower Canada, under such circumstances, as tend to create a reasonable suspicion, that the same is about to be driven, or transported into said province, every person so offending shall be liable to be apprehended without a warrant, and detained a reasonable time to procure a warrant, and then by virtue thereof be brought before any Justice of the peace in the county where such apprehension may be made, whose duty it shall be, on sufficient evidence of the circumstances aforesaid, to require of such offender a recognizance to the State's Treasurer with sufficient sureties, in a sum not less than five hundred dollars, nor less than double the value of such horses, Cattle, nor other property nor the person driving or transporting the same, shall go to be driven into said Province. And on failure to give such recognizance, such person may be imprisoned until a compliance with such sentence.

Sect. 3. *And it is hereby further enacted*, That if any person or persons shall drive any horses, or cattle, or transport any property towards said Province of Canada, with intent that the same shall get into the said Province of Canada, or if any horses, or cattle, or other property, shall be concealed near the said Province, with intent that the same may be driven or transported into the said Province, such property shall be forfeited, one half to the State Treasurer, the other half to the use of the person who shall seize and libel the same, before any three justices of the peace, one of who shall be a judge of the county court. . . . And every person offending against this third section of this act, on conviction thereof, shall be liable to the same penalties prescribed in the first section of this act.

Sect. 4. . . . And every Justice of the Peace within his Jurisdiction, shall have power, without warrant, to inspect the trunks or papers of every person travelling to, or from the Province of Canada (or elsewhere under suspicious circumstances) and open the same, if necessary, and fully ascertain whether such person shall be aiding in any Treasonable communications with the enemy, and on discovery of such aid, may cause process to issue, and the offender to be holden for trial before the Supreme Court. And such Justice may stop and detain all such letters and papers, as he shall deem improper to be carried either to or from said Province. *Provided*, That no dwelling house or other building shall be broken to make such inspection, without a warrant first and obtained according to law.

Sect. 5. *And it is hereby further enacted*, That all officers, civil and military of this State shall aid in carrying this act into full force. *Provided nevertheless*, That nothing in this act contained, shall be construed to effect persons acting under the authority of laws of the United States, or to prevent the marching of troops. *And Provided also*, That this act shall not extend beyond the present war.

Sect. 6. *And it is hereby further enacted*, That if any person shall actually drive or convey any horses, cattle, sheep or swine, or transport any property from this State into the said Province of Lower Canada, or shall be aiding or assisting therein, after the passing of this act, and shall be thereof convicted before the Supreme Court of Judicature of this State, such person so convicted shall forfeit and pay to the Treasurer of this State, a sum equal to double the value of the property driven, or transported as aforesaid—and shall be further liable to all the penalties and punishments contained in the first section of this act, and the value of

the property driven or transported as aforesaid, shall be found by the Jury, who shall return the same into court, at the time of conviction aforesaid.

Sect. 7. *And it is hereby further enacted*, That any Justice of the Peace or other officer, concerned in the execution of this act, shall have the right of calling to their aid, any of the citizens of this State, in the performance of the duties, required by this act, and in case any person or persons shall neglect or refuse to aid and assist such officer in the execution, of any of the duties required in this act when thereto requested, as aforesaid, such person or persons, on conviction before the Supreme Court of Judicature, shall forfeit and pay to the Treasurer of this State, a fine of not less than twenty dollars, no more than five hundred dollars, in the discretion of the court, before whom the trial is had.

Sect. 8. *And it is hereby further enacted*, That the Secretary be instructed, as soon as may be, to cause this act to be published, in all the news papers printed within this state.

STATE OF VERMONT
Secretary of State's Office,
Passed, Nov. 9, 1812

Source: *Acts and Laws Passed by the Legislature of the State of Vermont . . . 1812* (Danville, Vt.: n. p., 1812), pp. 141-146.

DOCUMENT 12

Sketches of Epidemic Diseases in the State of Vermont (1812-1813)
JOSEPH GALLUP

1813

The autumn of 1812, and winter of 1813, ushered in the most severe epidemic disease, that has ever afflicted the inhabitants of Vermont, the epidemic peripneumony, or disease of the lungs. It seemed to have the features of the disease, that had been in the state for about two years, called spotted fever; the chief difference seemed to be, that now the greatest force of local affection fell upon the lungs.

The disease appeared at the northward before it did in the county of Windsor, perhaps about one month. It appeared amongst the soldiers at Burlington, some weeks before it did amongst the inhabitants of that place. Very near the time it appeared at Burlington among the soldiers, it appeared also among the soldiers at Platsburg and Sacketts Harbour, and also in the camp at Greenbush, opposite Albany. No satisfactory account has ever been given the publick relative to the ravages of this disease at Burlington. I have solicted information from resident physicians there; but have received none. By information from some of the most respectable inhabitants of that place, and also from others residing there at that time, I am warranted in stating, that for some time, it was common for eight or twelve to die in a day. The whole number is said to be not less than seven or eight hundred in four months. Several dead bodies were carried through this place in sleighs, to be interred among their friends. The number of soldiers stationed at this encampment was about twenty-five or twenty-eight hundred.

Perhaps the fatigue and exposure of a camp life to men not accustomed to it, might have a share in rendering the soldiers the first victims of the disease. The depression of mind from a repulse immediately before under general Dearborn, in an attempt to invade Canada, may also be noticed.

The disease was not, however, confined to the camps. As the pestilential state of the atmosphere progressed to a degree of greater violence, the disease appeared among the inhabitants in the most comfortable condition; first in the northern section of the state, and immediately after in the middle, and southern sections. It is said to be about three weeks after it was very severe among the soldiers at Burlington, before the inhabitants were much affected. It, at length, became distressing and very mortal among the citizens of that place; and in about one month from its first appearance, it was pretty general over this and the adjoining states. The pestilential diathesis of the atmosphere, was not at its zenith until the first week in March. In this month, it raged with its greatest severity.

It is said, that many of the soldiers died in four or eight hours after the attack, and a few in two hours. It was fatal also in some places among the citizens, nearly in as short time. The common fatal period was about the fourth or fifth day. . . .

On account of the want of any regular returns of deaths in the towns in this state, it is impossible to ascertain the number that died of this disease. . . .

By the statement of Dr. Ware, of Pomfret, it appears that "In December last, the lung fever began, and continued until about the middle of May, 1813. Forty-four adults died with it in that time." The correctness of Dr. Ware will serve as a specimen for other towns, where the neglect of physicians has deprived us of any statement of this desease. He further observes, "where the practice of bleeding, puking, and purging was pursued, free expectoration promoted, and kept up, and heating stimulating means carefully avoided, the patients generally recovered. . . ."

Dr. Littlefield states, that the epidemic began at Arlington about the middle of January, and disappeared about the first of June. "It was not so fatal in this, and some of the adjacent towns, as in some other parts of the state. In Arlington, 10 deaths; In Sandgate, 20; in Sunderland, 1. From the best information, and some personal knowledge, I should say, in Manchester, 60 or 70; in Dorset, 40 or 50; in Rueport, 40 or 50; in Shaftsbury, 30; in Bennington, 70; in Pownal, 70 or 80. . . ."

Our correspondent further remarks, that previous to the first of March, he bled from two to four times, from 12 to 24 oz. each; his success was very great. But after this time he bled but little. In the latter period, the pulse was hardly perceptible; a sense of suffocation, the surface pale and cadaverous, or more commonly, a bloated purple colour, similar to a finger with a ligature on it; numbness, &c. From four to ten hours after the attack, the surface of the body would be often covered with spots or blotches like blood blisters; some of the bigness of a pea, others the size of a man's hand. Total loss of sight, insensibility, and other signs of approaching dissolution are mentioned. Sixteen adults died within six, or thirty hours after the attack, twelve of whom before any medical aid could be procured. It is further observed if the patient was put into a warm bed, &c. the fever arose with a pulse from 90 to 110 in a minute, bounding, but easily compressible. . . .

I very much regret my not being enabled to make a more particular statement. Great difference exists in the number of inhabitants in different towns, and also, the number of deaths by this disease. It must be considered a low estimate to day, that the towns throughout the state averaged 25 deaths. About 226 organized towns of six miles square, made 5,650 deaths. Add to this 750 soldiers, which makes the number of deaths by this disease alone 6,400, in about five months.— Census for 1810, 217,913 inhabitants.

The latter part of the summer and the first winter months, a considerable number of cases of typhus fever occurred. Also several cases of cholera infantum. This last disease has prevailed more or less almost every summer, although it has not been particularly noticed before now.

Source: Joseph A. Gallup, M.D., *Sketches of Epidemic Diseases in the State of Vermont* (Boston: T. B. Wait & Sons, 1815), pp. 69-75.

Document 13

Governor Martin Chittenden's Proclamation Recalling Vermont Troops from New York; Officers' Refusal to Obey (1813)

BY HIS EXCELLENCY
MARTIN CHITTENDEN, ESQUIRE
Governor, Captain General, and Commander in Chief, in and over the State of Vermont,
A PROCLAMATION

Whereas, it appears that the Third Brigade of the Third Division of the Militia of this State has been ordered from our frontiers to the defence of a neighbouring State: And whereas it further appears, to the extreme regret of the Captain General, that a part of this Militia of said Brigade have been placed under the command and at the disposal of an officer of the United States, out of the jurisdiction or control of the Executive of this State, and have been actually marched to the defence of a sister State, fully competent to all the purposes of self defence, whereby an extensive section of our own Frontier is left, in a measure, unprotected, and the peaceable good citizens thereof are put in great jeopardy, and exposed to the retaliatory incursions and ravages of an exasperated enemy: And whereas, disturbances of a very serious nature are believed to exist in consequence of a portion of the Militia having thus been ordered out of the State:

Therefore, to the end that these great evils may be provided against, and, as far as may be, prevented for the future:

Be it known—that such portion of the Militia of said Third Division, as may be now doing duty in the State of New York or elsewhere, beyond the limits of this State, both officers and men, are hereby ordered and directed, by the Captain General and Commander in Chief of the Militia of the State of Vermont, forthwith to return to the respective places of their usual residence, within the territorial limits of said Brigade, and there to hold themselves in constant readiness to act in obedience to the orders of Brigadier General JACOB DAVIS, who is appointed by the Legislature of this State, to command said Brigade.

And the said Brigadier General Davis is hereby ordered and directed, forthwith, to see that the Militia of his said Brigade be completely armed and equipped as the Law directs, and holden in constant readiness to march on the shortest notice to the defence of the Frontier; and, in case of actual invasion, without further orders, to march with his said Brigade, to act, either in cooperation with the troops of the United States, or separately, as circumstances may require, in repelling the enemy from our territory, and in protecting the good citizens of this State from their ravages or hostile incursions.

And in case of an event, so seriously to be deprecated, it is hoped and expected, that every citizen, without distinction of party, will fly at once to the nearest post of danger, and that the only rallying words will be—OUR COUNTRY.

Feeling, as the Captain General does, the weight of responsibility which rests upon him with regard to the constitutional duties of the Militia, and the sacred rights of our citizens to protection from this great class of community, so essentially necessary to all free countries—at a moment, too, when they are so imminently exposed to the dangers of hostile incursions, and domestic difficulties—he cannot conscientiously discharge the trust reposed in him by the voice of his fellow citizens, and the Constitution of this and the United States, without an unequivocal declaration, that, in his opinion, the Military strength and resources of this State must be reserved for its own defence and protection, *exclusively*—excepting in cases provided for by the Constitution of the U. States; and then, under orders derived *only* from the Commander in Chief [i.e., the president of the United States].

Given under my hand at Montpelier this 10th day of November in the year of our Lord One thousand

Eight hundred and thirteen; and of the Independence of the United States the Thirty eight.

MARTIN CHITTENDEN
By His Exy's Command, Samuel Swift, *Sec'ry.*

CANTONMENT, PLATTSBURGH, NOV. 15, 1813

To His Excellency, MARTIN CHITTENDEN, Esq., *Governor, Captain General, Commander in Chief, in and over the State of Vermont.*

SIR: A most novel and extraordinary Proclamation from your Excellency, "ordering and directing such portion of the Militia of the Third Brigade of the Third Division of the Militia of Vermont, now doing duty in the State of New York, both officers and men, forthwith to return to the respective places of their residence," has just been communicated to the undersigned officers of said Brigade. A measure so unexampled requires that we should state to your Excellency the reasons which induce us, and absolutely and positively, to refuse obedience to the order contained in your Excellency's Proclamation. With due deference to your Excellency's opinion, we humbly conceive, that when we are ordered into the service of the United States, it becomes our duty, when required, to march to the defence of any section of the Union. We are not of that class who believe that our duties as citizens or soldiers are circumscribed within the narrow limits of the Town or State in which we reside; but that we are under a paramount obligation to our common country, to the great confederation of States. We further conceive that, while we are in actual service, and during the period for which we were ordered into service, your Excellency's power over us, as Governor of the State of Vermont, is suspended.

If it is true, as your Excellency states, that we "are out of the jurisdiction or control of the Executive of Vermont," we would ask from whence your Excellency derives the *right* or presumes to exercise the *power* of ordering us to return from the service in which we are now engaged? If we were *legally* ordered into the service, our continuance in it is either voluntary or compulsory. If voluntary, it gives no one a right to remonstrate or complain; if compulsory we can appeal to the laws of our country for redress against those who illegally restrain us of our liberty. In *either* case we cannot conceive the right your Excellency has to interfere in the business. Viewing the subject in this light, we conceive it our duty to declare unequivocally to your Excellency, that we shall not obey your Excellency's order for returning; but shall continue in the service of our country until we are legally and honorably discharged. An invitation or order to desert the standard of our country will never be obeyed by us, although it proceeds from the Governor and Captain General of Vermont.

Perhaps it is proper that we should content ourselves with merely giving your Excellency the reasons which prevail upon us to disregard your proclamation; but we are impressed with the belief that our duty to ourselves, to the soldiers under our command, and to the public, require that we should expose to the world the motives which produced and the objects which were intended to be accomplished by such extraordinary proclamation. We shall take the liberty to state to your Excellency, plainly, our sentiments on this subject. We consider your proclamation as a gross insult to the officers and soldiers in service, inasmuch as it implies that they are so *ignorant* of their rights as to believe that you have authority to command them in their present situation, or so *abandoned* as to follow your insidious advice. We cannot regard your proclamation in any other light than as an unwarrantable stretch of executive authority, issued from the worst motives, to effect the basest purposes. It is, in our opinion, a renewed instance of that spirit of disorganization and anarchy which is carried on by a faction to overwhelm our country with ruin and disgrace. We cannot perceive what other object your Excellency could have in view than to embarrass the operations of the army, to excite mutiny and sedition among the soldiers and induce them to desert, that they might forfeit the wages to which they are entitled for their patriotic services.

We have, however, the satisfaction to inform your Excellency, that although your proclamations have been distributed among the soldiers by your agent delegated for that purpose, they have failed to produce the intended effect—and although it may appear *incredible* to your Excellency, *even soldiers* have discernment sufficient to perceive that the proclamation of a Governor when offered out of the line of his duty, is a harmless, inoffensive and nugatory document. They regard it with mingled emotions of pity and contempt for its author, and as a striking monument of his folly.

Before we conclude, we feel ourselves in justice to your Excellency bound to declare that a knowledge of your Excellency's character induces us to believe that the folly and infamy of the proclamation, to which your Excellency has *put your signature*, is not wholly to be ascribed to your Excellency, but chiefly to the evil advisers with whom we believe your Excellency is encompassed.

We are, with due respect, your Excellency's obedient servants,

Luther Dixon, Lieut. Col.	Daniel Dodge, Ensign.
Eligah Dee, Jun., Major.	Sanford Gadcomb, Captain.
Josiah Grout, Major.	James Fullington, Qr. Master.
Charles Bennet, Captain.	Shepard Beal, Lieutemant.
Eligah W. Wood, Captain.	John Fassett, Surgeon.
Elijah Birge, Captain.	Seth Clark, Jr., Surgeon's Mate.
Martin D. Follett, Captain.	Thomas Waterman, Captain.
Amasa Mansfield, Captain.	Benjamin Follett, Lieutenant.
T. H. Campbell, Lieutenant.	Hira Hill, Surgeon's Mate.

Source: E. P. Walton, ed., *Records of the Governor and Council of the State of Vermont,* Vol. 6 (Montpelier: Steam Press, 1878), pp. 492-494.

DOCUMENT 14

"Battle of Plattsburgh and Victory on Lake Champlain" (1814)

BATTLE OF PLATTSBURGH
AND
VICTORY ON LAKE CHAMPLAIN

In which 14,000 *British myrmidons* were defeated and put to flight by 5,000 *Yankees and Green-mountain Boys,* on the memorable Eleventh of Sept. 1814.

Tune - "Battle of the Kegs"
Sir George Prevost with all his host
March'd forth from Montreal, Sir,
Both he and they as blithe and gay
As going to a ball, Sir.
The troops he chose were all of those

That conquer'd Marshal Soult, Sir,
Who at *Garonne* (the fact is known)
Scarce brought them to a halt, Sir.

With troops like these he tho't with ease
To crush the Yankee faction:
His only thought was how he ought
To bring them into action.
Your very names, Sir George exclaims,
Without a gun or bay'net,
Will pierce like darts thro' Yankee hearts,
and all their spirits stagnate.

Oh how I dread, lest they have fled
And left their puny Fort, Sir,
For sure Macomb won't stay at home,
To afford us any sport, Sir.
Goodbye, he said to those that stay'd.
Keep close as mice, or rats snug,
We just run out upon a scout,
To burn the town of Plattsburgh.

Then up the *Champlain* with might & main
He march'd with dread array, Sir,
With Fife and Drum to scare Macomb,
And drive him quite away, Sir.
And side by side their nations pride,
Along the current beat, Sir,
Sworn not to sup 'till they eat up
Macdonough and his fleet, Sir.

Still onward came there men of fame
Resolv'd to give "no quarter!"
But to their cost found out at last
That they had caught a tartar.
At distance shot awhile they fought
By water and by land, Sir,
His *Knightship* ran from man to man,
And gave his dread command, Sir.

"*Britons*, strike home, this dog *Macomb*,
So well the fellow knows us—
Will just as soon jump o'er the moon
As venture to oppose us:
With quick dispatch light ev'ry match,
Man ev'ry gun and swivel,
Cross in a crack the *Saranack*,
And drive 'em to the Devil!"

The *Vermont* ranks that lin'd the banks,
Then pois'd the unerring rifle,
And to oppose their haught foes,
They found a perfect trifle.
Meanwhile the fort kept up such sport,
They thought the devil was in it;
They mighty train play'd off in vain—
'Twas silenc'd in a minute.

Sir George amas'd, so widely gaz'd,
Such frantic gambols acted,
Of all his men not one in ten,
But thought him quite distracted.
He curs'd and swore, his hair he tore,
Then jump'd upon his poney,
And galop'd off towards the bluff,
To look for Captain Downie.

But when he spy'd M'Donough ride,
In all the pomp of glory,
He hasten'd back to Saranac,
To tell the dismal story:
"My gallant crews, oh shocking news!
Are all kill'd or taken!
Except a few that just withdrew
In time to save their bacon.

Old England's pride must now subside,
Oh! how the news will shock her,
To have her fleet not only beat,
But sent to Davy's locker!
From this sad day let no one say,
Britannia rules the ocean,
We've dearly bought the humbling tho't
That this is all a notion.

With one to ten, I'd flight 'gainst men,
But these are Satan's legions,
With malice fraught, come piping hot
From Pluto's darkest regions!
Helas, mon Dieu! What shall we do,
I smell the burning sulphur,
Set Britain's isle all rank and file—
Such men would soon engulph her.

That's full as bad, oh! I'll run mad,
Those western hounds are summon'd;

[?]aines, Scott & Brown are coming down,
To serve me just like Drummond.
Thick too as bees the Vermontese,
Are swarming on the lake, sir;
And Izard's men come back again,
Lie hid in every brake, sir!

Good Brisbane, beat a quick retreat,
Before their forces join, sir.
For sure as fate they've laid a bait,
To catch us like Burgoyne, sir.
All round about, keep good look out,
We'll surely be surrounded,
Since I could crawl my gallant soul
Was never so astounded."

The rout began, Sir George led on,
His men ran helter skelter,
Each try'd his best to out run the rest
To gain a place of shelter;
To hide their fear they gave a cheer,
And thought it mighty cunning—
He'll fight, say they, another day,
Who saves himself by running!

Source: "Battle of Plattsburgh and Victory on Lake Champlain," 1814, Broadside, Special Collections, Bailey/Howe Library, University of Vermont.

DOCUMENT 15

Josiah Dunham and *The Hartford convention in an uproar! and The wise men of the East confounded!* (1815)

(depicted on facing page)

Source: Hector Benevolus, pseud. *The Hartford convention in an uproar! and The wise men of the East confounded! . . .* (Windsor, Vt.: n.p., 1815). Reprinted courtesy of Special Collections, University of Vermont Libraries.

Document 15

SECTION FIVE

1820-1850
An Era of Social Ferment

VERMONT VOICES

SECTION FIVE

1820-1850
An Era of Social Ferment

Introduction

After the War of 1812, Vermont entered an era of economic and social transformation. Acreage available for new settlement in the state diminished, real estate prices increased, and the attraction of cheaper, more fertile land on the western frontier grew, putting an end to the steady population expansion of previous decades. Many Vermonters, especially those of the younger generation, confronted what Randolph Roth calls a "crisis of proprietorship": the choice between abandoning the state, or staying, and forgoing the possibilities for self-employment. At the same time, Vermonters were experiencing a resurgence in religious fervor that brought forward new sects, expanded church membership rolls, and sent waves of revivalism across the state. This period of economic and religious turmoil—this "climate of confusion and strain," as Kevin Graffagnino has characterized it—provided fertile ground for a vigorous social and political ferment that, in turn, gave life to a flood of reform movements in the state.

Anti-slavery dominated this era of reformism. Vermont's record of opposition to "the peculiar institution" began with the Constitution of 1777, which prohibited adult slavery. In 1819-1820, the debates in the U.S. Congress over Missouri's application for acceptance into the Union as a pro-slavery state provided the occasion for another strong Vermont statement. The organized anti-slavery movement still lay in the future, but, as **Document 1** shows, the Vermont legislature adopted a report and resolutions denouncing the practice of slavery as "a moral and political evil" and requesting Vermont's congressmen to stop Missouri and its pro-slavery constitution.

In the 1820s, more troubling than slavery to most Vermonters was their awareness that although the nation as a whole was experiencing a period of prosperity, their own state's share of national markets in manufacturing and commerce was shrinking. Leading figures of the day believed that the cause lay in the state's relative geographic isolation, and that canal construction could be the solution. The Erie Canal, which opened the Great Lakes region to Atlantic shipping, had begun construction in 1817, and the nearby Champlain-Hudson Canal had been completed in 1823, linking Lake Champlain at its southern end to the Hudson River, New York City, and the West. **Document 2** is a broadside issued as part of an effort during July and August of 1825 to gather support for a projected canal connecting Lake Champlain with the Connecticut River along the route of the Winooski River valley. Its planners anticipated that a waterway traversing the Green Mountains could resolve the transport problems of inland farmers and bring prosperity to the region. The results of this and other "canal fever" plans for the state, however, proved disappointing. Inadequate financial support, the rugged terrain, and harsh winter weather posed such formidable obstacles that no Vermont canal project moved beyond the preliminary survey stage.

The difficult times that followed the War of 1812 brought into existence in Vermont and several other states a vigorous but short-lived protest organization known as the Working Men's movement. Its Green Mountain supporters, primarily struggling and discontented artisans living mainly in marketing towns, identified the source of their troubles as the maneuvers and plottings of "nonlaborers"—lawyers, merchants, and financiers—who they believed had used their economic power and professional authority to appropriate the wealth that rightly belonged to the "laboring class." **Document 3** describes a meeting of "the laboring class of the citizens of Woodstock," on July 17, 1830. The Woodstock-based *Working-Man's Gazette*, the movement's newspaper, published this account in its inaugural issue and also included a recently adopted constitution of the Working Men's Society of Woodstock. Although the movement waned by the mid-thirties it contributed momentum for a number of the era's other reform efforts.

The most popular protest movement that emerged from Vermont's postwar economic and social turmoil was Anti-Masonry. During the early years of the new American republic, most citizens viewed secret societies with disdain. Freemasons, however, had managed to avoid the reproach because of the eminent names on their membership lists which, in the past, had included

George Washington and a large number of other re-vered Revolutionary-era statesmen. That relative im-munity from criticism faded after the unexplained dis-appearance in 1826, in western New York State, of a former Mason who had been planning to publish an exposé of the order's secrets. The disappearance aroused deep suspicion and drew accusations that the Masons were anti-democratic, elitist, immoral, and—because so many of their members were leading po-litical figures—a threat to public institutions. Large areas of New England rapidly succumbed to Anti-Ma-son sentiment.

In Vermont, Anti-Masonry drew support from a wide range of groups and individuals, including many who were also attracted to the Working Men's move-ment. It divided communities, disrupted church con-gregations, and forced many of the state's Masonic lodges to yield up their charters. The movement took political form as the Anti-Mason Party, which exploited the slackening of traditional party loyalties in the state to win the governorship four times (1831-1835) for William Palmer, of Danville, and to carry all seven of Vermont's electoral ballots in 1832 for the Anti-Ma-son presidential candidate, William Wirt, his only elec-toral success. In **Document 4**, Samuel Elliot, a Mason from Brattleboro, proposes two possible courses of action to resolve the Masons' difficulties. Elliot's ap-peal appeared anonymously in a Brattleboro newspa-per in July of 1833 and was widely reprinted by other newspapers in the state.

The class-conscious themes that were apparent in the Anti-Masonry and Working Men's movements emerged, in part, from a growing concern over land-use trends in Vermont and northern New England in the years after the War of 1812. The Champlain-Hudson and Erie canals had lowered market prices for grain, the staple crop of many Green Mountain farmers, caus-ing them to turn to the raising of sheep, whose wool was in demand by southern New England textile mills. Small woolen mills had also begun to proliferate in Vermont. In this transition, wealthy farmers expanded their pasturage by buying up the smaller farms of their hard-pressed neighbors, prompting concern that the "sheep craze" was encouraging a pattern of land mo-nopoly and altering agricultural patterns and social relationships in destructive ways. The author of **Docu-ment 5**, who signed his name "Green Mountaineer" in

an article published in the *State Journal*, October 6, 1834, warns about possible effects of this trend and offers advice to the state's beleaguered small farmers.

The religious enthusiasm of evangelical Protestant-ism infused much of the era's reform spirit. David Ludlum identifies it as the central element in the era's "social ferment." The Green Mountains and much of the northeastern United States reverberated in the 1820s, 1830s, and 1840s with competing evangelistic impulses that, in Vermont, included the messages of Congregationalists, Unitarians, Free Will Baptists, and Methodist circuit riders, as well as the more offbeat ideas of Mormons, millennialists, Millerites, and the Perfectionist followers of John Humphrey Noyes. Of the period's numerous itinerant evangelists, Jedediah Burchard was considered by contemporaries to be one of the greatest, although his controversial methods an-gered many of the state's denominational leaders. In the fall of 1834, Burchard, a New Yorker, brought his "protracted meetings," or multi-day revivals, to sev-eral Vermont communities, including Middlebury, Shoreham, Cornwall, Woodstock, Royalton, Spring-field, and Burlington; and he claimed dozens of con-versions at each of his stops. In **Document 6**, Russell Streeter, pastor of the Universalist Society of Woodstock, attempts to discredit Burchard as a "dis-ruptive fanatic" who uses theatrics to play upon the "weak" and "superstitious" and the young. The excerpts are from a lengthy denunciation published by Streeter following Burchard's twenty-six-day meeting in Woodstock in February of 1835.

Evangelical Protestants provided much of the zeal for Vermont's early anti-slavery activism. Although it was not until the mid-1840s that opposition to slavery acquired a significant organized following in the state, the movement gained momentum a decade earlier with the formation in 1834 of the Vermont Anti-Slavery So-ciety at a meeting in Middlebury. Membership in local chapters grew rapidly after that, influenced not only by religious fervor but by the agenda of the radical abolitionist and onetime Vermont newspaper editor William Lloyd Garrison. Defining slavery as a "fla-grant sin," the Society called for immediate and un-conditional emancipation that would be achieved through "moral suasion," and it made a special point of denouncing the large number of clergymen in the state who embraced the less resolute "gradualist" goals proposed by the Vermont Colonization Society. The "immediatist" advocacy of the Anti-Slavery Society caused its public meetings to be disrupted occasionally by violent mobs or unruly individuals who did not want the issue to be agitated at all. **Document 7** provides excerpts from the Society's *First Annual Report*, presented at a meeting in Middlebury in February of 1835.

Aspects of the social transformation underway in Vermont during these years are depicted in **Document 8**, Nathaniel Hawthorne's brief description of Burlington's busy Lake Champlain waterfront in the summer of 1835. Much of the account is taken up with his observations of Irish immigrants, who had begun appearing in Burlington and Vermont's other larger towns in the 1820s and 1830s, and who were the first sizable group of non-English immigrants to enter the Green Mountain State. For many Vermonters, this gradually emerging alien presence in their midst brought a new awareness of class that linked ethnicity with poverty, disease, alcoholism, and—because most were of Catholic background—with anti-Protestantism.

It was not until the onset of Vermont's railroad era, a few years later, however, that Irish immigrants actually began entering the state in large numbers, drawn by the prospect of jobs on the large railroad construction projects. The beginning of that era is visible in **Document 9**, a circular dated December 21, 1835, announcing a "convention" in Windsor to plan construction of a railway across Vermont. By the 1830s, enthusiasm for railroads had replaced "canal fever" as the hoped-for method of breaking the state's physical isolation and infusing new vigor into the economy. This document announces a citizens' meeting of the kind that typified many such efforts in behalf of various rail schemes during the decade. Wealthy entrepreneurs and promoters led the call for railroad construction, but ordinary Vermonters, aroused by mass public meetings, yielded to "railroad fever" as well, sending a steady flow of petitions to the state legislature. Raising capital proved difficult for the projects' sponsors, however, and laying steel rails across the state's rugged terrain presented another daunting challenge. Although the Vermont legislature granted charters to three railroads in 1835, it took another decade for the first construction to begin, and three additional years before locomotives finally began rolling on Vermont tracks.

Another outlet for the era's reform impulse was the Patriote uprising in Lower Canada in 1837-1838. French-speaking Canadians, calling themselves *patriotes*, led this armed rebellion intended to expand popular control in the British colony and loosen the royal governor's grip on power. In December 1837, after the British regular garrison crushed the uprising, many of the insurgents fled across the border into New York and Vermont. Sympathizers in several Vermont towns, especially border communities, eagerly adopted the Patriote cause, seeing parallels with the United States' own war of independence against Great Britain and holding mass meetings in support of the refugees' struggle. To the dismay of Canadian officials, many of these meetings adopted resolutions condemning the Canadian government's treatment of the Patriotes and calling for United States intervention in their behalf. Other Vermont citizens assisted the rebels' efforts to prepare a new offensive. **Document 10** provides three public statements on the Patriote issue. The first one is an open letter, dated December 12, 1837, by a group of distinguished Burlington citizens. The letter, excerpted here, calls on Governor Silas H. Jenison to instruct Vermonters on the need for caution and strict neutrality. The next statement is Jenison's proclamation, issued on December 13. The third statement is the record, excerpted, of a meeting of "the Young Men of Middlebury," on December 20, published in the *Burlington Sentinel*, in which the governor's call for caution is essentially ignored and the distinguished citizens' letter is subjected to ridicule. The documents together invite comparisons of the conflicting principles and interests that motivated Vermonters during the Lower Canada events. The controversy and the public clamor over the Patriote rebellion continued into 1838. By November, however, the last of the Patriotes' military forays had failed and the excitement of Vermont sympathizers faded.

The staunch concern for political rights demonstrated by Vermonters in regard to their Canadian neighbors was not in evidence when the legal and political rights at issue related to their own state's female citizens. In the 1820s and 1830s, Vermont women, as with women in other states, enjoyed few legal rights in such areas as property, child custody, or inheritance. They could not vote and did not often speak or act in public. One place where the constraints began to loosen, however, was the Vermont Anti-Slavery Society, which, unlike its own national organization, allowed women full membership. **Document 11** provides excerpts from an anonymous Vermont female abolitionist's denunciation of those who doubt that women have a role in the lofty cause of abolition; she calls on the "females of the North" to help put an end to slavery. In a note on the publication's title page, the author writes that her message "eminated from the pen *and heart of a woman*—one who feels deeply for the degradation and misery of one portion of her sisters, and laments the apathy of another."

With the slackening of Anti-Masonic sentiment after 1835, Vermont politics gradually settled into a pattern of less volatile party relationships. Most Anti-Mason followers moved into the new Whig Party, and a few joined the Jacksonians in the national Democratic Party. These two groups, at the state level, shared much in common. For the Whigs, however, who maintained a tenuous control over state politics from the mid-1830s until 1853, national tariff protection became the central issue. The tariff directly affected the wool market, and when the Whig ticket of William Henry Harrison and John Tyler won the presidency in 1840, Vermonters hoped that tariff gains for sheep growers and a lift out of the doldrums for the state's economy would soon follow. Instead, big cuts in the tariff rate in 1841 and 1842 contributed, along with increases in western competition, to a significant drop in wool prices. The intense Whig discomfort so delighted Burlington poet John Godfrey Saxe, an activist Democrat, that he composed a poem, **Document 12**, for use in the state's Democratic newspapers. Another drop in the tariff in 1846, coupled with a gradual increase in wool production in the West, caused sheep-raising to become no longer a paying enterprise for many Vermont farmers. The "sheep craze," after peaking in the period 1830-1845, gradually declined over the next twenty years, and the number of Vermont factories making woolen goods fell with it.

Anti-slavery activists, in large numbers, participated also in the temperance crusade. Advocates of this moral reform, who tended to blame alcohol for the general decline they perceived around them during the years after the War of 1812, formed the Vermont Society for the Promotion of Temperance in 1828, and thereafter local chapters quickly spread across the state.

"Temperance" was the goal, and "moral suasion" the preferred means of achieving it. During the next decade, however, many activists, including large numbers of Vermont women, came to embrace the goal of total prohibition, to be accomplished by legislation. In 1844 the Vermont legislature enacted a local option plan, prohibiting licensing of the sale of alcoholic beverages in towns that had not formally authorized a board of county commissioners as grantor of licenses. **Document 13**, an appeal "To the Freemen of Chittenden County," is a product of the successful campaign in that county to elect anti-license commissioners on polling day, January 2, 1845. Two years later, temperance forces pushed through legislation that barred any town from licensing liquor sales unless a majority of the state's towns approved licensing. The licensing issues remained at the center of temperance discussions until 1852, when Vermont legislators enacted a version of the famous Maine Law, which outlawed the sale and manufacture of alcoholic beverages outright.

Many temperance boosters believed that Irish immigrants provided especially good examples of the evil effects of alcohol on individual behavior. The Irish newcomers' ranks had grown rapidly after the mid-1840s, and railroad labor contractors, undeterred by temperance skeptics, eagerly recruited Irish men as day laborers because of their willingness to toil long hours under poor conditions for low wages. On the job, however, their railroad employers often did not pay them on time, or did not pay them at all. It was the latter—a failure to receive wages—that produced the infamous "Bolton War" of July 1846, the first significant labor strike in Vermont history. After not being paid for three months, Irish workers laying rails for the Central Vermont Railroad through Bolton Flats, between Waterbury and Burlington, refused to continue working and seized a labor foreman as a hostage, with the promise that he would be released in exchange for their pay. A Chittenden County sheriff responded by dispatching a militia company and an armed volunteer fire brigade to the scene from Burlington, "to maintain the supremacy of the law" and force the Irish men back to work. **Document 14** is an account of this incident, published in the *Burlington Free Press* on July 10, 1846. Written by the newspaper's editor, DeWitt Clinton Clarke, it presents an unexpectedly sympathetic treatment of the Irish workers' plight.

The large railroad construction projects that began in the 1840s triggered fundamental alterations in Vermont's man-made and natural landscape. The state's forest land—already decimated during the sheep boom, to make pastures—was one of the natural resources most affected. Railroads energized the timber industry by providing increased forest access, serving as efficient haulers of lumber and logs, and, through their steam locomotives, becoming enormous consumers of wood fuel until the move to coal in the early 1860s. Generally assumed by farmers to be an inexhaustible resource, forests nevertheless shrank rapidly. In **Document 15**, George P. Marsh, of Woodstock, provides an early warning of the dangers of abusing Vermont's water and forest resources, and makes the case for preservation of nature's delicate balance. The document is excerpted from a speech Marsh delivered on September 30, 1847, before the Agricultural Society of Rutland. Marsh was U.S. representative from Vermont's Third District at the time. His book, *Man and Nature; Or Physical Geography as Modified by Human Action* (1864), which expands on themes of his 1847 speech, became in later years a chief resource of the environmentalist movement in the United States.

Although Vermont acquired the reputation as the most anti-slavery state in the nation, it was not until the late 1840s that the movement could claim the support of overwhelming numbers of Green Mountain state residents, including the rank and file of both the Democratic and Whig parties. The two parties, however, also continued to endorse their national organizations' presidential tickets and platforms, which invariably embraced positions of compromise on the slavery issue. As a consequence, both suffered heavy losses in party cohesiveness during the decade, with many defectors shifting to the Free Soilers in search of a stronger anti-slavery commitment. The dilemma was especially vexing for Democrats, whose national leadership had presided over the "slaver's war" with Mexico (1846-1848) and opposed the Wilmot Proviso, a legislative amendment barring slavery in territories that might be acquired from Mexico. **Document 16**, an account of the Democratic convention at Montpelier in July 1848, provides a vivid picture of a fragmenting party unable to reconcile the volatile politics of anti-slavery with competing desires to maintain patronage links with its southern-dominated national organization. The factional participants in this internecine struggle borrowed nicknames that derived from a similar party split in New York: Vermont's "Barnburners" represented the party's progressive wing, who opposed the extension of slavery; its "old Hunkers," or conservative wing, opposed anti-slavery agitation. Disaffected Barnburner Democrats who walked out of this July meeting in Montpelier met in Middlebury a few days later, where they played a central role in organizing the state Free Soil convention.

At mid-century, Vermonters found themselves being buffeted by changes, many of which were not only unwelcome but seemed beyond their capacity to control. The population exodus to the western frontier and to industrial southern New England caused the state's population growth to be the lowest in the nation during the 1840s; profits from sheep farming continued to plummet; manufacturing remained flat; and churches, confronted by a waning of revivalist zeal and weakened by continuing emigration, faced shrinking membership rolls and community influence; most of the diverse reform impulses of the era became subsumed in the growing fervor of anti-slavery. Vermonters were heading into a time of uncertainty. How might these factors have influenced the creation of the concluding document in this section, **Document 17**, a town ordinance enacted by Burlington selectmen in 1849? The ordinance attempts to restrict the entrance from Lake Champlain, through the port of Burlington, of "foreign immigrants, subjects of Great Britain." Confronted with evidence of a possible cholera epidemic, the town fathers, in a particularly mean-spirited act, singled out Irish Catholic immigrants as the source of their difficulties and concluded that the best solution was to keep them out.

DOCUMENT 1

Resolutions on the Missouri Question (1820)

STATE OF VERMONT
In General Assembly, Nov. 15, 1820

The Committee, to whom was referred so much of his excellency's speech, as relates to the admission of the Territory of Missouri into the Union, as a State, submit the following REPORT. The history of nations demonstrates, that involuntary servitude not only plunges the slave into the depths of misery, but renders a great proportion of community dependant and wretched, and the remainder tyranic and indolent. Opulence, acquired by the slavery of others, degenerates its possessors, and destroys the physical powers of government. Principles so degrading, are inconsistent with the primitive dignity of man, and his natural rights.

Slavery is incompatible with the vital principles of all free governments, and tends to their ruin. It paralyzes industry, the greatest source of national wealth, stifles the love of freedom, and endangers the safety of the nation. It is prohibited by the laws of nature; which are equally binding on governments and individuals. The right to introduce and establish slavery, in a free government, does not exist.

The declaration of Independence, declares, as *self-evident truths*, "That all men are created equal—that they are endowed by their Creator with certain unalienable rights; that among these are life, liberty, and the pursuit of happiness. That to secure these rights, governments are instituted among men, deriving their just powers from the governed: That whenever any form of government becomes destructive of these ends, it is the right of the people to alter or abolish it."

The Constitution of the United States, and of the several States, have recognized these principles as the basis of their governments: and have expressly inhibited the introduction or extension of slavery, or impliedly disavowed the right.

The power of congress to require the prohibition of slavery in the constitution of a state, to be admitted as one of the United States, is confirmed by the admission of new states according to the ordinance of 1787—and by a constitutional "guarantee to every state in the Union of a *republican form of government*." This power in Congress is also admitted in the act of March 6, 1820, which declares, that in all that territory ceded, under the name of Louisiana, which lies north of 36 deg. 30 min. north latitude, "slavery and involuntary servitude shall be forever prohibited."

Where slavery existed in the states, at the time of the adoption of the constitution of the United States, a spirit of compromise, or painful necessity, may have excused its continuance; but can never justify its introduction into a State to be admitted from the territories of the United States. . . .

It is apparent that servitude produces in the slaveholding states, peculiar feelings, local attachments, and separate interests:—and should it be extended into new states, "it will have a tendency to form a combination of power, which will control the measures of the general government;" and which cannot be resisted, except by the physical force of the nation. . . .

From information, it is to be seriously apprehended that Missouri will present to congress, for their approbation, a constitution which declares—that "the General Assembly shall have *no power* to pass laws—First, for the emancipation of slaves, without the consent of their owners, or without paying them, before emancipation, a full equivalent for such slaves, so emancipated"—and, "secondly" to prevent emigrants from bringing slaves into said state, so long as slavery is legalized therein. It is also made the imperious duty of its legislature, to pass laws, as soon as may be "To prevent free negroes and mulattoes from coming to, and settling in that state, under any pretence whatever."

These powers, restrictions, and provisions, to legalize and perpetuate slavery, and to prevent citizens of the United States, on account of their origin, color or features, from emigrating to Missouri, are repugnant to a republican government, and in direct violation of the constitution of the United States.

If Missouri be permitted to introduce and legalize slavery by her constitution, and we consent to her admission, we shall justly incur the charge of insincerity in our civil institutions, and in all our professions of attachment to liberty. It will bring upon the constitution and declaration of independence, a deep stain which cannot be forgotten, or blotted out! "It will deeply affect the union in its resources, political interests, and character."

The admission of another new state into the union, with a constitution which guarantees security and protection to slavery, and the cruel and unnatural traffic of any portion of the human race, will be an error which the union cannot correct, and an evil which may endanger the freedom of the nation. . . .

The committee therefore submit, for the consideration of the General Assembly, the following resolutions, viz.

Resolved, That, in the opinion of this legislature, slavery, or involuntary servitude, in any of the United States, is a moral and political evil; and that its continuance can be justified by necessity alone.

That congress has a right to inhibit any further introduction, or extension of slavery, as one of the conditions upon which any new state shall be admitted into the union.

Resolved, That this legislature views with regret and alarm, the attempt of the inhabitants of Missouri, to obtain admission into the union as one of the United States, under a constitution which legalizes and secures the introduction and continuance of slavery—and also contains provisions to prevent freemen of the United States from emigrating to, and settling in Missouri, on account of their origin, color and features. And that, in the opinion of this legislature, these principles, powers and restrictions, contained in the reputed constitution of Missouri, are anti-republican, and repugnant to the constitution of the United States, and subversive of the unalienable rights of man.

Resolved, That the senators from this state in the congress of the United States, be instructed, and the representatives requested, to exert their influence and use all legal measures to prevent the admission of Missouri, as a State, into the union of the United States, with those anti-republican features, and powers in their constitution. . . .

Source: *Acts Passed by the Legislature of the State of Vermont, At Their October Session, 1820* (Middlebury, Vt.: Copeland and Allen), pp. 48-52.

DOCUMENT 2

Subscription Appeal for the Proposed Connecticut River and Champlain Canal (1825)

TO the Inhabitants of the several towns in Washington, Chittenden, Orange, Windsor and Caledonia Counties, and all other persons interested.

AGREEABLY to previous notice, delegates from several of the towns in Calendonia, Orange, Washington and Chittenden Counties, assembled at the State-House in Montpelier on the 30th June last, for the purpose of "adopting suitable measures to explore and survey a route or routes, for a Canal connecting the waters of Lake Champlain with the Connecticut River, through the valley of Onion River"—at which meeting the following Resolutions were unanimously adopted, viz: —

1. *Resolved,* That the connexion of the waters of Lake Champlain with Connecticut river, by means of a navigable Canal through the valley of Onion river, is an object of great public importance, and that prompt and efficient measures ought to be taken, to secure the vast and permanent benefits, which would necessarily result from a water communication thus formed through the centre of the State, and through a fertile, populous, and wealthy section of country.

2. *Resolved,* That his Excellency the Governor be requested to apply to the Secretary of the War Department of the United States, for instructions to De Witt Clinton, Jr. Esq. the Engineer acting under the direction of that department in this State, or to some other United States' Engineer, to explore and survey, before the next session of Congress, a route for a Canal from Lake Champlain to Connecticut river, through the valley of Onion river—and that three Commissioners be appointed on the part of this Convention, whose duty it shall be to make known to the Governor the object of this resolution; and to act in conjunction with such Engineer as may be appointed under the same, and render him all necessary assistance therein.

3. *Resolved,* That it shall also be the duty of said Commissioners, immediately to explore the several routes

contemplated, and to take the most effectual measures to procure a survey of the same as soon as practicable. . . .

4. *Resolved*, That a committee of five be appointed to prepare subscription papers, and to appoint such persons, as sub-committees, as they deem proper, to obtain subscriptions in such towns as feel interested in the proposed object; and to take all other suitable and efficient measures to procure subscriptions to defray the expenses of said survey. . . .

The Convention then appointed Araunah Waterman, Esq. of Montpelier, John L. Woods, Esq. of Newbury, and John Downer, Esq. of Hartford, Commissioners.

The Committee appointed under the 4th resolution were, Messrs. SAMUEL PRENTISS, TIMOTHY MERRILL, JEDUTHUN LOOMIS, JOSHUA Y. VAIL, and JOSEPH HOWES.

The Committee in obedience to said resolution, earnestly request the attention of their fellow citizens to be subject of the above resolutions. It will be seen that the present object is solely to raise, by subscription, a sum of money, sufficient to procure the necessary surveys, so that further measures may be taken early in the fall. The sum required for this purpose is estimated at from **300** to **500** Dollars.

In an undertaking so vast, as that of constructing a Canal, and which requires so great pecuniary resources, the committee are fully aware of the obstacles which must be encountered; They are sensible, also, that prejudices and sentiments exist in the minds of a few respectable and intelligent citizens, adverse to an enterprize of this kind—and by some of these it may be considered visionary and impracticable—But they fully believe, that a nearer and more attentive view of the subject, will lessen these obstacles, and overcome and dissipate these prejudices and feelings, which are founded upon mistaken views, or have been produced by a very cursory examination of the subject.

The exertions which are now making in Massachusetts and New-Hampshire, leave little room to doubt, that the waters of the Connecticut and Atlantic, will, at no distant period, mingle together at Boston or Portsmouth—and whenever this takes place, Vermont will present the only obstruction to a water communication, through the western lakes, from Boston to New-Orleans. This consideration, alone, it would seem, would be decisive of the question respecting the utility of such a work. The advantages which would result from it to the United States, are very great; but to Vermont, and this section, particularly, they are incalculable. But with respect to the importance of the work, with a very few exceptions, there is but one opinion.

As the *practicability* and *means* of accomplishing it, it is not surprising that there has existed some difference of opinion.

The committee consider that the question, whether a Canal be practicable, has been settled in the affirmative beyond doubt, by the examination, and partial survey of a former committee, whose report has been recently published.

"Our mountains," to use the language of one of the ablest engineers in our country, "so far from being barriers," to the work, as many have supposed, "are rather to be considered the great laboratories of that element which is necessary to its execution,"—and there can be no doubt that the face and natural productions of our country offer facilities, equal, if not superior, to many places where canals have been made, or are now in rapid execution.

If, then, the practicability and utility of the work be thus apparent, may we not with propriety ask, Have we not remained long enough, inactive? Can any one contemplate the permanent and progressive benefits it would produce,—upon the increase of population,—of agricultural products,—of industry in general,—upon the development of those resources and means of profit, which a bountiful Providence has placed within our reach—and feel no desire for its accomplishment?

To the question, Where shall we obtain the means? we answer, The national government is awake to the subject of internal improvements, and will probably listen to our application for aid;—if not, it should be recollected that there is in our country, a vast capital unemployed, which we confidently believe may be called to our assistance, when the actual surveys and estimates shall have been completed—But above all, we would rely, upon that spirit of enterprize, which has distinguished the citizens of Vermont, and which has always been found adequate to the execution of any undertaking, dictated by public utility. To this spirit we address ourselves—and feel a confidence that our appeal will not be unavailing; but will be met by a zeal and liberality corresponding to the great subject in which we are engaged.

Montpelier, July 4, 1825.

Source: "Connecticut River and Champlain Canal," 1825, Broadside, Special Collections, Bailey/Howe Library, University of Vermont.

DOCUMENT 3

"Meeting of the Laboring Class of the Citizens of Woodstock" (1830)

WORKING-MAN'S GAZETTE

At a meeting of the working class held by adjournment at the Court-house, on the 17th of July last, Deac. Elias Thomas was chosen Moderator.

Voted, to hear the report of the committee chosen at the last meeting, which report was read as follows:

Report

The committee chosen at the last meeting of the laboring class of the citizens of Woodstock, to consider of existing grievances, have attended to that duty, and beg leave to report: —

That there is an inequality between the condition of the laborers and non-laborers amongst us, is too plain to be disputed. Industry does not receive its proportionate reward; for while those of the former class are becoming poorer, the latter are growing rich on the toils of those who labor. The experience of every day will convince us of these truths. But these evils are not confined to this place, or to this State. In every quarter of the Union have complaints arisen that the poorer class are becoming enslaved. These evils can no longer be endured—further forbearance would be a crime to American freemen. The standard of Independence is reared, and already we hear that the laboring class are asserting their rights in all parts of the land. In Pennsylvania, in New-York, in Massachusetts, and other places, the flame is spreading, and in all probability, will soon pervade the whole Union. The laborers, or those who produce the wealth of the country, will no longer be controlled by the drones or those who consume that wealth; and in the cause of liberty, Vermont will not be idle.

Your Committee are of opinion that the best and most effectual method of diminishing the number of the non-laborers, is to take away the means by which they live. If their number can be reduced, some benefit to community must ensue. As one means of effecting the great object, your Committee would urge the necessity of making a united exertion to do away the present universal system of credit, especially on small sums. This extensive practice of credit is ruinous. It has been computed that goods are sold in this village to the amount of seventy-five thousand dollars annually. Is not this great sum larger than real necessity demands? Would not ready pay diminish one fourth of this great sum? And when we consider that in consequence of the baleful system of credit, a large proportion of this great amount is collected by means of writs and executions, with cost so heaped upon cost, that it will frequently amount to more than the original debt, the reflecting mind becomes paralyzed with astonishment at the vast sums lost to community in consequence of this evil. By being indulged with credit, the purchaser buys more than is necessary, and pays much more for his goods than they are worth.—It is incumbent then on the laboring class to apply a remedy for this evil. Individual exertion will compass nothing—but united exertion will effect every thing.

But not only are we opposed in a pecuniary point of view but our rights as freemen are infringed. We have been fast verging towards an aristocracy. One class amongst us seem to think they have an exclusive claim to offices of trust and profit, and an exclusive claim to make and administer laws. It cannot be denied that lawyers have an undue share of public offices. We wish to proscribe no man, nor any class of men, from public office—we will allow to lawyers their proportional share, but no more. By allowing them to monopolize office, and by submitting to their extravagant fees we submit to an aristocracy in *fact*, if it is not so in name. It also tends to their rapid and unnecessary increase amongst us. Young men whether with talents or without, on choosing an occupation to follow through life, finding on the one hand, the choice of any mechanic art will lead to obscurity, contempt and poverty;—while on the other hand, the choice of a profession will consequently lead to fame, preferment and wealth, will naturally, and with good reason choose the latter. And if all our youths choose professions, what will then produce the wealth?

That we have reason to complain of this increase may be inferred from the fact, that when any particular class of laborers become too numerous, there will be a consequent reduction in the price of their labor, and in the articles of their manufacture. But the reverse of this is the case with professional men. Experience teaches us, that the more numerous they become, the higher will be their charges, as they *must* live. By allowing them therefore to monopolize all public employments, we help to forge the chains by which we are enslaved. . . .

Your committee would beg leave to point out some laws which are impolitic in their tendency[,] unjust in their operation, and apparently intended to enrich one class at the expense of the other—The most apparent of these is the law allowing imprisonment for debt. Here is a law which directly defeats its ostensible object. No man can earn money when shut up in prison. But on this subject, public opinion is setting so strongly against it, that it is not necessary to enlarge. And when we consider that every successive Gov. of this state and almost every Governor in New-England have for years denounced it in their annual messages, and urged that this relic of barbarism should be blotted from our statute books, while no solitary voice is raised in its defence—nay while even its constitutionality is doubted, and no one is able to place his finger on that page of our constitution which sanctions this monstrous injustice—it may be thought unaccountable that it should be retained. But there are some who are interested in its continuance, there is a secret influence among us, which works behind the curtain, and controls our reason and interest. Your committee would recommend instructions to our representative, and a petition to the Legislature for the repeal of the law allowing imprisonment for debt, unconnected and unshackled with any other subject whatever. The constitution declares that *all men shall be protected in the enjoyment of life, LIBERTY, and property*—let us not therefore, beg the repeal of this obnoxious law as a boon, but *demand it as a right.*

Your committee would further recommend as a means of redoing this legal tax on community, such an alternation in the laws as would make one attachment on property answer for all creditors who would file their claims and obtain judgment for the same, previous to the sale of the property so attached, thereby making an equal division according to the amount, without regard to priority of attachment. This would prevent the cost on half the suits which are now issued and would be more just in its operations. . . .

We are willing that property should always be held answerable for debts—but wish that done with the least possible loss. The only objection to the system now proposed is, that it will reduce the lawyer's and sheriff's business and consequently injure them. But what of that? Who ever refused his exertions to stop the conflagration of a building, from the consideration that the carpenter would be benefitted from its destruction? Who ever thought of neglecting the use of all means to stop the ravages of the yellow fever, or any alarming epidemic, from the consideration that physicians would lose employment?

Your committee believe that there are some other laws, which bear harder upon one class than the other, and to which they would wish to call your attention. Such are the laws incorporating banks and other companies where the private property of the stockholders is not holden for its debts. Of the injustice of this law, we have had an example in our very neighborhood. Further the law holds the mechanic answerable for all mistakes in his business, and that he must make good to his customers all losses which may ensue through his negligence or ignorance. How is it with the lawyer? Is he under similar responsibility? We think not. It does happen that after actions have progressed some length, and cost has accumulated to a great amount, there will be discovered a flaw in the writ, or some other technical informality, which will be judged sufficient to quash the whole proceeding.—Does the lawyer pay the cost in this case? By no means—his unfortunate client must foot the bill.

Furthermore, there is an inequality either in the laws or in the administration of the laws respecting nonattachable property. With commendable liberality the law says that a mechanic shall have tools sufficient to carry on his business. But a farmer's plough and cart, are said not be be exempted, although absolutely necessary. In spite of the law allowing a mechanic his tools, we have seen them taken from him, and decided that his tools were not tools, on the ground that he was an artist, or some other pretext equally frivolous. However such things may be sanctioned by law, or rather by the construction of the law, they are directly opposed to common sense, and ought to be put down.

In order to bring the two classes more on a level, your committee would recommend a reduction of lawyers' and sheriff's fees, as well as the charges of professional men generally. There is no reason or justice that a lawyer or a doctor should be allowed to charge and collect for a few hour's services more than the laboring man can make in as many weeks. . . .

The committee would wish not to be misunderstood. They would not make an indiscriminate attack upon professional men, or to divest them of their rights. It is only when they are too numerous that we complain of them. There are amongst us, lawyers of exalted talents, and honorable feelings—and instead of decrying them, we would bear testimony to their worth.

In conclusion, the committee would observe they are aware of the opposition to be encountered in taking this stand in defence of our rights. Already is misrepresentation busy in distorting our motives. We are charged with being office-seekers—but those making the charge do not come with such clean hands as might be expected. We are charged with being Deists and Infidels. On one hand it is alleged we are under Masonic influence—on the other hand it is said as confidently we are all Anti-Masons. We are charged with being Agrarians and Levellers, and that we intend to use the guillotine. Of such charges let our consciences acquit us, and let our conduct to the world give the lie to such base and unfounded calumnies. Let us go forward with a steady pace in defence of our rights,—paying no attention to the different parties or sects in our way remembering that "united we stand or divided we fall." Let us not desist till the laborer is restored to his just and proper influence in society, and man is, as of right he ought to be, free, equal, and independent.

In view of this, the committee propose the adoption of the following resolutions:

Resolved, That imprisonment for debt is a relic of barbarism, opposed to the spirit of the Constitution, which declares that "all men shall be protected in the enjoyment of life, *liberty*, and property," and ought to be abolished.

Resolved, That such an alteration should be made in the laws of attachment that one writ will hold good for all creditors.

Resolved, That no company or banking institution should be incorporated, unless the stockholders' private property is holden for its debts.

Resolved, That we consider that professional men, particularly lawyers, hold more than a due share of public office.

Resolved, That we will hereafter use all honorable exertions to contest public opinion on this subject, and to inculcate the doctrine that claims for office shall be founded only on merit.

Resolved, That in our dealings with professional men, we will use our endeavors to reduce their fees to a fair level with the wages of a laboring man.

Voted to accept said report and resolutions accompanying it.

Source: *Working-Man's Gazette* (Woodstock, Vt.), 23 September 1830.

DOCUMENT 4

"To the Masonic Brethren of Vermont and the Union" (1833)
SAMUEL ELLIOT

Through the medium of the public papers, I submit to your notice and consideration, some hints and propositions, having in view the *reform* or *abandonment of our institution*, with some reasons which I think ought to induce your undivided co-operation.

We all know that in consequence of the barbarous conduct of some of our *nominal* brethren in the state of New York, and the exposure of certain obligations and phraseology, said to be used by the Fraternity in their initiations and other ceremonies, and even from the well known SECRECY attached to the Order, that a deep & abiding distrust and prejudice hangs over our Institution, in the public feeling, which renders it not only unpopular, but nearly useless. And the extent or duration of this suspicion and public odium, is beyond human calculation. It *may* become general and overwhelming; or it *may* die away like other excitements, in our day and generation.

Upon the most serious and mature reflection upon this state of things I enter upon this business, having long been convinced, even before the existence of this excitement, that some revision and improvement ought to be adopted by the brethren in America, to meet the taste and feelings of the age and country, and to do away much of the ponderous matter of ceremony and labor in the Lodge; and to confine the institution more simply and strictly to its leading principles—*extending and cultivating honorable friendship—comforting and relieving the needy and unfortunate, more especially brethren—advancing the cause of liberal sentiment and mental improvement—handing down to posterity memorials of the age we live in, by the formal dedication of public edifices with suitable deposits of various coins, and brief memoranda of the names of the architects, distinguished characters and prominent events of the Epoch, in the well known* CORNER STONE—*and observing appropriate funeral ceremonies, and the ancient mode of conducting lodges with significant tools and implements—and all this in the spirit of love and unity, without interfering in the party or controversial affairs of men.*

It is from such considerations and motives, that I present this project to the masonic brotherhood of Vermont and the World, wishing that some state, and hoping that Vermont will have the disposition and independence to lead in this highly necessary and pacific enterprise. And I hereby earnestly request that you would bring the subject before the Grand Lodge in October next, where I would cheerfully advocate the measure, and more fully, and I trust satisfactorily, explain the practicability and utility of the plan, if I may be permitted, and should be able to attend. My project, in short, is, to move directly and boldly to the work, of either abandoning the Institution altogether, or stripping it of every suspicious feature and needless ceremony. I know their general principles are good, but I want it to be, like Caesar's wife, above suspicion. It ought, (if continued) to be divested of SECRECY, and its obligations reduced to a simple honorary pledge to support the principles of the Order, and these ought to be definitely explained. One general pledge might suffice for all the degrees, and these degrees or steps condensed or simplified; and above all, *every word and ceremony which can bear a construction in the least reprehensible or disgusting to the purest taste or sternest virtue, should be discarded as unworthy the Institution.*

In the present state of Freemasonry, how few will undergo the toil and vexation of lumbering their heads with an ordinary knowledge of its forms and labour?

We simplify every thing else, why not this? Why overload a good thing with such a mass of machinery and suspicion? Will it be said that *Secrecy*, and this complication of ancient and *foreign* ceremonies, are necessary to preserve it? If it cannot exist without such appendages, *let it cease*. But the experiment has not been tested, and there is no reason in the objection.

My Countrymen! This is no trifling movement in the present state of things, whatever you may think of it; and it is due to . . . the feelings and taste of the people and the times; and I hope it will soon be adopted . . . to the general satisfaction of our citizens. Be assured, that nothing will prevent it, but a false dread of touching a subject of such long and high standing, as the Masonic Institution. Let our *Green Mountain Boys* dare any thing for the welfare and improvement of mankind. . . I hope that measures will immediately be adopted by an application of the State Lodges to the General Royal Arch Lodge of the United States, or by an arrangement among the State Lodges, for the appointment of an able and independent Committee, or calling a Convention, say one from each State, to mature all necessary measures, either for abolishing the Institutions, or for adapting it to the taste and feelings of the enlightened age and country we live in.

Let not Masons or Antimasons hastily condemn this measure, before they have seriously examined it in all its bearings. Hasty conclusions are often the subjects of regret and repentance.

The Institution once freed from Secrecy, would be freed of suspicion and odium, and of at least half its tedious ceremonies; and would again share the public favor. The whole regulations and ceremonies might be essentially reduced, and easily understood and retained, and more time would be spared for interesting business & moral improvement. Members might invite their friends into the meetings, as in other societies. Less time ought to be spent in the business; two or four meetings a year would be sufficient, & those should be made interesting, and promotive of some active, practical good. For one, I am confident this can, and ought to be done, for our good, and to undeceive a prejudiced world as to the general principles and conduct of masons. I am not disposed, for my few remaining days, to be under the ban of public suspicion, nor do I wish my children and friends thus to be placed. Nor am I disposed to yield up my rights and privileges, at the bidding of any popular call, through fear or pusillanimity. I had rather meet a contest as long as the *Punic Wars of Rome*. But we can, as the Tariff advocates have done in Congress, generously adopt a measure of our own, with a due regard to the feelings of our opponents and the World, that shall restore good feeling, and result in our own permanent good, and our Country's peace and glory.

This business, if my life and health is spared, I am determined shall undergo public examination, and receive the public verdict, either for or against it. I therefore request the printer at *Brattleboro'* to publish this communication, and I hope it will be published by the printers generally, in the full belief that it will meet the sincere approbation of most of our countrymen, draw public attention to the subject, and eventuate in the most salutary results.

Brattleboro', Vt. July 17, 1833.

A ROYAL ARCH MASON

Source: Samuel Elliot, *A Voice from the Green Mountains, on the Subject of Masonry & Antimasonry* (Brattleboro, Vt.: George W. Nichols, 1834), pp. 4-6.

DOCUMENT 5

"To the Farmers of Vermont" (1834)
GREEN MOUNTAINEER

A just appreciation of the advantages which fall to our lot, is the dictate of wisdom. It is especially connected with contentment and gratitude. Every portion of the habitable earth possesses advantages and disadvantages, in some degree peculiar to itself. The principal things which affect the comfort of life, so far as natural advantages are concerned, are climate, soil, water and facilities of commerce. It is believed that, in regard to these, Vermont possesses advantages sufficient to render it a highly desirable place of abode. Its soil is not indeed the most fertile, but sufficiently so to reward the laborer with an abundant supply of the supports of life. Its facilities of commerce are less than those of almost any other State in the Union; yet every article which can be spared finds a cheap conveyance to market, while its climate is highly salubrious, and its water the best in the world. Our winters are cold, and long; but our forests supply an abundance of fuel, and the

snow renders travelling delightful, and the transportation of heavy articles easy and cheap. With these advantages, and blessed with the means of scientific and religious knowledge, nothing need prevent the farmers of Vermont from being as intelligent, respectable, virtuous and happy, as any body of people on the globe.

One of the excellent features of society in New-England, and pre-eminently in Vermont, is the general distribution of property, and especially of real estate. Almost every individual is lord of the soil on which he lives, and is able, by a course of persevering industry, to provide well for himself and his dependents. But there is a tendency to a different state of things. Many of the most wealthy portion of the community are engaging in manufacturing business, which requires a large number of hired laborers. Others are increasing their real estate by buying the small farms of their neighbors. By these processes, the number of land owners is diminishing, and the number of dependent tenants and hired laborers is increasing. It is easy to see that, in this way, will be produced a wealthy aristocracy, and a poor, dependent peasantry. The tendency of this is increased by the "spirit of emigration." Let the farmers of Vermont beware. Who that possesses a benevolent spirit is willing that the charming state of society which has existed here for fifty years, where every man is a free, independent landlord, thinks himself, while pursuing a virtuous cause, as good as his neighbor, and asks none but his Maker leave to live and thrive, should be exchanged for a community composed of purse-proud landlords and servile tenants?

Sons of the Green Mountains! Maintain your independence. We can spare a portion of our young men, every year, to settle in the wilds of the West, and aid in establishing, in those fertile regions, the institutions and habits of New England; but we cannot, without deadly injury to ourselves, spare our enterprising and industrious farmers, to sell their snug farms to their wealthier neighbors for sheep pastures, and go off to Michigan or Illinois. The good of society and of posterity requires that we keep the land divided, as at present, into small farms. It were better that the largest should be divided between three or four sons, than that the smallest should be purchased up by rich speculators, to be cultivated by tenants or hired laborers. By the influx of foreigners, and the overflowing tide of emigration, the good lands of the West will in a few years be settled, or in the hands of speculators, to be sold at a price above the reach of industrious young men who are without capital. If the lands of New England get into the hands of the wealthy few, when the West shall cease to invite emigration, what will then be the condition and prospects of the swarms that will be annually furnished by the New England hive? I say, then, to my brethren of the Green Mountains, Hold on to your farms! Instead of selling them because they are small, or less fertile than others, endeavor to acquire greater skill in the management of them; and render them, as you may do, doubly productive, by a higher state of cultivation. Few of you, probably, are fully aware how small a portion of land, skillfully cultivated, will support a family. Study the *New England Farmer*. Every farmer in New England can afford to take that paper. By the aid of its light on the various branches of agriculture, he may increase the yearly income of his farm more than ten times the cost of that interesting periodical.

Beware of the "western lever," and above all, *sell not your farms to your rich neighbors for sheep pastures.*

Green Mountaineer

Source: *Vermont Chronicle*, 17 October 1834.

DOCUMENT 6

Mirror of Calvinistic Fanaticism, or Jedediah Burchard & Co. During a Protracted Meeting of Twenty-Six Days in Woodstock, Vermont (1835)

RUSSELL STREETER

. . . Anxious Seats

Preparatory to getting the people into what are called *anxious seats*, in the meeting-house, Mr. B. entraps them in the following manner. He asks "*every man, woman and child*," to rise, "who believe that there is a God, that they may be prayed for." The audience, generally, rise immediately. But instead of praying the manager compliments them and, says, "take your seats, if you please." They do it. He then makes some curious remarks, and invites "every man, woman and child" "to rise up at once, who desires salvation through Jesus Christ," and flatteringly adds "you *all wish* to be saved. Rise up, *rise up*." As before, those who do not understand the plot, rise; and though a considerable number keep their seats, Mr. B. says, "all have risen; take your seats—sit down." Down they go again. He then manoeuvres in the same way again, and calls upon "every man, woman and child who is willing, or has no objections, to be prayed for," to rise. Of course, the unsuspecting, "up again;" and again they are seated.— Mr. B. then artfully says, that all who rose, who are not converted, *pledged* themselves to come forward, after the usual exercises are over, and be prayed for. This is the first suspicion that most of them have, that he had been throwing a "net" around them. The meeting goes on by prayer and singing, and the sermon, &c. as usual; but at last the preacher calls upon those who have no objections to be prayed for, to come into the front seats, which are cleared for that purpose. Then every convert from abroad, old and young, begins to urge others to come forward. Mr. B. tells the congregation that there is nothing in those vacant pews different from any others in the house; but that it is more convenient to have all the anxious together. He appeals to the common sense of his audience, whether it can hurt them to take a different seat? Then goes on the work of persuasion, and to set the wheels in motion, young converts take as many with them as possible, and march to the front pews. Every minister, and deacon, and zealot, after the first exhibition, flies about the house, urging, pulling, and hauling people forward. The lads and others are invited from the gallery to come right down, and corporals are stationed in suitable places, to hurry them onward. Without reflection they come rushing down, by scores; tittering and skipping along, as though on the road to muster. Mr. B. orders the people in the aisles to make way for those lads and young men and women. If more room is needed, he says, "get out of the way, old christians, and let these young sinners have a chance to be saved. Don't stand about here, you old gray-headed professors, *go out doors and stand in the snow*; it won't hurt you. Don't block up the way so that these unconverted sinners can't get to heaven.—Go out into the snow, I tell you." And if need be, "the pope" is obeyed. Such a rushing, scrambling, and hauling as takes place, cannot be conceived.

Mr. Burchard comes out of the desk, with the light tread of a cat, and the cunning of a fox; races about the house, through the aisles, over the pews, and on the *tops* of the pews, crying, "come every man, woman, and child, and be prayed for; come forward, come right forward, young friends, don't be afraid,—there, do step aside, brother, and let that daughter go out—lead her up,—come, come, there yet is room—the door of salvation is open—sing, sing there—'Come holy Spirit heavenly Dove,'—Sir,—do go forward, it won't hurt you at all. What are you doing here, brethren, why don't you exert yourselves,—the Holy Ghost is in our midst—God knows it,—O poor sinners, do escape from hell, now the spirit is moving."

Now, reader, all this, and a world more of the same sort, is uttered by Mr. B. as fast and earnest as ever an auctioneer spoke when in the midst of sharpbidding; and with a variation of tones, nearly equal to a ventriloquist.

Having coaxed, and frightened, and dragged his company into the forward pews, he would have some intervening exercises, some dolorous ode or something else, to give himself time to breathe, and eat "rock candy," (or as *some say*, a preparation of *opium*,) and then after others had prayed, drop upon his knees before them in the broad aisle, and scream just as loud as he could for his life—leaning at least half way back to his heels— telling God what the scriptures say about agonizing and groaning in prayer, and in what book and chapter he could find it!—This exercise was called *praying*; but if it were so, it must have been in conformity to the directions of Elijah, for there is no other scripture, so much to the point. "Cry aloud; either he is talking, or he is pursuing, or he on a journey, or peradventure he sleepeth, and must be awaked." (1 Kings xviii. 27.)—Never did I hear a crazy New-Light blunder together such a blustering, disconnected compound of words and phrases; for they could not be called sentences. . . .

Conclusion

I have a few words to add, to put the public upon their guard against the plots and impositions of J. Burchard and Co. A better service I could not render my friends, brethren and the cause of religion in general.

(1.) Let not an intelligent community be deceived by the rumors of Mr. B's success, in this place, as well as others. For, considering the duration of the meeting, the efforts that were put forth, and the circumstances of the case, it was "a mountain in labor." There are, in this town and those adjoining, *ten thousand* souls. The weather and sleighing were excellent, during the whole 26 or 27 days, and people came from various directions, in the circumference of more than an hundred miles in diameter.—Whole families of children, from three or four years old and upwards, were put under Mr. and Mrs. Burchard's care, to manage or mangle them, as they pleased; and all who could be made to *say* that they "gave their hearts to God," were reckoned as converts. Some of them, as facts declare, only said it, to get out of the clutches of the inquisitor. Well, instead of *thousands*, the braggadocio reported only *four hundred*, not half of whom can now be produced. And, although people were hurried into the churches, before they got cold, (lest, as Mr. B. said, the devil should catch more than half of them,) including unstable youth, and little, inexperienced children, yet the whole number amounted to only 120!

Why, a Mormonite, with half the advantages that Mr. B. had, would make *three* converts to his *one*.

(2.) The most proper course, is, to keep away from the money-making impostor. *Burchard* is joined to his idols; let him alone. He says he is now a "blind, miserable sinner, and was, till 24 years old, a most abominable rebel." One of the clergymen of Albany, (N. Y.) responds, that every word of his confession is true, and intimates that Mr. B. has violated both the laws of God and man, since that time, and to such an extent, that, it would not be well for him to make that city a visitation. "There is no peace to the wicked, saith my God."

People of different denominations at Strafford, (Vt.) acted the wise and christian part. Most of them treated him with neglect, as they would a worthless fortune-teller; and such as attended his meeting, were not flattered nor frightened out of their senses. They held the Mirror up before him, and he shrunk from his own visage, and ran away. His *failure* was complete. Amen! Glory to God!

(3.) The *anxious seats, and the inquiry rooms*, are the principle means of Mr. B's success. Young people who seek those places, are as lambs seeking the slaughter-house. The management on those occasions is Jesuitical and mean, in the extreme. Treat the invitations to take the *anxious seats*, or to go into the *inquiry* meeting, as you should temptations to visit a gambling-house, of any other description. People should not be themselves, nor suffer their children to be, coaxed off to meeting, by *Burchard's slaves*, whatsoever the color, who are sent out to collect audiences, with carriages &c. for their sovereign master.

(4.) Let a judicious public be upon the guard against the *great stories* which Burchard and his slaves report of his successes.—They are calculated to deceive. He cries off as many converts as he pleases; for no one will be at the trouble of hunting the country over, to ascertain the exact facts.

We have omitted Mr. B's ridiculous account of the *alarm-bell of hell*, or the great clock, ticking, *eternity, eternity!!* also his abusive treatment of a young lady from Strafford, and his denouncing Dea. Elias Thomas and wife, of the Christian order, as hell deserving sinners. Nothing has been said of his going into the inquiry meeting in the vestry or hall, and, shrinking as though expecting to receive his deserts, saying "he had rather God Almighty would put twenty-five stripes upon his naked back, than to come to that place;" nor of his telling a young Christian lady that "he had as lives have the prayers of a damned spirit in hell," as hers. It is too painful to a serious, devout mind, to record, an hundredth part of similar abominations.

Let the foregoing suffice, and serve as a warning to all of every persuasion, whither these pages shall come, to avoid BURCHARDISM as they would a *spasmodic* disease. It is ruinous to the best interests of religion. Many of the most talented and pious of the Congregational order as well as others, deprecate Mr. B.'s rash adventurers.

Towards the close of Mr. B.'s labors in this place, he recommended, for the first time, a perusal of the scriptures; and that Trinitarians should treat others with courtesy and respect; and, though inconsistent with his own conduct, we shall rejoice to see them follow his precepts, rather than his examples.

Source: Russell Streeter, *Mirror of Calvinistic Fanaticism, or Jedediah Burchard & Co. During a Protracted Meeting of Twenty-Six Days in Woodstock, Vermont* (Woodstock, Vt.: Nahum Haskell, 1835), pp. 117-121, 165-168.

Document 7

First Annual Report of the Vermont Anti-Slavery Society (1835)

. . . The Vermont Anti-Slavery Society was organized on the first day of May, 1834, about one hundred delegates being present, from thirty different towns. Since that time a travelling agent has been employed, five months, who has delivered from eighty to ninety lectures, and formed auxiliary Societies in ten or twelve towns, which, with those previously formed, make thirty town Societies in the State. The way is preparing for forming many more auxiliaries. One thousand copies of a circular were distributed in June, addressed to the clergy of this State, it being the report of a committee of the State Convention, on colonization, designed to disabuse the people on that subject. We are sure the effort was not lost. Five hundred copies of Mr. [James G.] Birney's Letter, printed in New-York, have been circulated by this Society and many more by its auxiliaries. The effect of these in opening eyes to the colonization delusion [of the American Colonization Society], has been most salutary. Three local agents have been appointed, who have lectured to some extent. By such means as these, this Society, in the nine months of its existence, has brought thousands to examine the great subject of slavery and emancipation, hundreds of whom have enrolled their names to support our cause. . . .

Among the important occurrences of a few months past, there is one too infamously important to be left unnoticed; we refer to the mobbing and violence that is so widely obtaining, trampling down the constitution of our State and of the United States, and making war upon the very genius of liberty. These riots are the legitimate fruits of that spirit of slavery that has ever been diffusing itself throughout this Republic. . . .

Vermont is the wrong place for mobism. The wolves that prey upon our flocks by night, may find a retreat in our Green Mountains; but they who tread under their feet our constitution, and wage war upon discussion, the citadel of our liberties—whether the lawless rabble, or those who set them on—will find themselves whelmed in public indignation.

There is great complaint, because we oppose the Colonization Society. But what has been the character of our opposition? Have we shown ourselves immoral? Do we oppose the Temperance Society? What have been our weapons? Have we used clubs and brick-bats? Have we stirred up mobs? No. Nothing like it. Had we used brute violence against that Society, its friends would have had a right to complain; but we have had nothing to do with that sort of argument—it all comes from the other side. . . .

We come now to make a plain declaration of our principles and designs, in regard to the colored population of our country. It will be brief. It can be told in a few words. Our principles are intuitive, common-sense principles, written in the Book of God, and engraved on the hearts of men. Our practices shall comport with our principles.

Viewing slavery, as we do, to be a crime of the deepest dye before God—not less wrong in practice than in principle—dangerous to republican government—daily and hourly weakening the bonds of our national union; as accountable beings, as men, and as Americans, we call for its *immediate abandonment*. This demand we have a right to make—it is just—it is reasonable. It will be a vain thing for any man or set of men, at the North or at the South, to tell us that this is an excessive demand—that it is treasonable or seditious. We are a component part of the physical power of this nation, that sustains slavery, and of the moral power, that is able to crush it. The aristocratic, the time-serving, the man-fearing, ask what right we have to interfere. What right, we ask, had the bystanders to interfere when the ruffian undertook to assassinate the Chief Magistrate of this nation? What right have we to interfere when our neighbors cry from their chamber-windows, their houses being wrapped in flames around them? We are not of the number who confound *right* with *might*.

We are told when we call for immediate abolition, that our work must be a work of time. So we are not to call for the immediate rescue of the drowning man, because it will be a work of time to get to him! Preachers of righteousness, temperance, and judgment, are not to urge immediate heed to the divine requirements, because it will be a work of time to gain the ears and hearts of the depraved! If we only require of the slave-holder that he reform when he finds it expedient, because he will not at once listen to the doctrine of immediate reformation, we may pursue the same course with the robber and adulterer, for the same reason. Nothing can be effectual, short of laying hold of his

conscience, and this can never be reached by compromising with him in his wrong doing. He must be made to feel that slavery is a *sin*--then he will repent. Grant him his own time to dispose of the matter, undisturbed, is all he asks. That time will be the latest day of his life, and his last act concerning it will be, to "entail the evil" on the next generation; and the next generation will demand their own time, and plead innocence because the system was entailed upon them.

Much alarm is expressed, lest we agitate the South. (How is this to be reconciled with the statement that our labor here will be lost, because we are situated so far from the evil?) We are not afraid of disturbing the South. We aim to disturb them—not to injure them, but—they must be disturbed. They are sleeping on a volcano; the surface now heaves under them! The judgments of Heaven hang over them; the arrows of retributive justice already begin to fall! It is our bounden duty to lift up our voices together, and swell them to a tempest—if possible we may awake them to a sense of their guilt, their folly, and their danger—a duty owed to ourselves, to our children, to the oppressor and the oppressed, to Christianity, to the cause of freedom. As for our being heard in the South, there is nothing to prevent. Intelligence knows no geographical boundaries; it does not stop on Mason and Dixon's line; it circulates through this nation, as blood through the animal system. The same conveyance that brings to Vermont Governor McDuffie's doctrine, that slavery is necessary to the perpetuity of our liberties,(!) will carry to South Carolina our doctrine, that slavery is the most *dangerous foe* to our liberties; and the latter will be read with equal avidity as the former, will produce discussion, discussion will elicit truth, and truth will make free. Do not the people of the South hear what we have to say on all other great questions of common interest? and will they be less heedful of what is going on in respect to what they deem their *peculiar* interest? They will eagerly seize and devour every page of anti-slavery matter that falls in their reach. What means the growling in the den? Light is breaking in upon the monster. Our Thomes and our Birneys, seized with sympathy, are spreading the kind contagion. Our Evangelists are kindling a moral blaze in every Seminary and every Synod. Our Emancipators are so many flaming torches, and our Liberators so many bursts of boiling lava, lighting up fires throughout all the dark valley of prejudice and oppression. The cry of Fire!—Fire!! from the watchmen of oppression, already meets us on every southern breeze, and every move they make but fans the flame. The tocsin of slavery sounds but to marshal and encourage its enemies—to confuse and dishearten its friends.

Let those who are alarmed at these things, point out a better way. Let that way be any other than *letting alone* this growing evil, this Boa-constrictor, tightening his folds around the neck of this nation. It has been let alone long enough. The spirit of slavery has diffused itself extensively enough. Danger! Danger! Let those who make this cry, before they run, look around and find where the danger lies. Is there no danger in goading men, already armed with despair? Is there less danger to be apprehended from the slaves, than from those who are employed in holding them? The Union is in danger! The chivalrous men of the South will declare "war to the knife!" And what is the present attitude of these men who are supposed to be for war? Are they prepared for a war of invasion? Every man of them is on sentry at home, and their foes are of their own house. If a Chinese wall could be built between them and us, the knives would be at their throats in less than one week, and they know it. In the name of reason and honor, we beseech the good people of the North not to be over-much frightened. A terrible thing to emancipate two millions of slaves! If there would be difficulty with two millions to-day, what, with two millions and two hundred to-morrow? with two millions and seventy thousand next year? with three millions, fifteen years hence? We pray those who have hitherto looked at the consequence of doing right, to dare for once to look at the consequence of continuing in the wrong.

We now appeal to the understanding and conscience of this nation. We cite the South to their own desolation and wretchedness. We ask them why the wolf now howls in certain portions of Virginia, where were once fertile plantations? Why is that State now the *fourth* or *fifth* in the Union, in point of wealth and population, whereas one it was the *first*? Why is Maryland now less than a *thirtieth* of the population of the United States, whereas, in 1790, it was an *eleventh*? Why does the slightest breeze make them tremble like an aspen? To the North we appeal, in the name of more than two millions, whose blood is as water, and whose grief as wind—in the name of the best interests of this republic—in the name of freedom—in the name of Christianity—in the name of earth and Heaven. Slavery must

be abolished. As sure as there is any virtue in moral power—any might in truth—any brotherly love, any common humanity, any sense of shame, any fear of retribution, any regard for justice, in Americans—it will be done speedily and peacefully. What American, what Christian, what human being, will not now come forward, lay aside for a moment differences in politics and religion, and all meaner things, and make common cause against a common enemy? Then what shall hinder us? Justice, and reason, and humanity are on our side; our parent-country has led the way and sent the noblest of her victors to help us; God and angels are with us. Onward! to the bloodless strife! Onward!—stare tyranny in the face—rouse the church—wake the nation. Onward! until cart-whips no longer tear human flesh—until the woe and waste of slavery cease. Onward! until the groans of the oppressed be turned into songs of liberty, and the foulest stigma be removed from a nation calling itself free!

Source: *First Annual Report of the Vermont Anti-Slavery Society, 1835* (Montpelier: Knapp and Jewett, 1835), pp. 9, 12-13, 17-20.

DOCUMENT 8

"The Inland Port" (1835)
NATHANIEL HAWTHORNE

It was a bright forenoon, when I set foot on the beach at Burlington, and took leave of the two boatmen, in whose little skiff I had voyaged since daylight from Peru. Not that we had come that morning from South America, but only from the New-York shore of Lake Champlain. The highlands of the coast behind us stretched north and south, in a double range of bold, blue peaks, gazing over each other's shoulders at the Green Mountains of Vermont. The latter are far the loftiest, and, from the opposite side of the lake, had displayed a more striking outline. We were now almost at their feet, and could see only a sandy beach, sweeping beneath a woody bank, around the semi-circular bay of Burlington. The painted light-house, on a small green island, the wharves and warehouses, with sloops and schooners moored alongside, or at anchor, or spreading their canvass to the wind, and boats rowing from point to point, reminded me of some fishing town on the sea-coast.

But I had no need of tasting the water to convince myself that Lake Champlain was not an arm of the sea; its quality was evident, both by its silvery surface, when unruffled, and a faint, but unpleasant and sickly smell, forever steaming up in the sunshine. One breeze from the Atlantic, with its briny fragrance, would be worth more to these inland people than all the perfumes of Arabia. On closer inspection, the vessels at the wharves looked hardly sea-worthy — there being a great lack of tar about the seams and rigging, and perhaps other deficiencies, quite as much to the purpose. I observed not a single sailor in the port. There were men, indeed, in blue jackets and trowsers, but not of the true nautical fashion, such as dangle before slop-shops; others wore tight pantaloons and coats preponderously long-tailed—cutting very queer figures at the mast-head; and, in short, these fresh-water fellows had about the same analogy to the real "old salt," with his tarpaulin, pea-jacket and sailor-cloth trowsers, as a lake fish to a Newfoundland cod.

Nothing struck me more, in Burlington, than the great number of Irish emigrants. They have filled the British provinces to the brim, and still continue to ascend the St. Lawrence, in infinite tribes, overflowing by every outlet into the States. At Burlington, they swarm in huts and mean dwellings near the lake, lounge about the wharves, and elbow the native citizens entirely out of competition in their own line. Every species of mere bodily labor is the prerogative of these Irish. Such is their multitude, in comparison with any possible demand for their services, that it is difficult to conceive how a third part of them should earn even a daily glass of whiskey, which is doubtless their first necessary of life—daily bread being only the second. Some were angling in the lake, but had caught only a few perch, which little fishes, without a miracle, would be nothing among so many. A miracle there certainly must have been, and a daily one, for the subsistence of these wandering hordes. The men exhibit a lazy strength and careless merriment, as if they had fed well hitherto, and meant to feed better hereafter; the women strode about, uncovered in the open air, with far plumper waists and brawnier limbs, as well as bolder faces, than our shy and slender females; and their progeny, which was innumerable, had the reddest and the roundest cheeks of any children in America.

While we stood at the wharf, the bell of a steamboat gave two preliminary peals, and she dashed away for Plattsburgh, leaving a trail of smoky breath behind, and breaking the glassy surface of the lake before her. Our next movement brought us into a handsome and busy square, the sides of which were filled up with white houses, brick stores, a church, a court-house, and a bank. Some of these edifices had roofs of tin, in the fashion of Montreal, and glittered in the sun with cheerful splendor, imparting a lively effect to the whole square. One brick building, designated in large letters as the custom-house, reminded us that this inland village is a port of entry, largely concerned in foreign trade, and holding daily intercourse with the British empire. In this border country, the Canadian bank-notes circulate as freely as our own, and British and America coin are jumbled into the same pocket, the effigies of the king of England being made to kiss those of the goddess of liberty. Perhaps there was an emblem in the involuntary contact. There was a pleasant mixture of people in the square of Burlington, such as cannot be seen elsewhere, at one view: merchants from Montreal, British officers from the frontier garrisons, French Canadians, wandering Irish, Scotchmen of a better class, gentlemen of the south on a pleasure-tour, country 'squires on business; and a great throng of Green Mountain boys, with their horse-wagons and ox-teams, true Yankees in aspect, and looking more superlatively so, by contrast with such a variety of foreigners.

Source: Nathaniel Hawthorne, *The Snow-Image and Uncollected Tales* (Columbus: Ohio State University Press, 1974), pp. 298-301. Reprinted with permission of the Ohio State University Press.

DOCUMENT 9

Announcement of a "Railroad Convention" (1835)

CIRCULAR

At a meeting of citizens of Windsor, 16th Dec. inst., it was resolved, in accordance with suggestions from the North and the South, to call a general Convention, to take measures to construct the contemplated Rail Road through the Valley of the Connecticut to the St.

Lawrence, connecting with New Haven and New York. The place designated was Windsor, Vt., and the time, Jan. 20th, 1836.

Among the reasons for this movement are the following: —

1. The Legislature of Vermont, at its late session, granted an act of incorporation for a Rail Road from the south line of the State, in Windham County, to the north line, in Orleans County.

2. It is understood that petitions are about to be presented to the Parliament of Lower Canada for the charter of Rail Roads from Lake Memphremagog in two directions, viz. to Montreal and Quebec, prospectively to connect with the Connecticut River Rail Road. It is also understood that a lively interest is felt in Canada in this enterprise, and, that a convention of delegates from the towns on the respective routes in Canada, and in the valley of the Passumpsic, in Vermont, is appointed to be holden at Derby Line on the 31st instant.

3. It is understood that a fresh interest is awakened among the friends of the enterprise on the southern part of the route.

4. The time has unquestionably arrived when a convention of citizens, from the towns on the whole route, can no longer be delayed, without manifest detriment to great and important interests.

The objects of the measures to be taken at the Convention are these:—

1. To obtain charters for those parts of the route not yet granted.

2. To procure a survey of the whole route, with estimates of the expense.

3. To collect and arrange facts concerning the amount of business that may be expected on the route.

4. By these and other means, to present to the public such a report as shall induce capitalists to make investments in the stock.

The great importance of this enterprise is obvious on a moment's reflection.

The AGRICULTURAL SUSCEPTIBILITIES of this whole route are very great—second to none in New England.

The WATER PRIVILEGES and powers of manufacture are immense.

As a THOROUGHFARE of business and pleasure, the route is unrivalled.

It will connect the great cities of New York and Canada, and bring them within twenty-four hours' ride of each other.

The country is singularly adapted for the construction of a Rail Road—no point, it is believed, will require a stationary engine.

The greatest activity prevails among the friends of other kindred enterprises in New England. If the people on this route do not now put forth their best efforts in the accomplishment of this object, they will tamely give into the hands of others the advantages which nature has put into their own.

These considerations, it is confidently believed, will insure, at this Convention, a general attendance of delegates from all the towns on the route; and gentlemen into whose hands this Circular may fall, are earnestly requested to use their influence to cause the appointment of the same.

Gentlemen who may attend, are requested to bring with them as much statistical and other information, on the objects above specified, as possible.

Committee:
THOMAS EMERSON
ALLEN WARDNER
CARLOS COOLIDGE
JOHN RICHARDS
I.W. HUBBARD
Windsor, Vt., Dec. 21, 1835.

INFORMATION ON THE FOLLOWING POINTS WOULD BE PARTICULARLY ACCEPTABLE AT THE CONVENTION.

1. What is the present population of your town?

2. What number of manufacturing establishments—particularizing the largest, also mills of all descriptions?

3. Amount of capital employed in manufactures, trade, and agriculture—distinguishing between each?

4. The different kinds, quantity, and value, of or each kind of article annually manufactured?

5. What number of stores and ware-houses of all descriptions?
6. Cattle, horses, &c., also agricultural products and manufactured articles, sent to market annually—specifying the quantity of each kind?
7. What number of passengers arrive and depart at your place annually?
8. Number of tons transportation annually to and from your place in all directions—specifying places and amounts, and distinguishing between exports and imports?
9. Quantity of flour imported?

ADD ANY THING ELSE
YOU MAY DEEM IMPORTANT.

Source: "Connecticut River and St. Lawrence Rail Road," 1835, Broadside, Special Collections, Bailey/Howe Library, University of Vermont.

DOCUMENT 10

Vermont Reactions to the Patriote Rebellion (1837)

TO HIS EXCELLENCY THE GOVERNOR OF VERMONT
[EXCERPTED]

The subscribers have learned with great concern, that a portion of the public press and many of the citizens in the northern part of this state are advocating and adopting measures in relation to the existing difficulties in the Province of Lower Canada, which the undersigned conceive to be not only of most evil example and mischievous tendency, but in direct contradiction to every sound principle of public morals.

The newspapers have been filled with exciting rumours and inflammatory articles in favor of the so called patriots; they have solicited contributions in aid of their cause; public meetings have been had, and encouragement of countenance and assistance held out to the insurgents, and it is even credibly reported that they have been gratuitously furnished by citizens of Vermont with arms and munitions of war.

The rule of noninterference in the internal dissensions of other nations, has been always professed and generally observed by the American Government, and the justice, wisdom and propriety of this course of policy rest upon grounds so strong, that extreme cases alone can excuse a departure from it. That the struggle in Canada presents one of those cases, we by no means believe. We have now been independent of the British empire for more than threescore years, and with the exception of short periods of interruption, have sustained friendly relations with that power ever since the close of the revolutionary war. The prejudices, the jealousies and the embittered feelings engendered by that contest and by the war of 1812, may be supposed to have subsided, and we ought now to hold the British nation in common with the rest of the world, *in war indeed, as enemies, but in peace as friends.* With the Provinces of Canada our intercourse has been nearly as free as that among the states of our confederacy, and a mutually beneficial and highly important commerce has grown up between the citizens of those provinces and the inhabitants of the valley of Lake Champlain and the northern frontier. The provincial government in all its departments has treated our people with uniform justice, liberality, and even courtesy, and few instances in modern history have occurred of so free and friendly an intercourse between contiguous nations. Every principle of justice and national comity therefore binds us to refrain from all unnecessary acts which may tend to the injury of a government and people to whom we have so long sustained the most friendly relations.

We do not propose to enter upon the discussion of the questions now pending between the British government and a portion of the people of Canada, but it may not be impertinent to observe that the grievances complained of by the malcontents amount to no invasion of the sacred rights of life, and personal liberty, no impeachment of the freedom of opinion and discussion, no spoiling of the fruits of humble labor or the profits of honest industry, no denial of justice in the legal tribunals of the land, or want of protection against foreign aggressions or domestic violence, & in short, to no such grinding oppressions as must enlist the sympathies of every friend of humanity; but they resolve themselves into a bare question concerning certain alledged political rights, the exercise whereof is said to be denied to the Canadian people, and the demands of the insurgents involve such changes in the frame of government, as would not fail to end in the separation of the province from the British empire. . . .

The blessings of order and law are certain—the benefits of revolution are always before hand doubtful. . . . The question of interference is one, on which the action of the government should precede that of individuals. With both it ought to be a matter of duty, and while none pretend that the insurgents have a right to demand our aid, we ought to be extremely cautious that an illjudged sympathy does not betray us into acts neither just nor politic, and which must result in great evil to our own best interests, if not to those whom we may design to serve.

We have thus far treated this matter as a question of right, and we believe that upon this high moral ground alone it ought to turn. But we cannot forbear to suggest, that any interference in the affairs of Canada by American citizens, must inevitably produce serious mischief. It is not to be expected, that the British government will quietly suffer their North American provinces to be wrested from them, or that they will tamely allow us to lend countenance and support to those whom they regard as rebels. If supplies of arms, munitions, or men are furnished to the insurgents by our people, it is idle to hope that a border warfare can be avoided, or that, that can fail to end in a formal declaration of hostilities, to say nothing of the lesser evils of restrictions of trade, and of the freedom of general intercourse with Canada which will inevitably follow any manifestations of the public sympathy of our people with the insurgent cause.

The subscribers believe that if these considerations be suggested to the people by the authorities they have been accustomed to respect, their own good sense, love of impartial justice, and regard for the laws of the land, will induce them to refrain from any interference in matters that so little concern them, as the disputes now agitating the minds and disturbing the tranquility of our citizens.

The undersigned therefore beg leave to suggest to your Excellency the propriety of issuing an executive proclamation requiring the good people of this State to observe that strict neutrality between the contending parties which the principles of national right, the laws of the land and the public morals manifestly demand.

Burlington, Dec. 12, 1837.
[Signed by 23 citizens]

Source: *Burlington Free Press*, 14 December 1837.

STATE OF VERMONT. A PROCLAMATION BY THE GOVERNOR.

It is known to my fellow citizens that disturbances have broken out in the neighboring province of LOWER CANADA, which have resulted in bloodshed. The head of the Provincial Government has issued his proclamation declaring martial law in the district of Montreal.

This state of things necessarily changes the relations which have heretofore existed between the inhabitants of this State and that Province, and the possibility that any, through the influence of ardent feelings, may be betrayed into acts of unauthorized interference induces me to call the attention of my fellow citizens to the subject.

With the kingdom of Great Britain we are in a state of profound peace. We have treaties with that government which it is our duty, and I trust our desire, to fulfil to the letter.

It is obvious that as a nation we have no right to intermeddle with the constitution of any neighboring power.—While as republicans we prefer that form of government under which it is our happiness to live, a decent regard for the opinion of others, will prevent all dictation as to the form of their government.

Principles which have been admitted for ages, forbid all national interference unless in the character of allies, and it is scarcely necessary to add that individuals should not do that which the government *cannot—must* not do.

It has been represented to me that in some few instances arms have been furnished, and hostile forces organized within this state. No one can be ignorant of the consequences of such a state of things if allowed. Such forces may be repelled, and our territory be made the theatre of active warfare.—This is not to be tolerated for a moment, and every good citizen will appreciate the importance of rebuking all such acts as may tend to produce it.

That comity which binds nations to each other condemns all interference in their intestine broils, and the laws of Congress are explicit in their denunciation, subjecting those who improperly interfere to heavy penalties and imprisonment.

Under these circumstances and with these feelings, I have thought it my duty to issue THIS MY PROCLAMATION, cautioning my fellow citizens against all acts, that may subject them to penalties, or in any way compromise the government.

Our first duty is to our own government; and the greatest benefit we can confer on the world is by giving them a perfect example in the action of that government. With other nations our conduct should be regulated by the principles of an enlarged and enlightened philanthropy. In war we may treat them as enemies; but in peace they are to be regarded as friends. In the present posture of affairs our duty is manifest—that of a strict neutrality—neither lending such aid to either as would be inconsistent with that character, nor denying the rights of hospitality to either, so long as they are within our borders, and maintain the character of quiet and peaceable citizens.

My fellow citizens will appreciate the feelings by which I am actuated.—The nation's honour cannot be confided to better hands than their own. Their zeal in the cause of liberty was never doubted. It is only necessary to caution them against such interference with the rights of others as might jeopardize the peace of our country.

Given under my hand this 13th day of December, A.D. 1837, and of the Independence of the United States the sixty second.

S. H. JENISON

By the Governor,

G.B. Manser, Secretary

Source: *Burlington Free Press*, 14 December 1837.

PUBLIC MEETING AT MIDDLEBURY [EXCERPTED]

The adjourned meeting of the Young Men of Middlebury was holden in the Town Room on Wednesday evening the 20th instant. . . . Mr. B. [E. D. Barber] on taking the chair [as presiding officer] addressed the meeting in eloquent terms, at considerable length, stating the object of the meeting, and defending the right and propriety of the citizens of the United States, expressing their sympathies for the cause of the Canadian patriots and extending their encouragement to them.

On motion, E. R. Jewett was appointed to invite Gen. T. S. Brown [Patriote military leader] to attend the meeting. Judge Wooster moved that the invitation be extended to Mr. [Louis] Perrault [publisher of the Patriote newspaper, *The Vindicator*]. When they made their appearance, they were received with enthusiastic applause.

A. Spencer, Jr., from the committee on resolutions, reported the following, which were unanimously adopted:

WHEREAS, The late and glorious attempt of the Patriots of the Canadas to throw off the yoke of oppressive government, and to endeavor to obtain that place among nations to which they are so justly entitled, has called forth the opinions and views of many young men of our State; and whereas we, the young men of Middlebury, in accordance with these noble principles of constitutional liberty which guarantee to us the freedom of opinion and of speech, deem it a duty as well as privilege to express our sentiments in relation to the Canadian revolution and to extend to the suffering "Sons of Liberty" that sympathy which our fathers found among the patriotic and enlightened of the civilized world —

THEREFORE,

1. Resolved, That inasmuch as our country has ever been distinguished as the asylum of the oppressed, especially since the establishment of our national independence, we consider ourselves bound by every principle of humanity, hospitality and republicanism to receive and protect those who, fleeing from the exactions and tyranny of their own governments, seek refuge and a home within our borders.

2. That in accordance with the principles upon which our government has been wisely and honorably conducted, of giving no offense *to* and submitting to no insults *from* any foreign power, it is our duty as citizens, in no wise to compromise or embarrass the government of this Union; but that nevertheless whenever a people, whether they be the subjects of Russia, of Turkey, of Great Britain, or of any other nation, whether of nations sufficiently strong to make war upon us, or too weak to seek revenge, are forced by tyrannical usurpations to rise in arms in freedom's cause, for the protection of their lives, their liberties or their honor, it becomes us as American freemen, who once claimed the sympathy of our fellowmen, openly and manfully to express our

liveliest interest in the success of their endeavors.

3. That with every desire to cultivate and continue the happy relations of amity and commerce now subsisting between our Government and that of Great Britain, we should not forget that with every other nation in the world, we have, from the day of our independence, arranged our national disputes by friendly negotiations—by Great Britain alone have we been compelled to resort to violence and the sword, in the maintenance of our national honor.

4. That though the existing treaties between the United States and Great Britain enjoin upon our government a strict neutrality in the pending controversy with her colonies, the right publicly to express our opinions and to extend our sympathies never *has* been and never *can* be surrendered, without abridging the freedom of speech and of the press; and accordingly exercising this right as American citizens, we most cordially proffer our sympathies to the Patriots of the Canadas, now struggling for their independence.

5. That we consider it the duty of American young men to manifest their attachment and veneration for humanity, by an unreserved and manly expression of their abhorrence of British oppression, as exhibited in depriving the Patriots of Canada of the sacred rights of life and personal liberty, and especially of the inalienable privilege of free discussion. . . .

7. That the threatened attack of the Tory party in Canada on some of our border towns for harboring and protecting Patriots proscribed by their tyranny has, to use the language of one of their own writers, "and that we view all such bravado with sovereign contempt, as the miserable subterfuge of a bad cause."

8. That if their rashness and folly should carry them so far as to execute their threats, we will give them a reception as warm as their ancestors have several times met with from our fathers. . . .

12. That those gentlemen of Burlington, who *"have learned with great concern that a portion of the public press and many of the citizens in the northern part of the state are advocating and adopting measures in relation to the existing dif-* *ficulties in the Province of Lower Canada, which (they) conceive to be not only of most evil example and mischievous tendency, but in direct contradiction to every sound principle and public morals,"* are pre-eminently entitled to our *supreme respect and veneration, for their marvelous attachment to the cause of* PUBLIC MORALITY!!!. . . .

15. That it is our hearts' desire and prayer to heaven, that the noble struggle already commenced in the Canadas, may eventuate in the establishment of a government in those Provinces on principles of the purest Republicanism—a government, effectually securing every individual in the enjoyment of person, property and character—a government affording protection to virtuous industry and encouragement to honorable enterprise—a government which guarantees the sacred rights of conscience, and the inestimable privilege of acquiring knowledge to all—a government, in short, which sanctions no privileged orders, confers no exclusive rights, no hereditary distinctions, and no ancient and time-honored abuses to curb the spirit and paralyse the energies of a generous and gallant people.

16. That we admire the spirit manifested by our frontier brethren, and heartily approve the measures they have adopted to show their contempt for the threats of the loyalists, and their devotion to the cause of the patriots.

17. That the "Sons of Liberty," who have taken refuge in our own community, are entitled to our hospitality, our friendship and our protection.

Source: *Burlington Sentinel*, 29 December 1837.

DOCUMENT 11

An Appeal to Females of the North, on the Subject of Slavery by a Female of Vermont (1838)

As there has been much that was excellent and convincing said and written, relative to slavery, I should deem it quite superfluous, to add my mite to the already abundant fund, were it not that a feeling of duty and an increasing interest in the cause of oppressed and degraded human nature, constrain me thus to appeal to the benevolence and religious sensibility of my sisters; if happily by "importunity" their slumbering energies may be awakened to efficient effort for the peaceful and speedy overthrow of a system so entirely at variance with the precepts of the gospel.

I am aware that it requires no small degree of moral courage to enable our sex to appear as the friends of the slave. We must dare to exercise those powers of mind which the Almighty has bestowed upon us, or we shall be driven from this position by the objections and entreaties of those whose views are in opposition to ours. The most formidable barrier that is presented before us is the *political bearing of slavery.*—We are gravely told that on this account it is exceedingly unfeminine and intrusive for us to advocate the cause of the enslaved; and that retirement is more congenial with our capacities and habits. This is a specious argument; but, unhappily for those who advance it, it appears to have been coined for this exigency, and applied exclusively to this question,—for we know that the sphere of female action has not always been thus circumscribed. We know that the sympathy and the co-operation of females are solicited in aid of missionary operations—that women are now urged by all that is beneficent in their nature to assist in sending the teacher of Christianity to heathen India—even when they are assured that the doctrines he will declare are directly opposed to the political organization, the established customs and long-cherished prejudices of the nation to whom he will go. They are not now cautioned against an interference with the rights of others, and warned of the revolution and bloodshed that may result from the promulgation of these doctrines. No, they are commended for the sacrifices they are making in support of the cause, and told that the blessings of these benighted souls will rest upon them. The alarming thought is not suggested to them, that if these doctrines should prevail, and the Chinese be induced to consign their multiplicity of idols to the flames, this teacher of Christianity may possibly be regarded as an incendiary, by those who derive their gain from the sale of images, and forfeit his life by his temerity. No, those who are thus anxious to benefit the distant heathen do not in this case consult consequences; they act upon the im-

mutable principle *that it is right to do our duty*, and leave the event with Him who can overrule all for good.

And women have been, and still are, appealed to, as co-workers with their brethren in the cause of Temperance. Their influence is sought in diffusing the doctrines of Peace. And, astonishing as it may now seem, their aid was once invoked in behalf of Greece and Poland, when their sons were waging physical warfare against their oppressors! It was not then viewed as a derogation from their delicacy, nor their dignity, to commingle feelings with their fathers and brothers, or even to transmit the token of their sympathy to those who were contending for freedom. They were not then reproved for meddling with the affairs of rulers and their subjects. Oh, no, they were admired for their zeal, and eulogized as angels of mercy, commissioned to bear the balm of hope to desponding breasts!

It is truly surprising that the acute discerners of feminine impropriety have not, ere this late hour, discovered that a participation in these enterprizes was an aberration from female decorum, and kindly remanded woman to the quiet routine of domestic avocations. Such a course would have been in consonance with their present assertions, and might have saved them from the mortification produced by our indiscretion! But the undisguised truth is, that the opponents of Abolitionism have not been actuated so much by a sense of our departure from correctness of conduct, as by an apprehension that the principles of universal love and equity must ultimately triumph over hatred and oppression, unless the discussion of this question could be checked. They are convinced that woman's voice has not been powerless when raised in behalf of virtue, and therefore, impotent as they may affect to consider our efforts in this cause, it has been their policy to divert our attention from this momentous subject, and thus prevent a concentration of our influence. This must be obvious to every unprejudiced mind—for if the exertions of women, in the instances enumerated, were irreproachable, it surely cannot now reflect indelicacy nor indignity upon us to "remember those in" our midst who are in "bonds, as bound with them," unless it can be clearly demonstrated that our benevolence derives its angelic hue from the remoteness of the object which elicits it, and that the inhabitants of the "isles afar off" have stronger claims upon our sympathy, than the thousands, aye, millions, who are perishing at our very threshold! Alas! it is pride, it is bitter, cruel prejudice, united with selfishness, that would bind us to their wants and close our ears to the recital of their wrongs. . . .

Our sisters of England have done nobly in the cause of Emancipation, and the effects of their labors afford ample and encouraging proof that they have not spent their "strength for nought." Shall we imitate their bright example, or content ourselves with idle admiration of their zeal and firmness? Let us be willing to act in behalf of the oppressed, though the wise and prudent of this world deride us. "It is enough for the disciple that he be as his master;" and if so let us cheerfully submit to have our names cast out as evil.

But perhaps some may despair of our accomplishing anything by our labors, because we do not participate in the government of our country. We possess the power to accomplish much, if that power is rightly applied. It is acknowledged that we have influence in private life; and as it is from amongst those who compose the fireside circle that our statesmen are chosen—our fathers, brothers and husbands, we can, (if our own views are rectified,) while reclining beneath our vine of domestic enjoyment, remind them of the two and a half millions of immortal beings now pining in hopeless bondage, and so enlist their sympathies as to secure their exertions in their behalf. We can labor to eradicate that deep-rooted and unrighteous prejudice against a skin not colored like our own. And we can, in our neighborhood-intercourse dare to vindicate the aspersed character of our colored brethren. We who are mothers, can effectually though unobtrusively aid the cause of the oppressed, by instilling into the minds of our precious children an abhorrence of the sin of oppression and impressing upon their hearts the important truth that all mankind are the children of one common father, and therefore equally the objects of His love and mercy. We exert an influence over our sons and daughters that may yet affect the happiness of thousands; and let us not prove unworthy of this noble trust, but by every possible means endeavor to excite their interest in behalf of this outcast and degraded portion of our fellow creatures. We can diffuse information relative to this wide-spreading sin. We can implore Divine strength to endure with humility the reproach cast upon us by reason of our efforts; and if thus mercifully aided, we can continue to intercede for the deliverance of this people, until our country shall be cleansed from the guilt and disgrace which now pollute it. Thus, through different mediums we may operate upon the moral sense of the nation, and contribute to the purification of public sentiment from the leprosy that has long disfigured and enfeebled it. —Oh! if the multiplied and unequalled horrors of this modern Aceldama could be suddenly revealed to our view, they would startle the most indifferent and stimulate them to untiring exertions for the removal of this appalling source of corruption and death from the land. We may now endeavor to excuse ourselves from this labor, and offer what we may deem satisfactory the reasons for our idleness; but they will avail us nothing with Him whose requirements are plain and easily understood, and who "will reward" us "according to our works." We cannot believe that the redeemed soul of the now despised captive will be presented less spotless before the Father's throne, because the prison house of clay from which it had been liberated was of darker hue than that in which we tabernacled while on earth; and if not, then in *that* soul will the Omniscient Judge acknowledge an heir of God,—while to us may be addressed the awfully impressive language, **"Inasmuch as ye did it NOT unto one of the least of these my brethren, ye did it not unto me."**

Source: *An Appeal to Females of the North, on the Subject of Slavery by a Female of Vermont* (Brandon, Vt.: Telegraph Press, 1838), pp. 3-4, 7-8. Reprinted with permission of the Rokeby Museum, Ferrisburgh, Vermont.

DOCUMENT 12

"The Whig's Lament" (c. 1841)

JOHN GODFREY SAXE

Oh dear! Oh dear! The times, the times —
When will the story end.
In spite of Tip and Tyler Too[1]
The times refuse to mend.
We ask for change of government —
Alas! the cry was rash —
For though we've got a change in men —
We've got no *change* in cash.

In old Vermont-mont-mont
We're in a dreadful *state*.
Instead of fifty cents for wool
We can't get thirty-eight.
They promised if we'ed vote for Tip
That wool would surely rise;
But all they've done with wool has been
To pull it o'er our eyes.

Source: Mary Sollace Saxe, "A Vermont Bard," *Vermonter*, 7, no. 5 (1899): 424.

DOCUMENT 13

"To the Freemen of Chittenden County" (1844)

A TEMPERANCE CIRCULAR

FELLOW CITIZENS:

As the time appointed for the election of County Commissioners, under an act, passed at the last session of our state legislature, is approaching, and deeming it all important that a full expression of the views of the freemen of this county, should be had upon the

---

[1]In the 1840 presidential campaign, Whigs had hailed William Henry Harrison as "the Hero of Tippecanoe," in reference to his role, while govenor of Indiana Territory, as leader of the forces that engaged the Swawnee chief Tecumseh in the 1811 battle at Tippecanoe. "Tippecanoe and Tyler too!" became a popular slogan of the Whig campaign.

system of licensing, we have thought proper to call your attention to the subject in a short address. In order that you may vote understandingly, it becomes necessary that you should fully weigh the claims of the conflicting parties to your support, and for this purpose, we propose to examine briefly the principles for which each contend.

That the dealing in intoxicating liquors does not rest on the same basis with other traffics is self-evident. Disabilities have ever been thrown around it by law. If it is not an injurious and pernicious practice, why has not one citizen as good a right to engage in it as another? and why has the law ever required *a bonus* from the rumseller, before it would permit him to engage in the traffic? Yet so it has always been, and never have we heard the dealers complaining of this, as an infringement of their liberties. Why is this? The answer is plain—*it is immoral—it is pernicious—it is injurious*, and the law has a right to throw as many obstacles as possible in the way of those about to become dealers in the article.

This is not jumping to a conclusion; "the tree is known by its fruit:" consequences always determine the character of actions. The use of ardent spirits is pregnant with iniquity and crime. Abolish their use, and you almost abolish our criminal code, for nine-tenths of our criminals, date their fall from virtue to infamy, at the time when they first put the rum glass to their lips. From the fashionable potation at the splendid bar, the drunkard gradually descends to the three-cent grog shop, where he commits the deed, which either consigns him to the walls of the state's prison or a murderer's grave. The strongest advocates of the practice dare not assert that men are made more moral or more upright by drunkenness. Shall we then in vain implore the aid of the moralist or the Christian?

In our pecuniary affairs the evil is scarcely less alarming—the amount of liquor annually consumed in this county alone, exceeds in expense the sum paid during the same time for flour, one of the necessaries of life. The facts presented to us by the increasing importations of flour are brought home to every man, and the necessity of raising enough for our own supply and thereby retaining at home the thousands of which we are yearly drained is every day becoming more and more apparent. But look now at the cost of the rum importations for our own consumption. Is 300 hogsheads a high estimate for this county? Statistics show that it is not. The average price for which this is sold cannot be less than seventy-five cents per gallon—which gives us the alarming account of twenty seven thousand dollars, expended every year, not for food, not for necessities, but for a public and private curse, and rendered ten times more deadly, by the poisonous drugs with which all liquors are now adulterated.

In view of these stubborn facts, will not every person who has an interest in the public morals and private property, refuse to sustain or support men, who foster and cherish this degrading, devouring and demoralizing evil? Will the christian or philanthropist vote for a system which will surely make its brutes and demons? In the name of christianity, philanthropy and patriotism, we conjure them not to.

If the traffic in, and use of, ardent spirits be an evil, it certainly follows that it is wrong to license men to commit this evil. Shall we be asked to sanction infamy, countenance crime, and make the right to sin a matter of bargain and sale. If so, then we have receded in philanthropy and enlightenment, from the barbarians of the middle ages.

But there is a higher responsibility resting upon the freemen of this county, than upon any other in the state. While other counties are only chargeable with the amount actually consumed within their borders, it is a notorious fact, that Burlington alone, yearly inundates at least one-fourth part of the state with alcohol, producing drunkenness and pauperism. Washington, Lamoille, Caledonia, Franklin and Orleans Counties look here for the means of sustaining the traffic; and the flood-gates once shut down, by the voice of the freemen of this county, they would abolish the trade almost from necessity. Are we not then justly chargeable with all the iniquity and ruin, which are the legitimate offspring of this traffic, if now, while the means are in our power, we do not use every honorable exertion to put an end to it?

The time has now come when the honesty of those who have heretofore professed an adherence to the cause of temperance is to be put to the test. There are many who oppose the course pursued by the advocates of the anti-license system, because, say they, we are *too ultra* in our notions. To such we appeal in a spirit of kindness, and ask them, to let the principles we advocate be once carried out, and then if their operation is not beneficial, immediately to withdraw their support from our ticket. We are not warring against liberty—we would set the intemperate free from an enslaving vice, and remove the tyrant of temptation.

Freemen of Chittenden county—a heavy responsibility is now resting upon you. The election which you have just passed through shrinks into insignificance, when compared with the importance of the one upon which you are entering. You are to decide by your votes, whether you will continue to foster and nourish drunkenness, at an annual expense of nearly thirty thousand dollars—whether a few rumsellers shall continue to fatten upon the moral and physical destruction of their victims; whether peace, plenty and prosperity shall dwell among us; or whether they shall be supplanted by poverty, misery and ruin.

In the language of our brethren in an adjoining county, we "call upon all classes to arise and rush to the rescue of all that is dear. We call upon clergymen, as the teachers of a pure religion, and the bearers to the people of 'good tidings,' to do their duty! Let Physicians, the guardians of our health, speak and act! We look to Fathers and Mothers and entreat them to cast their whole weight of influence for the well being of their sons and daughters! In a word, we invite all who can *speak or write*, or *weep*, to stir up the Freemen of this county to right ACTION.

"Let every tax payer say, '*I will not be taxed without my own consent.*' And let every freeman declare 'As for me and mine, WE WILL NOT BE SLAVES!'"

John Herrick, Lyman Burgess, William Weston,
County Committee

N.B. Time of election, second day of January, 1845

Source: "To the Freemen of Chittenden County," 1844, Broadside, Special Collections, Bailey/Howe Library, University of Vermont.

DOCUMENT 14

"Disturbance on the Railroad" (1846)

BURLINGTON FREE PRESS [DEWITT CLINTON CLARKE]

Considerable excitement was aroused in our town, on Friday last, by the sudden requisition of the Sheriff, Mr. Ferris, for an *armed* force, to aid him in the execution of legal process, which had been forcibly resisted by the laborers on the Central Railroad, near Richmond in this County. The principal facts in the case, as we learn them from the Sheriff, are these:

On Friday morning last, information was communicated to the Sheriff, by Mr. Deputy Gleason of Richmond, that the laborers on the Railroad, (some 200 in number) about three miles east of Huntington's tavern, had suspended work, and having collected together, were engaged in disturbing the peace in various ways—that they had thrown impediments in the way of the mail stages running between Burlington and Montpelier—and with violent language and demeanor had attempted completely to prevent the free use and occupation of the road by the public—and finally that they were holding in duress, Mr. Barker, one of the principal Contractors, peremptorily refusing to liberate him.

The Sheriff promptly repaired to the scene of the outrages, accompanied by two of his deputies and Mr. Church, Constable of Burlington, and by peaceful means endeavored to cause the rioters to disperse.—His Proclamation to this effect was utterly disregarded, and his attempt to release Mr. Barker forcibly and successfully resisted. Obtaining the necessary warrant for the arrest of the supposed ring-leaders, he again encountered resistance, and the individuals arrested were *rescued* by force from his custody.

Under these circumstances the requisition for an *armed force*, above alluded to, was promptly resorted to by the Sheriff.—The Light Infantry Co. in Burlington were called out, and the Company of Firemen immediately and unanimously tendered their services to maintain the supremacy of the law, and were furnished by the Sheriff with arms and ammunition.

With this force, amounting to seventy-five or eighty men, the Sheriff again reached Richmond, on Friday evening, accompanied also by a number of our most respectable citizens. On Saturday morning, either intimidated by the presence of an armed body of men, or otherwise awakened to a conviction of the fruitlessness, as well as the criminality, of further resistance, the Disturbers had mostly dispersed. Mr. Barker was released, some ten or twelve were arrested and lodged in jail in Burlington, and thus the affair terminated—fortunately without bloodshed or further outrage.

One word respecting the *causes* of this disturbance, and we leave the topic. It appears that the ground of complaint on the part of the laborers was that *they were not paid for their labor*, & that they had received no pay for several weeks. Their language to the Sheriff was, "give us our pay and we will disperse—this is all we ask, and this *we will have*." Now these were poor men, earning their daily bread by the sweat of their faces, and *they ought to have been promptly paid*. Holding all resistance to the LAWS, and all illegal combinations for the purpose of redressing even *real* wrongs, in utter abhorrence, and believing that they should be suppressed, promptly and if necessary, by armed force, we yet unhesitatingly affirm that these laborers, indefensible as their conduct became, were NOT *the first wrongdoers*. That sin must lie at the doors of those who, knowing their necessities, continued to receive the benefit of their unrewarded labor.

We know how easily these sentiments may be misconstrued and misrepresented. But we cannot help *that*. Those who, by injustice, incite others to a violation of the laws of the land, should and will, in the estimation of good men and merciful judges, share the responsibility of the *crime*, however unequal may be the *legal* allotment of *punishment*. "Be just and fear not" is an admirable maxim; but "Be just and you will have nothing to fear" is a much more practical truth.

We understand that those who employed these men, are Messrs. Smith & Co., *subcontractors in the 4th remove*. The Directors of the Company will undoubtedly take such steps as will be likely, hereafter, to prevent irresponsible men from having it in their power to involve the community in difficulty and danger by unjustly withholding from the laborer his hire.

Source: *Burlington Free Press*, 10 July 1846.

Address to the Agricultural Society of Rutland County (1847)

GEORGE P. MARSH

. . . There are certain other improvements connected with agriculture, to which I desire to draw your special attention. One of these is the introduction of a better economy in the management of our forest lands. The increasing value of timber and fuel ought to teach us, that trees are no longer what they were in our fathers' time, an incumbrance. We have undoubtedly already a larger proportion of cleared land in Vermont than would be required, with proper culture, for the support of a much greater population than we now possess, and every additional acre both lessens our means for thorough husbandry, by disproportionately extending its area, and deprives succeeding generations of what, though comparatively worthless to us, would be of great value to them. The functions of the forest, besides supplying timber and fuel, are very various. The conducting powers of trees render them highly useful in restoring the disturbed equilibrium of the electric fluid, they are of great value in sheltering and protecting more tender vegetables against the destructive effects of bleak or parching winds, and the annual deposit of the foliage of deciduous trees, and the decomposition of their decaying trunks, form an accumulation of vegetable mould, which gives the greatest fertility to the often originally barren soils on which they grow, and enriches lower grounds by the wash from rains and the melting snows. The inconveniences resulting from a want of foresight in the economy of the forest are already severely felt in many parts of New England, and even in some of the older towns in Vermont. Steep hill-sides and rocky ledges are well suited to the permanent growth of wood, but when in the rage for improvement they are improvidently stripped of this protection, the action of sun and wind and rain soon deprives them of their thin coating of vegetable mould, and this, when exhausted, cannot be restored by ordinary husbandry. They remain therefore barren and unsightly blots, producing neither grain nor grass, and yielding no crop but a harvest of noxious weeds, to infest with their scattered seeds the richer arable grounds below.

But this is by no means the only evil resulting from the injudicious destruction of the woods. Forests serve as reservoirs and equalizers of humidity. In wet seasons, the decayed leaves and spongy soil of woodlands retain a large proportion of the falling rains, and give back the moisture in time of drought, by evaporation or through the medium of springs. They thus both check the sudden flow of water from the surface into the streams and low grounds, and prevent the droughts of summer from parching our pastures and drying up the rivulets which water them. On the other hand, where too large a proportion of the surface is bared of wood, the action of the summer sun and wind scorches the hills which are no longer shaded or sheltered by trees, the springs and rivulets that found their supply in the bibulous soil of the forest disappear, and the farmer is obliged to surrender his meadows to his cattle, which can no longer find food in his pastures, and sometime even to drive them miles for water. Again, the vernal and autumnal rains, and the melting snows of winter, no longer intercepted and absorbed by the leaves or the open soil of the woods, but falling everywhere upon a comparatively hard and even surface, flow swiftly over the smooth ground, washing away the vegetable mould as they seek their natural outlets, fill every ravine with a torrent, and convert every river into an ocean. The suddenness and violence of our freshets increases in proportion as the soil is cleared; bridges are washed away, meadows swept of their crops and fences, and covered with barren sand, or themselves abraded by the fury of the current, and there is reason to fear that the valleys of many of our streams will soon be converted from smiling meadows into broad wastes of shingle and gravel and pebbles, deserts in summer, and seas in autumn and spring. The changes, which these causes have wrought in the physical geography of Vermont, within a single generation, are too striking to have escaped the attention of any observing person, and every middle-aged man who revisits his birth-place after a few years of absence, looks upon another landscape than that which formed the theatre of his youthful toils and pleasures. The signs of artificial improvement are mingled with the tokens of improvident waste, and the bald and barren hills, the dry beds of the smaller streams, the ravines furrowed out by the torrents of spring and the diminished thread of interval that skirts the widened channel of the rivers, seem sad substitutes for the pleasant groves and brooks and broad meadows of his ancient paternal domain. If the present value of timber and land will not justify the artificial replanting of grounds injudiciously cleared, at least nature ought to be allowed to reclothe them with a spontaneous growth of wood, and in our future husbandry a more careful selection should be made of land for permanent improvement. It has long been a practice in many parts of Europe, as well as in our older settlements, to cut the forests reserved for timber and fuel at stated intervals. It is quite time that this practice should be introduced among us. After the first felling of the original forest it is indeed a long time before its place is supplied, because the roots of old and full grown trees seldom throw up shoots, but when the second growth is once established, it may be cut with great advantage, at periods of about twenty-five years, and yields a material, in every respect but size, far superior to the wood of the primitive tree. In many European countries, the economy of the forest is regulated by law; but here, where public opinion determines, or rather in practice constitutes law, we can only appeal to an enlightened self-interest to introduce the reforms, check the abuses, and preserve us from an increase of the evils I have mentioned. . . .

Source: George P. Marsh, *Address Delivered before the Agricultural Society of Rutland County, Sept. 30, 1847* (Rutland, Vt.: Rutland Herald, 1848), pp. 17-19.

DOCUMENT 16

Democratic State Convention (1848)
VERMONT WATCHMAN & STATE JOURNAL

This Convention came off formally on Tuesday; but the battle began at a preliminary meeting on Monday evening—a second edition in miniature of the Baltimore Convention [The Democratic National Convention, held in May 1848, which selected Michigan's U.S. Senator Lewis Cass, the favorite of the party's southern wing, as its candidate for president], bordering very nearly at times upon a general row. In short, for the first time in Vermont, there was a public demonstration of division in the democratic ranks—a recognition of *two* democracies, called in New York by the euphonious names of Old Hunkers and Barnburners. Stephen S. Brown of St. Albans, E.D. Barber of Middlebury, Lucius E. Chittenden of Burlington, and a gentleman from Milton, whose name we do not know, took strong grounds for the Wilmot proviso [which called for the banning of slavery in territories that might be acquired from Mexico] and denounced GEN. CASS. We did not hear Mr. Brown's opening, which was said to be very strong. Mr. Barber argued the matter well: he regarded the question to be simply this—whether the democracy must support CASS and sacrifice all their principles in reference to the extension of Slavery—or abandon Cass and stick to their principles. This was the issue forced upon them by the South, and by Gen. Cass himself in the Nicholson letter [in which Cass asserted Congress lacked authority to regulate slavery in the western territories]. The Baltimore Convention might have avoided it; might, and in his judgment ought, to have presented a candidate unshackled, and left the question to Congress—just as the Whigs have done, thought we: but they had forced a choice between Cass and principle—and he was for sticking to principle. Mr. B. was interrupted, in no friendly way: but it only stirred up the fire within him, and elicited a fine peroration which carried the house by storm, and brought out a grand burst of applause, even against the prevailing under current of feeling. Mr. Chittenden spoke very handsomely, and argued the Wilmot proviso with a good deal of ability—effectively quoting and contrasting the opinions of men learned in constitutional law with the positions of the Nicholson letter. The founders of the Constitution, nearly all our Presidents, and jurists such as [John] MARSHALL, [James] KENT and [Joseph] STORY, all had affirmed the power of Congress to the fullest extent over federal territory; and it had remained for *Lewis Cass* to swallow his own speeches and announce the entirely new discovery that Congress had *no* constitutional power to act at all. Then, said he, as an honest man—as a man bound by the solemn sanctions of his official oath—Lewis Cass as President would be bound to veto any act prohibiting slavery in territory now free; and is the very man of whom Mr. [Paul] Dillingham [Jr.] in October last said, and solemnly invoked God to witness the declaration, that no Northern Democrat could ever support him.

On the Hunker side, Judge [Levi B.] Vilas of Chelsea, Judge [Daniel] Cobb of Strafford, and Judge

[David P.] Noyes of Morristown, were conspicuous. They contented themselves with advocating the necessity of adhering to the party, and endeavored as well as they could to dodge the Slavery question, by such stuff as is to be found in any late number of the *Patriot*: but the spider's webs were demolished without mercy. The speakers endeavored to be courteous; and the Chairman (Mr. [Jefferson P.] Kidder of Orange Co.) tried to keep order; but the Barnburners were grossly insulted, particularly by Judge Cobb, who denied their right to sit in the Convention and advised them to join the Whigs. These and like insults only provoked still stronger declaration of resistance to Cass from the other side. Finally, one of the Hunkers rose for a third time, to support the "hero of Hull's surrender," and the audience by consent quit the house.

Thus ended the first chapter.

The second chapter was like unto the first, and so on until the end. Tuesday morning the Convention opened in form, and (evidently by a preconcerted movement,) Hon. Levi B. Vilas (old Hunker) was put into the chair. We pass over the formal business and deal only with the cream of the matter.

Hon. Paul Dillingham Jr. took the floor, and in a brief speech declined running as a candidate for Governor, it would interfere with his business; but besides that he didn't agree with the Democracy on certain important points. In the main he accorded with the sentiments of MARTIN VAN BUREN.

Sundry of the old Hunkers deprecated this movement of Paul's; if he didn't exactly stick to all the notions of the party, they would stick to him.

S.H. Price Esq. of Windsor spoke ably for an hour and a half. The Wilmot proviso was the great question of the day, absorbing all others; and if Gen. Cass and the Democratic party are faithless to the country in this emergency, he must and would quit both.

Hon. Stephen S. Brown of St. Albans, was a Barnburner too, and stood on the same ground. He warned the Democracy that if the Rubicon is passed now there would be no return. He said that Gen. Cass could not get forty votes in the town of St. Albans.

In the afternoon a long and bitter fight ensued about delegates from Swanton. There were two sets, Barnburners and Old Hunkers. It had been whispered by the Old Hunker leaders, and especially by the Patriot Junto, that every Barnburner was to be ousted—

"we'll put our foot upon their necks," said they. But it was awkward ousting men who had regular credentials. Swanton, however, had two sets of men and two sets of credentials—so here was a fair chance for Old Hunker vengeance. A committee was raised and reported to admit the Hunkers alone—thus rejecting the Barnburners. Messrs. [Norman L.] Whittemore, Chittenden, and Barber defended the Barnburner delegation; they were the true representatives of Swanton—a town where Cass men are scarce; while the Hunkers, they insisted, were a spurious set, appointed at a secret meeting but done in the custom house. But in vain; Messrs. [Isaac B.] Bowdish, Judge Noyes, Judge [Calvin] Blodgett and Judge Cobb said the custom-house delegation must come in; and so said a majority of the Convention. The democracy of Swanton are really in a pickle: if they won't have Cass to rule them, they are forced to succumb to the custom house. Shouldn't wonder if they have a word to say about the business.

The next interesting demonstration was from Mr. Barber. He introduced a resolution, declaring substantially *that Congress has the constitutional power to prohibit Slavery in newly acquired territory, and ought to exercise it immediately*. A Hunker met this with a motion to *lay it on the table*. Bradley Barlow and Judge Noyes were for thus killing the unwelcome intruder. Messrs. Barber and Chittenden however compelled the Convention to face the music: if they laid the resolution upon the table, they declared that it would be regarded as a rejection, and the friend of freedom must bolt. This settled the hash—the motion to lay upon the table was withdrawn, and a direct vote forced. The ayes were loud—some twenty or thirty uttered a strong *No*; and the resolution was declared Carried amidst a storm of hisses from one side and cheers from the other.

Mr. Barber was not slow to avail himself of this temporary advantage gained by the Barnburners. You have solemnly resolved, said he, that Congress has the power and ought to exercise it—now do you mean to stultify yourselves by voting for LEWIS CASS—the man who denies this power and pledges himself to Veto any exercise of it? True enough—stultify. But the Hunker's denied that this was Cass's position, whereupon Mr. Barber just read from the Nicholson letter the very words of Cass denying the power in question, and eloquently invoked the Convention not to be so grossly inconsistent as to denounce his doctrines and yet sustain the man—Veto and all. In one of his speeches Mr. B. introduced a letter showing that Hon. John Kellogg of Benson, and his son Loyal C. are opposed to Cass; whereupon Mr. [John C.] Sawyer vouched that Rutland County Democrats are unanimous—the Kelloggs not being of them, but old National Republicans.

This scene ended the nominations were made: Dillingham for Governor—Charles K. Field for Lieut. Governor and J.T. Marston for Treasurer.

The resolutions followed quietly after the old sort, until up came one ratifying the nomination of CASS and [William O.] BUTLER. Mr. Barber rose—the gag was at once applied, in shape of *the previous question.* Withdrawn after hard begging, and Mr. B. proceeded to speak against Cass. Hon. S.S. Brown took the floor—but the gag was applied in his case unrelentingly—so also in the case of Mr. Poland of Lamoille County. The Barnburners having been thus choked off, the question was put, and greeted by the Hunkers with a fierce yell in the affirmative. The noes were called—the Barnburners yelled defiance in a round *No.* The resolution was declared to be carried amid another storm of hisses and cheers; and at once a goodly portion of the Barnburners took their hats and *retired from the Convention.*

Electors at large were nominated (L.B. Vilas and John S. Robinson, we believe); Mr. Dillingham swallowed his morning's speech and came out for Cass and Butler; a few Hunkers tried to smooth over matters, and then the Convention adjourned.

At times, the Convention was something like pandemonium—hisses, cheers, and curses, mingled in strange confusion—and the President (a delegate to Baltimore), naively remarked that it was *very much like the Baltimore Convention, only it was not quite so bad.*

We guess *both* will prove sore jobs for the dough faces.

Some of the Hunkers were mortified at the position in which Mr. Barber has placed them, and moved *to reconsider the vote*; but they dare not try it. More will yet be mortified; but "what's done can't be helped." The Old Hunker democracy has effectually stultified itself, as Mr. Barber justly remarked.

Source:*Vermont Watchman & State Journal*, 13 July 1848.

Document 17

Burlington's Anti-Irish Ordinances (c. 1849)

Whereas the indiscriminate importation and landing at this Port of foreign immigrants, subjects of Great Britain, in the large and crowded masses in which it is now and for some weeks past has been accustomed by Masters of vessels on Lake Champlain, large numbers of which immigrants are both paupers and diseased, and become a charge upon the Town, and a cause of sickness, and a source of danger to the public health: and as we adjud[g]e it to be necessary for the public health and safety to make some regulations concerning the same it is therefore ordered that there be established the following

Regulations

1. That _____ is hereby appointed Inspecting Physician for the purposes herein named.

2. All Masters of vessels arriving at this port from any port in Canada, are forbidden to land or set on shore any foreign immigrant subject of Great Britain without the consent of the Inspecting Physician.

3. The Inspecting Physician will be on the docks at the usual landing places of the several Steam Boats, at the time of their arrival as near as may be, so as to cause no unnecessary delay, and in case of arrival [of] two vessels together, it will be his duty to inspect the boat that first touches the dock; the other boat to wait if need be until he is ready to board her.

4. The Inspector will not allow any such person to land unless they appear to be in good health, unless in his discretion he deems it safe for the public health; all others, the Masters of such vessels will be required to retain on board.

5. If such vessel shall afterwards arrive here from any other place, the Masters thereof are forbidden to land any person so previously rejected by the Inspector.

6. Every Master of a vessel whether steam or other vessel, who shall violate any of these regulations, will forfeit for each offence one hundred dollars, and said penalty will be rigidly enforced as provided by Law.

Source: City of Burlington Papers, Special Collections, Bailey/Howe Library, University of Vermont.

SECTION SIX

1850-1870
Emergence of a Mature Society

VERMONT VOICES

SECTION SIX

1850-1870
Emergence of a Mature Society

Introduction

By the 1850s, much of the turbulence and instability of Vermont's earlier years had subsided. The "youthful energies" of the 1820s-1840s that "flowed swiftly," according to David Ludlum, into myriad social and religious reform efforts became largely absorbed by the overriding issue of anti-slavery. Multiparty political conflict gave way to the stabilizing one-party dominance of emergent Republicanism. Economically, the state moved beyond the stage of land settling, farm making, and road clearing, to an era characterized increasingly by farm consolidation and specialization, innovative village industrialism, and the railroad. In Ludlum's words, by the mid-1850s Vermont had "reached maturity."

The coming of the railroad affected life in Vermont more than any other single development in the nineteenth century. In 1850 the state's two most important rail lines, the Vermont Central and the Rutland Road, were in their first year of full operation, and a third, the Connecticut & Passumpsic Rivers Railroad, was under construction. By 1855, five hundred miles of track had been laid, and within another fifteen years most railroad building in the state was completed.

The railroads provided Vermont with direct links to the regional and national markets that previously had been blocked by rugged Green Mountain barriers, and raised hopes in towns along the routes that trade and jobs would increase. Agricultural markets in fact did expand, the value of nearby farms increased, and the isolation of many hinterland communities was permanently pierced. There were drawbacks, as well, however. After southern New England established rail connections in the West, farmers in Vermont and the rest of northern New England began experiencing stiff competition from that region's cheap agricultural goods. In addition, the lower-priced products shipped into the state from large manufacturing centers to the south drove out of business many of Vermont's small local industries such as wood and flax mills, foundries, tanneries, and starch factories. The railroads also facilitated Vermonters' out-migration to eastern cities or the western frontier, and from small hill farms to valley villages and towns, by making the move less time-consuming and expensive.

Document 1 is a broadside circulated in 1851 by the Connecticut & Passumpsic Rivers Railroad extolling the convenience and ease of overland passenger travel within, as well as beyond, the Green Mountains. The state's railroad companies initially lured passengers with offers of free rides and half fares; by the early 1850s enterprising managers introduced the use of coupons enabling a traveler to more conveniently transfer from one line to another, on an extended trip. Passenger travel, nevertheless, remained routinely uncomfortable and inconvenient, with poor connections and overnight stops. It is not surprising that in 1860 the income from the Vermont Central's freight business was almost double that of its passenger returns.

Document 2 is an excerpt from the recollections of Jonas Wilder, a Massachusetts-born pioneer of Vermont's early railroad era, who claimed to have conceived the idea of the passenger coupon. Wilder describes his involvement in the development of two of Vermont's first railways and the struggles to turn those early roads into profitable enterprises through such innovations as the refrigerator car for butter and cheese producers, and freight rate concessions for industrial shippers, as well as the coupon ticket for passenger travel.

Although Vermont's economy remained heavily dependent on agriculture, the railroad symbolized a new direction in the state's growth. The ease in transport of goods and products by rail renewed interest in manufacturing and industrial development. A handful of factory towns, including St. Johnsbury, Colchester, and Bennington, surged in growth, and Rutland-area marble and slate quarries accelerated production. The hub of Vermont's nineteenth-century small-town industrialism, however, was the Connecticut River village of Windsor, which emerged to play an influential national and international role in machine-tool and firearms manufacturing. A central figure in Windsor's early machine-tool development was Richard Smith Lawrence. Born in Chester, Vermont, in 1817, Lawrence combined mechanical and business ingenuity. By the early 1850s, his techniques in the manufacture of rifles brought worldwide fame to the Robbins and Lawrence Armory and Machine Shop. **Document 3** provides excerpts from Lawrence's memoir of those formative early years of industrial Windsor.

Among the issues that occupied Vermonters' attention at mid-century, women's rights received scant notice. This was so despite the increased public participation by women in broad-based popular movements such as anti-slavery and temperance. Clarina I. H. Nichols' accomplishments consequently were remarkable for her time. Born in Townshend, Vermont, in 1812, she was a divorced mother with three children when she married Brattleboro newspaper publisher George W. Nichols. She took control of, and edited for ten years, her husband's *Windham County Democrat*, and also stumped the Green Mountains speaking out for causes ranging from temperance and abolitionism to the social reformism of Charles Fourier. Women's rights was her greatest interest, however, and she was the most outspoken and eloquent advocate for the interests of women in the state until 1853, when the *Democrat* folded and the Nichols family emigrated to Kansas to join that territory's struggle over slavery. She later wrote of hoping to find in Kansas territory less resistance to progress for women than "in conservative old Vermont, whose prejudices were so much stronger than its convictions, that justice to women must stand a criminal trial in every Court of the State to win, and then pay the costs." Although the main focus of Nichols' attacks was the legal and property restrictions of married women, she began in 1849 to advocate woman suffrage as the method for ending such restrictions. In an unprecedented appearance before a joint session of the Vermont General Assembly in 1852, she proposed a bill granting women the right to vote in school meetings. It was the first public call for woman suffrage in the state. Legislators did not support her request, responding in a committee report that "the other sex can best discharge their duties as educators, at the fireside or in the school room." **Document 4** is a speech Clarina Nichols delivered in September 1853, at the Woman's Rights Convention in New York City.

Native Americans seeking redress of grievances fared no better in Vermont than advocates of women's rights. As early as 1798 (see Section 4, Document 5), and again in 1812 and 1826, the Iroquois nations of Canada submitted petitions to the Vermont legislature, without success, requesting compensation for hunting grounds taken from them in the state. When the Iroquois chiefs pressed their petition again in 1853, the legislature referred the matter to Governor John C. Robinson, who appointed Timothy P. Redfield, a Montpelier lawyer, to investigate the claims. **Document 5** is Redfield's report, filed with the General Assembly in 1854. Legislators found it sufficiently persuasive to request the governor to appoint yet another commissioner, to negotiate the claim directly with the Iroquois representatives. In 1855 the state senate passed a bill granting the modest sum of five thousand dollars in final settlement of the Iroquois petition; the house, however, decisively rejected it. A disappointed editor of the *Burlington Free Press* futilely called on house legislators to reverse their stand and accept the "sense of justice" on which the senate bill had been based, warning that "the future historian" would otherwise "say that Vermont was ready enough to demand justice for her own people and to insist upon its being done by others to all men; but when the red men petitioned for justice to be done them, her heart was hard and her ears were deaf."

Issues of Iroquois claims and women's rights may not have attracted the interest of Vermont's political parties, but anti-slavery did. In fact, by the early 1850s, the deepening sentiment for abolition had thoroughly undermined both the Whigs' and Democrats' stability. Portraying themselves as earnest opponents of the "peculiar institution," the two parties nevertheless alienated supporters by continuing to go along with the compromising ways, on this issue, of their national organizations. The Vermont Free Soil Party was also in a weakened condition, having in 1853 entered into a coalition with the morally compromised Democrats to oust the Whigs from their hold on state power. By 1854, consequently, the old ties of all three Vermont parties seemed no longer binding, a fact made clear in local responses to the Kansas-Nebraska bill, maneuvered through the U.S. Congress by the Vermont-born senator from Illinois, Stephen A. Douglas. Signed into law on May 30, the bill contained provisions replacing the Missouri Compromise with the concept of "popular sovereignty" in determining whether new territories in the West would be slave or free. Popular sovereignty allowed residents in each western territory to decide the status of slavery for themselves. Anti-slavery spokesmen across the North denounced the legislation, and in Vermont, Whigs, Free Soilers, and some restless Democrats united in their condemnation of the bill.

Circumstances were right for a new party, and at a mass convention in Montpelier, on July 13, 1854, a group of six hundred to eight hundred people—frustrated by the three-way state political struggles of the recent past and drawn by the moral issue of slavery—formed themselves into a coalition of voters to "be known as Republicans." Over the next year this union of former Whigs, Democrats, Free Soilers, temperance enthusiasts, and assorted other interests solidified as a permanent party. The July 1854 meeting in Montpelier preceded by two years the organizing of the national Republican Party. **Document 6** contains excerpts from the "Platform and Resolutions" of the historic mass convention.

The new Republican Party faced an early challenge from the Know-Nothing Party (also known as the American Party) of Vermont, a group animated by anti-Catholic, anti-Irish hostility. In the mid-1850s, Vermont became one of several states—most of them in the Northeast—where such nativist sentiment gained a strong, however short-lived, grip. Know-Nothingism attracted many of the state's principal leaders. Ryland Fletcher, of Cavendish, after winning election in 1854 as lieutenant governor on the Republican/Whig slate, attended the Know-Nothings' National Council meeting in Philadelphia in 1855 as a Vermont delegate. In 1856 the Vermont Know-Nothings made him their candidate for governor. A few weeks after this designation, Fletcher attended the Republican Party's first national convention and accepted the Vermont Republicans' nomination for governor in a pairing with lieutenant governor nominee James M. Slade, who as president of the Know-Nothing State Council was the movement's leading Vermont spokesman. In the fall elections the two men easily won, each of them attracting more than 70 percent of the votes cast.

As Fletcher's experience indicates, the Republican Party leaders' method for dealing with the Know-Nothings was to absorb them into the new party's already eclectic constituent mix. While publicly criticizing the secrecy of Know-Nothing methods, they avoided direct conflicts and made clear their support for nativist "convictions." **Document 7** is a private letter written in April 1855 by U.S. Congressman George P. Marsh to former Whig governor (and future Republican governor) Erastus Fairbanks. This communica-

tion between two of the state's most prominent Republicans provides evidence of the strong influence of anti-Catholic sentiment at the highest levels of the new party's leadership.

During the 1850s, "emigration fever" continued to absorb Vermonters. Broadsides and advertisements in newspapers proclaimed the transportation conveniences and lowered departure expenses made possible through the state's new railroads and—in summer months—on regularly scheduled packet lines in all-water routes through Lake Champlain and the Great Lakes. **Document 8** is a broadside promoting the advantages of organized group migration. Although most emigrants journeyed individually or in small informal parties, some signed on with groups such as the Vermont Emigrant Association, which was organized by Rutland residents in the spring of 1855. Between one hundred and two hundred men and their families responded to the association's appeal. This group's ultimate destination turned out to be land owned by the Illinois Central Railroad in La Salle County, Illinois, southwest of Chicago, and these Green Mountain frontiersmen gave the name "New Rutland" to their new community. Many non-migrating Vermonters, however, reacted bitterly to group efforts such as those of the Vermont Emigrant Association to induce residents to abandon the state, one Windsor newspaper editor even going so far as to demand that organizers of emigration colonies be charged with treason.

During the 1840s and 1850s the Vermont General Assembly repeatedly returned to the issue of slavery, passing resolutions and legislation aimed at encouraging a national commitment to restriction by every means legally available. The Montpelier enactments included a "personal liberty" bill in 1843 barring Vermont's courts and magistrates from issuing warrants for the arrest of fugitive slaves and a pronouncement in 1849 that slavery was a "crime against humanity." Such legislative declarations became so well-known beyond the state that national abolitionist crusader James G. Birney asserted he had never seen the anti-slavery cause "stand on such high ground among political men as it does among those of the Vermont Legislature." **Document 9** is that body's reaction to the U.S. Supreme Court's decision in 1857, in the famous case of *Scott* v. *Sanford*. At issue was the freedom of the slave Dred Scott, but the court's decision also had large implications for the spread of slavery into the western territories and elsewhere. The Vermont legislature passed joint resolutions denouncing the decision. Legislators then followed up these resolutions by enacting a bill declaring that no person "within this State" should be considered as property, and that every slave who came into the state, voluntarily or involuntarily, was to be free.

The Civil War began in April of 1861, and Vermonters responded readily in defense of "the Union, the Constitution, and the integrity of the United States Government," as Governor Erastus Fairbanks characterized the conflict. During the devastating four-year military struggle that followed, Vermont underwent immediate and far-reaching changes. In the short term the war had a unifying effect as Vermonters temporarily set aside divisive local concerns and rallied to the larger cause of union. "All partizan differences are ignored and lost in the higher principle of patriotism," Governor Fairbanks proclaimed. The conflict also provided a vigorous economic stimulus felt primarily in the larger towns, as war-driven needs resulted in lucrative contracts for Green Mountain manufacturers of rifles, gunpowder, and woolen cloth; and in expanded sales for producers of lumber, blankets, uniforms, and hardware. State government, too, enlarged its scope of activities, taking on the role of managing the Vermont war effort—raising, equipping, and sustaining troops until they officially entered federal service.

On April 24, 1861, eight days after President Abraham Lincoln's nationwide call for troops, Governor Fairbanks convened a special joint session of the Vermont General Assembly. **Document 10** is the speech Fairbanks presented to legislators on that occasion, in which he pledged that "the United States Government must be sustained and the rebellion suppressed, at whatever cost of men and treasure." The General Assembly demonstrated its agreement by appropriating one million dollars and authorizing the raising and equipping of six military regiments, although Lincoln had asked Vermont for only one.

Vermont's young men enthusiastically answered the call for volunteers, drawing broad support from their communities. One employer, Charles Clement, a marble dealer, told his enlisting employees, as they departed for military encampment, that should they die, he would allow their families to remain in their tenements, rent-free, until the war's end. "All we ask in return," he told

them, is that when engaging the Confederates, "you make a market for all the gravestones possible."

Despite a militia that had been in organizational disarray for years, Vermont's young recruits brought skill as well as enthusiasm to their soldiering tasks. Three of the new Union Army's eighteen elite companies of superior marksmen known as the U.S. Sharpshooters were composed of Vermonters. Recruiters for these companies staged sharpshooter tryouts at a number of sites around the state, including one held on August 27, 1861, at Bellows Falls, as is indicated in the broadside announcement in **Document 11**. **Document 12**, also a recruiting advertisement, unambiguously defines the war's goal as "putting down treason" and emphasizes the remunerative features of the volunteer's military service.

In all, more than 34,000 Vermont men eventually served in the war, 5,200 of whom, or 15 percent, lost their lives, either from wounds, disease, or accidents. Many of those who served left written accounts of their experiences, in letters, diaries, and memoirs. **Document 13** presents excerpts from the diary of Rutland volunteer William H. Jackson, who after the war went on to a distinguished career as a photographer of the American West. Jackson recorded these diary entries during his Vermont camp days in Rutland and at Camp Holbrook near Brattleboro, with Company K of the Twelfth Vermont Regiment, prior to his being shipped out of state. The Twelfth Vermont Regiment eventually became part of the Second Vermont Brigade, whose most notable engagement came in July 1863 at the Battle of Gettysburg. **Document 14** provides excerpts from a firsthand account of Vermont soldiers' central role in turning back Pickett's Charge, one of the most dramatic battlefield encounters of the war. By war's end, two-fifths of the men of the Second Vermont Regiment had been killed or wounded. **Document 15**, an 1864 recruiting broadside announcing the organization of a new regiment, the Seventeenth Vermont Regiment, provides evidence of the difficulties state authorities experienced in obtaining recruits after three years of carnage. The Seventeenth Regiment, organized in February and March of 1864, was the last that the state of Vermont provided in the long struggle.

The hostilities did not all occur in distant locations; on October 19, 1864, St. Albans, Vermont, became the scene of the Civil War's northernmost military action.

Document 16 is an eyewitness account, by a local citizen, of the "St. Albans Raid," as the infamous event came to be known. The raiders, about two dozen Confederate followers, launched their attack from across the Canadian border with the immediate goal of robbing the town's banks and escaping back into Canada. They hoped as well that this northern display of southern military strength might cause Lincoln to divert Union troops to Vermont in numbers sufficient to relieve some of Grant's relentless pressure on the Southern front. They believed the incident might also provoke a retaliatory attack by Vermonters into Canada that would bring Great Britain into the war against the North. Only the bank-robbing goal was achieved. As the raiders retreated back across the border, Canadian officials took most of them into custody, but to Vermonters' dismay, their court cases ended indecisively, and after a year in Canadian jails authorities freed the Confederates to return south.

The most immediate reaction by Vermonters to the St. Albans event was to hurriedly establish a provisional military force to guard against further attacks from the north. William W. Grout, of Barton, a future Vermont congressman, issued the broadside that is **Document 17**, appealing for help to "every man who has a musket or rifle," and he initially commanded the frontier cavalry "division" that responded to his call. This provisional body eventually was formed into companies that operated as part of the Twenty-sixth New York Cavalry, defending New York and Vermont territory along the Canadian border until the war's end in May of 1865.

With the war securely in the past, divisive state-level concerns again pushed to the surface. Tensions between a continuing spirit of reform and the forces of conservative caution characterized this immediate post-war period. The changed conditions were clearly visible in the re-emergence of the issue of woman suffrage. Introduced initially by Clarina Nichols in 1852, it had briefly regained attention in 1858 when delegates at a "Free Convention," held in Rutland, adopted a resolution declaring "that immediate steps should be taken to . . . place Woman politically, educationally, industrially, and socially, on perfect equality with Man." The Republican Party, which by this time had established its hegemony in state politics, held a conservative position on woman suffrage, as it did on most issues. In addition, the *Burlington Free Press* routinely trumpeted the view that most Vermonters, including most women, were not yet ready for votes for women. Consequently, when a three-man study committee of the Vermont Council of Censors, in July 1869, recommended extending "the right of suffrage to all citizens of the State, without regard to sex," an intense rhetorical battle was joined. The Censors' proposal asserted that "even-handed justice, a fair application of the principles of the Declaration of Independence and of our State Convention . . . give woman the ballot, and do not shut out from it one-half of the intelligence and more than one-half of the moral power of the people. Custom and prejudice alone stand in the way." Opponents' criticism of this view included the speech excerpted in **Document 18**, by Charles C. Dewey, whose perspective ultimately carried the day. At the constitutional convention that was convened in 1870 for the purpose of acting on proposals by the Censors, the elected delegates sent woman suffrage down to a crushing 233-1 defeat.

Document 1

Advertisement for Connecticut & Passumpsic Rivers Railroad (1851)

(depicted on facing page)

Source: Advertisement for Connecticut & Passumpsic Rivers Railroad, 1851, Broadside, Special Collections, Bailey/Howe Library, University of Vermont. Reprinted courtesy of Special Collections, UVM Libraries.

Document 2

Journal of a Vermont Railroad Pioneer (c. 1850)

Jonas Wilder

. . . At this time railroad building had got a start. The Boston & Albany R. R. was built and in operation. The Fitchburg Road was running from Boston to Fitchburg. The Lowell & Boston was completed to Lowell. The Boston & Providence was running. Some disconnected roads were running between Albany & Buffalo. This was about all the roads we had, but other roads were being constructed to make through lines. The Central Vermont R. R. had begun grading.

I was offered good pay, ($50 a month) to take charge of the commissary and supply departments on the Central Vermont construction.

We finished the eastern division to Montpelier, Vt., but funds ran short and we had to hold up. We moved over to New York and graded 30 miles of the Ogdensburgh R. R., then the Central had raised more funds, and we came back and finished grading. They wanted to push the work and divided up into four divisions of about 12 miles each. I was placed in charge of one division, the president another, and the superintendent and engineer each a section. I still had the care of the supplies. I finished my grading nearly two months before the others. When track laying began they asked me to go into the operating department, and gave me the management of the freight, tickets, and the organi-

zation of the stations on the western division. As the track was laid to them, I was to employ the men and an agent to manage, when I moved up to the next station.

We reached the last station before Burlington, our terminal, some two and one-half miles distant, and had to wait there nearly a year to take out a deep cut. I built a temporary station beyond, which reduced the distance to one mile.

A little out of the village on the R. R. was a lime kiln with fine quality of inexhaustible lime stone, owned by Judge Underwood. He was a rather easy going business man, but very social; he often came into my office. One day I asked him to give me 15 or 20 barrels of lime and I would ship them free to the important towns on the line, such as Concord, Manchester, Lawrence, Nashua, and Lowell, and then have the station agent give them to the best builders, and to the Lowell and Pepperell Bleacheries. This he agreed to. I wrote the agents to find the price of lime at their place and write me, and if any one wished to buy, to put me in communication with them. The scheme worked and orders came in and the result was that he had to build six more kilns and gave the R. R. line nearly a $1,000 freight per month.

Another, The Peck Co., were wholesale heavy hardware and grocery merchants in Burlington and had a warehouse on the lake dock. A schooner from Canada left with them some 16,000 feet of fine Canada pine lumber to sell; it was the best quality. Deacon Chase of Nashua came up to buy iron, nails, and some kinds of groceries; he had a sash and door factory and kept a store. When down to the storehouse, Peck showed him the lumber; he was pleased with it and the price was very low, but said he could not buy because the freight would prevent. Peck asked him to ride over and see me; they came in and Peck made known the business. It went through my mind like electricity that if we could start a trade in that Canada pine it would add largely to our earnings. I said to the Deacon, "I will ship the lumber at your own price." He replied, "That ain't quite fair; I have no idea what you can afford; make some suggestions."

I said, "How would $4 per thousand do?" He asked, "Will you take it at that rate?" I replied, "Yes." Turning to Peck, he said, "I will take it."

Some three weeks later a man came into my office, said his name was Barns, asked me if I had

Document 1

shipped some pine lumber to Mr. Chase of Nashua at $4 a thousand. I said yes: he then asked if I would ship for him at the same rates (he was a lumber merchant). I said, yes, all you wish.

He told me he was started for Canada to buy lumber, if he could get those rates. I told him I would extend it at same rates to Manchester, Lawrence, Nashua, Lowell, and Boston. That settled it for Burlington to be a lumber market; in four years, Burlington was only third lumber market in the states.

The road had all it could handle and its competitor, the Rutland & Burlington R. R., had to come to the relief to handle the lumber; that price remained till 1863. In war time it was raised to $5 but since came back to $4.

I mention these circumstances to show the importance of R. R. management being ever on the watch to assist in developing new business, and do it at once.

. . .

We got into Burlington late in the spring of 1850. The Ogdensburgh R. R. was completed and operating. Freight began to come from the west through the Welland Canal, over the Ogdensburgh Road to Rouse's Point, and we had a steamboat that brought it to Burlington, thence by rail to Boston and all parts east.

The Vermont & Canada was nearly completed giving railroad connection with the Ogdensburgh R. R. at Rouse's Point by a bridge across the foot of Lake Champlain. The bridge was expected to be done for winter use, but there was a delay and the lake froze. But freight continued to come. The Ogdensburgh Station was filled, and the elevator filled with grain; then the big station at the lake was filled with flour, and no way of getting it across to the railroad.

The president asked me if I had men that could run the Burlington station; I told him I had. He then said he wanted me to go to Rouse's Point and get the freight over, either by keeping the ice cut to run the boat, or team it across. I found it impossible to keep the boat running, so I hired teams and sledded it across on the ice. It was a hard winter's work and cars were scarce; I could have loaded more if I had had cars. The Boston merchants had drafts coming due on the freight consigned, and to keep them pacified was worse than the work, but I succeeded and the company made me a present of $200 extra for the winter's work. . . .

When east my headquarters were at Rouse's Point. I was in on a vacation about the first of June. I met the superintendent one evening and suggested to him to fit up refrigerator cars. I had been studying up the matter, as St. Lawrence County was a great butter district, with fine butter, but they had to keep it till cool weather and then got only 12 1/2 cents per pound, while such butter in fine condition was selling in Boston from 18 to 20 cents.

The supt. took onto it and ordered the master mechanic to fit up what I wanted under my direction. I advertised it at every station when it would start and that it would run every Monday, also got them to consign to a man in Boston that went from that county. I notified him.

The first car we ran had eight tons. They fitted up eight cars and they ran three and four every week. The rates were just double, but the farmers got four and five cents more for their butter than ever before. This was the first start of refrigerator cars, built and run. . . .

February 13, 1852, I took my position as supt. of the Rutland & Washington R. R. It was not open for business but the track was laid 63 miles connecting with the Troy and Boston R. R. at Eagle Bridge. The working train was working with force to fit it for operating.

March 18th. I made my first time table for opening, but with only one passenger train each way and freight down one day and return the next.

In June I put on an express in connection with the Hudson River Railroad and connecting roads north, making daily service between New York and Montreal each way.

One of the directors was to be what is called general manager. He had no railroad experience, but took upon himself many duties that he little understood; one was to arrange freights for the slate and marble business. These quarries had begun to be developed; their existence on the line was the original inducement to build the road. This manager, like some other railroad men, started in on the principle, "I have got you and you must ship by us," one of the great mistakes in railroading. He organized on the plan of a long road with business developed; we needed more cars and engines. The company issued $300,000 of second mortgage bonds (there were only $200,000 first bonds) to sell, in order to buy cars and engines and finish the track. The bonds could be sold in New York for 90 cents cash, but the Boston Treasurer wanted to sell them in Boston and agreed to furnish the money as wanted. My duties were circumscribed to the running of the trains and charge of the general accounting, but he let me buy the freight cars and I built 20 refrigerator cars, in all 300; he bought the engines and passenger coaches. He bought seven, we had three, seven was all we needed, but like many others at that day that acted as if there was no bottom to the railroad purse, he was proud of his engines and allowed the master mechanic to trim them up with brass, which cost much labor to keep them shining. The money was furnished as agreed, but not a bond sold. Money was obtained from banks and bonds placed for security. Four-month notes, when due, were renewed with interest added or hired to take up the notes; it was like starting a snow ball in a damp snow.

About this time occurred the [Robert] Schuyler fraud of the over-issue of the New York & New Haven R. R. which knocked railroad securities flat; the bonds could not be sold and it resulted in bankruptcy of our road. Slate and marble did not develop as expected, the owners of the quarries were at war with the manager, and the earnings were light, track neglected; it looked like utter ruin. Finally there was a committee appointed to try for an adjustment and start anew. They issued 1,000,000 bonds, settled with old bond-holders, gave two for one, and exchanged bonds for the notes; appointed three trustees, one in Boston, one in New York, and a Vermont lawyer to be managing Trustee; they appointed me agent and supt., no treasurer, directors or president. The Vermont man was a good man, he had no railroad experience; he knew it, and left the business to me. The whole was in bad condition: iron rails bruised on account of neglect, bad ties, and cars and engines needed repairs and no money or credit, with only $8,000 or $10,000 earnings per month. To add to this, Russell Sage had a mortgage on the rolling stock of over $100,000 to be paid by installments, beginning with $3,000 per month and increasing every quarter till paid.

With all this it was not a bright outlook, but I had faith that the road would be paying if the business was properly handled.

First I organized by reducing the expenses as much as I could, having but two prominent officers: a master mechanic to take charge of the repair shops and employ the men—engineers and firemen; the other to take charge of the road bed and employ the men to do the work. All other business I assumed: freight and passenger business, purchasing and supervision of the general office, station agents, and conductors.

The next thing to do, I saw, was that the marble and slate business must be developed to make a success. To do this I called the principal men in the business together and asked them to make a tariff that they would be able to push their business, that their quarries were worthless without the R. R. and the R. R. worthless without the developing of the quarries. We were really partners, and, as business men, should make a fair division of the business. It surprised them that a R. R. should make such a proposition.

They made up a tariff and presented it to me; I looked it over and was satisfied and accepted it. That ended the war between them and the railroad, and the railroad never had any more trouble. The men took hold with courage and the business increased. In other ways I helped to develop business and the earnings increased.

I then went to work to develop the passenger business. The Boston & Albany R. R. was older than the western business from Boston to the west, which was very large at that time. We had a line from Boston to Albany which was 30 miles longer, but made the same price; we got a very small share.

Then single tickets were sold at Boston to Albany; the Fitchburg R. R. conductor took up the ticket and gave his check and so on the passenger was checked through.

I conceived the idea of a coupon ticket, sold at Boston through to destination, and each road take up a coupon; it would be more easily settled between the roads and better for the passenger. I had some samples printed and started west to see if the roads west would accept them.

At Buffalo I saw the supt. of the Lake Shore and presented my plan and the samples; he readily approved of them and said you can go home, I will see that they are good to Sundown, or as far as the railroads are finished and keep me advised how far I could ticket. I arranged in the same way with the Great Western (now Grand Trunk); I printed my tickets to read from Rutland, Vt., our eastern terminal, and placed our tickets in the Fitchburg Station at Boston and the principal stations between Boston and Rutland, they selling their own to Rutland and ours to destination.

I soon found we were getting western passengers, sometimes from 10 to 15. I then got out a map of the line and advertisements and framed them, sent one of the conductors west to distribute them and arranged with the western roads to ticket back over our road in same way; the roads adopted the plan and soon we had passengers from the west, and it grew up to a large business. The Boston & Albany saw we were drawing on their passenger traffic and adopted the coupon ticket. The Fitchburg Road began to use their own tickets and put them to stations in Maine; finally railroads in general adopted the coupon ticket.

Our business increased from $8,000 and $10,000 per month to $30,000, but it was hard struggle the first year to make ends meet. I put the track in fine condition, repaired cars and engines, and all buildings, put all in fine condition and paid off the Sage debt . . . .

Source:*Vermont Quarterly* 14 (July 1946): 122-129.

DOCUMENT 3

Memoirs of a Vermont Mechanic (c. 1850)

RICHARD S. LAWRENCE

. . . Being in my 21st year I thought it time to settle on something in a larger field than found in Brownsville [N.Y.]. Thought I would start for Vermont. . . . took Canal boat for Albany, thence by stage over the Green Mountains to Windsor.

I found Windsor Village a dull place. . . . Found my friends all glad to see me. Visited with them for several weeks. While with Doct. Story found he had two Rifles, one made by his Brother, Asa Story, who had a gun shop close by. This he called his Turkey Rifle, the other was an old Pennsylvania Rifle, full stock, barrel 4 feet long, all rusty. The Doctor said it had been one of the best. He had killed many a deer with it.

I asked him to let me repair the rifle and put on a peep sight. He had heard of this sight but had never seen one. Was very much interested about the sight but did not dare let me repair the Rifle for fear I would spoil it. After a while he consented to let me make the

trial and went over with me to his brother's shop and obtained his consent to let me use his shop and tools. I went to work, took the gun all apart, leaded out the barrel, forged out the sight, finished it and put it on the gun. His brother watched me all day. He had never seen a peep sight and a mere boy handling tools and forging out work as I did was a little astonishing to him. On the Doctor's return from his daily trip he made for the shop to see what I had done with his Rifle. He found it in such nice shape that he could not say too much in my praise.

He made an appointment for a trial the next day as to the shooting qualities. I had most of the day to give the Rifle a trial and adjust the sights. We went out, he paced off 12 rods from a maple tree which had a 3/4 auger hole in (made for sap spill). He said to fire at that. I found a good rest, lay down on the ground and fired. . . . After the third shot I went up to the tree to investigate, and all of the tree balls which I had fired were found in the auger hole.

The Doct. was astonished—dumbfounded. Said he never heard of such shooting. We spent half of the night talking about guns. He said we must go down to Windsor Prison where N. Kendall & Co. were making guns. They must know about the peep sights. Mine was the first ever seen in that section.

We went down to the Prison the next day. The Doct. told them all about the sight and his Rifle. The Company hired me at once for the term of two years at about $100 per year and board. My first work was stocking rifles (short stocks, their rifles were stocked only on the breech). The first day I put on five stocks, all hand work. The next morning Mr. Smith, one of the Company, came along and looked the work over. Said the work was done well but it would never do to rush work as I had, for I would soon gunstock them out of town— must hold up a little and take it more easy. After a few days I was put on iron work.

I made it a point not to let anything be done in the shop that I did not make myself familiar with, and soon found myself capable of doing the best work. . . . At the end of six months from beginning was put in charge of the shop, much to the dislike of the older hands, but I carried the work along without any trouble, to the satisfaction of all. . . .

I continued work at the Prison. This was in 1842. During this year the Co. gave up the gun business. I then engaged with the State as foreman in the carriage department, continued in this position for about one and one-half years, then in company with N. Kendall, hired a shop in Windsor Village on Mill River and started the Custom Gun Works and Jobbing. Carried on the business for about one year, done a fair business.

One day in the winter of 1844 Mr. S. E. Robbins came into the shop and spoke of the Government asking for bids for Rifles. We talked the business over and decided to put in a bid for 10,000 U.S. Rifles. Mr. Robbins, with a friend Price, went on to Washington to put in a bid for the Rifles at $10.90 each, appendages extra. This was 10 cents below any other bid. The contract was awarded to Robbins, Kendall & Lawrence. This was in the time of the Mexican War and the Government was very much in want of Rifles. We made the contract to finish the job in three years. Guns were not made at this day very fast. We had nothing to start with—building or capital. We had much opposition from all the Government Gun Contractors. They said we could never do the work.

We had nerve and pluck and were determined to carry out the contract. The real work fell upon myself, Robbins not being a mechanic and Kendall not exactly calculated for such nice work, made it hard for me. We went to work with a will—bought land, built factories, bought and made machinery with determined will. We started the business in good shape. Soon after finishing the Rifles, Robbins and myself bought out Kendall. Robbins then said to me, "Lawrence, if it were not for you as a mechanic and by your attention to business we could never go along with the heavy outlay (debts) on our hands." We finished the contract 18 months inside of the time. Made a nice thing out of the job.

Went on to Washington. The Ordinance Board (Gen. Talcott) told us that ours was the only Gun Contract ever finished within the contract time. He said, "What do you want now? You have done well and finished." We said, "We want another contract for Rifles." He said, "Come with me over to the Secretary of War's Office" (Sec. Marcy). Gen. Talcott told the Secretary all about our work and wants. The Secretary said they would see about it. On our way back to Gen. Talcott's office he saw that we were a little disappointed. He said, "Go right home and a contract will be sent to you in a few days." The contract came for 15,000 Rifles, which placed us above board.

In manufacturing Govt. Rifles a loss of about 38% was considered for bad material and workmanship. About this time the California Gold excitement was raging. Guns were in great demand. We sold all of our second quality work and good mixt with it, anything to make up the gun for full Govt. price. This was a great relief every way. Things looked very bright. This was in 1849-50.

About this time we contracted with Courtland C. Palmer for the manufacture of 5,000 of the Jennings Rifles, now the Winchester (improved). This required new buildings and machinery. We made the guns. Before this date we were very unfortunately situated about freight, as no Rail Road passed through Windsor. Most of our freight came by team from Boston. About this time the Rail Road was built through Windsor, which put us in the market much to our advantage. The Rail Road contractor, Mr. S. F. Belknap, came to us and wanted to start the car business with us, led us to believe that he could control all the Rail Road car work in that section. We went into the business with him. He put in $20,000 as a silent partner.

We went to a large outlay, and about the time we finished the first cars, Belknap had a quarrel with the President of the Road and we could not sell a car when we expected to sell. We sold the cars to the Rutland and Burlington Road, took stock and lost every dollar. to the tune of $40,000. Then we sold $14,000 to Boston, Concord & Montreal Road, lost it all; $5,000 to Sullivan Road, $75,000 to Vermont Central. This total loss of $134,000 was a drain on the gun work and cramped us terribly.

About this time Belknap died. In settling his estate they brought in a charge of $105,000 against Robbins & Lawrence as money lent. This I knew nothing about. As near as I could learn Belknap & Robbins lost this money in stocks in Boston. We had to pay the charge, which made a total loss up to this time of $239,000, all paid from gun shop business. We gave up the car business after a while. It was a mistake in ever going into this business. . . .

When we first commenced the gun business at Windsor we commenced building nice machinery, made many machines for other gun makers. Made at Windsor for the English Government most of their gun machines for the Enfield armory. We ran a regular machine shop also. . . . I introduced the first edging machine ever in use, on the Sharps gun in Windsor. The principle of this machine is now in general use. Also introduced the first machine for pressing on car wheels on a taper without splining or keying. This was done at Windsor. This principle has since been used in all Rail Road shops. Made a great mistake in not securing patents on both of the above. . . . Introduced the principle of lubricating the bullet for breach loading guns which was the salvation of breach loading guns. The guns were of no use before this. This was done in the winter of 1850.

Source: Joseph Wickham Roe, *English and American Tool Builders* (New Haven, Conn.: Yale University Press, 1916), pp. 283-287, 289-291. Note that in the original, this document appears without paragraphing.

DOCUMENT 4

Speech at the Woman's Rights Convention, New York City (1853)
CLARINA I. H. NICHOLS

Mrs. C. I. H. NICHOLS, editress of the *Windham County Democrat* being introduced, spoke thus:—To establish woman's right to vote, should not, it might naturally be supposed, be a matter of so much difficulty, when we consider the extent to which, in matters of weighty importance, that right has been already conceded to her. In our country we have many private corporations, banks, stock companies, railroad companies, manufacturing companies, in which women are shareholders, and thus have the right, which none dispute, to vote upon questions affecting the interests of those companies. The same is the case in the Bank of England, that great money institution, which could, with a breath, shake every European throne. There, women, as shareholders, have an equal right to vote with them. In the East India company, which holds in its hands the destinies of the millions of Hindostan, woman's pecuniary interest gives her a like control with man over these countless human beings. Inasmuch, then, as woman, where her pecuniary interests are concerned, has found a way that is admitted to be womanly enough of expressing her feelings, I also take it for granted

that she will find a right womanly way of expressing her feelings on those great questions which involve her moral, intellectual, and social, as well as her commercial interests.

Now I will state my reason for desiring to vote—my reason for maintaining that women should have the right to vote; and it is this, that she may have a due control over her own moral, intellectual, and social interests. I want to have this power, because, in not having it, I am deprived of the power of protecting myself and my children, because I do not possess the power which ought to belong to me as a mother.

It is an undisputed fact that, if women were allowed to vote, the best measures for the good of the community would be carried. As it is, when a petition goes up to a legislature, the signatures are reckoned, and it is said, "so many are voters, and so many are women." No one denies that, if women had votes on temperance laws, and such moral reforms, the majority of women would be in favor of them. Friends, I want the right to vote, so that my name, when it appears on a petition, may be reckoned as that of a voter, whether or not I exercise the franchise.

Through the affections of the mother, men have controlled the actions of woman. Woman stands before you, with all the wants of man, and also with all the capability of man to provide for these wants; but the present laws have disowned the capacity of woman from her necessities. From woman all the sphere for the development of her capacities has been taken away; by law and custom she is regarded as dead, she has been legally executed. It is said woman should not go to the polls—she would meet rowdies, the purity of her nature would be sullied by the base contact into which the exercise of political rights would bring her. I maintain, on the contrary, that her going there would have a good effect, and instead of her purity being soiled by the place, the place would receive a purification from her presence. How is it in all the walks where woman now meets man? Whether is *she* lowered, or *he* raised by the contact? In the railroad car, the steamboat, are not the rudenesses of man's nature laid aside when woman enters? Do not courtesy and refinement enter with her, and sanctify the place while she remains? No; the argument is a fallacy, and what it urges as an objection, would really be a strong recommendation. I think I have shown it is not good for men and women to be alone. [Cheers, apparently ironical, and meant to create a disturbance, here interrupted the speaker.]

As I have only twenty minutes to speak, may I beg that you will be good enough to spare your plaudits. I will better occupy my time in explaining my views, than in receiving your demonstrations of applause.

Woman's property is given by the laws to her husband; her children belong to, and can be claimed by, their father, however brutal and degraded that father may have become. Man takes from her her right in property—her right over her own earnings, and offspring and services, and then, to compensate her for the robbery, enacts that she shall be held under no obligation to support her children. Women are not permitted to be, are not, by the law, regarded as fit to be, the guardians of their children, after the death of their husbands; if there be any person to offer opposition to their being so, the guardianship is taken from them. But when a wife dies, the husband becomes, as a matter of course, the legal guardian of the children. If a women marries a second time, she has no power to support her children by a former marriage. Let her bring to her second husband a dower ever so princely, and she cannot *claim* support for her offspring by her former marriage; nay, the second husband can, if he choose, demand a compensation for supporting them.

As widows, too, the law bears heavily on women. If her children have property, she is adjudged unworthy of their guardianship; and although the decree of God has made her the true and natural guardian of her children, she is obliged to pay from her scanty means to be constituted so by the law.

I have conversed with judges and legislators, and tried to learn a reason for these things, but failed to find it. A nobleman once gave me what he probably thought was a good one. "Women," he said to me, "cannot earn as much as men!" We say they should be allowed to earn as much. They have the ability, and the means should not be shut out from them. I have heard of another man who held woman's industrial ability at a low rate. "His wife," he said, "had never been able to do anything but attend to her children." "How many have you?" he was asked; and the answer was—"Nine." Nine children to attend to!—nine children cared for!—and she could do nothing more, the wife of this most reasonable man. Now, which is of more importance to the community, the property which that reasonable

husband made, or the nine children whom that mother brought, with affectionate and tender toil, through the perils of infancy and youth, until they were men and women? Which was of more importance to this land—the property which the father of George Washington amassed, or the George Washington whom a noble mother gave to his country? The name of Washington, his glorious deeds, and the enduring benefits he secured for us, still remain, and will, long after the estates of Washington have passed from his name for ever!

In the State of Vermont, a wife sought a divorce from her husband on the ground of his *intemperance*. They were persons moving among our highest circles—wealthy people; and the wife knew that she could, through the aid of her friends and relations, with the influence and sympathy of the community, obtain a divorce, and a support for her children. That father carried away into Canada one child, a little girl, and paid three hundred dollars to a low, vile Frenchman, that he might keep her from her mother and friends. Three times her almost heart-broken mother went in search of her; twice in vain, but, the third time, she was found. So badly had the poor child been treated in the vile hands in which her father had placed her, that, when recovered, she was almost insensible; and when, by her mother's nursing care, her intelligence was at length restored, her joy at seeing her mother was so violent, that it was feared its excess might prove fatal. The cause came into Court, and the judge decided that the two daughters should be given to their mother, but that the custody of the son should be given to the father. She was acquitted of the least impropriety or indiscretion: yet, though the obscenity and profanity of her husband in his own family was shocking; and it was in the last degree painful to that high-minded woman to see her son brought up under the charge of such a man, the law decided that the unworthy father was the more proper guardian for the boy!

In the Green Mountain State a great many sermons have lately been preached on the text, "*Wives submit yourselves to your husbands.*" The remaining words, "*in the Lord,*" are generally omitted; so that the text is made to appear like an injunction that the wives should submit to their husbands, whether they were in the Lord or in the devil. And the best of all is, that we are told that, although we should be submissive, we could change our husbands from devils into angels. . . .

As to the text which says that woman must obey her husband, surely that is no reason why she should obey all the bachelors and other women's husbands in the community. My husband would have me advocate the claims I do, therefore, by the logic of our opponents, as I should obey him, I should vote, and they should not hinder me.

Source: *Proceedings of the Woman's Rights Convention, Held at Broadway Tabernacle, New York City, Sept. 6 and 7, 1853* (New York: Fowler and Wells, 1853), pp. 57-60, 75-76.

DOCUMENT 5

Report on the Claim of the Iroquois Indians upon the State of Vermont, for Their "Hunting Ground" (1854)
TIMOTHY REDFIELD

To His Excellency Stephen Royce:

On the 14th of June last, I was appointed by the Governor to discharge the duties imposed by the resolution of the last Legislature:

> That his Excellency the Governor be requested to take such measures to ascertain the claims of the Iroquois Indians to compensation for lands in this state, as he shall see fit in his discretion, and cause the result of such examination to be laid before the General Assembly of this State, at the next session.

And I now submit to you "the result of such examination" as I have been able to make.

The Iroquois, who represent the ancient confederacy of "the Six Nations," assert a claim to compensation for lands in this State, with these bounds:

> beginning on the east side of Ticonderoga, from thence to the great Falls, on Otter Creek, and continuing the same course to the height of land that divides the streams between Lake Champlain and Connecticut river, thence along the height of land opposite to Missisquoi, and thence to the Bay.

There seems no reason to doubt that the Iroquois had possession of these lands and exercised dominion over the same, until dispossessed by the encroachments of civilization; and had what has been treated by the United States government, in other cases, *title* to these lands; and have never parted with that title by any treaty or compact, to which they, as a tribe or nation, have been a party.

The Chiefs representing the "Six Nations," A.D. 1798, appeared before the Legislature of this State, then sitting at Vergennes, and preferred their claim to compensation for lands situate within this State, defining the boundaries as they now do. The matter was brought to the attention of the Legislature by a communication from Governor Tichenor, and the Legislature made a small appropriation for their expenses while attending upon the Legislature, and one hundred dollars as a gratuity and token of friendship; and the Governor was empowered to examine their claim, whether the same were founded in justice and equity.

Governor Tichenor made a report against the claim to the next Legislature, A.D. 1799; and the claim was again presented in A.D. 1800, 1812, and 1826, and has been at all times rejected.

It seems not to have been denied, but substantially conceded, that the claimants, prior to the treaty between Great Britain and France, A.D. 1763, had possession of the lands described as their "hunting ground," and such title as Great Britain and the United States have uniformly treated with respect in their intercourse with the Indian tribes.

It will be seen, by the accompanying papers, that the authorities of this State have, at different times, insisted, that they could not treat with the Iroquois without the consent of Congress; that it would be deemed an agreement or compact with a foreign power,—and thus within the prohibition of the tenth section of the first article of the Constitution. At other times it has been claimed that any agreement touching this claim would be in violation of the act of Congress entitled "an act regulating trade and intercourse with Indian tribes," passed July 22, A.D. 1790—which declares: "That no sale of lands made by any Indians, or any nation or tribe of Indians, within the United States, shall be valid to any person or persons; or to any state, whether having the right of preemption to such lands or not, unless the same shall be made and duly executed at some public treaty held under the authority of the United States."

If this were a proposition strictly to *purchase lands* of a tribe of Indians residing within the jurisdiction of a foreign power, by which the Indian yielded his title and possession upon receiving the stipulated consideration, or the assurance therefor, it would obviously be in conflict with the law of Congress, and doubtless obnoxious to that provision of the Constitution. But inasmuch as the jurisdiction of the State over the territory is not disputed, and the lands have been in the peaceable possession of the citizens of this State for more than a half century, with undoubted title to the same, it is submitted that the State might act in the premises; and, if the Legislature should deem that the Iroquois were entitled, in the "*forum of conscience*," to some *remuneration* for lands long since *granted* and appropriated by the State, and should make appropriation for such remuneration, that such proceeding would neither conflict with the provisions of the act of Congress nor the Constitution. If, however, there were scruples on this point, it would seem obvious that, if it were conceded that there was a *duty* upon the State to pay for these lands, it would be no less a duty upon the State to provide the legitimate channel, through which such compensation could reach the recipients.

The main objection, however, to the allowance of this claim has heretofore been, that the lands were granted by the King of Great Britain without reservation of Indian titles,—and that the Iroquois were then subjects of the King, and that, by the treaty of 1783, by which jurisdiction to this territory was ceded to the United States, the Indian title became extinguished.

It has also been claimed that the Iroquois were allies of the King of France, in the war between Great Britain and France, which resulted in the conquest of Canada by the former power, and hence, by the treaty of 1763, this claim was extinguished.

The Six Nations, during the "French War" and also the war of the Revolution, seem, in the main, to have been attached to the crown of England; although great efforts were made by the French to obtain their alliance during the former war, which at some times and to some extent was successful. Yet it is not obvious upon what principle, if it be conceded that the Iroquois were allies of France, the cession of Canada to the crown of England should extinguish the Indian title to lands situate within the British colonies. It is quite certain that the King of England did not so regard it; for there is abundant documentary and incontestable evidence, that from A.D. 1763 until A.D. 1783, the British Sovereign, by his agents, did negotiate with the Chiefs of the Six Nations, and did hold council with them respecting their lands, and, at all times, they were treated as having the undisputed title.

It has also been insisted that the Iroquois lost their title by the treaty between the United States and Great Britain, A.D. 1783,—and this, upon the ground that the Iroquois were not only allies but *subjects* of the Crown of England—and hence that treaty, ratified by the Sovereign, was binding upon all the subjects of the Crown and upon the Iroquois. Yet there seems to be no warrant for asserting that the British Crown did ever assume to convey the Indians' land, or extinguish their title, either by treaty or by grant, without their consent, or that they were regarded as the *subjects* of the Crown. They were the friends of the Sovereign in peace—his allies in war—and as the Crown did treat with them, as an independent power, before the treaty of 1783, so have the United States, since that time.

On the 31st day of May, A.D. 1796, the authorities of New York, through the intervention of Abraham Ogden, a Commissioner appointed by the authority of the United States, concluded a treaty with the Iroquois, then denominating themselves "the Seven Nations," which was duly ratified, and proclamation thereof made on the 31st day of January, A.D. 1797. By this treaty, the "Seven Nations" ceded to the people of the State of New York all title to their adjacent lands situate within the limits and jurisdiction of the State of New York,—and in consideration therefor, said State paid the sum of one thousand four hundred and forty-seven pounds, one shilling, four pence; and made the further stipulation to pay them annually, thereafter, two hundred and twelve pounds, six shillings, eight pence.

It is said by Governor Tichenor, in his report to the Legislature, that in the grants, by the Crown of England, of lands in New York, there was a reservation of the Indian title, while in the grants of *these* lands there was no such reservation, and hence a distinction might well be taken. But it is submitted that the Crown, previous to the Revolution, and the United States since, have never assumed to convey the unencumbered *fee* of the land while in the occupancy of the Indian tribes;

but the grantee took the fee, encumbered with the right of Indian occupancy, and the sole right to extinguish the Indian title.

The Supreme Court of the United States say, in the case Clark vs. Smith, 13 Peters' Reports, 195:

> The ultimate fee, encumbered with the right of Indian occupancy, was in the Crown previous to the Revolution, and in the States of the Union afterwards, and subject to grant. This right of occupancy was protected by the political powers, and respected by the Courts, until extinguished, when the patentee took the unencumbered fee. So the Supreme Court, and State Courts, have uniformly held.

In the case United States vs. Clark, 9 Peters' Reports, the same Court say:

> One uniform rule seems to have prevailed in the British provinces in America, by which Indian lands were held and sold from the first settlement, as appears by their laws; that friendly Indians were protected in the possession of lands they occupied, and were considered as owning them, by a perpetual right of possession in the tribe or nation inhabiting them as their common property, from generation to generation, not as the right of individuals located on particular spots. Subject to this right of possession, the ultimate fee was in the Crown and its grantees.

> Indian possession was considered in reference to their habits and modes of life; their hunting grounds were as much in their actual possession, as the cultivated fields of the whites, and their right to its exclusive enjoyment, in their own way, and for their own purposes, were as much respected until they abandoned them, made a cession to the government, or an authorised sale to individuals.

The rule seems to have been uniform that discovery vested in the Sovereign the absolute title to lands as against other powers, but subject to the Indian right of occupancy; and the several Sovereigns of Europe and the United States have ever assumed to grant only what they had obtained. And hence it would seem that Great Britain, by the treaty of 1783, yielded to the United States her claim to *sovereignty* over these lands, and remitted to the latter the same rights that she had claimed to herself. And so far as the Crown had granted these lands prior to the Revolution, the grantee obtained the title, subject to the Indian right of occupancy, and the sole right to extinguish that claim.

If the Iroquois have been divested of their title, it would seem more legitimate to say that they had been divested, and the title obtained, *by conquest.*

That that ancient and powerful confederacy, which claims to have given the model to our own, have retired before the advancing empire of another great confederacy, and surrendered their lands and *themselves* to its dominion, is confessedly true. Their very weakness, however, is sufficient guaranty that they will be heard. That they will be heard by the representatives of a people whose attribute is justice, is the warrant that their cause will be decided justly.

The early settlers of this State won laurels on the field of Bennington, which have now become the common property of the Union, and there made expenditures which should have long since been replaced from the national treasury; yet the State can forego her claim if she elects so to do. But when a claim is made to *her* sense of justice, by a people having no power to enforce it, and which rests solely in her will and discretion, I doubt not it will be met in the spirit of magnanimity and kindness.

I have gathered such facts as could be readily obtained, and submitted such reflections as have occurred to me, and it remains for your Excellency to act in the premises as to you shall seem meet.

All which is very
Respectfully submitted,
Timothy P. Redfield

Source: Timothy Redfield, *Report on the Claim of the Iroquois Indians upon the State of Vermont, for Their "Hunting Ground"* (Montpelier: E. P. Walton, 1854), pp. 3-13.

Platform and Resolutions
of a Mass Convention in Montpelier
(1854)

The Freemen of Vermont assembled in Convention, in pursuance of a spontaneous call emanating from various parts of the State, and embracing men of all political parties, to consider upon the measures which duty demands of us as citizens of a Free State, in the present crisis in reference to the late acts of Congress, on the subject of Slavery and its anticipated further extension, viz:

For the protection of Free States from Southern aggression and Northern treachery;

For the recovery of the rights of the Free States as an integral part of the Union; and

For the rescue of the General Government from the control of the Slave power:

. . . *Resolved*, That henceforth all compromises with Slavery are at an end, and one rallying cry shall henceforth be the repeal of the Fugitive Slave law, and of the inter-state slave trade, the abolition of slavery in the District of Columbia, the prohibition of Slavery in all the Territories of the United States, and the admission of no more Slave States into the Union.

Resolved, 1, That we pledge ourselves to the extent of our power to the repeal of the Fugitive Slave Bill.

2, To resist the admission of Utah and New Mexico as States, without Constitutions excluding Slavery.

3, To the restriction of Slavery to the States in which it exists.

4, To the exclusion of Slavery at the earliest practicable moment, by all constitutional means, from the federal territory, Nebraska, Kansas and the District of Columbia inclusive.

5, To oppose the admission into the Union of any new State, tolerating Slavery, whether it be formed from territory belonging to Texas or elsewhere.

6, To resist the acquisition of any new territory wherein Slavery exists, unless the prohibition of Slavery shall first have been provided for.

7, To encourage immigration into the territories of freemen, pledged irrevocably to the cause of Freedom.

8, That the Nebraska bill is only one of a series of aggressive pro-slavery measures, each depending on preceding measures of the same kind and manifesting the natural tendency of slavery. Had the annexation of Texas or the Fugitive Slave Bill, been resisted, the Nebraska bill would never have been proposed. The issue should have [been decided] many years ago, between extension and non-extension of Slavery. Let us make it now.

9, We hereby avow our determined purpose not to support for the office of President or Vice President, or Senator or Representative in Congress, or Governor, or Lieut. Governor, or Treasurer of the State, or member of the State Legislature, any man of whatever party, not known to be in favor of the purposes above avowed.

Resolved, That inasmuch as there are now no great measures of Legislation or administrative policy, dividing political parties, except that of slavery, and harmony is absolutely essential to successful resistance to the alarming aggressions of the slave power, we do as Whigs, Free Soilers, and Democrats, freely relinquish our former party associations and ties, to form a new party organization, having for its object to secure the blessings of liberty to ourselves and to our posterity, and also a wise, just and economical administration of the Government: and as the principles for which we are contending, lie at the foundation of Republicanism, as proclaimed by our fathers, we propose and respectfully recommend to the friends of freedom in other States to co-operate, and be known as *Republicans*.

Resolved, That we hold the following general principles as essential to the just and proper administration of the Government.

1. A rigid accountability and economy, in the administration of the government.
2. Retrenchment of the patronage of the President by the election of postmasters, and all other civil officers by the people, as far as the same may be practicable.
3. Cheap postage for the people, and the abolition of the franking privilege by members of Congress.
4. A judicious system of River and Harbor improvements by the government, whenever demanded for the safety and convenience of commerce with foreign nations, or among the several states.

5. A Tariff for revenue with proper discrimination in favor of American industry.
6. The free grant of homesteads to actual settlers in consideration of labor and privation incurred in making settlements in the wilderness, with just reservations of the public lands, regarded as the common property of all the States.

Resolved, That we recommend the calling of a general Convention of the Free States and such of the Slave holding States or portions thereof, as may desire to be represented for the purpose of forming a national organization, opposed to the aggressions of Slavery, and for the adoption of other and more effectual measures of resistance to such aggression, and that in anticipation of such action, this Convention appoint delegates equal in number to the Senators and Representatives of this State in Congress, and that such delegates be a Committee of Correspondence on that subject with our friends in other States.

Resolved, That the enactment of the law of 1852, known as "An act to prevent traffic in intoxicating liquors for the purpose of drinking," and its subsequent enforcement, has been of vast pecuniary, social and moral benefit to the people of Vermont, and the continuance and ardent support and execution of that law is demanded by the public welfare and the public sentiment, and none but its firm and consistent supporters should be elected to offices of trust and honor.

Source: *Burlington Free Press*, 18 July 1854.

DOCUMENT 7

Letter on the Know-Nothing Movement in Vermont (1855)
GEORGE P. MARSH

Private
Burlington, April 19, 1855

My dear sir

I have been so much occupied since the receipt of yours of April 9 that I have not until this moment found a leisure moment to reply.

No man can be better convinced than I of the impropriety and danger of all secret combinations and organizations whatever for political purposes, and indeed for any other object, and if I could be persuaded, that the Know Nothings were likely to retain that objectionable feature as a part of their policy, I should be ready to take any lawful measure almost to resist them. I believe, however, that they must and will abandon their whole foolish machinery of lodges & wigwams, sachems, oaths, secrets, and all the like silliness, which, coupled with such insanity as that of _____ & his colleagues, will otherwise infallibly destroy the party.

For the present, therefore, I do not believe in the necessity of any special effort to resist the movements of the party, and, committed as I have publicly been for more than twenty years to their avowed principles—which I understand to be repeal or at least restriction of the right of naturalization, and resistance to catholic commandments—I cannot participate in any steps which would expose me to the suspicion of having abandoned these *principles*, barely because I disapprove the *means* which are resorted to to advance them.

In my judgment, our liberties are in greater danger from the political influence of catholicism than from any other cause whatsoever, and I cannot act with any party which I believe to be, I will not say friendly to that influence, but indifferent to that danger. It is certainly much to be deplored, that a party organized for such objects should adopt so miserable a policy in effecting them, & I cannot but hope, that the American people will adopt their principles and repudiate their tactics.

I am aware that the position of the K. N. on the slavery question is a bad, or at least an equivocal one, but if one may judge by several late articles in the N. York Times on the Cuba question, the leading opponents of the K. N. in N. York are preparing to go over to the South on that question & thus to sacrifice our free soil and our free religion together.

Very truly yours,
Geo. P. Marsh

Mr. Erastus Fairbanks

Source: Erastus Fairbanks Papers, Doc. Box 95, Vermont Historical Society, Montpelier, Vermont.

DOCUMENT 8

Advertisement for the Vermont Emigrant Association (1855)

Dr. H. D. Allen, President   Dr. O. Cook, Secretary
Wm. W. Ingraham,   J. B. Kirkaldie, Treasurer
Vice President

Board of Directors

H. D. Allen	Dr. E. C. Lewis	Hosea Pelsue
J. M. Southwick	William Kent	J. B. Kirkaldie
Wm. B. Burns	O. Cook	A. L. Brown
Wm. W. Ingraham	Dr. J. Ross	O. L. Allen
	Mr. __ Parsons	

Locating Committee

H. D. Allen   Wm. Kent   Wm. B. Burns

An Association has been formed in Rutland, Vt., for the purpose of forming a settlement in the most favorable part of the West, comprised of enterprising men from Vermont, to emigrate where the country and climate is good, and where social, civil, and religious privileges may be established and enjoyed. The object of this Company is to occupy a tract of land, favorably situated, in the best possible location, as near as may be ascertained, to or on some great thoroughfare. The locating committee are now canvassing the country, and will probably determine on some one of the points contemplated in the State of Iowa. They will purchase a tract of land for a City site, and obligate themselves to deed to each member his lot when called for after due arrangements are made. The City will be laid out with streets, parks, and sites for public buildings, in a systematical manner.

This location will be in the midst of Government Land, and of excellent quality. The country is unquestionably one of the finest in the world, and quite as productive. The rolling prairie abounds and is extremely fertile; the climate good and healthy.

The advantages of such an Association are readily seen by all. The farmer procures a farm for a small amount of money, as good as lays out doors, and is at once in the midst of a good society, of Vermont character, and in no other way can these blessings be procured. A village is started on short notice, and the member gets the rise of the lot as well as the farm.

The object of this Association is not a piece of wild speculation on the part of the officers; equal rights and privileges to all the members. This Association is now organized with about fifty enterprising Vermonters, and with great encouragements of great numbers to take hold of the same enterprise. We cordially invite farmers, mechanics, and business men of all professions, that possess good moral character, to enlist in this enterprise and emigrate with us.

Source: Advertisement for the Vermont Emigrant Association, 1855, Broadside Collection, Vermont Historical Society, Montpelier, Vermont.

DOCUMENT 9

Resolutions and Legislation Relating to Slavery and the U. S. Supreme Court's Decision in the Dred Scott Case (1858)

Resolved, by the Senate and the House of Representatives of the State of Vermont:—

That the Constitution of the United States invests Congress with the sole power to govern the territories,—a power always exercised, and never questioned by any department of the government, for more than sixty years after the adoption of the Constitution.

Resolved further, That, in the exercise of this power, Congress has the same right to exclude slavery, or any other evil, from the territories of the United States, that the States have, by State legislation, to prohibit the same in the States; and, as guardians of the public interests, it is the duty of Congress to exercise this right.

Resolved, That Vermont will continue to resist the admission of new slave States into this Union, and the extension of slavery into the territories of the United States; and, now as ever, will seek the abolition of slavery at the national capital, and in all places under federal jurisdiction.

Resolved, That all laws of Congress which recognize the right of property in man, or deprive any person of liberty without due process of law and a jury trial, or provide that any person shall be delivered up, as owing service to another, without such trial, are unconstitutional, void, and of no effect.

Resolved, That property in slaves exists only by the positive law of force in the States creating it. The moment it passes from under the operation of these laws, it is property no longer.

And whereas, the present federal administration and judiciary have denied to the government and people of the United States the right, which the Constitution guarantees to them, of prohibiting the introduction of slavery into the territories; and have denied the right of the citizens of the independent States of this Union to protect their liberties or property, by instituting suits in the courts of the United States; therefore,—

Resolved further, by the Senate and House of Representatives, That the doctrine maintained by a majority of the judges of the Supreme Court, in the case of Dred Scott, that slavery now exists, by virtue of the Constitution of the United States, in all the territories, and in all places where the Federal Government has jurisdiction—that the Constitution carries slavery wherever it extends—has no warrant in the Constitution, or in the legislative or judicial history of this country.

Resolved, That these extra-judicial opinions of the Supreme Court of the United States are a dangerous usurpation of power, and have no binding authority upon Vermont, or the people of the United States.

Resolved, That no ingenious sophistry of the judges of that court can make it appear that the citizens of each State are not citizens of the United States, and citizens *when in the other States*; and entitled, as such, to all rights and privileges of citizens in the several States.

Resolved, That, whenever the government or judiciary of the United States refuses or neglects to protect the citizens of each State in their lives or liberty, when in another State or territory, it becomes the duty of the sovereign and independent States of this Union to protect their own citizens, at whatever hazard or cost.

Resolved, That the senators in Congress from this State be directed, and our representatives requested, to use their utmost endeavors to induce Congress to propose amendments to the Constitution of the United States, so that the President and Vice President of the United States be elected every fourth year, by the ballots of the legal voters in the States,—a majority of all the votes cast at said election, in all the States, constituting a choice.

Resolved, That, in case of no election of President or Vice-President, in the manner prescribed in the preceding resolution, they should then be chosen, as such officers are now chosen, by Congress.

Resolved, That the Governor of the State be, and he is hereby, requested to transmit a copy of these resolutions to the governors of the several States, and to each of our senators and representatives in Congress.

G. F. EDMUNDS,   BURNAM MARTIN
Speaker of the House   President of the Senate
of Representatives

Source: *Acts and Resolves Passed by the General Assembly of the State of Vermont at the October Session, 1858*, (Bradford, Vt.: Joseph D. Clark), pp. 66-69.

DOCUMENT 10

Address to the Special Joint Session of the Vermont General Assembly (1861)
ERASTUS FAIRBANKS

Gentlemen of the Senate and House of Representatives:

We are convened to-day in view of events of an extraordinary and very alarming character. The element of disunion which, in a portion of the United States, for many years, vented itself in threats and menaces, has culminated in open rebellion; and an unnatural and causeless civil war has been precipitated against the General Government.

Unprincipled and ambitious men have organized a despotism and an armed force, for the purpose of overthrowing that Government which the American people have formed for themselves, and of destroying that constitutional frame-work, under which we have enjoyed peace and prosperity, and, from a small and feeble people, grown and expanded to a rank among the first nations of the earth.

The enormity of this rebellion is heightened by the consideration that no valid cause exists for it. The history of the civilized world does not furnish an instance where a revolution was attempted for such slight causes. No act of oppression, no attempted or threatened invasion of the rights of the revolting states, has existed, either on the part of the General Government, or of the loyal states; but the principle has been recognized and observed, that the right of each and every state to regulate its domestic institutions, should remain inviolate.

The inception and progress of this rebellion have been remarkable; and characterized, at every stage, by a total absence of any high honorable principle or motive in its leaders.

Its master spirits are composed, essentially, of men who have been in high official position in the General Government; and it has transpired that members of the late Cabinet at Washington, while in the exercise of their official functions, were engaged in treasonable plots for seizing the public property and subverting the United States Government.

Conventions of delegates in the revolting states, chosen, in some instances, by a minority of the legal voters in those States, have, with indecent haste, adopted ordinances of secession, which ordinances have in no instance been submitted to the people for their ratification.

These proceedings have been followed by a convention of delegates from the several revolting states, which convention has organized a confederate government, adopted a constitution, elected its executive officers and subordinate functionaries, constituted itself into a legislative body, and enacted a code of laws,—all which proceedings have been independent of any action of the people of those states.

The authorities of the revolting States, and subsequently that of their confederacy, have proceeded to acts of robbery and theft upon the property of the United States, within their limits. Forts, arsenals, arms, military stores, and other public property, have been seized and appropriated for use against the power of the General Government; and custom houses and mints in Southern cities, with large amounts of treasure, have been feloniously robbed.

These acts have been followed by military demonstrations and strategetical operations against the United States forts at Pensacola and Charleston, the latter of which, under its gallant commander, Major Anderson, after a bombardment of thirty-four hours, from beleaguering batteries of the insurgents, was evacuated on the 13th instant, and the flag of the Union withdrawn. But the crowning act of perfidy, on the part of the conspirators, is the proclamation of Jefferson Davis, styling himself the President of the Southern confederacy, "inviting all those who may desire, by service in private armed vessels on the high seas, to aid his government, to make application for commissions, or letters of Marque or Reprisal": thus instituting a grand scheme of piracy on the high seas, against the lives and private property of peaceful citizens.

These acts of outrage and daring rebellion have been equalled only by the forbearance of the General Government. Unwilling to precipitate a conflict which must involve the country in all the calamities of civil war, the present government of the United States has exhausted every effort for peace, and every measure for bringing back to their allegiance the disaffected and misguided States.

The duty of protecting the forts and government property not possessed by the insurgents, was imperative upon the administration; but further than this, no measures for coercing the revolting States into obedience to the constitution and the laws were adopted; and in the matter of the beleaguered forts, the government acted only on the defensive, until the conflict was commenced by the insurgents.

Such forbearance on the part of the Government, while it has served to place the conspirators in a moral wrong, is no longer justifiable; and the country hails, with entire unanimity, and with ardent enthusiasm the decision of the President to call into requisition the whole power of the nation for suppressing the rebellion and repelling threatened aggressions.

From every part of the country, in all the loyal states, there is one united voice for sustaining the Union, the Constitution, and the integrity of the United States Government. All partizan differences are ignored and lost in the higher principle of patriotism. In this patriotic enthusiasm, Vermont eminently participates. Her citizens, always loyal to the Union, will, in this hour of peril, nobly rally for the protection of the Government and the Constitution.

On the fifteenth instant, the President of the United States issued his Proclamation, "calling forth the militia of the several states of the Union, to the aggregate number of seventy-five thousand, in order to suppress treasonable combinations, and cause the laws to be duly executed."

The quota required of Vermont, for immediate service, is one regiment of seven hundred and eighty officers and privates.

On receiving the requisition from the Secretary of War, for this regiment, I ordered the Adjutant and Inspector General to adopt the proper measures for calling into service such of the volunteer companies as are necessary to make up the complement; and the Quarter Master General was directed to procure, with the least possible delay, the requisite outfit of knapsacks, overcoats, blankets and other equipments; which duty he has performed.

Having adopted the foregoing preliminary measures, for responding to the call of the President, I availed myself of the Constitutional provision for convening the General Assembly in an Extra Session; not doubting that you, gentlemen, representing the universally expressed patriotism of the citizens of this State, will make all necessary appropriations and provisions for defraying the expenses already incurred and carrying into execution further measures for placing our Military quota at the service of the General Government.

Conceiving it imminently probable that, at an early day, further calls will be made upon this State for troops, I respectfully call your attention to the importance of adopting immediate measures for a more efficient organization of the military arm of the State.

During the long interval of peace which we have enjoyed, while our citizens have been uninterrupted in their lawful industrial pursuits, the importance of a military organization and discipline has been lost sight of. Our laws in relation to the militia have been subjected, during nearly a quarter of a century, to numerous isolated amendments and alterations, until as a code, they are disjointed, complicated, and altogether too cumbrous for the basis of a regular and effective organization. I therefore recommend that the Legislature should promptly remedy these defects, and adopt such enactments as shall provide, effectively, for organizing, arming and equipping the militia of the State, and for reasonably compensating the officers and pri-

vates, when required to meet for exercise and drill.

I desire, also, to urge upon you the duty of making contingent appropriations of money, to be expended under the direction of the Executive, for the outfit of any additional military forces which may be called for by the General Government.

The occasion is an extraordinary one. Intelligence reaches us, that the Virginia convention of delegates, elected under the express provision that any ordinance adopted by them, should be submitted to the people for their approval or rejection, has, in secret session, passed an ordinance of secession, and that the Governor of the State has assumed to order the seizure of the United States forts, arsenal and vessels within the limits of that State.

The Federal capital is menaced by an imposing and well armed military force, and the Government itself, and the national archives, are in imminent peril.

Such is the emergency, in view of which I invoke your immediate action. The Legislatures of other States have made liberal appropriations and extensive military arrangements for aiding the Government, and their citizens are hastening to the rescue of our country's flag. We shall discredit our past history should we, in this crisis, suffer Vermont to be behind her sister States, in her patriotic sacrifices for the preservation of the Union and the Constitution.

I feel assured, Gentlemen, that you will best reflect the sentiments and wishes of your constituents, by emulating, in your legislative action, the patriotism and liberality of the noble States which have already responded to the call of the Government.

It is devoutly to be hoped that the mad ambition of the secession leaders may be restrained, and the impending sanguinary conflict averted. But a hesitating, half-way policy, on the part of the administration of the loyal States, will not avail to produce such a result.

The United States Government must be sustained and the rebellion suppressed, at whatever cost of men and treasure; and it remains to be seen whether the vigorous preparations that are being made and the immense military force called into service by the President, are not the most probable and certain measures for a speedy and successful solution of the question.

May that Divine Being, who rules among the nations, and directs the affairs of men, interpose by His merciful

Providence, and restore to us again the blessings of peace, under the aegis of our national constitution.

Erastus Fairbanks

Source: *Journal of the House of Representatives of the State of Vermont*, Extra Session (Montpelier: E. P. Walton, 1861), pp. 18-22.

DOCUMENT 11

"To the Sharp Shooters of Windham County!" (1861)

(depicted on following page)

Source: "To the Sharpshooters of Windham County!," 1861, Broadside Collection, Vermont Historical Society, Montpelier, Vermont.

DOCUMENT 12

"The Seventh Vermont Regiment, 'Now is the Day, Now is the Hour'" (1861)

(depicted on second page following)

Source: "The Seventh Vermont Regiment, 'Now is the Day, Now is the Hour,'" 1861, Broadside Collection, Vermont Historical Society, Montpelier, Vermont.

DOCUMENT 13

Civil War Diary (1862)

WILLIAM H. JACKSON

Monday, Aug. 8, 1862. Applied for membership in the Rutland Light Guard. Capt. Kingsley commanding. I had been thinking the matter over for some time and had come to the conclusion it was my duty to enlist.

The country needs more men urgently and every one who can possibly go should do so—The sooner the better—and it will be better to enlist voluntarily than to be dragged in as a conscript. Nothing to me would appear more disgracing, but I am glad the draft has been decided upon. It is plain to be seen that if we do not bring men forward more rapidly we shall soon loose all we have won and more besides. An order for the draft will stimulate enlistment and it may be that in some parts of the country it can be avoided but in other less patriotic sections they will wait until forced to go— Then sullenly—unwillingly, a nuisance to their camarads and a drawback upon the Government.

Tues. Aug. 17th. This evening at a meeting of the Light Guard at their armory in the Town Hall, I was elected a member of the Company and signed the By Laws.—Thus enrolling myself effectually. Our services were formally offered to the Government in response to the recent call for 300,000 men to serve for a period of nine months.

Thurs. Aug. 21. Took train for Home (Troy) at 3p.m. and arrived there at 8—surprising the folks very much as they had not heard of my recent move. Some time previously I had written them on the subject of enlistment & had been advised to wait—that I might get some better office than as a private and that there might be no draft, but that in any case I must act on my own judgment. Have made up my mind however to go now.

Monday Aug. 25. Have been purchasing some some [*sic*] little knick-knacks and conveniences to take with me.

1st	a little rubber ink bottle	37cts.
2d	Portfolio	45cts.
3d	5 quires paper	75cts.
4t	stick of India ink	18cts.
	Total	176

Thurs. 28. Arrived back in Rutland at 11.30 this evening. Eliza has made me a nice dressing case.

Monday Sep 1. Commenced drilling this morning at 9 o'clock until 11. Found Abe Burnett in the ranks— was on my left in the drill. Were instructed in facing & in marching.

Wednesday Sep 3d. Company inspected today by Dr. Adams was passed as all right.

Friday Sep 5. This evening just after supper I was much surprised to see brother Ed walk into the house,

TO THE
SHARP SHOOTERS
OF WINDHAM COUNTY!

Your Country Calls!! Will you Respond?

CAPT. WESTON has been authorized to raise a Company of Green Mountain Boys for Col. Berdan's Regiment of Sharp Shooters which has been accepted by the War Department to serve for three years, or during the war. Capt. Weston desires to have Windham County represented in his Company.

The Sharp Shooters of Windham County and vicinity who are willing to serve their country in this time of need and peril, are requested to meet at the ISLAND HOUSE in Bellows Falls, on TUESDAY, the 27th inst., at 1 o'clock, P. M., for the purpose of testing their skill in TARGET SHOOTING. There are great inducements to join this celebrated Regiment, destined to be the most important and popular in the Service.

No person will be enlisted who cannot when firing at the distance of 200 yards, at a rest, put ten consecutive shots in a target, the average distance not to exceed five inches from the centre of the bull's eye to the centre of the ball.

GREEN MOUNTAIN BOYS!

"Rally for the support of the Stars and Stripes!"

YOU ARE INVITED TO BRING YOUR RIFLES.

F. F. STREETER, Supt. of Trial.

BELLOWS FALLS, VT., August 19, 1861.

Phenix Job Office, Bellows Falls.

Document 11

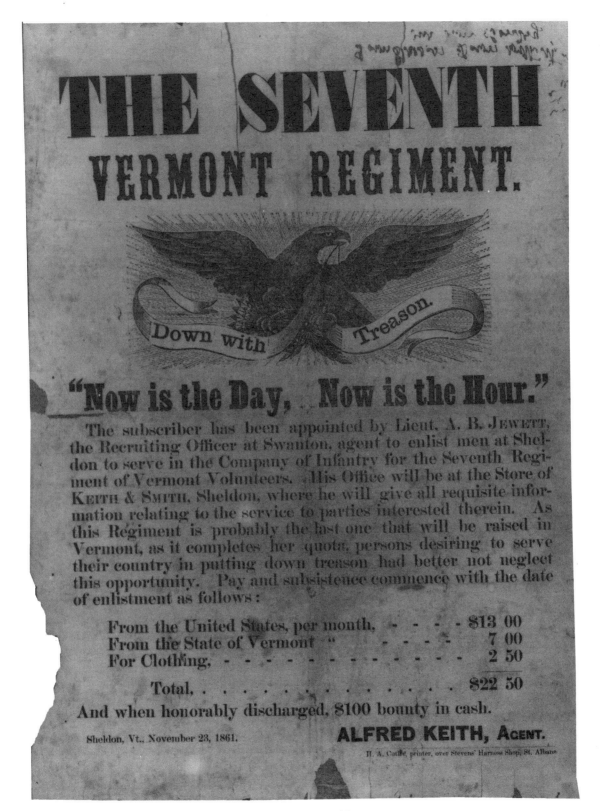

THE SEVENTH VERMONT REGIMENT.

"Down with Treason."

"Now is the Day, Now is the Hour."

The subscriber has been appointed by Lieut. A. B. JEWETT, the Recruiting Officer at Swanton, agent to enlist men at Sheldon to serve in the Company of Infantry for the Seventh Regiment of Vermont Volunteers. His Office will be at the Store of KEITH & SMITH, Sheldon, where he will give all requisite information relating to the service to parties interested therein. As this Regiment is probably the last one that will be raised in Vermont, as it completes her quota, persons desiring to serve their country in putting down treason had better not neglect this opportunity. Pay and subsistence commence with the date of enlistment as follows:

From the United States, per month, - - - -	$13 00
From the State of Vermont " - - - -	7 00
For Clothing, - - - - - - - - - - - -	2 50
Total, ...	$22 50

And when honorably discharged, $100 bounty in cash.

Sheldon, Vt., November 23, 1861.

ALFRED KEITH, Agent.

H. A. Cutler, printer, over Stevens' Harness Shop, St. Albans.

Document 12

as he was entirely unexpected. Said he had come up to enlist. Had written him several days before about his chances for joining the Sharp Shooters as we thought he could not go with me in the Light Guard as the Company was full. Being on the ground now however we went around to see the Captain & found there were some vacancies due to dismissals on acct of inspection.

Thurs. 6th. Ed passed the examination by Dr. Adams & is now fully enrolled. Commenced drilling today.

Friday Sep 19th. We have now been drilling for some two weeks and are making good proficiency in the marches by the flank and front, with other movements. Lately they have been putting us through the manual of arms; it is more tiresome work by far than marching. At first we were required to stand still while going thro' the manipulations, and it was no easy matter to hand handle a musket around for two hours at a stretch in one position. Latterly we have gone thro' the manual marching & it comes much easier. A week ago last Wednesday Ed got a furlough for us both to go home for a short visit. Started off at once, arriving in Troy at 8 p.m., much surprised the folks who had no word of our coming. Had a very enjoyable time visiting acquaintances.

Since my enlistment have received a number of presents from my friends: a revolver from Sam Tappan; a bowie knife from Ira Johnson Frank Hiams All Hayward, Sam Tappan and Ed, and a combination knife fork and spoon from Mowry.

Uncle Sam seems to be short on blankets. In an order from the Adj. Genl's office it said that owing to the very great demand the Government is unable at present to furnish volunteers with blankets, and advises that they purchase these for themselves if they wish [to] make themselves comfortable while in camp. Don't know what to do about it as I haven't money enough to buy them and do not know of any friends who have any to spare. Have written home to see what they can do for us. Yesterday I bought two flannel shirts for 3.75. Had some pockets put in and changed the buttons about. They are grey flannel trimmed with red tape. There is some prospect of our soon leaving Rutland for the Rendezvous camp at Brattleboro. Capt. Kingsley says we leave next week Thursday the 25th.

About the first of the week five more men were detailed from the Co. to go to Brattleboro and help build Barracks. Abe Burnett was one of them.

Have been doing some work for Mowry since my enlistment. Today I painted two pictures, a cabinet and a whole sign, and made good things of them.

Friday Sep. 26. We are at last in camp at Brattleboro and as I now write the confusion of hundreds of voices and the noisy clatter of the hammers of the carpenters who are putting the finishing touches to our quarters—makes a very bedlam. The last day or two has been one of continuous excitement. Yesterday morning I made my appearance at the Armory in uniform . . . coats & pants only being furnished now. At a quarter of eleven we left the rooms for the station, where we met two other companies from Burlington & Brandon. Were soon aboard the cars and off after a few hurried and tearful leave takings. While on the road the boys made themselves as joyful as possible, singing and sky-larking to their fullest extent. At Bellows Falls we met the rest of the regiment and after fifteen minutes delay proceeded on our way and in an hour or so arrived at Brattleboro. On disbarking we were formed in line by our colonel (whose appearance by the way impressed us all most favorably) and marched to the Campground about a mile distant. Dust.! Talk about dust! I never knew what dust meant until we made that march. It was almost impossible to breathe and when we arrived at the camp several of the boys were so weak they had to be carried into their quarters and one of them fainted outright.

Were lined up again and after a few formalities were marched by companies to our respective quarters and told to pick out our bunks. From a big stack of straw outside we got enough to make a comfortable bed & on this spread our rubber & then our woolen blankets. (Blankets were issued to us here, contrary to expectations, including a rubber blanket; so we will have to return the ones we brought with us.) This matter attended to, we were marched out to supper about half a mile distant. It was nearly dark by this time & no lights in the bare barracks of a room but we managed nevertheless to make out a good meal of bread & butter & beef & coffee. Returning to our quarters we retired at once for the night.

This morning were formed in line at 7, and half an hour later had breakfast, and a good one it was too—would never ask for better.

Saturday Sep. 27. Yesterday afternoon we received our muskets. The Captain said before issuing them that he had never seen better rifled muskets and they really were fine looking—very smoothly & finely polished and A No. 1, in every respect. After supper were out on dress parade and I must say we made a fine appearance. This morning directly after breakfast we proceeded to elect a captain and Lieutenant caused by the promotion of Capt. Kingsley to be Major of the regiment. The Lieut. Colonel presided over the proceedings which resulted in moving up the present officers— 1st Lieut. W. C. Langdon to Capt. 2d Lieut. Staly to 1st Lieut. and Ord. Sergt. Rounds to be 2d Lieut. Changes were heartily approved, not from any dislike of Capt. Kingsley for if we had our own way he would remain Capt. Had another medical inspection. All passed except B. B. Thrall but do not know for what reason—

Sunday. Reveille beat this morning at 6—breakfast at 7. Directly afterwards packed up our traps and proceeded to move to new quarters in accordance with the assignment of our Co. to its place in the regimental line. This order follows the rank of the Capt. commanding each Co., the oldest commission being Co. A, and as our present Capt. is the last one appointed we are therefore Co. K. Today men have been detailed to dig ditches—four men and a corporal going from our Co. This afternoon a smart rainstorm drove in the ditch-diggers. This has been Sunday in name only. Hundreds of men have been busy battening up their quarters, arranging bunks & all the other things needed to make camp comfortable. Take it all in all it has been a very busy day. Have been at work on the Capt.'s quarters doing some carpentering. Dress parade at 6. A fine drizzling rain at the time & the parade was of short duration. When assembled on our own parade ground the Capt. took us to task for our appearance, said it was too irregular—that we must always keep eyes straight to front & remain immovable. We needed the lecture all right.

Monday Sep. 29. In morning was detailed to clean up ground in front of our quarters. Had blistered hands from unaccustomed use of shovel. In the afternoon worked hard at boarding up the roof & sides of some of the barracks buildings.

Tuesday Sep. 30. Detailed for guard duty—in second relief on beat no. 9. Went on first at 11 a.m. & was relieved at 1. Witnessed a battalion drill in which our

reg. took part, during the time I was off duty. Movements were performed very well indeed much better than I thought they would do with so little drilling. Went on guard again at 5 p.m. All went well until about 7 when four soldiers attempted to run past my line. They separated so that I could hold up only one of them. All four were members of our Co. Was relieved a little after 7, and after getting supper slept away the time in the guard-house until 11, when I went on again for another two hours. Nothing of note occurred & when relieved went back to the guard-house for another nap until I should go on again at 5. The interior of the guard-house presented a curious appearance. Sleeping guardsmen covered the floor completely, on the benches and under the benches as well, and as one of the soldiers said, they seemed to be lying four-deep. Found a resting place among them somewhere and slept soundly until I was roused for another two hours duty.

Saturday Oct. 4. The last few days we have received about all our equipment. Knapsacks, haversacks, cartridge & cap boxes and clothing. On Friday the 3d we were brought out on dress parade fully equipped. This was the first time we had shouldered our knapsacks and when first put on were pronounced very light and easy to carry. Then we were taken out on the parade ground and drilled for about an hour, and at the end the knapsacks were thought to be decidedly heavy, two or three of the boys leaving the ranks on account of fatigue. It was very severe—our muskets were carried constantly at shoulder-arms and that alone was enough to tire us pretty well. This morning at 10 were again under arm burdens with addition of knife fork cup & plate in our knapsacks, for final inspection by Maj. Austin, Col. Stoughton & others. Got through about noon. At 2 in afternoon were formally mustered into the U.S. Service by Maj. Austin of the Regular Army.

Monday Oct. 6t. Were paid our bounty of $100. and back State's pay, amount to $10.70. Makes some of us feel pretty rich to have so much money in our pockets at once. Sent $40. to Mrs. Fisher for board and $70. home.

Tuesday Oct. 7t. Started today for "Dixie." The morning was occupied in breaking camp. Formed in line at 11 and marched downtown & up around by the Governor's house: most of the time at quick step & once in a while at double quick. It came rather hard with our heavy knapsacks. When we got to the station found cars were not ready, and had to lie around waiting until 8 in the evening when we were hustled aboard in quick order.

Source: William Henry Jackson Diary. 1862-63. Manuscripts and Archives Division, The New York Public Library, Astor, Lenox and Tilden Foundations. Reprinted with permission of The New York Public Library.

DOCUMENT 14

A Vermonter's Account of Events during the Battle of Gettysburg (1863)

GEORGE GRENVILLE BENEDICT

Headquarters Second Vt. Brigade,
    Battlefield of Gettysburg, July 4, 1863
Dear Free Press:

The scene has shifted since I wrote you last from the shores of the Occoquan to the fields of Pennsylvania, from pleasant camp life to scenes of battle and frightful bloodshed. My last letter was hardly closed when we got the exciting news that Lee's army was in full march to the north, through the Shenandoah Valley, and that the Army of the Potomac was on its way north to protect the National Capital—news soon confirmed by the appearance of troops of contrabands and long columns of the cavalry and infantry of three army corps, with forty batteries of the reserve artillery, which came streaming past for four days and as many nights.

On the 23rd of June General Stannard received notice that his brigade had been attached to the Third division of the First Army Corps; that it was to hold the line of the Occoquan till the main army had passed, and then was to follow the corps and join it if possible before the great battle which was expected. On the 25th ult. the brigade started. . . .

The first news that the great battle we were expecting had begun reached us about noon of Wednesday, July 1, when a courier, spurring a tired horse, met General Stannard riding at the head of his brigade, eight or nine miles south of Gettysburg, with word from General Doubleday that a big fight was in progress at Gettysburg; that General Reynolds had been killed and he had succeeded to the command of the First corps; that the corps and cavalry were fighting a large part of the rebel army and having hard work to hold their ground, and that Stannard must hasten forward as fast as possible. . . .

The second day of the battle opened on Thursday without firing, save now and then a shot from the pickets, but we saw considerable moving of troops on our side behind the low ridge which concealed us from the enemy, and doubtless the same process was going on, on their side, unseen by us. The batteries alone on the crests of the ridges menaced each other, like grim bulldogs, in silence.

The three regiments present of our brigade . . . were placed behind Cemetery Hill, a round hill crowned by a cemetery laid out with an amount of taste unusual in a place of the size of Gettysburg; and General Stannard was notified that he was in command of the infantry supports of the batteries upon the left of the hill, and would be held responsible for their safety.

Our batteries were planted, not actually upon the graves but close to them within the cemetery—such are the necessities of war. Our regiments lay behind the hill through the forenoon, the men lounging on the grass, till about 3 o'clock, when the ball opened by the whizzing of shell around our ears . . . . We were told by the old warriors that this thundering of cannon must be the prelude to a charge upon our lines, and all watched to see where it would come. About six, the nearing of musketry firing to our left indicated the spot, and in a few minutes we heard, above the din, the yell with which the rebels charge. There was scarce time to think what it meant, when orders came for our brigade to hurry to the left, where the lines were now being borne back by the enemy. Several regiments had broken for the rear; a battery had been taken, and our brigade was called for to fill the gap. Five companies of the Thirteenth, under Colonel Randall, led the advance on the double quick. The left wing of the regiment, under Lieut. Col. Munson, had been supporting a battery to the right and brought up the rear of the column. General Hancock was rallying the troops on the spot. "Can you retake that battery, Colonel?" was his question, as they came up. "Forward, boys," was the reply, and in they went. Captain

Lonergan's company of "bould soldier boys" took the lead and rushed at the battery with their Irish yell. Colonel Randall's gray horse fell under him, shot through the shoulder, and he went on, on foot. The guns were reached, wheeled round and passed to the rear, and pressing on, the boys of the Thirteenth took two rebel guns with some eighty odd of the "graybacks" who were supporting them. This ended the fighting for the night. The Thirteenth fell back to the main line, which, thus restored by the Vermonters, was held by our brigade to the close of the battle, at the point on the left centre at and around which the hardest fighting of the next day took place. . . .

Our men slept Thursday night upon their arms. . . . The artillery fire was quite sharp for a while in the morning [Friday] from the rebel batteries opposite us, but died away in an hour or so. It was perhaps intended to divert attention while the enemy was preparing a desperate attack upon our extreme right. Gen. Stannard adjusted a little the positions of his regiments. The Sixteenth was on the skirmish line in front. The Fourteenth was moved forward several rods to a line where some scattered trees and bushes afforded a partial cover. The Thirteenth was placed to the right and a little to the rear of the Fourteenth. No troops were in front of us. The ground had been fought over the day before, and a number of the dead of both armies lay scattered upon it. . . .

Gen. Lee, as it turned out, was collecting his batteries behind the crest of the ridge over against us. The ground here is a broad open stretch of meadow land, sloping away from the ridge on which our batteries were placed, in front of which, further down the slope, our infantry lay in three lines of battle perhaps 50 yards apart, and then rising to a rounded ridge over against us, from half to three-fourths of a mile away, which was held by the enemy. Our men improved the lull to make a little protection by collecting the rails which had been fences a day or two before, and piling them in a low breastwork perhaps two feet high. This would of course be a very slight protection for men standing; but for men lying prostrate they proved a valuable cover, and we found we needed every such assistance before night.

About one o'clock a couple of guns from the enemy gave the signal; from seventy-five to a hundred guns (one hundred and fifty guns were employed by General Lee in this cannonade) were run out upon the ridge right over against us, and for an hour and a half, what old veterans pronounce the severest cannonade of the war was opened directly upon us. The air seemed to be literally filled with flying missiles. Shells whizzed and popped on every side. Spherical case exploded over our heads and rained iron bullets upon us; the Whitworth solid shot, easily distinguished by their clear musical ring, flew singing by; grape hurtled around us or rattled in an iron storm against the low protections of rails, and round shot ploughed up the ground before and behind us. The men needed no caution to hug the ground closely. All lay motionless, heads to the front and faces to the ground. Though most of the shells went over us, occasionally a man would be struck. The wounded men invariably received their injuries without outcry, and lay and bled quietly in their places. They understood that for their comrades to attempt to remove them would be almost certain death, and waited patiently till the close of the fight should allow them to be cared for. The general and his staff alone stood erect or passed up and down the lines, and kept a close watch to the front for the first indication of the expected charge. Of course our batteries were not silent. They fired rapidly and well, but the enemy seemed to fire two guns to our one. . . .

About four o'clock, the shout, "There they come" from our watchful general, brought every man's arms into his hands, and many a man's heart to his mouth. Two long and heavy lines came over the opposite ridge and advanced upon us. Down they came to about half the distance between our lines and their batteries, when our Thirteenth and Fourteenth regiments were ordered up, and rose in a close and steady line. At the sight the rebel column seemed to halt for an instant, then turned at a right angle and marched across the front of our brigade, then turning again at a right angle, came in on the charge, a few rods to the right of our brigade. The troops holding the lines there met the rebels with a line of fire; but the gray masses still came on, with unearthly yells, led by an officer on horseback who rode back and forth waving a red battle flag and cheering on his men. They had nearly reached the Union bayonets, and it began to be a question how lines of battle but two men deep could stand the onset of a massed column, when a new and unlooked for arrangement changed the appearance of things. The point of attack had no sooner become evident, than General Stannard ordered forward the Thirteenth and Sixteenth regiments to take the enemy on the flank. The Vermonters marched a few rods to the right, and then, changing front, swung out at right angles to the main line, close upon the flank of the charging column, and opened fire. This was more than the rebels had counted on. They began to break and scatter from the rear in less than five minutes, and in ten more it was an utter rout. A portion made their way back to their own side; but fully two-thirds, I should think, of their number, dropped their arms and came in as prisoners. Of course they suffered terribly in killed and wounded. The Fourteenth had kept up a constant fire upon them, and a line of dead bodies marked their line of march across its front, while where their column came in on the charge their dead literally strewed the ground.

It was a savage onset and a glorious repulse; but it did not end the fight on the left centre. Veazey and Randall and their men were occupied with the agreeable duty of receiving colonels' and majors' swords, when the order came to "about face" and meet another charge. A body of the enemy, evidently the supporting body of the main rebel column, was coming down to the left of us, apparently aiming at the position of the Fourteenth. The same mode of treatment was applied to their case, with the happiest result. The Fourteenth met them with a hot fire in front, and Colonel Veazey with the Sixteenth, hurrying back on the double quick, took them on the flank and bagged about a brigade of them. . . . With these repulses of the enemy the big fight in effect closed. There was some skirmishing on our left, but no more hard fighting. At dark I was sent out with a detail of men, and stationed a picket line across the front of our brigade, and at 9 o'clock our Vermont regiments were relieved from their position in the front line and allowed to find rest and comparative relief from care a little distance in the rear.

I cannot give the loss of the brigade, as the list of casualties has not yet been prepared. It cannot be much less than 300 killed and wounded. The list of missing will be small. I did not at any time see a man of the brigade making for the rear.

The length of this hurried letter compels me to leave undescribed many an interesting incident of the fight, some of which I may perhaps describe in a future letter. One or two, however, must not be passed over.

Gen. Hancock was shot from his horse while he was talking to Gen. Stannard. I helped the latter to bandage Hancock's wound and his blood stained my hands. I might say *stains* my hands, for there has been no water to wash with, and not much to drink, where we have been on this field.

During the last sharp shower of grape and shell, with which the enemy strove to cover their retreat, Gen. Stannard was wounded in the right leg by a shrapnel ball, which passed down for three inches into the muscle of the thigh. The wound was very painful until a surgeon came and removed the ball, but the general refused to leave the field, though urged to go by Gen. Doubleday. He kept up till the regiments had marched back and till the wounded had been removed and then sank fainting on the ground and was taken to the rear.

He was about the coolest man I saw on the field, exposing himself in a way that would have been rashness, were it not the need he felt of animating his men by his example. He was a constant mark for the enemy's sharpshooters, but nothing daunted or disconcerted him. To his presence of mind and timely orders is largely due the glorious success of yesterday. The general is proud of his troops and they of him; and Vermont may well be proud of both.

The brigade, or the three regiments engaged, is still on the battlefield. We have no tents, no fires and nothing to cook if we had. The men stand or sit in knots near their stacked arms, worn, hungry and battlestained; but a better feeling body of men one does not often see. The big battle is over; and every man is glad to have had a part in it.

Yours, B.

Source: George Grenville Benedict, *Army Life in Virginia* (Burlington, Vt.: Free Press Association, 1895), pp. 159-60, 163, 166-70, 173-81.

DOCUMENT 15

"To the Selectmen of the Several Towns in the State; to Recruiting Officers; and to All Patriotic and Loyal Citizens!" (1864)

Six months ago, in pursuance with an order from the War Department, the State authorities commenced to raise a Regiment to be called the Seventeenth Vermont Volunteers (Veterans), with a prospect that the same would in a few weeks be filled; but various circumstances have combined to retard enlistments in said Regiment, so that to-day four hundred men are lacking to fill the same. The great obstacles in filling this Regiment have been that larger bounties have been paid to men to enlist in old Regiments, and men enlisted for this Regiment were not credited to towns on their quotas, which is not now the case. The men already raised for said Regiment are idle, and must be until the Regiment is filled. The several towns in the State are in arrears of men sufficient to fill this Regiment, and probably a good deal more. The Government is demanding the raising of these men, and until the 1st of March pay a

BOUNTY OF THREE HUNDRED DOLLARS,
to raw recruits, and
FOUR HUNDRED DOLLARS

to Veterans, after which a draft will be ordered to raise them. It is apparent that the towns can much easier raise their deficiencies, aided by the Government bounties. It can easily be done if towns will take ho'd of the matter in earnest. Don't let us keep the Seventeenth Regiment longer as a public charge, but fill it, that it may be off, doing service in the cause of the right. I make this as a personal appeal, for I am anxious to be in the field with this Regiment, where the Government will very soon so much need us. You are imperatively called on for these men. Let us have them and avoid a draft.

As many men are ready to enlist from towns whose quotas are full, provided they can get a town bounty, such towns as are paying a town bounty as will notify me of about how many men they need, I can aid them in procuring them. And to men who are desirous to enlist and obtain town bounties, if they will enlist with the selectmen of the towns, or with any recruiting officer for the Seventeenth Regiment, leaving the place of their residence blank, and have the officer enlisting them notify me, I will have them credited to a town that will pay them a town bounty, until all such towns are filled. The town bounties are in most towns three hundred dollars, where they have voted bounties at all. True economy demands that this Regiment be filled at once. Men must enlist before the 1st day of March to secure the Government bounties, but if they do not state their residence I can assign them to towns that pay a bounty after that date, so as to secure for them town bounties.

F. V. Randall,
Col. 17th Regiment Vt. Vols.,
Montpelier, Feb. 15th, 1864.

Source: "To the Selectmen of the Several Towns in the State," 1864, Broadside, Special Collections, Bailey/Howe Library, University of Vermont.

DOCUMENT 16

"The Invasion of St. Albans" (1864)
St. Albans Messenger

St. Albans has been surprised—excited. At about half-past three o'clock yesterday, our peaceable community was taken somewhat aback to find in our streets a company of some twenty or thirty armed horsemen. The meaning of it, it was impossible to divine. Men rushed from their stores and offices, not, perhaps, paralyzed with fear, but with wonderment. One enquired of another, "what does this mean?" "They are armed with revolvers!" "It is a rebel raid;" "They mean to destroy the village," were the exclamations that greeted us on all sides as we entered the street. We knew not ourself what it meant, and the neighbors, of whom we enquired, were equally ignorant. We saw men proceeding from the livery establishment of Wm. & E. D. Fuller, with horses, unharnessed, led by the ostler of the establishment, who said he would ride them—"No," said the men who ordered them, "We will take care of our own horses." Jumping on to them with impetuous haste, large navy revolvers showed themselves in the hands of all the mounted men. Mr. E. D. Fuller, who was then approaching the "scene" exclaimed: "what does this mean"; "take back those horses." "God d__m you, if you don't keep still we will shoot you," producing their revolvers. The next part of the programme was the appearance of Fuller with a poor six shooter. He stood near the shoe shop of Mr. Bildad Paul, and tried to shoot his gun, but for three consecutive times the 'thing' failed to give other utterance than a 'click.' Mr. E. J. Morrison, the contractor for our large hotel, was standing on the steps of Miss Beattie's shop, just one door north of the *Messenger* office, with hand on the latch of the door, and received a shot through his right hand, which was in his pocket passing through his bowels. He staggered to the stairway of the *Messenger* office, exclaiming, "I'm shot," pressing his hand at the same time upon his stomach. One or two of the *Messenger* hands immediately assisted him to the Drug Store of L. L. Dutcher & Son, where medical help was immediately summoned.

While this was going on, the more Southern part of Main Street was in great excitement. As we looked down the street, we saw armed horsemen shooting their guns with the greatest impunity. Our citizens stood silent, and almost speechless. A man came running up the street, exclaiming, "All the banks are robbed." "What shall we do?" "What can we do?" was the universal answer. About that moment appeared Captain George R. Conger, of the 1st Vermont cavalry, who urged the citizens to arm themselves with anything, even with broomsticks. "We have a lot of rebel riders upon us," he emphatically exclaimed, and "let us catch them." During the first ten minutes time, the raiders were entering our banks, stealing horses, and awing our citizens in the most frightful manner. Their first descent was upon the National Bank. They entered it without any resistance—and it was impossible to make any. They took $29,650 in 7 3-10 Treasury bonds, in denominations of 50's, 100's, 500's and 1,000's; $10,000 in 5 per cent legal tender coupon notes; $5,000 legal tender interest bearing notes; $8,000 in currency on N. E. Banks and green backs. On entering the Franklin County Bank the cashier, Mr. Beardsley, and a man by the name of Clark, with whom the cashier was settling for some work he had been doing for him, were unceremoniously shoved into the bank safe, and the key turned upon them. The raiders, of course, then

helped themselves to all the visible funds there were. The amount taken from the bank was about $20,000. Mr. J. R. Armington, coming into the bank a few minutes after, finding it apparently vacant, and mistrusting something, asked, "Who's here?" when Mr. Beardsley, from his 'closely confined den,' said, "let us out." The safe was opened, and out came the imprisoned, somewhat alarmed, as may be readily supposed. The St. Albans Bank was the next operation of the raiders. Quietly they entered it and the tellers, Messrs. Bishop and Seymour, were compelled to take the Confederate oath, much to the disgust of these loyal and respectable men. Mr. Breck, of the firm of Breck & Wetherbee, coming into the bank at this time with $400 in hand to deposit, was insolently informed by one of the raiders that he "took deposits," and seized the money from him. The raiders then proceeded to ransack "the money department" of the bank, and succeeded in carrying off a large amount.

Our citizens about this time commenced realizing their position. They felt that the town was invaded in earnest. All went in search of arms—and, indeed, few there were in town; horses were in great requisition, as were shot guns and revolvers. The raiders, marauders, or confederate thieves quietly proceeded northward. In twenty minutes or less, a company of horsemen to the number of about forty, we should judge, was organized by Capts. Mewton and Stranaham and others. The brave Capt. Conger and a few others having preceded them—which immediately started in pursuit. The pursuers kept close to the marauders, who on their arrival in Sheldon set fire to the bridge, also barn of Mr. Alfred Keith, but the fire was promptly extinguished. Being closely pursued by the party from here they had no time to rob the bank at Sheldon, and the raiders thence went directly towards Canada to Slab city, where the "advance guard" of the pursuers reached them. Some jumped from their horses, in the greatest haste, and "took" for the woods. On application to the Canadian authorities, two of the robbers were arrested and put in irons. The Canadian authorities, then with commendable energy, went in search of the robbers. At this writing we learn there have been arrested at Slab city or near that place three, and six at Stanbridge, where fifty thousand dollars were also recovered.

Our town is most thoroughly organized. Never before has the excitement been so great in this section of the country; and the presence of militia from Burlington, Montpelier, and Brattleboro is a safeguard of security. An attempt was made by the marauders to fire several of our buildings. An attempt was made to fire the American Hotel last night,—or rather it was discovered after the villains had left, but the fire was extinguished. This Thursday morning, Mr. Atwood on attempting to open his store found that a portion of it was ignited with phosphorus. Along our streets we cannot fail to see the bullet holes. In front and on all sides we observe the attempts of the rebels to kill and murder.

In the window of A. H. Munyan, are three or four bullet holes to be seen; it was near this point that C. H. Huntington received his wound, the shot being occasioned by his determined persistence to stop the operation of the raiders. We are glad to be able to say that Mr. Huntington is likely to recover.

The appearance of the military here last evening, commanded by Lt. Col. Benton, somewhat aided our citizens in preserving order, and the orderly manner of the soldiers during the night and to-day, attached much credit to Col. Benton, Maj. Barstow, and Lt. Burnett.

We have much more to say concerning this "raid," but the shortness of compositors compels us here to stop. At one time during the day we were fearful that we should not be able to issue a paper, so great is the prevailing excitement.

Source: *St. Albans Daily Messenger*, 20 October 1864.

DOCUMENT 17

"Orleans County Awake; Rebels in Vermont!" (1864)

(depicted on following page)

Source: "Orleans County Awake; Rebels in Vermont!," 1864, Broadside Collection, Vermont Historical Society, Montpelier, Vermont.

DOCUMENT 18

On Woman Suffrage in Vermont (1869)

CHARLES C. DEWEY

. . . Mr. President, am I asked at this stage of the discussion if there be *any* rights which I accord to woman? One who thus asks must still have a very confused notion of the meaning of the word. Yes, sir, I accord to woman not only the right, but the duty, to fill the sphere for which she was created. I deny to the planet Venus, the goddess of beauty, the right to fill the orbit of Saturn, the god of war; but I accord to her the right to move in her own divine orbit. I do not want to see discord and confusion introduced into the motions of the earthly bodies any more than I desire to see it in the heavenly.

The report of your Committee on Suffrage represents our wives as being under our feet, and we are frantically asked to step off their necks and permit them to stand at our sides; which means, when transmuted from its sublimated nonsense into solid foolishness, give her the ballot! Sir, our wives *do* stand in freedom at our sides to-day; but not equal in stature or in physical strength. While her limbs are cast in a delicate mould, and her skin is as soft as the silken violet, the limbs of the man are framed for war, a heavy beard covers his square cut chin, and his body is shagged, like the lion, with hair. Before his exerted strength she would be crushed like the moth; before his stubborn will she would be powerless as the prey in the talons of the eagle. But, on the other hand, before her divine love, exerted in the appropriate sphere of woman, this monarch of the physical world will be moulded in the spirit of his temper and obedience to the likeness and image of a fawning and obedient babe in the arms of this angelic being! Am I, then, denying to woman any place in this poor world of ours? Sir, each sex is supreme in the sphere made for each. . . .

A few observations by way of improvement will serve to close my discourse.

1. We can not fail, sir, to perceive that this movement has its origin in unchastened ambition for the high places of worldly honor. The love of office has depraved the moral sense and blunted the otherwise keen sagac-

ORLEANS COUNTY
AWAKE

REBELS IN VERMONT!

St. Johnsbury, Oct. 19, 1864.
By Telegraph from Montpelier to Col. Grout:

Lieut. Col. Wm. W. Grout will immediately proceed to take such measures as may be necessary to organise and arm such force as may be necessary to protect the Banks at Irasburgh and Derby Line, from a

REBEL RAID NOW BEING MADE IN VERMONT!

and is hereby authorised to take command of all forces which he may raise. He will report to this office as often as possible. By order of the Governor.

P. T. WASHBURN,
Adjutant and Inspector General.

The above telegram was received by me
at 12 o'clock last night, and the special messenger who brought it from St. Johnsbury, also brought the rumor that a rebel raiding party from Canada had

Entered St. Albans,

and murdered her citizens, and in obedience to the above order I call upon every man who has a musket or rifle to

REPORT AT ONCE

for military duty during this emergency. Bring powder and ball. Those in Irasburgh and vicinity will report at Irasburgh to Rev. J. H. Woodward, whose orders they will obey. Those in Derby and vicinity will report at Derby Line to Col. B. H. Steele, whose orders they will obey. Those in Barton and vicinity will report at Barton to Capt. George H. Blake, whose orders they will obey. Those in Newport and vicinity will report at Newport to Capt. L. H. Bisbee, whose orders they will obey. Those in Troy and vicinity will report at North Troy to Hon. A. J. Rowell, whose orders they will obey.

BARTON, OCTOBER 20, 1864.

WM. W. GROUT,
Commanding Provisional Forces.

Document 17

ity of our people. It is the bane and may be the cause of the downfall of the Republic. Sir, this love of office should be eradicated from the breasts of our young men. And who could better do it than our mothers, our wives and daughters? But how, pray, if they get bewitched for it themselves? . . . Let the women, then, chasten the worldly ambition of their sons, by precept and example, and thus will they conserve the best interests of the Republic. . . .

3. Much criticism is bestowed upon the feudal system of our ancestors in connection with the wrongs of woman, the application of which to the subject in hand is not perceived. That our ancestors in Great Britain based marriage upon the Bible doctrine, is true. They called it a sacrament. They made man and wife one flesh, and they carried this divine theory into all their laws governing the family relation. Their property was commingled into a common mass. The husband was by law made her protector and defender. If her property became his, so did her liabilities. He was made responsible for her misdoings. Divorces were not granted except for adultery, in accordance with the Scriptural injunction. Sir, I do not accord wisdom to the modern legislation upon this subject. We are already reaping its baleful fruits. In theory it is attractive, in practice it is wretched. It weakens the ligatures of the marriage relation. It untwists the strands which unite the husband to the wife. Divorces are multiplied to a painful extent. Infidelity is terribly on the increase.

Thus, while we are legislating for the supposed *separate* interests of the wife, we are forgetful of the awful consequences that follow from disregarding the divine law, which can never be disregarded by either individuals or governments without incurring the divine wrath and punishment.

4. It is urged that woman may exercise the function of voting without going out of her natural sphere, and that she will carry into its performance all the divine attributes of her nature, and thus throw a good influence around the polls. What an assumption! It is belied by the experience of all history, and is contrary to nature. Voting is a function, not a natural right. It is a power exerted, as much as the thrust of a bayonet. It calls up, in its exercise, all the passions of the human heart, on its side of will and force, as completely as does an engagement in battle. And, sir, it is not merely the casting of the ballot, which in the glowing language of your committee, is said to fall like a pure snow-flake upon the breast of the earth, that constitutes the entire performance of this function. It is what precedes it. It is the long political campaign, in which the worst human passions get aroused. It is the political caucus and convention, it is the prior private discussion, the personal rivalries, growing day by day in bitterness, breaking out in family feuds that last for life, and descend to the children, even unto the third and fourth generation, that make up the inherent evil of the elective system of government. In her own station, woman may allay much of this excitement. She may allay the passions of man with her own sweet nature, and subdue him to the dominion of the pure influences of her gentle heart. But can she do this by participating with him in the excitement, the wrangling, the bitter partizanship of the strife? Will not her more susceptible nature be more easily excited, and her passions be more uncontrolled than his own? Witness the French Revolution! Women led the column of those who shouted in frenzy for blood, and they paddled their feet in fiendish delight in the blood that flowed from the guillotine! Sir, within her own sphere, she may control the destinies of the nation through the ballot. She may *muster* voters; she may send them to the polls filled with patriotism, as a Roman mother sent her son to the war, with a shield, saying, "This, or on this."

5. It is said that woman has shown her capacity to rule, as illustrated in the lives of the Queens who have occasionally filled the thrones of the empires of the world. I deny it. Under the wise theory of the governments over which they have reigned, they were not, by the general rule, recognized as being in the line of monarchs. They were permitted to reign as a necessary evil, to fill up a gap in the line of male descent. Some of them, by the aid of wise male counselors, have made a respectable figure in history. Most of them have been lamentable failures.

6. Sir, nowhere in any bill of rights is the ballot defined to be a natural right. The right to vote is not born with the person, as is the right to life and liberty, and the right of self-defence. . . . Sir, it seems to be logical, that if women are to claim the right to vote, as being a natural right, it follows that she ought also to bear arms, as that is declared by the Constitution to be an inherent right. And, sir, so believing, I offered a resolution instructing the Committee on Suffrage to enquire

into the expediency of so amending the Constitution as to compel women to bear arms as well as men. . . . I claim, sir, that the ballot and the bayonet go together. Without the one, the other would be useless. It is no answer to say that the duty to bear arms is not, by our law, made co-extensive with the right to vote. There is no general rule without its exception, and the exception proves the rule. Age and physical infirmity only constitute the exception. . . .

Mr. President, there is one department of human government in which I would permit women to have a controlling voice. To gain it does not require the giving her the ballot. She should have a controlling voice in the management of the schools and seminaries of learning, in the management of the hospitals and institutions of public charity. . . . For these, sir, are but the adjuncts, the nurseries of the family; love and obedience and purity preside in them, and no bitter political contests need be involved in their management. Sir, the men are ready to concede these places to women. No amendment of the Constitution is needed to this end. The spirit of Christianity has already laid the path open to her, and she has but to walk therein.

Mr. President, permit me to say, that this, to me, is a strange spectacle! . . . Shall we, by proposing this amendment to the Constitution, invite the army of harpies, representing all the forms of infidelity which afflict the age, free love, woman suffrage, and the kindred fruits which hang from a common stem, to come into this little State of Vermont and make it, for the next two years, the battle ground of these pestiferous *isms*? Shall they come in swarms, as they are anxiously waiting to do, and come on *our* invitation, to debauch the hearts of our wives and daughters, and draw them from that sphere in which they now move, the admiration and the hope of the world? Sir, I have five little girls, growing into womanhood: may my tongue cleave to the roof of my mouth, and my right arm wither, before I will consent to expose them to be devoured by these ravenous wolves. In their tenderness they may be misled, through appeals to their vanity, their love of pleasure, and of conspicuous places. Sir, I would invite the Serpent again into the garden of Eden as soon as I would invite these emissaries of his design into this State. . . .

Hence it is, Mr. President, that all the right minded women in the land, look upon this movement with the utmost aversion and loathing. It is confined, sir, to a few eccentric females, and to a class of politicians who can hope for no repute in treading the old ways. They are like the Athenians and strangers whom Paul met on Mars-hill, who spent their time in nothing else but either to tell or to hear some new thing, and whom Paul addressed in that most wonderful of all oratorical productions: "Ye men of Athens, I perceive that in all things ye are too superstitious; whom ye *ignorantly* worship, him declare I unto you." It was an old truth which Paul laid before these Athenians. It is an old truth I have laid before you today.

Sir, if we visit the places of the entombment of the dead empires of the world, we shall find upon the monuments which commemorate them, this inscription: "Perished, because, though the Word of God is sure and steadfast, and a never failing source of personal and national glory and endurance, yet hath man turned away from it, and sought out many inventions!" How long shall poor, weak man continue to seek out these "many inventions" under the name of "human rights" and "liberty," in whose sacred name only too many crimes have already been committed? God has given the woodpecker the instinct to build its nest as perfectly on the first trial, as when, in the morning of the creation, it first rattled its music to the rising sun. Man, being an accountable creature, God has given to him a law of conduct as binding and as perfect and unerring as the instinct of the bird, but in his blind ambition he has sought out many inventions, and hence he learns only by mistakes. Experience means the knowledge of failure. If man would only foll[o]w the eternal ordinances of God as unerringly as the feathered songster follows its God-given instincts; if he would only learn, after six thousand years of miserable failure, to leave off making his foolish inventions, and calling them "Human Progress, number one millionth, patent applied for by Lucy Stone;" then would the Kingdom of God and His glorious Millenium be ushered in. But until then, we must wait in patience and in prayer and in hope, and struggle manfully against the sad procession of the errors and follies of our still unregenerate race.

Source: Charles C. Dewey, *Woman Suffrage, Speech . . . Delivered in the Council of Censors, Montpelier, August 4th, 1869* (Montpelier: Journal Press, 1869), pp. 19-29.

SECTION SEVEN

1870-1896
Old Ideals and New Ideas

Section Seven

1870-1896
Old Ideals and New Ideas

Introduction

The breakdown of isolation in the lives of Vermont people and communities that began in the 1830s and 1840s gained momentum in the last three decades of the nineteenth century. Spurred by advances in communications, an impulse toward organization, and practical necessity, Vermonters in growing numbers turned to formal groups and associations to share information and to deal with their common problems. Contemporaneously, state government activity continued to expand, so that despite strong traditions of localism and individualism, Vermont found itself in the forefront of a consolidating, centralizing trend of state governments nationally. Many of these initiatives were driven by the triple challenge of rural poverty, emigration, and the rapid pace of economic change. Vermonters, while not backing away from long-cherished Green Mountain values of individualism and independence, signaled, in diverse ways, a readiness for new approaches to the task of preserving traditional interests and ideals from end-of-century threats.

Concern for Vermont's rural and agricultural future was a dominating theme of the period. This worry prompted state legislators in 1870 to create the Board of Agriculture, Manufactures, and Mining, an agency that, despite its title, focused almost wholly on trying to save Vermont farms. The board and its several successors over the next thirty years gathered statistics, published and disseminated periodic reports, sponsored meetings, and issued advice about new crops and agricultural techniques. **Document 1** is an excerpt from "Vermont as a Home," a paper presented in 1872 by Zuar E. Jameson, an Irasburg farmer and schoolteacher, at a meeting of the state Board of Agriculture in St. Johnsbury. Jameson expresses a broadly shared frustration over the continued loss of farmers from the state, makes the case for Vermont farming as a profitable and fulfilling way of life, and laments that so many of his fellow citizens have been misled by the "false promise" of the West. Despite such arguments, and the board's activities, however, the out-migration continued, as did population shifts within the state, to towns and away from the less productive hill farms and villages, with a result that Vermont's rural population dropped by one third in the half century after 1850.

Farmers who remained in Vermont during the extended nineteenth-century population exodus nevertheless did not avoid having to cope with the challenge of change, and, in fact, responded to the era's altering circumstances with considerable versatility and resilience. In their pragmatic search for reliable profits, Vermont's farmers, over a seventy-five-year period, embraced successively, as their primary agricultural commodities, wheat and corn, then sheep, before finally settling on dairying after the Civil War. The adjustment from sheep to the more stable-priced products of dairy farming was completed between 1870 and 1890, a period in which the number of cows in the state doubled, enabling Vermont to take the lead among New England farmers in butter and cheese production. **Document 2** traces the nineteenth-century evolution of the profitable butter market in St. Albans, whose creamery, according to local claims, produced more butter than any other plant in the world. The document is excerpted from a speech delivered in March of 1872 by Dr. R. R. Sherman, of St. Albans, before the Board of Agriculture.

The steady growth of industrial towns after the Civil War provided a powerful signal of Vermont's declining economic and cultural homogeneity. In 1880, Rutland overtook Burlington as the state's largest city, aided by its location as an important railroad center and by the large population of wage workers drawn to the area's expanding marble quarrying excavations. By 1886, employees in Rutland County marble works had acquired sufficient collective strength to form a chapter of Terence Powderly's national worker organization, the Knights of Labor. Powderly's goal, to bring into his union everyone who "toiled" (excluding only bankers, lawyers, gamblers, speculators, and liquor salesmen), was reminiscent of Vermont's Working Men's movement of the 1830s in its definition of "producers" and its adversarial relationship to special privilege and monopoly. The Knights were at the pinnacle of their national strength in 1886, and the organization's presence in Rutland represented a multilayered challenge to the authority of former Vermont governor Redfield Proctor and his Vermont Marble Company, the state's largest corporation at the time. With a membership mostly of immigrants or the sons of immigrants, the Rutland Knights sought not only to improve workers' economic well-being but also to provide a mechanism for their entrance into local politics. In September of 1886 they formed an alliance with small businessmen, fielding a ticket of "independent labor" candidates that swept the election and gave Rutland its first Irish-American and French-Canadian officeholders. This community alliance controlled town politics for the next ten years, putting an end to the closed, self-selected structure of political leadership that had governed Rutland for years. **Document 3**, excerpted from an article published in the *Rutland Herald* on January 29, 1886, contains the first public announcement of the Knights' presence in the city.

Group problem-solving also attracted the interest of Vermont's ruggedly independent farmers in this period. The uneven, disappointing performance of the Board of Agriculture hastened the formation of private organizations by such specialized agricultural groups as Morgan horse farmers, dairymen, sheep farmers, and maple sugar makers. The largest and most active of these agricultural organizations was the Patrons of Husbandry (Grange), founded in 1871. Although its leaders repeatedly stated that their group was "not political in any sense," the Vermont Grange lobbied the state legislature on behalf of tax reform, railroad regulation, and a law barring the sale of oleomargarine, and it spoke out against "monopolies and combinations that are in antagonism to the well being and advancement of our order." In its most ambitious political battle the Grange took on the state's railroad corporations, primarily the Central Vermont and Rutland roads, and achieved modest success in 1886 with legislation creating a three-person state board of railroad commissioners. Railroad-friendly state legislators managed to resist further regulatory advances despite election-year commitments to Grange goals by the state Republican Party and Governors Ebenezer Ormsbee and William P. Dillingham. **Document 4** is an excerpt from a speech in 1887 by Alpha Messer, head of the Vermont State Grange, protesting the legislative favoritism enjoyed by the railroads, the railroads' own industrial customer favoritism, and the excessively high local freight rates, which he depicted as a discouragement to the state's industrial growth.

The state Grange was unusual in Victorian Vermont in the wide latitude it offered for the participation of women in its activities. For many middle- and upper-class Vermont women in towns and cities, however, it was the issue of liquor prohibition that provided the largest opportunity for making use of their talent, and their activism on this issue ignited a renewed effort for voting rights in the state. In the early 1870s, Vermont churchwomen began a crusade for more rigorous enforcement of the state's 1852 prohibitory law. As a part of this effort, in 1874, a group of activists formed the Vermont chapter of the Women's Christian Temperance Union (WCTU). WCTU's leaders soon concluded that in order to forward the anti-liquor cause, their all-female organization would need more direct political involvement. In 1879 the Union played an instrumental role in gaining legislation permitting tax-paying women to vote at school district meetings and to hold the office of school commissioner. Many Vermont women, however, opposed WCTU's move toward political activism, and when delegates at the annual state meeting in September 1888 adopted resolutions (**Document 5**) that included an endorsement of full woman's suffrage and strong positions on other non-liquor-related reform causes, the action opened a deep fissure within the Union's membership. A few weeks later the Vermont House of Representatives rejected a bill granting women the franchise in municipal elections by a resounding 192-37 vote, and Vermont's WCTU chapter soon thereafter abandoned the woman's suffrage issue.

In the post-Civil War years, responsibility for Vermont's poor citizens remained a local matter, and the relief they received, in almost all instances, was inadequate. The state's ongoing economic difficulties pushed many unfortunate farm families into indigent status. They were joined by sizable numbers of Irish and French-Canadian immigrants, especially in the larger towns. **Document 6** provides descriptions, excerpted from nineteenth-century town history accounts, of the varied attempts by two Vermont towns, Newbury and Stowe, to cope with their infirm and indigent poor. Upbeat assessments of such efforts, as in the description of Stowe's poor farm, should be balanced by other local perceptions. In the 1870s one fearful resident of Stowe, Seth Chase, wrote, "I'll starve or freeze to death there [in the woods] before I will go to that accursed poorhouse." In 1876, nevertheless, the luckless Chase died at the Stowe poor farm. It was not until the mid-twentieth century, with the emergence of a federal commitment to welfare, that the poor farm and its ancillary methods of caring for the needy faded completely from the Vermont landscape.

By 1880 the state government had become essentially indistinguishable from the Republican Party. Between 1854 and the end of the century, Republicans won majorities in every statewide election and carried the state's electoral votes for all of its presidential candidates. Democrats were little more than patronage-seekers, leaving political competition and policy debate to be subsumed within the Republican organization. Republicans, meanwhile, sought to minimize factionalism through a mechanism known as the "mountain rule" that apportioned statewide offices between the east side and the west side of the Green Mountains in an informal rotating system. In 1890, despite mounting their strongest post-Civil War electoral challenge, Democrats still fell 110 votes short of a majority in the house, and acquired only one of thirty senate seats. **Document 7** is an article by C. H. Davenport, "The Future of Democracy in Vermont," published on the eve of the 1890 election. In it, Davenport, editor of the *Windham County Reformer*, anticipates a Democratic resurgence in Vermont. He recounts his party's difficult past and calls on individual voters to begin applying, again, the "Democratic idea of the diffusion of powers" in both the public and private sector, rather than allowing the continued accumulation of Republican spoils and of monopoly power in the hands of Vermont's railroads and other corporate interests.

In the late 1880s, Vermont legislators again turned their attention to the continuing problem of native sons' and daughters' emigration from the state, and the mounting number of abandoned hill farms. Governor William P. Dillingham, acting under legislative mandate to gain information and devise strategies for repopulating the hill country farm areas, appointed Alonzo B. Valentine, a wealthy Bennington businessman, to take on the task. **Document 8** is Dillingham's assessment of the migration issue. It is excerpted from his address to the Vermont General Assembly on October 2, 1890. Valentine approached the repopulation challenge by looking abroad to find individuals who might be willing to accept the special hardships of hill country life. He had in mind not more immigrants from Ireland or French Canada but instead the "industrious" and Anglo-Saxon-appearing North Europeans— Swedes in particular—whom the state of Maine had enjoyed some success in recruiting a few years earlier, in a repopulation program of its own. Valentine sent a recruiting agent to Sweden, and he also provided information on Vermont's unoccupied farms to the United States minister there. These efforts nevertheless attracted fewer than thirty migrant families to the state, most of whom settled in the small towns of Wilmington and Weston. The state legislature did not authorize funds for the continuation of Valentine's work, and by 1892 several of the new Swedish arrivals had already abandoned Wilmington and Weston in search of economic betterment elsewhere.

In the 1890s the state's economic performance continued a sluggish pattern. In search of revenue sources, several leading Vermonters embraced the view that the Green Mountains' tranquil rural scenery and bountiful supply of fish and game might be a means for enticing summer visitors and thus enhancing the state's prosperity and general well-being. Earlier in the century numerous mineral water resorts and large lakeside hotels had been a lure for travelers and tourists, but Vermont's share in New England's tourist trade always remained modest. Officials now began efforts not only to systematically promote tourism but to "keep up our attractions" through legislative mandates for environmental conservation and "resupply." In **Document 9**, John W. Titcomb, secretary of the private, politically influential Vermont Fish and Game League, specifically links prospects for tourist trade success with expanded state responsibility for natural resources conservation. Titcomb's assessment was published in the state Board of Agriculture's annual report in 1892, shortly before his appointment to the position of Vermont Fish and Game commissioner.

By the 1890s Vermont's immigrant population had grown to more than 13 percent of the state's residents, and French Canadians had replaced the Irish as the dominant newcomer group. French-Canadian assimilation into the mainstream of Vermont life, however, remained limited. Most lived in the state's northern tier of counties, clung to their distinctive identity, and made frequent return visits to their Canadian homes of origin. Measured by occupation, they stayed generally in the lower strata of Vermont's society, drawn to the sorts of nonpermanent and seasonal employment that, at mid-century, had been identified with the Irish. In **Document 10**, Rowland E. Robinson makes clear his view that the state's French-Canadian population was an alien, discordant, and unwelcome element. Robinson, whose father had been a prominent Vermont abolitionist and agent of the underground railroad, managed the family farm near Ferrisburgh and enjoyed a reputation as an able regional writer, popular for his nostalgic depictions of rural Vermont life. In this document, excerpted from *Vermont: A Study of Independence* (1892), his widely read history of the Green Mountain state, Robinson records his doubts that French Canadians can adequately replace Vermont sons and daughters migrating West, or that they are competent to perpetuate the traditions and values he believed critical to Vermont identity.

The effort to attract tourists mentioned by John W. Titcomb in Document 9, was part of a broad new program directed by the Board of Agriculture in the "selling of Vermont." The Swedish immigrant project and a campaign to market the vacant hillside farm structures to city people for summer homes were other parts of the program. It was the summer home initiative that led the board to the concept of the "farm vacation": that the fresh air and solitude of Vermont's pastoral landscape could become a profitable enticement for those wanting a summertime escape from the city, or who were simply impelled by nostalgia for rural life. Victor I. Spear, statistical secretary of the Board of Agriculture, directed the program. **Document 11** is an excerpt from a speech Spear presented in 1893 to a farm audience at Brattleboro. In it he depicts the summer tourist as a new specialty "cash crop" and calls on Vermont's farmers to cultivate this "crop" by becoming summer hosts to city visitors, boarding and feeding them in their farm homes, and providing them with an authentic rural experience. Spear saw the "farm vacation" plan as an important contribution toward preserving the future of the Vermont farm.

As the century neared its end, no Vermont community presented a larger challenge to Rowland E.

Robinson's nostalgic vision of the state than did Barre. After the Central Vermont Railroad built a spur line linking the town to the main line at Montpelier Junction, in 1875, Barre and its granite industry underwent a rapid expansion. The number of granite companies more than doubled, to a total of 146, and Barre became, for a few years, the second leading industrial center in the state, after Burlington. Its workforce, composed largely of new arrivals from Scotland, northern Italy, Spain, Ireland, and elsewhere in Europe, encompassed diverse traditions and customs that transformed Barre into a cosmopolitan mixing-bowl community. Political views shaped by bitter old-country experiences informed the local dialogue. By 1900, ninety percent of area workers in quarries and sheds belonged to one of fifteen local unions, and many of them identified themselves politically as socialists or anarchists. **Document 12** provides a description of the difficult conditions of life and employment on Barre's Millstone Hill in the period of most rapid expansion. George Ellsworth Hooker wrote this excerpted commentary in 1895, when Millstone Hill provided living quarters for two thousand persons, and six hundred men were employed in its quarries.

The continuing loss of population in Vermont's rural areas and the ominous implications of this trend for the state's economic and social future remained a major concern among state leaders as the end of the century approached. In **Document 13**, Harriet M. Rice considers ways to persuade young Vermont women to remain in their farm homes even though their lives might be isolated and lonely and their prospects bleak. A number of familiar themes come together in the essay, either explicitly or implicitly. The contrast between the uncertain "promise" pursued by the out-migrant and the blessings of "Vermont as a Home," is certainly one. Others include the appropriateness of responsibility by state government, the community, and the individual in efforts to raise the quality of rural life; the ongoing need for school improvement; the double-edged impact of education in a rural setting; and woman's place.

DOCUMENT 1

"Vermont as a Home" (1872)

ZUAR E. JAMESON

The love of home is an affection that should exist in the minds of the majority of the citizens in every prosperous country. It aids in bearing with patience the disagreeable circumstances that will cross the lives of all. It tends to contentment and happiness. It is the battle cry of nations, and inspires the soldier to deeds of valor and daring. It exists in the minds of children; a glorious halo seems to rest around the memory of the old hearthstone, brothers, sisters, and especially parents; the fields, flocks, herds, fowls, as well as our favorite play grounds, all rise up in found recollections. We sympathize with a true love of home, even by those who have left homes of want and oppression. . . .

But I fear in Vermont but a small portion have a sincere respect and affection for the place of their nativity, regarding it so lightly that, as the spaniel shakes from him the superfluous water and hides away after a cooling bath in some other brook, so the Vermonter with the same carefulness shakes himself free from home, relatives, and all early associations, and seeks new scenes. Old parents are in loneliness, wearing life away. Children early throw off restraint, and the man who so easily divorces himself from other ties, does not always hesitate to sever the marriage relation. The item is afloat that "three hundred divorces were given in Vermont last year," and at the West who can number them? It is a by-word and a reproach.

We infer that the love of home is not deep-seated in Vermont, because her rural towns are losing in population. One writer puts the loss at 30,000 from the agricultural districts. Referring to Windham county, he says: "In every direction we find the relics of an ancient household, a few decaying timbers, an old cellar, and the crumbling chimney." An old school teacher says that when a young man he taught a school of seventy scholars in one district on this hill. In this district there is now no school, no scholars, and only two houses inhabited. In another district adjoining, in which there is not a single house standing, he taught a school of sixty scholars.

Thirteen towns in Caledonia county have lost in the last decade an average of over one hundred each; the town of Waterford two hundred and ninety-four, and Danville three hundred and twenty-seven. If I may judge these towns by Irasburgh, that lost only forty-six, I should believe that in many instances the deserted farms had been joined to others, so that what was once several homesteads is now one large farm. It is an easy matter to count a dozen homesteads thus given up in almost any of our towns, and as many of these are well situated, with fertile soil, we infer that the love of home was not a prominent virtue in those who left them.

Now what do we know? We know there are many people in the state that do not make necessary improvements and repairs, because they are intending to sell the first chance they get, and therefore are afraid it won't pay. We know there are others who are making improvements and repairs on purpose to sell, and believe it will pay. We know there is a large class that believe if they were out West they would be much better off, and no matter how low Vermont is rated by returned travelers, they will not resent any insult heaped upon the State or its people. . . .

No country can stand the continuous drain of both young men and capital, that has been going on in Vermont the past years. There has doubtless been over $150,000 carried West from my own native town within fifteen years. Who can estimate the amount carried from the whole State? Who can value the educated minds, the productive power and enterprise, that are lost by the removal of our young men? Mountains covered with timber, full of iron, copper, marble and slate, water power to turn machinery, fertile meadows and hillsides that should yield abundantly of all vegetable growth that sustains life, all is of little value without men to move these treasures and utilize these forces.

Some speak with contempt of the increase of population at Rutland, Burlington, and St. Albans, saying it is of an illiterate and transient character, and therefore of little value to the State. But not so, for at the head of these enterprises are men of intelligence, who by their planning and direction cause a thousand arms and hands to do their bidding, thus making them like their own hands increased a thousand fold in power. An ignorant, unskilled workman wandering loose in society may be a source of weakness, but when his whole strength is engaged by the ablest talent in the country, his productive power is of more value probably than the self-directed efforts of an ordinary man.

A writer from Illinois estimates the value of Chinamen to the State at $2,000 each, the moment they are landed in their midst. The conclusions are that every home broken up in Vermont and transferred to the West is a loss to us of all the money carried away, and certainly $2,000 for each individual. Notwithstanding our regrets for the depopulation of the State; it is very right and proper for it to continue if there is no merit in our soil, climate or surroundings. If straight, practical farming, that basis of true prosperity, *cannot be made profitable*, it is useless to try and stop the outgoing tide of emigration. We should rather hasten the departure of all that are able to go. . . . How does Vermont compare with other sections? By referring to the reports of the Agricultural Department at Washington, I find that in 1867, only two States in the Union raised more wheat per acre, and only one State raised more corn per acre. In 1868, no State raised as much wheat per acre, and only one State more corn. In 1869, two States gave a heavier yield per acre, and four States more corn per acre. In 1870, Vermont is ahead of all the States on corn, and there are eight States where the price of corn was less than fifty cents per bushel. In four States the yield of wheat is more, while eight States yield less than ten bushels per acre.

I am aware that in other States more acres are cultivated on each farm than is the practice in Vermont. But the figures brought to your attention show the fertility of our soil, and capabilities of our climate. Consider also that the ordinary hay crop is worth as much per acre here as the corn crop at the West, and in the hay crop is where our acres tell. In Iowa, 32 bushels of corn per acre at 34 cents, is $10.83 per acre; a ton of hay in Vermont more than equals it in value.

But let us drop details, and admit that the farmer in Iowa can plow his farm of, say, 100 acres, and raise 3,200 bushels of corn that would bring him 34 cents per bushel. To balance this, the Vermont farmer on 100 cleared acres can keep fifteen cows that will yield as much profit; for his butter averages higher per pound than the Iowan's corn per bushel.

A farm at the West devoted to raising grain for market does not improve in value. There are usually very poor accommodations for storing crops. The grain is sold, and nothing remains behind, with no other source of income. But upon a Vermont dairy farm run to its full capacity, there are many other items of income such as calves, pigs, pork, poultry, sugar from the woodland, and then the large quantities of manure cause abundant crops from which a surplus is often spared. I have the statistics of over 700 farms in Orleans county where all items of produce are given by the farmer himself, but it is useless for me to give you the items of his income, for I doubt not every farmer among this audience knows of many instances where men have bought farms on credit, and from the produce have paid debts, supported families, built good buildings, filled their houses with comforts, educated their children, and improved their farm and stock. If this is so, as I know it is, then we can say farming, plain, simple, practical, legitimate farming, pays in Vermont. Yes, pays, notwithstanding the constant draining away of strength and capital to the West. If Vermont was constantly receiving a tide of young, healthy emigrants, with thousands of dollars to invest in our various industries, I doubt not our prosperity would excite the wonder and admiration of other States and nations.

Let us now consider one of the principal causes of the popularity of the West. 1st. The rise of real estate. It is said that a man with a few thousands of dollars can go out there and buy land and not lift his finger to work, yet will increase in wealth faster than he can in Vermont with all his industry. . . .

A former resident of Orleans county came from Illinois last year. He went there with one thousand dollars fifteen years ago. He recently buried his wife, (an event that frequently happens to our western emigrants,) sold out, and was worth $10,000. He says, "I did not make it by raising corn at eight cents a bushel, as I have sold it at that price, and burned it for fuel all winter. I made my money by rise of land, and shall now go West and invest it again." This rise in real estate depends upon the direction new comers take. There are settlements in Wisconsin that at this time are disconsolate because they are in debt. Their crops were partly destroyed by storms, and at the low price hardly paid for the necessary help to harvest them. Money commands a high rate of interest, and no one comes to pay them double the price they paid, and they look with the greatest interest and anxiety to see if Congress and eastern capitalists will build a railroad to bring men and women to their relief.

We freely admit that land does rise in value at the West. Its first cost is nothing. A homestead for $15.00!

But how is it in Vermont? At one time I set myself to compiling an array of statistics to show that the good farms that pay debts and support families do at the same time rise in value. But I found the proof so plenty that it seems useless to make a statement. On every road, in every town, there are cases in point. A friend from Craftsbury writes me that farms have advanced in ten years, on an average, 30 per cent and in some cases much more, where no permanent improvements had been made except in fencing. He gives the following from many instances of farms sold:

One in 1854, for $1100; in 1857, $1600; in 1867, $2500. Keeps six cows and team.

One in 1854, $1600; in 1863, $2500; in 1866, $3000. Keeps twelve to fourteen cows and team.

One in 1854, $1400; in 1860, $1800; worth 1870, $3500.

In Irasburgh one farm of 220 acres cost in 1858, $6000. In 1868, 170 acres were added at a cost of $2500, making a total cost of $8500. It is now worth, $16,000.

Another farmer paid in 1850, for 220 acres, $3500. It was worth in 1870, $12,000.

A farm of 60 acres in 20 years has advanced from $500 to $3000.

But why should I enumerate instances? Wherever a man farms to make himself a desirable and profitable home, his land rises. Where men avoid making necessary repairs, because they intend to sell soon, their farms do not rise rapidly.

By the reports gathered by the Agricultural Department in 1867, lands had then advanced from five to thirty per cent all through New England since 1860. They did not bound upward as the price of gold rapidly advanced, neither did land recede to its former price as gold approached par value. In most cases the rise must be attributed to the improvements upon the land, the improvements in prices of produce and improvements in methods of cultivation, so that larger incomes are received from the lands and they therefore become desirable. We have reason to believe that if the capital gained in Vermont can be in a good degree kept here, our prosperity is but begun. The hundred years of labor and sacrifice incident to the early settlement of a country should not eclipse in glory the one hundred years succeeding, that may be likened to those years of strength and vigor of youth passing to manhood.

But such results will not be realized if all our thoughts and care are chiefly to build up the West. Railroad men invest their fortunes in its new lines, farmers send their sons with all their strength and talent, and all the money they can raise, and their fathers move into our villages and tell other young men of the prosperity of their sons, and while the money is freely spent at the West for churches, schools, ware-houses, the fathers at home, (blessed be the memory of their industry and frugality,) have passed their days of production and live to save and spend grudgingly, and seldom favor improvements of public buildings, sidewalks, roads and schools. Then our institutions of learning, literary and scientific, seem to feel that it is not for Vermont that they labor, as this leading idea in the report of the Trustees of the Vermont Agricultural College for 1869, shows; "There are indications that there will be an increasing demand for instruction in these courses. The vast expansion of the American railroad system, and the rapid development of the *western* mines, call for a large number of thoroughly trained men in civil and mining engineering." If Vermont was crowded and hundreds of hands hanging in idleness, it surely would be more justifiable to so educate the young that they might go abroad.

Of the social, educational, and religious privileges of Vermont, I cannot boast. Many neighborhoods are so bare of young people, that stillness and dullness and almost a mouldiness rests upon the community. Churches are without pastors, and pastors are without proper and adequate support. Common schools are small, and academies, with their apparatus, and museums, and libraries, fall into dilapidation.

For myself, I was born upon a farm that my father had tilled for nearly fifty years. Within twenty rods of my birthplace my own home stands, where by farming I intend to share the fortunes of Vermont farmers, believing that the beautiful valley of Black river, containing thousands of acres of land (of which my farm is a part,) free from stone, rich in the elements of plant food, is as favorable for the home of a prosperous and contented people as any section of this wide country.

Source: Zuar E. Jameson, "Vermont as a Home," *Vermont Legislative Documents and Official Reports Made to the General Assembly, 1872*, Vol. 3 (Montpelier: 1872), pp. 553-562.

Document 2

"Origin of the St. Albans Butter Market" (1872)

R. R. Sherman

In order to bring the subject before you in its proper light, it may be necessary to draw comparisons between the past and the present, or in other words, compare the market as it was up to a certain period, with what it has been since and now is.

Franklin county is composed at present of fourteen small towns, each being about six miles square. St. Albans, although situated on the extreme west side of the county, is the shire town. Fifty years ago the dairy products of the county were but small. The farmers who kept more than eight or ten cows each were then very few, and a dairy of twenty cows was nearly unknown. Butter brought but ten to twelve and cheese four to five cents a pound, and was often a drug in the market at that. Very little of the dairy products of the county found their way to Boston or New York prior to 1840. Up to that time Montreal was almost the only market that the farmers of Northern Vermont could use for the sale of their surplus products, and poor enough it was, too.

Then, during the summer, no butter nor cheese was sold. When the St. Lawrence was frozen the farmers loaded into their double sleighs their dressed hogs, butter and skim-milk cheese (which the frost could only mellow and improve) and started for Montreal. Seldom less than a week was consumed in marketing the load and returning home. Think of it—a week in selling for scarcely $100 what can now be marketed in half a day, bringing from $300 to $400!

About 1840, the tide began to change and farm products began to float the other way. Boston and New York began to seek for them to supply the manufacturing districts that were springing up throughout New England and the Middle States, and as these and other internal improvements advanced, butter and cheese became to be more in demand and at better prices. But they could only be sent to market in the fall, and by water. Buyers then went through the county and bought the butter and cheese to be delivered at St. Albans Bay, which remained the port for the shipment of nearly all the farm products of the county until the completion of the Vermont Central and Vermont and Canada Railroads in 1850.

Then commenced what is commonly called the "St. Albans Butter Market." In one sense such a "Market" has no existence; that is, there is no regularly organized market or exchange, regulated by rules and by-laws, as such markets are elsewhere. Everybody buys that wishes to, and there is nothing to pay for the privilege. Farmers bring their produce here to sell because the buyers are here, and the buyers are here because here are the railroads and the banks.

Previous to the time when refrigerator cars for conveying butter were put on the road, there was not even a "butter day" here. Butter was received and shipped on all days, though more perhaps on Mondays and Tuesdays. But when, in 1854, the Vermont Central Railroad commenced running its butter cars, supplied with ice, once a week during the summer months, between St. Albans and Boston, Tuesday was the day selected as the most convenient day for all concerned.

During the hot weather butter is mostly brought in early in the morning, and by noon the market is closed. St. Albans presents a lively appearance on Tuesday, during the spring, summer and fall. From early morn till near noon teams laden with butter and cheese are coming in from all directions, as they file in down Lake street toward the depot, that street becomes packed in one dense mass of horses and wagons. Teams are hitched at every post on Main street; the hotel barns and yards are full; the hotels are full, and the farmers—I mean their pockets—are full. Butter is King.

The prominent buyers now in business are J. H. Pease of North Fairfax; H. H. Bowman, H. B. Soule and S. C. Noble & Co., of St. Albans; R. B. B. Kinnerson and F. H. Marshall, of Boston; J. E. Toof and E. L. Hibbard, of Franklin; John H. Draper of Sheldon, and some others, all of whom stand well as fair dealing and honorable men. Some of them have followed the business since the market was opened (now over twenty years). The scene, when the buyers, crowding in among the teams in the streets, are engaged in buying the butter and cheese of the farmers, is a very exciting one.

At first, for some years, most of the butter and cheese bought at this market was consigned to commission merchants in Boston. But for a few years past it had been bought at a commission by these buyers, for Boston dealers. The usual commission for buying is one cent a pound. It requires great experience and skill to be a good butter buyer, and many fail in this respect. It takes years to educate the senses of taste and smell up to the standard of a first rate judge of butter.

There is usually a friendly feeling existing, both among the buyers themselves and between them and the farmers. There has never been but one attempt to "make a corner" in butter in this market. In 1856, B. F. Rugg, who was then engaged largely in the produce trade, (and who has been the heaviest dealer in the county and State, though now retired with a handsome fortune,) undertook to carry out a plan for controlling the Boston butter market. Boston, during the hot weather, is very largely supplied with butter from the country, and to keep back a large quantity of it has the effect to advance the price. This Mr. R. well understood, and having brains and energy, with unbounded confidence in his own ability to carry out so gigantic a scheme, as well as excellent credit, he made his arrangements at the various banks in the county for an unlimited supply of means. He began buying toward the last of June when butter was low, and quietly stored it away in cellars. This he continued through July and August, sending to market only a small supply from week to week.

Before August was past, in consequence of keeping this large amount out of the market, butter began to advance in price. Mr. Rugg still continued to buy, and when he could buy no more, advised the farmers that still had butter to hold on for higher prices. This they are only too willing to do on a rising market, and their prices became so extravagant that buyers could not buy. Now he had them. Boston had to submit to St. Albans. The profits of this little speculation amounted to the snug little sum of $18,000; so says the gentleman himself, and nobody doubts it. The next year (1857,) he attempted to repeat the operation, but the disastrous financial crisis of that year interrupted his plans, and although he did not fail, he probably lost quite as much as he had made the previous year. The following figures show the progress of the butter business in St. Albans during the last twenty-one years:

	Cheese, lbs.	Butter, lbs.
1851	555,228	1,192,967
1852	601,969	1,149,225
1853	1,122,703	1,939,354
1854	1,035,376	1,712,404
1855	966,287	1,715,127
1856	1,228,128	2,293,568
1857	825,162	2,364,745
1858	1,294,393	2,713,309
1859	1,247,288	2,424,969
1860	1,984,000	2,566,700
1861	1,481,716	2,732,209
1862	1,281,602	2,420,370
1863	911,842	2,863,576
1864	923,210	2,472,854
1865	1,174,261	3,035,257
1866	882,495	2,617,095
1867	925,357	2,720,284
1868	948,276	2,606,880
1869	736,920	2,875,060
1870	——	2,945,450
1871	435,000	3,270,182

The total quantity of butter shipped since 1851 in thus seen to amount to 50,631,595 pounds, or about one million tubs. At 30 cents a pound this would amount to $15,189,478. The cheese shipped in the same time (estimating 1870, for which the figures are not given,) would be about 21,000,000 pounds, which at 14 cents would come to $2,940,000; the total of butter and cheese being thus $18,129,478. The butter in tubs set side by side would reach 230 miles, or counting 40 tubs to a load, the teams required to draw it would cover 150 miles of road.

Source: R. R. Sherman, "Origin of the St. Albans Butter Market," *First Annual Report of the Vermont State Board of Agriculture, Manufactures and Mining, 1872* (Montpelier: J. & J. M. Poland's Steam Printing Establishment, 1872), pp. 158-163.

The Knights of Labor Gain a Foothold in Rutland (1886)

RUTLAND HERALD

For several weeks, workmen interested in labor organizations have been visiting persons employed in the corporations here in the interest of the Knights of Labor. The work was done secretly in order to avoid opposition which they feared from certain employers and the meetings have been held without attracting notice. The cigar makers in town are all members of a labor union, and knowing its methods, have been able to enlighten members on the workings of the organization and there are several persons in town who have been initiated into the order of the Knights of Labor in other states. When enough persons had been secured to assure the success of the society, organizer J. J. Largan of Boston came and formally initiated candidates into an assembly here, which has since met and organized with the election of officers and committees. When the assembly was fully started Largan left for other fields and it is understood that he will organize assemblies of the Knights in Burlington, Brattleboro, St. Albans and Montpelier so that a district may be built up in this state, it requiring five assemblies to form one.

A representative of the *Herald* called on one of the prominent members of the organization yesterday to learn something of the membership and objects of the society in Rutland. "We have been working in secret," said the Knight, "for we knew that if the suspicions of some capitalists were aroused before our organization was complete they would attempt to crush it out, and would probably have succeeded in doing it at first. But now that we are sure of our ground and have members in every department of labor in Rutland we have nothing to fear as we are strong enough to resist and maintain our independence. Yet the employers do not know now how many of their men have been initiated into the order and it is for our interest to keep quiet for awhile. No, the organization is not started to get on a strike. Workingmen here are pretty well satisfied now and the order endeavors to avoid strikes by arbitration whenever this can be done and still maintain the interest of the employee. We want Rutland capitalists, however, to recognize the organization, and we also want to help forward the cause all over the country, by sympathy with its principles and contributing funds when it is necessary to advance its interests. Our great object here at that will be to interest workingmen in movements for their betterment and there will probably be no call for violent measures. I can't tell you how many members we have got here, and I am forbidden by the obligations I have taken to name any of them. But I can soon prove to you how strong we are if you will pledge yourself not to reveal any names you may get of me." He then took the reporter to a secret place of meeting and soon convinced him of the foothold the order had already got in Rutland. By working quietly but persistently a remarkable number of workingmen representing almost every department of work in town had been enlisted, and by meetings held in various parts of the town, groups of workingmen had been initiated into the secrecy of the society. . . .

[T]he candidate gives his pledge not to reveal to any person or persons any of the signs, mysteries, arts, privileges or benefits of the order, nor the name or person of any of its members to any employer or any person. He is told . . . that the order means no conflict with legitimate enterprise, nor any antagonism to necessary capital, but that it intends to fight men who in their haste and greed, blinded by self-interests, overlook the interests of others and violate the rights of those whom they deem helpless. "With all our strength," says the grand officer, "we will introduce and support laws made to harmonize the interest of labor and capital." . . .

"Doesn't the Catholic church object to its members joining you on the ground of secrecy?" [he] was asked. "No, the officers of the Catholic church have satisfied themselves that there is nothing in our teachings that will interfere with religion and they encourage rather than hinder us." . . . "As to our organization . . . [i]n Rutland we only have a charter for a mixed assembly, but we hope that it will become the mother of a number of trade assemblies. The `working' of an assembly combines the mysticism of the masonic lodge with the beneficiary element and defensive purposes of a trade union after the old English pattern, while those who believe in the ballot for relief from oppressive laws find ample opportunity to make known their views in the debate on 'labor in all its Interests' which, by the Constitution, must be discussed for at least 10 minutes at every meeting. . . ."

"Isn't the order in danger of falling into the hands of political managers?" was asked. "No," the Knight replied, "no professional politicians are admitted. . . . We also exclude lawyers, gamblers, liquor sellers and all banking men, but our order embraces members of every other honorable profession. . . . About our principles, I cannot state them better than they are stated in the preamble to the constitution, a copy of which you may have to make public if you like. It may help the order here and it will certainly attract attention to the society, and now that we are firmly entrenched we have no fear in doing that." Pocketing the constitution, the reporter was let out of a private entrance, amazed at what had been going on in our very midst, while few besides the initiated knew of it.

Source: *Rutland Herald*, 27 August 1886.

DOCUMENT 4

Address to the Annual Meeting of the Vermont State Grange (1887)

ALPHA MESSER

The subject of transportation is so intimately connected with the material prosperity of the people of this country that it has engaged the earnest attention of politicians, statesmen and political economists for many years. The rapid development of the country, and the consequent demand for means of transportation, necessitated the building of lines of railroads in all directions to supply the demand. The producers of the country have been so anxious for ready and quick facilities for transportation that in many instances they have not only granted charters and all the concessions asked by corporations for building and equipping the roads, but they have also contributed largely for their construction. In return for the magnanimity and liberality thus shown them, many of these corporations have seen fit to absorb all the capital invested and then establish rates of transportation which are manifestly unreasonable and unjust, denying at the same time all

the natural and lawful rights and privileges of those who gave them existence and who furnish the products for transportation without which they could not, as corporations, for a moment exist. The railroads in Vermont are not in this respect different from roads elsewhere. They obtained valuable franchises from the people and pecuniary aid in their construction in proportion to the ability of the people to contribute in this direction. These roads receive all the surplus products of the State for transportation, and their charges for the same are such as to oppress the people and depress agriculture, which is by far the leading industry in the State. By reason of exorbitant rates of transportation within the State, manufacturers have, to a large extent, been virtually prohibited from using the unrivaled water-power which is furnished by our mountain streams, thus depriving farmers of home markets for much of the product of their farms. Thus it is that these high rates of transportation have been a prominent factor in the great depreciation of real estate in Vermont.

The Courts having decided that States had no power to regulate inter-State traffic, and that this power was vested in Congress alone, that body, in compliance with the direct demands of farmers, passed the inter-State Commerce act, which was intended to correct many of the existing evils of railroad management and relieve the people, to some extent, of unjust discriminations and exorbitant rates of transportation, especially those on the short-haul traffic. For many years the Central Vermont railroad has charged more for transporting farm products and merchandise from this State to Boston, and *vice versa*, than to and from the distant points of Detroit and Chicago, thereby discriminating most unjustly against the shippers in this State, and, by arbitrary methods, virtually placing Vermont farmers further from Boston and other New England markets than their competitors on the fertile and easily tilled farms of the West. As the inter-State Commerce law was intended to correct flagrant abuses of this kind, as soon as opportunity was presented the State Grange entered a complaint to the inter-State Commission against the Central Vermont railroad for direct violation of the long and short-haul clause of the law, and petitioned the Governor of the State, in behalf of the farmers, to appoint counsel in the case, under section 148 of the Revised Laws, which is as follows:—"The Governor may employ counsel in behalf of the State when, in his judgment, the rights of the State demand it." The Governor appointed Kittredge Haskins, of Brattleboro, to present the case. In the meantime, efforts were made to secure the eminent legal services of Senator George F. Edmunds to assist in the case. In view of its importance to the farmers of the State, and because of his high sense of justice and right, the Senator most generously consented to argue the case for the Grange free of cost. At the time the complaint was entered the rates on six classes of freight from St. Albans to Boston and over the reverse route, were as follows:— 60, 50, 40, 27, 24, 17 cents per hundred pounds. The rate on the same classes of freight from Detroit to Boston *via* Ogdensburgh and the steamboats owned by the Central Vermont company, was 41, 36, 29, 20 17, 14 cents per hundred pounds—almost 33 1/3 per cent less for the long than for the short haul. The hearing was called at Rutland, September 1, before the full Board of Commissioners, and lasted three days. The decision of the Commissioners, which was given later, fully justified the State Grange in making the complaint, and also sustained it by ordering "the Central Vermont and the other defendants concerned with it in inter-State traffic between St. Albans and Boston, and Ogdensburgh, respectively, including these points, must wholly cease and desist from charging or receiving, in respect to any part of such traffic, a greater compensation for transportation of a like kind of property for a shorter than for a longer distance over the same line in the same direction, the shorter being included in the longer distance." . . .

But as this decision affects only inter-State traffic, it has nothing to do with the local traffic, which is entirely within the control of the State and subject to such restrictions in discriminations and rates of freight and passenger transportation as the Legislature may deem proper and just in the premises. That the local rates of freight charged by the railroads in this State are unreasonable, unjust and actually oppressive to the people, is an established fact beyond dispute. The President of the Central Vermont railroad, in his testimony before the inter-State Commission at Rutland, virtually admitted this fact when, in reply to a question of Senator Edmunds, he stated that he thought his road "could live without the local traffic." Vermont farmers do not ask the roads to carry freight at a loss; they only ask that the rate shall be reasonable for the service rendered.

During the years that are past they have repeatedly asked the Legislature to enact such laws as would compel the roads to desist from unjust discriminations, and conform to a reasonable rate. But by paid lobbies and other well-known means, the roads have defeated the will of the people and made the Legislature bend to their own dominant power. But the people are not discouraged by repeated failure or overawed by the power and arrogance of these corporations. They will renew these demands to the Legislature for the enactment of such laws as will compel the roads to cease from oppressing the people by a form of taxation for private gain which is so manifestly unreasonable and unjust. In these demands they will ask for the abolition of the free pass, for equal facilities for transportation, a reduced rate of transportation between points in the State and from points in the State to Boston and other New England points, and a publicity of all rates: the application of the long and short-haul principle on all roads in this State; the reduction of passenger rates so as not to exceed 2 1/2 cents per mile; and the amendment of the present laws establishing the railroad commission so as to give the commission greater powers and means for compelling a strict compliance with their orders. These reforms are absolutely needed by the farmers of this State, and I would urge the State Grange of Vermont to take measures to bring the whole subject of railroad reform before the people, and, by continued discussion and agitation, induce them to elect a Legislature none of whose members will bend the knee to corporate power, but stand for the right and act in accordance with the will of their constituents.

Source: *Journal of Proceedings, Seventh Annual Session, Vermont State Grange, 1887* (Montpelier: Argus and Patriot, 1888), pp. 8-11.

Resolutions Relating to Women's Rights, Temperance, and Other Reforms (1888)

WOMEN'S CHRISTIAN TEMPERANCE UNION OF VERMONT

The report of the Committee on Resolutions was called for, and was read by Mrs. S. E. Blodgett as follows:

RESOLUTIONS

1. *Resolved*, That with reverence we recognize God our Supreme Ruler, as the foundation of all true government and reform; and remembering with gratitude His guiding hand during our past year's work, we consecrate ourselves anew to our Master's service.

2. *Resolved*, That we ever keep in front Christ's gospel, and that in the coming year we recommend that some method be adopted whereby our State Superintendent of Evangelistic Work may be enabled to do the needed work in every County; and believing Evangelistic Work to be the underlying principle of reform, we urge upon our Unions the necessity of the work of this department.

3. *Resolved*, That we believe all ecclesiastical disabilities should be removed from women, and applaud the action of the M. E. [Methodist Episcopal] General Conference in submitting to that great church the question of opening the doors of its highest council to the representatives of the sex that form two thirds its membership.

4. *Resolved*, That we commend the work of the National Social Purity department in defence of the "White Slaves" of the northern woods of Michigan, and urge its continuance; we also appeal to our members throughout the State to push the department of Social Purity in their several localities.

5. Believing the use of tobacco to be one of the great evils of our times, and only second to the liquor traffic in its baneful effects upon the young men of our nation, Therefore, be it *Resolved*, That we petition the next legislature of Vermont to make the sale or giving of tobacco in any form to minors, a criminal offense.

6. *Resolved*, That we desire to express our appreciation of the services of our Health Superintendent, and pledge her our assistance in the sale of the Health Calendar.

7. *Resolved*, That we recognize the importance of sustaining OUR HOME GUARDS, and urge local unions to increase their subscription lists.

8. *Whereas*, The earliest days of life are the best days in which to train the young in the principles of temperance, and to form character, *Resolved*, That the work for the children in our State under school age, shall be organized under the mother's covenant work, also that we will endeavor to create a sentiment for the Kindergarten in the public schools.

9. *Whereas*, The non attendance at school of many of the children of our State, is primarily the cause of much of the ignorance and vice prevalent in our large towns, Therefore, *Resolved*, That we endeavor to win the children to our public schools, and that we earnestly request our Superintendent of Juvenile Work to make efforts in this direction.

10. Most thoroughly believing the fact stated by Gov. [Ebenezer] Ormsbee, namely, "That the laws upon this subject (Prohibition) are openly violated and flagrantly disregarded, and that in some instances, too numerous to be contemplated without concern, those upon whom has been and is imposed the sworn duty of its faithful execution, are its violators, and are blind and indifferent to its violation in others," Therefore, be it *Resolved*, That we record our emphatic denunciation of the conduct of all officials, who according to the testimony of the governor of the State, do thus neglect their sworn duty.

11. *Resolved*, That the decision of the U.S. Supreme Court in the case of Bowman versus the Chicago & Northwestern Railroad Co., proves beyond question that the prohibition of the liquor traffic is a national issue.

12. *Resolved*, That the success of municipal suffrage in Kansas, convinces us that no stronger weapon has been hurled against the liquor power, and as the Republican Party in Vermont in their platform have declared their willingness to grant municipal suffrage to women when they desire it,

we therefore urge upon our members the importance of trying to secure this power, in our State where there is a prospect of success in such an undertaking.

13. *Resolved,* That we re-affirm our loyalty to the Prohibition Party, in State and Nation, and thank our generous brothers at the Indianapolis National Convention, for standing so strongly by the plank for the enfranchisement of women as a means of home protection.

14. *Resolved,* That we tender our hearty thanks to the Rutland W. C. T. U. and all citizens for their untiring efforts to provide for all our needs, to the trustees of the Congregational church for the use of their beautiful edifice, to the pastors for their presence and assistance, to the White Ribbon Quartette for their sweet music, to the Loyal Temperance Legion for the fine exercises of Wednesday evening, to the officers of the House of Correction for so kindly showing our ladies through that institution, and to the railroad companies for the courtesy of half fare on all roads. A motion to accept them as a whole was withdrawn, and they were voted on one by one. All but 12 and 13 passed unanimously.

Source: *Fourteenth Annual Report of the Women's Christian Temperance Union of Vermont, 1888,* (Brattleboro, Vt.: Press of Frank E. Housh & Co., 1889), pp. 20-22.

DOCUMENT 6

Care of the Poor (c. 1880s)

FREDERIC P. WELLS; ABBY M. HEMENWAY

Newbury

The poor and unfortunate we have always had with us, and the money expended for their support would amount to a larger sum than people suppose. The town [of Newbury] had not been long settled before there were people needing aid, and in 1771, Jacob Bayley, Jacob Kent and John Haseltine were chosen "poormasters." Who were the objects of their care, or what the expense to the town, we do not know. It is probable that such aid was in the shape of provisions and medical attendance. The officers do not seem to

have had much to do, as the same persons were also chosen as "supervisors," "commissioners," and the like for many years. Usually there is no mention of any overseer of the poor in the record of town meetings. There were poor people, however, who had to be helped and . . . such public expense was much the same in its details as now—aid to the physically and mentally infirm, help in sickness, burial of the dead, and the care of orphan children.

No person is entitled to expect relief from a town unless he is a resident of it, and to determine what constitutes residence has always been a perplexing question, and has given rise to more lawsuits between towns than almost anything else, and various laws have been passed, and decisions of the Supreme Court handed down, which bear upon this question. There was, formerly, a law, in most of the New England states, which provided a way by which towns could prevent any newcomer, from gaining residence, and thus freeing the town from responsibility for support of such person. The process was called "warning out of town," and consisted in the reading in the hearing of such a person, by a constable, or by leaving a copy of a warrant, issued by the selectmen, of which the following is a specimen.

State of Vermont}   *To the first Constable of*
Orange County, ss.}   *Newbury in sd County*
Greetings. By the authority of the State of Vermont, you are hereby required to warn A.B. and family, now residing in Newbury to depart sd. Town. Hereof fail not, but of this precept and your doings due return make according to law. Given under our hands this 27th day of December, 1814.

    Asa Tenney,}   *Selectmen*
    Joshua Hale,}   *of*
    Jonas Tucker,}   *Newbury*

State of Vermont} Newbury, Jan. 6, 1815
Orange Co. ss.}
I then served this precept by leaving a true and attested copy with the said A.B. and family. Attest, Abner Bayler, Constable.
    Fees
Travel 10 miles, .60   Newbury Town Clerk's office
Copy,   .17   Jan. 10, 1813.
       .67 [sic] Recd and recorded,*
        I. Bayley, Town Clerk

This thing was quite profitable for others, if rather unpleasant for the person who thus received a hint that his residence was not desired, as there was a fee for the selectmen who prepared the warrant, another for the constable, and another for the clerk. There are 112 such warnings recorded in the first book of [Newbury] town proceedings. The first is dated January 5, 1787; the second, July 20, 1806; and the last, November 12, 1816, when the law was repealed. One of these warrants includes twenty-four families.

In 1823 it was voted, "not to build a poorhouse." It was the custom for many years to "sell the poor at auction," as it was called. The support of the homeless poor was set up at auction, in town-meeting and struck off to the lowest bidder. This was quite apt to be some sordid soul, who pinched and starved the unfortunate beings, who were thus at his mercy. This gave rise to some scandals, which may as well not be recalled.

In 1837, the "surplus money," from the United States, was divided among the towns, and Newbury received $5,376.03, and with a portion of this the town bought the Simon Blake farm at West Newbury, for a town farm. . . . This was the last earthly home of many unfortunates, during the twenty-nine years it was thus occupied. No record was ever kept of the deaths that occurred there. In 1846 there were eleven persons whose ages averaged 76 years. . . . The present farm was bought . . . in 1867, and the main part of the present structure was built, and the barns remodelled, in 1885. . . . The deaths at the present farm have been forty. The system of herding all the helpless beings of a whole county under one roof never has been adopted in Vermont.

Source: Frederic P. Wells, *History of Newbury, Vermont* (St. Johnsbury, Vt.: The Caledonia Co., 1902), pp. 285-287.

Stowe

In 1859, Stowe united with Morristown and Johnson, in the purchase of a poor-farm, under an arrangement that all the paupers of both towns should be supported on the farm, at a common expense, which should be borne in the proportion of their respective grand lists. An excellent farm, convenient for the purpose, was purchased in Morristown, about five miles from the center village of Stowe, and, lying on the main road from Stowe to Morristown, one of the most de-lightful farm situations in the whole county. The buildings were fitted up, and prepared for occupation for such a purpose, and the intended inmates removed to the premises.

The success of the scheme depended much on procuring the right kind of man to superintend the carrying on of the farm, and managing the persons who came there to reside. The towns, thus far, have been very fortunate in securing superintendents, well fitted for the place, and it is thought that the arrangement is given excellent satisfaction to all parties interested. It is quite obvious to the most hasty observer, that the poor are much better provided for, and are much more happy and contented, than they were when often removed;— a consideration which every humane person would regard as of the first importance: and hitherto, it is understood that the joint expenses to the town, has not exceeded, if it has equalled, that which they incurred under the old practice. When the plan was first proposed, it was strongly objected to by some, as unkind to the poor, as, in some instances, it took them out of towns in which they had long resided, and away from families with which they were connected. These considerations were to be weighed. There are some inconveniences in being poor; especially, in being so poor as to be dependent on the public for support. But, on the other side, there were considerations which experience well confirms. At the farm, the poor are furnished with all the usual comforts, and even luxuries, of families well-to-do in the world,—good comfortable habitations, good clothing, good food, good nursing, and an assurance that, so long as they remain dependent, even if for their whole life, they will not be compelled to change their home and its conveniences and comforts. Under such circumstances it would soon have many of the attractions of home.

Source: Abby M. Hemenway, ed., *The Vermont Historical Gazetteer*, Vol. 2 (Burlington, Vt.: A. M. Hemenway, 1871), p. 709.

DOCUMENT 7

"The Future of Democracy in Vermont" (1890)

C. H. DAVENPORT

The question of the future of democracy in Vermont is illuminated by the facts and causes of the decline in the past.

From 1804 to 1824 the State was Democratic, so far as present names can be applied to the organizations of that time, giving an adherence, which finally became almost unanimous, to the great party that has, in spite of all its errors and wanderings, maintained a continuous and unbroken organization ever since the adoption of the constitution. The State's electoral vote was given to Jefferson for his second term and to Madison and Monroe for both their terms. It was the only New England State that held firmly to the Jeffersonian faith through this period. . . .The hardy and self-reliant character of our people, all the principles and traditions of the struggle of the Green Mountain Boys for independence, naturally brought Vermonters into line with the anti-centralization ideas of Jeffersonism as soon as these ideas came to be understood. . . .

The anti-Masonic party appeared in 1829, drove the National Republicans and Masons into alliance, threw the election of Governor into the legislature in 1830, and in 1831 put Governor Palmer into the executive chair. For several years the anti-Masons controlled the State and gave its electoral vote to Wirt in 1832. The democratic was the only distinctively political organization that could stand up against them. The Whig lines were reformed largely out of anti-Masonry, but the Whig majorities were kept down to 2500 to 4000 until the Harrison flood of 1840. . . .

An analysis of the above quadrennial periods shows that from 1840 to 1850, the Vermont democracy almost held its own, though it was the time when the Whigs waxed strongest in the nation, carrying two out of the three presidential elections. The next decade was a Democratic one, nationally, but in Vermont Democratic losses came thicker and faster, as the dominant wing of the party was more and more clearly seen to be that of Slaveocracy. In the rancorous split of 1860 between the [Stephen A.] Douglas and [John C.]

Breckinridge factions, though the Douglas men found themselves in a majority of nearly five to one, the two tickets between them mustered only a little over 10,000 votes. The issues of the war increased the rout and demoralization. A recovery began in 1868, increased slowly up to 1884, and if the opportunities had been rightly improved, large results of good might have been accomplished. Instead there has been retrogression. While the party has been gaining strength everywhere else in the nation, while several States have been revolutionized against odds as great as ours, while right across the lines to the East of us, South of us and West of us there is growth and progress, while all the rest of New England, except perhaps Maine, is counted upon to soon swing into the Democratic column, it remains for Vermont alone to tell the story of decadence.

The cause for this condition of affairs may be said to be several, but really resolve themselves into one. The people of the State are peculiarly moveable by the force of moral ideas. They live largely upon the patriotic memories of the war. With the true mountaineer's hatred of slavery they remember the time when the Democratic Samson was beguiled into the lap of the Delilah of the South, and it has not been brought home to them that the Democracy of today stands for anything better. So far as has been shown to them the party in the State lives only to hold Federal offices when there is a Democratic administration. They have seen it as an organization steadily kept as an appendage to a Republican machine. They have seen it tagging along behind the reforms that have been partially wrought out in State affairs, in taxation and in the proper control of the corporate creatures of the State,—reforms that were peculiarly Democratic in idea, and were wrought out, albeit incompletely, because, though unrecognized and repudiated by the party in the State, these Democratic ideas had taken hold of the popular thought.

In a word the trouble has been a total lack of organized application of the Democratic philosophy to State and local offices. The error probably began far back among men sincerely anxious to promote the cause in a national sense who thought it politic to avoid any pronounced position on State issues. The next step, as power was felt to be slipping away and as the spoils system developed in politics in the evolution of the boss, was easy and well nigh inevitable. The decline in strength has been coincident and kept almost even pace with the boss power. It is not necessary to attack the men personally who have held this position, for among them have been some very able and worthy men. But a boss-ship that is the product of such conditions, is necessarily enervating. It has no direct responsibility to the people. It exists by favor in the shape of patronage which the people have only a remote hand in controlling, and it is only human nature that it should seek to perpetuate itself in the distribution of patronage. It was this tendency to live alone upon the offices, to reduce the leadership to office holders or office distributors that caused the subservient following of the administrations from 1852 to 1860, in disregard of all the feelings and convictions of the people of Vermont, and culminated in the break-up of 1860.

Spoils politics of this kind are exceedingly apt to run into a rut where there is no genuine conflict of parties but where a minority is in alliance with a faction of a majority, where it is arranged that the federal and local patronage shall all be "kept in the crowd" no matter which side wins, and where it is almost impossible for the voter to strike a blow that will have any effect. The combinations of Tammany and the Republican custom house ring in New York City have repeatedly illustrated this. It was his Republican support that several times saved Tweed from overthrow at the hands of the Tilden or Young Democracy in the New York legislature. It took an earthquake of popular wrath to upset this combination, which, however, quickly reappeared after the storm had blown over. We have had for years just such a combination in Vermont, because of the lack of a positive, aggressive, clearly defined Democracy in State politics. The spoils are always weakening to the parties, ever tending to make mercenaries of fighters, and when a party is largely in the minority they hopelessly emasculate it. If there were not a possibility of such a thing as getting a federal office the effect would at once be vastly invigorating to the Green Mountain Democracy.

While there is always danger of partisanship going too far in State and local affairs in making political spoils of places of local trust, the Democratic idea of the diffusion of powers, of hinging them down as close as possible to the people, of delegating nothing to the nation that it is in the power of the States to properly perform, nothing to the States that concerns the county, town or school district alone, and nothing to any power whatever except what is necessary to secure the rights of all, is one of whose applications we have every day need. Government constantly tends towards schemes of socialism and paternalism, towards adopting the notion that nothing can be trusted to the uplifting forces of christian and moral progress as regards the individual, but that he must be legislatured into goodness, or what the law making power regards as such. Our prohibitory legislation is an illustration with the extravagances it has had to adopt to maintain itself, violative of the very primary principles of free as distinguished from despotic government. Any number of other instances will occur to lawyers where this gospel of meddlesomeness has been imbedded in our statutes. There is constant need of the Democratic idea to teach that there are some things in which the citizen can be trusted to take care of himself and that government has done its duty when it has prevented him from encroaching upon the rights of others. There is pressing need for restraint of the public powers, which, in the necessities of modern government, have been delegated to corporations. There is hardly a State in the Union that has such shiftless safeguards against encroachments of this kind as Vermont, or that has made less progress towards a solution of the difficult problem of the relation of railroads to the State. In taxation, also, only a beginning towards reform has been made. Discriminations exist that cannot be justified on any ground of principle, and that involve the plan of subsidy, the burdening of the many for the benefit of the few, which it ought always to be the mission of Democracy to fight. Methods exist which involve needless stretches of authority and are self-defeating.

There is vitality, energy, development, broadening power, progress and prosperity in the Democratic Idea, and all the indications are that the time is rapidly approaching when it is again to bless Vermont. The people are as much Democratic in sentiment now as they were seventy-five years ago. All that is necessary is to convince them that the party of today represents the idea in some reasonable degree, and the first step to that end is to make that part of the party that is before them in their own State entirely worthy of their respect. Vermont's interest in the tariff question is very strongly on the Democratic side. So with the public land question and the evil effects Vermonters have felt from the over-development of the west by means of government subsidies: Vermonters have always believed in the blessings of simple and frugal government, carefully limited to its necessary functions, rather than one that is bloated with all sorts of absorptions, with high taxes and with all the artificial distinctions that have their root in the subsidy principle. The abuses and extravagances that have now reached such an enormous aggregate in State expenses in spite of all efforts at improvement are a daily demonstration of the need of returning to sound theories, diametrically opposed to those of Republicanism.

The Vermont Democracy has at last aroused to its duty and opportunity, and the writer thoroughly believes that the next four years are to witness some surprising changes in Vermont.

Source: C. H. Davenport, "The Future of Democracy in Vermont," *Quill* (September 1890): 50-58.

DOCUMENT 8
Address to the Joint Assembly of the Vermont Legislature (1890)
GOVERNOR WILLIAM P. DILLINGHAM

. . . When the legislature of 1888 assembled, there was, as now, a well-settled conviction that the resources of Vermont, both as a manufacturing and agricultural State, were too little known to the world, and that means should be devised to advertise the advantages which the State offers to those seeking to make new homes. Legislative thought finally took form in No. 110 of the laws of 1888, entitled "an act providing for the appointment of a commissioner to investigate the agricultural and manufacturing interests of the State, and devise means to develop the same." Realizing the importance of selecting for the position of commissioner a man of sound judgment, experienced in business, of good general information, I finally selected Hon. A. B. Valentine of Bennington, and after considerable importunity induced him to accept the position. . . .

His report, embodying the result of his own observation and study, is exceedingly valuable, and well calculated to arouse thought on the part of those most interested in the State's welfare. . . .

You will observe that a considerable portion of his report pertains to the scheme inaugurated to induce the best class of Swedish emigrants to come to Vermont and settle upon what are known as unoccupied or abandoned farms, and you will read the same with lively interest.

The question he presents to your consideration relates to the continuance or abandonment of the experiment already inaugurated, but not yet fully solved, to induce a good class of emigrants to purchase lands and make homes in our midst, thus ministering to the wealth and prosperity of our State. In considering the question it will be well to remember that for a good many years there has been a constant depreciation in farm values. In every section of our own country, and in all parts of the world, agricultural interests have suffered a severe depression. In a new and growing country like our own, there have been opportunities for young men who were strong, temperate, intelligent, industrious, enterprising and ambitious to seek and make fortunes in the commercial and manufacturing centres, and in those portions of the west where speculative values have afforded opportunity for the exercise of sagacity and sound judgment. Vermont has reared more than her share of this class of men, and the result has been that they have taken advantage of the opportunities so offered, and in all portions of our land business and professional circles have been enriched by the addition of young men with sound minds in sound bodies whom we have sent out. . . . That this exodus proceeded from the more purely agricultural towns is, I think, generally admitted. . . In the county of Addison, one of the finest for agricultural purposes in the State, though her villages increased in population and importance, there was between 1830 and 1880 a decrease in her population of about 750. In 1830 Bennington county had 17,468 inhabitants; ten years later, in 1840, only 16,872, but through a growth in manufactures and the opening up of quarries her population in 1880 had come to be 21,950. In Caledonia county the population, which in 1830 was 20,967, had come in 1880 to be 23,607, a gain largely accounted for in the growth of two or three of her larger villages. In 1830 Chittenden county had a population of 21,765; in 1850, 29,036; and in 1880, 32,792; a growth largely attributable to Burlington's prosperity. In Orange county, which is peculiarly an agricultural region, but which possesses several prosperous and growing villages, the population decreased between 1830 and 1880 from 27,285 to 23,525. The population of grand old Rutland county also decreased in the ten years between 1830 and 1840, but on the opening of her quarries and the establishment of manufacturing industries her population began to increase, and between 1840 and 1880 she had made a gain of about 11,000. In Washington county the gain of 4,000 between 1830 and 1880 was largely in the villages, and the gain during the last ten years (the greatest of that in any county in the State) has been mainly in Barre and Montpelier, and is the direct result of the opening of a large number of granite quarries at the former place. Notwithstanding the growth and prosperity of Brattleboro and Bellows Falls, the loss of population in Windham county between 1830 and 1880 amounted to 1,985, while in Windsor county, with some of our finest and most prosperous villages in her midst, the falling off during the same time amounted to more than 5,000.

All of our counties have suffered from the removal to other States of young men from the ranks of our farmers, and the impression which has generally prevailed, that only the back towns have been affected, is, in my judgment, unfounded. I am strongly of the opinion that the exodus began from the towns more favorably located with reference to railroads and other great thoroughfares, but was not so noticeable as it would otherwise have been for the reason that emigration from other States and countries poured in to take the places of those who had gone out. Connected with the building of our early railroads a large immigration from Ireland was induced, and as these new comers became acquainted with the existing condition of things, and saw the facilities here offered for obtaining homes, they had the courage and foresight to buy and cultivate lands and to encourage their friends abroad to immigrate to Vermont for the same purposes; and in this way it has come about that in many of our best towns our Irish fellow-citizens have become the owners of a large proportion of the farm property, and are highly esteemed for their intelligence and success. With the increase of manufactures in our larger towns, and the development of our lumber interests in different sections of the State, there have also come to us large numbers or industrious persons from British America, and while a good many of them have purchased land and are engaged in

its cultivation, it is probably true that the greater number of them are gathered in the business centres.

But for the introduction of these new elements into the State, I apprehend that the condition we are now called upon to face would have appeared much earlier; and the fact that in ten years intervening between 1870 and 1880 the number of foreign-born residents in Vermont decreased from 47,155 to 40,959, indicates that the tide upon which we had come to depend, and which had ministered so much to the prosperity of the towns affected by it, had ceased to flow. The extent to which this and other depressing influences have operated is shown by the statement of the Commissioner that nearly one-tenth of the acreage of the State is either unoccupied or indifferently cultivated, though a large portion of the soil is very good, not worn out, and can be made as fruitful as other lands lying contiguous which are now successfully cultivated. The towns where these lands are mainly found are what are known as back towns, or, from their situation, are at some distance from the railroads or manufacturing centers. Aside from the value of their real estate, there is, comparatively speaking, little personal property with which to swell the size of their grand lists, and as values and population have gradually lessened, the rate of taxation has correspondingly increased until now, in many places, it has come to be a serious burden to our farmers, and a grave industrial problem has been presented for solution. This condition of things cannot, in my judgment, be attributed either to a free trade policy in the past or to the protective tariff of the present, nor is it to be presumed for an instant that the lands in question are poor or valueless. They are, as stated by the Commissioner, of good quality and not worn out. Many of them have buildings in a fair state of repair, and at the price at which they can be purchased are undoubtedly as good an investment for those desiring to make homes as can be found in any part of the United States; but the fact exists that in a nation affording so many avenues to wealth as are open in the United States, and which offers so many temptations to young men of enterprise and ambition to engage in more remunerative pursuits, there is a tendency on the part of American boys in every part of our land to abandon small farming. So far is this true that almost every State in the Union has been obliged to look to foreign fields for material with which to make up or replenish its farm population.

It is evident to my mind that the enterprising youth whose exodus from our State helped to produce the present condition of affairs, will not return to again join the ranks of our husbandmen. It is true also that the sons of our foreign-born population have, in a large degree, imbibed the spirit of enterprise that has inspired the action of native Americans, and they too are pushing out into mercantile, manufacturing and professional pursuit, with an energy that is most commendable, but which reminds us that they cannot be depended upon to maintain the number of our farmers.

If our sparsely settled towns are to be re-populated, and the farms now unoccupied are to be restored and brought into a higher state of cultivation, we too must look abroad for the material with which to accomplish this result. Almost every State in the Union has been compelled to adopt this policy, and to this end bureaus of immigration have been maintained, and agents have been sent to all parts of Europe for recruits. What is true in Vermont is true in every part of the land; farms are waiting for purchasers, and the State that makes the most intelligent and well-sustained effort is the one that brings emigration to her doors. This was the thought that inspired the legislation under which the Commissioner was appointed, and that impelled him in his effort to direct the tide of foreign emigration to our State.

After much thought I am unable to avoid the conclusion that the only plan of relief for the overburdened farmer in sparsely-populated towns, that offers any hope of success, lies in the direction of this experiment.

In the Swedes who have been induced to settle here, the Commissioner is confident a beginning has been made which will eventually result in a great and lasting benefit to the State; and after a careful personal examination of the colonies at Wilmington and Weston, I am of the opinion that the experimental action so begun should be continued during the biennial period upon which we are now entering. Through the favorable reports of those now among us, supplemented by other judicious effort, he hopes and expects to reach others of the same class who have means sufficient to enable them to make advance payments upon farms they may purchase, and who will enter vigorously upon their cultivation.

Source: Address to Joint Session of Vermont General Assembly by Governor William P. Dillingham, October 2, 1890, *Journal of the Senate* (Montpelier: 1890): 306-310.

DOCUMENT 9

"The Fish and Game Supply of Vermont" (1892)

JOHN W. TITCOMB

United States Commissioner McDonald, having occasion to look into the leases of some Scotch rivers, reported that the Tay alone rented for £40,000. It is said that $140,000 of this represents rod privileges.

While our fishing is in a broad sense free, this statement illustrates to what extent fisherman will loosen their purse strings for the enjoyment of this invigorating sport. We have no river Tay stocked with salmon, but nestling among our green hills are between four and five hundred ponds and lakes with a total area of some 125,000 acres. As tributaries or outlets to these bodies of water, we have innumerable mountain streams which broaden into rivers as they flow into and through the valleys fertilized by them.

The majority of these waters are the native haunts of the speckled trout. In addition to the trout many of our waters abound in a great variety of fish, the leading ones being bass, land-locked salmon, salmon trout [longe, or great lake trout], pike, pike perch [white perch], and pickerel.

On our western border, and more than half of it within our limits, is historic Lake Champlain, noted for its beauty and remarkable for its varieties of fish. Many sportsmen are attracted to its shores by the abundance of aquatic birds in the vicinity. This may be said also of Lake Memphremagog on our northern border. For the hunter, partridges will always be the game which gives the most sport and the best results as a food supply. Nearly all the large game native to our forests has become extinct, but deer are increasing rapidly, as evidenced by the frequent reports of their being seen in our rural districts. Under the wise law enacted by our last Legislature, their protection from slaughter has been continued until November 1, 1900. At present they are very tame, and it is a question whether it will not be advisable to continue their protection for an indefinite period, as they would be quickly exterminated if the fostering care of the State were withdrawn.

Woodcock furnishes as good sport as in other States of New England. Quail have been introduced several times, but it appears doubtful if they can endure the severity of our winters.

English pheasants have recently been introduced by Dr. Webb at his Shelburne Farms, and the result of his experiment is watched with interest. Many new varieties of game birds would undoubtedly thrive in Vermont, and any efforts in this direction should receive the hearty endorsement of every one. Rabbits and squirrels, though decreasing in numbers, are still abundant, and are a source of much sport to the hunter.

I have attempted to briefly state our resources in the way of fish and game supply. It has been asserted by the authorities in the Fish Commission and Geological Survey of the United States, that within a century the waters of this country will supply as much food as the land produces, and by that time water farms will have become as plentiful as land farms. Water farming is far more profitable even now, for a given area, than the tilling of the most fertile soil. Were it possible to obtain an accurate report of the fish and game taken in Vermont during one season, the value as a food supply would doubtless be surprising. The chief value to our State, however, is not in the fish and game themselves, either for the market or consumption as food. It is in the attraction afforded not only to residents of our State, but to the thousands of summer visitors who flock to our lakes and hills every season, that our fish and game supply is becoming such an important factor in the economy of every rural community.

With the efforts being put forth by the railroad companies, and very generally by the inhabitants, to call outside attention to the attractions of Vermont, it is but natural to expect summer tourists in greater numbers each year. If we would retain our hold upon this desirable element in the economy of our State, we must keep up our attractions.

Farmers are not without some reason when they make some such remark as "Fisherman are a nuisance, anyway." But they must admit when taking a broad view of the question, that the fishermen patronize the railroads, and cause better accommodations for everybody. They cause hotels to be built, and bring their families. They hire boats and guides, and patronize the country stores. Last, but not least, they buy our much abused "abandoned hillside farms," and make summer homes of them. The farmer sells his chickens, eggs, butter, lambs, etc., and gets a better price at home than for-merly at a distant and uncertain market. It is the fisherman or summer tourist who creates the demand for what he raises, and he gets his pay in hard cash.

Clubs are being formed in various parts of the State, whose membership is made up largely of non-residents. These clubs are buying up land for fish and game preserves. By damming the brooks to form ponds or a series of pools, many of our abandoned farms can be turned into fish and game preserves, indirectly more productive to the wealth of the State than many more fertile farms now under a state of cultivation.

It has been demonstrated in other States that artificial propagation will do much towards restoring depleted waters to their former condition. The New York Commissioners, in a recent report, say that there is better fishing to-day than when the Commission was organized some twenty years ago. There is nowhere a more practical illustration of the effects of restocking streams, perhaps, than in Rutland County, where some twelve years ago a few thousand rainbow trout escaped from a private pond into East Creek. About one in three trout now taken from this stream are the rainbow variety. Previous to this event the rainbow trout was unknown to our local fishermen. Several have been taken this year ranging in weight from one to three pounds. There is probably no State in New England in which so little practical attention has been paid, either to preserving what fish and game we have, or to restocking our woods and waters, as in Vermont. The Legislature has never made any appropriations which would permit a commission to devote its time to the subject of fish and game preservation and propagation. At the last session, however, in addition to the regular allowance to the commission, an appropriation was made sufficient to provide for the construction and maintenance of a hatchery. It is hoped that this will soon be "hatched," that we may lose no time in replenishing our depleted waters, and introduce new varieties for which our streams are so well adapted.

At the same session of the Legislature, the Vermont Fish and Game League was incorporated. Starting off with one hundred and twelve charter members, its numbers have steadily increased. It is a State institution, working for the benefit of all its inhabitants. Its membership roll is open to all citizens interested in the welfare of Vermont.

We have fish and game laws, too many of them, but they exist in many sections only to be disregarded.

As in other States, the greatest difficulties in the way of successful protection of fish and game are conflicting and misleading laws and ignorance of them. Experience in other States goes to show that a more proper observance of the laws follows the erection of a hatchery. Apparently influenced by the work of our own State in this matter, Congress made a liberal appropriation with which to purchase a site, and establish a U.S. hatchery within our limits. Thus with two hatcheries within the State, it only remains to secure proper legislation to protect our fry and young fish and see that the laws are enforced.

One of the most crying evils to-day and one which on certain streams would accomplish more by prevention than the hatcheries will accomplish by propagation, is the reckless discharge of sawdust, lime, refuse from gas houses, etc., into streams which would otherwise abound in fish. If the State engages in fish culture and would make a success of it, this evil must be corrected.

This article is written from a purely economic and business stand point. I will not enter into the details of the pleasure to be derived from fishing and shooting, or the recreation coming from such pure out-door sports. Our own citizens would be benefited if they would spare more time to themselves and encourage our youth in these healthful amusements.

With all the gifts of nature at our doors, let us show our appreciation of them. With a proper attention to our roads, a wise protection of our forests and a faithful attention to the work just inaugurated to increase our fish and game supply, Vermont will be truly called the Arcadia of America.

Source: John W. Titcomb, "The Fish and Game Supply of Vermont," *Twelfth Vermont Agricultural Report by the State Board of Agriculture for the Years 1891-92* (Burlington, Vt.: Free Press Association, 1892), pp. 156-160.

DOCUMENT 10

Vermont: A Study of Independence (1892)

ROWLAND E. ROBINSON

To fill the place left by this constant drain on its population, the State has for the most part received a foreign element, which, though it keeps her numbers good, poorly compensates for her loss.

Invasions of Vermont from Canada did not cease with the War of the Revolution, nor with the later war with Great Britain. On the contrary, an insidious and continuous invasion began with the establishment of commercial and friendly relations between the State and the Province. Early in the century, a few French Canadians, seeking the small fortune of better wages, came over the border, and along the grand waterway which their noble countryman had discovered and given his name, and over which so many armies of their people had passed, sometimes in the stealth of maraud, sometimes in all the glorious pomp of war. At first the few new-comers were tenants of the farmers, for whom they worked by the day or month at fair wages, for the men were expert axemen, familiar with all the labors of land-clearing, and as handy as Yankees with scythe and sickle; while their weather-browned wives and grown-up daughters could reap and bind as well as they, and did not hold themselves above any outdoor work.

After a while some acquired small holdings of a few acres, or less than one, and built thereon log-houses, that with eaves of notched shingles and whitewashed outer walls, with the pungent odor of onions and pitch-pine fires, looked and smelled as if they had been transplanted from Canada with their owners.

When the acreage of meadow land and grain-field had broadened beyond ready harvesting by the resident yeomen, swarms of Canadian laborers came flocking over the border in gangs of two or three, baggy-breeched and moccasined habitants, embarked in rude carts drawn by shaggy Canadian ponies. After a month or two of haymaking and harvesting, they jogged homeward with their earnings, whereunto were often added some small pilferings, for their fingers were as light as their hearts. This annual wave of inundation from the north ceased to flow with the general introduction of the mowing-machine; and the place in the meadow once held by the rank of habitants picturesque in garb, swinging their scythes in unison to some old song sung centuries ago in France, has been usurped by the utilitarian device that, with incessant chirr as of ten thousand sharded wings, mingling with the music of the bobolinks, sweeps down the broad acres of daisies, herdsgrass, and clover.

Many Canadians returned with their families to live in the land which they had spied out in their summer incursions, and so in one way and another the influx continued till they have become the most numerous of Vermont's foreign population.

For years the State was infested with an inferior class of these people, who plied the vocation of professional beggars. They made regular trips through the country in bands consisting of one or more families, with horses, carts, and ricketty wagons, and a retinue of curs, soliciting alms of pork, potatoes, and breadstuffs at every farmhouse they came to, and pilfering when opportunity offered. In the large towns there were depots where the proceeds of their beggary and theft were disposed of. They were an abominable crew of vagabonds, robust, lazy men and boys, slatternly women with litters of filthy brats, and all as detestable as they were uninteresting. They worked their beats successfully, till their pitiful tales of sickness, burnings-out, and journeyings to friends in distant towns were worn threadbare, and then they gradually disappeared, no one knows whither.

Almost to a man, the Canadians who settled in Vermont were devout Catholics when they came; but after they had been scattered for a few years among such a preponderant Protestant community, most of them were held very loosely by the bonds of mother church. Except they were residents of the larger towns they seldom saw a priest, and enjoyed a comfortable immunity from fasting, penance, and all ecclesiastic exactions on stomach or purse. On New Year's Day, perhaps the members of the family confessed to the venerable grandsire, but after that suffered no religious inconvenience until the close of the year. Now and then one strayed quite out of the fold and took his place boldly among the heretics, and apparently did not thereby forfeit the fellowship of his more faithful compatriots. But when the flock had become large enough to pay for the shearing, shepherds of the true faith were

not wanting. With that steadfast devotion to the interests of their church which has always characterized the Catholic priesthood, these men began their work without ostentation, and have succeeded in drawing into the domination of their church a large majority of the Canadian-born inhabitants of Vermont and of their descendants, as completely as if they were yet citizens of the province, which Parkman truly says, is "one of the most priest-ridden communities of the modern world."

What this leaven may finally work in the Protestant mass with which it has become incorporated is a question that demands more attention than it has yet received.

The character of these people is not such as to inspire the highest hope for the future of Vermont, if they should become the most numerous of its population. The affiliation with Anglo-Americans of a race so different in traits, in traditions, and in religion must necessarily be slow, and may never be complete.

No great love for their adopted country can be expected of a people that evinces so little for that of its origin as lightly to cast aside names that proudly blazon the pages of French history for poor translations or weak imitations of them in English, nor can broad enlightenment be hoped for of a race so dominated by its priesthood.

Vermont, as may be seen, has given of her best for the building of new commonwealths, to her own loss of such material as has made her all that her sons, wherever found, are so proud of,—material whose place no alien drift from northward or over seas can ever fill.

Source: Rowland E. Robinson, *Vermont: A Study of Independence* (Boston: Houghton Mifflin, 1892), pp. 328-332.

DOCUMENT 11

". . . No Crop More Profitable Than This Crop from the City" (1893)
VICTOR I. SPEAR

. . . I believe, as I have said, that we are adapted to dairying. . . . We have decided it, we have been pitted against the world and have held our reputation. We are adapted here for raising fruit and the markets of the world have been a witness to our success. We are adapted in Vermont to the production of the finest horses that have ever been put in the harness. The man who loves horses has a pride in Vermont. Vermont is adapted to raising sheep, and as we go back 50 years in Vermont history and see the conclusive results that have come from the efforts of Vermonters in developing the Spanish Merino sheep, we find sufficient evidence of what can be done by her breeders for this animal. We are adapted to the production of maple sugar in the highest quality and in the greatest quantity. We are adapted to the raising of almost every farm crop. And there is one thing more that we have all neglected; we are adapted here in Vermont to taking into our State every year thousands upon thousands of city people, and taking them into our homes. I want to impress upon you the importance and necessity of this industry. There have been efforts made by our railroads and by the Board of Agriculture to stir up the people to this new industry, and to the advantages that Vermont has as a summer home. Now, as a result, the people are already sufficiently stirred up on this point, and the difficulty that is next to be overcome is to prepare a place for them to rendezvous. Last summer I took reports from many of the places where we had comfortable quarters, and found that they had more of these people than they could accommodate. Now there is no crop more profitable than this crop from the city, and it is one that comes directly to the farmer, and he should encourage and promote this visiting from our city cousins. They are willing to pay, they don't care for fishing grounds, they don't care for hunting; they don't care for boating, but they do care for good roads; they want a little good food, they want a little milk to drink that has not been skimmed; they want a little good butter that they can swear by, and when they come to Vermont they can find it; they want to get out of the city, and the children are the ones that the people are the most interested to find a place for, where they can stay through the summer. This is not perhaps exactly on the line of my remarks but that does not matter, it is a subject I wish to call your attention to and say to you that by proper attention on the part of our citizens, by their taking proper interest in this matter and providing places where these people may be entertained we may find in Vermont, in a very few years, that the most profitable crop will be these city visitors. They have al-

ready come here, and one cannot come to Vermont and spend the summer and forget it, those who have been here wish to come again, and they will bring others with them. I will leave this thought with you. Let us see if next season we can not make more here and thereby benefit ourselves and do good to others. It will do them good to breathe a little Vermont air, and get an inspiration from our mountains.

Source: Victor I. Spear, "Farm Management," *Thirteenth Vermont Agricultural Report by the State Board of Agriculture for the Year 1893* (Burlington, Vt.: Free Press Association, 1893), pp. 56-57.

DOCUMENT 12

"Labor and Life at the Barre Granite Quarries " (1895)

GEORGE ELLSWORTH HOOKER

Millstone Hill? What is it?

Earlier in the century, superior grinding stones were cut from the exposed granite ledges. Hence its name. To the ordinary inhabitant of the dependent and newly incorporated city of Barre, it is, under its more familiar title of "the hill," or "the quarries," a place from which has come already an industrial development so considerable as to have transformed a quiet Vermont village into the third largest city in the State. To the social inquirer, on the other hand, "the hill" is primarily the workshop of 600 men, and the abode, isolated and crude, of about 2,000 people.

Only the business interpretation, however, of the quarry district, has thus far really touched the popular imagination. Length of obelisk, clarity of stock, volume of shipments, capital extension, land values, scales of wages, have been gravely discussed or enthusiastically heralded. Boarding house life, however, obstacles in the way of acquiring homes, dispersion of the inhabitants owing to land speculation, abuses of renting, lack of sanitary, intellectual, recreative institutions, have had no critic and no serious recognition.

The advent of the railroad into Barre two decades ago, marks the beginning of a steady and rapid development, both in its quarrying branch on "the hill" and in its finishing branch at Barre village, of what had before been a straggling industry employing only ten or twenty men. A dozen years later the "sky route" was carried from the village to the very top of "the hill," nearly five miles distant, and local transportation thus became largely a matter of the loco[mo]tive instead of the ox teams, and trains of 20 to 30 horses of preceding days.

The output of the forty quarries now operated in the district goes chiefly for monumental purposes, and has extended its market to the pacific slopes. Its distinctive feature is eveness of texture. Shafts forty or fifty feet long are absolutely free, over their entire length, from spot or cloud. In color it is light gray, and dark or blue gray, takes a high polish and is wrought into all monumental effects as well as into statues. . . .

Of the six hundred men employed in the busy half of the year, a number, varying from twenty five to one hundred, are paving cutters, about seventy are blacksmiths, steam drill men, engineers and foremen, and the balance are quarrymen. The last get $1.75 to $2.25 per day, perhaps an average of $1.85. Steam drill operators get $2.50, blacksmiths $2.75, paving cutters, by the piece from $2.50 to $5.00 per day. Engineers receive $50.00 to $60.00 per month and foremen from $90.00 to $150.00 per month. Lack of employment is not a serious problem in the district, neither are low wages. Quarrying, however, is a specially hazardous employment, not only from the use of explosives, but even more because of the heavy material dealt with and the tremendous strain upon machinery. An obelisk lately quarried weighed 100 tons in the rough and 60 tons when dressed for shipment. Seven or eight fatal accidents and many more serious ones have occurred in recent years. One superintendent explained that he avoided accidents by refusing to employ careless men. "If I saw a man go under that stone," he said, pointing to one suspended at the moment by the derrick, "I would discharge him." No special employer's liability legislation exists in Vermont, and if an employee is injured through the negligence of a fellow workman he has no redress. In any case his only recourse is a suit for damages, which is somewhat dubious expedient; for, not only are eye witnesses tempted to favor their employer in order to hold down their jobs, but the costs and delays of litigation are such that the plaintiff, to quote a local engineer, "unless he's a stayer and got money, might jest as well git out."

Labor at the Barre quarries proceeds at a comparatively high tension. Men from quarrying districts in Maine contrast the easy pace there with uninterrupted and rapid movement here: and when compared to the old country the contrast is still sharper. Were he to count, the observer would be surprised at the rapidity with which blows rain down upon the drills. The heavy, eight-pound sledge, swung with both hands while the drill is held by a third man, falls about 40 times per minute, and the 3 1/2 pound hammer, swung with one hand while the drill is held by the other, averages double that rate. Shifting drills, driving wedges, hitching chains, vary the exercise, but the physical expenditure of energy in the 9 hour day is heavy. No Saturday half-holiday obtains, as in the old country throughout the year and as in the finishing trade at Barre during the summer. Many Scotchmen have come here from the granite industry in Aberdeen, Scotland. Some of these express the opinion that as compared with the old country the men here work harder, receive higher wages, spend more money and are no happier. A man, however, is alleged to have "more freedom with his employers" here, and can, if a complaint arises against him, be "heard to state his case," whereas there he would more likely receive a peremptory "go."

A preference exists among the men for having the day's leisure massed at its close. Accordingly work begins early. Not only is "hill" time one half hour ahead of standard time, but even then some quarriers commense in summer at 6:30 a.m.

The noon whistle precipitates a lively scene. Clicking hammer and creaking derrick cease on the instant, and before the whistle's note is finished some of the men are half way across the quarry. An hour is too short a period in the case of many for them to reach their regular tables, eat in comfort and return on time. Hence the frequent "dinner pail gang." A typical dinner pail contains two large, thick slices of bread buttered, a slice of cold meat or of cheese, one doughnut, one slice of cake, two cookies, two pieces of pie, and two cups of tea or coffee.

In the social development of the district the chief difficulties in the way have been (1) mixture and transiency of population, and (2) real estate speculation.

Compounded as local society mainly is of four nationalities, Scotch, French Canadians, Irish, and Americans, associated effort is much hindered by this racial diversity. Religious separation is the most vital. No local A.P.A. [American Protective Association] lodge exists, but the feeling has run high, that a society of Orangemen is being organized. The Roman Catholic contingent comprises from one-third to one-half of the entire population. Association of work, at table, in Unions, and especially at school, tends, however, to mollify religious suspicion.

Furthermore, the population is constantly shifting. Apart from ordinary coming and going there is the annual migration to the lumbering camps as winter, with its contraction of work, approaches. Paving cutters too are an especially unstable class. They must go where contracts go. If these are short, moves must be frequent and perhaps from Maine to Georgia and then back again. Their high wages are sometimes entirely consumed thus. This explains the remark of one cutter on receiving $100.00 for his work last July, that he could "not afford to marry."

A salient feature of the workers as a whole is their youthfulness. Probably they would not average above 28 years of age. They are, to a large extent, a body upon whom the cares of life sit lightly. Their conscious wants are not numerous and their wages are amply sufficient for these. Thrift is quite apt to characterize the head of a family, especially if he has a prudent wife. But in a great number of cases, when the month's pay comes to a single man, he settles his board bill, squares up at the store and livery stable, and then as for the balance, "rolls it lively." It may go for a suit of clothes, or to cover poker chips, or to be stolen from him in a spree. He is often "strapped" within a few days, whereupon he goes stolidly on in his strapped condition until the next pay day. His code of honor on the subject of debt paying, however, is, as a rule, high. "There are few succors or skins in the hill," said a local livery stable keeper, "and very few who can't get credit."

Nearly all trade is done on a credit basis. "Gut 'ny 5 cent tablets?" inquired a tiny pink-clad school girl of the general store clerk. "Yes," he replied, and handed her one. "Put't on'e book," she called out as she disappeared through the door.

"Is that the way most of your business is done?" asked a by-stander. "Yes, most of it," answered the clerk: "Settle once a month."

Concerning the personal characteristics of the people, many outsiders conceive "the hill" to be "a terrible place." Distance, however, lends much of this terror. True, many of the refinements of life are absent. Men go to their table in their shirt sleeves. They disfigure a hall floor pretty badly at an entertainment. They swear in a most senseless manner. They rarely quarrel, sometimes gamble, and ofttimes get drunk. On the other hand, it is, as elsewhere, the minority who thus greatly discredit local life and defy the better judgment of the community. With a large section of the population historical training even more than appetite stands opposed to the prohibitory legislation of the state. Evasion, therefore, is far from unusual, and is enhanced by that dangerous few whose greed for the enormous profits of illegal selling leads them more or less openly to press their trade. The "boys" call it "going after the sewing machine" when they drive to Barre to fetch a consignment of whiskey from outside the state. This is then quickly peddled out at a profit of from 150% to 300%. "Salting the colt" is going back into the country of a Sunday and celebrating with a jug of cider procured from some farmer.

Boarding is the lot of more than half the men. The two largest boarding houses can accommodate 60 to 70 each, but are rarely full. Numerous smaller houses have from 5 to 20 boarders. A boarder's room is ordinarily about 9 feet square, having a shade at the window, a double bed, a chair or two, a little stand in one corner embellished with a line of pipes, an assortment of tobacco, a few writing materials, perhaps a handful of books and maybe a Bible. On the opposite wall hangs a motley display of coats, hats and trousers, while underneath is lined up a collection of foot gear. This is particularly his sleeping room. The "bar room" below is his sitting room, where he deposits his outside garments, chats, reads, smokes or plays cards. Except in the small groups the family in the house know little about him. He has his own outside entrance and mingles little with them. General conditions are improving in that the boarding house is steadily yielding to the fireside. About one-half of the men in the district are married. Of the more than two hundred houses, a least two-fifths are owned by the occupants. Comfortable homes and normal family circles are increasing in number.

A book agent who has been making periodical visits to the place for two years, affirms that, within that time, he has sold there $2,000.00 worth of books, principally the standard novelists. Some men indeed are reading Ruskin and Carlyle. A large amount of mail matter comes to the district. Men could be found taking two daily papers, and many households receive nearly an average of one weekly a day. Of the scattering ones who, perhaps owing to hard conditions in early life, can neither read nor write, three, at least, have lately applied to a friend to be taught. The three public schools of the district, with their enrollment of as many hundred children, ought indeed to be supplemented by at least one night school for adults.

Of the four religious bodies established in the locality, the Roman Catholic surpass the three Protestant organizations combined, both in numbers and in cost of plant.

The Good Templars' lodge has a flourishing membership of 100, meets weekly and is an influence in local life. The Forresters' lodge is smaller.

For enlivening daily routine, the arrival of the stage coach from Barre, at 6 P.M., is the chief event. From 75 to 150 men crowd the Post Office store and steps, pending the distribution of the mail. This finished, they drift away, some to billiard tables, some to each other's rooms, some to an evening of whist, some to "see their girls," some to sit on the fence and play a harmonica and sing songs, some to their books or newspapers.

Recreative opportunities are sorely meagre. After supper, in Summer time, a group of men may often be found in front of the livery stable, pitching quoits, or putting the shot, and a little baseball is played at times. Any proper organization of outdoor sports, however, is prevented by the lack of a Saturday half-holiday.

Separated, as the people are at the quarries, from the more variegated and engrossing life of the neighboring young city, the absence of adequate diversion and sparkly in their experience, undoubtedly tends to provoke them to coarse substitutes and to render them prosy, unimaginative, and sometimes morose. "What do people do up here to have a good time?" was recently asked of a number of persons on the spot. It was put to one man who, compelled to loaf for the day on account of his proprietor's death, had "cleaned up" and was sitting on the back piazza of his boarding house, while a pool of sewage below was spreading its odors through the air. "What do they do?" he replied. "Nothing as I know, 'cept to sleep, and eat an' work." To the same query a very intelligent engineer answered, "They hire a team, drive to Barre, get drunk, smash the wagon,

pay a fine or go to jail." "Them as sez they have a good time," answered a young man of Methodist proclivities, "comes back to the quarry on Monday morning an' tells how as they went off with a team, day before, an' got drunk. But the fact is, they don't have no good time." In full agreement, an officer of one of the unions re-iterated, "They don't have any good times;" and one of the pioneer residents added, "There aint no amusements." To the same interrogatory, however, a clergyman answered, "Oh they dance." For a very considerable portion of the population the promiscuous dance is certainly the favorite amusement, a masquerade ball being the brilliant acme of local recreation.

The realization of a proper social existence at the quarries has been chiefly hindered by land speculation. By preventing people from living where they wished to live, this has prevented a natural development of community life, and thwarted or impeded the normal functions of that little social body. When about fifteen years ago, the steady expansion of the quarrying industry became assured, three wealthy men, one residing in Barre, one in Montpelier, and one in Albany, N.Y. bought up most of the desirable land in the district. One of these proceeded to erect upon a portion of his land a score or more of small houses, little better than shanties, containing one room below, and an attic above, the water supply being from a tub in the general area. This group of red huts bears the aristocratic title of "Stovepipe City." The houses rent for $3.00 per month for four winter months and at double that rate for the rest of the year. The income is perhaps from 20% to 35% upon the investment. Having gone thus far, this owner rested and simply "held" his land. The holdings of the other two men included entirely and precisely the area forming the natural site of the town. This area, however, they have kept out of the market, declining either to sell or lease on reasonable terms. Working men have thus been compelled to go afield for habitable houses to rent or suitable lots on which to buy. The result is, not only that nooks and corners, knowls and sidehills, have been resorted to as building sites, but, still worse, the people are most injuriously scattered. Their dwellings straggle through five distinct settlements, which ramble over a distance of more than two miles.

From the standpoint of sanitary needs this has been a serious disadvantage. The area has been so great and the population so sparse, that no proper water or drainage facilities have been afforded. Sewage is nowhere cared for, and two of the settlements, including the principal one of all, depends entirely upon shallow wells for water, though springs of ample flow might be available for a larger and more urgent demand.

From the standpoint of access to work, to the Post Office, to stores, churches, lodges, social events, this dispersion is most unfortunate, and thereby the entire collective life of the people has been permanently handicapped. The Post Office and the trading center are not in the middle of these settlements, but at one of the extreme edges. The Roman Catholic church, in seeking to be central, was obliged to choose an unsettled locality, without so much as a farm house close at hand. Distance, thus, from each other, especially in view of the severe weather during much of the year, and the lack of sidewalks, results in isolation and monotony which would have been greatly lessened had people been allowed to group themselves naturally, according to convenience for work and for social contact.

To the social student, such a development as has taken place in this quarry district, has a unique value. Being so rapid, it epitomises a series of events which, in other cases, extend over long periods. Where a community takes fifty years to grow from 200 to 2,000, the people have time to re-adjust themselves to abnormal conditions. Consequently the abnormality is never glaring, and may be almost completely disguised. When, however, as is true of Millstone Hill, a single decade changes 200 to 2,000, the situation will be less conventional and less the product of artificial re-adjustment. Unnatural constraints can then be more clearly perceived.

In accord with this fact, the most urgent truth which the quarry life illustrates is that of the irresponsible and selfish power and the injurious influence which land speculation may exercise, particularly in small and remote centers, over the life of an entire community. The speculators themselves are in no sense improvers. They do not reside on the spot; they spend none of their profits there; they assume no responsibility for the welfare of the people; they simply regard the growing community as their promising Milch cow. Any idea that such land-owning is a trusteeship, primarily in behalf of those locally concerned, is entirely out of

mind. The exigencies of prospective values preclude the social growth of the community. This is the most obstructive fact which meets the student of life at the Barre Granite Quarries.

Source: George Ellsworth Hooker, "Labor and Life at the Barre Granite Quarries; A Brief Survey of Social Conditions on Millstone Hill, Barre, Vermont, in the Autumn of 1895," November 1895, typescript at Vermont Historical Society, Montpelier, Vermont.

DOCUMENT 13

"The Young Women and the Farm" (1896)

HARRIET M. RICE

In considering this subject, we may well ask, "Why are there so few young women on the farms?" Why do so many of our bright Vermont girls go to the city to obtain work, instead of remaining in their native town? Are the cities and villages the only desirable places of residence nowadays? Is the country only a good place to emigrate from? Why is it that there should be abandoned farms? Let us try to answer some of these questions.

With too many of the farmers, life becomes a sort of routine. There are heavy debts to be lifted and so they work early and late, taking but little time for recreation. Many times they think that the boys and girls ought to do the same. In one of last week's papers I noticed the following:

"Farmer's boy — Father, kin I go to the minstrels to-night with Hiram Homespun?

Farmer—Naw. 'Tain't more'n a month since yer went to the top of the hill to see the eclipse of the moon. Pears to me yew wanter be on the go the hull time."

While this is exaggerated, is it not an illustration of the spirit shown by too many of the tillers of the soil? Often they are thoughtless in their demands, but the young folks make up their minds that life on the farm is nothing but work, that the good times are few and far between,—and so they decide that just as soon as they are old enough they will go away "for a change."

Then, too, young people want society. They want to know what other young people are doing. They *need* to come in contact with minds wiser and better than their own to broaden their ideas and stimulate them to do their best. One of the great objections to life on a farm is the long distances from neighbors. This is especially hard for the women. The men's work takes them away from home,—there is feed, wood, and coal to be drawn, usually milk to be carried to the creamery, pork and other products to be marketed, and even when they are at work on their land, often they can call to their neighbors at work on the other side of the fence. But with the women it is different. Their duties compel them to stay at home much of the time. There are the three meals a day to be prepared, dishes and milk things to be washed, the house to be kept clean and in order, washing, ironing and sewing to be done, and often it is about impossible to get help. After the necessary work of the day is done, they feel too tired to walk to a neighbor's, and wish they might live where neighbors weren't so far away, and they could see somebody once in a while.

It is pleasant, too, to attend church regularly as well as to go to prayer-meetings, sociables, or lectures, but for weeks together, the condition of the roads make it well nigh impossible to go far from home. . . . For weeks in the spring and fall almost all business must be suspended till "the going improves," and the daughter of the house stays at home day after day waiting for the mud to dry up; for what fun is there in visiting a friend three or four miles away, when at least two hours must be spent on the road, wondering whether you can ever get out of this "Slough of Despond." Truly such a trip is indeed a "pleasure exertion," as Samantha Allen says.

The difficulty of communication is another great disadvantage. I dare say that there are thousands of homes in Vermont where the mail does not come, on an average, oftener than once a week. With the going so bad that the horses must not be taken out except on the most urgent business, when but few except those that can walk attend even the Sunday services at the churches, and with no communication with the outside world oftener than once a week, is it any wonder that the daily round of duties begins to seem monotonous and the house almost like a prison.

Again, too few of the farmers or their wives have much education, and to the young people comes a desire to have more. This desire is entirely praiseworthy and should be encouraged, but too often the district schools are poor, even the common branches being taught in a half-hearted and slip-shod way. So the girls and boys must be sent away from home if they are to learn much beyond the three R's.

Another reason why the young folks go away from home, is the hope of making more money. We all know that fortunes are not made very fast on the farm.

But the great reason why the average American girl leaves her home to earn her own living, in city and country alike, is that she wants to be independent. If she has a letter to mail she doesn't want to have to ask Pa for the necessary two cents. She doesn't want to be obliged to *tease* for a new dress, a new hat, or a new pair of shoes. She wants a little money to do just what she pleases with, without any questions from anybody. Few farmers allow their wives or daughters much money which they can call their own.

So in the face of all these disadvantages—life a humdrum sameness, without much society, and with but poor opportunities for education, money scarce, and a little often grudgingly given—is it much wonder that many of our bright, talented, intelligent girls leave the farm and educate themselves for positions of trust and honor, as teachers, type-writers, stenographers, book-keepers, telegraph operators, doctors and lawyers, and that others, thinking that anything is better than life on a farm, become servant girls, seamstresses, waitresses, clerks, etc.? Sometimes it is doubtless better for them, too.

What, then, is the remedy? How shall life in the country be made so pleasant and attractive that people in general, and the young woman in particular, shall prefer it to life in the city?

I think the remedy lies largely with the individual family. Don't work too hard and take a vacation once or twice a year, if possible. The old saying is, "All work and no play makes Jack a dull boy," and I suppose it would be equally true if we were to make it read thus: "All work and no play makes Jill a dull girl." So let the girls have time for an occasional visit of a week or two. Then, when the horses are not too busy, let them go for a ride once in a while. Farmers sometimes say, "My horse needs exercise. I have been so busy lately I haven't had time to drive him." Teach the girls to drive properly and then in a busy time they can often save much inconvenience by taking the horse to be shod, the tools to be mended, etc. But perhaps some girl will say, "I should like to do this, but when I am ready there is no one about to harness for me." Harness the horse yourself, and if there is none in the barn go to the pasture and catch one.

If the horses are busy and you want to go to a place two or three miles away, why walk. I believe that no investment of time can be made to yield a larger amount of pleasure and vigor, than a half hour a day spent in the open air. It is said that the women of England think nothing of walking five or ten miles at a stretch, and their health is much better than that of their American sisters. But exercise to be of value must be begun gradually and persisted in, not overdone one day and neglected the next.

Then let the daughter of the house have some particular duties of her own to do. Many mothers prefer to do all the work themselves so that their daughters can have an easy time. This is not wise. "All play and no work" would probably make Jill "a mere shirk," and that isn't the kind of young women that are wanted anywhere. . . .

Scientific farming is the order of the day. Why should not scientific housekeeping be also? Is there any more need of science in feeding cattle and horses than in providing food for human beings? Practical physiology should be studied not only in the schools, but by those who have the charge of the family cooking, and let labor-saving machinery be used indoors as well as out-doors to lighten drudgery. The right kind of papers and books are a great help, and often pay for themselves many times over. There is no place so good as the country to learn housekeeping, for in an emergency you must depend upon your own ingenuity, and not the baker's. Learn everything you can about everything, whether it be to make a salad or a loaf of bread, to trim a hat or darn a stocking, to arrange flowers or to wash dishes. You will probably find a use sometime for all your accomplishments, if not for yourself, for others. If the work is done intelligently, and in co-operation, some time will doubtless be found for mental improvement. Many of the best books are now sold at such a low price as to be within the reach of all. When oppressed by loneliness, as we all are more or less, books will often drive away the blues, and speak to us of higher living. . . . Reading aloud will help to pass away pleasantly and profitably many a long win-

ter evening. The people in a neighborhood may form a reading-circle, and have a good time as well as gain instruction. Even two or three who are interested can read or study the same thing and then meet once in awhile to compare notes. "Where there's a will there's a way."

Let me also suggest a few public improvements which seem to me desirable.

First, let us have better roads, so that we shall not need to be shut out from communication with the outside world, and with each other, for so large a part of the year. Let the mail facilities be extended and bettered. If all the families in this country were to unite to demand free delivery of mails, it would doubtless be accomplished before many years. Why should the dweller in the city, who lives within two minutes walk of the post-office, be entitled to have his mail brought to his door while the farmer must go for his letters and papers from one to six miles? Is not one a citizen of the United States as well as the other, and should he not therefore have the same rights? May the time be hastened when this shall be done!

In the meantime, let new post offices be established, or let those in a community club together and engage some one to deliver their mail every day. If all would do this the expense need not be so very great. Then, every family could, if it chose, take a daily paper, and be as well posted as anyone.

Let the citizens of the town establish a public library. Then its young people could have plenty of good wholesome reading, and need not have recourse to dime novels.

Then, too, we ought to have better schools. Perhaps, as a teacher, it is hardly the thing to say, "Let us have better teachers." But do let us have more general interest in the cause of education. Let the parents visit the schools oftener, and know what is being done. . . . Let the school grounds be made beautiful and attractive. Let the laws against truancy be so well enforced that every child of school age shall be in school and *attend regularly*, instead of doing as some do now,— go one day, and stay out the next. . . .

It seems to me that if these things could be done in this town, and every other, there would be less ignorance and vice, the schools would be improved, and into the minds of all would be infused more respect for law and order, and a deeper love of knowledge. The work of teaching in the country would attract more intelligent teachers and no one would need to go away to get a thorough knowledge of the common school studies; while if central high schools were established, more than are now able to do so could take the higher branches of study. The school commissioners should have the active support of every good citizen in their efforts to improve the schools.

As to the improvements suggested, you will say, "Yes, these things are all very well to talk about, but they cost too much." Have you ever seen anything worth having that didn't cost something, either of money, time or effort?

We often read in the agricultural papers this sentence, "Give the boys a chance" as referring to financial matters. I agree with that fully, but would add this, "Give the girls a chance, too." Let them have a chance to earn a little money for themselves.

Perhaps you will ask, "What are some of the ways in which a girl can earn money on the farm?" One of the most common is by keeping poultry. A flock of from twenty to fifty hens will afford considerable spending money, if properly cared for. Farmers sometimes say, "If there is anything I hate, it is a hen." Others think that it is better to buy eggs and chickens than to take time to produce them. Such could give the charge of them to the women of the household, furnishing feed in return for eggs consumed at home. Two ladies in this State, with whom I am acquainted, made over two hundred dollars in one year from their poultry, besides doing all the work for a family of five.

A considerable sum may sometimes be made by raising vegetables, berries, and fruit. The prices for vegetables are, of course, not so remunerative as in a large city, but fruits and berries meet with a ready sale even in the country. After the first year, currants, grapes, pears, plums or cherries do not require any great amount of attention, and would be likely to prove a good investment.

A young woman living near a city might raise flowers and plants for sale. This has been proved successful by many.

The field of literature, too, is open to all in country as well as city.

Seamstresses and dressmakers are always in demand, and when compared with the cost of living, the prices paid do not differ very much from those paid in cities.

The girls who have had a musical education can teach music, and others can prepare for the noble work of the common school teacher and often find employment in their own neighborhood.

But perhaps the most satisfactory plan for those who have neither the time or the talents for any of the things mentioned, would be to receive a regular allowance for their services. Even though it were not so much as they would otherwise get, they would feel a sense of independence, and would take pride in making it go as far as possible, perhaps even saving a little toward a bank account.

By the way, the amount actually saved by the city girl is often not large. The one who earns six or eight dollars a week may seem to be getting good pay, but her board costs probably more than half it, and after she has clothed herself, she hasn't a great deal left.

First and foremost among the blessing to be gained by the farmer's girl in staying on the old homestead, is the blessing of home. Many of those who leave this secure haven for the tempestuous ocean of city life, find that the things for which they sought are as far off as ever, and if they had worked half as hard at home as they have since, they would be better off in every way. In her father's house the young woman may become as the light of the household, relieving her tired mother of many burdens, filling the old rooms with music, giving many pretty touches to the house, and encouraging and helping her brothers and sisters. In the neighborhood and town in which she lives there is always need of her help in church and society. Is not this a broad enough field of usefulness?

Then, too, she need not be so far behind her city cousins in manners and dress. Most of these get much information from books and magazines. Why may she not do the same? She, too, if she has skill with her needle, can, with the aid of paper patterns and the printed directions, have her gowns made in the prevailing mode.

Let her have as good an education as possible, and then make use of it to help those who are not so fortunate.

Where could she find a more beautiful place to live than this grand old Green Mountain State? The poet says:

Breathes there a man with soul so dead,
Who never to himself has said,
This is my own, my native land?

The fertile valleys and rounded hills with their magnificent background of mountains, ever changing in color, sometimes a pale, hazy blue, sometimes changed to red and purple and gold by the setting sun, in winter robed in snowy white, standing from year to year unmoved, should all speak to her of their unchanging Creator. David, "the sweet singer of Israel," says: "I will lift up my eyes unto the hills from whence cometh my help," and is there not an inspiration to nobler ideals in the very sight of the mountains?

Vermont has always been noted for the high character of its men and women. Let the young of to-day strive to be worthy successors of those who have gone before. Happy shall be the young woman who shall so improve the golden present and the future years that she may be, like Abraham, a blessing to all with whom she comes in contact, whether she be rich or poor, or her home in city or country.

Source: Harriet M. Rice, "The Young Women and the Farm," *Sixteenth Vermont Agricultural Report by the State Board of Agriculture for the Year 1896* (Burlington, Vt.: Free Press Association, 1896), pp. 193-201.

SECTION EIGHT

1896-1917
Pastoral Politics

VERMONT VOICES

SECTION EIGHT

1896-1917
Pastoral Politics

Introduction

W ell before the close of the nineteenth century, Republicanism in Vermont had become more than a political party. For many it had achieved the status of a civic religion. Non-Republicans, sometimes calling themselves Democrats, occasionally won election, but never to major office. Republicans so dominated the state, they boasted generations of the state's business and professional leaders and could frequently claim all 30 senators as well as over 200 town representatives during any given legislative session. Threats to Republican hegemony therefore were feared not merely as the potential loss of political power but also as a repudiation of the state's social and moral ethos.

Josiah Grout's inaugural address suggests such a concern.Grout was a battle-scarred veteran of seventeen Civil War engagements who returned to Vermont after the war to practice law and politics. A younger brother of long-time Congressman William Grout, Josiah served multiple terms in the state legislature, two as speaker, before he was elected governor. **Document 1**, an excerpt from his inaugural address, outlines the responsibilities of state government at the close of the nineteenth century. While Grout's celebration of the prohibitory law may ring hollow to modern ears, his rationales for state financing of schools and roads have since proved more popular in concept than in execution.

Redfield Proctor served simultaneously as Vermont's premier industrialist and most influential politician. Like Grout a Civil War veteran, he founded the Vermont Marble Company and a political dynasty that included two sons and a grandson who became governor. Redfield's own political career encompassed service in the state legislature, a term as governor, and appointment to the position of secretary of war in President Benjamin Harrison's cabinet. In 1891 he succeeded George Edmunds as senator and remained in the Senate until his death in 1911.

In 1898 he visited Cuba to assess conditions there in light of widespread assertions that Spanish control over Cuba had broken down and that while attempting to suppress the Cuban revolution, General Valeriano Weyler had devastated the countryside. Upon his return to the United States, Proctor delivered the address to the Senate excerpted here as **Document 2.** Proctor, regarded as both a military expert and an anti-imperialist, made a deep impression on the nation with this address and converted many skeptics to the view that Cuba should be rescued from Spanish rule.

Public perceptions of Proctor as an anti-imperialist were probably misplaced. Theodore Roosevelt thought him "very ardent for war," and Proctor had interceded directly with President William McKinley to secure command of the Asiatic Squadron for Montpelier native Commodore George Dewey prior to the outbreak of the Spanish-American war. Dewey's subsequent victory over the Spanish fleet in the Battle of Manila Bay broke the Spanish hold on the Philippines and led to American occupation of the islands. Manila Bay thrust Dewey into the front ranks of American war heroes. He was plied with adulation, memorialized by triumphal arches, and celebrated in song. **Document 3**, "King of the Sea," is a representative song.

During 1902, Vermont experienced what was arguably its most tumultuous gubernatorial campaign. Fed by objections to the prohibitory act and demands for local option under which individual towns decided whether to license the sale of intoxicating liquors, the local option movement was led by *Rutland Herald* publisher Percival Clement. Clement had been proposing local option since at least 1890, and Governor Grout's defense of statewide prohibition (see Document 1) was in part to rebut Clement's charges. By 1902, Clement had succeeded in making local option the primary political issue, and he announced his intention to seek the Republican gubernatorial nomination. **Document 4**, which served as his formal announcement, gives his reason for seeking the nomination. The state convention adopted a platform plank advocating a local option referendum but denied Clement the nomination. Clement bolted the convention to campaign as a local option candidate on an independent ticket. His candidacy was the first serious threat to a Republican gubernatorial candidate since the birth of the Republican Party, and **Document 5** was distributed by the Republican State Committee in response to that threat. In addition to denouncing Clement and appealing to party loyalty, the "Address" most significantly alleged that state taxes had risen not through waste or inefficiency but because the state had assumed financial burdens of local operation from the towns.

The Republican candidate John McCullough won a plurality, but Clement votes along with those of the Democratic candidate were sufficient to deny him the popular majority required for election by the Vermont Constitution. The 1902 legislature promptly elected McCullough governor and shortly thereafter passed a referendum by which a popular majority voted local option.

Document 6 is from Governor McCullough's inaugural address. Delivered to the legislature prior to its deliberations over the local option bill, its detailed recommendations reflect prohibitionist concern over the licentiousness they feared might accompany adoption. McCullough's address is also engaging as an example of a paean to Vermont towns, a tribute that became increasingly popular, even though, as the Republican State Committee noted (in Document 5), the "settled policy of the state regardless of party" was to shift burdens from the towns to the state. Even more bizarre, McCullough's support of the state road tax and a primary law further restricted town autonomy.

Document 7, *The Status of Rural Vermont*, deals with a third point raised by McCullough, the condition of the state's Anglo-Saxon heritage. This document, excerpted from a report by the State Agricultural Commission, chronicles a decline in the quantity and quality of the state's rural population in the context of a worldwide rural depression. The author, like Governor McCullough, extols the character of Vermont's original settlers but confronts the reality that their descendants were emigrating from the state in large numbers to be replaced by a foreign-born population, often Catholics. In the author's judgment, shared by popular writers such as Rowland Robinson (see Section 7, Document 10), "on the whole the swapping of inhabitants tended to create a lower average character status for rural Vermont." One cannot help but speculate as to how the author determined character status.

The exodus of native-born Vermonters to the West and out-of-state urban centers inspired more ballads than even the exploits of Admiral Dewey. Nostalgic yearnings for bygone days in an idyllic habitat were not limited to transplanted Vermonters, as is attested by official state songs such as Virginia's "Carry Me Back to Old Virginny," and Indiana's "On the Banks of the Wabash." Nonetheless, Vermont cultivated its allure as home sweet home to thousands of expatriates through pageants, parades, "old home weeks," Vermont clubs, and, of course, song. Dozens celebrated their composer's reverence for Vermont, but none achieved the popularity of their Virginia and Indiana counterparts. **Document 8**, "Take Me Back to Old Vermont," is a sentimental ballad typical of its genre and most notable for its evocation of Vermont symbols.

Woman suffrage was a visible force in Vermont politics as early as 1870, when a constitutional convention voted 233 to 1 against a suffrage amendment (See Section 6, Document 18). Undaunted, suffragettes continued their efforts, suffering defeat after defeat in the state legislature. Annette W. Parmalee was one such relentless crusader, and through private correspondence and public addresses she canvassed the state for her cause. That her efforts were not always appreciated is evident from **Document 9**, responses to Parmalee from a Mrs. H. W. Abbott. **Document 10**, generated seven years after Mrs. Abbott's responses, reveals Mrs. Parmalee still actively pursuing the suffrage cause in a speech in Randolph. Within two months of the Randolph address, suffragettes celebrated a major victory when the governor signed into law a bill permitting women to vote in municipal elections (they could already hold municipal office).

As is clear from Annettee Parmalee's address, the Green Mountain state was not immune to the reform impulses that were sweeping the nation. During the first decade of the twentieth century the state legislature enacted a list of Progressive initiatives that included judicial reorganization, the adoption by state government of scientific management principles, the creation and strengthening of state regulatory commissions, the mandating of weekly wage payments, and incremental concessions to woman suffrage. Notably absent from the state's list of major reforms was the adoption of a direct primary.

Document 11, an editorial supporting the direct primary, argues that by promoting greater participation, the primary would wrest control of candidate selection from party bosses. In it the editorial writer rejects the objection that the primary would create "practically, another general election." This objection, however, cannot be dismissed so summarily. Vermont law mandated that nominations for most political offices be by majority vote. If no candidate at a caucus received a majority on the first ballot, a common occurrence, another ballot would be held; a primary in which the leading candidate led by a plurality and not a majority would require scheduling a second election.

Document 12, excerpted from "Vermont: Designed by the Creator for the Playground of the Continent," is a tract fashioned by the state's publicity bureau and distributed by the secretary of state's office to advertise Vermont. It stands as an implicit acknowledgment of the expanded role of state government. In this instance it assumed the responsibility from private enterprises for attracting tourists, with the larger objective of bolstering the state's economy. Also note the author's approval of the state "taking over more of the burden of maintenance of the roads" from the towns.

Document 13 consists of two publications issued by the Vermont Progressive Republican League. They reveal that in the spring of 1912, a Progressive element hoped to gain control of the state Republican Party to legislate a broad reform agenda that included a direct primary as the first order of business. Also seeking like-minded national candidates, in early June the League endorsed Ernest W. Gibson, the author of one of the primary bills cited in Document 11, for the Republican nomination to Congress.

These efforts were abandoned later that month after the Republican National Convention in Chicago renominated William Howard Taft for president and Theodore Roosevelt bolted to run on a Progressive ticket. Contrary to original intent the League reorganized into the Progressive Party to support Roosevelt and nominated a slate for state and local office. Although they failed to carry the state for Roosevelt (Vermont was one of only two states to cast its electoral votes for the Republican candidate), the Progressives did manage to deny the Republican state ticket a popular majority. For only the second time since the inception of the Republican Party, the election was decided in the legislature; Allen Fletcher, the Republican candidate who received a plurality of the popular vote, was elected governor.

If Ernest Gibson personified the Vermont Progressive, Edward Curtis Smith was his conservative counterpart. The son of J. Gregory Smith, a former governor and first president of the Northern Pacific Railroad, Edward followed family tradition, also serving as governor and railroad president. **Document 14**, "State Expenditures," provides excerpts from his speech to the Greater Vermont Association, an organization of state business leaders. Smith was alarmed by the growth of state government and the rise in state expenditures, and he attributed it to the legislature having shifted the largest burden of state financing from property to corporate taxes.

Like Smith, Allen Fletcher remained a loyal Republican throughout the Progressive insurgency. Facing opposition by Progressive and Democratic candidates in his 1912 race for governor, as noted above, he was elected by the legislature after receiving a plurality of the popular vote. As governor, however, he proved more susceptible to Progressive initiatives than the more traditionalist Smith, and compiled a record that satisfied a number of reform objectives.

It was not until 1915, however, and only after a titanic struggle among Republicans, that Vermont passed a direct primary law. In 1916, the year it went into effect, Allen Fletcher sought unsuccessfully the Republican nomination for the U.S. Senate. **Document 15** provides the text of a campaign pamphlet Fletcher addressed to Vermont's industrial labor force. It is one of the earliest of such direct appeals, marking Vermont's changing demographic and economic landscape and suggesting a new departure for Vermont politics.

Document 1

Inaugural Address (1896)

GOVERNOR JOSIAH GROUT

Gentlemen of the Senate and House of Representatives:

Elected and sworn to be governor of the state, I humbly enter upon the duties of the office, impressed with the importance of the trust:

In so doing I would gratefully and appreciatingly acknowledge the honor conferred, craving the kind forbearance of all. Good government depends upon wise laws faithfully executed. We are assembled in regular biennial session to assist each other in encouraging such government in Vermont and under Divine guidance let us enter upon the work of such an undertaking. . . .

Finances

This is probably the most interesting subject, all in all, you will consider, and from time immemorial has been instinctively accorded first position among the message topics of my honored predecessors.

Receipts, disbursement, resources, and liabilities are words suggesting the ins, outs, reliability, and emergency of the exchequer. They are the ways and means language of public financing; four words in the Treasurer's report, to which your most careful attention is directed, standing for revenue, appropriations, dependence, and credit.

The money supply now occupying so much thought invites an equally earnest consideration of its use, wherein lies its value. In raising and appropriating the public moneys be just and prudent; avoid both extravagance and parsimony; keep the resources secure and the credit firm.

Taxation

Our revenue flows into the treasury from various sources and out in various ways. . . .

CORPORATION TAXES AND TAX COMMISSIONER'S REPORT

Thirteen annual taxes have been collected under the corporation tax law; the first in 1883 amounting to $196,678.51 and the last in 1895 amounting to $376,723.04. The tax for the last biennial period was $734,582.81, being $42,351.62 more than for the preceding biennial period. These taxes, show a uniform increase, are cheerfully paid and are important to the state. They should be so assessed and collected as to deal justly by the corporations paying them and at the same time so as to realize for the state in proportion to the protection afforded. An inquiry into the equality of assessment is suggested as a proper investigation.

The assessment and collection of the corporation taxes, constituting nearly 75 percent of the state's revenue, is a very important official duty. The faithfulness with which the work is done signifies much to the treasury. Your attention is directed to the Commissioner's report for the information it affords concerning this source of income.

THE FIVE PERCENT STATE TAXES

These taxes are equalizers of the school and highway burdens in the different towns of the state. They are drafts upon the stronger in favor of the weaker. Steps in the direction of true democracy calculated to strengthen our education and improve our roads.

This plan for upbuilding the state, always acceptable to the poorer, is generally agreeable to the wealthier towns, for they well know any excess they pay, inures to the benefit of the state as a whole. All, believing in Vermont, recognize that doing it to the least is doing it to the greatest, and so welcome the 5 percent state taxes. Whether this step in the right direction should be lengthened is a question for you to decide. Road improvement can profitably use more money and incorporated school districts are reminders that the poorer communities have a right to equality in school burdens. . . .

State Expenses

Next in importance to income are expenditures.

A contented treasury must receive more than it disburses. The income should be sufficient to meet the proper needs of the state. In representing the wishes of the people, you will be safe in avoiding new ways of expense and providing for existing ways with reasonable economy.

The biennial term just closed records an expense of $1,140,097.56, being the largest in our history. The preceding term cost $920,397.48 and the term preceding that cost $1,031,710.92. These are large biennial expenditures. They should be decreased rather than increased. The expenses of the state have gradually augmented during the last twenty-five years; so have our public gratuities and institutions. The increase of expenses I apprehend has been principally occasioned by the creation and maintenance of the multiplied institutions.

The Reform School, the House of Correction, the Soldiers' Home, the Waterbury Asylum, the Fish Hatchery, the State Board of Health, the Normal Schools, donations to the colleges, the Experiment Station, the Railroad Commission, the Grand Isle County Bridges, and the Gettysburg Monument are reminders, in part, of the consideration for which the people have exchanged their money.

To denominate such expenditures extravagance is a misnomer. The state has value received and in most, if not all instances, the investments were wise, patriotic, in the interest of better government and of humanity. The money was in large part for higher improvements, which mark our progress and adorn our better civilization. Without prejudice to the past or allowing it to influence the present, let us discriminately consider the various expenses of the state and according to the times, fearlessly and fairly adjust each item.

Previous to 1880, our state tax averaged about 63 cents for the biennial term and since it has averaged about 14 cents. The direct tax burdens to the people have not increased and while we have expended more money it has been for what we needed. . . .

Roads and the State Road Commission

Good roads are an index of civilization and poor roads are a heavy tax upon any community. A general interest in road improvements exists throughout the states. Early in our history national appropriations were made for interstate turnpikes, then came railroad building, absorbing all thought concerning traveled ways, and now we are returning to first principles in which the better road figures conspicuously.

Vermont is interested in all her roads alike, and encouraged by the progress made it is hoped she will extend the system of permanent road improvement already so successfully begun. The 5 percent state tax and any enlargement of it should be exclusively expended in aid of this system. Successful road improvement has been accomplished in other states through individual contribution from the locality to be directly benefited.

A measure authorizing competitive subscriptions from neighborhoods asking the state tax and awarding the tax to the locality offering the largest local contribution would carry out this thought and would materially aid in realizing the object sought. Expensive road building should be avoided and the minimum, not the maximum, cost of a good road should be the guide in carrying out the reform. Probably no one thing will attract temporary and permanent dwellers to the state more than good roads.

If the policy of permanent improvement is continued by means of state funds there should be a state supervision of their expenditure and perhaps this can not be provided for any better than to make a permanent State Road Commission, giving it more voice in determining the character and location of the reform. Regarding this subject nearer than almost any other to the material prosperity of the state it is consigned to your care. . . .

The Prohibitory Law

For nearly half a century prohibition has been an omnipresent theme with the people of Vermont and a study of temperance has become a feature of our educational system. It has stood and stands a bulwark between brutality and home, order and riot, the better and the worse in all things. The prohibitory law has occupied a conspicuous place upon our statutes and signally aided the cause of temperance.

It has not exterminated for our society all disposition to violate its provisions nor does any law destroy the germ of transgression, but it has to a very satisfactory extent restrained the offender, making rum selling unprofitable and a reproach. Violations are the exception and confined mostly to the larger places.

The general temperance of our people is superior to that of any sister state. Our prohibitory law insures a better home for the laboring man and his family here in Vermont than in any other community of its size on the face of the earth. We have reason to congratulate ourselves upon many things but upon no one thing more than the character which has become a part of our life since prohibition has guarded the avenues of our society.

With these and other considerations in full view we are confronted by the usual biennial inquiry, shall the prohibitory law make way for high license [local option], or shall the law be more carefully enforced? . . .

Public sentiment in many localities regard the enforcement of the prohibitory law differently from the enforcement of other law and in my opinion you should provide better pay to the officers called upon to enforce it. . . .

Officers cannot nurse crime in Vermont for the fees derivable from prosecuting it unless the people are willing. Interest the prosecuting officer and make it an object for him to do his work, if you would be sure of the best service. Pursuing and punishing crime as a work of love cannot always be relied upon. . . .

Source: *Journal of the Senate*, October 8, 1896 (Montpelier: 1896): 342-352.

DOCUMENT 2

Speech to the U.S. Senate on Conditions in Cuba (1898)

SENATOR REDFIELD PROCTOR

Mr. President, more importance seems to be attached by others to my recent visit to Cuba than I have given it. . . .

My trip was entirely unofficial and of my own motion, not suggested by anyone. The only mention I made of it to the President was to say to him that I contemplated such a trip and to ask him if there was any objection to it; to which he replied that he could see none. No one but myself, therefore, is responsible for anything in this statement. . . .

There are six provinces in Cuba. . . . My observations were confined to the four western provinces, which constitute about one-half of the island. The two eastern ones are practically in the hands of the insurgents, except the few fortified towns. These two large provinces are spoken of today as "Cuba Libre."

Habana, the great city and capital of the island, is, in the eyes of the Spaniards and many Cubans, all Cuba, as much as Paris is France. . . . Everything seems to go on much as usual in Habana. Quiet prevails, and except for the frequent squads of soldiers marching to guard and police duty and their abounding presence in all public places, one sees few signs of war.

Outside Habana all is changed. It is not peace nor is it war. It is desolation and distress, misery and star-

vation. Every town and village is surrounded by a "trocha" (trench), a sort of rifle pit, but constructed on a plan new to me, the dirt being thrown up on the inside and a barbed-wire fence on the outer side of the trench. These trochas have at every corner and at frequent intervals along the sides what are there called forts, but which are really small blockhouses, many of them more like large sentry boxes, loopholed for musketry, and with a guard of from two to ten soldiers each.

The purpose of these trochas is to keep the reconcentrados in as well as to keep the insurgents out. From all the surrounding country the people have been driven in to these fortified towns and held there to subsist as they can. They are virtually prison yards, and not unlike one in general appearance, except that the walls are not so high and strong; but they suffice, where every point is in range of a soldier's rifle. . . .

There are no domestic animals or crops on the rich fields and pastures except such as are under guard in the immediate vicinity of the towns. . . . Every man, woman, and child, and every domestic animal . . . is under guard and within their so-called fortifications. To describe one place is to describe all. To repeat, it is neither peace nor war. It is concentration and desolation. This is the "pacified" condition of the four western provinces. . . .

Nearly all the sugar mills are destroyed between Habana and Sagua. Two or three were standing in the vicinity of Sagua, and in part running, surrounded, as are the villages, by trochas and "forts" or palisades of the royal palm, and fully guarded. Toward and near Cienfuegos there were more mills running, but all with the same protection. It is said that the owners of these mills near Cienfuegos have been able to obtain special favors of the Spanish Government in the way of a large force of soldiers, but that they also, as well as all the railroads, pay taxes to the Cubans for immunity. I had no means of verifying this. It is the common talk among those who have better means of knowledge.

The Reconcentrados—The Country People

All the country people in the four western provinces, about 400,000 in number, remaining outside the fortified towns when [General Valeriano] Weyler's order was made were driven into these towns, and these are the reconcentrados. They were the peasantry, many of them farmers, some landowners, other renting lands and owning more or less stock, others working on estates and cultivating small patches; and even a small patch in that fruitful clime will support a family.

It is but fair to say that the normal condition of these people was very different from what prevails in this country. Their standard of comfort and prosperity was not high measured by ours. But according to their standards and requirements their conditions of life were satisfactory. . . .

The first clause of Weyler's order reads as follows:

I ORDER AND COMMAND

First. All the inhabitants of the country or outside of the line of fortifications of the towns shall, within the period of eight days, concentrate themselves in the towns occupied by the troops. Any individual who, after the expiration of this period, if found in the uninhabited parts will be considered a rebel and tried as such.

The other three sections forbid the transportation of provisions from one town to another without permission of the military authority, direct the owners of cattle to bring them into the towns, prescribe that the eight days shall be counted from the publication of the proclamation in the head town of the municipal district, and state that if news is furnished of the enemy which can be made use of, it will serve as a "recommendation."

Many, doubtless, did not learn of this order. Others failed to grasp its terrible meaning. Its execution was left largely to the guerrillas to drive in all that had not obeyed, and I was informed that in many cases the torch was applied to their homes with no notice, and the inmates fled with such clothing as they might have on, their stock and other belongings being appropriated by the guerrillas. When they reached the towns, they were allowed to build huts of palm leaves in the suburbs and vacant places within the trochas, and left to live, if they could. . . .

[The] commonest sanitary provisions are impossible. Conditions are unmentionable in this respect. Torn from their homes, with foul earth, foul air, foul water, and foul food or none, what wonder that one-half have died and that one-quarter of the living are so diseased that they can not be saved? A form of dropsy is a common disorder resulting from these conditions. Little children are still walking about with arms and chest terribly emaciated, eyes swollen, and abdomen bloated to three times the natural size. The physicians say these cases are hopeless.

Deaths in the streets have not been uncommon. I was told by one of our consuls that they have been found dead about the markets in the morning, where they had crawled, hoping to get some stray bits of food from the early hucksters, and that there had been cases where they had dropped dead inside the market surrounded by food. Before Weyler's order, these people were independent and self-supporting. . . .

The Hospitals

Of these I need not speak. Others have described their condition far better than I can. It is not within the narrow limits of my vocabulary to portray it. I went to Cuba with a strong conviction that the picture had been overdrawn; that a few cases of starvation and suffering had inspired and stimulated the press correspondents, and that they had given free play to a strong, natural, and highly cultivated imagination. . . .

I could not believe that out of a population of 1,600,000, two hundred thousand had died within these Spanish forts, practically prison walls, within a few months past from actual starvation and diseases caused by insufficient and improper food. My inquiries were entirely outside of sensational sources. They were made of our medical officers, of our consuls, of city alcaldes (mayors), of relief committees, of leading merchants and bankers, physicians, and lawyers. Several of my informants were Spanish born, but every time the answer was that the case had not been overstated. What I saw I can not tell so that others can see it. It must be seen with one's own eyes to be realized. . . .

The Spaniard

I had little time to study the race questions, and have read nothing on it, so can only give hasty impressions. It is said that there are nearly 200,000 Spaniards in Cuba out of a total population of 1,600,000. They live principally in the towns and cities. The small shopkeepers in the towns and their clerks are mostly Spaniards. Much of the larger business, too, and of the property in the cities, and in a less degree in the country, is in their hands. They have an eye to thrift, and as everything possible in the way of trade and legalized monopolies, in which the country abounds, is given to them by the Government, many of them acquire property. I did not learn that the Spanish residents of the island had contributed largely in blood or treasure to suppress the insurrection.

The Cuban

There are, or were before the war, about 1,000,000 Cubans on the island, 200,000 Spaniards (which means those born in Spain), and less than half a million of negroes and mixed bloods. The Cuban whites are of pure Spanish blood and, like the Spaniards, dark in complexion, but oftener light or blond, so far as I noticed. The percentage of colored to white has been steadily diminishing for more than fifty years, and is not now over 25 percent of the total. In fact, the number of colored people has been actually diminishing for nearly that time. The Cuban farmer and laborer is by nature peaceable, kindly, gay, hospitable, light-hearted, and improvident. There is a proverb among the Cubans that "Spanish bulls can not be bred in Cuba"—that is, the Cubans, though they are of Spanish blood, are less excitable and of a quieter temperament. . . . One thing that was new to me was to learn the superiority of the well-to-do Cuban over the Spaniard in the matter of education. Among those in good circumstances there can be not doubt that the Cuban is far superior in this respect. And the reason of it is easy to see. They have been educated in England, France, or this country, while the Spaniard has such education as his own country furnishes.

The Negro

The colored people seem to me by nature quite the equal mentally and physically of the race in this country. Certainly physically they are by far the larger and stronger race on the island. There is little or no race prejudice, and this has doubtless been greatly to their advantage. Eight-five years ago there were one-half as many free negroes as slaves, and this proportion slowly increased until emancipation.

The Military Situation

It is said that there are about 60,000 Spanish soldiers now in Cuba fit for duty out of the more than 200,000 that have been sent there. The rest have died, have been sent home sick, or are in hospitals, and some have been killed, notwithstanding the official reports. They are conscripts, many of them very young, and generally small men. One hundred and thirty pounds is a fair estimate of their average weight. They are quiet and obedient, and if well drilled and led, I believe would fight fairly well, but not at all equal to our men. Much more would depend on the leadership than with us. The officer must lead well and be one in whom they have confidence, and this applies to both sides alike. As I saw no drills or regular formation, I inquired about them of many persons, and was informed that they had never seen a drill. I saw perhaps 10,000 Spanish troops, but not a piece of artillery or a tent. They live in barracks in the towns, and are seldom out for more than the day, returning to town at night.

They have little or no equipment for supply trains or for a field campaign such as we have. Their cavalry horses are scrubby little native ponies, weighing not over 800 pounds, tough and hardy, but for the most part in wretched condition, reminding one of the mount of Don Quixote. Some of the officers, however, have good horses, mostly American, I think. On both sides cavalry is considered the favorite and the dangerous fighting arm. . . .

Having called on Governor and Captain-General Blanco and received his courteous call in return, I could not with propriety seek communication with insurgents. I had plenty of offers of safe conduct to Gomez's camp, and was told that if I would write him, an answer would be returned safely within ten days at most.

I saw several who had visited the insurgent camps, and was sought out by an insurgent field officer, who gave me the best information received as to the insurgent force. His statements were moderate, and I was credibly informed that he was entirely reliable. He claimed that the Cubans had about 30,000 men now in the field. . . .

Cubans are well armed, but very poorly supplied with ammunition. They are not allowed to carry many cartridges; sometimes not more than one or two. The infantry, especially, are poorly clad. Two small squads of prisoners which I saw, however, one of half a dozen in the streets of Habana, and one of three on the cars, wore better clothes than the average Spanish soldier. . . . About one third of the Cuban army are colored, mostly in the infantry, as the cavalry furnished their own horses. This field officer, an American from a

Southern State, spoke in the highest terms of the conduct of these colored soldiers; that they were as good fighters and had more endurance than the whites; could keep up with the cavalry on a long march and come in fresh at night.

The Political Situation

The dividing lines between parties are the straightest and clearest cut that have ever come to my knowledge. The division in our war was by no means so clearly defined. It is Cuban against Spaniard. It is practically the entire Cuban population on one side and the Spanish army and Spanish citizens on the other. . . . I have endeavored to state in not intemperate mood what I saw and heard, and to make no argument thereon, but leave everyone to draw his own conclusions. To me the strongest appeal is not the barbarity practiced by Weyler nor the loss of the *Maine*, if our worst fears should prove true, terrible as are both of these incidents, but the spectacle of a million and a half of people, the entire native population of Cuba, struggling for freedom and deliverance from the worst misgovernment of which I ever had knowledge. But whether our action ought to be influenced by any one or all these things, and, if so, how far, is another question.

I am not in favor of annexation; not because I would apprehend any particular trouble from it, but because it is not wise policy to take in any people of foreign tongue and training, and without any strong guiding American element. . . .

But it is not my purpose at this time, nor do I consider it my province, to suggest any plan. I merely speak of the symptoms as I saw them, but do not undertake to prescribe. Such remedial steps as may be required may safely be left to an American President and the American people.

Source: *Congressional Record*, 55th Cong., 2nd sess., 31: 2916-2919.

DOCUMENT 3

"King of the Sea" (1900)

(depicted on following pages)

Source: Sheet Music Collection, Special Collections, Bailey/Howe Library, University of Vermont.

DOCUMENT 4

Letter on the Prohibitory Act (1902)
PERCIVAL CLEMENT

Gentlemen: In response to your question as to a license and local option campaign this year, permit me to say to you and through you to other republican voters who have mentioned my name in connection with the governorship, that I welcome any opportunity to discuss the prohibitory law.

In the march of social improvement and education upon the subject of temperance, our state has been left 50 years behind the times. At a special election in February, 1853, at the end of a temperance revival which swept the state, the prohibitory act was approved by a majority of 1,171 votes in a total of 43,259 votes cast. It was a grotesque piece of legislation among the enactments of that day.

Its advocates, recognizing the evils of intemperance, undoubtedly expected that the law would bring on the millennium, but in that they were disappointed. A man has never been made temperate in what he eats or drinks by legislative enactment, and the law reenacted and amended and made more stringent at subsequent sessions of the Legislature, remains a wart upon the public statutes.

It makes it a crime to deal in alcohol, in its various forms, an article of commerce which the rest of the civilized world says may be properly dealt in between man and man and used with propriety. It gives almost unlimited powers in certain directions, to courts and officers of the law, which are outrageously abused.

It encourages the cupidity of officers employed for its enforcement by liberal allowances for costs, following fines imposed upon its offenders, and it entirely fails to suppress the evils of intemperance, but rather increases them, and creates others which are greater.

There is more intoxicating liquor, adulterated and highly injurious, sold in Vermont than in any other state in the Union according to population. It is also true that there is more morphine, chloral, opium and kindred drugs consumed in our state per capita than in any other state in the Union.

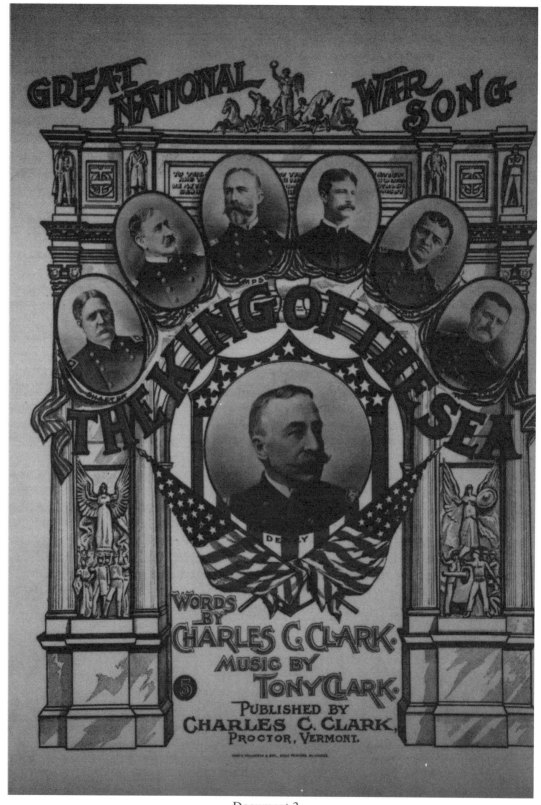

Document 3

THE KING OF THE SEA.

Words by CHARLES C. CLARK.

Music by TONY CLARK.

Tempo di Marcia.

1. Oh, the king of the sea Is our Ad - mi - ral Dew - ey, The world has ac-knowl-edged his fame, And the men by his side, No
2. Just look at our war - ships, So vi - ci - ous in bat - tle, Their e - qual was ne'er seen be - fore, Yet old Spain in her pride, Thought no
3. We have great gen - er - als, He - roes like Ad - m'ral Dew - ey; With our Shaf-ter, Schley and Samp - son, And Hob - son, that's a fact: The only
4. Roose-velt and rough rid - ers, Are home from o - ver the sea; With fight - ing Bob, and his I-rish boys; Now beat them if you can; It's a

The King of the Sea.—3—1.

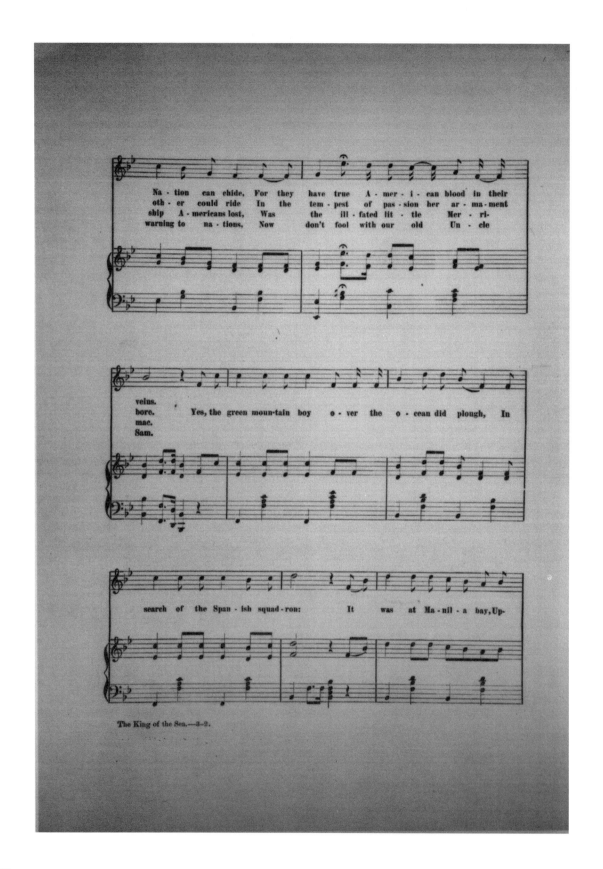

The King of the Sea.—3—2.

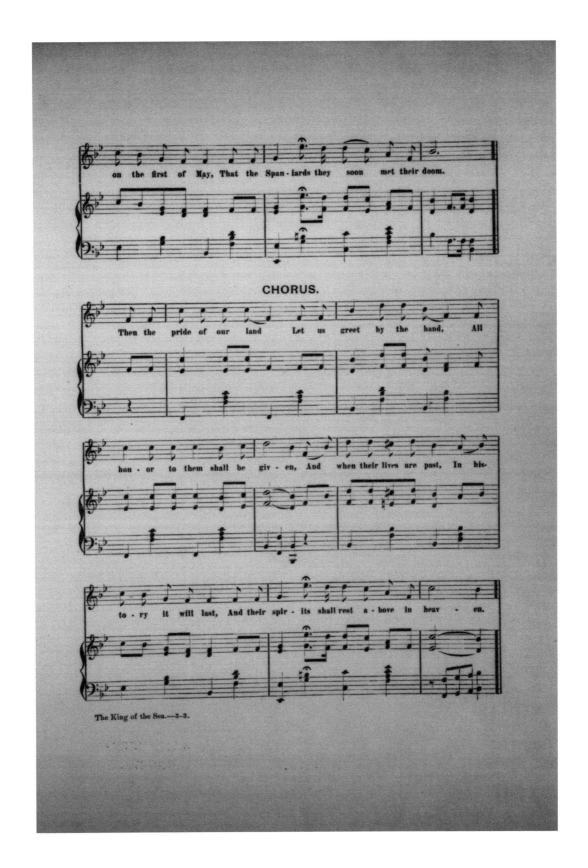

The whole effect of the law is pernicious and it has retarded the natural development of our state, and rests as a curse upon us, in so far as it breeds hypocrisy, perjury and lying,—evils even greater than intemperance itself. Liquors are sold by the towns and we are all made parties to the transaction, but there is little or no profit to the town or the state.

The law is drastic in its provisions and rotten in its execution, and, as a knowledge of its workings spreads, a feeling of disgust comes over every man who cares for the honor of our state. I stand with any man for law, order and good government. I am against any law which relies for its enforcement not upon a healthy public sentiment, but upon the large fines and fees which public officers are able to extort from their victims and put to the credit of their own bank accounts—a law which is commonly used for the purpose of blackmail.

We license advocates believe in a law which will permit the sale of intoxicating liquors, when a town so orders it, under regulations, which, from experience, we know do in other states reduce the evils of intemperance to a minimum and return immense revenue to the towns.

Such a law has been drawn and presented to the Legislature many times within the past few years; but the political machine, which controls the destinies of Vermont legislation and Vermont politicians, has every time put obstructions in the way of the passage of such an act and would not even permit it to be presented to the people of the state for their approval or rejection, lest in the change of sentiment, which must inevitably take place, were such a measure presented to every voter in the state for his consideration, it would lose the reins of government.

For 40 years Vermont has stood for the principles of the republican party in national affairs, and in that no one glories more than I, but in state affairs we have had no politics.

A few men have controlled official positions and legislation and have traded out the various offices from governor down, year after year, saying, "You support me this time and I will support you next," and upon that platform they have gone through the state with their strikers, hat in hand, begging votes.

I believe the time has come when the people of this state are anxious to take hold and assume their proper place in the government. I believe that the affairs of the state should be run on a business basis. If nominated, I will stand for high license and local option and a real retrenchment in state expenses and honesty in the administration of state affairs. I will use my best efforts to win out for the cause and work for the repeal of the prohibitory law and the enactment of real temperance legislation in its place and for the honest and faithful administration of public affairs.

Thanking you for the interest you have shown in this matter, I remain

Yours very sincerely,
Percival W. Clement

Source: Mason A. Green, *Nineteen-Two in Vermont: The Fight for Local Option* (Rutland, Vt.: Marble City Press, 1912), pp. 11-14.

DOCUMENT 5

"An Address to the Republican Party of Vermont" (1902)
REPUBLICAN STATE COMMITTEE

To the Republicans of Vermont,

Since 1855 the Republican party of Vermont has marched from its Convention hall to the polls with unbroken ranks and loyal hearts to win constant victories for its chosen standard bearers and its exalted principles. Its devotion and fealty to principles and candidates have given it national honor, distinction and importance and have secured for Vermont the proud cognomen of the "Star that never sets," while the long line of illustrious men who have represented it in the Halls of Congress, who have been its chief Executives, together with the marked civic virtue of its legislators and officials, with entire absence of public scandals and freedom from all taint of corruption, have reflected peculiar credit, luster and honor upon our beloved State until the name of Vermont has become a national synonym for political honesty and integrity. . . .

No one denies that the state expenses have largely increased during the years of Republican ascendancy, but it is because of the settled policy of the state, regardless of party, requiring such expenditures and shifting large burdens of expense from the towns to the state and not through corruption, inefficiency, prodigality or mis-management.

Which part of this settled policy would Mr. Clement repudiate?

We have now a hospital for the insane owned and equipped by the state, equipped with modern conveniences and conducted in accordance with advanced and approved methods for the safety and recovery of these unfortunate members of our society, answering the proper demands of a sympathetic and philanthropic people.

We have a House of Correction for the less incorrigible law breaker where reformation may be secured; we have the Industrial School for the young where virtuous manhood and womanhood may be wrought out of what would otherwise become fixtures among the criminal classes. Our colleges are aided from our state treasury in order that poverty shall not prevent the ambitious youth from obtaining broad and thorough culture. We provide instruction for the blind, the mute and the weak minded. We raise a 5 percent State tax to distribute among our towns which are richer in road mileage than in grand list. We equalize in a degree the burden of school taxation by an 8 percent State tax. We care for the insane poor at the state's expense and thus relieve each town of this burden and secure better treatment and care. We expend a considerable amount upon our State Militia and our Soldier's Home.

All this and much more is done because the state has approved of it and yet this large expenditure has been so provided for by our system of corporation taxes that the state tax assessed upon the grand list is less than it was twenty years ago. Undoubtedly this method of corporation taxation can be improved upon and extended and the State tax be still further lessened and even entirely dispensed with.

A Commission reporting when Mr. Clement was in the Senate that the corporations were bearing only about one-fourth of their fair share of the burden of taxation, an effort was made to increase corporate taxation, but Mr. Clement was strenuous in opposition and it was defeated. He was then President of the Rutland Railroad system. He now asserts that no State tax was needed and that he voted against increased corporation taxation because no additional revenue was required, but as the chairman of the Senate Finance com-

mittee of 1900, he in fact recommended the very day he brought about the defeat of the corporation tax bill, the very tax which you are now paying.

He decries the method of liquor law enforcement in his city and draws many illustrations therefrom. He has for many years been an influential citizen of Rutland and has been its Mayor and yet these abuses continued without correction when he had official power, and without rebuke from him as a man.

Mr. Clement alleges that he doubts the sincerity of the Republican party of Vermont in its plank concerning the submission of the license local option law to the vote of the people and seeks thus to justify his secession. But when was the Republican party of Vermont or of the nation untrue to its pledges? From its inception to the present hour—as the party of liberty under Fremont, of the Constitution and Union under Lincoln and Grant, of sound money and protection to American industries under Hayes, Garfield, Arthur, Harrison and McKinley, crowned by its honorable and philanthropic position towards Cuba and the Philippines—when and wherein has it in either state or nation betrayed its trust or wandered from the paths of honor, justice and rectitude? In the light of its history then, he who would impugn the honor and good faith of the Republic party impeaches his own. . . .

We confidently appeal to the men of Vermont who see in the Republican party and its achievements the unexampled glory and prosperity of our state and country, who are proud of their little state which has borne no mean and trivial part in the progress of our nation; who believe, as rightfully they may, and should, and believing exult that during all this time they have lived in the cleanest state in the Union where corruption in the legislature, in the judiciary and in the executive offices has been unknown and who would retain untarnished the fair fame of the state.

We appeal to all such to indignantly repudiate and condemn the man who in the blindness and wickedness of his own selfseeking does not hesitate to publish and proclaim to the world, foul slanders upon the integrity and honor of Old Vermont.

We confidently appeal to all who love the party for its state and national issues of far reaching importance, who have gloried in its achievements, who are devoted to its principles, who believe them paramount to any single state issue, who believe that all these are best gained and best maintained within and not without the party, who love its leaders, who look forward to a national triumph in 1904, that we may continue our present prosperity and national grandeur; all such we appeal by their voice and by their ballots to keep secure our State in the front rank of the Republican party in 1902.

No greater disaster could come upon the Republican party or the Nation than the removal of Vermont this year from the Republican column. A broken party in 1902 means a broken party in 1904 and broken Republicanism in Vermont would most signally aid to break its hold upon the country and to end the marvellous prosperity which has come under the Republican rule. Vote then for the men whose defeat our enemy seeks. Vote for the regular Republican candidates for town, for county and state offices. Vote for McCullough and Stanton, plain men of the people, strong, clean, incorruptible, clear headed and warm hearted; for men who can look upon the strongest and best, level eyed and clear, and in their regard for labor and its rights, in devotion to our interests, our institutions and our industries, in intellectual and moral stature and in all that goes to make true Vermonters are in the front rank among the most trusted leaders of our state.

Lead on, men of Vermont, to your accustomed sweeping victory which shall cheer the hearts of your political friends from Maine to California, shall presage and assist a like sweeping National triumph in November and pave the way for Republicans and Roosevelt in 1904.

Source: "An Address to the Republican Party of Vermont by the State Committee," pp. 3-15; Special Collections, Bailey/Howe Library, University of Vermont.

Document 6

Inaugural Address (1902)
Governor John G. McCullough

Gentlemen of the Senate and House of Representatives:

We have come together in obedience to the requirements of the Constitution. This Government is, however, essentially a people's Government. In Vermont the Governor is the titular head of the State. He is expected to represent her at public functions. His duties, unless in some great national crisis or convulsion, are neither many nor arduous.

In Vermont, too, we are fortunate that the powers of the Legislature itself, the law making department of every representative government, are only called into exercise in the mildest degree.

The people govern themselves.

A State whose citizens have mastered the problem of self-government is best governed when least governed. From its first settlement, through the stormy period of its Colonial life, during the Revolutionary era, as an independent Republic for thirteen years, as a member of the Federal Union for over a century, Vermont has been educated in a school of self-reliant manhood. That the majority should rule, that the rights of the minority must not be infringed, that liberty regulated by law must prevail, are the lessons that have been so well learned by the citizens of Vermont as to be, and have become, a part of their very being.

The civilization of this people that had its origin in Lower Germany centuries ago, that crossed the Channel and sprouted and grew slowly with the ages amid and against countless obstacles from within and without on the British Isles, that budded at Hastings and Runnymede, at Lewes and Naseby, that blossomed at Bunker Hill and Bennington and Yorktown, at Gettysburg and Appomattox, needs no guiding hand to instruct its subjects in the matters best suited for their welfare and government.

Your ancestors who founded this little mountain commonwealth struck off your first Constitution in 1777 in the midst of war, and with the enemy upon your borders declared Vermont a "free and independent State." And under its rule, and as revised in 1786, for thirteen years maintained an independent existence; and after admission into the Federal Union established the Constitution of 1793, under whose beneficent provisions, and the amendments from time to time adopted, you and your ancestors for over a century have enjoyed the blessings of free government; and, so far as human wisdom can foresee, you and your posterity will continue for other centuries to enjoy the multiplied and multiplying blessing of even a freer government. . . .

Our town system existed before the State. It is the inheritance and the growth of the ages of Anglo-Saxon uplifting. It was simply recognized in our Constitution.

These republics in one form or other have always had their Legislatures. In their annual March meetings, or at other sessions regularly called, they select their rulers for the year and discuss all public questions and decide what is for the best good of the community and the State; and that judgment expressed at the general election is reflected in the persons of the two hundred and forty-six Representatives standing for these little republics and in the persons of the thirty Senators representing the counties.

The duty and the responsibility of any needed legislation rests almost wholly on you; the function of the Executive being advisory. . . .

Temperance Legislation

The verdict of the freemen of the State on September 2d last was in favor of the General Assembly framing a local option and high license law and submitting the same to the people for their adoption or rejection. This duty will require the very best efforts and the most intelligent consideration of the members of the Assembly.

For fifty years prohibition has been the policy of the State. The mandate comes up now from the people to their legislators commanding them to formulate and to submit to them for their decisions some other system. This is the Anglo-Saxon, the American method. It is the rule of the majority.

And primarily, on this subject, it must be borne in mind that all sumptuary legislation must be supported by public sentiment to be effectual. In framing a statute the General Assembly will have the benefit of the legislation on the subject of eight or ten of the other States. Experience is the very best guide. . . .

Different States and different parts of the same State may require different treatment. Unlike most of the States, Vermont has few manufacturing centers or large municipalities; the great majority of her towns are rural and agricultural. Massachusetts is more nearly similar to Vermont than any other State, and from her legislation probably more valuable suggestions will be derived than from any other source.

But in the legislation of no one State, only, should we look for the best and wisest provisions, and those most suitable to the circumstances of our people. . . .

As to the licensing body or authorities, it has been well said that judicial purity and reputation for purity are far more important than discreet licensing. It is of the utmost importance that courts and judges should be kept as far removed from politics as possible.

This matter of licensing, therefore, should be entrusted to some other department or to boards specially raised up for that purpose, and which boards should have stability and independence.

There should be several grades of license fees depending on the size and population of the towns or cities; and the traffic should be made to raise large revenues for both the State and the towns or municipalities.

Every license should be restricted from selling to minors or intoxicated persons, or on Sundays, election days, or any legal holidays, nor should he be allowed to furnish musical entertainment of any kind or billiards or cards or any game whatever; and the place should be wide open to inspection from the street or highway, and the hours should be strictly limited, and the shorter the better, provided public sentiment supports these restrictions.

If druggists' licenses are to be granted at all, they should be entrusted only to registered pharmacists who should be authorized to sell only in small quantities and only on the written prescription of a physician not interested in the store. These suggestions, gathered from many sources, may be of some value in formulating a proper statute to be submitted to the people for their adoption or rejection.

Primary Election Law

Many of the other States have such laws, and the enactment of a similar statute by Vermont would tend to secure purity in nominations. The caucus should be surrounded by the same safe-guards as the election. The primary election should be held on the same day and hour throughout the State; check lists should be provided; the choice should be by ballot; and all the precautions of the general election law should be extended to the primary election.

Good Roads

In view of the agitation on this subject for the past ten years or more in this country, and of the advanced action taken in many of the States, and of what has already been done in this State, it cannot be necessary for me at any length to urge consideration and action on your part.

Nothing can add more to the prosperity of the State, nothing can serve to lift farm values so materially, nothing can bring summer tourists and residents to settle and beautify and enrich our valleys so much as permanent road building.

I would not only urge the continuance of the present State tax, but I would advise an increase of the same, and even more liberal treatment. And in this connection, and as a corollary, I would recommend that the State begin a system of elimination of grade crossings of both steam and electric roads and the highways.

The laws of Massachusetts and New York furnish desirable methods. Proceed slowly, but make a beginning.

It seems to me, without unjustly or improperly burdening any interest, that all the expenses of the State government can be raised by indirect taxation, and relieve real estate entirely, and I commend this subject to the intelligent consideration of the Legislature.

In conclusion, permit me to express the hope and the expectation, that you will prosecute your legislative labors with all diligence, and that the results may be the passage of a few wise and well considered measures redounding to the welfare and prosperity of the State whose best interests we are all anxious to promote.

John G. McCullough
October 3, 1902.

Source: *Journal of the Senate,* October 3, 1902, (Montpelier: 1902): 484-489.

DOCUMENT 7

The Status of Rural Vermont (1903)
GEORGE F. WELLS

V. THE CHARACTER STATUS OF RURAL VERMONT

The character standing of a community is essentially its religious standing. Intellectual or moral life is generally expressed through church and religious customs and ideals.

The first point in measuring the character status of rural Vermont is an absolute one. Rural Vermont has diminished territorially. Consequently, then, so much cannot be expected of the rural part of the State as formerly.

Condition of Vermont Churches

The Congregational church since its organization in Vermont in 1762 has enjoyed an almost continuous growth in membership. From 1890 to 1900 it gained 6 percent. The Methodist church has had a similar growth since 1796, gaining 6 percent during the last census decade. The Baptist church in the State has slightly decreased in membership in each of the last two decades. The Protestant Episcopal church shows a gain of 15 percent in ten years. The total increase in Protestant churches in ten years has been 5 percent in number of churches, 9 percent in number of ministers, and 5 percent in membership.

But the above figures are for Vermont as a whole, with no reference to the rural sections. In most of the Protestant churches, if not in all of them, there has been a falling off in membership in the more rural sections, while there has been a gain in the cities. Rev. C. H. Merrill D. D., of St. Johnsbury, said, in 1900 giving data as to Congregational membership: "The southern and eastern parts of the State in the farming regions lost, while the western and northern parts gained." The diminishing populations of many small towns have brought about the extinction of a large number of churches during the last eighty years. In speaking of Congregational churches which had become extinct, Rev. Henry Fairbanks of St. Johnsbury said in 1889: "There were some sixty-five of these churches that have died, or been united to others, probably as many Methodist, and a Baptist brother refers to a list of 160 of that denomination that have been given up. This does not indicate any corresponding loss, but is often due to the mere shifting of business centers." But rural Vermont has suffered in consequence, nevertheless. It must be confessed that in both financial and membership standing the rural churches have declined.

The first Catholic edifice in Vermont was built in Burlington in 1831. The growth of this church in the State, though almost entirely from immigration, has been exceedingly rapid. The 1900 Census gives the Catholic population (no membership being reported) as 57,000, a gain of 11,000 over 1890. Rev. L. H. Eliott says, from data obtained by actual canvass: "About 25 percent of the population claim to be Roman Catholics." Bishop Michaud in the "Vermonter" for January, 1903, says: "Vermont today has a Catholic population of 70,000." Since this church does not tend toward unifying the society of the commonwealth its numerical increase is out of proportion to the effect exerted upon the character status of the State.

The Unchurched Masses

Another condition to be reckoned with is the large mass of the rural inhabitants who are unchurched. Rev. Henry Fairbanks has reported the following facts for about the year 1885: In 44 towns in five counties actually canvassed only 49 percent of the number found by the canvassers, or 44 percent of the total population of the towns, call themselves church attendants, either Protestant or Catholic. "A majority of our people are never at church. Of those living two miles or more from church, only about one-third attend church." For the whole State Mr. Fairbanks reported from reliable statistics that more than 125,000 never hear the gospel preached. "A majority of more than six to five, 183,000 in the State, do not even call themselves church attendants. In the rural districts of New England and New York, from which the strongest men in the cities and the west are coming, more than half of the people are not only unreached, but are absolutely unapproached by any direct Christian efforts." That these facts are relatively accurate, and that the conditions are about the same today is shown by the report of Rev. L. H. Eliott in February, 1903, from an actual canvass by the Vermont Bible Society. He says: "Of the Protestant element only about 55 percent claim to attend church, and in some towns less than 40 percent."

Influence of Emigration

The change of population elements has greatly affected the character status of rural Vermont. In 1900 nearly 41 percent of the native born Vermonters were living outside of the State. On the other hand, in 1880 12.3 percent of the total population of the State were foreign born, in 1890 13.3 percent, and in 1900 13 percent. In 1900 19.3 percent of the males of voting age were foreign born. The western emigration and the Civil War started the exodus of the most enterprising of Vermonters from our farming towns; and the urban fever continues the same skimming process. The material

which is left is being diluted by the incoming foreign element. The farming towns receive their share of these as well as the manufacturing towns. The incoming of the French Canadians, the Irish and other nationalities has brought in new religious sects, and the old have had to die. But this situation must not be viewed narrowly. Not all of the best native stuff has emigrated. Moral and social stagnation hold too large a part of the once best original stock. A part of the incoming element is being assimilated and becoming the most enterprising and industrious members of some of our communities. But on the whole the swapping of inhabitants has tended to create a lower average character status for rural Vermont.

Minor Conditions

Other minor conditions affect the character status. Some of these are the rapid rise of the young people's societies in the churches; the addition to the church edifices of lecture rooms, parlors, and kitchens; the awakening of the rural churches to the advanced thought and missionary interests of the age; and the increasing freedom from bigotry, narrowness and denominational zeal. These things are all encouraging. The more thorough system of free common and high schools; the greater recognition of the value of college training; the increase of magazine reading and use of free public libraries; the highly developed, trolley, telephone, and mail service; all of these agencies tend toward lessening rural isolation, and are both tokens and promises of a better day. That the rural districts desire a clergy equipped on a par with the urban clergy is a good indication, even though the ministers are required to live on the meager rural charities. That so much essential morality, and almost Christianity, is just outside of the churches is another condition and problem which demands special thought.

Summary

It is hard to say, for a general conclusion, that the character status for rural Vermont is lowering. Neither do we say it. Some sections have held their own, and much more; but many have not. The communities far from churches in particular are on a very low character level. It is very certain that the improvement in character has not kept pace with that of the economic growth, even though nearly every important agency for raising the character status is in a healthy condition. On the whole there has been a great change in the character conditions.

VI. THE CAUSES OF SOCIAL CHANGE
The Industrial Civilization

The rural depression which to a greater or less extent has permeated all civilization during the last few decades has but one main cause. A knowledge of this will make clear nearly the whole rural problem. This cause is the steam engine; the predominance of mind power working through machinery over muscle power or hand labor. This cause has operated in three leading directions.

1. It has created the factory system in manufacturing. This has made possible the rapid increase of wealth which is used as capital, and too, the redistribution of populations and their collection near the factories in the industrial centers.

2. Steam power applied to commerce has brought about cheap and rapid transportation, which, with the monopoly system of production, has created the world market. Cheap transportation means cheap travel, which has greatly hastened the rural exodus.

3. A new agriculture is not the least of the results of the great invention. Machine labor has displaced hand labor upon the farms, thus sending the laboring population, to a large extent, to the towns and cities. The use of machinery has made possible the opening of new and broader fields for farming which, by natural competition, has led to the abandonment of the less favorable farming lands upon the mountain sides. The intensive methods of farming have made possible a supply of agricultural products far in excess of the demand for them. Farming is now carried on under the organized scientific methods employed in manufacturing.

So we live today in a period of social readjustment. The conflict between labor and capital, the rural exodus, and the urban congestion are the stresses and clashes of reconstruction. We look forward to the time when these conflicting elements, become settled and quiet in their normal state of maturity.

Rural Vermont has undergone a profound economic change. This change is simply the normal transition from an agricultural to an industrial civilization. No longer does each community produce to supply its own needs and no more. Farmers grow now what they can grow best, sending the product to the cities or to other countries, and receiving in return urban or foreign products. Mind power, as expressed by the steam engine and the factory, is at the bottom of all this change. . . .

VII. CONCLUSION

Popular public opinion points to the continuing decline of the rural sections of Vermont. When rural Vermont is properly defined and the truth known, this judgment cannot stand. Facts speak more loudly than opinions.

The population, economic, and character conditions present changes sufficiently marked to prove the displacement of the agricultural by the industrial civilization. The change is especially felt during the latter part of the last fifty years. The mountain side, isolated sections of rural Vermont are declining, and ought, many of them, in the light of the industrial spirit of today, for the economic and social good of the people, to be turned into carefully managed timber orchards. The agricultural industries of the state are growing rapidly. The character status has been somewhat lowered by the national and international exchange of population elements, and by the uneven distribution of the churches; but this change is being counteracted. Moral reaction takes place slowly but surely. Our temporary sacrifice is our permanent gain.

Vermont is on a par with any other part of the civilized world with equal natural advantages, and at no less distance from the world's centers of power. The factory, the railroad, the bank, the telephone, the co-operative creamery, the rural high school, and the community church are factors in its life today. The world is so small nowadays that every part of it influences every other part. Economic and moral forces work side by side toward a common end. Vermont keeps pace with the world in many things, and leads it in some things; and few if any sections territorially so small are more productive of civilizing influences.

Source: George F. Wells, *The Status of Rural Vermont* (St. Albans: Vermont State Agricultural Commission, 1903), pp. 29-35.

DOCUMENT 8

"Take Me Back to Old Vermont" (1907)

(depicted on following pages)

Source: Vermont Historical Society, Montpelier, Vermont.

DOCUMENT 9

Letters on Woman's Suffrage (1910)
MRS. H. W. ABBOTT TO MRS. ANNETTE W. PARMALEE

Landgrove, Vt.
Nov. 10, 1910

Mrs. Parmalee,

Madame: I rec'd papers from you this morning, relating to womans suffrage. This is the way I feel about it. First I consider it an insult, and I think that a woman who will lower her self enough to want to vote, does not deserve to be called woman. And I sincerely hope that if they ever pass such a law that, (the women?) no they won't be women when they get down low enough to vote, will be compelled to pay a poll tax, just as much as the men. I should be ashamed to be called woman if the Legislature ever gives women the right, that you want them to have, there will be nothing right or just about it.

I don't believe the Creator intended that woman should have that right. If a woman attends to her house duties as she ought too, that is enough law making for her.

Respectfully,
Mrs. H.W. Abbott

Post-Office Londonderry, Vt.
Nov. 23, 1910

Mrs. Parmalee,

A Suffragette is a being who has ceased to be a lady and is no gentleman. People who want and try to be anybody do not believe in any such things. And a woman who does believe will drink just as much as the lowest man. And a woman who will slip up and hug a man stranger as you might say) in public, so that it is floating in all the papers, (*isn't much*) and is pretty brazen faced. I understand *you done this*. I don't believe _____ Legislature are bought to kill the bill. But they would be *fools* if they didn't kill them.

I have heard your name used as a by word in several different places. I should hate to have my name used so, and I think anyone would, who cared anything for humanity. Anyone who could believe as you do about the matter must be pretty easily led astray. Yes the Creator blessed both man and woman and bid them subdue the earth, but he didn't tell the women to wear the pants. If he had wanted them to do this, he never would have created woman. But I notice that there is once in a while a woman, who thinks she knows it all, that wants and tries to wear them. This is the way with the suffrage women.

These women that have to pay taxes, have a right to vote on school affairs and that is enough. And a good share of them wouldn't have to pay any tax, if they want. So fond of wearing the pants for the sake of saying they had so much property in their own names. I think the greatest percent of the men are capable of running business without their wives sticking their noses into affairs in any way shape or form. And any woman who does not thinks so, isn't fit to get married.

I can't see as there is any Golden Rule about *your letter*. Beauty is only skin deep, but the brazen side of the question is still deeper. Hope next time you write you will pay the postage, as I don't consider your letters worth my paying postage on. I had to pay postage on the one I rec'd this time, but shall not do it again as they are not worth noticing.

In some places it may be as you say about men owning their children and selling, giving or willing them away, but I don't believe it was ever done in the State of Vermont. I am not so easily frightened as that. I have noticed a good many times that some men will talk that they believe in woman's suffrage when they are in company with the women. And as soon as the women are gone they talk altogether different.

I think that is the way with the men who have allowed their names to be printed on this circular. I am glad my husband has got brains enough to run his own business, and isn't soft enough to vote for

Document 8

2

TAKE ME BACK TO OLD VERMONT

I
I long to wander o'er the fields
Where my childhood days were spent,
And climb the nearby rugged hills
And mountains' steep ascent.
To tramp beside the meadow streams
With my fav'rite rod and fly,
And try my luck and skill again
On the speckled beauties shy.

II
I long to meet my old schoolmates
Who played truant oft with me;
And raid once more the sugar camps
When the sap is running free;
To ramble through the woodland wild
And the birds and game surprise;
And from the green hills just beyond
Behold nature's paradise.

III
I long to join the happy throng
At the shady swimming pool,
And hear the ringing of the bell
Of the dear old district school;
To make the farmers one more call
And invade their orchards rare
And pick the choisest fruit in sight
Be it apple, plum or pear.

IV
I long to visit the old store
And the ancient tavern near
And hear again those stirring tales
By some hoary pioneer;
To loiter 'round the old grist mill
When the farmers gather there,
And join my comrades for a lark
At the circus or the fair.

CHORUS
Take me back to old Vermont
Where plenty smiles on every want.
Amid her winding vales, there let me roam,
By her famous pools and rills,
Marble, slate and granite hills,
And best of all, my old green mountain home.

BY MAIL 25 cts.

THE VERMONT MUSIC COMPANY
  RUTLAND, VERMONT

3

TAKE ME BACK TO OLD VERMONT.

Words by J.C. JONES.

Music by H.F. STAFFORD.

Published for Band and Orchestra

Copyright 1907 by Jones & Stafford

4

climb the near-by rug-ged hills, _____ And the mountains' steep as-
raid, once more the su - gar camps, _____ When the sap is run - ning

cent. _____ To tramp be - side the meadow streams _____ With my
free. _____ To ram - ble thro' the woodland wild _____ And the

fav - 'rite rod and fly, _____ And try my luck and skill a-
birds and game sur - prise _____ And from the green hills just be-

gain _____ On the speck - led beau - ties shy. _____
yond _____ Be - hold na - ture's par - a - dise. _____

Take Me 3

CHORUS

Tempo di Marcia

Take me back to old Ver - mont _____ Where plenty smiles on ev - 'ry

want _____ A - mid her wind-ing vales there let me roam _____ By her

famous pools and rills _____ Marble, slate, and granite hills _____ And

best of all my old green moun - tain home. _____ Take me home. _____

Take Me 8

C.F. W. Schirmer Music Press, Boston, Mass.

woman's suffrage. And a man that will let a woman run them and doesn't dare to say their soul's their own, is lacking something somewhere.

I am not the only one that is against this dirty low work.

Respectfully,
Mrs. H.W. Abbott

Source: Vermont League of Women Voters Papers, Vermont Historical Society, Montpelier, Vermont.

Document 10

"Woman's Place Defined" (1917)
Mrs. Annette W. Parmalee

Chelsea Herald, Feb. 8, 1917

Randolph has survived the shock occasioned by the holding, at the high school auditorium last Friday evening, of its first public meeting for disseminating equal suffrage wisdom. Mrs. Annette W. Parmelee [*sic*] of Enosburg Falls and Mrs. Julia Ashley Pierce of Rochester being the speakers. Principal Ham of the high school presided, and previous to the suffrage talk Miss Julia Cummings gave a piano solo, Miss Victoria Morse a monologue, "Sally Ann's Experience," and Mrs. E. J. O'Brien a song, "The Flower Girl," kindly responding to an encore.

Mrs. Pierce touched briefly upon the growth of the movement in Vermont since the first suffrage convention was held in St. Johnsbury, Nov. 8, 1883, and introduced Mrs. Parmelee, who said in part: —

"Women would seem to be the most interesting creatures ever created, for men have had much to say about us ever since Mother Eve manifested a desire for knowledge. Some have called us superlative beings, some household queens, but the last census report lists us a home-keepers, persons of no occupation, in fact. This may account for my presence here tonight.

"Men have written many learned articles on women's sphere. Some have placed us as fit to occupy a pedestal in some man's parlor, while others say our place is rocking the cradle in some man's kitchen. If every woman's place is 'in the home' why have not all

women been given decent homes and decent husbands? It seems a pity, too, that many unfortunate men cannot have good competent wives to care for them.

"There is one big sphere, that of usefulness, belonging to men and women alike. God placed men and women here to be co-workers in the great world's work. Go back to the foundation of home-life, and of civics, and you will fail to find any place where it is recorded that men were given exclusive right to rule. 'Male and female created He them,' equal in brain power, ability, health and endurance, yet differing in function. He blessed both and said unto them, 'Be fruitful, multiply and replenish the earth.' Together they were to control and subdue it; together they were to have dominion over every living thing. Both sinned, and thus destroyed the Creator's original plan.

"Men have tried to 'control and subdue the earth' with brute force, by bullets, by education, by ballots, and by the principles which Jesus taught, but the world is not yet subdued. Throughout the ages a prophet of God or a bearer of unvarnished truth has been deemed sensational, crazy, a crank.

"Men have killed truth's advocates, but what is right in the sight of God has thundered down the ages until an answer has been given that has satisfied. Back of every revolution has been a truth which could no longer be suppressed or held in check.

"History records that queens as well as kings were divinely appointed, and the most brilliant period in England's history was during the reign of Queen Victoria.

"Much has been said and written of the progress of moral reform and civic righteousness, but until recently little credit has been accorded to women; yet almost invariably, if one investigates, he will find there was a woman somewhere behind the man. As she has been persistently denied direct influence upon public matters, she has unceasingly in season and out of season expressed her mind with varying degrees of intensity, and after a time things have come to pass. I have no hesitation in affirming that the work of women challenges comparison with that of men in all ages and under all conditions. Yet not many medals are struck or monuments erected to commemorate the deeds of the mother.

"In the early days there was only one line of work open to daughters outside the home, and that was teaching. Susan B. Anthony was, when teaching, compelled to build her own fires and shovel paths to the school house. One day she asked why if she did a man's work she was not entitled to a man's pay. That question cost her her position, the committee declaring that a woman who will ask such a question 'knows altogether too much to keep school.'

"There is on record in a town meeting held in Connecticut a motion made, seconded and carried in effect that it would be a waste of public funds to attempt to teach girls the back part of the arithmetic, as they could never comprehend 'figgers' to any great extent. The first woman graduate of Oberlin college was not permitted to have her name appear upon the commencement program, nor was her name listed among the graduates in the school catalogue. Her alma mater, however, has recently conferred upon her a degree.

"The first women clerks in St. Albans shocked the whole surrounding county and women for a time boycotted stores where women were employed. Less than 75 years ago pulpit and press combined to silence the speech of women in public.

"When Lucy Stone expressed a wish to enter college, where she later graduated, her father exclaimed, 'Is she crazy! Her business is to keep house and raise babies, and she don't need any education for that.' She later became one of the great pioneers of the suffrage cause. 'Three old crows to speak' is the way a Vermont newspaper announced a meeting to be addresssed by Lucy Stone, Mary Livermore and Julia Ward Howe. All these women were refined homekeepers, women of noble presence and had a command of language and dignity of expression which held their hearers spellbound. Because they advocated higher education for women they were criticised, and almost mobbed, but, as Mary Lyon said, 'They paved the way for Mt. Holyoke college and every other college for women.' Except Oberlin, not a college was open to women before the organized movement for suffrage.

"Less than 30 years ago a Massachusetts senator opposed female suffrage on school matters, saying, 'If we make this experiment we shall destory the race and it will be blasted by the vengeance of Almighty God.' What commendable caution!

"Women today read, write, think, speak from the same platform as men, and are listened to with equal courtesy. Women today, in nearly one-half the area of this great country, thirteen states, are voting upon equal terms with men, considering all public questions with equal intelligence. They are sitting in the same legislatures in some of these states, making and amending laws, working in entire harmony with the men. Miss Jeannette Rankin of Montana will be the first woman in this country to occupy a seat in the National Congress at Washington to represent her constituents, both men and women. In the Oregon legislature a woman was recently called to the chair to preside in the absence of the speaker, being accorded every courtesy. And why not?

"Woman is fast emerging from ignorance into knowledge, from slavery to near freedom, from impotence to power, due to Christianity and education. Today nine million women are engaged in over 400 professions and industries. Nearly 4,000 women are practicing law, 10,000 women are practicing medicine, because women have long been deceived regarding the cause of many of their illnesses and operations. Women are conducting great hospitals in all parts of the world with eminent success. The first assistant to America's greatest surgeon is a women, as is the first assistant to the United States district attorney of California. Women are holding important positions under the government, among those recently appointed being Ida Tarbell to the tariff commission.

"The best illustration of good government, however, is the Christian home where father and mother have equal power and where both are working for the general good of the family, as wherever you find a home with one dominating party you will usually find a master and a slave. Equal rights mean equal responsibility, equal justice to working men and women, equal pay for women who do work equal to that of men; in fact, the conservation of the human race. Women have only half fulfilled their mission when they have fitted their children for the world—they should have a part in fitting the world for their children."

Source: Vermont League of Women Voters Papers, Vermont Historical Society, Montpelier, Vermont.

"A Primary Election Law" (1910)

VERMONTER

No one can raise any objection to the two basic principles upon which such a law is founded. First, the individual expression of each voter, by ballot, for his own personal choice for a candidate for public office. Second, prohibiting the use of money by any person to aid or promote his own nomination to a public office.

Two primary elections bills were presented to the last General Assembly for its consideration, one introduced in the Senate by Senator [Ernest W.] Gibson and the other in the House by Representative [Frank E.] Howe of Bennington. Senator Gibson's bill passed the Senate after some amendments were made. Both bills received but scant attention in the House, the sentiment, apparently, being overwhelmingly against the passage of any such bills. The principle objection heard was that it created, practically, another general election.

What is the situation at the present time in regard to the interest manifested in the caucus and the attendance? About five percent of the whole number of voters attend the caucus, unless two local political leaders get into a "scrap" and proceed to call out their respective followers. Under such a condition as this would it be expedient or wise to have another so called general election in June of each biennial year? No.

But how can we bring about a change in the situation and get a larger attendance at the caucus? Some measure must be looked for to relieve the monotony of this non-attendance at the caucus and cause the average voter to take more interest in the question as to who shall be the candidates for public office, or in the language of the street to cause him to "sit up and think."

Under the present system has the average voter anything to do at the caucus, except to consent to the putting through of some "cut and dried" plan of a local political boss? To do this hurts the pride of a great many of the voters and, therefore, they stay away.

If this influence of the local political boss could be removed would not the average voter begin to take more interest in the candidates for public office? If all the local barriers were removed would there not be a much larger attendance of voters at the caucus or primary election and thereby procure a much greater individual expression in regard to the candidates? In order to produce this much needed result what better remedy can you propose than a primary election law?

What is it that is becoming a stench to the nostrils of every true Vermonter? Need you answer when you hear the remark made so often that a man must have a "fat pocket book" in order to be Governor.

Windsor county has an able man and one of considerable legislative experience who would make a most excellent governor. In a former campaign he was accused of getting "cold feet" upon the gubernatorial proposition. It, perhaps, was for the reason that he as well as other able men hesitate in financing the proposition of procuring the nomination. This hesitation is, probably, caused by reason of their disgust in viewing the alacrity with which the "boys" proceed to get in upon the ground floor with the candidate who has a "barrel" and who of course must pay for all legitimate (?) services and expenses.

Is it not time to call a halt through some radical measure? Can you suggest any better remedial legislation to combat the present lethargic situation than a primary election law?

Source: *Vermonter* 15 (February 1910): 62.

"The Playground of the Continent" (1911)

GUY BAILEY

When the moisture laden winds with healing in their wings, sweeping inland from their wide surge over the North Atlantic, encounter their first obstacle, the mountain range that divides Vermont, they distill to earth a portion of their aqueous burden, and this stimulates and sustains the verdure of the hills which from their first discovery have given Vermont its name, the Green Mountain State, Verd Mont.

Few sections of the country are so well watered as Vermont. Lying between Lake Champlain and the Connecticut River, it is traversed by hundreds of streams, large and small, and dotted with innumerable lakes and ponds. Yet its altitude is such, its drainage to the valleys so perfect, that the air is dry rather than surcharged with moisture. Altitude, atmosphere, climatic conditions, the absence of congested centers of population, combine to make Vermont one of the most healthful sections of the country. . . .

Vermont puts forth no claim as a universal sanitarium, but it is so elevated, watered and aerated that its healthful conditions must command attention.

Most visitors who have written anything about the State have used such adulatory terms as to make what they have written seem like exaggeration. From Henry Ward Beecher to Ambassador James Bryce superlatives have been squandered in efforts to depict the natural beauties of the State, and Vermonters, believing that they live in the finest country on earth, have accepted and echoed such statements. . . .

Medicinal springs are . . . numerous in many parts of the State and afford a cure for many diseases. Analysis shows some of them to closely resemble some of the famous German spas, while others differ little from such English springs as those at Harrowgate or the Ballcastle and Castlemain springs in Ireland. . . .

No mountain peaks rear their heads in rugged, barren grandeur as in the Rockies or in such imposing loftiness as the Presidential range, but all about are graceful, green clad elevations, accessible without the aid of a cog wheel railway, from which may be seen a wonderful panoramic combination of wilderness and civilization.

Mansfield, the highest peak, 4369 feet above the sea, has a well equipped hotel at the summit and is easily climbed by carriage or on foot. Looking west the eye roams over an expanse of forest, over a broad and fertile valley divided by the sinuous Winooski, on to Burlington and its green slopes, to Lake Champlain dotted with many islands, and further in the blue distance the Adirondacks range before the vision.

Travelers have said that the view from the summit of Mansfield presents a more varied and attractive combination of scenery than they have discovered in this country or abroad. So, too, they have said that sunset on Lake Champlain, viewed from Battery Park in Burlington, surpassed anything in Switzerland.

Development of the outdoor spirit among Americans in recent years is bringing a better appreciation of the natural beauties of our own country.

Mansfield is reached by a regular stage line in summer. Camel's Hump (Le Lion Couchant), a near neighbor and but little lower, must be climbed on foot, but an easy trail leads to the summit. No hotel has been erected there, but a club of public spirited gentlemen maintains a shelter on the summit, with a caretaker in charge, where the visitor may buy his meals or have the use of culinary utensils to provide his own.

Ascutney overlooks the Connecticut valley, affording a wonderful view to the north and far into Massachusetts to the south. Directly across the river is the famous Cornish, N.H., summer colony of artists and writers. . . .

Killington and Pico in the west, Jay Peak in the north, Wantastiquet and Equinox in the south, and half a hundred others of varying elevations, all have their charms and points of interest, varying the appearance of the landscape and furnishing extensive views for those who care to climb to their summits.

The Green Mountain Club, organized last year by some prominent people in the State, plans to make the various peaks more accessible and to furnish shelter and accommodations such as visitors may require. It proposes to cut a trail along the summits of the Green Mountain range which traverses the State from north to south.

The State is entering on a policy of forest reserves which is being aided by private individuals, and some of these are on the mountain summits, set aside under conditions that will keep them forever free from the devastation of the lumberman's axe. . . .

Champlain and the larger lakes afford ample opportunities for boating and there are yacht clubs at Burlington and Newport with large membership and commodious club houses, supporting a considerable fleet, while motor boats ply the ponds and streams in all sections. . . .

The fishing season for trout opens in the streams on April 15 and in the ponds on May 1. The bass season opens June 15, affording the fish time to finish their duties on the spawning beds and seek their summer feeding grounds.

Vermont ponds and streams are natural trout water and some of the stories told of the catching of fish by early settlers are almost unbelievable. As in other States various causes have operated to deplete the supply of fish to some extent, but a plentiful restocking is gradually going on, so that there is probably as good fishing to be found in Vermont today as in any other State, though the man who knows will not expect to find this in public waters close by the larger villages. . . .

Brook trout are caught almost everywhere, in some streams apparently too small to afford them room to turn around, and intelligent and effective efforts are being made to keep up the supply. . . .

Probably no eastern water affords better bass fishing than the Great Back Bay of Lake Champlain. It is an ideal breeding and feeding ground and for years seining has been prohibited in the lake, so the bass, sturdy fish and well able to care for themselves, maintain their numbers and promise a continuance of sport for many years to come.

Arrangements are being made for the artificial propagation of sturgeon, of which there are now a considerable number in Lake Champlain. These fish, weighing sometimes 100 pounds or more, are not easily taken with ordinary tackle and can hardly be classed as game fish. Much so-called Russian caviar is made from American sturgeon roe.

The United States government maintains at Swanton a hatchery for wall-eyed pike, or pike perch, and the fry of these is distributed by the million in public waters not inhabited by trout. They reach a weight of several pounds in a few years, and while not accounted a game fish are always welcome on the table.

Campers and tourists seeking an addition to their menu will find in all parts of the State an abundance of yellow perch, always easily caught and one of the most toothsome of fresh water fishes when properly dressed. Perch weighing a pound and a half are frequently taken in the larger lakes, but elsewhere they run a little above half to three quarters of a pound.

The forests furnish a variety of sport for the hunter. Deer are taken by the hundred every season. Having been protected for twenty years they have become comparatively tame, and every year are seen in the streets of villages and cities. Some are shot every year within the city limits of Montpelier, the capital.

Hunting of moose and caribou is prohibited. There is a herd of moose in Essex county steadily growing in size. As the moose is a migratory animal the hunting of it will probably be permitted in a few years. Only occasionally have any caribou been seen in the State for years.

Gray squirrels are numerous in years when nuts are plenty and hares and rabbits afford good sport. Partridge and woodcock are as plentiful as can be expected in a thickly settled country. Wild duck and geese are taken in large numbers during the season of flight and snipe and plover are plentiful. English pheasants and capercailie, which have been placed in some coverts, are protected until 1913 when they are expected to furnish good shooting.

The necessity for going over or around so many hills has given Vermont a large highway mileage in proportion to its area. Maintenance imposes a heavy burden on the small towns, where in some cases road mileage is out of all proportion to area or population, and some of the highways there are not kept up as they should be. The State, by extending financial aid and increasing the authority of its highway commissioner, is gradually taking over more of the burden of maintenance. Already the main highways are in excellent condition, and the Munsey automobile tourists last year declared that the roads of Vermont were as good as those of any states through which they passed. More than a million dollars will be spent on the highways of the State this year. This fund is distributed by the State highway commissioner and county supervisors in accordance with improved modern methods. These and other officials work so far as possible with automobilists and officials of the automobile club, and without burdening the State with debt the highways are being placed in excellent condition. Macadam is used in places where traffic is heavy enough to require it, and in the country districts a high quality of gravel road is constructed. Many of the cities use some tar compound to surface their roads and keep down the dust, while treatment with crude oil has been very effective on dirt roads.

Automobilists receive reciprocal courtesies and privileges, they find here good roads, hotels equal to any in the country in quality if not in size that make their interests a special care, and State officials who have no disposition to impose upon them any restrictions beyond those of the statute, which automobilists admit are reasonable and satisfactory. The Munsey automobile tourists passed through the State last year and were greatly pleased with the treatment they received, and the Glidden Reciprocity tourists will travel almost the entire length of the State this season.

To the tourist, whether by automobile, on foot, by carriage or train, to the camper, the fisherman or the hunter, the mountain climber, the scientist, the seeker for natural curiosities, the artist and the photographer Vermont offers wondrous scenery, clear air, pure water, healthful conditions, a delightfully equable climate, good roads, and opportunities for varied amusements.

At Brattleboro, Bellows Falls, White River Junction, Woodstock, Montpelier, Waterbury, Burlington, Swanton, St. Albans, Rutland, Lake Bomoseen, Manchester, Bennington and other places are large and commodious hotels making special provision for summer guests. Smaller and less pretentious resorts are scattered about the State, there are numerous camps along the lake shores, which may be leased for the season or for a few weeks, and boarding houses that furnish ideal summer accommodations, while many private houses are opened for a few visitors.

First class train accommodations enable one to reach all the more important points in Vermont with ease and comfort, while branch lines and a dozen or more lines of electric road make a large part of the State readily accessible. The Boston and Maine railroad follows the course of the Connecticut river on the eastern side, with a branch division reaching across the State; the Central Vermont traverses the central portion and the New England States Limited over its line is one of the finest trains running out of Boston. The Rutland road connects with Boston trains at Bellows Falls and with the Delaware and Hudson and New York Central at Rutland, running south to Bennington and through Massachusetts and north through the islands of Lake Champlain to Montreal. These three great systems with their branch lines, and the other roads that enter the State for a few miles at points not otherwise covered make all the more desirable resorts of Vermont easy of access.

Fully detailed information as to the best trains and most convenient means of reaching any desired point will be furnished to any one who will address,

Guy W. Bailey,
Secretary of State,
Essex Junction, Vt.

Source: "Vermont: Designed by the Creator for the Playground of the Continent" (Vermont Bureau of Publicity, 1911), pp. 5-12.

DOCUMENT 13

Declaration of Principles and Platform (1912)

VERMONT PROGRESSIVE REPUBLICAN LEAGUE

Meeting at St. Johnsbury. The Platform Adopted.
Next Meeting at Montpelier,
Wednesday, May 22, at 7:30 p.m.
All Progressive Republicans
Invited to be Present.

At Montpelier. Vermont
Progressive Republican League
Adopts Platform at St. Johnsbury.
Adjourns to May 22.

About 50 progressive Republicans from different sections of the State met Thursday evening at Pythian hall, St. Johnsbury, to hear a report of the committee on platform for the Vermont Progressive Republican League.

Dr. T. R. Stiles of St. Johnsbury was chosen president and Samuel E. Abbott of Bethel was chosen secretary, L. P. Thayer of Morrisville read a report of the committee on platform. The name in the resolutions was the Vermont Progressive Republican League.

The following "Declaration of Principles" was unanimously adopted, subject of course to amendment at any future meeting:

Declaration of Principles.

Whereas, This is a government of the people, dedicated forever to the principles of truth, justice and human liberty, sanctified by the sacrifice and devotion of those heroic men and women who founded this State and Nation, therefore be it

Resolved, That we, the members of the Vermont Progressive Republican League, reaffirm those cardinal principles and pledge anew our earnest purpose to reduce those principles into practice as living issues of today.

Resolved, That to the end that the people may again resume their rightful sovereignty as it was exercised by their forefathers, to control the government of this country, we are in favor of

1 — A simple, direct primary for the nomination of all public officials.

2 — The choice of United States Senators by direct preferential ballot.

3 — A revision of the system of taxation so that all will be taxed alike.

4 — That every citizen have the privilege of borrowing or loaning money on the same conditions as the banks.

5 — Full publicity of all campaign expenses.

6 — No man is fit to be entrusted with making laws; no man is fit to be entrusted with executing laws; and no man is fit to be entrusted with construing laws, unless he himself wholeheartedly is willing to live up not only to the letter but to the spirit of the law.

It was expected that a permanent organization would be formed at this time, but after discussion it was decided that the wiser course would be to form a permanent organization at a meeting more generally attended and that had been as widely advertised as possible. L. P. Thayer of Morrisville, William Beane of Newport and L. M. Hayes of Essex Junction were appointed a committee on publicity and to have published the resolutions and to call a general meeting to be held at some central place. The committee retired and later reported that the next meeting would be held for the permanent organization of the Vermont Progressive Republican League at Montpelier on Wednesday, May 22, at 7:30 p.m. and that all people interested in the progressive principles be invited to attend.

The organization does not aim to promote any candidate for the governorship or any state office but to work for the election of progressive men to the legislature, and the success of the republican, state and national tickets on the lives of the old Young Men's Republican Club.

New Vermont Platform (1912)
Ernest W. Gibson

TO THE PEOPLE:

I am a candidate to bring the following ideas to results, and if elected to represent this district at Washington, I will pull off my coat, work early and late until they are accomplished:

1. A NATIONAL LAW providing for the nomination of candidates for president and vice-president by a direct vote of the people. Such a law would insure the selection of the choice of the people on a day certain, and put an end to the selection by party bosses.

2. I SHALL WORK to secure such amendments to the Postal Savings Law, and for such provisions in the so-called Monetary Bill as will provide for the loaning of postal savings funds so they may be applied to the development of local industries and the encouragement of local agricultural interests. We have sent too much money out of the state for the development of other sections of our country, and kept too little for home development. In the same connection I favor a provision that national banks loan to a greater extent with special reference to seasonal needs of agriculturists, so that the crops of farms can be moved with the greatest economy and advantage to the producer and the consequent advantage to the consumer. I would have an investigation and report upon co-operative land, mortgage banks which have proved such a help in developing the intensive agriculture of Europe. In other words, I would turn local accumulated money to home advantage.

3. (a) AS DIRECTLY HELPING this District, I would secure a soil survey made so that each farmer may know the crops his land will best handle. This is already provided for and the survey is now being carried on in twenty-six different states, but not in Vermont. It can be had for this state with energetic demand. It would save our farmers $200,000 in fertilizer bills alone, and double returns from farm products.

(b) I would secure from the Good Roads Bureau of the Department of Agriculture the detail of one of the road building experts connected with that bureau and have him travel from county to county to give advice and assist in the building of roads, especially in the poorer towns.

(c) I would secure from the Department of Agriculture the stationing in this District of an expert who would devote all of this time to seed testing, aiding in increasing the productivity of the soil and in exterminating such pests as the farmer has to contend with. Even many southern sections are profiting by the work of these experts but not Vermont.

4. THE TAX on oleomargarine must be large enough to fully protect dairy interests. This district is the principal dairying section of New England. Oleomargarine should not be placed in competition with butter. I am opposed to the Lever Bill which aims a fatal blow at our dairy interests.

5. THE HIGH COST of living is a grave problem. It concerns every man, woman and child. How a man of ordinary income can support his family under present conditions, is almost beyond comprehension. Without abandoning the principle of protection, I favor such a tariff revision as will aid and protect the poor man in his struggle of life. In that way one of the causes of the high cost of living will be removed.

6. I WOULD ENDEAVOR to secure for all the manufacturers of the district, through the Interstate Commerce Commission, the advantage of Boston freight rates. Such rates would stimulate manufacturing and add to the prosperity of our people.

I submit this platform concerning matters directly affecting interests of this district to the careful consideration of the people. If it appeals to you, vote for it and for the one you believe will secure these benefits.

I do not want a vote unless that vote represents just what the voter believes. I do not care for votes obtained by "gum shoe" methods. My campaign will be in the open. I want votes in the open.

Respectfully,
E. W. GIBSON
Brattleboro, Vt., June 7, 1912.

Source: Fraser Metzger Papers, Box 1, Folder 2; Special Collections, Bailey/Howe Library, University of Vermont.

DOCUMENT 14

"State Expenditures" (1916)
EDWARD CURTIS SMITH

The success of a state or a nation depends upon the character and morality of its citizens. These two—character and morality—have their foundation in the divine law. Constitutions, the common law, statutes as enacted by states and nations, are merely human efforts looking towards the expression of that law. The degree in which such expressions are carried out, the quality of the impetus of advancement in civilization, the degree of the appreciation of the rights of the individuals who make up society, the conformity to the duty imposed by these rights between the members of a community, these measure the progress of the state to the ideal perfection. The constant aim of a state should be the just recognition of those rights and the accomplishment of that duty. To depart from those ideals leads in the end to disaster, to temporize with them postpones their fulfillment.

I take it that the purpose of this organization [Greater Vermont Association] is to develop a greater Vermont along these lines. . . . This organization looks to a truly greater Vermont whose object is to hold the people of this State steady to the purposes of our fathers, and to make a Vermont greater in the elements of character and morality, which are in truth the only sure and safe foundation on which to raise a material prosperity. . . .

Now, the first essential of success in the organization of a community is a basis for taxation that is fair and sane. . . . The constitution of the state provides:

"That every member of society hath a right to be protected in the enjoyment of life, liberty and property, and therefore is bound to contribute his proportion towards the expense of that protection."

Until the year 1880 the state lived up to the profession of its faith as embodied in that provision, and followed the principle of fairness as nearly as was possible, in the basis of taxation adopted for raising state revenue. The burden of supporting the state was then borne *ratably by all* the citizens of the state; but about that time a different policy was adopted and the state departed from its long time system of levying a general property tax to provide the expenses of the state, in which all the people shared the burden of the state government ratably, and inaugurated a new system of making one portion of the members of society bear the burden of the balance of the members. Certain of the corporations of the state were thereafter taxed to pay state expenses, and gradually the other members of society were relieved from paying their proportions. From that day until the present by inevitable logic, the expenses of government have increased, at first slowly but as time progressed with increasing momentum, until during the past year the volume of state expenses has increased over three hundred percent above what it was ten years ago, and the end is not yet. The practice of making one branch of society carry the expense of the state organization for all its members is precisely tantamount to the proposition of living on other people's money. Living on other people's money inevitably leads to extravagance and extravagance inevitably leads to waste. It was precisely at the point of departure from the spirit of the constitution, which I have quoted, that the trouble started, and then the evil grew and increased. The legislature found it comfortable and satisfactory to vote appropriations, and these appropriations increased from year to year. It became easier and easier to add to the expense of the various branches of the government on the one hand, and that course forced the necessity for increasing the volume of revenue on the other hand. The scrutiny of expenses through personal interests by the citizens gradually faded away, because it was not their money that was being spent; the spirit of economy that had always prompted hesitation and deliberation in the expenditure of the state's money, gave way to indifference: the term of the biennial sessions was gradually lengthened, and the whole governmental expenditure loosened up, and all because money which is the result of other people's thrift is always easier to spend than the money one has to earn himself. The changed condition is clearly traceable to the fact that the state had departed from a right principle and has adopted a wrong one. . . .

The period when this policy seems to have gathered its greatest momentum extends from 1901 to the present day. For my part I have searched in vain to discover any other explanation than that above to justify or excuse the situation. The population of the state has not increased during the past fifteen years, materi-

ally. There have been no great public works to call for the expenditure of large sums of money. I except, of course, the most creditable improvement in our highways, for the reason that this improvement has largely been paid out of special sources of revenue, and does not come altogether from the corporations and is in fact largely self-supporting. Nor does a comparison of the real necessities of Vermont's 360,000 inhabitants fifteen years ago, with the real necessities of the same people today, indicate a state of affairs that would demand an additional expenditure of $1,500,000 to support the same people in 1916. It does not seem to me that the social condition of the state in 1901 was three hundred percent worse than it is today. But yet all this is precisely what the record of state expenditures would indicate, unless the cause I have mentioned is admitted to be the true cause of the changed conditions.

Just compare the figures: In 1901 the total expenditures for state government was $750,000. During the twelve succeeding years it grew by leaps and bounds until in 1914 it had reached the sum of $2,145,000,— an increase of nearly 300 percent. An analysis of the details will show that in 1901 legislative expenses were only $61,979, but these arose in 1913 to $190,579. The expenses of the various commissions appointed by the legislature have jumped from $21,264 in 1901, to $143,462 in 1914. Annual appropriations for colleges and schools have run up from $46,000 in 1901 to $317,590 in 1914. Even the expense for the administration of justice has swollen from $246,000 in 1901 to $388,000 in 1914. . . . To my way of thinking the condition indicates a decided tendency to extravagance that should be checked.

I want to emphasize the statement that no one who knows the officials of the state would question for a moment the strict integrity and honesty of every one of them. The fault does not lie at their doors, but solely in the system under which they are working. There can be no fairly debatable question of the fact that there has been during these years, waste, inevitable waste in the state expenditure and there is today. . . .

A condition of the result of this policy to those who "pay the price" of this condition of affairs is interesting.

I leave out that portion of the state's revenue which is derived from licenses, inheritance tax and the fees from the administration of justice, for the reason that, being in the nature of taxes on privileges, they properly belong to the state's treasury in any event, whatever the basis of taxation, and I am considering only the effect on those members of society who contribute the balance of the revenue. This is furnished by the corporations, and constitutes about 65 percent of the total. It constitutes the entire state revenue after deducting the taxes on privileges mentioned above. None of the other citizens of the state have contributed, during the period from 1901 to 1912, one penny towards the expense of the state.

The amount paid into the state treasury by banks ran up from $252,000 in 1901 to $704,949 in 1914, about 300 percent increase. The railroads paid to the state $140,306 in 1901, and they were taxed in 1914, $548,000, about 400 percent increase. Insurance companies were increased from $54,000 to $168,000, 300 percent, and telephone and telegraph companies from $5,900 to $30,486—500 percent. It will no doubt be claimed as a justification for all this rapid and startling increase in the volume of taxes collected annually from corporations, and for the increasing expenditures by the state, that the whole proposition is, after all, a normal one; that modern methods demand expansion and improvement, that the corporations are rich and can stand the tax and, therefore, the state in its expenditures must keep abreast of the time. But I submit that an expansion of expenditure without tangible and profitable results is waste, and that "keeping abreast of the times" without anything to show for it, is extravagance, or what is worse, is pandering to pride of position. Waste is unforgivable anywhere and at all times, and whether the corporations involved, are able to respond to the contribution demanded by the legislature as I have indicated or not, does not justify the collection of one penny of the state for extravagance or waste or pride of position.

Therefore, whether these corporations are rich or poor they should not be asked to contribute one five cent piece to the expenses of the state organization that is not justified under the provisions of the constitution which says that "they shall contribute their proportion," and that means only their proportion, towards paying for the protection they receive from the state. That some of the corporations are not able to bear the burden as it exists today I know.

I am President of the Central Vermont Railway Company. . . . In 1901 the state taxes paid by the Central Vermont were $53,000 or 31 percent of its net revenue. When the demands for more money to run the state, increased, the taxes paid by the road were increased. In 1909 they had reached the amount of $93,000 or 96 percent of the net revenue for that year. In 1913 they had climbed to $120,000—that year the percentage of the net was 108 percent. The road's entire net revenue and more was taken to meet the increased demand for state expenditure. In 1915 the taxes were $138,000 or 90 percent of the net revenue. It strikes me that this is an exorbitant tax on net income and wholly unjustifiable, when one considers the obligations of a railroad manager to provide out of the insignificant amount remaining in the treasury after payment of taxes, new rails, new bridges, a safe track for the public to travel over, new equipment for the public to ride in, to meet the increasing demands of labor, and at the same time with no advance in rates for handling passengers or freight to offset the increased demand for taxes. And yet these are the facts. There is no question for debate about them. They are the plain truth. I confess that my efforts to reconcile a proper justification for a seizure like the above, with the language of our constitution I have quoted, have impressed me a good deal like trying to fit a square peg in a round hole. It cannot be done.

This state of affairs on its face is bad enough but there is more to the proposition. The state has taken a hand in the operation of the railroads. The elimination of highway crossings is unquestionably in the interest of humanity and should be accomplished with all the haste possible. The railroads should respond with their share of the expense, but the public and the state should be equally interested in the protection of the citizens and should contribute toward the accomplishment of this desirable end equally with the railroads. . . .

With the enormous growth in this country in wealth and population and developing resources, Vermont by comparison is growing smaller and there never was a time in history when greater heed should be given to the words of St. Paul "Prove all things, hold fast to that which is good." Vermont can never be a greater Vermont if its natural strength is wasted, and its sinews of power are prostrated. Today is no time for a change in the established order of its political procedure. . . .

Source:*Vermonter* 21 (Autumn 1916): 197-204.

DOCUMENT 15

"A Brief History of the Record of Allen M. Fletcher

on Subjects of Labor While Serving as Governor of Vermont, 1912-1913" (1916)

TO THE WORKING MAN.

In presenting this booklet to the voters of the State, the Allen M. Fletcher Senatorial Club hopes you will give it your careful perusal.

If Mr. Fletcher's labor record meets with your approval you can show your appreciation at the primaries in September by casting your ballot for him for United States Senator for Vermont.

ELECT YOUR FRIENDS AND DEFEAT YOUR ENEMIES!

———————

Ex-Governor Allen M. Fletcher's Labor Record

First—He signed the Factory Inspection Bill, favored by labor, even though opposed by the manufacturing interests from every part of the State. This great measure has been one of the most beneficial from a physical and moral viewpoint that was ever placed on the statute books of Vermont. Since the introduction of the law, toilets, fire escapes, water bubblers, guards on machinery, dust removers, etc. have been placed in nearly every mill and factory in the State and the good work is still going on.

Second—He signed the 58-hour law for women and minors engaged in manufacturing or mechanical establishments. This measure was favored by labor and solidly opposed by the great textile interests of the State. Before the passage of this humane law young women from 16 years of age to 20 years of age toiled in the mills of Vermont from 65 to 83 hours per week and in some cases 18 hours in a single day. THESE ARE FACTS—WE HAVE THE PROOFS.

Third—He signed the Trustee Process law which was favored by labor. This measure was the first of its kind in Vermont. It provides that ten dollars of a workman's wages are exempt when an attachment has been placed on his earnings, thus affording him the opportunity to at least supply himself and family with the necessities of life. Earnings of minors or married women are exempt after the law. Wage earners agree that the measure has acted as a buffer between them and the cheap grade process server. Certainly, a progressive advance over the old way, when by attachment every dollar of the man's wages were taken.

Fourth—He signed the Conciliation and Arbitration act, which was favored by labor, and in preference to having a compulsory measure saddled upon the workers he appointed a member of organized labor on the board. The measure has not been operative during the past two years, the present governor failing to appoint a new board even when so requested by labor. Labor disputes in Washington and Rutland counties might have been adjusted had the board been in existence.

Fifth—He signed the act relating to the heating and ventilating of factories, which was favored by labor. This measure is under the supervision of the State Board of Health and it has made commendable efforts to improve the surroundings of Vermont's wage earners.

Sixth—He favored the Workmen's Compensation law and worked hard to have the necessary amendments made to the common law and placed before the people of Vermont. After approval was made by the people, he appointed a commission to investigate the subject of workmen's compensation, its aims and objects. Later, in his retiring message, he urged the incoming Legislature to enact a proper and beneficial law. This is what he said:

> The commission which the last Legislature created to consider this subject will present a bill for your consideration. As a matter of State policy I believe the principle of workmen's compensation and employers' liability should be adopted by you.

GOVERNOR FLETCHER SIGNED MORE LEGISLATION IN BEHALF OF THE WORKING MEN AND WOMEN OF VERMONT THAN HAD BEEN PREVIOUSLY PLACED IN THE STATUTE BOOKS OF THE STATE.

He was made an honorary member of the Vermont State Branch of the American Federation of Labor in recognition of his efforts in the interests of labor. . . .

This little booklet has presented the record of Governor Fletcher on labor.

It has also given you the labor record of Senator Page at Washington on labor. He has a labor record in Vermont. It will be presented to you later in the campaign.

The question may well be asked, "Who, Fletcher or Page, has proven himself the friend of labor?" And again: "Who will best represent you at Washington!"

<u>YOUR VOTE MAY BE THE DECIDING ONE. CAST IT RIGHT AND IN YOUR INTEREST BY VOTING FOR MR. FLETCHER.</u>

[Union Water-Marked Paper]

Source: Republican Senate Primary Material, 1916, pp. 3-6, 9; Political Ephemera Collection, Special Collections, Bailey/Howe Library, University of Vermont.

SECTION NINE

1917-1941
Serpents in the Garden

VERMONT VOICES

SECTION NINE

1917-1941
Serpents in the Garden

Introduction

Vermont responded to Congress' April 6, 1917, declaration of war against Germany with its customary patriotic fervor, as evidenced by **Document 1**. More than 16,000 Vermonters served with the military and almost as great a number served in some capacity mobilizing citizens for "home front" duty. Early in 1918, at the suggestion of the Vermont Committee of Public Safety (an umbrella civil defense organization created by the governor), the state Board of Education issued the message to Vermont's youth excerpted in **Document 2**. Essentially a call for Vermont's school-aged children to help finance the war's cost by buying war stamps, its depiction of the German government is particularly worth noting. Reference to *The War Book* was extensive and former teachers and students recalled its rhetoric and demonizing over half a century later. Exposure to it arguably provided the one common war experience that touched more Vermonters than any other. By November 11, when the armistice ending the war was signed, the state had recorded 650 military deaths due to enemy action and disease, more from the latter than the former.

Fortunate to have escaped the war with such relatively light losses, the state turned to domestic concerns. Two causes stimulated by the war, prohibition and women's suffrage, by January 1919 were implemented by constitutional amendment. Vermont ratified neither. Having experienced prohibition throughout the second half of the nineteenth century, most Vermonters were not eager to see it restored.

The Nineteenth Amendment to the U.S. Constitution, declared ratified on August 26, 1920 (without Vermont's support), permitted women to participate in the 1920 elections. Edna Beard gained the distinction of becoming the first woman elected to the Vermont legislature, while other women (over 28,000 registered to vote) experienced their political baptism. Among the latter was Bernice Bromley, who remained active in Republican organizational and electoral politics for the next thirty years. **Document 3** is an excerpt from her reminiscences.

Although Vermont is frequently promoted as a rural paradise, it has experienced interludes of industrial violence, with strikes of considerable magnitude by workers in the railroad construction, copper mining, marble, and granite industries. **Document 4** provides excerpts from interviews with observers of a 1922 strike by Barre granite workers, collected by the Works Progress Administration Federal Writers Project Life History Narratives. The interviewer, Mari Tomasi, a Montpelier native, later gained fame as the author of *Like Lesser Gods*, a novel about Barre granite workers and their families. Although Ms. Tomasi did not date these interviews, they were presumably conducted during 1938 and 1939.

Populated in large number by Italian, Spanish, and Irish immigrants, Barre continued to serve traditionalists as a symbol of unwanted change that was overtaking their state. Rural lifestyles were being superseded by more urban fashions, as emigration by descendants of earlier settlers and their replacement by non-Protestant arrivals persisted. Earlier commentators such as Rowland Robinson (Section 7, Document 10) and George F. Wells (Section 8, Document 7) had associated this shift with an alleged decline in the "character level" in some regions of the state. Proponents found confirmation for this view from statistics gathered during the processing of recruits for military service, noting that "only one other state had so large a proportion of its young men of draft age rejected because of physical and mental defects." Efforts to counter this distressing situation elicited recommendations from a variety of sources, with the most systematic and ultimately the most notorious coming from the Eugenics Survey. The Vermont affiliate of the national eugenics movement, which operated from 1925 through 1936, was directed by a University of Vermont zoology professor. **Document 5** is an excerpt from the Vermont group's initial report; its principal welfare reform proposals, not included in this report but following national trends, were a marriage restriction and a sterilization law. The sterilization law was adopted by the legislature in 1931, making Vermont the twenty-fifth, but not the last, state to adopt such a law.

A natural disaster, however, precipitated an even more profound reshaping of the state's material, political, and social environment. On November 3 and 4, 1927, New England experienced a severe rainfall that, preceded by an abnormally wet autumn that had already saturated the ground, caused extensive flooding. Vermont was especially hard hit as rivers overflowed, 84 lives were lost, and homes, livestock, farmlands, industrial sites, and much of the state's communication and transportation network were destroyed. Reconstruction was a massive undertaking and the state acted promptly. Even before the floodwaters had abated, Governor John Weeks convened a special session of the state legislature to deliberate over a detailed plan that he presented and that was adopted in a marathon thirteen-hour-and-twenty-minute session. Prepared by the state Highway Department with aid from the federal Bureau of Public Roads, the plan envisioned a transportation network more dependent on motor transport and less on railroads, and its implementation required heavy borrowing to finance what was until then the largest public works project in Vermont history. While Montpelier was adopting the governor's reconstruction plan and abandoning its pay-as-you-go philosophy in order to expedite highway funding, Vermont's Washington delegation was appealing to Congress for flood relief funds. **Document 6** provides excerpts from Congressman Elbert Brigham's justification for that request. Congress voted for the appropriation and President Calvin Coolidge promptly signed the bill and dispatched the funds.

Vermonters seldom summon up images of their congressional delegation securing its $2,600,000 highway reconstruction appropriation or their governor accepting a $600,000 relief check from the Red Cross. They do, however, frequently recall that no appropriation was requested for private and business property losses and that the costs were borne largely by individuals. In that spirit they invoke the words President Coolidge uttered when he visited his native state the year following the flood. Printed as **Document 7**, they are probably the proudest tribute ever bestowed upon the state. They have since been inscribed on a wall of the Montpelier statehouse and lend substance to the oft-repeated claim that Vermonters sought help from no one.

Document 8, Governor Stanley Wilson's second inaugural address, was delivered during the depths of the Great Depression and in the interregnum between Franklin D. Roosevelt's November 1932 election and his March 1933 inaugural. The excerpts selected suggest, with some accuracy, that the extent to which Vermont was rural and isolated from industrialization cushioned

it from some of the worst extremes of the Depression. One wag suggested, "Vermont didn't have a depression. It went through the weakest boom in many many years." Industrial communities such as Rutland, Barre, and Winooski, however, suffered far greater deprivations than their rural counterparts.

Winooski, a one-mile-square city carved from the town of Colchester in 1920, was peopled principally by French Canadians who worked in the local textile mills. In 1928, having voted for the Democratic candidates for president and governor, it was castigated by the press as a "foreign island surrounded by Republican Vermont." By the 1930s, Winooski's ethnic consciousness was expressed increasingly through the election of community and state leaders. Russell Niquette was one of the earliest and most powerful of these political leaders, and the portion of his oral history that recounts his entry into politics is reproduced as **Document 9**.

Document 10, "The Conservation of Vermont Traditions and Ideals," excerpted from *Rural Vermont: A Program for the Future*, provided a blueprint for state planning that historian Kevin Dann described as prophesying "to an astonishing effect. . . the direction the state would take in the next half century." Written and published by the Vermont Commission on Country Life, which was composed of two hundred prestigious Vermonters loosely associated with the Eugenics Survey, *Rural Vermont* proposed "scientific planning" so that Vermont might achieve "higher goals." Rejecting the idea that Vermont could ever become industrialized and seeing the greatest opportunity for economic advancement through the recreation industry (pre-skiing), its 385 pages include recommendations for state land-use planning, banning billboards, cleaning polluted waters, reforestation of abandoned farms, enhanced tourist facilities, a state police force, and construction of scenic highways. As is evident from the excerpt chosen, the commission celebrated and hoped to achieve this by preserving Vermont as an Anglo-Saxon community nurtured on rural values.

Not all commission recommendations were accepted, and the one that raised the greatest controversy and ultimately divided even commission members was the plan for a federally funded Green Mountain Parkway. The parkway was envisioned as a 260-mile scenic highway running along the spine of the Green Mountains from Massachusetts to Canada. It initially received support from the Vermont Country Life Commission, the state Chamber of Commerce, and Governor Stanley Wilson, and it gained the preliminary approval of President Franklin Roosevelt. Opposition originated among members of the Green Mountain Club, guardians of the Long Trail along which much of the highway would run, and spread rapidly throughout the state. In 1935 the state senate approved the plan by a narrow vote, and the house by an even narrower margin rejected it. To settle the issue, Governor Charles Smith convened a special session of the legislature that scheduled a statewide referendum for March 1936 town meeting day. **Documents 11** and **12**, excerpts from articles by Ernest H. Bancroft and Arthur Wallace Peach, were contributions to the referendum debate by Country Life Commission members. Bancroft, favoring the parkway, was chairman of the Subcommittee on Dairy Problems, and Peach, opposing the parkway, was chairman of the Committee on Vermont Traditions and Ideals (see Document 10). The parkway was defeated by a 42,873-to-30,795 vote.

While the state debated how best to assure an arcadian future, Vermont's most infamous industrial dispute took place in the Rutland area over efforts to unionize workers of the Vermont Marble Company. Organized by Redfield Proctor shortly after the Civil War, the company had grown to become Vermont's largest employer, with quarries, offices, and factories in other states as well. The basis for the Proctor family's economic and political fortunes, the company countered declining revenues during the Depression by cutting working hours and distributing the available work without dismissing employees. The employees, already subjected to a low wage rate, sought organization by national unions. In the course of the ensuing strike, disclosures that the company maintained its stock dividend levels and that special deputies hired by Proctor Marble to break the strike had been supplemented with additional deputies at state expense, engendered out-of-state sympathy for the strikers. A fund-raising committee was started at Dartmouth College and was joined by groups at Bennington College, Skidmore College, and the University of Wisconsin. An umbrella organization, the United Committee to Aid the Vermont Marble Workers, was established in New York City, and the proceedings of a hearing it held in West Rutland are excerpted as **Document 13**. Although the work of the committee was widely reported, it had no influence on the outcome of the strike, which ended in a complete victory for management.

Lieutenant Governor George Aiken was among those who deplored state government's deference to industrial management in general and to the Proctors in particular. Elected governor in November 1936, in the midst of overwhelming national Democratic victories, he demonstrated a sympathy and restraint in dealing with labor disputes that initiated a more evenhanded era in Vermont's industrial relations that earned him organized labor's long-term support. He contended that the Republican Party's dedication to the primacy of property rights and its leaders' obsession with maintaining control over the party machinery discredited it as a viable alternative to Roosevelt's New Deal. As governor of one of the only two states that had remained loyal to the GOP in the 1936 elections, he took advantage of his status to plead for a reformed Republican Party. **Document 14**, an open letter to the Republican National Committee, sets forth his proposals.

As is apparent from the conclusion of Aiken's letter, the deteriorating international situation had become an increasing concern. By September 1939, Europe was at war, and after May 1940, when France fell to Germany, a debate raged in the United States over whether it should convert itself into an "Arsenal of Democracy" to supply Great Britain in her struggle against Hitler. Ernest W. Gibson, Jr., was Vermont's and arguably the nation's foremost proponent of this cause.

Upon the death of Senator Ernest W. Gibson, Sr., in May 1940, Governor George Aiken appointed Gibson, Jr., as interim senator. Gibson did not seek election and was succeeded by Aiken. On December 15, 1940, Gibson gave his last formal speech as senator, in which he appealed for greater aid to Great Britain. **Document 15** provides excerpts from that speech. Shortly after leaving the Senate, Gibson was appointed director of the Committee to Defend America by Aiding the Allies, serving as a zealous spokesperson for approval of aid to Great Britain. Repeating the arguments and rhetoric from his December 15 speech at public rallies, on radio broadcasts, and for newsreel film clips that were played in movie theaters, he toured the nation until Congress voted the adoption of Lend-Lease in March 1941.

DOCUMENT 1

Recruiting Poster (1917)

(depicted on opposite page)

Source: Vermont Historical Society, Montpelier, Vermont.

DOCUMENT 2

The War Book (1918)

VERMONT STATE BOARD OF EDUCATION

Boys and Girls of Vermont:

The United States is at war. At war with an enemy ruthless, relentless and merciless. An enemy who will fight to the utmost, disregarding all neutral rights, mindful of no feelings of humanity. Its every resource must be exhausted, its last man drawn into the swirling vortex of war, the ultimate strength of each human unit made to yield to a superior force, the only god the imperial German government knows, before peace will come.

Upon such an undertaking has our nation entered. The ultimate victory must be ours, but it will not be ours until by sacrifice we shall gain the right to be called victors. Money and material are but the least that must be given. The blood of our best young men, the promise of American life, must freely flow on the fair fields of France ere democracy, through the supreme sacrifice, is made secure.

You have learned how the war came to America, why America fights, the real problems of raising an army and navy, of manufacturing and furnishing them supplies and of helping supply our allies, of building a fleet of merchant and transport ships sufficient to balance the toll of the deadly submarine, of producing and conserving sufficient food to insure that not only our allies but we ourselves may be kept free from the pangs of hunger and threatening starvation. How the mere money cost of it all must be met by each individual's saving, thrift and doing without has been explained in the account of the war savings stamps and thrift stamps by means of which every man and woman, boy and girl may become a real enemy of the German kaiser, an actual defender of American liberty and American right, a fighter in the cause of democracy.

Never before in the history of our country or of any country has there been offered to every citizen, even our school boys and girls, an opportunity such as is now laid before you. Yours is the privilege of practicing the homely virtue of thrift, of doing without the unessential things, of saving your nickels and your dimes for the purchase of war savings stamps. By your sacrifice our armies can be equipped and the forces of our allies supplied. In the victory that must be ours you will have nobly done your share.

Boys and girls of Vermont, sons and daughters of a state that has never yet failed our nation in time of need, lead on to victory!

Source: Clyde M. Hill and John M. Avery, *The War Book* (Montpelier: Vermont State Board of Education, 1918), pp. 76-78.

DOCUMENT 3

On Women Entering Politics (1920)

BERNICE BROMLEY

Interviewee: Bernice Bromley
Interviewer: Samuel B. Hand
Date: July 1981
Place: Ormand Beach, Florida

I became involved [in politics] in 1920 when Mr. James Hartness announced his candidacy for governor. We were living in Springfield and Mr. Bromley was working at the Jones & Lamson. Mr. Hartness was the president and he had been very sympathetic to Jim's problems as they dealt with a widowed mother and the responsibilities attendant thereto. And Jim had felt a great feeling of gratitude for Mr. Hartness so he suggested that possibly we could offer our services in some way in his candidacy. So I went to the office and offered my services as a volunteer, and they were pleased I guess to have me.

Anyway, I did volunteer my services and it was my first insight into a political statewide campaign. I realized Mr. Hartness was a political neophyte, that he

President WILSON ISSUES CALL FOR MEN

To Fill Emergency Allowance of Navy

AT ONCE!

Nation's First Line of Defense to be Fully Prepared for all Emergencies

Thousands of Young Men between 17 and 30 years of age wanted

A Call to "GREEN MOUNTAIN BOYS" to "RALLY ROUND THE FLAG"

Your Postmaster is Waiting to Give You Information

Navy Recruiting Stations at
**P. O. BLDG., Burlington, Vt.
7 UNION BLOCK, Montpelier, Vt.
51½ Merchant's Row, Rutland, Vt.**

Young Men: "Heed that Call One and All"

Document 1

had never participated in any politics, even in the town. He was a man of great fame and renown because he was an inventor and been in the machine tool business all his life. He was so respected and loved that I expect that that is the thing that seemed to transfer itself into the various communities where we were looking for help. . . . He was the victor over three opponents and then, of course, was elected in the November election.

Mr. Hartness was a man that gave orders and did not take them, and what he didn't realize was that he was going to encounter a very strong political machine in Montpelier that was going to try to avoid any changes which he might make. He was—it must have been a dream of his—I never realized why he wanted to be governor, what he had in mind, but whatever it was he had difficulty from the very beginning. It was a very stormy time for him because, as I say, those men who dominated the state political scene were not willing to give in to him. But he served his . . . one term, with distinction and honor and was perfectly satisfied that he had attained what he wanted to accomplish and resorted to his telescope and observatory which was very famous in the Springfield area. He was very much interested in astronomy, as well as the machine tool. And personally I feel that probably he was one of the outstanding, honest, and I will emphasize honest, governors that the state had.

I think the way the campaign for governor was run must have made a very lasting impression on me and really it heated my blood. Observing what was good in politics, and from there I tried to take an interest locally. I was on a committee of fifteen which studied the articles for the town meeting, and that in those days was a real spectacle. Battle lines were drawn and the pros and cons hurled and assaulted each other. And [I] loved it, and I said it—and I know that it went on for years, and then finally, Springfield adopted a town manager's system and that seemed to alleviate a lot of that bad blood.

And then I rang door bells for the Women's Republican Club. It was more active at that time than the town Republican Committee and I was trying to get memberships for twenty-five cents, and I know I had all sorts of experiences. One woman told me that politics was a dirty word. And another woman told me that a woman's place was in her home. And then a woman said to me, "Now who are you?" And I said, "I'm Bernice Bromley." She says, "Oh, you're a politician, what do you want to get out of this." And I said, "I just want to keep the Republican Party alive." Then I left her. And those were the days that women had to be coerced into politics. I'll put it that way, I don't know how else to say it. They were very indifferent. But still they complained about the way the men ran it, they weren't willing to participate.

And then Mrs. I. R. Doane and I were elected by the town committee to be delegates in Burlington at the state convention. Now I don't remember the date, but we went and we heard by accident that there was to be a county caucus and we hadn't been notified, but we decided we would go and we had our first introduction to the term so frequently used by politicians "smoke-filled room," and when we went in we weren't too welcomed. We were the only two women there. But after a while they extended us the courtesy of seating us and making us feel that we were a part of the meeting. And the next morning when we went to the convention hall we stood beside two men; one of them tore his ticket in two to make the other candidate a delegate so that he could be seated, and we kind of raised our eyebrows at that. There wasn't too much that interested us in this state convention, because we didn't know very much about it, but a floor fight developed for national committeeman and we were interested in that. And then we were known to be present because somebody wanted our vote. And, of course, we supported the man from Windsor County, Mr. James Dewey.

In 1937 we moved to Ascutney Village. My sister and I had been interested in a very attractive house there, really an old landmark that had been very well preserved, and we had in mind having our guest house—which is a glorified name for a tourist home— and when it went on the market we prevailed upon my father, Charles Vail, and my husband, Jim Bromley, to finance us. And so we went into the business. And, aside from our activity in the church, we didn't do much for two or three years because we were busy establishing our business. Fortunately at that time we could get very good help. Finally we went to town meetings, and they had a moderator that would recognize you if you would observe the three S's: speak up, shut up and sit down. And I would speak up but not always shut up, and then I would have the gavel rapped and tell me I was out of order. And then, I became known I guess of my habit of trying to stress a point, possibly beyond reasoning, but I was built that way. . . . One day I saw in the paper where there was to be a Republican town caucus for the purpose of electing delegates to the state convention. And I said to my sister, "I believe I will go." It was to be held in Perkinsville at the town office at two o'clock. So, I took myself over there and went in and there was nobody there. But presently a man came in and introduced himself as Mr. John Hicks, chairman of the town Republican committee. And after a very short time he said I don't believe anybody else is going to come to this meeting, so I will call it to order and will nominate you as a delegate to the state convention. And I said, "Well, Mr. Hicks, you can't really do that can you?" And he said, "Oh yes, I can and I do." And I said, "Well in that case I could nominate you and I do." So with that he said that there's no more business to come before the meeting and he adjourned it.

Then we were protested very vigorously by several townspeople who were not sufficiently interested to attend the meeting but . . . wanted to do something about us nominating ourselves to be delegates. But after some embarrassment and humiliation we were seated at the convention. And from then on I began to wonder why people were not interested in the town Republican committee. So, I got after the people in Ascutney and got them to attend meetings and to show some interest, and they did. They were good Republicans, they just felt, I guess, that their services weren't required. There was a great deal of disinterest, not only in Weathersfield but all over the state of Vermont. Not too much active participation in the Republican party.

As I look back I don't know how these things happened, but I was elected by the Town Republican Committee as a member of the County Committee. And I served on that committee for some time and eventually was elected to the State Committee. I served two years as secretary, and one year on the Executive Board, and I'm under the impression that it was something like ten years that I was on that committee. . . . I served until I saw some manifestation of interest on the part of another woman to take my place. I felt that I had served long enough and was perfectly willing to have somebody else take my place, but I hadn't seen any indication of anyone being interested. And then I did

find some interest, so I nominated Margaret Hammond of Baltimore, a very outstanding legislator, to take my place on the State Committee. . . .

Source: Transcript, "Bernice Vail Bromley Oral History," pp. 1-5, Folklore and Oral History Collection, Special Collections, Bailey/Howe Library, University of Vermont. Reprinted courtesy of Special Collections, UVM Libraries.

DOCUMENT 4

The Barre Granite Strike (1922)

Labor troubles were very much on the minds of Barre residents. In the three interviews that follow, the widow of a granite cutter, a rank-and-file union militant, and the grande dame of Barre each spoke of "the big strike" of 1922. During the early months of the strike, quarry owners brought in hundreds of poor French-Canadian farmers as strike-breakers. They were paraded up Main Street to the music of bands and fed free Sunday dinners of chicken and ice cream. Eventually the quarry owners succeeded in breaking the strike and it took the unions of Barre years to recover.

— Ann Banks

Mrs. Lachance

I don't know much about the big strike. My husband struck along with the rest of them. I used to hear him talk about it a lot, but you hear so little about it now that I've forgotten. I *do* remember my husband saying that some of the unskilled French who came in to break the strike could be excused. That was quite a statement from my husband; he was as much against them as anybody. One of those strike-breakers was a friend of his. They'd grown up together in Chambly, good friend. He hadn't seen or heard from him for years, then all of a sudden he sees him parading through town with the rest of them. My husband was dazed; he could hardly believe it. This friend, Pete was his name, came up to the house to see my husband the next day. His farm, like so many other French farms that year, wasn't paying. The crops amounted to nothing. He had a wife and three children to feed. He could see no signs of work for him in Chambly. Then this opportunity for work in Barre came to him. Work meant keeping his family together.

Can you blame him for accepting it? I don't. He'd never worked in granite. He'd heard, of course, of Barre and the granite workers. But he knew of them vaguely, just as he knew of miners and steelworkers. I mean, how hard the work was, and dangerous. But he had to be amongst the workers, live with them and do their work, before he could really appreciate the fact that they needed a strike to better their conditions. I haven't seen much of him since my husband died. But I know he's a union man now, and a good one.

— Mari Tomasi

Manuel Terel

Of the some 150 non-union men in the Barre district, most of them are French. I ought to know. A bunch of squawkers and suckers. They've come up to me and pulled their sob story. "Look," they complain, "my work is as good as So-and-so's. He gets his eight-fifty a day, I get only five dollars. I'm worth as much as he is. I put in just as much time. You've got to help me. What can I do about it?" I should tell them to go to hell. I should say: "You were satisfied to sneak up to some shed boss behind the union's back and get your miserable five or six dollars a day. You've got no right to bellyache now. Get out." I *should* tell them that. But the union has rules. I have to stick to them. O.K., I tell them, you've been working for five dollars a day for a year, huh? O.K. then, pay up the union dues for that period and you'll get your union wages.

Those French spoiled everything for us back in '22. We'd have a lot more today if it hadn't been for those strike-breaking rats. Farmers, bakers, anyone who had hands to work with. Some of 'em had never seen granite, I bet.

You know what we should have done? We should have massed together, all of us, down at the Montpelier railroad station, and the Barre station. We should have met them at the train. Warned them to keep out. We'd have kept them out. It wouldn't have come to a good fight. They're too yellow for that. But the union wasn't so strong then, it wasn't what it is today. Today it would be easy.

— Mari Tomasi

Miss Wheaton
(fictitious name)

Living quietly here as I do, I know little of labor troubles and less of the granite industry.

I remember little of the strike of '22. I often sit by the window, and I did those days, but I remember no parade and no militia. There was a feeling of oppression in the air, and I felt that plans were being laid in secret. Plans that we outside the granite industry knew nothing of. I saw clusters of men, groups of them hurrying along the street on their way to various halls where they held meetings. Their voices were loud and harsh, raised in anger. They waved their arms and shook their fists. It was all very disturbing. My mother was alive then. Just she, and the housekeeper and myself in the house. The strike made no disorder or confusion in our tenor of living. Not during the day. At night we heard the tramp-tramp of feet on the pavement outside the house. There was much shouting. Cars kept roaring by, going I don't know where. In spite of locked doors and windows, I found it all very disconcerting. I had no inclination to sleep.

I remember vaguely of workers being injured during the strike, and of riots, but I have forgotten the details. I do know that the last granite strike caused a great deal of temporary poverty and need. One Barre charitable organization that I am acquainted with reported thirty new families added to their lists for temporary assistance. Most of the aid was in the form of food; a few families accepted clothing that had been contributed by various ladies of the organization.

It seems to me that if strikes in attaining their end must cause such need and injury, then certainly they are no solution to labor conditions. Perhaps the granite workers were justified in asking for more pay and less hours. It's hard work, and injurious to health. I know that many of these workers have good-sized families. I'm not well acquainted with them. I don't have to be to know that death from stonecutters' tuberculosis has struck members of several of these families. For about fifty years I have read the same pitiful stories repeated in the obituaries in the Barre *Daily Times*:

"Mr. A_____, aged fifty, died today after an illness of several months. Since coming to this country he has been employed as stonecutter in the local sheds. He was a member of the Granite Cutters' Union. Surviving him are his wife, three sons, and a daughter."

— Mari Tomasi

Source: Ann Banks, ed., *First-Person America* (New York: Alfred A. Knopf, 1980; revised ed., New York: W. W. Norton, 1990), pp. 109-113. Interviews conducted in 1938 and 1939. Reprinted with permission of Ann Banks.

DOCUMENT 5

"Review of Eugenics in Vermont" (1926)

HENRY F. PERKINS

The casual reader sometimes gets the idea that advocates of Eugenics are confirmed pessimists looking on the dark side of life, and foreseeing nothing but degeneration and final ruin. Of course the constant study of bad conditions amongst people does tend to depress anyone, unless he can look beyond the immediate state of things and see some chance for improvement. The best thing about Eugenics is just that chance for improvement; and it is the duty and pleasure of everyone interested in the subject to point out possible chances for improvement in particular communities.

The fine old stock of original settlers in Vermont, Warner and the Allens and their ilk, were amongst the best human material that was at hand when the new Republic was formed. We are tempted to ask what has become of that fine old stock. Isn't there any of it left here in Vermont? Of course there is, lots of it—I almost said plenty of it, but that would not be true. There is not enough to guarantee the continuance of the old ideals, the old energy. If Vermont is to be a safe place for Vermonters, indeed if she is to be the mother of statesmen and presidents and other national leaders, the "good stock" must be increased. There is no need of its being the "good *old* stock" providing the additions that are made are of the right sort. Good blood, from whatever country, added to and mixed with the good Yankee blood which is to be found in every community, makes for better communities, a better Vermont. Modern science, in the guise of Eugenics, offers us of Vermont, a simple and practical means of continuing the splendid traditions of pioneer days. There are more Vermonters now, with the grit, the intelligence, the unselfish devotion of our first pioneers, than there were a hundred and fifty years ago. The trouble is that the less valuable element in the population has increased much more than the good element.

Almost every thinking person has devised his own explanation for the running down hill that seems to be observable in our Vermont population. The student of the problem asks some pertinent questions, such as:

"Is it true that the population of Vermont is going down hill in quality?" "What are some of the apparent reasons for this condition, if it is true?" "What would check the downward progress?" "Is there any chance that remedies could be made to seem official enough to bring about their adoption?"

The war draft examiners turned in some very unpleasant figures to Washington. . . . The Draft Boards found an excessive amount of feeble mindedness, and other mental defects amongst our men. A number of physical defects like spinal curvature, eye troubles and asthma (which is perhaps not a physical defect), were also found in excessive numbers of the applicants for draft examinations. Only one other state had so large a proportion of its young men of draft age rejected because of physical and mental defects. . . .

[One possible reason it] showed up badly is that Vermont is constantly skimming off the cream of her younger population . . . the taste for city life has been the cause of a great deal of emigration from Vermont. Either actually or apparently, young men and young women can find better chances for making their way in the cities than in the country. Those who stay in Vermont do so for one of these reasons: circumstances offer them a good chance for a livelihood and self-improvement; or home ties, dependent and aged relatives make it seem wrong for them to move away, or ambition is lacking. Undoubtedly the last reason is the one that keeps a good many of the less well equipped bodies and minds here in Vermont, while those who are more ambitious and fit, physically and mentally, move out and find openings elsewhere. Were it not for the home ties, and the ability to recognize and make the most of good opportunities at home, Vermont would soon be drained of all her best blood. Already too much of it has slowed into other channels.

The two ways of improving the population are, first to encourage larger families amongst the physically and mentally fit; . . . second, to bring about, by one means or another, a less rapid increase in the "unfit" part of our population—those who are unable, through misfortune or depravity, to bear their share of the community burden, or even maintain themselves and their children. No doubt we all have a more or less definite idea that a large part of the money paid into the state and town treasuries in taxes, has to go for the support of dependents and criminals. Probably most of us would do well to find out more exactly where our tax money really does go. Is there not a way of looking at the matter from a commercial angle? Cannot the number of tax payers be increased rather than the number of absorbers be decreased? Various communities have attempted some sort of study of the conditions governing these problems. Usually some prison commission or other official organization, more or less connected with state politics, makes some attempt to analyze the social and non-social elements in the state or area under consideration. Here in Vermont a somewhat unique experiment has been carried on during the past year, an experiment conducted by entirely non-partisan and unofficial workers, and financed by private means. While this study has not been ambitious in its extent or in its aims, some highly interesting information has been collected, and some rather definite proposals for improving the population of Vermont can be made as a result. . . .

The results of the investigation are briefly and partially as follows:

1. There are comparatively few families in Vermont—and we have studied fifteen of them with considerable thoroughness—that have contributed very heavily in the wrong direction. They may have been the cause of heavy expense to the state instead of a source of financial or moral help to it. This expense has been in court costs, through the arrest, trials and commitment of criminals; the damage to property done, without running into the clutches of the law, by petty thieving, willful destruction of property, fishing and hunting contrary to law, and many other minor offenses, the total of which is formidable. The heaviest charge against these families is that they have cost the tax payers of the State large sums for maintenance in prisons, jails, asylums and Reform Schools. They have cost the towns large sums for their maintenance in poor houses or as recipients of help from the poor master.

The financial cost to the state of certain single families has been rather carefully worked out and it appears that in the case of at least three families not less than one-half a million dollars has been drawn from the public funds to combat the deficiency and delinquency of their members. The estimating of such costs is a matter for experts in economics. It is highly important that such a study should be made on the basis of the information accumulated by this Survey. Plainly, how-

ever, no more exact figures are really needed to persuade us that we, the tax payers, are contributing pretty heavily for the benefit of a few degraded families. Those who have fallen upon hard times and misfortunes, and are in need of help through no fault of their own or ours, should, or course, be supported,—and the poor we have with us always. It is in the preventing of these cases that the Survey is interested.

In the course of our study of certain selected families it has come to light that certain outstanding characteristics can be assigned to practically every family. There are what may be called undertones of defectiveness or criminality or disease, but in most cases a single peculiarity seems to have been responsible for a large part of the bad history of the tribe, and appears to be very strongly inherited.

Family A, for example, comes of a strain . . . of a mixed ancestry with apparently very strong doses of Indian and Negro. This whole family numbering well over 150 individuals retains its ancestor's roving or Gypsy tendency. They are horse traders, fortune tellers and basket makers.

Family B, is characterized by Huntington's Chorea. There are a number of other families from which some hereditable defect comes to light at frequent intervals. This defect may not be the cause of the poor record but rather a result of the same cause. At any rate, if it is nothing more than a label, it serves to bring about an unfortunate state of things that is bound to continue as a hindrance and an expense to the community.

If a railroad accident occurs, the first thing to do is to give first aid to the injured and clear away the wreckage. After that everyone wants to know what happened, how it happened and how similar accidents can be prevented in the future. That is the only way any progess in measures of safety has been accomplished. After such a study as had been made during this survey it is impossible to avoid raising the question, after we have given first aid to the injured and cleared away some of the wreckage: Is there some way of preventing similar accidents in the future? The way of modern enlightened philanthropy is to look beyond the segregation and training of mental defectives and the custody of criminals and to see whether there is any scientifically approved method of checking the reoccurance of such calamities. While it is the sole purpose of the Eugenics

Survey of Vermont to get hold of a reasonable amount of reasonably accurate information bearing upon the mental and physical status of the population, certain rather definite recommendations have inevitably occurred to the members of the Advisory Committee. . . .

In conclusion, the Survey has fulfilled its purpose which was to gather information and make it available for future use. It paves the way for constructive legislation and community service.

Source: *Vermont Review*, 1 (September-October 1926): 56-59.

DOCUMENT 6

Speech to Congress on the 1927 Flood (1928)

REPRESENTATIVE ELBERT S. BRIGHAM

Mr. Speaker, H.R. 9767, introduced by my colleague, Mr. Gibson, and reported favorably by the Committee on Roads, authorizes an appropriation of $2,654,000 for the relief of Vermont in the matter of highways damaged by flood. It is my purpose to outline briefly the reasons why representatives of Vermont are asking for this appropriation.

The newspapers have carried such a complete story of the flood which descended upon Vermont in November, 1927, that you are probably already somewhat familiar with the destruction of property which it caused and the toil of human life which it levied. The people of Vermont are now face to face with the difficult problem of rehabilitation.

The legislative reference service of the Library of Congress has compiled a list of the acts passed by the Congress for the relief of those who have suffered from calamities of various kinds. These acts go back to 1803 and revised to date would include [two Mississippi Valley flood relief] bill[s] passed in the opening days of this session of Congress . . . .

If you will go through this list of acts, going back a century and a quarter, you will find none for the relief of the State of Vermont or of any political subdivision thereof. I believe that this is the first time that representatives of Vermont in the 136 years of its membership in the Union have appeared before a committee of Congress, asking for relief. Such calamities as we have had heretofore have been within the capacity of our self-reliant people to meet. I assure you that we appear here now only because a disaster has befallen our State so overwhelming that it is without parallel in her history.

We are accustomed these days to think of things in terms of size. Because of this the attention of the Nation is, and has been for months, centered upon the flood disaster in the valley of the Mississippi. I wish in no way to minimize the terrible disaster which has overtaken our people in the Mississippi Valley. Figures as well as pictures tell a story of appalling destruction there. Nor do I question their dire need of assistance nor the wisdom of an emergency measure which carried with it the expenditure of $7,000,000 in their behalf, but it does give me confidence to bring our needs to your attention, and it does give me the hope that in proportion as our needs equal theirs we may look for like assistance. Let us, then, in order to grasp the extent of the Vermont flood disaster compare for a moment the damage done to our little State with the damage done to the several States which suffered from the Mississippi flood. This comparison should, I think, be made in terms of relative population and wealth, so the problems presented to the people and the government of each of the several afflicted States may by comparison be made more clear.

The following table shows the relative population, area, and total flood damage done to the Mississippi Valley States and to Vermont and translates these losses in terms of their meaning to the persons involved and their ability to meet them:

(see next page for table)

You will see from this comparison that only the three lower Mississippi Valley States of Arkansas, Mississippi, and Louisiana suffered a total flood damage exceeding that of Vermont. You will see also that the damage per person in Vermont was more than three times the damage per person in the average of the Mississippi States worst afflicted, and the damage per million dollars of State wealth, which means capacity to meet loss, in Vermont is more than twice that suffered by Arkansas, more than three times that suffered by Louisiana, and is more than one-half greater than that suffered by the State of Missis-

State	Population, 1920	Area in square miles	Flood damage, 1927	Wealth in thousands, 1922	Par capita flood damage	Flood damage per million dollars of State wealth
Arkansas............................	1,752,204	53,335	37,948,919	2,599,617	21.66	14,600
Illinois................................	6,485,280	56,665	16,765,465	22,232,794	2.59	750
Kentucky............................	2,416,630	40,598	3,295,750	3,582,391	1.37	674
Louisiana...........................	1,798,509	48,506	38,389,814	3,416,860	21.35	11,240
Mississippi........................	1,790,618	46,865	45,931,294	2,177,690	25.65	21,090
Missouri.............................	3,404,055	69,420	7,691,265	9,981,409	2.26	770
Tennessee..........................	2,416,630	42,022	5,958,950	4,228,251	2.47	1,410
Vermont.............................	352,428	9,564	30,435,299	842,040	86.35	36,146

sippi—the three States sustaining the greatest flood damage in the Mississippi Valley.

This, I think, will make clear to the membership of the House what a flood loss of $30,435,299 visited upon a small rural State with a small population, means to the people of that State, and will explain why we, as representatives of that State, are here asking you to pass a bill which will grant help from the Federal Government to our people in meeting a difficult problem.

Relief Limited to Public Works

Our request for relief is limited to the rehabilitation of public works—namely, roads. Our losses to private property have borne heavily upon farmers, business men, and corporations. One of our main railroad lines is in the hands of a receiver and will probably not resume normal operations for months to come. Other lines have spent millions to repair damages. Many farmers and business men have lost their savings of a lifetime and are being assisted to carry on by the Red Cross, by private gifts, by loans from the Vermont flood corporations, from banks, and from various other sources. We are asking for no appropriation to help our people meet losses of this kind. You can readily see, however, that the tax-paying ability of our people is greatly impaired, and it is extremely difficult for a small State to meet the tremendous burden imposed and, for years to come, next to impossible for it unassisted to carry on its normal activities.

Vermont is, as you know, a mountainous State. Its river valleys as they cut across or run parallel to the mountain ranges are for the most part narrow and hemmed in by hills on either side. The main roads are located in these valleys and received the full force of the rushing water, which could be likened in its fury but to a storm at sea. When the flood waters receded Vermont found herself practically without a road system in large areas of the State. Roads and bridges which it had taken a century to construct were destroyed in one short day. Photographs well illustrate this.

As soon as the extent of the damage was known the State highway department laid plans for making temporary repairs in order to make it possible to deliver the mails and to transport food and supplies to the towns and cities which were cut off from rail transportation. The cooperation of local town officials in this work was splendid. I heard an Army engineer pay tribute to the resourcefulness of Vermont town officials who in a remarkably short space of time threw temporary bridges of logs and plank across rivers and smaller streams and filled great gullies in roads so that traffic could get through. I am informed that the temporary road repairs alone will cost nearly $1,000,000.

Then came the problem of permanent reconstruction. . . .

Vermont's Highway Problem

The highway problem in Vermont has been the subject of a recent cooperative study by the United States Bureau of Public Roads and the Vermont highway department. This bureau in conjunction with the State highway department made a survey of traffic on the Vermont highways in 1926. Upon this survey and upon predictions as to future needs, recommendations were made in a report recently released as to what Vermont should do in the way of future road construction. Up to 1923 roads constructed in Vermont were principally of gravel surfaces. They were not in all cases the best roads but they were such as we could pay for. It became apparent, however, that on our main routes, including the Federal-aid designated system and some of the State roads a surface superior to gravel was necessary because traffic had increased to the point where the cost of maintenance of gravel surfaces made the construction of a surface superior to gravel necessary. The report recommends a construction program for the years 1927-1931 of 275 miles of surface superior to gravel on the principal routes, which are Federal-aid routes, with a probable cost of another $12,000,000. The regular annual Federal-aid allotment for Vermont is $365,000. This 10-year program would cost a total of $24,000,000. This program of construction was entered upon by the Vermont Legislature of 1927, and during the last year 47.2 miles of hard-surface roads have been constructed at a cost of $1,877,247.

Now, this survey also shows that Vermont roads— and I presume this is true of the roads of all the States — have taken on an interstate and international character. It showed that on our Federal-aid routes and on nearly 1,000 miles of our State-aid system about 35.6 per cent of total passenger-car traffic and 9.6 per cent of the truck traffic was foreign traffic. . . .The burden thrown upon Vermont roads by this foreign traffic is indicated by the paragraph from the report:

The large volume of foreign traffic on Vermont highways adds considerable to the cost of providing highway service on the main routes of travel. This volume of foreign traffic, in addition to local Vermont traffic, results in increased maintenance costs on present improvements, which are loaded beyond their economic capacity, and makes necessary earlier improvements or reconstruction of these routes by the construction of surfaces superior to gravel. The present contribution of foreign traffic to Vermont highways revenue is limited very largely to that derived from the taxation of gasoline sold to operators of foreign cars, and it is doubtful if this revenue is at all commensurate with the increased cost of providing highway service caused by foreign traffic.

Now, Vermont wants to keep her place with her sister States in the line of progress. She wants to provide roads for foreign traffic as well as for her own people, and her policies were being formulated to that end before the recent disaster overtook her.

Vermont is a dairy State, marketing her products in the form of milk and cream. According to a recent survey, made by the United States Department of Agriculture, Boston depends upon Vermont for 62 per cent of her milk and 50 per cent of her cream supply. Other New England cities and New York also obtain from our dairies substantial quantities. These products are perishable and must move from farm to market every day. Unless our roads are restored these cities will obtain with difficulty an essential food supply and the main business of our State will be disrupted.

From the figures presented as to cost of rehabilitating our highway system, you will see that the State of Vermont will have to pay more than seven and three-fourths millions of dollars for permanent reconstruction, in addition to nearly a million dollars already spent for temporary construction. This is more than a small State like ours can bear and expect to do anything in the way of new construction. Therefore we are asking the Federal Government in this bill to assume the cost of reconstructing that part of our highways known as the Federal-aid system.

Source: *Congressional Record,* 70th Cong., 1st Sess., 69: 4880-4881.

Document 7

"Vermont Is a State I Love" (1928)

President Calvin Coolidge

Vermont is a state I love. I could not look upon the peaks of Ascutney, Killington, Mansfield and Equinox without being moved in a way that no other scene could move me.

It was here that I first saw the light of day; here I received my bride; here my dead lie pillowed on the loving breast of our everlasting hills. I love Vermont because of her hills and valleys, her scenery and invigorating climate, but most of all, because of her indomitable people. They are a race of pioneers who have almost beggared themselves to serve others. If the spirit of liberty should vanish in other parts of the union and support of our institutions should languish, it could all be replenished from the generous store held by the people of this brave little state of Vermont.

Bennington, Vermont, September 21, 1928

Source: Reprint of extract of speech, undated, Calvin Coolidge ephemera file, Special Collections, Bailey/Howe Library, University of Vermont.

DOCUMENT 8

Inaugural Address (1933)

GOVERNOR STANLEY WILSON

Vermont has suffered from unemployment and consequent necessity for poor relief less than most states. This does not mean, however, that we have been immune. In 1931 I appointed a State Committee on unemployment which acted in conjunction with President Hoover's Unemployment Committee, largely as a fact finding commission and a clearing house for information and suggested relief.

In 1932 we effected a coordination of several of the public relief and unemployment agencies including the above, the Mayors Committee, the Share-the-Work Committee, the Red Cross, the Committee for Trade Recovery, and representatives of the local overseers of the poor. The work has been quietly organized and apportioned. Improved methods of poor relief to avoid doles, eliminate frauds, spread work and create new work have been put in operation wherever cooperation could be secured.

The state itself through the highway department and the forestry department have aided materially in furnishing employment to those in need. . . .

The banking record of Vermont is unique in that during the past two years no bank in the state has closed its doors. The record is a strong testimonial to the stability of our financial institutions, the conservatism of our bankers and the good sense of our people who own the deposits in our banks. . . . Banks are a great benefit to the state and to the communities in which they are located. Our people rely upon them for the protection of their savings, for a convenient and safe medium of commercial transactions involving money payments, and for the credit facilities needed for the conduct of business. A great part of the loans of our banks are made upon mortgages on the farms and homes of our own people. It is also to be remembered that the banks contribute annually over a million dollars to our state treasury in taxes.

General business conditions during the past three years have made it difficult for banks as well as for individuals. When individuals, because of reduced earning, do not have money to pay their loans, the banks do not have those funds to finance other individuals. . . . In times of depression it is natural that bank depositors desire to draw upon their savings for use. . . . Throughout the country, due largely to the present abnormal conditions, there have been a great many bank failures. . . . In view of the misfortunes which have come to the banking institutions in many states and the serious financial conditions which prevail the country over, we will be derelict in our duty if we fail to provide every reasonable safeguard for our banking institutions. . . .

I believe governmental costs should be reduced. I believe the cost of town and city government should be reduced. To shift burdens from the towns to the state does not relieve the burden of taxation, although it may effect a different distribution of that burden and may secure greater efficiency. To cut off a state endeavor that is deemed essential will not relieve the burden. It will simply cast it on the several communities.

Probably we have no state endeavors that do not have merit. Some are absolutely essential to the continuance of our functioning as a state. Others are essential according to modern standards. We must reduce our expenditures both state and local to reduce taxes . . . with estimated annual revenues more than a million dollars below the annual appropriations . . . we must reduce expenditures to balance the budget.

Your work as legislators is especially important this session. Legislative action will be watched this year by the people as seldom before. These times of depression have brought forth a multitude of radical suggestions the country over. You will doubtless have some presented to you.

Source: *Journal of the Senate*, January 5, 1933 (Montpelier, 1933): 500-517.

DOCUMENT 9

Ethnic Politics in Winooski (1935)

RUSSELL NIQUETTE

Interviewee: Russell Niquette
Interviewer: Samuel B. Hand
Date: July 14, 1980
Place: Russell Niquette's Law Office in Winooski, Vermont

H. [Nineteen] thirty-five you became Winooski city attorney?

N. First of all, I graduated from law school in nineteen hundred and thirty-three. I was admitted to the bar in nineteen hundred and thirty-four. And in 1935 I got into my first political fight. The city council of the city of Winooski—Winooski is a very small city, you'll notice, it is only 7,000 people—and the peculiar thing is that it was just about that in nineteen hundred and thirty-five. It hasn't grown because of the fact it is so small and it hasn't any place to expand. It's only 850 acres—one square mile. It has only about eleven miles of street which is very little. A lot of people say eleven miles sounds a lot to them, but there are hundreds of miles in practically every town in the state of Vermont let alone cities. In nineteen hundred and thirty-five I was elected city attorney after a very bitter fight among four councilmen and the mayor. At that time it was Mayor [John E.] Kelty, who is still living. He lives up here next to the French church on Weaver Street. Now, the city attorney at the time was Allen [H. A.] Bailey, a well-known fellow in the state of Vermont, a well-known politician. And he lived in Winooski, born here, his family lived here—he was a Yankee, a real Yankee, and I say that because Winooski, you know, used to be all Yankee once upon a time, although it turned to be all French later. But H. A. Bailey, by the way, is the man who married Consuelo Northrop, and Consuelo Northrop had a great history of her own in the legislature, state's attorney and otherwise running for office—for national office.

  Now, I was elected city attorney by a close vote of two-to-two on the city council at that time. Two of them being for Mr. Bailey to be reelected because he was then the city attorney, and two of them for me, and those two were two Frenchmen. And that's the reason why. They voted for another Frenchman, me.

H. Bailey was a Republican?

N. Bailey was a *strong*, conservative Republican and so was his wife Consuelo, who was his second wife, by the way. His first wife—I knew her too—a very fine woman. H. A. Bailey — was a very fine man. He died—he was sick for a long time because he had what you called that sleeping sickness, whatever that is, you know, that you close your eyes practically all the time [Parkinson's disease]. It was really pitiful to watch him during his later years of life.

  Well anyhow, the mayor stood for one hour, you wouldn't believe this, without saying a word, and the whole council waiting for his vote. I was not there. Didn't want to be there. Didn't care about the office of city attorney. I was just a graduate of law school only a year and I wanted more experience, especially being a Frenchman, I needed more experience because all of my high school and all of my college years were done in St. Hyacinthe, Quebec, in a French school. And the only English that I had up there was one hour a week. And so when I got back here and was ready to go to law school, I thought I should go to some school and learn English, and I went to Burlington Business College—that's all before my becoming city attorney or a lawyer. And they had special courses in grammar, special courses in English and in history. Strange as it may seem, I had just barely had a history of the United States having been to Montreal five long years, six long years. I say Montreal, but St. Hyacinthe is thirty miles east of Montreal—it's a real educational city, very fine city, too.

  I give you that because it was my first political fight where I really had no interest in it at all. It was between the council people instead. And so after an hour or so and John Kelty voted for Russell Niquette and that made it three to two and Bailey got right up — he sat there all through that hour, he did—and got up immediately and ran right across the street, and I don't think he ever spoke to John Kelty after that. It seems that John Kelty had promised him his vote. But I've never known that. I let that sleep.

Why is that important? Now why that is important is because as I told you a minute ago, being the city attorney for the city of Winooski was different than being a city attorney of the city of Burlington, and why? It is different because Winooski has on the city council people who probably had graduated—lucky if they had graduated from grammar school—so they knew very little about city business let alone politics. But they had been involved in these general politics—general politicians. Winooski being very much a French town, the whole town was probably uneducated any more than eight years, some of them high school, but not many of them. Any people going to high school thought they were going to [the equivalent of] college at that time. So they went right to work. They had to in order to maintain and help big families that they belonged to.

So the city attorney became the pivot point of the operations of the city council and all the city business. The mayor would not do a thing unless they called the city attorney. So I tried to do my best to try to remain friends with all of them the best I could without taking sides. And by doing that, of course, I got their friendship throughout—I never had anybody run against me all through the twenty-two years — and I gave it up after twenty-two years in order to allow the young attorney, Bill O'Brien from Winooski, to go in as city attorney. I guess he did and he stayed there a couple of years, and his mother never could thank me enough for helping a young lawyer like I did. Nobody else would do it, she said. . . .

Now that's the first twenty-two years of my life. . . . The same two Frenchmen who were on the city council were so glad and so proud that they were able to elect a Frenchman at that time as city attorney—the first for the city of Winooski. By the way, I was the first French lawyer in Winooski.

H. You have anticipated so many questions.

N. Two years after that in nineteen hundred and thirty-seven the two same Frenchmen came to see me and they said now they had another job for me. And what was that? And they said, "Representa-tive in the General Assembly in the state of Vermont." Well, they said I had to go. They claimed that a Frenchman hadn't been there for a long time, but I had to go to represent the people of Winooski, at least the French population which was ninety-five percent of the population of Winooski at that time.

And so as much as I didn't want to go: why, in the first place because I was poor, and in the second place I wanted more experience as a lawyer and as a city attorney, although I was going to remain the city attorney just the same. I couldn't refuse because it was probably the one opportunity knocking at the door in my life that I probably would never forget if I did refuse it. And especially because I couldn't afford it I said, it paid $300 a year, a session, how could I live—my family—with that, although at that time I had no children as yet. But I got married in 1937 in the very first year that I represented Winooski up there, in August, August the 10th I was married.

Now that was the beginning, of course, of my first experience in the legislature, and I was a greenhorn. I didn't go up there as a Democrat although I was a Democrat here. My father and folks were all Democrats and to my way of thinking it was just like a religion. I'm a Catholic and that was just another religion I belonged too—the Democrats. And so I remained Democrat all through my life. . . .

Source: Transcript, "Russell Niquette Oral History," pp. 1-4, Folklore and Oral History Collection, Special Collections, Bailey/Howe Library, University of Vermont. Reprinted with permission of Russell Niquette, Jr.

DOCUMENT 10

"The Conservation of Vermont Traditions and Ideals" (1931)

VERMONT COMMISSION ON COUNTRY LIFE

"If the spirit of liberty should vanish in other parts of the Union, and support of our institutions should languish, it could all be replenished from the generous store held by the people of the brave little State of Vermont." This sentence from ex-President Coolidge's "Bennington Address," now widely known, might well be taken as the keynote of a wide range of literature of varied kinds and types, including letters, journals, diaries, historical and social documents, novels, essays, poems, orations and speeches, in which the authors have praised various attributes and characteristics of the state and its people. The amount of such material, merely suggested here, is decidedly impressive; and much of it was written and spoken by men and women with no ties of allegiance to the state—in many cases by those who were in actual intent and purpose hostile, or, at least, unsympathetic toward Vermont.

The student of the subject might begin with the yellowing pages of a magazine published in Philadelphia in 1792, in which an unknown writer wrote of the state's people as those "who enjoy a liberty as pure as the air they breathe, which is not excelled on the globe. Health reigns and cheerfulness and vigor, those greatest of earthly treasures." Pondering a hundred references and more on his journey toward the present, the interested student might linger a moment on this statement by George Washington: "The country is very mountainous, full of defiles, and very strong. The inhabitants a hardy race, composed of that kind of people who are best calculated for soldiers; in truth who *are* soldiers," and close his study after covering a century and a half with the words of Sinclair Lewis, famous for his unhesitating directness and frankness of utterance: "I have never spent more than eight months in any one place, have traveled through thirty-six states and lived in eight or ten in addition to visiting eighteen foreign countries, but Vermont is the first place I have seen where I really wanted to have my home—a place to spend the rest of my life."

Though the emphasis on the characteristics of the people of the state can be directly or indirectly phrased, the total evidence, briefly indicated here, of appreciations of the state is significant, and must be accepted by the unbiased student as indicating values in *Green Mountain life and ways that merit consideration in any study of the problems of the state's future well-being.* The reasons for the existence to this day of pronounced traditional and idealistic qualities of mind and heart that give Vermont and Vermont folk their particular significance can be stated with some assurance of accuracy . . . the following factors would probably have their place: Factors of environment with elements of isolation, factors of association and heredity involving the "will-to-do" of a hardy, independent, liberty-loving, brave and individualistic people, still as stubborn as were their fathers in opposition to what they consider to be against their rights or whatever fails to appeal to their judgment and common sense.

The particular problem which the Committee on Traditions and Ideals faced was to find ways and means of preserving the distinctive values, repeatedly emphasized in the state's past and present, which have to do largely with immaterial rather than material possessions of any kind, and which are easily recognized in the history, literature, and the general life of the people. . .

[Our challenge is to combat] successfully the ceaseless change that in many of its aspects in this day and generation seems to be destroying so much of the life of the state that is traditional and idealistic. One of the problems lies in the very nature of the work to be done. Home, one of our Vermont poets has suggested, was never really *home* to the pioneer woman until she had her flower garden by the homestead door. Surely, one could not easily chart by any known technique the value of such flower gardens through the years to Vermont and Vermont people, yet only the thoughtless would argue that such gardens have had and do have no real value in creating something fine, even if intangible, in the lives of those touched by the gardens. Vermont was never a homeland, one of our essayists suggests, until on some pine-topped knoll or in some lot by road or lane, the pioneer laid his loved ones in their last sleep. This deep attachment, powerful as it is, escapes the analyst who would reduce it to a working formula and list it side by side with the findings of economic research. The values are there, nevertheless, and the problem.

Interesting and suggestive as a statement of the whole question are the words of the late Senator Frank L. Greene:

You and I as toilers in the treadmill of publicity, used to the drab and shabby and seamy side of human nature as well as to the brilliant spectacle now and then, know full well how far short of its ideals our race and its civilization fall. Sometimes, I have no doubt you feel as I do, that perhaps the present-day generation is not quite as keenly alive to the sentimental influence of the old traditions about some things as its fathers and mothers used to be, and that, too, making all allowance for the customary distrust of the rising generation in every period that is so characteristic of men in a generation that is no longer "rising."

Sometimes, we are moved to wonder whether our people are actually losing something of their ancient attachment to institutional life and forms and rituals (I mean the healthy part of them that makes for steadfastness and loyalty to something definite and worthy) and are drifting carelessly and flippantly along with the current, and nothing more. Sometimes we are moved to wonder whether the ancient Green Mountain Boys' tradition and all that it meant to their day and down to the present time is in this period a living, inspiring influence in the minds of most men and women we meet on the streets.

. . . The effort to recreate, to vivify, to clarify, and then to conserve. . . the traditions and ideals of the state must be only a part in a program that gathers strength from every fibre of its texture. Such a program, the present writer assumes, should emerge from the work of the committees under the Vermont Commission; and the program involves, in the last analysis, the question of leadership. To quote from President [John M.] Thomas [Middlebury College]:

It is not beyond reason to hope that the tides of population may be turned back again to the fields, that the old towns of the State, which have been losing ground for half a century, may regain their prestige, and that the State as a whole, instead of being saved from actual loss only by the commercial centers and the quarrying towns, may take her place again as one of the most healthfully vigorous and progressive of the American nation. The task is not more difficult than that which confronted the first leaders of Vermont, when a State on either side of us lusted for our territory, when a dallying Congress parried over our claims, when the army of England hung on our northern border—that glorious day of the independent republic of Vermont.

"When thy young flag was suddenly unfurled,
And thy lone eagle left his stormy nest,
Soaring above grim Mansfield's darkening crest,
And screamed defiance to the whole armed world."

The old stock is here still, in greater proportion to the total population than in any other commonwealth of the north. The old spirit is by no means dead. All we need is organization, the power and habit of working together for a fixed and determined purpose. And all we need for organization is leadership—leaders who see the goal plan, and who will consecrate themselves to its attaining in high patriotic devotion.

―――――――

Prepared for the Commission by its Committee on Vermont Traditions and Ideals.

Arthur W. Peach, Chairman

Sarah Cleghorn	Helen Hartness Flanders
Walter J. Coates	Bertha Oppenheim
Walter H. Crockett	J. D. Shannon
Zephine Humphrey Fahnestock	Mary Spargo
	Frederick Tupper

Dorothy Canfield Fisher

Source: Two Hundred Vermonters, *Rural Vermont: A Program for the Future* (Burlington, Vt.: Vermont Commission on Country Life, 1931), pp. 371-372, 383-385.

DOCUMENT 11

"Why People Should Favor the Green Mountain Parkway" (1936)

ERNEST H. BANCROFT

The question of whether or not the State of Vermont should cooperate with the Federal government to the extent of providing the right-of-way for a National Parkway to extend along the Green Mountain Range for the entire length of the state, will be settled by the freeman voters of the state in town meetings on the first Tuesday in March. I believe this is one of the most important questions that the voters of Vermont have been called upon to decide in many years. The decision that will be made at that time, I believe, will be far-reaching in its effect upon the future prosperity of the state and its people. . . .

I am . . . convinced that the construction of this proposed Green Mountain Parkway by the Federal government along the Green Mountain Range is one of those really great opportunities that is rarely presented to a state and its people. I will attempt briefly to state the reasons that caused me to arrive at this conclusion.

On June 15th, 1933, the Congress of the United States passed a National Appropriation Bill which provided three billion, three hundred million dollars for a Public Works Program. A year ago the Work Relief bill with another sum nearly 50% greater was enacted. There can be no question in anybody's mind but that Vermont must and will contribute her share through Federal Taxes to these tremendous appropriations and without regard to the amount of Public Works that will be undertaken within this state.

With the exception of the cost of the right-of-way . . . not to exceed five hundred thousand dollars, the tax burden upon the citizens of Vermont will be just as great if the eighteen million dollars estimated cost of construction is expended in some other state, as it surely will be if Vermont turns down this opportunity. The expenditure of this vast sum of money . . . in the towns and cities throughout the state, will certainly add a stimulus to business of all kinds that will be felt long after the last mile of construction is completed.

I think that we have every reason to believe that this scenic highway, if it is constructed, will when completed, be something in which the citizens of Vermont would forever take pride, that this would be true is no longer a matter of conjecture for we have the experience of other states who have already taken advantage of the Federal government's program of parkway construction. . . .

Virginia has completed and has in use sixty-four miles of the three hundred and forty-five miles which the state will have when the [Skyline Drive] is completed and . . . [the drive has already] proven to the people of Virginia to have been a highly successful venture and this conclusion seems to be borne out by the reports of our own citizens who have visited Virginia recently. . . . Those who have visited Virginia's beautiful "Skyline Drive" and have talked with the people report that there is general satisfaction and enthusiasm expressed by them and that the hotel people and proprietors of roadside camps are especially enthusiastic about the benefits that have accrued to them, because of the construction of this mountain highway. . . . How long are we going to continue to see Vermont money used to help develop and build prosperity in other states and refuse to take advantage of an opportunity to participate in it ourselves? How long are we going to listen to that siren song about keeping Vermont unspoiled, and shall we later complain when we see the youth of Vermont follow our money to more progressive states to establish there, their homes and live their lives?

Vermont, because of its location, will never become a great industrial state and it must fight desperately to maintain its present agricultural position. Our only opportunity for a greater degree of prosperity and greater opportunities for our youth seems to lie almost entirely in the direction of the development and extension of our tourist, recreational and summer house business, and I believe this Parkway offers an excellent opportunity to promote such a development in a big way. It has been argued that tourists will drive through the state along the Parkway and that traffic will be diverted from the regular trunk-line highways. This has not, however, proven to be the case in states that already have parkways and I believe that if Vermont secures this proposed parkway, that of the great number of people who will come here to drive over it, a large percent of them, after having looked out upon the marvellous panorama of mountains, valleys, lakes and villages and the unsurpassing scenic beauty of the state, will go down into the valleys and visit places of interest. They will stay at the hotels and roadside camps and many of them will eventually purchase summer homes. I believe that a very large number of the abandoned farms of Vermont would be developed as summer residences by these people, thereby increasing the grand list of the back towns and sharing to a substantial extent, the burden of the over-taxed farmer. . . .

There are those who are bitterly opposed to any co-operation whatever with the Federal Government. We Vermonters are apt to pride ourselves on our rugged independence, but pray let us not forget that there is a point where independence ceases to be a virtue. History shows us that progress has never been made except that it first had to overcome the obstacles and arguments that were thrown in its way by the ultra conservatives. . . . Many of us can remember the arguments made against the automobile when it first made its appearance and also against the expenditure of money to improve our highways. . . .

Undoubtedly the state's unbalanced budget, the crying need of new sources of taxation, which the special session of the legislature failed to provide, will be the "red herring" that the opponents of the Parkway will use to divert the thinking of the citizens before town meeting day. The voters of the state know that they cannot escape the ever-increasing burden of taxation. What they sorely need is the source of income that will enable them to live comfortably and pay their taxes. The laborer wants a job and a weekly pay check, the merchant and the manufacturer need the purchasing power of the farmer and the laborer. The small towns need the development of summer homes within their borders, to increase the amount of their grand list and share with their citizens the tax burden.

I think that it will be difficult to make a Vermont Yankee think that he isn't getting a good trade if the state spends five hundred thousand dollars, or twice that for that matter, and in return gets from the Federal government an expenditure of at least eighteen million dollars within this state in the construction of this Parkway which the Federal government, through the National park service cares for and maintains, landscapes, polices, in fact, carries the entire burden of upkeep, while the state of Vermont retains and has jurisdiction

over the land so held by the United States; for the purpose of requiring the registration of motor vehicles and the imposition and collection of a tax on gasoline in accordance with the laws of the state. . . . It has been estimated by a competent engineer that Vermont will get back in the vicinity of three hundred thousand dollars in truck registration and gasoline taxes during the construction period and I do not think that anyone can successfully argue that the increased earnings in gasoline taxes that will accrue to the state annually after the Parkway is completed will not far more than retire these bonds over the period of time that they extend, so that the people of Vermont will enjoy all the benefits of this Parkway without any cost to themselves whatsoever.

It is a fact that some of the summer people who are already with us object strenuously to anything that will tend to bring others into the state and there are those who would keep our mountains and the unsurpassing views to be had from their summits only for the limited number who have the time, physical strength and endurance to cover the "Long Trail." I believe that the average citizen is entitled to enjoy the unequalled scenic grandeur that can be had from the crest of our Green Mountain Range. . . . I believe that partisan politics has absolutely no place in this issue. We should keep in mind only the welfare of our state and its citizens without regard to politics.

The question may be raised as to the possibility of securing this parkway if we should vote "yes" in this referendum. One thing is sure, we won't get it if the majority vote "no." If we want it, the first thing to do is to vote "yes" and if the vote is favorable to the Parkway, the next thing to do is to go after it vigorously. One should not forget that the Green Mountain Parkway is not an isolated project, but has a definite relation in the National Park Program of the National Park Service. That in connection with its program, of locating public works of national character in the various states, the Federal government appropriated to the National Park Service of the Department of the Interior, the sum of fifty thousand dollars for a study of the Green Mountains of Vermont as the possible location for a great National Parkway. A reconnaissance survey has already been made. I believe that it is a matter of general knowledge that the authorities at Washington have looked with favor upon this project, if Vermont desired it. If we do want it, the least we can do is go after it vigorously.

I hope that every Vermonter who is eligible to vote on this question will realize its tremendous importance to the future of the state and its people and will make every effort to cast his vote, that he will give careful study to the whole matter so as to vote intelligently and that he will not be influenced by prejudice or partisan politics, but will vote for what he honestly believes will be for the best interests of the average citizen of the state.

Source: *Vermonter* 41 (January-February 1936): 5-8.

DOCUMENT 12

"Proposed Parkway a Threat to the State's Well Being" (1936)

ARTHUR WALLACE PEACH

I

Since I believe the building of the Green Mountain Parkway would be a tragic mistake, a blunder whose destructive consequences would reach far into the future of Vermont, I was willing to undertake to offer to the readers of *The Vermonter*, at the editor's request, an outline of my convictions and the grounds on which they rest. . . . I believe that my conclusions as to the Parkway are based on a careful study of every phase of the question, beginning with a first favorable impression and deepening to a final conviction which this discussion will develop. I should like to emphasize the fact that I am representing no group, no individual, no organization of any kind, that I am writing as a Vermonter who sees in the Parkway scheme a threat to his state's well-being; its individuality, its fine old spirit of independent living, its peace and charm, and other assets that have come to be known as "Vermontish."

What is the Parkway? . . .

II

First, we should notice that this Parkway does not begin in southern Vermont but in Massachusetts, that "it will extend the entire length of the state of Vermont through the Green Mountains and their adjacent ranges and foothills," that "it will extend to the Canadian boundary, where there will be a park of 20,000 acres, and include several peaks of the Jay group." The Parkway will be 260 miles long; and "There are within an automobile driving radius of about 200 miles or less from the Parkway some twelve to fourteen millions of people living in urban communities."

The MINIMUM right of way will be 1,000 feet "which will give approximately 500 feet of forest and park land on either side of the Parkway road," but we should notice this casual statement, that "at numerous places this width will be expanded into park area including whole lakes and their shores, stream valleys, and their adjacent hillsides and entire mountains or groups of mountains." In other words this Parkway is not a highway through the State with a right of way of 1,000 feet, but it takes in Vermont land to the tune of 50,000 acres, and reaches a width of seven miles in one spot. Here is another statement in the report, usually overlooked by the Parkway prophets: "It is not proposed to provide facilities for such service [lodging, meals, and motor service facilities] except at the development in the wilderness park near Jay Peak and possibly at one or two intermediate points." Here is still another significant sentence: "No trucks or other commercial traffic will be permitted on the Parkway road and the parkway traffic will be at all times under the supervision of Parkway police and rangers."

. . . I should in fairness point out that the Parkway will be maintained by the Federal Government, that grades will be easy, that it will be free from grade crossings, that no advertising or hot-dog stands will be permitted along it. We can assume that the Parkway will be competently built and managed, and that it will make available scenes of surpassing beauty. This latter argument for the Parkway is unquestionably sound. . . but suppose we look at the whole picture and what it signifies to our state in the present and future; then we note the following unhappy facts:

1. This Parkway will cut the state completely in two by a strip of land 1,000 feet to several miles wide, running from Massachusetts to Canada, "with no way around the ends," as the former Attorney-General of the United States, John G. Sargent says, "except into another state at one end, and out of the United States at the other, and no way across it except as some United States Government official

graciously grants permission." In blunt terms, it will break Vermont into two parts, from border to border, and do it forever.

2. It will include whole lakes and shores, mountains and groups of mountains and take them forever out of grand lists and out of any possible future development by Vermonters for the benefit of themselves and the state. A man must be quite a seer if he is willing to say that these 50,000 acres can never be developed by Vermont—in her own way, under her own ownership, to her own reward.

3. In Jay Park area there are to be hotel accommodations and motor service and "possibly at one or two intermediate points." A road 260 miles long without a garage would hold dire prospects for many motorists; and it is commonsense that somewhere along such a road there should be accommodations for meals and lodgings. Such a situation really means that thousands of motorists and their parties can enter the state from a Massachusetts through road, drive the entire length of the state, stay overnight, and drive back without leaving a dime in Vermont jeans, although the visitors are riding on a Parkway that Vermonters bought with $500,000 of their hard-earned money. . . .

4. "No trucks or commercial traffic will be permitted." There is sound wisdom in this rule; nevertheless, though the Parkway cuts through valuable timberland and several farms, no farmer or lumberman will be allowed to drive his truck on it; although when the Park Service cuts timber its representatives will drive trucks thereon and place the product on the market in competition with Vermont lumbermen. The Vermont farmer referred to is simply out of luck.

III

I have listed above three items that lie under the pretty picture. There are others, but I see no logic in too close an examination by either side of the minutia of the issue. . . . There are, however, some other vital points that a Vermonter should consider; and I list them herewith in a suggestive rather than complete form;

1. It is estimated that it will cost $500,000 to buy the 50,000 acres. One of the leading members of the House committee which rejected the Parkway scheme said it might cost $750,000 or $1,000,000. By the time titles have been searched, condemna-

tion suits have been fought—one farmer has threatened to carry his case to the United States Supreme Court before he surrenders his ancestral home—it seems reasonable that costs will mount.

2. This money must be raised by Vermont in a time of depression, when new taxes are even now being talked of to meet a deficit of nearly $500,000; and whether by bonding or otherwise, it will come out of Vermont pockets, soon or late. . . . Even in prosperous times the expenditure of such a sum in the state would be a serious matter.

3. Even though Vermont should buy at heavy cost the land needed, I believe there would be no certainty or guarantee that this Parkway, requiring $18,000,000 for the work according to the latest estimate, would be completed. It may be true that the Federal Government carries out its promises as our Parkway friends argue; but no sane man or woman, it seems to me, can reasonably say that the Federal Government today carries out all its plans. Facing the situation it does, the present administration might well find it necessary to limit activities such as this Parkway dream; and I doubt if a Republican administration would be eager to carry out Democratic plans that run into millions. . . .

4. We should keep in mind the fact that able constitutional lawyers in the Vermont House questioned the constitutionality of any law that would involve condemning Vermont land for the purpose of the Parkway....

IV

If hosts of tourists are to come over the Parkway from the crowded places, it would mean in the end the destruction of values that Vermonters hold most dear. I cannot see how intelligent Vermonters would wish to run the risk of creating in Vermont conditions similar to those in the Catskills, at certain beaches on the Maine coast and in certain localities in the White Mountains. A leading attorney of Buffalo, a native of Vermont, who bought an old Vermont place renovated it and brought in friends who did likewise, says "We desire freedom from the very things this Parkway will bring. . . ."

Lieut. Governor [George] Aiken's studies of summer home development in the state are amply fortified by my own data. Vermont can easily become the great summer home state of the east, and do it without cost if the state will follow its traditional lines of growth, not the lure of some spectacular project, golden in promise and not much else. Vermont's taxes are lower than in other New England states; men in business, men seeking homes, are coming steadily. Build the Parkway, lift taxes, flood the state with any kind of people, particularly those attracted by the spectacular, and the tide will turn. We know there are certain types of people who are destructive of values we want to preserve in Vermont: why not be honest about it? Other states have been ballyhooing for these people; let 'em have 'em. . . . Perhaps those who love serenity and simplicity of living must in the end go down to defeat, but there is one stubborn Vermonter who intends to do battle to the end for what he conceives to be a Vermont way of life. . . .

We are informed that building the Parkway will relieve unemployment, but we were warned at the Montpelier hearings that at best only 1,500 men could be employed at one period, that no contractor could be compelled to employ Vermont labor—a reasonable position, for no contractor is running a charity or missionary enterprise, and he would prefer to employ his own experienced men. In any event, to spend $500,000 to take a small per cent of Vermont men from the relief rolls does not make startling sense. As for the "grab all the funds we can" argument, I find it amusing. The Vermont newspaper which argued this—its theme song for many months—will lambast the Democratic Administration in one column for its spendthrift attitude and in the next column argue that Vermont should grab this $18,000,000 while the grabbing is good—a typical example of the logic of some of our Parkway friends. . . .

VI

In conclusion I think we should remember that one of the strongest committees of the Vermont House of Representatives, with every facility for securing all information available about the Parkway, turned the project down. When forced to a vote by a group of men who seem determined to bring this Parkway to Vermont, it was defeated by the House, only to bob up again through action by the Senate; again it was rejected by the House with a larger vote against it than in the first instance. Thus, Vermont representatives on three occasions, after hearing all sides of the question discussed, spoke decisively against the Parkway. Facing continuous pressure that ranged from argument to

belittlement at the hands of a Parkway lobby, these Vermonters stood fast by what I maintain are the traditions and ideals of their state.

Now, for the fourth time, the same group of Parkway enthusiasts have forced the issue to a vote at the coming town meetings. I have faith in the judgment of Vermont voters, but I do not dodge the fact that they are face to face with an issue on which many of them will not have adequate information, yet they must vote on a scheme that will, if adopted, change the entire geographical arrangement of the State and, I believe, change its fundamental character. . . .

Whether the Parkway is created or not by a Vermont referendum, underneath this controversy there will still be a deeper question. I think we are watching the dark emergence of a state philosophy alien to Vermont for a century and more. I take from an editorial in the *Vergennes Enterprise* a clean-cut statement of what I have in mind, and I quote it, changing only the tense of the verbs: "The issue is fundamentally a contest between two opposing schools of thought. The proponents of the Parkway want to carry Vermont into an intense commercialization of its mountain scenery and summer attractions. The opponents represent a school of thought which prefers to have the state's development follow along more traditional lines." Vermont must, before many moons, choose between the leaders of these two schools, and the decision will be a fateful one for the State.

It is along traditional lines that I believe the State should move for many reasons. In a day when there is confusion, clamor, and uproar all around us, we should cling to our traditional peace; in a day when wise men from New York and Burlington are telling us how to be saved, we should stick to our old faith that men are saved by calm consideration of what actually is and not what others promise us shall be; in a day when fever is in the air, we should keep our temperatures down; in a day when men are inclined to follow loud voices promising and prophesying golden things, we should listen to the cautious, careful leaders whose voices are not loud, and keep in mind the warning of the western cattleman that when a herd is stampeding, the real leaders are never in front—they are back in the herd because they cannot see what all the racket is about; and, as a last hint, we might as well remember what our fathers learned among these Vermont hills long ago—that there are no new roads to Paradise—not even a Parkway.

Source: *Vermonter* 41 (January-February 1936): 9-13.

Document 13

Public Hearing on the Strike by the Vermont Marble Workers (1936)

United Committee to Aid Vermont Marble Workers

Held in the Town Hall, West Rutland, Vermont, Saturday, February 29, 1936
Chairman of Hearing Committee: Mr. Rockwell Kent
Counsel for the Committee: Mr. I. Polier
Chairman of the Session: Mr. Tredwell Smith

The session was opened at 2 P.M. by Mr. Alan Raycraft. . . [who introduced] Norman Tallentire, who represents the United Committee to Help the Vermont Marble Strikers.

Mr. Tallentire: Brother Raycraft, Citizens of Rutland and vicinity, and delegates: It is my duty just to acquaint you as far as possible with the personnel, the people who are present here on the platform from outside your county. . . . There are some on the platform with whom you are already acquainted, . . .

We have on the delegation representatives from New York City representing different viewpoints, in the labor world, in the newspaper world, in the arts and in the press. . . . There are also delegations from Barre, and delegations from Albany [N.Y.] in which are included four representatives of the Central Labor Union of that town; a delegation from Bennington College, a delegation from Dartmouth College, a delegation from Boston is on the way, and I believe there is a delegation from Middlebury due here in the course of the afternoon. . . .

It is my duty and pleasure now to introduce the chairman of this delegation who is well known to many people in Vermont, having been a resident of your state on several occasions. Not only is he known in this regard, but . . . [also as] a writer and an artist. . . . It is my pleasure to introduce to you the Chairman of the Committee to Investigate the strike of the marble workers, Mr. Rockwell Kent.

Mr. Kent: In the Rutland paper of today there is a very decent, fine, fair editorial about this committee of outsiders coming here to the city of Rutland to inquire into this strike, its causes and the conditions that prevail today. Everyone should realize that America today has gotten to be a country in which the interests of every citizen are wider than the little community in which he lives, the city, the county, the state in which he lives. Our interests are at least national. . . .

It is our duty, the duty of every American-born and everyone who comes here and takes up citizenship in this country—it is his business to see that life, liberty and the pursuit of happiness are enjoyed in this country. And it is only when every living soul in this country enjoys life, liberty and the pursuit of happiness that we can quit work.

And if we in New York State learn that a group, a crowd, a class of people in California, or in Texas, or in Arizona or anywhere else, are not getting those things this country was established for, it is our duty to go there and if possible help them to get it. We are not outsiders intruding upon a Vermont situation. We are Americans doing what we are pledged to do, what is called our right and duty to do. If we find that you people, you marble workers, are enjoying life, liberty and the pursuit of happiness, if you are dwelling in marble halls, then we will congratulate you and go on. But if we find that is not so, we will fight tooth and nail to help you. . . . We want to find out what this strike is about. We want to be fair to every side. I have in my own heart and brain my own convictions; I can't state them until we hear from the other side.

To return to that charge about the sympathizers from outside who intrude themselves on local disputes—I want to tell you that this chairman of your meeting today is a man who cannot be accused on those grounds. It is our good fortune to have a son of Vermont, a man who helped make this marble industry what it is. I am going to introduce as your chairman Professor [F.] Tredwell Smith.

(Applause)

Professor Smith: In beginning the formal business of our meeting this afternoon, I want to make certain things clear as chairman, and give you an idea of how this meeting is to proceed. In the first place, speaking as chairman and member of the Investigating Committee from the outside, I want to make it clear that we come from various groups and points of view at the request of this committee of sympathizers, in order to get an impartial hearing. We are here to call on testimony from many different sources, and we intend to weigh that testimony as fairly and objectively as possible

I want to say a word before we begin with an analysis of the situation. I would like to say that I have always wanted to get into this Town Hall, and this is the first time I have ever been here. The reason I wanted to get in here is that my great-grandfather, many years ago when the town was being laid out, said, "This is the logical place for the Town Hall. . . ." And he was the man, I believe, who set out the trees that are still standing out there around the Town Hall.

Just before coming in here I went by the cemetery at West Rutland where there are a great many of my ancestors, and I went outside the town of West Rutland where there used to be a Congregational Church—I suppose you remember my father, he has his lot in the town of Castleton, and my great-grandfather who came across from Randolph driving his cows. As a self-educated geologist, he opened the first marble quarry on the hills in the days when the Irish were the first workmen to do the excavating. That is sufficient, I think, for me to indicate a connection and a reason why I am interested in coming up from New York to act as chairman here. There are a good many connections; I could bring out connections with the Proctor family by way stages, and with the towns of Rutland, West Rutland, and so forth . . . .

After the hearing has been concluded, the investigating committee on the platform will retire for its own meeting to weigh the evidence and prepare for a report tonight at the meeting; also to collect the reports of the delegations who have been out in the small committees seeing various factors in this particular situation which, I hardly need remind you, is getting the attention now of the entire United States. Interest in what is happening here today is intense in many parts of the United States, and what is done today will be reported in many parts of the United States. We have here our own stenographer to take down accurately the proceedings. . . . [Inquiries from the chairman revealed there were no representatives from the Vermont Marble Company or town officials present and willing to testify.]

Chairman Smith proceeded: Are there any representatives of the Marble Workers Union and the Quarrymen's Union prepared to testify?

Eugene Petersen, President of the Quarrymen's Union announced his presence and readiness to testify; he reported that James R. Gallagher, chairman of the Rutland Local of the Marble Workers Union would arrive later.

Chairman Smith: Are there any other representatives here of the men on strike?

Alan Raycraft, President of the International Marble Workers Union: I am here to testify.

Chairman Smith: Any others representative of the strike? Are there any representatives of other workers in the marble industry?

James Falzo of Danby responded present.

Chairman Smith: Are there any representatives of the community or citizens of the community not involved in the strike who wish to testify as to conditions before and during the strike, as to the situation of work, or of living conditions, or of maintenance of order, of civil liberties or of administration of relief—any members of the community who wish to speak other than the strikers?

There was no response from the meeting.

Chairman Smith: Are there any women, housewives or members of families of workers who wish to testify this afternoon?

Mrs. George Felyeo: Yes, I will.

Counsel I. Polier: We might save time if I could call the names we received from the union this afternoon as to who would testify for the union.

Eugene Petersen was then summoned to the platform to testify.

Mr. Polier: . . . Mr. Petersen, you are, I understand, the President of the Quarry Workers Union?

Mr. Petersen: Yes, the West Rutland branch.

Mr. Polier: Is the Quarry Workers Union affiliated with the American Federation of Labor?

Mr. Petersen: It is.

Mr. Polier: Would you be good enough to tell us when the strike started, what happened before the strike and what has happened during the strike? Take as long as you want to, and not more than a half hour!

Mr. Petersen: Mr. Chairman, brother delegates and friends: Of course we have to go way back, two years, before we can get started. But as you all know, we organized in February, 1934. Immediately the Vermont Marble Company tried to hoist what you call a company union on us. But it didn't work. So in July of 1934 we wrote to the Vermont Marble Company and requested a conference, which was granted on August 1, 1934. We continued those negotiations until we were called before the Regional Labor Board in Boston in December, 1934. We were ordered to go back and try to reach an agreement with the company. We started all over again negotiating until February, 1935. In this hall we took a strike vote and the men voted almost unanimously to go on strike for failure by the company to reach an agreement with us.

Then we were immediately called by the Regional Labor Board in Boston again. We spent two days before the Board. They handed down two decisions, one against the company in our favor regarding the company union. The second one they claimed the company was not discriminating, because of the hard times, the slackness of business. And the company immediately came out and said the Board gave them a perfect whitewash. You all remember that, lots of you people around here.

Then the Wagner Bill was declared unconstitutional [sic], and of course that broke off all negotiations because we were afraid if we went over there without any law to protect us we would have been heaved out the window. So we waited until Congress enacted the Labor Disputes Bill.

We met so many times I have lost track of it, until in October last year Danby walked out. It happened that the company posted a notice on the timeclock at the quarries in Danby that they would be working only three weeks a month. And the men claimed they couldn't live on that, so they walked out.

We had seven conferences with the company, and we almost reached an agreement when the men in Rutland and West Rutland and Central Rutland and Florence decided to walk out on November 4th. They declared a holiday. We met the company that week and they told us they would not talk to us under any circumstances until this violence had stopped. And there was no violence whatever. True, we chased a couple of scabs around the streets, but nobody got hurt. And still we had to promise to be good boys, and we did promise.

When we came up Monday morning the Vermont Marble Company had 86 what you call deputy sheriffs on the job. We presented the agreement which had been accepted by the men at the mass meeting. We told the company these conditions were absolutely agreeable and acceptable to the men. They said there was nothing there they could sign and put into effect.

We begged them to raise the wages of the lower paid workers two cents. They said no. We said would they raise it a couple cents and sign an agreement to come back here the first of the year and take up the wage question then. They said no. We said give them a little now and let it stand till April, 1936. They said no.

There was nothing to do but come back to the men and tell them. And they voted unanimously to strike. That was November 11th last year, and they are still on strike.

Since the strike it has been a hard time to feed all these people. We tried and have been successful to a certain extent to get some town aid—work on the road, PWA and such projects as that for some of our men. But in other places, the people from Danby and so forth can testify to what assistance they have been getting down there. But we have been fortunate in West Rutland in getting a little relief.

We have been accused of starting fights with the deputy sheriffs. I don't know of any single instance when any of our men has ever attacked a deputy sheriff. Because we have always preached for the men to keep quiet, peaceful and orderly. These men are not a bunch of ruffians. They are decent American workmen. They obey the law. They have never broken the law that I know of. But one morning, last January 7th, when we were on the streets here picketing; and they were loading some carloads of marble, the men were picketing up and down the railroad track, quietly, never saying a word. The company had 75 to 80 deputy sheriffs around the plant, trying to start a fight with us. After the riot started the men come back to the town, they stood around on the sidewalks. Immediately a superintendent drove them through—nobody touched him or anything; there were about 150 men standing around there. Then three carloads left the office; one contained two men who had been working on the marble up around there, and the other two cars were full of deputy sheriffs. The cars immediately stopped and circled around the leading car. And the deputy in the leading car steps out and gives them the signal three times with his hands to pile out of the car. The deputies walked over to those men and started slugging them down without any proclamation or orders to disperse or anything—just slugging them down in cold blood. They knocked out five men unconscious; these men had to be sewed up in the hospital. I will say for our credit that they knocked out five men and the men laid out eleven deputy sheriffs along with them. . . .

It may interest you to know that several of those deputy sheriffs have been discharged since then, and arrested for drunkenness and fined. It is on record. It has been proven they were drunk on the job. I went on the picket line one night and when I passed one of the deputies the smell of liquor was strong enough to knock you down. And he was on duty swinging a club and looking for trouble. They are looking for trouble so they can get the National Guard in here and open these plants. That is what we have to put up with here in town. They are kind of sore at us because we won't quit. And we are not going to quit. We are not going to quit until the Vermont Marble Company sits down and signs that agreement they drew up with us (interruption by applause from the meeting) because 80% of that agreement was dictated to us by the Vermont Marble Company and it was accepted by the men at a mass meeting, and then they said there was nothing there in writing they could put into effect. The full agreement appeared in the *Rutland Herald* November 12, 13 of last year. There is nothing in the agreement to be afraid of. The only thing the Vermont Company is refusing is they don't want no organized labor in here. Why, I don't know.

If there is anything else the committee would like to know, I would be glad to answer it. . . .

Source: Report of Public Hearing, Strike of Vermont Marble Company Workers, West Rutland, Vt., February 29, 1936, pp. 1-6, 34-35, Special Collections, Bailey/Howe LIbrary, University of Vermont.

DOCUMENT 14

Open Letter to the Republican National Committee (1937)

GOVERNOR GEORGE D. AIKEN

Gentlemen:

The State of Vermont deserves the respect and attention of the Republican National Committee. With our sister State of Maine, alone of all the forty-eight States of the Union, we returned a majority for our Party in the last national campaign. As elected leader of the Republican Party in this one of the remaining Republican States, it is my duty to inform you that, in my judgment, neither in Vermont nor elsewhere in the Union will we, as a national party, again receive the support of a voting majority unless your body recognizes the necessity of reorganizing and becomes responsive to the enlightened opinion of the voters whom you profess to serve.

America faces a crisis. The Democratic Party, swept into power on the wave of the depression, has now ruled our nation for several years. During this time a large part of the vaunted liberty of our citizens, won at the cost of a century and a half of struggle and sacrifice, has been wiped away. Our children's children have been bonded to pay the costs of inefficiency; small business has been stifled; the ranks of labor have been sundered; confusion has increased, and hope has been largely superseded by despair; for millions, centralized paternalism has supplanted self-reliance, and a virtual dictatorship over a hundred thirty million educated and erstwhile free Americans is being seriously proposed and sought.

But there is still in the hearts of the great majority of our citizens a love of liberty that does not die, a desire to bring order out of this confusion, a will to make workable those proposals upon which the spotlight of time focuses our attention as desirable, and the courage to discard the great mass of unworkable or premature theories, dreamed by dreamers and seized upon by opportunists as a vehicle on which they may ride into power.

Ordinarily, patriotic citizens would turn to the Republican Party as a means of combating the insidious changes coming over our form of government, but they are not doing so today. They see no hope in a party offering no constructive policy or program, a party whose leaders are apparently more concerned with controlling the party machinery than in American welfare, a party so torn by internal bickering, hopeless ambitions and lack of direction, as to be in a nearly complete state of demoralization. The body politic of American citizens demands a party of integrity and ability to which it may give allegiance. The Republican Party has a last opportunity—it may become the grand new Party of America, or it may *not*.

After consultation with leaders of opinion in the Republican Party in this State, and with their advice and encouragement, I make three demands with reference to your organization.

The first demand is that at the earliest opportunity the National Committee be purged of the baneful influence of the Southern Committeemen who represent no one except themselves and their allied officeholders, past and present—mostly past. Nourished on political patronage alone and used as a tool for controlling the Party, this body of committeemen is your organization's greatest liability. The character of their representation is such as to preclude any possibility of securing the cooperation of the millions of patriotic fellow-citizens south of the Potomac and the Ohio; and their prominence in party councils repels right-minded voters everywhere.

I suggest that each committee member be alloted a vote equal to the proportion which the Republican vote in his State bore to the total vote in that State cast for president in the last national election. The enforcement of this rule would do more than deprive a group of opportunists of unearned and misused power. It would make the position of committee member attractive only to men and women who are convinced of the possibility of building up the Party in Democratic territory and are determined so to build it.

My second demand is that the National Committee set before itself, as a major aim, the winning to the Party of the youth of the nation, and the placing upon it of the serious responsibilities of party leadership. We have become a party of old men. Unless we can become also a party of and for young men and young women the party will die—and the processes of dissolution have already begun. It is obviously necessary not only to draw the younger party members into counsel, but necessary that there be a program for party policy and later for party platforms which appeals to the keenest intelligence and highest aspirations of American youth.

My third demand is the immediate preparation of an affirmative program. Among the points acceptable in such a program I suggest the following:

1. Accept in general the social aims which the opposing party has had the wisdom to adopt, but has lacked the ability to put into efficient operation.

2. Reject decisively the use of enormous expenditures and special benefits as a political expedient for attaching agriculture, industrial groups, and other workers to our Party. We can never outbide our opponents and we should be ashamed to try. Our claim for support must be made on higher grounds.

3. Instead of offering a place at the feed-troughs, invite the youth of the nation in all occupations and in all walks of life to work together to produce and distribute, by the labor of head and hand, a larger volume of goods and services for more people of this nation. Emphasize what we can give and do—not what we can get.

4. For the sake of all of us, recognize both the fundamental importance and the peculiar difficulties of the business of agriculture. Encourage the farmer in self-support and in the preservation of the fertility of his soil, provide means for carrying over the surplus of bumper years into the lean years, and on crops whose prices are made in the world market provide a subsidy on domestic consumption that is the equivalent of the tariff subsidy available for manufactured goods. I believe that all this can be done without detriment to the annual purchasing power of the industrial worker, without imposing production control on the farmer, and without destroying the foreign market for his surplus. We can surely avoid in this last respect the mistakes of the present administration whose policies have

dangerously crippled our farm market abroad, and have so done in the face of the obvious failure of similar experiments with British rubber and Brazilian coffee.

5. The industrial worker must be assured of his fair share of the nation's production. We ask as the main objective to this end an expansion of employment and increase of production. The consequent demand for his services will assure him of both an increased pay envelope and increased actual purchasing power for the enjoyment of himself and his family. Everything has been tried but this, and nothing but this will serve the worker's needs.

In the interest of the small business man upon whom the perpetuation of free competition depends, we demand the restriction of monopolies and a minimum of regulation. When regulation seems necessary the government should bear in mind the difference between large and small industries and their respective abilities to bear regulatory burdens. Free competition fosters personal initiative, aids the smaller communities and also reacts to the benefit of the consumer.

6. For all workers, whether in industry, agriculture, or the service occupations, we further demand the coordination into a national system of our present unrelated policies of governmental borrowing, expenditure, employment and relief on the one hand, and private employment, taxation and debt repayment on the other.

7. The neglected element in the preceding demands is a proper relationship between government and business. It is imperative that government shall look upon business as the source of production, employment, and consumption, and that private industry be fostered to this end. It is the corresponding duty and interest of business to meet more than halfway the honest overtures of an honest government. On this mutual respect and understanding of business and government depend the solutions of most of our yet unsolved problems. A more profitable and active private business can and will pay larger

real wages, make a better market for the farmer's produce, draw into its workshops the surplus population of the farms and thereby reduce the surplus farm production and raise farm prices. And a prosperous business can and will, through higher wages, salaries, and dividends, pay the taxes needed for the maintenance of our social program and reduction of our public debt to a point where national credit can safely withstand a peace or wartime emergency. No other source of financial support is available.

8. We must defend the rightful sovereignty of the States, not because of our attachment to some outworn doctrine of States' rights, but because the well-being of the people demands that we do so. The shift to Federal rule results in an unwise relinquishment of local responsibility. The process is insidious. First we exchange self-reliance for dependence on local and State government, then we yield local and State responsibility to the Federal government. Such yielding in the majority of cases induces a weakness of character in our citizenship which our Party must make every effort to prevent, whether among our own members or in the body politic at large. It is particularly necessary that young men and young women be infused with the sense of personal responsibility for local government. The other aspect of this problem is that the Federal government is taking on itself powers too great and too complicated to be successfully used. As a result, we are now on the pont of legislative and administrative breakdown, a situation whose consequence we scarcely dare imagine.

9. Finally, we must preserve all useful elements in our form of government and change only by constitutional means those whose usefulness has ended. We must return to Congress its legislative and deliberative functions. We must perserve the authority, integrity and independence of our courts. We must refuse to the presidency a blanket grant of power by methods or for purposes unauthorized by law and unrevealed before the elections, but should strengthen it and its supporting staff in the

gathering of information and the making of wise and constructive recommendations.

With the breakdown of parliamentary governments and the growth of personal power and rule in Europe as our warning, and with the harassed state of the peoples living under them as our warrant, we must sound a trumpet call to the citizenship of America, young and old, to take upon itself the responsibility for making this nation truly great and its government truly a minister to the needs of its people; and that trumpet call must summon them not merely to legislative halls and to the polls, it must summon them as well to farm, store, and factory.

To purge the Party organization of its reactionary and unfair elements, to focus its forces on the recognition of the youth of our nation, to prepare immediately an affirmative program—that is the demand which the Republican leadership of Vermont makes on the Republican leadership of the nation.

If that demand is not met, we must look elsewhere for an organization through which thoughtful and devoted Americans of North and South, East and West, can join together to work for the good of all.

> Sincerely yours,
> George D. Aiken

Source: George D. Aiken, *Speaking from Vermont* (New York: Frederick A. Stokes Co., 1938), pp. 216-223. Reprinted with permission of Lola Aiken.

DOCUMENT 15

"America's Part in the Defense of Democracy" (1940)
SENATOR ERNEST W. GIBSON, JR.

This is a matter very close to my heart: a matter in which I have taken an active part trying to formulate opinion; a matter which I believe must be made alive, warm and real to you and to me, to everyone who lives in this country and wants to continue to live as free men. This issue, this question, is America's part in the Defense of Democracy.

Here in America we are still a Democracy. Here in America we can go our own way, do as we please—within certain very broad limitations. Here in America we let the will of the majority of the people of America set the rules by which you and I are to live. Through these rules we have the greatest liberties; the greatest freedom of any people living in the world today. . . .

In Europe today . . . [people are] slaves driven by the masters who believe they themselves are the chosen ones to rule the world and the rest of us are the ones to be ridden. He cannot even worship the God of his own choice. If we are to continue to live as free men under our own rules, it is time that every man, woman and child in this country seriously considers America's place in the Defense of Democracy. . . .

Today Europe is a totalitarian state, and Asia is practically that. If England is conquered, four-fifths of this world will be governed by totalitarian autocrats. . . . Now let us seriously examine America's position in this world if England is conquered, and if four-fifths of this world is under these dictators. . . .

If England is conquered, we will have Hitler for our next door neighbor: he will attempt to assume domination over the English colonies in our hemisphere, and we will be in the position of having to do business daily with a man who you and I know is unscrupulous and dishonest. Not only will we have to do business daily with Hitler but the chances are pretty certain that we will have to do business on Hitler's terms! Heretofore this country has been able to do business with many countries. There has been competition, but if Hitler conquers England he will practically control all of the world outside of the Western Hemisphere.

Our labor in this country will have to compete with slave labor in the rest of the world. Our economic system could not stand this. Our industry could not survive under those conditions. Laborer and industrialist, farmer, professional man and preacher will be reduced to the slavery that we see in Europe today. How would business men in ordinary every day business pursuits enjoy having to conduct business with a man whose words you know you cannot trust—with a man to whom honesty means nothing; to whom promises are only something to be broken the instant advantage can be gained by doing so—with a man you knew was eternally scheming and conniving to make you his slave?

If Germany conquers England, will it not be vitally necessary for this country, among other things, to seize the Island of Bermuda, the English West Indies and Greenland? That in and of itself will undoubtedly embroil us in war because Hitler will want those possessions if he conquers England. We cannot let Hitler have them if we hope successfully to defend ourselves in the years to come.

Some people say that if England is conquered, the English will never surrender their navy to Hitler—that the worst that could happen would be that it would be scuttled. Churchill probably never would surrender the English Navy to the Germans but if England is conquered it will not be when Churchill is the head of the Government of England. In his place will be someone desiring to appease and make peace with Hitler. The English people will be told then by a controlled press and a controlled radio that they have had to make peace because America would not help further. The English people will hold the same feeling against America that the French held against England when France made its armistice.

No, we are leaning on a slim reed when we say that the English fleet will never be surrendered or turned over to Hitler. We hope such will never happen, but we must not count on it if we are to protect ourselves as free men.

If England is defeated, our relations with Canada would be of an uncertain nature. England would have a Hitler dominated government, a government that would demand the loyalty of the Canadian government just as the Hitler-dominated French government demands the loyalty of its African colonies. . . .

If England is defeated can anyone say that we will not have to maintain a standing army of millions of men? This in itself is repugnant to you and me, who have lived in a free country. This in itself has inherent dangers to freedom. This in itself is a costly burden to place upon the people, but we will have no other alternative if England is defeated. . . .

But we are not ready for war—we are just at the beginning of our preparation to defend ourselves from invasion. . . .

Then what can we do for Democracy? . . . The first thing we can do, and we must do, is for all Americans to be convinced of what this Revolution is all about. To be convinced that this Revolution involves an issue to be fought in the hard and stony passes of the human spirit—an issue between the frenzy on the one side of a herded, whipped-up crowd begotten cause, and on the other side a simple man's belief in liberty of mind and spirit in gayety, joyousness and humility; in

his willingness to sacrifice his goods, his comforts, his earnings for this free spirit's sake.

This issue must be made stark clear to the whole people of America. It must be made a real living, warm issue if we are to become a united nation in this struggle. . . .

I am a great believer that America's part in the fight for Democracy is to aid England. It matters not what England's past history may have been. It matters not whether England may have been the aggressor nation in the past. It matters not who urges our giving aid to England because though the devil urge it if it be to our advantage, if it be to the advantage of Democracy that we aid England, we should not hesitate. If we can turn the industrial activity of this country into the proper and efficient channels for the manufacture of materials of war, if we can ship those materials across to England, this war may be kept from our shores. If Hitler knows we propose to send ships and then more ships, to send planes and then more planes, to send all manner of material of war in great quantities to England, then Hitler will know that Democracy means more to us than merely the rapid production of goods and then more goods; than merely a life of greater ease for all. Hitler will not be so sure of himself. Peace may come the sooner. . . .

Americans and Englishmen are sons of a common land. This day the English fight for liberty: this day they fight for their very freedom. The German Fuehrer has, they know, a mighty army. They do not disguise its strength. His army, his allies he has collected together by promising to each a share in the spoils of the world. But Hitler cannot offer to his greatest chief gifts nobler than those we offer our lowliest free man, liberty and right and law in the soil of his father.

The English are fighting as brothers under the eyes of their fathers and chosen chiefs. They fight for the women they would save from the ravisher; they fight for the children they would guard from eternal bondage; they fight for the altars which the swastika would darken.

No Englishman dreams of retreat. Some day in the not far distant future you and I—this whole country—may be forced to fight for Democracy—for our freedom of spirit and our liberty of mind.

In future times and in strange lands the lowly and humble, the proud and the might shall praise England's brave men and women for their valiant deeds wrought in such a holy cause. They will say in the great and glorious future when some brave man does some valiant deed—he was brave as those who fought for freedom by the side of Churchill, and swept from this earth those gangster dictators who placed themselves on a higher throne than that of Almighty God—who worshipped the cross that was not the cross of Christ. If the time ever comes in America when we face an invasion by those who worship not the cross of Christ, if the time ever comes when this country faces the last bitter test of Democracy, may we here in America be invested with that unconquerable spirit—the love of Freedom.

Source: *Vermonter* 45 (December 1940): 274-280.

SECTION TEN

1941-1966
The Emergence
of Modern Vermont

VERMONT VOICES

SECTION TEN

1941-1966
The Emergence of Modern Vermont

Introduction

Vermonters committed to the citizen-soldier tradition and to upholding a cherished reputation for resisting tyranny reveled in Ernest W. Gibson, Jr.'s denunciations of Nazi Germany. (See Section 9, Document 15 and Section 10, Document 5.) It is, however, a legislative resolution adopted September 16, 1941, almost three months before Pearl Harbor, and since celebrated as Vermont's "Declaration of War," that has come to symbolize the state's determined opposition to aggression.

The incentive for the resolution was concern for fellow citizens called to active military service. September 16 marked the anniversary of the first peacetime draft in American history, but an even more substantial number of Vermonters had been called to active military duty the previous February, when units of the Vermont National Guard were activated. Boasting 1,700 men and 27 units from 18 different towns, its roster included men in mid-career and pillars of their communities. The ranking Vermont officer (Leonard "Red" Wing) was a partner in the state's most prestigious law firm and Ernest W. Gibson, Jr. joined the unit (172nd Infantry Regiment) after the enactment of Lend-Lease. As **Document 1**, a *Burlington Free Press* editorial, makes clear, the resolution was adopted to facilitate bonus payments to men on active military duty. It was conceived as a gesture of encouragement and support, and Governor William Wills attributed it to Vermont's being "temperamentally and traditionally the very opposite of nazism."

Although defense contracts brought prosperity to some Vermont industries (machine tool factories in Springfield, for example) as early as 1940, it was not until after Pearl Harbor that the impact of World War II was widely felt. Thirty-eight thousand Vermont men and women ultimately served on active duty, with twelve hundred killed or reported missing in action. For many who remained at home, wartime prosperity brought greater material comforts despite rationing and shortages. The war also brought greater federal and state regulation over an average citizen's daily activities than Vermonters had ever before experienced.

Document 2, an excerpt from a *Burlington Free Press* feature article, discusses the most visible state presence, the Vermont Council of Safety (VCS). Created by Governor Wills, the VCS coordinated such activities as the training of spotters to identify enemy aircraft (Springfield was alleged to be a prime German target) and served as the state agency for cooperating with the federal government to implement such activities as food and fuel rationing. While in retrospect a disproportionate share of the council's efforts promoted vigilance against unlikely enemy air attacks, the VCS also organized thousands of volunteers for more mundane nonmilitary efforts. **Document 3** provides Ralph Locke's lyrics to "Making Maple Syrup," to be sung during the 1942 sugaring season by high school students recruited by the council to help alleviate the state's farm labor shortage.

At about the same time Ralph Locke was drafting his lyrics, Norman Rockwell, an Arlington, Vermont, artist most famous for his magazine covers, was pondering how he might best contribute to the war effort. He hoped to make "some statement about why the country was fighting the war," but his muse eluded him until, as he noted in his autobiography:

> [O]ne night as I was tossing in bed . . . rejecting one idea after another and getting more and more discouraged as the minutes ticked by . . . I suddenly remembered how Jim Edgerton had stood up in town meeting and said something that everybody else disagreed with. But they had let him have his say. No one had shouted him down. My gosh, I thought, that's it. There it is. Freedom of Speech. I'll illustrate the Four Freedoms using my Vermont neighbors as models. [1]

Rockwell's illustrations were published in early 1943 in the *Saturday Evening Post* with astonishing results. Reprint requests flooded the *Post* offices, and government and private organizations distributed reprints throughout the world. As the centerpieces of an art show that toured the nation while selling war bonds, they attracted 1,222,000 viewers. **Document 4**, *Freedom of Speech*, remains the most celebrated and best

---

[1] Norman Rockwell, *My Adventures as an Illustrator* (New York: Harry N. Abrams, 1988), p. 313.

recognized of Rockwell's "Four Freedoms" paintings and also the image most closely associated with Vermont.

Rockwell and Locke provided inspiration by invoking traditional values, but Vermonters also confronted new realities. Government and industry reflected those realities by incorporating a broader spectrum of citizens into their leadership. The military draft along with an increase in available jobs produced a labor shortage that enhanced the economic bargaining power of labor unions and individual workers alike. At the war's end, they, along with newly organized veterans' organizations, became a major force in the politics of the dominant Republican Party.

This changing of the guard was illustrated in the 1946 Republican primary, in which returning veteran Ernest W. Gibson, Jr. defeated incumbent Governor Mortimer R. Proctor. Proctor, heir to a political and industrial dynasty, was the fourth member of his family to occupy the governor's office. He had toiled in the party's political vineyards, serving his political apprenticeship in the house and senate and as lieutenant governor. Gibson also carried a grand family name and had served six months as Vermont's interim U.S. senator after the death of his father in 1940, but he had never before sought statewide elective office. Assisted by his ally, U.S. Senator George Aiken, Gibson argued that the traditional apprenticeship system was outmoded and denied returning veterans opportunities to exercise political leadership. Further, as is apparent from **Document 5**, excerpted from a 1946 Gibson for Governor campaign flyer, Gibson advocated a larger and more active government than Proctor, whose more traditional Vermont philosophy was "our ability to do is limited by our ability to pay."

Document 6, "Vermont Goes Radical," is excerpted from an article by William Gilman that appeared in *Collier's*, a popular national magazine, in April 1947. The national elections had produced the first Republican majorities in Congress since before the Democratic New Deal, and Gilman, profiling Aiken, Gibson, and newly elected U.S. Senator Ralph Flanders, concluded that Republican victories hardly denoted a repudiation of the objectives of the New Deal.

Reelected in 1948, Gibson served until January 1950, when he resigned to accept appointment by President Harry S. Truman as judge of the Vermont Federal District Court. While granting so rich a patronage plum to a Republican outraged Vermont Democrats and signified Truman's disapproval of the state's Democratic organization, it also signified his approval of Gibson's legislative agenda. Governor Gibson was able to secure a progressive income tax, the creation of a state police system, and higher teacher salaries and benefits, but he also met disappointments. Chief among these was the legislature's rejection of a Vermont Power Authority and the defeat of his plan for mobile health units.

Lee Emerson, who as lieutenant governor cast the deciding vote against Gibson's health plan, was elected governor in 1950. More fervently committed to "fiscal responsibility" and less confident than Gibson in the ability of federal and state government to resolve social problems, Emerson, who took office during the Korean War (June 1950-July 1953), was among Vermont's most zealous anti-Communists. **Document 7**, the initial section of Emerson's first inaugural address, calls for extraordinary measures to combat world Communism. Along with millions of other Americans, Emerson believed the preservation of their freedoms required resistance to external aggression by the Soviet Union combined with a constant vigil against internal subversion. Hosts of private, state, and federal investigators, the most notorious being U.S. Senator Joseph McCarthy of Wisconsin, sought alleged American Communists and former Communists.

While the ostensible Communist menace dominated the political agenda, trends threatening other customary political behaviors went relatively unobserved. Most notable of these was the increase in female legislators. Fifty-two women, then a record, served in the 1953 Vermont House of Representatives and helped elect Consuelo Northrop Bailey the first and only woman speaker of the Vermont house. In 1954, Bailey, a Republican lawyer active in politics since the 1920s, went on to become the first elected woman lieutenant governor in the United States, although the grand prize of governor eluded her. **Document 8** contains the remarks Bailey made after formal announcement of her victory as speaker.

Later that same spring the U.S. Senate Internal Security Subcommittee (Jenner Committee) called University of Vermont (UVM) biochemistry professor Alex Novikoff to Washington. Novikoff was questioned about whether he had ever been a Communist and about his political associations when he was a member of the Brooklyn College faculty in the 1930s and 1940s. By taking the Fifth Amendment and refusing to answer questions about his pre-UVM activities, Novikoff precipitated the convening of a 23-person faculty-trustee board of review. **Document 9** contains excerpts from a transcript of that hearing. Subsequent to the hearing, the board of trustees, with Governor Lee Emerson in attendance, dismissed Novikoff from his university position.

After his dismissal, and partly on the recommendation of Albert Einstein, Novikoff was given a position at the Albert Einstein Medical School. There, continuing cancer research he had been conducting at UVM, he won international recognition. In 1983 the University of Vermont acknowledged Novikoff's research accomplishments by awarding him an honorary degree.

If Vermonters sometimes succumbed to McCarthyism, they also demonstrated the courage to oppose it. Senator Ralph Flanders had expressed his reservations regarding Senator McCarthy as early as 1950, but it was not until the spring of 1954 that he launched a frontal attack upon the Wisconsin senator. In June, after a series of direct confrontations, including one in which Flanders referred to his colleague as Dennis the Menace, Flanders offered the resolution that led directly to the Senate condemnation of McCarthy later that year.

Document 10 provides excerpts from "Vermont: Where Are All Those Yankees?" a bittersweet portrayal that appeared in *Harper's Magazine* in December 1957. Its author, Miriam Chapin, a sixth-generation Vermonter, chronicled the passing of the Vermont of legend even while acknowledging that it probably never really existed. Chapin particularly lamented the decline of family farms and the rise of urban values, asserting that Vermont has been "annexed" by Bronxville and Brooklyn. Written before the construction of what she saw as a "badly needed highway program," her observations highlight the dilemma between development and preservation that Vermonters would experience even more intensely in subsequent decades.

Document 11 is a *Rutland Herald* editorial responding to the election of Philip Hoff, the first Democrat to serve as governor since 1853, before the founding of the Republican Party. Garnering a smaller percentage of Democratic votes than his 1958 predecessor candidate, Hoff, as noted by the *Herald*, managed sufficient independent votes to win 50.5 percent of the popular vote. While questions about the relative importance of the various factors that contributed to Hoff's victory are still debated, there is agreement that one consequence of the 1962 Democratic victory was to revitalize Vermont's two-party system.

The final selection in this chapter, **Document 12**, is an article by Rockwell Stephens that appeared in *Vermont Life*. Stephens, returning to the dilemma between preservation and development, welcomed the federal interstate highway system as a marriage of convenience with safety that would showcase Vermont's scenic splendor by providing "quicker and easier access" to its mountains, country roads, villages, and farms. Opponents countered that the interstate route threatened the remoteness that had kept Vermont "unspoiled," but they never constituted a serious threat to the project. Unlike their predecessors who had contested the construction of the Green Mountain Parkway, they could not hold off what most Vermonters had come to regard as progress.

"Vermont Declares War" (1941)
BURLINGTON FREE PRESS

Most spectacular of the acts of the Vermont General Assembly in its closing hours yesterday was what amounts to a declaration of war, or at least a declaration that a state of war exists between the United States and Germany. Congress probably will sit up and take notice when this news reaches Washington, since that body has always considered that it alone of all the legislative bodies in the United States had power to determine the issue of peace and war.

After the house military affairs committee had reported adversely on the bill passed by the senate to pay the $10-per-month soldier bonus, and the house had followed that report and killed the bill, it appears that a considerable number of the legislators had a change of heart and decided that the boys ought to have the bonus.

So the military affairs committee sponsored a resolution which declared that President Roosevelt's order of last week to the navy to shoot at belligerent ships on sight really put this country in a state of armed conflict, so that the bonus should be paid under the law passed at the regular session last spring.

Some Vermonters may have a little difficulty in following the course of events on this issue. But the explanation of it seems to be that the majority of the legislators didn't want to pay the soldiers a bonus in peace time, but thought they ought to have it, so decided to define "armed conflict" as used in the law now on the books, so that it would be possible to pay the bonus without any new law.

Governor Wills seems to have been uncertain about signing the resolution, probably because no provision was made for additional revenue to pay the bonus. But he did sign it. So the soldiers will get their bonus — when they complete their service in the army or reenlist at the end of their present term.

Source: *Burlington Free Press*, 17 September 1941. Reprinted with permission of the *Burlington Free Press*.

"Vermont Council of Safety Is Now Busy Day and Night to Protect Lives and Property of People of the State" (1942)
BURLINGTON FREE PRESS

Montpelier, March 8. Two days after Pearl Harbor Gov. William H. Wills was in session with the Vermont Council of Safety in the executive office at the State House. The clock on the wall registered exactly 12:52 as the ringing of the phone bell interrupted the serious discussion in progress.

"Gentlemen," said the governor quietly as he put down the receiver, "that was an air raid warning from Boston. All New England is now on yellow." Yellow, in the new parlance of air-raid wardens, is the first stage of an air raid warning. Then they really went to work. Within 10 minutes every community in the state of 2,000 or more population had been notified by telephone. There was no going out to lunch that noon for the governor and the members of the council. At 1:55 came the "all clear."

Its Duty

Speaking that same day to the people of his state, by radio, Governor Wills stated: "Today, in the crisis with which our country is faced, I repeat the words of my predecessor, Gov. Erastus Fairbanks to President Lincoln during another national crisis: "Vermont will do its duty."

That today Vermont is doing its duty in the matter of civilian defense is evident from a visit to the executive chambers, where frequent conferences on the subject are in progress, and to the third floor of the State House, where the staffs of the Council of Safety and its related activities have their headquarters. Here is a veritable bee-hive of activity throughout the day. Here the lights burn far in the night. Here two offices are devoted to the work of the Council of Safety, one to rationing, one to salvage and one to the American Red Cross. From here lines of activity radiate to every corner of the state with more than 8,000 persons working under the direction of the council for the safety and protection of every community in Vermont.

Legalized Body

The Vermont Council of Safety is no mere extra-legal body, without official status and without authority. No, it was legalized under that name by the special session of the 1941 General Assembly on Sept. 13 by request of the governor and authorized to "prepare, put into effect and supervise the operation of plans for civilian defense throughout the state, to act as the state agency for cooperation with the federal government in all civilian defense matters and to direct the organization of, and supervise and coordinate the civilian defense activities of counties and municipalities."

Preliminary Steps

Long before the Council of Safety was given legislative status, however, it was busily at work on preliminary steps for a unified civilian defense program. Shortly after his inauguration in Jan. 1941, Governor Wills went to work on building up an adequate defense program for the state.

Mindful of the early settlers of the state who, during previous trying days, had formed councils of safety for their own protection, the existing State Council of Defense was renamed Vermont Council of Safety and given official status. The governor was made chairman ex officio and he named Albert A. Cree of Rutland, executive vice chairman. . . .

Survey of Industries

Early in Jan., 1941, the council secured the cooperation of industry in making a survey of all industries of the state. In May a study of farm labor needs was undertaken and that same month the council was asked to organize air-raid warning services. Through the cooperation of the American Legion, which had already done some of this work, 4,000 volunteers were secured to man 260 aircraft warning posts throughout the state.

By the end of May President Roosevelt had organized the Office of Civilian Defense and the country as a whole first began to hear of civilian protection units. Under date of June 14, 1941, Governor Wills issued Memorandum No. 1 to the executive officers of all Vermont communities, in which he called attention to the responsibilities of local officials for the protection of the persons and property in their communities. He urged that local police, fire fighting and medical aid services be augmented by the recruiting of volunteers for emergency work. That summer came the aluminum collection campaign in which the council played

a directing role and later, Secretary Ickes' "gas curfew," during which Governor Wills set up the state fuel board to make a survey of Vermont's solid and liquid fuel needs. That survey is now almost completed.

Rationing Duties

The coming of rationing placed on the council the duty of first organizing this work. Later Fred S. Brynne was appointed by the federal government as state rationing administrator. He works in cooperation with the council and is an associate member of the council. The "Salvage for Victory" program is another interest of the council of safety with A. Vail Allen, chairman of the state salvage committee, as associate member of the council, although the executive secretary of the committee is a federal employee.

Air Raid Warning

Any successful air raid warning system is dependent on prompt and efficient communication at all hours between various points. Such a system was established by the council, according to plans prepared by Albert A. Cree, executive vice chairman of the council in charge of communications. In accordance with this plan the state was divided into 10 districts, based on telephone rather than geographical or political lines. Each of the districts has a district warning center from which lines of communication "fan-out" to cover the entire district. In addition the army has installed special receiving phones in four main district centers: Burlington, Rutland, White River Junction and Bellows Falls. These district centers will be notified directly from the army information center at Albany, N.Y. The result is an effective air raid warning system through which the army will notify the state, the state will warn the communities and the communities will notify the people by a standard air raid warning signal. All communities can be notified within 10 minutes.

Red Cross Agreement

Through the council the state has entered into an agreement with the American Red Cross whereby the Red Cross had undertaken to give more first aid instruction and thus provide the state with an expanding list of first aid instructors. By this agreement the Red Cross has undertaken to equip ambulances and provide surgical dressings and bandages and to provide complete care of all non-medical casualties. E.E. LeMasters, director of the American Red Cross Emergency Field office, has been provided with office facilities in the State House and made an associate member of the council.

Volunteer Offices

Mrs. Marjorie Conzelman of Barre has been placed in charge of the volunteer offices with the purpose of setting up a volunteer office in each community where volunteer workers for all kinds of defense services will be able to register.

In addition to all this specific work, the council has in general engaged in the work of educating the public through newspaper and radio publicity, the issuance of numerous bulletins, leaflets and pamphlets, holding instructors' schools and sending men to government sponsored schools for civilian protective services. Council members have addressed numerous meetings and aided in establishing local defense set-ups in accordance with a general pattern.

Is all this activity tantamount to setting up a straw man? There are those who say: "It's a waste of time. Vermont will never experience an enemy air raid." To such people the governor's reply is: "I hope they are right. I hope the people of Vermont never have to experience the death and destruction resulting from air raids and bombings. But it is better to take out insurance before the fire breaks out, to lock the barn before the horse is stolen. It is true this is no time for hysteria, and the work of the Council of Safety is designed not to create but to allay hysteria. However, I have in mind two words which are filled with tragedy for those to whose action they were applied. The words are . . . too late!"

What Total War Means

"Let us resolve, even at this late date, that they can never be applied to actions of Vermonters. We love liberty and freedom too dearly to watch them be taken from us through our inaction. Today total war includes attack on civilian population as well as on the military and naval forces. To meet total war, a nation must prepare not only adequate fighting forces and their services of supply, but also it must have its civilian population so organized and trained that breakdown on the home front will not defeat its armed forces.

"Now that we appreciate the dangers with which our country is confronted, I feel sure we will go forward with great strides. I feel that when any call is made upon Vermont, or when I am asked as its governor, what the nation may expect from us, that I can answer with Erastus Fairbanks: Vermont will do its duty."

Source: *Burlington Free Press*, 9 March 1942. Reprinted with permission of the *Burlington Free Press*.

DOCUMENT 3

"Making Maple Sugar" (1942)
[tune of "Working on the Railroad"]
WORDS BY RALPH LOCKE

We are making maple sugar
 Boiling night and day.
We are making maple sugar,
 in the good old Yankee way.
Can't you see the steam arising
 through the open roof?
Can't you hear the pan aboiling
 You don't need more proof.

2

We are making maple sugar
 Helping on the the farm.
We are making maple sugar
 work that builds a husky arm.
Can't you smell the sap aboiling?
 Hear the roaring arch?
We will fight the sugar shortage
 Youth is on the march.

Source: William Wills Papers, c. March 1942, Vermont State Archives, Secretary of State's office, Montpelier, Vermont.

DOCUMENT 4

Freedom of Speech (1943)
NORMAN ROCKWELL

(Depicted on facing page)

Source: Printed by permission of the Norman Rockwell Family Trust. Copyright © 1943 the Norman Rockwell Family Trust.

Document 4

DOCUMENT 5

"Gibson for Governor" (1946)

Ernest Gibson's life has been marked by service to the people — of his own state and of the nation at large. Vermont-born and bred, he has already been quick to grasp the needs and problems of his state and to safeguard its natural resources and promote its industries.

For a generation Ernest Gibson's name has been uppermost in any endeavor or movement aiming at the improvement of the social, cultural, educational, economic and health conditions of the Vermonter. Yet his public life and his mental horizon have not been bounded by the Green and the White Mountains. His public-spirited activities have been of national scope. It was he who in 1941 succeeded the late William Allen White as a national chairman of the chairman of the Committee to Defend America by Aiding the Allies.

That was only natural since, a whole year before, Ernest Gibson's voice was pleading in the United States Senate for preparedness and selective service. His memorable speech on the subject, which Alben Barkley, the Majority leader, described as one of the ablest he had ever heard in the Senate, helped rouse complacent Americans to the danger their nation was facing.

Ernest Gibson follows his words with deeds. His passionate pleas for preparedness he translated into action by joining the armed forces, well ahead of Pearl Harbor. Assigned to the famed 43rd division under the illustrious General Leonard F. Wing, Colonel Gibson shipped overseas with advanced detachments in 1942. After participation in the campaigns on Guadalcanal and the New Georgia group, for which he was decorated with the Silver Star and the Legion of Merit, a wound received at Rendova necessitated his return to the United States. He was assigned to General Staff duty in Washington, where during the critical final stages of the war, he was Deputy Director of Military Intelligence, a task of far-reaching importance, for which he received a War Department Citation.

Returning to civilian life in September, 1945, Ernest Gibson, now older and his hair grayer, immediately turned his attention to the pressing post-war problems of his state, among them the safeguarding of precious Vermont farm lands and the intensification of the dairy, maple sugar, and other specialized Vermont industries, as well as the utilization of large tracts of idle, unproductive land.

Nor has Ernest Gibson forgotten for one moment that Vermont's greatest wealth is its people. As the father of four Vermont-born children —Pvt. Ernest W. 3rd, 18; Grace, 16; Robert, 14, and David, 10—he considers the health, education, and economic well being of the Vermonter as his primary concern.

VERMONT is at the Crossroads
Follow these Guide Posts to a Better Vermont
Under the Aggressive Leadership of
ERNEST W. GIBSON

1. Stop flooding Fertile Land
2. Guard the Health of All the Children
3. Keep Young Vermonters in Vermont
4. Remember that Better Teachers + Better Training = Better Children
5. Develop Our Vast Acreage of Idle Land
6. Help Our Farmers to Market Crops More Profitably
7. Increase the Use Value of Our Natural Resources
8. Flow the Millions of Recreational Dollars into Vermont's Year-Round Recreational Climate
9. Attract the Kinds of Industry to Our State that Fit Our Needs
10. Make Good Our Promises to Our Veterans

Vote on August 13   Ernest W. Gibson for Governor

Source:Gibson for Governor campaign flyer, 1946, Political Ephemera collection, Special Collections, Bailey/Howe Library, University of Vermont.

DOCUMENT 6

"Vermont Goes Radical" (1947)
WILLIAM GILMAN

No other state has voted Republican so consistently as Vermont, but the same kind of independence that made her declare war on the Axis three months ahead of the rest of the U.S. has modernized that Republicanism into a new progressive pattern.

Since the first World War the rest of the country has been standing still in its notions about Vermont, and Vermont hasn't been standing still at all. Today's natives are mighty tired of being forever posed against their tilted landscape and captioned as quaint characters. When a photograph was published some time ago of a "typical Vermonter"—a hillbilly guy with whiskers to his knees and galluses hanging down his unbuttoned pants—aroused citizens didn't rest until they proved he was a wandering wood chopper from New Hampshire.

Moreover, Vermont challenges any other state to match the liberalism of its top-tier political spokesmen—its veteran senator George D. Aiken, its new Senator Ralph E. Flanders, its new Governor Ernest W. Gibson. Being Vermonters these men don't wear out the microphone. And being Vermonters they are Republicans. But each, by no coincidence, happens to be a well-documented progressive. And don't forget that what's liberal elsewhere has been considered downright radical for Vermont.

There are reasons for its special status. Boil down the Vermonters and you'll likely find a God-fearing farmer or small-towner. His roots grow deep and he claims to be more purely Anglo-Saxon than any other New Englander. He still lives in the house where he was born. A Vermont realtor, unrolling blueprints, explains:

"Two tracts I'm turning into developments. One's been in my family since 1768. The other's more recent—1796."

Isolationism has been almost a way of life in this very model Republican state. Back in the days of the Revolution, Ethan Allen's Green Mountain Boys outfought everybody else. They resisted King George, New York, New Hampshire and the Continental Congress, and ran their own ornery republic for 14 years until they deigned to join the Union in 1791.

But now, with a frightening war behind and the Atomic Era ahead, Vermonters say simply, "We can't go it alone. . . ."

Of course the state's geography and history have given it peculiarities which won't be changed overnight. One of them is the state's unswerving loyalty to the Republican party. When your Vermonter votes, he's more or less following principle, and definitely following habit. Back in the good old days when "a barrel of beer and a jug of buttermilk" elected a man to state legislature, Vermont also took a deep swig of Republicanism. To this day, it has refused to elect a Democratic governor, senator or President. . . .

Unlike "progressive" Wisconsin, another state strong in dairying and farm co-op movements, "hidebound" Vermont went all the way with Wendell Willkie—cheering both his Bull Moose Republicanism and his One World dream. The Vermonter saw nothing contradictory in wanting One World and marching off to set the world right, while warning outsiders not to interfere with him. One of his governors explained it a century ago when he declared that "hostility to slavery is an instinct" with Vermonters.

In those days the state was a thorn in the flesh of tyranny. It backed faraway Hungary and Greece in their fights for freedom. It helped Canada revolt against Britain. It needled the South's slaveholders so savagely that Georgia's exasperated legislature called on the President "to employ a sufficient number of able-bodied Irishmen to proceed to the State of Vermont, dig a ditch around the limits of the same, and float 'the thing' into the Atlantic."

Apparently, Vermont figured it had set the world right and went into hibernation after the Civil War. It has now decided the job has to be done again, and that's the setting which explains what has been happening. . . .

Perhaps the best illustration of the trend is in the power climb of those two freewheeling Republicans, Senator George Aiken and Governor Ernest Gibson.

As a young fellow, Gibson spent some time working as a Coast and Geodetic Survey mathematician in Washington, where his father, Ernest, Sr., was Vermont's congressman—and later its senator.

Aiken was originally an energetic farmer. His raspberry patch got out of control and he thinned it out. That left him extra plants which, if he hadn't been a Vermonter, he'd probably have tossed over the bank. Instead he found a customer for them. Berries led to shrubs, shrubs to Christmas wreaths—and Aiken set up a nursery in the near-by village of Putney.

Then Gibson returned to Brattleboro and hung out his law shingle. His first client happened to be Aiken with a fistful of unpaid nursery bills he wanted collected. That's how the two men first met.

A political bug bit Aiken in 1930 and he went to the state legislature at Montpelier as Putney's representative. There he started right off fighting the utilities and, in general, speaking for the farm bloc. Shortly before the 1932 election, he confided to friend Gibson that he was thinking of running for the state senate. Gibson suggested a higher goal. It worked out. Aiken got re-elected to the House and bid boldly for the speakership. His opponent was a banker. Bankers were unpopular then. Aiken became speaker.

In two more campaigns he moved to lieutenant governor and governor. He had climbed from the bottom of the ladder to its top in six years.

Gibson was named secretary of the state senate. In 1940 when Gibson's father died, Aiken appointed the son to step into his father's senatorial shoes until a special election could be held. There, carrying the ball for Willkie Republicans, the freshman made a speech for Lend-Lease which Democratic Leader Alben Barkley praised as "one of the ablest I have heard in many years."

That same fall Aiken ran for the Senate and won. In Washington he voted as he pleased. Vermont's newspapers were leery, but their readers stampeded for this mugwump in his 1944 re-election campaign. He has gone on to establish a pro-labor voting record which anguishes Ohio's conservative-Republican Bob Taft, delights the C.I.O.'s Philip Murray and doesn't irritate Aiken's farmer supporters, whose interests he watches like a mother hen.

Meanwhile, Roosevelt had privately approved Gibson to succeed William Allen White as chairman of the Committee to Defend American by Aiding the Allies. Gibson scourged America Firsters for a while but didn't like the pretense that we weren't in war. He went into the Army in May, 1941, and saw action in the South Pacific as an Intelligence officer. Later, as a full colonel, he was sent to Washington to direct U.S. spies and fight snafu as Deputy Director of Military Intelligence. When he returned to Brattleboro in September, 1945, he found Aiken and his other friends looking blue.

Nationally, Aiken was pleading for a Republican bloc "to preserve what liberal element the party has left in Congress." And Vermont, he reported, had slipped back into Old Guard hands. He figured that the state would rally behind Gibson for governor. When Farm Bureau heads joined in the urging, Gibson agreed, although he didn't expect he could win.

Tradition was against him. He had never run for state office before, and Vermont prefers advancing a man step by step. Tradition also dictated that incumbent Governor Mortimer Proctor be renominated in the 1946 primary for a second term of two years. Behind him also was the power of the Old Guard—Vermont's hierarchy of utilities, insurance companies and Proctor's own big business, the Vermont Marble Company. To cap it all was the resounding family name— his grandfather, father and uncle had all been Vermont governors. Against this dynasty, Gibson had only one illustrious ghost on his side—that of his father, the late senator. But he also had crusading energy. He rode the R.F.D. circuit and didn't miss the Rotary Clubs. . . . Proctor, a well-meaning standpatter, didn't smart under much worse invective than hearing his record dismissed as A Study in Still Life. Vermonters flocked to the rebel banner and Gibson kidnapped the nomination comfortably, 32,166 to 24,170. After that, he trounced the Democratic candidate in November by the usual four-to-one.

In winning, young Ernest, who was 45 and prematurely gray, admittedly had a war record and a face that many women consider the handsomest of them all. But it was his pledge to be an "aggressive, progressive leader" that brought him the majority among the farmers, workers, small-towners and the new voters called veterans.

You spot a Gibson supporter in the fellow back from agricultural college, who takes on a couple of ghost farms in addition to his father's, mechanizes everything he can touch and proudly recites the butterfat record of his purebred Ayrshires. And there's the agile old-timer, stoutly supporting the program to restore the timber he knew as a boy.

In a town you come upon a mill worker and an employer, both against anything that might stir up labor trouble, like the "anticoercion" bill which almost slipped through the Proctor legislature.

"Our workingmen are solid citizens, not thugs and not Communists," says the boss. "That bill would only have made labor mad. If we have strikes, the usual law against assault and battery can handle any picket who doesn't behave himself."

Over to Brattleboro, Gibson speaks for himself. Dapperly dressed, sprawling comfortably in his main-street law office, guarded by a pretty red-haired secretary, he tells how he blitzed the Old Guard. He serves notice that he intends to be heard in the national arena where he'll demand a liberal Republican candidate for 1948's Presidential fracas. . . .

Gibson wants to modernize the colonial house called Vermont but retain its "character." He plans development of the state's natural resources and wants to give veterans a start on reborn farms and in small, new industries. He urges cheaper electric power. Vermont, he says, should capitalize on its chance to become a Switzerland for vacationists.

To Combat Physical Unfitness

As an urgent "must" he wants more and better-paid teachers, and one of his pet projects is to have mobile health units visit schools regularly. Vermonters were startled to learn what kind of youngsters they had been raising when Selective Service headquarters disclosed that the state had the worst 4F record in New England, and one of the worst in the nation. Its percentage of physical unfits placed it down in the cellar with eight Southern states.

Young Ernest didn't wait until his inauguration day to get started. On the day after election he called on the state party chairman to resign, informing that senior Republican that he was "entirely out of touch with the times and was living in the good old days of the 1920s."

Ten miles north of Brattleboro is the Aiken Nurseries, where you'll find Vermont's senior senator in his jam-packed little office tacked on to the greenhouse. Fifteen years of politics have fashioned George Aiken into a ministerial-looking farmer-statesman of fifty-four—a soft speaker who is stubborn and canny. His oldest energy is what he calls the Power Trust, and his pet project is the St. Lawrence Seaway. Currently, his big interest is in joining hands with other Republican liberals to thwart the forces behind Bob Taft. . . .

Dispatches from Washington inform him that he's being branded a renegade, but he continues speaking his piece:

"This is the first time I know of when a party took power without one constructive idea to offer. The Old Guard isn't interested in fighting labor's unreasonable demands—it's fighting labor. It mustn't try to turn the clock back—everywhere I go, the people want a better way of life and will refuse to give up the social gains of the past 15 years."

He's basically optimistic, willing to go fast slowly, and chuckles, "Things are changing. Even the Old Guard isn't as Old Guardish as it used to be."

Up the road 25 miles more is the busy industrial town of Springfield, home of Jones & Lamson Machine Company. Its president, Ralph E. Flanders, 65, is the new junior senator from Vermont whom Willkie Republicans would like named Secretary of Commerce after 1948 and whom philosopher John Dewey called "the most enlightened industrialist I have ever met."

Vermont expects a national vote of thanks when this versatile teamworker gets going on Capitol Hill. As head of the New England Council, he was called the country's liveliest regional organizer. He was president of the Federal Reserve Bank of Boston. His able hand is credited with guiding the Bretton Woods agreement, straightening out war-production jams, keeping N.R.A. from going wild. In his election campaign, he had the C.I.O. seal of approval.

Flanders is the poor boy who became an inventor, then grew wealthy and wise. . . . One clue to his ideology was his call on New England businessmen to accept fully the aims of the New Deal without necessarily swallowing its methods. . . .

Voice of the True Faith

There are many Vermonters who haven't the vision of Flanders, Aiken and Gibson. But the bulk of their constituents chose them; they didn't win office through accident or passing Pappy's biscuits. And right now, Vermont's progressive Republicans claim the right to discuss what the G.O.P.'s national party line should be. Taft's Ohio and Stassen's Minnesota speak with some authority, but Vermont's voice seems to be that of the true faith—there's no blot on her G.O.P. escutcheon. Teaming with Maine, she entered the only nay to F.D.R. in 1936. Back in 1912, she and Utah stood alone for William Howard Taft. Therefore, when this state now prescribes the shorter skirts of liberalism, it's the dowager of the party speaking.

But she speaks still with her own Yankee twang. When Aiken was lieutenant governor, the legislature rejected a federal parkway through the Green Mountains, tossing the $18,000,000 back into the astonished Washington's lap. Modern Ethan Allens refused to allow "a strip of foreign territory" to cross the state.

When Aiken was governor, he welcomed the Rural Electrification Administration but declined to allow Rex Tugwell's Resettlement Administration boys in the state, asserting that Vermont didn't want its hill-and-valley folk resettled, and merely shrugged when told that Vermont was the only state so balky. Then he slapped down a flood-control project, notifying the White House that Vermont's permission hadn't been asked.

And right now, though he won't concede the recent G.O.P. sweep was a mandate for reaction, he says a cleanup was due: "Responsibility had drifted too far away. We'll have more social legislation going back under state control—with the states, of course, discovering they'll have to put up more of the money."

As Vermont goes, so goes the nation? Sometimes. As Vermont goes, so goes the Republican party? Well, say its Young Turks, the G.O.P. could do a lot worse. They don't believe that Democrats should have a vested interest in liberalism, and won't agree that all Republicans are congenital Tories.

What party line should the G.O.P. follow to win friends and influence America's voters? Up speaks a Vermonter just back from a trip to Canada:

"They've got a party up there with an interesting label. It's called the Progressive Conservatives."

Source: *Collier's* (April 19, 1947): 12-14, 104-105.

DOCUMENT 7

Inaugural Address (1951)

GOVERNOR LEE EMERSON

TO THE GENERAL ASSEMBLY AND PEOPLE OF VERMONT:

As we enter upon the deliberations of this Legislature, it is well to pause and take brief account of stock so that we may know and appreciate the job which lies ahead of us. The little segment of time with which we deal will be an important link in the chain of history of our nation and our state.

The times are ominous and uncertain. The world is in turmoil. It is peopled by a vast majority who have been taught not to like us and who are jealous of our democracy and what it has been able to accomplish. To many of these people, a crust of bread or a bowl of rice is a prize to be coveted. To many of these people, Communism is attractive because they have been falsely persuaded it offers a better way of life than the misery and degradation they have heretofore lived under. Communistic leadership is utterly ruthless. It seeks to destroy democracy as a way of life just the same as the Huns and Vandals of an earlier day sought to destroy the superior civilization created by the Roman Empire. The fate of the Roman Empire, gone soft, is one of the milestones of history known to us all. Let it be said of us we are determined that history shall not repeat itself. Those who do not know and take heed of history suffer by repeating its mistakes.

But the task which lies ahead is great. We have committed ourselves wholeheartedly to the cause of peace through the medium of the United Nations. In a world today that knows only force, we are the only nation with sufficient potentiality to oppose force with force. In Korea our force has not been sufficient to put into effect a United Nations edict. It must be made sufficient. In a world grown small because of the airplane and the atomic bomb, to think that we can carry on continually seeking the good things of life first and military and home front preparedness second is to court disaster. . . .

EXTRAORDINARY MEASURES

Communism. We here in Vermont believe in democracy, and its most important attributes such as the right to free speech, freedom of religious worship, freedom of assemblage and a free press. However, we do not want to see this democracy imperiled by the advocacy, through the medium of any political party, of the overthrow of our government by force. Any party having such a principle as a part of its platform should be outlawed in Vermont. Furthermore, I call your attention to the fact that the United States is not technically in a state of war at the present time. Chapter 306 of the Vermont Statutes known as the Sabotage Prevention Act comes into force and effect only when the United States is so engaged. I believe this chapter dealing with acts of sabotage in time of war should be so amended as to make it applicable under present day conditions.

Civil Defense. No. 251 of the Acts of 1949 sets up a civil defense agency within the Department of Public Safety. This Act provides for a council which is charged with the duty of adopting a plan contemplating the coordination to the maximum extent of all civil defense functions of the state with the comparable functions of the Federal government. This Council should be made answerable to the Governor. The Act should be clarified and enlarged to fully meet the conditions we are faced with. Plans for all kinds of disaster relief which may not have been contemplated at the time the Act was drawn, including the care of refugees who may come to our State from bombed metropolitan areas should be detailed therein. As a matter of patriotism it behooves the citizen for his own self-protection to give freely of his time and effort so that an adequate civil defense set up may cover the state. The work should be kept upon a volunteer rather than a paid basis as much as possible. We must all volunteer willingly for this work and be willing to do or perform whatever tasks may be assigned to us to accomplish. Many local civil defense setups are rapidly being put into effect and commendation is due for the spirit and leadership which has made this possible. An appropriation for this activity will be recommended in the budget.

War Powers Act. The Legislature of 1943 adopted a measure, No. 6 of the Acts of 1943, known as the "State Emergency War Powers Act of 1943." Such an act, with modifications to bring it up to present day situations, should in my opinion be re-adopted by this legislature, the act to be put into effect in the event of war between our country and any foreign nation or to be put into effect in the event of any surprise acts of aggression against our country by any foreign power before a formal declaration of war can be made. In this connection attention is called to the fact that during the last year there was a threatened strike of electric utility workers in the Newport area because of a failure of the workers and the employer utility to get together on the matter of pay. A strike by the workers of an electric utility might cause the crippling or shutting down of plant activities thereby resulting in possible grave injury to the people of the area serviced by it. The same situation might arise in connection with the operation of other utilities whose work is of a semi-public nature. It would appear as though, to meet any such possible conditions arising and disrupting our normal economy, that the governor should be implemented with power to seize and take over the property of the affected utility and provide for its temporary emergency operation until such time as the dif-

ferences between management and labor could be ironed out. This grant of power could very well be useful not only in the unusual circumstances under which we live today, but as a permanent addition to our statutory law under normal conditions.

State Guard. In view of the fact that most of our National Guard has been activated into Federal service and other remaining National Guard units in the state have been alerted, the state will be in the position of not having adequate military forces available in the event of major disasters or emergencies confronting us. I, therefore, recommend the setting up of a State Guard substantially along the lines provided for by No. 180 of the Acts of 1941, which act first created a State Guard in this state.

Soldiers Bonus. Although there has been no formal declaration of war, we are at the present time engaged in armed conflict with the North Korean forces and the armies of Communist China. Vermont boys are giving their lives and their service to the cause of the United Nations on the battlefields of Korea. I recommend that members of the armed services during the period of armed conflict of war be paid a bonus the same as the veterans of World War I and World War II have been in this state. An appropriation to implement this recommendation is provided for in the budget.

Aviation. No one can gainsay the fact the aviation will play an important part in any emergency which war conditions may thrust upon us. Likewise its usefulness in aiding the development of recreational and business activity in the state has been slowly but steadily improving.

The money we have been appropriating for airport development is, under existing statutes, permitted to be used only for airport construction. Federal funds on a matching basis have been available for construction work, but not for maintenance. There is not as great a demand upon this fund for airport construction as there has been, and although the Federal government does not match money we spend for maintenance, still I feel that the State should permit the use of some portion of this fund for such purpose because this is becoming an increasingly more pressing problem at the twenty-two airports in the state.

An equitable formula should be worked out whereby the state could render some assistance in the matter of snow removal and repairs to these airports so that they may be kept in a proper and usable state at all times.

In common with eleven other states, in 1923 Vermont adopted a statute holding the owner or pilot of an aircraft doing damage absolutely liable as the result of flight or accident. Most of the states which adopted this legislation are now doing away with it or modifying it to a considerable degree and are now providing that liability be predicated solely upon the basis of negligence, the same as in automobile accident cases. I recommend that Vermont do likewise.

Voting. I further recommend that the legislature give careful consideration to the amendment of our election laws to permit to the fullest extent possible voting by members of the armed services in local, state and national elections they might desire to participate in. . . .

Source: *Journal of the Senate,* Biennial Session, 1951 (Montpelier: Capital City Press, 1951): 692-695.

DOCUMENT 8

Speaker's Remarks (1953)
CONSUELO NORTHROP BAILEY

Members of the Legislature of 1953:

First of all, I want to thank each and every one of the members of this House for their great and generous expression of confidence which you have placed in me today. I also want to thank each and all of you who have extended the kindness and the courtesy of your homes when I have been privileged to visit you.

I want to congratulate each and every one of you. I congratulate you because your electorates have given you the blessed privilege of serving the people of this great State.

Thirdly, I want to take you into my confidence long enough to say, at this point, that I cannot help but think of the Legislature of 1900 and the member of Fairfield in that Legislature. I speak, of course, of my father, our father, because my sister, representing the same town, is occupying the same seat that my father, the late Peter Bent Brigham Northrop, occupied in the session of 1900.

I hope that when the people of this state notice the first sentence of the first Article of the Constitution of the State of Vermont and they read that "all men are created equally free and independent" that those words will take on a brighter, a more complete meaning for the women not only of this House, but also of the women of Vermont.

Because someone said in the House this morning that I am the first woman speaker in this country, I feel that it should be called to your attention at this point that this is an incorrect statement. There was a lady by the name of Minnie Craig of the State of North Dakota who served as speaker of the House of that State in the Legislature of 1933.

I want to tell you, as I told some of you folks last night, a little incident, which I will not elaborate on at this time because the hour is late, that when Calvin Coolidge said that he was going to appoint a woman to the United States Customs Court of New York City he was told that no woman had ever held the post and he replied, "No one will ever say that again." I cannot tell you how much I appreciate the honor that you have placed upon me, but I want you to thoroughly understand from now on that I realize that this honor is completely outweighed by the responsibility which you have given me. You know, in referring to Calvin Coolidge, I can't help but say this, I think if he were here today that he would say to us that the State of Vermont needs and deserves the very best that every one of us two hundred and forty-six people can give the State and he would point out to you that as he used to watch a pair of strong horses pulling a heavy load of logs up a hill in Plymouth, that unless they pulled together, they just could not make the grade. So I ask all of you in that spirit to work together. I shall need the help of every single one of you who have so generously and graciously retired in my behalf today. I know that all of you would have made splendid, efficient, competent speakers.

I do appreciate what you have done and in closing I want to say that this now is no time for any of us to think of anything except one thing at all times. I hope you will bear it in mind from now until the close of this session. There should be only one question in our minds. In other words, we should put aside all unsatisfied desires and ambitions and keep before us at all times the one paramount issue—what is best for the State of Vermont.

Thank you very much.

Source: *Journal of the House*, Biennial Session, 1953, (Montpelier, 1953): 11-12.

DOCUMENT 9

Proceedings of University of Vermont Faculty-Trustees Board of Review of Dr. Alex B. Novikoff (1953)

Three charges were made:

1. That Dr. Alex B. Novikoff is guilty of conduct which justifies his discharge, in that when summoned to testify before a sub-committee of the United States Senate Judiciary Committee, investigating the subversive influence in the educational process, he testified freely concerning his activities since coming to the University in 1948, but when questioned concerning his connections with the Communist Party, if any, prior to 1948, he claimed privilege under the Fifth Amendment.

2. That Dr. Novikoff is guilt of conduct which justifies his discharge, in that when summoned to testify before a sub-committee of the United States Senate Judiciary Committee investigating the subversive influence in the educational process, he improperly invoked the Fifth Amendment for the protection of others and not for his own protection.

3. That Dr. Novikoff was guilty of conduct which justifies his discharge in that he has refused to disclose fully his connections with the Communist Party prior to 1948, if any. . . .

Examination by Mr. [Francis] Peisch [attorney for Professor Novikoff]

MR. PEISCH: What is your name, sir?

A   Dr. W.E. Brown.

Q   Are you dean of the University of Vermont Medical School, sir?

A   I am not now. I am the retired dean.

Q   During what period were you dean, sir?

A   I was dean from August-September 1st, 1945 through September 1st, 1952.

Q   Were you dean of the University of Vermont Medical School at the time Dr. Alex Novikoff was retained?

A   I was.

Q   Would you tell this Board, very briefly, what the circumstances of his hiring were?

A   Dr. Novikoff was brought for an interview to my office . . . [with] the idea that he would become a special research worker in the field of cancer and also that he might teach in the Department of Biochemistry. As I always did with any prospective employee of the University, I explained to him the rules of tenure which are always given to individuals when they are employed, as I always felt it was important for them to know what those rules were. I also explained to him, as I did to every other candidate, that he would be required to sign a teacher's oath, and that that was a notarized oath in which he agreed to uphold the Constitution of the United States, the laws of the United States and the laws of the State of Vermont. Dr. Novikoff left my office and later accepted the offer made to him. That was in, as I recall, in the Spring of 1948 and he was employed as of the first of July, 1948.

Q   Dean Brown, excuse me, was this the Oath: "I do solemnly swear and affirm that I will support the Constitution of the United States and of the State of Vermont and the laws of the United States and of the State of Vermont. So help me God."

A   Yes. With the addition that at the end of it there is a place to be notarized and they were always notarized by my secretary, who is a notary public.

Q   And was that done?

A   That is always done as soon as the individual comes and the oath is put on file. At the same time he came he was given a copy of the rules of tenure which we always give. . . .

Q   Do you have an opinion, sir, as to his loyalty to this country and this state during the time that you were Dean of the Medical School?

A   Yes, I do.

Q   Would you give that opinion to this Board and the reasons for it?

A   Well, in the first place, when an individual takes an oath, such as we require, to me that is prima facie evidence of loyalty. Now, if an individual subsequent to taking that oath ever gave evidence that he was not keeping or that he was violating the oath, then I would feel called upon to call him in. But at no time during my administration as Dean, and if my mathematics are correct Dr. Novikoff was there during my administration for four years, did I ever have so much as a whisper that Dr. Novikoff was anything but a very loyal citizen of the United States, a loyal citizen of the State of Vermont and loyal to the University.

Q Did you ask him if he was or ever had been a Communist?

A I didn't, any more than I would have asked President Borgmann when he came whether he had been a Communist. I felt it was not my duty to ask individuals what their race or religion, creeds or politics were. I didn't hire individuals on any of those bases.

Q Would you care to make an observation to this Board as to his professional competence?

A Yes, while I feel, if I may inject this, that his professional competence is not important at all in this hearing because I would come as his witness if he were the poorest faculty member that we had, I feel that he is a very competent individual, who has made and is making very great contribution in the field of cancer. However, I should say that if I thought he was guilty of any subversive acts I would be the first one to proceed against him despite his ability. . . .

Examination by Mr. [Louis] Lisman [counsel to the University]

Q Dr. Brown, you don't mind answering my questions, do you?

A Not at all.

Q Doctor, at the time that you were considering Dr. Novikoff's employment did you get in touch with the head of his department at Brooklyn College where he had formerly been employed?

A No, I did not for the simple reason that is the departmental head's prerogative, his duty.

Q You, yourself, were not in touch with Professor [Earl] Martin, who was the head of the Department of Biology at Brooklyn College at the time?

A No.

Q So that you are not aware of what Professor Martin's opinion at the time was of Dr. Novikoff's trustworthiness—you heard nothing of that?

A I heard nothing of that, and I have not reviewed the letters which we had from Brooklyn College, but I may say that the letters which we had in support of Dr. Novikoff mentioned nothing of the sort.

Q You heard nothing, for example, and had nothing in these letters about Dr. Novikoff's connection with a certain local of the Teachers' Union?

MR. PEISCH: I object to this question. Dr. Novikoff has already stated that he has no knowledge of any correspondence. Now, that should end it.

MR. LISMAN: I don't think Dr. Brown would mind answering the question.

A I had no such knowledge. . . .

Q Would it make a difference to you if you had learned that the same Union had been expelled from the American Federation of Labor because of Communist domination?

A Then I would have questioned him about whether or not he was still a Communist. Had he told me he was not a Communist, he had seen the error of his ways, I would still have thought he was eligible for employment.

Q But, Dr. Brown, you had none of this information about which I have questioned . . . .Dr. Novikoff, so far as you have known, has always been a loyal citizen, and you have told me that you have no knowledge or have had no knowledge of these things I have asked you about . . . . In other words, this connection, this leadership in the Communist dominated Teachers' Local of the Teachers' Union at Brooklyn College is something you learned about since?

A Yes.

Q And you have learned since that Dr. Novikoff was a leader in that group?

A Yes.

Q And you have learned that since the time he was employed that the head of his department of Brooklyn College considered him not to be a trustworthy person?

A No.

Q That you did not—

A That I did not know.

MR. PEISCH: I object to this line of questioning. This is McCarthyism. . . .

MR. LISMAN: Mr. Chairman . . . I'm going to address myself directly to the charges. We have had a lot of eloquence this afternoon. We've had a great deal of "beating about the bush." If I am guilty of eloquence from now on it is wholly unintentional. If I do any "beating about the bush" that, too, is unintentional.

I am going to address myself to the first charge, that Dr. Novikoff is guilty of conduct which justifies his discharge in that when summoned to testify before a sub-committee of the United States Senate Judiciary Committee investigating the subversive influence in the educational process . . . he claimed privilege under the Fifth Amendment.

This morning and this afternoon we have heard testimony, though it hasn't come from Dr. Novikoff, he declined to testify as to anything that happened prior to 1948 . . . we heard from others, witnesses whom he produced, that he was a Communist at one time. And it didn't stop there. There was positive evidence that he was the leader of a Communist dominated union.

This board, certainly the Board of Trustees, feels that the mere fact that a man claims privilege under the Fifth Amendment should not in and of itself warrant his discharge from the University. But Dr. Novikoff is charged with something more than claiming privilege in and of itself. Dr. Novikoff . . . was a leader of one of the Communist fronts, a Communist dominated teacher's union. Does not such a man have a greater obligation to this country than any other? Does not such a man, in view of what we all know of the Communist conspiracy in this country, does not such a man have a duty to disclose the information which he gained as a leader? Such a man if discharged from the University faculty is not being discharged for the claim of privilege in and of itself. He is being discharged because, having knowledge, particular knowledge, knowledge not available to the ordinary Communist even, of activities inimical to the security of this country nevertheless refuses in an investigation of the subversive influence in the educational process to give to a Congressional Committee the benefit of his knowledge.

In my opinion such conduct constitutes moral turpitude. In my opinion you are not only justified in discharging Dr. Novikoff under the first charge, but further you are justified in discharging him on the ground of moral turpitude under the first charge.

As to the second charge that he improperly invoked the Fifth Amendment. . . . I submit that that [the evidence] shows Dr. Novikoff did not claim his privilege in good faith; that he was not fearful of incriminating himself; or else that he was not fearful of involving others; and whatever his reason for having claimed the benefit of the Fifth Amendment he has not yet given it to us. On the contrary his evasiveness, his loss of memory tend to show that he had a reason which was not a good reason, whatever it may have been.

And now I come to the last charge which, in my opinion, is the one that Dr. Novikoff has himself most clearly proved. . . .

Had Dr. Novikoff taken the stand and testified freely and fully before the Jenner Committee we wouldn't be here. But we haven't required that he do that entirely. Up until today we said that the mere fact that he didn't claim his privilege wouldn't matter. I've asked you to consider, however, what has happened today; I asked you to consider that we know now something that we never knew before, that he was a leader in this movement; that he was a leader of the Communist conspiracy; he was a leader of a Communist dominated union. Now, I ask you to consider something further—I ask you to consider his attitude today. Regardless of all else he certainly owes the Board of Trustees and to its agencies a duty of frankness, forthrightness and candor. . . .

I consider, and I believe you will, that his refusal to cooperate with the Board of Trustees and with the Board of Review is evidence in support of the third charge. It is evidence that shows that Dr. Novikoff right along has refused to disclose fully his connections with the Communist Party prior to 1948. That's what the third charge is. I feel, Ladies and Gentlemen, that when you have given this matter due consideration you will decide that Dr. Novikoff is guilty of conduct which justifies his discharge. And I am inclined to think you will go further and find that that conduct constitutes moral turpitude. . . .

Source: Transcript of Proceedings, University of Vermont Faculty-Trustees Board of Review of Dr. Alex B. Novikoff, 8/29/53, University of Vermont Archives, pp. 6-7, 34-38, 102-106. Reprinted courtesy of Special Collections, UVM Libraries.

Document 10

"Vermont: Where Are All Those Yankees?" (1957)

Miriam Chapin

A strictly non-maple syrup account—by a Vermonter in good (up to now) standing—of the professional quaintery of Vermont and its imitation Yankees.

Vermont is the most beautiful state in the Union. As a sixth-generation Vermonter, I put that axiom at the head of my credo. It is also more full of assorted baloney, hokum about unspoiled Vermont, snobbery about ancestry, guff about noble Vermonters, maple syrup, and Calvin Coolidge, general antiquery, than any other state with the possible exception of Virginia. Probably the last genuine old-time Vermonter went out to Utah to found the Church of the Latter-Day Saints. Those who stayed were sick, riddled with tuberculosis. In my grandfather's family twelve out of thirteen died of "consumption" before they reached thirty. He, the youngest, bought a substitute to fight the Civil War for him and die in Andersonville, and lived to seventy-eight, superintendent of the local Sunday School and the crankiest old man I ever encountered.

Perhaps there has been at some time a Vermont according to the legend. . . . That Vermont, and there never was much of it, has been conquered by the cities. Its present citizens use the slogan of quaintness as tourist bait, and collaborate with the conquerors. Vermont is a fief of Boston and New York. It is about time Vermonters came out from behind the maple sugar bush, out from under the covered bridge, took off their patchwork quilts, and looked themselves in the eye. Vermonters are much like other people, not much better, not much worse. In fact, a great many of them *are* other people, who came from Kansas and Quebec, Milan and Bratislava.

The process of taking over the Green Mountains as an annex of Bronxville and Brooklyn has been going on for considerably more than fifty years, but since 1945 it has been precipitous. The figures don't tell the whole story, but they indicate it. In 1900 five million acres of Vermont land were in farms, real farms, run to

make a living. Much of it ought never to have been cleared of forest, but it was. In 1954 just over three million acres were farmed. In 1900 there were 33,000 farms; in 1945, they were down to 26,500; in 1954, only 16,000. The acreage is a little more than half what it was fifty years ago, the farms fewer than half as many, but bigger. They produce as much, but they support a smaller number of families. At the four-corners a half-mile from my home, there used to be a schoolhouse where fifty children went to school. It was torn down forty years ago. . . .

In a new guise, the family farm creeps back, but as a home, not as practical enterprise. Johnny Wimett (Ouimet, I presume), who lives a mile down my road, could not make a living on a place that will keep only eight or nine cows. So he took a job, driving twenty miles each way, at a plant in Rutland, where he puts in an eight-hour day at a machine. When he gets home, he does a few chores; weekends he hays or chops wood. He works seven days a week, long hours, and his wife and children help with the chores, so that he can stay on the land and still pay for his car and gasoline, keep up the installments on the television set and the refrigerator. In another variation, Al Parks, who is a high-school principal in Worcester, bought a run-down old place and gets enormous satisfaction out of raising a garden, painting the house, putting in his own plumbing, taking his kids swimming where he has built a dam in the brook. He keeps no stock, and if he has any plowing done, he hires someone to do it, but the house is lived in part of the year. Neither of these establishments, though listed as a farm, is one in any true financial sense.

City-Bred Farmers

From my window, high in the back-country hills and looking toward the main range of the Green Mountains, I can count eleven farmhouses. Only one is still occupied by a farmer who actually makes part of his living from a dozen cows, none pure-bred. He couldn't possibly support his family on them alone; it is doubtful if they really pay their way. He makes out by cutting pulpwood on his own land and for other men, hauls it to the paper mill ninety miles away, does haying for the summer people round about, who pay him to cut their fields so they will not grow up to brush—though they have no use for the hay. Nobody has much use for hay unless it grows on a meadow flat enough for the baler to be used. Pitching hay, riding the big, loose load into the barn, is as obsolete as the hand scythe and is seen only far back in the mountains.

Of the other houses in my view, one is inhabited by a couple who are dancers, who hope their latest television show will pay for a septic tank. Higher up on the mountain opposite is a magazine-cover artist, over by the lake are a couple of writers and some college professors, down in the hollow are a retired businessman and two engineers who work in a factory twenty miles away. That big house in a fold of the hills belongs to an ex-editor of *Fortune* who is able to spend much of the year in it. . . .

Vermont has only two colonies of the very rich, Manchester and Woodstock . . . and a few isolated big estates. Most of its farms have gone to professional people and the middle classes. None of them has any real contact with the local people, none of them knows what it is like to live all winter in a house heated by wood stoves, all are distrusted in greater or less degree by their native neighbors. . . .

The remaining big farmers, who are in dairying as a business, necessarily have a very sizable investment. A few are city men who hire an agricultural college graduate to run their place while they come on weekends to show to guests their fancy stock. . . . But mostly the farmers are local men who have inherited or bought farms now grown large by acquisition and built up by hard work. They need to have at least fifty milch cows, well-built barns, milking machines, cooling stations, sterilizing plants, tractors and trucks and field machines, training in agriculture, carefully kept record books.

The small farmer cannot meet the requirements, stricter each year, of the sanitary inspection, the whitewashed barns, the drains, the curried cattle, the bacterial count. The Vermont dairy industry operates under the control of Boston, except for a few west-side districts which ship to New York. It deals in fluid milk. Butter is seldom profitable. . . . Vermonters eat twice as much margarine as butter, sold in the chain stores where they buy their chemicalized bread and frozen orange juice. The federal administrator in Boston sets the price for milk to be paid the out-of-Massachusetts producer; the Vermont Milk Board sets it for the local delivery. Out of what he gets the farmer must buy his western grain and pay his help, with the aid of what he can make by selling surplus stock. The unpaid labor of women and children becomes less essential as the small farms vanish, though it is still a factor.

The creamery, often a co-operative, that collects and ships the milk, must make its profit between two fixed rates, which vary according to the season, the cost of grain, and the howls of the consumer. Its margin and that of the farmer are both precarious. Cows are stubborn, atavistic beasts, and even when induced to give birth in November instead of May as their instinct tells them to, they retaliate by producing far less milk in the cold winter months when they are shut in the barn than in June off the green pastures. So the creamery or pasteurizing plant, which also requires a big investment, must dispose of a surplus in summer months. It makes cheese, powdered milk, ice-cream mix to freeze in storage; it separates cream and sells skim milk back to feed the farmer's calves, evaporates and condenses milk, experiments constantly with new outlets. No one has yet succeeded in canning milk without changing its taste, but they keep trying. Apple and chicken farms follow similar patterns, are equally dependent on the metropolis.

The New Overlords

Not only are the farms adjuncts of Boston and New York, not only are the summer owners increasing each year, but the big corporations are happily moving in. Right after the war Vermont was losing about four thousand people a year, mostly young men and women who saw no future at home. That drain has been checked, but at the cost of a greater dependence on outside interests. Now when the Army cuts back its production, and GE lays off five hundred men in Burlington, the state's economy shudders. GE, IBM, half a dozen other giants, have branch plants in Vermont, whose young executives delight in fixing up old houses for their homes. But they can have no real stake in the community, since they know well they may be sent to another plant halfway round the world on a month's notice. Each new factory links the state more closely to the financial centers, makes it more dependent on continued national prosperity, less cushioned against depression. . . .

Vermont used to be ruled by the Proctor dynasty, who owned the Vermont Marble Company, an indigenous industry using foreign labor to work native rock.

It blossomed with Senators, Congressmen, Governors. The power-tools industry of Springfield came next, and the day of the public utilities, which, except for some small co-operatives and municipal plants, are owned outside the state. So are the main communications systems and the railways, which must now depend on freight, not passengers, for profit. The big industrial corporations will have their turn, and when the badly needed highway program with federal aid is completed, more will flock in, eagerly welcomed.

Since every town, whether it has fifty voters or fifteen thousand, has one representative in the legislature, this body is absurdly cumbersome and unrepresentative. Lobbying is intensive and effective. Town meetings—celebrated as the epitome of democracy—are often rigged. . . . The notables of the village, the storekeeper, some of the bigger landowners, the local lawyer and doctor if the place is big enough to have them, get together and decide who shall go to Montpelier as town representative, who shall be town clerk and who road commissioner or selectman. The word is passed around and the followers vote. When a man gets a toe-hold on a job, he can usually hang onto it. . . . Once in a long while the citizens revolt, over taxes or school questions usually, and once in a while they get concessions. Because Vermont has a poll tax which may run as high in some towns as eight or nine dollars . . . those residents who can't or won't pay are disfranchised in any election. About one per cent come under this ban. They can't get a license to drive a car either. Not in this cradle of democracy they can't. Before issuing a new card in some public libraries, the librarian will inquire softly, "May I see your poll-tax receipt?"

Vermont has problems of power development, rural slums, city ones too, low wages, uneven taxation burdens, management-labor relations (there have been terrible strikes in marble and granite) which it has not yet begun to look at squarely. Part of the reason is that they are screened behind the cloud of "unspoiled Vermont" vaporings. Too many Vermonters are bemused by their own publicity, flattered into complacency. Poems about the pure clear air of Vermont, read into the *Congressional Record*, printed in the papers, vials of said air sniffed by Vice President Nixon for the newsphoto men, don't do a thing for the little matter of sewage disposal. Many a Vermont stream is a stinking, filthy, open sewer, and the air above is not clear or fresh.

Burlington has at long last been obliged to take measures to avoid the pollution of the Lake Champlain beaches by the Winooski River. It might hurt the tourist trade. . . .

Hooks, Lines, and Sinkers

The collaborators, citizens who make a living out of visitors and new residents drawn by the loveliness of the mountain valleys, are of two kinds. There are the native Vermonters who seize the opportunity to drag out of their attics the spinning wheels and the bizchairs (predecessor of the bedpan), collect broken-down chairs and old dishes from their neighbors, set out the goods by the roadside and wait for the tourist. Or they sell real estate, start motels and snack bars, open a filling station. The immigrants do those things too, run bowling alleys for a New York chain, slash out ski trails often without heed for the dangers of erosion, and have adventures with the quaint natives. Then they write cute books, detailing their conversations with these characters and illustrating them with cute pictures. . . .

The cult of the antique requires serious psychological and sociological study, which no one has yet given it. The eager women who throng the auctions to bid on mortars and pestles, hair wreaths and Rogers groups, on grandfathers' clocks that will never be asked to tell time and teapots that will never brew tea again, who just love the old country stores and buy kerosene lamps to be fitted with wires for electricity, who drive up to the museums in Cadillacs to look at the surreys and pungs with laughter and nostalgia, of what are they in search? Are they in quest of an older time that they dream was happier and more secure, though it probably wasn't? Or is the vogue part of the ancestor worship by which the old New England families try to maintain a fragile and simulated superiority, while those of later arrival try to pretend to their background? Along with the Old Home Weeks, the back-country fairs, the exhibitions of old costumes, this nostalgia is a source of income to those who know how to use it. . . .

A very few of the native Vermonters do survive in pristine state. . . . In many towns a few families live in hovels on the back roads, live as their forefathers did. The men cut pulpwood because the work is paid by the cord and they don't have to punch a time clock. They earn enough to pay interest on the mortgage, and the taxes, or they let the taxes ride, since the town fathers know they can't collect. They get drunk on Saturday nights, pillage the empty summer camps in the fall, go to jail for driving their old cars without licenses, go fishing when they feel like it, pick berries, shoot deer and rabbits without too much care for the seasons set by the game laws. The game wardens don't bother them seriously, for they figure if a man needs meat and a deer walks past him it is asking too much of human nature not to pick up a rifle. They don't hog all the game, and they know every creature in the woods. They are, of course, looked down upon by the respectable, and they resent it. But in return they get a lot of amusement out of the behavior of the summer folks:

"That new fellow bought the Town Farm, he left his car out by the woods the other night, and the porcupines chewed every tire on it."

Within narrow limits, closing in each year, they preserve some freedom. Ethan Allen, that atheist rebel, would claim them as kindred souls, his spiritual descendants. So long as they have neither wife nor child, they can live their own lives, in some aspects ideal lives. But women suffer, living in leaky shacks, lugging water, walking miles for groceries. Illness is a calamity. In childbirth they have to depend on relatives. An aching tooth is pried out with a screwdriver, or yanked with pliers. Children get only enough schooling to learn to read and write a little. Pictures of their homes seldom appear in the books of colored photographs of the state—yet these individualists are part of the real Vermont and always have been.

Nowadays, however, their children are gathered in for a few months each year by the truant officer, looked over by the public health nurse, get hospital care in illness. Television, in every cabin that is within reach of electricity, "gives the kids ideas." The backwoods children I know all had Davy Crockett hats, not from coon and bear their fathers shot, as might well have happened, but bought in stores. They will leave their hills to work in shops and factories some day, and be none the happier.

The new Vermont offers little privacy any more. The machine age has come upon it before it was ready, and the state must grow used to public living and learn to regulate it. It has not yet. The seal of the city's conquest is the crowded air, the big transports growling in the sky day and night, so that there is seldom silence. The jets from the Army post a hundred miles away draw white lines across the blue from rocky peak to pine-stabbed horizon.

Neither my parents nor my grandparents, I'm sure, ever thought of sun-bathing in their back yard, but if they had wanted to they could surely have done it with no eye upon them. I like to, and since I have no near neighbors, I go down in my lower meadow on pleasant days to lie in the sun. One day a small plane from the commercial airport in the nearest city sputtered over me, then came back so close to the treetops that I hastily pulled on my terry coat. As it sailed off to the north, I saw a bit of white flutter down. I retrieved it from the bushes down the hill, a tiny parachute bearing a note wrapped around a bit of metal. It said:

"Lady, ain't you lonesome? Call Pete, M19-3924."

Ah, the noble Vermonter!

Source: *Harper's Magazine* (December 1957): 50-54.

DOCUMENT 11

Hoff's Upset of Keyser (1962)
RUTLAND HERALD

In a contest which was almost a replica of that in 1958, Philip Hoff, the young lawyer from Burlington, upset Gov. Ray Keyser on Tuesday and became the first Democratic governor-elect of Vermont since John S. Robinson of Bennington in 1853.

In 1958 Bernard Leddy, another Burlington lawyer, after a recount, lost to Robert Stafford, now congressman, by only 719 votes. This year the pattern was the same, with one exception. It was a tight race all the way, ending with Hoff the victor by almost exactly the same narrow margin, 759 votes, according to the unofficial returns reported on Wednesday.

Hoff will become the state's first Democratic governor ever elected by popular vote. In the 1853 election, Robinson was named governor by the Legislature.

The Democrats capitalized on dissatisfaction with the Keyser administration that was not reflected in the strong support for U.S. Sen. George D. Aiken and U.S. Rep. Stafford.

Democratic party leaders became confident early in the administration of Gov. Keyser that he could be upset, if they could find an attractive candidate and could overcome at least some of the resistance of Vermont Republicans to marking a ballot for a Democrat. Hoff proved to be the man. Filing as an Independent as well as on the Democratic ticket, he won enough Independent votes to produce his thin victory margin.

Comparing Keyser's performance with that of Stafford in 1958, the governor was cut in the Northeast Kingdom, and in the counties of Rutland, Bennington and Windham. His best showing, compared with Stafford's, was in Washington County.

Gov. Keyser decided on Wednesday that he would ask for a recount. Experience in 1958, however, showed how unlikely it is that a recount will change the results even of a close race. The complications of tabulating the Independent vote may be the soundest reason for having the count checked.

One of the sour notes in the election reporting was the refusal of the City of Winooski to release its figures on the governorship election. There is no good excuse for deliberate withholding of election figures in this manner. If it is a valid subject of legislation, the Assembly should take action to discourage such practices.

Gov.-elect Hoff faces a difficult situation at Montpelier. Presumably he has already done some preliminary planning about changes in personnel. He will be confronted by demands for a thorough house cleaning and by the need of maintaining in office the best of the capital's career officials.

The manner in which he approaches the personnel problem may well have much to do with his success or failure in dealing with the solidly Republican Legislature. This is important for any governor and particularly for the state's first Democratic governor in more than a century, if he wants to achieve any of the objectives of his administration program.

Source: *Rutland Herald*, 8 November 1962. Reprinted with permission of the *Rutland Herald*.

DOCUMENT 12

"Broad New Highways through Vermont" (1966)
ROCKWELL STEPHENS

Get forty acres of land (the forty acres and a mule that used to be the one man farm, but never mind the mule), stretch it, bulldoze and shape it into a Paul Bunyan size bowling alley. Add a few thousand tons of crushed rock, asphalt and concrete, and trainloads of miscellaneous condiments, including tons and tons of steel. Season with a million dollars, give or take a few hundred thousand, recruit economists, planners, lawyers, engineers, landscape architects and an army of truck drivers. Add another million dollars for assorted machinery and equipment. Boil about two years for construction and you'll have a mile of Interstate highway.

Banish all hot dogs stands and hamburg palaces, gas stations and used car lots, neon signs and billboards, stop lights and intersections and set your four lane highway on woodland or pasture, ridge crest or valley where the eye of the traveler can see and enjoy the countryside he may have come a thousand miles or more to find.

Link it with 320 similar miles made to the same prescription and you have the Vermont Interstate highway system, now sufficiently advanced to provide a good working sample of what lies ahead when completed in 1970.

Already the traveler coming into Vermont's southeast corner below Brattleboro will find more than fifty uninterrupted miles leading north from the Massachusetts line. Another forty-five miles links the capital at Montpelier to the state's largest city, Burlington, and swinging north makes a good start toward the Canadian line and Montreal. By the spring of 1967 it is expected that more than 120 of the 321 miles in the total system will be ready for the flow of traffic across the state to the Montreal exposition opening that summer.

Construction of the National System of Interstate and Defense Highways is a project to stagger the imagination. Under the Federal Highway Act of 1956 a 41,000 mile nationwide network of divided, controlled access highways was authorized, to be built at an estimated average cost of approximately a million dollars a mile to connect every major city and to be completed in 1972.

Furthermore, every mile was to be built to satisfy the anticipated needs of traffic for a period of twenty years.

The law created what is said to be the largest public works program ever attempted on earth, some thirty times greater than the combined construction of the Panama Canal, the St. Lawrence Seaway, and Grand Coulee Dam.

Though the Interstates represent only about one per cent of the federal highway system, they will carry twenty per cent of the nation's traffic. Vermont's 321 miles, less than one per cent of the national grid, account for more than fifteen per cent of the state's primary highways but are expected to carry a far larger share of the state's traffic load than the national average.

Geography, population and industrial economy dictated the location of Vermont's Interstate routes. The Connecticut river valley proved to be the natural channel to link population and industrial centers of Massachusetts and Connecticut and provide a nearly straight line to Canada. This is the route of I-91. At White River Junction, a bit more than a third of the way up the state and some 70 miles from the Massachusetts line, I-89 swings west and north to Montpelier, Burlington and the Canadian line and by a mammoth interchange takes traffic on 89 from the south-east across New Hampshire and the Boston megalopolis. Some sixty miles farther north another interchange near St. Johnsbury connects I-91 with I-93 in northern New Hampshire.

One must drive over a good portion of these new Vermont routes to sense the full impact of the Interstate concept. For these highways are not only freeing motor vehicles to serve their full economic and social potential, but are also, in inevitable consequence, expected to influence the development of the state no less significantly than the coming of the railroad.

Driving times are cut 25% or more. New York becomes four and a half hours instead of six hours distant, Boston three hours instead of four. More significant, perhaps, than main line travel is the new access to the state's more than 11,000 miles of local roads forming the happy hunting ground of travelers with the leisure to find the full flavor of the Vermont countryside. About 60% of the entire area of the state is within 20 miles of an Interstate interchange, and 80% of the state is only 30 miles distant, along present local roads.

The significance of this map shrinkage is obvious to the vacationer with a summer place back in the hills or the visitor with time to play shun-pike. The economic side of the picture is equally notable in the increased mobility of local labor and easier access to markets and materials.

Need for a major attack on the problems created by the spawning motor vehicle was obvious years ago. More than 49 million cars and trucks on the roads in 1950 became over 62 million in '55, 73 million by 1960, and more than 86 million in 1964. Vehicle travel increased astronomically from some 450 billion miles in 1950 to over 718 billion ten years later and nearly 840 billion in 1964.

Standard two lane highways for intercity travel with their theoretical capacity of 900 vehicles an hour under favorable conditions proved no answer. It was a long leap forward to the present Interstate design basis of four lanes engineered for safe travel at a speed limit of 65 miles an hour, and capable of carrying some 30,000 vehicles a day.

Experience has already demonstrated the relative safety of these new roads, with an accident rate one third that of highways with uncontrolled access. Nor have engineers overlooked the pounding they will take under bigger loads and higher speeds. A typical section of I-89 in the Burlington area, for example, starts with a thoroughly compacted sub-grade meaning everything under the pavement. Then are added six inches of sand, 18 inches of four and a half inch chunks of rock, then five inches of two and a half inch rock, and this is topped by three inches of hot mix black top,— more than 5000 tons of the latter to the mile. Built to last, these roads—for twenty years and more.

The road builder who gashes a destructive path through hill and valley, leaving two monotonous strips of raw concrete as his memorial, is dead as the dodo by Vermont standards. "Keep Vermont Beautiful" is a well nigh universal if not an official state slogan. It is no surprise, then, to find that the landscape engineer and the consulting landscape architect are important cogs in the machinery of the state highway department. As one of their engineers put it, "our job is to fit the highways into the hillsides with such success that they simply 'belong.' The builders work is not complete until the landscaper has added his art to the total job."

Nice sentiment, but the proof is in the seeing. Come up I-91 from the south. Ten minutes inside the state line and you know it's true; there's something different about the landscape they call Vermont. More to the point, the placement and width of the right of way lets you see more of it. Glimpses of the Connecticut valley become long vistas as the road takes a high line along the valley side; the two lanes spread wide apart as the median strip reveals rock outcrops and pinnacles and even part of a forest preserve. These and deep rock cuts, sweeping views of the pasture dotted hills ahead, banish "throughway blindness" and monotony-caused driver fatigue every mile of the first sixty in use since late fall.

"Scenic" is an overworked word that takes fresh luster when applied to the sweep of Interstate 89 between Montpelier and Burlington. There again deep rock cuts expose the bare bones of the hills, and in the contorted folds of the rock faces reveal the thrusting forces of geologic time that formed the panorama of valley, hill and mountain.

Vistas to gladden the eye and lift the spirit are too many to enumerate: the long sweeping curves of I-89 as it drops down from the west into the Winooski valley; the long view of valley and mountain with river, railroad and both new and old highways side by side on the valley floor through Bolton Gorge; glimpses of the Champlain Islands above Burlington, and the great sweep of the Adirondacks when approaching Burlington from the east.

Add to the other qualities of these new highways a new sense of spaciousness and freedom,—freedom to move, freedom to see. No, there's not a dull mile in a carload on Vermont's new Interstates.

Source: Rockwell Stephens, "Broad New Highways through Vermont," *Vermont Life* 20, no. 3 (Spring 1966): 12-16.

SECTION ELEVEN

Since 1965
Microchips and Maple Syrup

VERMONT VOICES

SECTION ELEVEN

Since 1965
Microchips and Maple Syrup

Introduction

In 1965, for the first time in history, Vermont cast its electoral votes for a Democratic president and ushered a Democratic state ticket into office. Governor Hoff used his second inaugural, **Document 1**, to urge sweeping changes in government. The most compelling, reapportionment of the house and senate on a one-person-one-vote basis, had been ordered by the federal courts, and Vermont reluctantly complied by accepting a 150-person house based on population and apportioning the senate without strict regard for county boundaries. Most other recommendations met stiff resistance. The most radical, a proposal to redraw the state's internal boundaries to facilitate the administration of services on a regional basis, stemmed from Governor Hoff's belief that town lines had become "barriers to efficient and effective public programs." Vermont's strong devotion to town government doomed the proposal.

Nevertheless, Great Society programs, most notably Medicare, Medicaid, and the War on Poverty, furthered unprecedented growth in state-administered services and in state employment rolls. Vermont's general approval of Great Society proposals crested with adoption of the Civil Rights Acts. Despite having the fewest and lowest percentage of nonwhites in the nation, the state prided itself on enlightened racial views and deplored the racism manifested in the Deep South. That Vermont's self-image might not comport with reality was suggested by resistance to the New York-Vermont program instituted by Governor Hoff and New York City Mayor John Lindsay for bringing urban black youths to summer in rural Vermont.

The "Irasburg Affair" provided a starker illustration of Vermont's racial ambivalence while attracting national attention. In 1968 a nightrider fired into the home of a newly arrived black family; the assailant was caught but law enforcement agencies seemed as determined to prosecute the victims as the perpetrator. **Document 2**, written by a black nationally syndicated columnist, appeared in the *Brattleboro Reformer* contemporaneously with the event. **Document 3**, a retrospective editorial, "Rehashing Irasburg," by *Rutland*

Herald publisher Robert Mitchell, appeared in 1979.

By 1970 the inherent dilemma in promoting economic development while preserving the state's pastoral environment became a matter of official concern. The greatest growth occurred in Chittenden County, where population increased by one third from 1960. A major contributor to this growth was IBM, which located in Essex Junction in 1957 with a workforce of 200 employees, grew to 3,900 employees by 1970, and peaked at 8,000 in the 1980s. **Document 4**, "IBM: Burden or Bonanza?" appeared in *Chittenden* magazine in 1969 and explores IBM's impact on the community in which it located.

Upon assuming office in 1969, Governor Deane C. Davis appointed an eighteen-member Commission on Environmental Control. Its report, excerpted in **Document 5**, led directly to Vermont's pioneering State Land Use and Development legislation (Act 250) and signaled the emergence of environmental protection as a major political issue. As the report discloses, the commission's specific recommendations were less a response to industrial development than to expanding ski areas and year-round vacation homes, which overnight had transformed the character of many of the state's small towns and rural landscapes. Growth in recreational facilities fostered rising land values and the sale of farm acreage, promoted strip development along major highways, and threatened to overwhelm municipal government resources.

By 1970 local concerns had become intertwined with the Vietnam War. As early as 1966, Senator George Aiken had expressed his deep reservations, and by 1970, town meetings, New England's prized bastions of direct democracy, were voting resolutions condemning government policy. Vermont's college anti-war elements were relatively subdued until the Ohio National Guard killed four and wounded eleven students at Kent State University. The Ohio governor had declared martial law after students protesting the U. S. invasion of Cambodia rioted in downtown Kent and firebombed the ROTC building. The killings, however, occurred on campus during a peaceful rally to protest the governor's action. **Document 6**, an editorial and two news items from the *Burlington Free Press*, chronicles the variety of local responses.

As the *Free Press* editorial writer makes clear, he feared that the politicizing of college campuses marked a departure from sound practices and threatened their intellectual integrity. New arrivals, often derided as hippies, who sought Vermont as fertile turf in which to live alternative lifestyles, also threatened traditional institutions. Many were attracted to ephemeral communes which they soon abandoned to pursue more orthodox living arrangements while continuing to communicate their disdain for conventional society through support of Vietnam War protests and third-party political movements. The most prominent among these former communards was Bernard Sanders, who, spurning affiliation with both major political parties, was subsequently elected Burlington mayor and United States congressman. **Document 7** is his account of his first statewide contest, in which he campaigned as the 1972 Liberty Union Party candidate for governor. Although he collected few votes, he garnered considerable name, face, and voice recognition.

Feminism provided still another perceived threat to cherished institutions. Few openly opposed the movement with the vehemence with which Mrs. H. W. Abbott opposed woman's suffrage (See Section 8, Document 10), but supporters sometimes encountered barriers of social convention and language that persisted until directly challenged. No one more exemplified successfully meeting that challenge than Madeleine Kunin, elected in 1984 as the state's first woman governor. **Document 8** provides excerpts from the first of her three inaugural addresses. She entered office with an ambitious agenda, and her inaugural message was particularly notable for its tribute to the openness of Vermont society. Like former Speaker and Lieutenant Governor Consuelo Northrop Bailey (see Section 10, Document 8), Kunin stressed female achievement, but unlike Bailey, who also celebrated her Vermont heritage, Kunin chose to recount her immigrant background.

Act 250 hardly ended the debate over environmental controls, and Governor Kunin's administration quickened a heated dialogue over regulatory processes that encompassed interrelated issues such as retaining family farms, ensuring employment opportunities,

achieving a balance between environmental and economic goals, and strengthening town and regional controls over the regulatory process. The most publicized disputes generally involved the construction of huge shopping centers or the expansion of ski resort areas. Proponents of expansion defended their proposals as environmentally sound and accused opponents of advancing their own personal tastes and economic interests rather than the best interest of Vermonters. Burlington Mayor Bernie Sanders' opposition to proposed construction of a large shopping mall in the neighboring town of Williston was criticized by proponents as influenced by his concern that the mall would displace Burlington's downtown retail center.

As was true in respect to the movement for Act 250, it was again ski resort expansion that captured the widest public concern in the regulatory debate. This time, along with concern over sewage disposal, there was also considerable public debate and court action over water sources for snowmaking. **Document 9**, excerpted from "The Mountains Are for Everyone," is an effort by Preston Smith, chief executive officer of Killington Ltd., and the initial developer of the Killington ski area, to assure the public of the soundness of Killington's expansion plans. Smith argued that his resort's sewage disposal system was environmentally sound and technologically superior to the systems employed by many of Vermont's cities and towns. Opponents raised technical objections to Smith's argument, but **Document 10** suggests they were particularly adept at less conventional debate. It should be noted that Killington received permits to use these systems but did not spray treated effluent on the ski slopes.

Document 11 is from the 1988 "Report of the Governor's Commission on Vermont's Future: Guidelines for Growth." The commission was created by Governor Kunin in 1987 to "assess the concerns of Vermont citizens on the issue of growth, to establish guidelines for growth, and to establish mechanisms to help plan Vermont's future." After reviewing written testimony and holding eleven public hearings at which three hundred persons testified, the commission recommended that towns and regions adopt more specific planning documents, essentially zoning blueprints, under state guidelines to improve the effectiveness of the regulatory process introduced through Act 250. The legislation adopted several of the commission's suggestions as Act 200, and Act 200 subsequently met fierce resistance by a property rights movement. **Document 12** is one expression of its opposition. The movement helped thwart hopes for a statewide development plan but failed to obtain the repeal of Act 200.

On several occasions prior to the Civil War, Native Americans presented legislative petitions and claims to the state of Vermont, each time without success (see Section 4, Document 5, and Section 6, Document 5). After the 1860s these efforts were abandoned until the second half of the twentieth century, when Indian claims were reasserted under different circumstances.

Historians had customarily written that when the first European settlers arrived in what has become Vermont, they found it a "no-man's land," virtually uninhabited, with no established villages. More recent scholarship refuted this contention with evidence that Abenakis did indeed inhabit Vermont. This evidence provided an opportunity for descendants of Abenakis who claimed continuous Vermont occupancy to secure federal recognition as an American Indian Tribe. **Document 13** is excerpted from a petition filed for that purpose, and readers will note references to the version of creation described in Section 1, Document 1. The Abenakis hoped to obtain significant economic and other advantages from federal recognition, but the petition was denied and subsequent efforts have also failed. For a short time, however, a Vermont court granted those who could demonstrate their Abenaki ancestry immunity from hunting and fishing regulations because they held "aboriginal title" to the land. The state appealed the decision, and in **Document 14**, *State of Vermont* v. *Raleigh Elliott, et al.*, the Vermont Supreme Court reversed the lower court decision, concluding all aboriginal rights had been extinguished when Vermont became a state.

In June 1993 the National Trust for Historic Preservation designated Vermont as one of America's eleven most "endangered historic places." A symbolic gesture without legal or other tangible effect, it nonetheless capsulated anxieties over Vermont's future that had motivated numerous state studies and provoked political controversies like the Green Mountain Parkway referendum, struggles to adopt Acts 250 and 200, and movements for their repeal. At one extreme are those who would open Vermont to unrestricted development, and at the other those who maintain that Vermont must preserve its quaint characteristics at whatever the economic cost. As a practical matter, proponents of neither extreme have governed the debate, and elements of both are incorporated in contemporary lifestyles. Noel Perrin caught this paradox in **Document 15**, "The Two Faces of Vermont," a 1964 article for *Vermont Life* that is as relevant today as when it first appeared. Perrin evokes traditional images of Vermont through allusions to stone fences, dirt roads, sugaring, and dairy farming, while contending that it is no longer possible to preserve maple groves and dairy farms operating on a traditional scale and without modern technology. This persisting cultural and economic dilemma, one that pits the profits of development against the perils of environmental deterioration, is intensified by the nostalgia Vermonters retain for the hard times that characterize so much of our past.

DOCUMENT 1

Second Inaugural Address (1965)

GOVERNOR PHILIP HOFF

We are assembled today at the direction of the people of Vermont to chart a new course in the history of our great State. I am convinced that Vermont is already feeling the stirrings of change that promise the greatest era of progress and development in our history. The forces at work in our world have created almost unparalled opportunities for Vermont and it is our responsibility to meet this challenge. We must act to control these changes and not be content merely to acknowledge them as inevitable.

Today, more than ever before, we must look outward to understand the changes that are taking place within our own society. Ours is a world of many quiet revolutions going on simultaneously. Some are easily noted. Others, perhaps more difficult to define, give promise of equally dramatic impact upon our lives. The revolution in communications and transportation has opened Vermont to the world in a way not imagined possible a generation ago. It demands we educate our children for living and working in one world. Population expansion and attendant problems of urbanization make the open space and untouched beauty of Vermont the envy of countless thousands. It would be naive to think that this population explosion will not have a tremendous impact upon our State. We must prepare now to preserve the untouched quality of Vermont from unplanned and uncontrolled urban growth.

The revolution in technology with its promise of a substantially reduced work week opens a new era where the effective utilization of free time will figure more and more in economic development and growth of our State. The revolution in knowledge makes education crucial in our planning for the future. These are but a sampling of the forces at work in our world today that require us to broaden our scope as citizens not only of Vermont but as citizens of a global community. . . .

Democracy is not neutral. It is not indifferent to the outcome of man's efforts to live meaningfully. It is firmly anchored on hope and faith in man's capacity to build the good life within a free society. It is an open system of values which embraces change and which weaves new events into the fabric of our life as free men. With this concept of democracy in mind, let us now consider specific proposals designed to meet the problems and to grasp the opportunities presented by the forces at work in our society. . . .

Reapportionment

Our first obligation is to meet the challenge of the 14th Amendment to provide equal protection to all citizens before the law. The Courts have told us what we all have suspected for many years. That is, of course, that our General Assembly is malapportioned and that we must reapportion it on the basis of one man, one vote. This then, is the Assembly's first and more urgent task. I urge you all to consider this simple fact. . . . If this Legislature fails to re-organize itself to extend the franchise so that it is equally shared by every citizen of Vermont, it will be done by the courts. I am confident that our record as independent and fair-minded citizens will not be stained by failure to accomplish this task.

Thus, our first responsibility here is to properly shape our Legislature, our basic instrument for enactment of public policy, to better meet the demands of our Democratic heritage and the needs of contemporary society. The United States Supreme Court has decreed it to be the law of the land that legislative bodies of the several States must provide for representation based on population. This principle cannot and it will not be compromised. . . . We do not seek to defy tradition. We seek only to breathe new vitality into aspirations that for too long have gathered dust in the public archives. If there is a single thread that links the world of today with the aspirations of those who charted Vermont's course as a State, it is the idea that government exists to serve the needs of the people when these needs cannot be better met by citizens acting in private concert. Similiarly, it is that government is viable and subject to modification as the needs of citizens change.

Let me quote from a man whose hands held the pulse of our State at its birth. . . . Ethan Allen said in an address to the people of Vermont:

> . . . All good and wise men, will exert themselves in establishing and supporting good government and order, which are inseparably connected together. Formed constitutions and modes of government may and undoubtedly

are, more or less imperfect; Yet they may, in future, be corrected and amended as time of leisure, cool deliberation, and experience may dictate.

Ethan Allen, of course, was not alone in his conviction that government is not simply the instrumentality of majority will, but the government's role is to transcribe public necessity into action to serve the greatest good for the greatest number of people. Equal representation in government does not pit town against town. Neither does it pit urban residents against rural residents, or those over twenty-one against those who have yet to reach their majority. Bearing this in mind and the many weeks of thoughtful study and planning that have already gone into solution of this problem, I am certain this task can and will be met with speed and with justice.

Differences of opinion still exist on this issue but I am confident that Vermonters as men of reason and good will are determined not to fail in this task. Rather than to delay or defy what we know must come to pass, I urge the members of this Assembly to face the task of reapportionment immediately and with determination to get the job done so that we can move forward in other areas where action, as we all know, is so urgently needed. In doing this I would certainly not oppose speedy submission of a reapportionment plan, or even several plans to the Courts for review. . . .

The Task Ahead

We are fortunate at the moment that we can pursue the task of reapportionment while also acting to move Vermont ahead in other areas. Two years ago I urged that we re-evaluate and reform our program of public service in light of the dramatic changes underway in our society and the people of Vermont have served notice that they want this done. Vermonters realize that we cannot divorce ourselves from the world, that the events in far-off corners of the globe directly affect our daily lives. This fact is one we cannot afford to state and then ignore. This fact must be reflected in our approach to education, to the conservation of our natural resources, to economic development and the very organization of our system of state and local government.

Vermont has a strong tradition of town government. Our town boundaries were drawn in colonial times roughly along lines six miles square. This was done arbitrarily and with the exception of major rivers, natural boundaries were frequently ignored. In the days of communication no more rapid than a horse and rider, our towns served as efficient and effective units for the control and operation of education, welfare, highways and other public programs.

But over the years these arbitrary town lines have increasingly become barriers to efficient and effective public programs. This has been recognized and some action has been taken to cross town lines in the administration of certain public services. Our administrative units have frequently been extended and expanded largely, however, on a haphazard basis and without regard to the overall needs of the people of the State. Progress in one area of the State has not always been matched in other areas.

A Regional Approach

We now have the information available to organize many of these services on a regional basis so that they can be more effectively administered for all the people of Vermont. To this end, I am calling for a regional approach to education, tax assessing, planning, development, probate courts, municipal courts, state's attorneys, and ultimately to our town and State aid system of roads, although here action may have to be deferred until 1966. This is the key to our present program of reorganization and revitalization of our governmental services. We aim to organize these services in districts that include the human and economic resources required to support them. This is the only feasible way for us to assure equality of educational and economic opportunity to all Vermonters regardless of the town in which they reside.

With imagination and the determination to creatively utilize our traditions and resources we can set the pace for progress in combatting educational deficiencies, poverty, and other problems. Vermont has the talent and the resources to achieve this goal. We also are small enough so that the magnitude of the problem can be clearly seen and our progress can be easily demonstrated.

Education

Our greatest resource and our greatest responsibility is the talent of our people. Two years ago I described education as the keystone to our future development. This is even more true today. We have made great progress in the past two years. State-aid has been increased and is now distributed on an equalized basis. Much remains to be done, however, before we can say to ourselves we are meeting the needs of today, much less the needs of tomorrow. For this reason I recommend an additional 1.5 million dollars in State-aid to local school districts in 1966 and 2.5 million in 1967, or a total of 4 million for the biennium. It is anticipated that the additional million in 1967 will be keyed to quality and/or reorganization. This will provide for total State-aid of approximately $9,000,000 in 1966 and $10,000,000 in 1967 . . .

Of equal importance in our endeavor to better educate our young people is the reorganization of our school districts so that they more adequately include the resources required for their support. I will submit to you a plan for regionalized districts that will accomplish this on a voluntary basis but which will not permit our residents to disregard the need for rapid progress in this area. This task requires additional money to strengthen the Department of Education, to finance more classes for the mentally retarded and the handicapped, for retraining and for vocational education as I will outline in my budget message. Ever increasing costs for top quality educational programs at the level beyond the high school must also be recognized.

We embarked upon a pilot program of State-guaranteed loans for college freshmen earlier this year. Despite predictions that there was no need for this, the program has already helped many, many young Vermonters finance their college education. This aid must be expanded. . . . Additional funds will be required also to strengthen the quality of educational programs at the University of Vermont and our State colleges. Authority will be sought to assist private colleges and secondary schools through State guarantee of loans for plant and capital improvements as is now authorized for industrial projects.

You will be asked to inaugurate an educational television network and to increase minimum salaries for Vermont public school teachers.

Courts

The concept of better organizing our resources in support of public enterprise and private well-being applies to the administration of justice. A district or regional organization of our Courts has had widespread support for many years. Certainly, this basic reform of our Courts is long overdue. In this age we need a system of District Courts presided over by full-time adequately paid judges and this should apply equally to our present Probate Courts as well as to our Municipal Courts.

Linked to this should be a network of full-time adequately paid district attorneys supervised by a strengthened Attorney General's office. No reform of our Court system will be complete without modification of our system for the selection of superior judges. . . .

Planning and Development

The concept of district reorganization is also essential for us to follow if we are to promote greater effectiveness at the least cost in the field of planning and development. We must structure our public services to more effectively reflect our changing population patterns.   Here again, I propose a new program of State assistance to local industrial development groups to stimulate regional planning and zoning. This will involve additional State personnel and grants to regional organizations that meet realistic standards. We must promote increased programs of research and development to assist the residents of every area in the State in reaching their maximum potential. This applies equally if our agricultural growth is to be more than a series of crisis situations. . .

Department of Labor

I recommend consolidation of the Department of Employment Security and the Department of Industrial Relations into a new Department of Labor. With this should be passed a Little Wagner Act. The extension of coverage of unemployment benefits as well as a strengthened program of workman's compensation are directly related to this development program. So too is continued provision for the manpower retraining program and increased emphasis on vocational training.

Natural Resources

Of equal importance to total development of our State is the conservation of our natural resources and the protection of our heritage of scenic beauty from the blight of uncontrolled urban sprawl. This will require increased State-aid for local pollution abatement programs. It will require broadening the State's land condemnation authority for certain public purposes. It will require minimum flow legislation and a long range program to assure every Vermonter an adequate water supply.

The cleaning up of our streams, the protection of our wealth of water resources should also include expansion of coordinated recreational facilities. In this regard, I will recommend increased bonding to finance State participation in developing Federal and State outdoor recreation programs. I anticipate great progress in this area within the next few years. Vermont and the nation are deeply committed to the planned public development of our forests, our parks and our unique natural geographic areas. This will increasingly involve State-Federal cooperation in multi-purpose development of our resources. It will also require that we move forward promptly to meet our need for regional zoning. . .

Health, Welfare, Safety

In the same manner we cannot separate highway safety and the expansion of our State police force from other programs designed to protect human resources. We cannot treat agriculture apart from the food stamp program we will recommend. These are merely facets of a single, far-reaching effort to move our State forward so that our people may enjoy a fuller, safer and healthier life. I will recommend an expansion in our welfare department, an expanded program of highway safety, and expansion of our State Police to include forty-two new troopers during the biennium. . . .

Stewards of Hope

Ours is a time not of triumph but of dedication. We meet here not as exponents of party but as stewards of hope. We share a sacred trust, the future of our great State. Let us draw that future in bold strokes with confidence in our mission and faith that men of reason and good will can chart a course of action that will serve humanity. Working together I am confident that with divine guidance, we will meet the test of our times. . . . That no man, however humble of origin, however remote his domicile be denied the opportunity to fully exploit and enjoy his status as a member of our free society. Thank you very much.

Source: *Journal of the Senate,* Biennial Session, 1965 (Montpelier: Capital City Press, 1965): 623-633.

Document 2

"A Black Man's Viewpoint" (1968)
Kenneth Wibecan

Last week a Vermont court determined that the price for firing a shotgun into the home of a black man is $500. The price is somewhat higher than that to be found in the State of Mississippi, but then this is the liberal north where racism is more subtle and not as honest or open as it is in the southern states.

The irony of life in America for a black man is that in the south murderers of Blacks are convicted of "violating their civil rights" while in Irasburg an attempted murder (court testimony called it an attempt to "scare") is somehow transformed into a "serious breach of peace." One can't help but wonder what the charge would have been if the Rev. Johnson or some member of his family had been killed by those well aimed shots.

In an attempt to offer some moral support to the Johnsons, and visit the scene of the crime, my wife and I—in the company of Dr. and Mrs. Lawrence McCror[e]y of Charlotte, Vt.—travelled to Irasburg on Saturday. Our interview with Rev. Johnson took place in the living room of his large, high-ceilinged house—the same room where his family huddled terror-stricken on the floor while shotgun pellets crashed through their windows on the night of July 19.

One thing remained very clear throughout our conversation, and that is the fact that the Johnson's civil rights have been violated. I am very concerned about the survival of this black family in such a hostile environment.

According to Rev. Johnson, only three families have stood by them throughout their troubles. They were grateful for the help of these people, but I was appalled at the lack of support from people throughout the state.

Only a few letters were received by the Johnsons and many of them were the traditional hate letters such as the one from Lyndonville, Vt. that read: "Get out of town you B____ B_____ before we b_____ you out." Or one letter postmarked Haverhill, Mass. which read, in part ". . . you should forgive this young soldier and not prosecute. He is right in trying to keep Vermont clean. You better go to Mississippi or Virginia and shine shoes or work in a factory. Don't try to preach to us whites—you have nothing to tell us."

While many white people may be horrified at these events, to black people incidents like these are part of the reality of being in black America. The sickening familiarity of many of the things Rev. Johnson told us about only served to re-emphasize the underlying racism in American society that the Kerner Commission made us aware of. To be called "Boy" by the police is nothing new to most black people—a black man can be 90 years old and still be called boy.

The blatant hostility of a police force united in its efforts to investigate the victim of a crime in an attempt to make the victim the criminal is a tactic that has been used to intimidate black people all over America. White Americans must realize that they are the victims of this type of oppression along with their black brothers. Any society that condones the prejudicial actions of the police and others is suffering from a sickness that affects all members of that society.

Rev. Johnson served this country in the Army for 25 years. He fought for democracy in Korea where he received three Bronze Stars and returned to this country to find bullets and hostility to greet his efforts. The damage that has been done to this family is irreversible.

During our interview Rev. Johnson sat in a chair facing the front windows where he felt he had to keep an eye on the police driving back and forth in front of his house. This is a sad commentary on the destiny of this black family.

It is interesting to note that the Johnsons arrived in Irasburg on July fourth, which happens to be Independence Day, a national holiday for white Americans. It is through incidents like this that one becomes increasingly aware that black Americans are still awaiting the day when they can celebrate their own Independence.

Source: *Brattleboro Reformer*, 28 August 1968. Reprinted with permission of the *Brattleboro Reformer*.

"Rehashing Irasburg" (1979)
RUTLAND HERALD

A state police investigation and the contested discharge of Public Safety Commissioner Frank Lynch by Gov. Snelling have served to resurrect the story of what happened at Irasburg in 1968 when the home of a newcomer from California was the target of a midnight attack by gunfire. Victims of the assault were David Lee Johnson, a black minister, his family and guests in the home.

Statewide controversy over the affair was caused when the state police who investigated became more diligent in pressing a charge of adultery against the black minister than they were in acting against the individual who launched the midnight attack. Intervention by Gov. Philip Hoff and Attorney General James Oakes was necessary before the police did their duty and arrested the perpetrator of the attack who first pleaded not guilty to a mild charge of breach of the peace then later did not contest the charge and was fined $500.

When Gov. Hoff directed Public Safety Commissioner Alexander to discipline three state police troopers involved in the Irasburg affair and the charge of adultery against Johnson, which was later dropped, Alexander refused to comply. The commissioner's conduct at the time seemed to establish a pattern in the department for maintaining that the police could do no wrong—a pattern which has emerged in the Lynch affair as well as in the case of Paul Lawrence, the police undercover agent who was convicted of framing innocent persons on drug charges.

There was an interesting review of the Irasburg affair this week in the Burlington *Free Press* under a headline saying "Vermont Tarnished by Irasburg Affair." The story was interesting even more for what it didn't say than for what it said. A notable omission concerned the part that was played by the press in the way the case was handled by the police—notably the *Free Press*, the now defunct Burlington *Sunday News* and the Newport *Daily Express*. All three papers supported the police mishandling of the case and either overtly or indirectly took the position that Johnson was an unwelcome intruder in the town of Irasburg and the state of Vermont who got no more than he deserved. All three publications in one way or another attempted to help the police dig up unfavorable information about Johnson in California. Without that kind of media support, it is doubtful that the police and other law-enforcement officers in the county would have sided so strongly against Johnson rather than against his assailant. It was a sad day for the cause of racial justice in Vermont, but perhaps even more was it a shameful episode in the annals of the Vermont press.

Eleven years after the event, there is a measure of reassurance in having the *Free Press* take a more enlightened view of what happened at Irasburg and of the way the affair was handled by the Public Safety Department.

Source: *Rutland Herald*, 29 August 1979. Reprinted with permission of the *Rutland Herald*.

DOCUMENT 4

"IBM: Burden or Bonanza?" (1969)
RUTH PAGE

Traffic jam? Long wait in the supermarket? School overcrowded and forever needing additions? Housing shortage? Beaches packed?

Everybody says, "It wasn't like this before IBM came. Too many people in too short a time, and their kids fill the schools and their cars fill the roads."

Some Chittenden County residents even say, "We were better off without them." Yet many of these also say, "Our own town needs a bit of industry, though—our tax base is too narrow."

How is it possible to measure the entire impact of the largest single industrial enterprise in the State of Vermont on the community and county in which it lives? And what of the impact of Vermont, and what we will we call the Greater Essex Area, on the industry?

No one can trace every thread of the complicated county web of life, commerce, and recreation of which IBM is an important part. But some of the major strands can be identified, and traced through the pattern, to show how this great industry has affected every life in the county.

Numbers

When International Business Machines decided to lease, and then purchase, the first Greater Burlington Industrial Corporation speculative building, the company was producing wire contact relays, and it hired some 500 employees the first year, 1957.

Since that time, the original building (40,000 sq. ft.) has much more than doubled in size, five more were added including laboratories, office space, and manufacturing facilities, additional offices were provided at Fort Ethan Allen and the A&P Shopping Center on Pearl Street in Essex. By the end of this year there will be nearly 3900 employees in almost a million square feet of space.

The company expects to have approximately a 300-employee increase per year until 1971, then a levelling off with an employment figure possibly up to 4,200 by 1972. Another manufacturing and service facility may be built for use by 1972.

The advantage of the growth to the workers and their families is that it is a highly stable industry, producing electronic components for computers and simultaneously researching new methods and parts; so it is in the vanguard of modern technology, and thus likely to remain healthy for uncounted years ahead.

Indeed, to "old-time" Vermonters there appears to be an anomaly: the little rural state which until recently had more cows than people now houses one of the most advanced modern technology facilities in the world.

The area's only other comparable industry is General Electric Co., which at its present peak in Burlington has some 3400 workers, many of them dependent on government wartime contracts for their jobs. GE has a past record of fluctuating employment, in 1964 having gone as low as 1000 employees.

Why Vermont?

Why did the state's biggest industry settle in what was then one of the state's small towns? (Essex Junction had about 5,000 residents in 1957. There are 8,400 now.)

There were several reasons. Because its product is tiny (the computer parts IBM makes here are minute chips of which it takes a hundred to cover the surface of a half-dollar), transportation was no problem. Therefore IBM could seek an attractive site, away from the rush and tangle of the great cities, and thus more attractive to employees.

They also found that schools in the Greater Burlington area were satisfactory; the University of Vermont offered a cultural resource, both educational and recreational, for employees; the great teaching hospitals assured fine health care; the lake and the snowy mountains offered both beauty and relaxation; and progress of the Interstate Highway System assured accessibility to all of New England and New York.

There was also a fairly large, well-trained, conscientious work force available. James J. Ritchie, now general manager of the plant, has said, "The people in this area take pride in their work and strive to do a good job. About 70 percent of our employees come from within the state. About 30 percent of our experienced professional college graduates are Vermonters. . . .We may, in fact, have a higher percentage of native Vermonters than would be reflected in the figures. We know that many of our people have returned to work at IBM after leaving Vermont to find work in other areas."

Impact

It has been estimated that for each 10 employees with families who move into an area, ten service employees spring up . . . the people who sell, provide laundry and cleaning service, mend shoes, cut hair, etc. This means that IBM is unquestionably responsible for a great deal of the growth in Chittenden County in the past ten years, though it is impossible to delineate it precisely because GE, the University, and the Medical Center Hospital have also attracted large numbers.

In Essex Junction, Essex Town, Underhill, Jericho, Milton, Williston, and Colchester, there is no question in old-time residents' minds whence both the affluence and the drawbacks of growth have sprung: It's these IBMers. "Hafta build a new school every two years to take care of all the kids, and all their taxes go the Essex Junction. 'Tain't fair."

They're right. 'Tain't fair, and IBM would be the first to agree. But IBM has not set up the tax system in Vermont, it merely pays its share—all to Essex Junction village, though the town indirectly gets its slice through the general fund to which villagers contribute 73%. Essex Junction's total taxes in 1969-70 are $1,756,980. IBM is paying $777,000 of this or 44.2%.

Meanwhile, many of the employees are living in other area towns, and while they are in most cases making a substantial contribution to the life of the community, working on school boards, libraries, recreation commissions, planning groups, study committees, and others; their parent company is not permitted or required to contribute to local coffers. And everyone knows that no house pays enough taxes to cover the cost of educating the children who live in it.

The county's towns were laid out, at least as to roads, in the last century. The combination of population increases and car-use increases would have made a traffic mess in Burlington, So. Burlington and Essex even without the big IBM plant—but no one denies that that compounds the problem. Not only does it put thousands of cars on the road between 7:30 and 8:30 each morning, all pouring into the village; and thousands more in the afternoon between 4 and 5; but it means traffic to and from all the car-washes, cleaneries, eateries, barber and beauty shops, and other businesses which mushroom in the purlieus of growth industries.

Thus Essex Junction is partly right in attributing its Five Corners traffic problem to IBM, and the motorists who wait out the 60-second light sequence there may be forgiven for muttering imprecations against the monolith; and users of Williston and Shelburne Roads, and Pearl Street, and Church Street, are right to give IBM a share in the blame for their slow-moving traffic . . . as well as a share of credit for the affluence of this county in which personal income growth has outstripped all the rest of the state.

IBM Benefits

Many residents of "Chittenden" do not realize how much IBM, both as a company and through its employees, does for the community directly and indirectly. This is partly the company's own fault, if it is a fault. There is a company policy, handed down from the top, of not advertising or publicizing the benefits the company brings to its community; "let the good we do be discovered, not advertised," is the principle.

A few of the obvious benefits are easy to list: the company and its employees gave $100,000 to the United Fund this year, the largest contribution ever made in the state by a single industry; they also gave 14% of the total Fanny Allen Hospital Building Fund goal of $300,000 and $15,000 to the Lund Home Capital Fund Drive, their largest donation ever.

IBM is also a leader in providing equal opportunity to women and to minority races, though in the latter there has been considerable lack of appreciation in Vermont, where there are still residents who consider the hiring of blacks "importing a problem."

While IBM is Essex Junction's main tax support, its direct demands on village services are as modest as full cooperation from the company can make them.

For example, IBM provides 370,000 gallons of water per day from its own wells, right on IBM property, and gets 125,000 from the village. Because the company expects to need additional water in coming years, it has taken an active interest in the Champlain Water District, and met with its officials.

The company has built all its own access roads at its own cost, and paid to widen a portion of Maple Street to provide for smooth traffic flow at the IBM turnoff. Its sewage plant, handling all company needs, is superior to the village plant, and the water it returns to the Winooski River is cleaner than the water it takes out. At present, the IBM plant provides both primary and secondary treatment of wastes, and there are now plans to spend another one and a half million dollars to add tertiary treatment.

Air pollution is combatted as a part of company policy. The IBM plant used to burn No. 6 (industrial) fuel, but when natural gas came to Essex it converted at great expense to gas, because of the superior cleanliness.

With the old fuel, the plant emitted some sulfur dioxide (about 2% or so of what the Burlington generating plant emits). With the gas, there is zero sulfur dioxide emission, and carbon (soot) emissions have been reduced in a ratio of 30 to 1 compared with the old fuel. "A negligible quantity" of soot escapes when the stacks are "blown" or cleaned now, according to William Lotz, senior associate facilities engineer in the Facilities Engineering Design department, and air pollution control coordinator for IBM Burlington. (We're sorry, but we asked for his full title.)

"The irony is," according to Community Relations Manager Edward H. Willard, "that when we had low stacks and were polluting the air to some extent, nobody said a word. But now that we have bought cleaner fuel and the problem is negligible, and we have put in

high stacks so that none of the emissions will lie in this area, the planners want us to have lower stacks."

When IBM first came to Essex, it brought a traffic light from Poughkeepsie which was installed at the corner of Park and River Streets. As traffic became greater, a more sophisticated light was put in by the village, which used the old one elsewhere in Essex Junction.

IBM has its own plant protection officers, and rarely has to call on local police for help, though the Essex Junction Police Cruiser does tour the plant area now and then to help keep an eye on things.

The plant does not have to call on the local fire department unless a major fire should occur. It has its own fire engine, and is far more likely to help the village department than vice versa. In addition, the emergency wagon which provides First Aid service and nourishment to firemen at serious fires, under the aegis of the Red Cross, is manned by IBMers, trained by their company.

IBM trains a corps in fire-fighting and first aid, and many of these men serve in their hometown volunteer fire departments, which are thus saved the time and expense of training them.

Some of the benefits of IBM to the ordinary guy-on-the-Chittenden-street may be considered drawbacks by older employers. IBM pays well, hires many, and offers excellent benefits to employees including free recreation, health and pension plans, sizable awards for innovative ideas, subsidies for cultural programs in the area, and many others. (IBM has no union workers—it is usually a jump ahead of union benefits.)

This has meant that other companies, small and large, have had to increase pay and benefits to their employees, and for some of the smaller concerns it has not been easy. Good secretaries are hard to find, and technicians trained in area businesses have a way of drifting IBM-wards from time to time.

Yet from the point of view of the entire public good, this rising tide is lifting most of the ships to prosperity, for well paid employees buy goods and services from everyone.

Both the Vermonters and the "outsiders" attracted by IBM have all kinds of skills and educational backgrounds of use in their hometown communities, another countywide gain which is hard to measure. These people, most of them young, have brought new life to some sleepy country towns (just try to find a sleepy town in Chittenden County now!) and while this isn't always welcomed by rockin' chair residents, it may be just the shot of new life which was needed to strengthen school boards, planning groups, church and women's clubs, service organizations, and local governments.

In Chittenden County, growth and action are everywhere, and part of the responsibility for both the headaches and the benefits of that fact lies with International Business Machines, Essex Plant.

Source: *Chittenden* 1 (December 1969): 10-15. Reprinted with permission of Ruth Page.

DOCUMENT 5

Report of Governor's Commission on Environmental Control (1970)

Current environmental factors causing widespread concern . . . may be grouped into two general categories: first, those factors affecting the environment in an esthetic sense, and secondly, those affecting the ecological balance and thus posing a threat to the survival of mankind. The former would comprise such elements as billboards, junk cars, roadside litter, architecture, slum housing, mass housing, and other factors usually termed "a blight upon the landscape." The latter would encompass such physical pollutants as pesticides and other chemicals, land misuse practices that contribute to erosion, excessive runoff, reduction of critical natural areas, and in general disturb the balance of nature. It is the latter category which has received the Commission's attention during the last few months because of high priority upon the environment of the State.

With regard to its detailed recommendations, the Commission wishes to point out certain basic goals which it feels the State should pursue. It feels that our overall objective should be to insure optimum use of the resources of the State, including land, water, people, and space. We still have more unspoiled resources than do most parts of the Eastern United States. Once destroyed or lost these resources may never be retrieved. Vermont is now enjoying the benefits of a substantial

economic development. The function of its government must be to build upon that economic opportunity while making full use of what has been learned from the failures and consequences of unplanned development elsewhere. Facing a period of substantial growth and intense development in the 1970's, we have the opportunity and hence the obligation to utilize the newer understanding of the science of ecology, and the improved knowledge concerning effective government organization, to provide a uniform, comprehensive approach by state government to assure development without destruction. A basic goal, therefore, should be the preparation of a comprehensive land use plan for the State of Vermont to be undertaken as soon as practical and completed within the period of one year. Secondly, such a plan and its subsequent administration should be the responsibility of an effective administrative unit clearly charged with the responsibility of protecting the environment, and clearly provided by the legislature with the authority and funds required to meet this responsibility. An agency or department of natural resources and environmental control, or a permanent environmental control commission, is essential in order that there may be centralized direction and coordinated administration of environmental management within the State. We should seek to effect the most practical use of our land, both private and public, by establishing standards for land use, and each water system should be classified for the use to which it is best suited, and standards set which will assure the maintenance of the suitability of that system for the use specified. We must establish control over any act which has an undue adverse effect on the public health and safety, or the right of people to enjoy an unpolluted environment.

Land Development

Large scale land development is taking place at an accelerated pace and creates an immediate problem which must be dealt with. In the last few months purchase of land for recreation, second homes, and vacation resorts has gone beyond the province of the individual entrepreneur, and has become a major activity of large corporations. Vermont has large areas of undeveloped land, much of it adjacent to ski and recreational resorts, and it is in these areas primarily that such development is now taking place. However, the attractiveness of the Vermont countryside and the improvement of our transportation facilities through improved air and highway transportation makes the whole state vulnerable to this type of development. Large scale development creates problems, not only ecological in nature but also directly affecting local town government. Much of it is taking place in our mountainous areas which are characterized by a fragile ecology, and in areas where the towns are of light population density and with low tax ratables and few municipal services. Unrestricted and unregulated development damages the landscape and the environment, and can add tremendous burdens to town governments. The fact that much of Vermont is forested and that large acreages are owned by large lumber companies who are interested in land development as a corollary activity makes us particularly vulnerable. This situation was brought to the attention of the Commission because of the very active real estate development operations in Windham County, and the announcement last summer of the projected development by the International Paper Company on 20,000 acres of what had been to date wilderness land in the Stratton and Winhall areas. Because of the immediate threat posed to the State's environment by this activity, the Commission made this a first order of business. . . .

Under the provisions of the Vermont Planning Act there is no mechanism by which municipalities can adopt subdivision regulations without first having adopted a comprehensive plan. While this is good procedure from the theoretical planning standpoint, it results in a long interval between the time of development taking place and the opportunity to adopt such regulations. . . .

It is the purpose of subdivision regulations to direct that development take place in a manner which will serve the best interests of the community. They are most effective when complementary to an effective zoning ordinance. Each supplements the other. Considering the rate at which development is taking place in Vermont there is an emergency which requires that subdivision regulations be available to our rural towns immediately to supplement any existing powers such as zoning, and to protect health, safety, and the general welfare. With developers starting now to subdivide thousands of acres of land, much of it on mountains and in areas where subdivision regulations are not in existence, towns cannot wait upon the completion of comprehensive plans in order to establish such regulations. Furthermore, much of the planning legislation in the United States does not require a comprehensive plan as the basis for the exercise of subdivision control. . . .

As a result of his analysis of the powers of the various departments of the state government to regulate land development, the Commission counsel recommended that . . . the Health Department has sufficient authority to issue the necessary regulations to exercise control. . . .

However, the concerns expressed about improper land development go beyond the possible threat to public health, and therefore the regulation of land development should be based upon a much broader concern. Such concerns involve disciplines other than those found in the traditional Health agencies. We therefore recommend that the regulation of land development be not based upon the regulatory powers of the Board of Health but incorporated into an administrative body that is concerned with a total environmental concern.

Source: State of Vermont, Governor's Commission on Environmental Control, Reports to Governor: January 19, 1970-May 18, 1970, Deane C. Davis Papers, carton 3A, folder 3, pp. 1-4; Vermont State Archives, Secretary of State's office, Montpelier, Vermont.

Document 6

Kent State (1970)
Burlington Free Press

UVM Students Gather to Protest Slayings at Kent State University [May 5, 1970]

A group of several hundred University of Vermont students joined in a hastily organized but very peaceful march to the university's Ira Allen Chapel at midnight Monday in response to the slaying of four Kent State University students Monday afternoon.

The University of Vermont students started talking about a march to the chapel in several dormitories early in the evening but the march itself didn't get under way until just a few minutes before midnight when students started leaving the dormitory complexes on the campus proper and the Redstone residential campus. Many of the students carried candles as part of the march or vigilance in memory of the students and in protest over the slayings. Burlington City Police, Vermont State Police and the University of Vermont security police were all watching the march at the university Monday evening.

Burlington police said they were notified of the march by the university and were on standby in case of trouble; they in turn notified the state police. Traffic at the intersection of Main and Prospect Streets was held up for several minutes as a large group of students from the Redstone campus made their way to the chapel. The students walked several deep down Prospect Street, some overflowing into the road and slowing traffic, but the students did not appear to be deliberately trying to hold up the cars.

Brooks McCabe, former Student Association president, made opening remarks at the chapel stating his feelings on the slayings and the feelings of the students in general. Several other students expressed their feelings of dismay and sadness about the killings. The atmosphere at the gathering was very subdued and the students obeyed the requests of the campus security officers without any incident when it came to forming and marching.

There was considerable talk early Tuesday of a boycott of examinations as part of the student strike which is being called for by student governments across the nation. Further activity is expected today as students were preparing signs early today for a massive rally slated for the UVM green at 3 p.m. The rally was originally planned for a discussion of the United States' intervention in Cambodia, but it is expected much of the student interest will be focused on the Kent State antiwar protest which included the deaths of the four students.

John Phillips, Student Association president, will return to Burlington from Washington, D.C. today after meeting with National Student Association representatives who have formulated a position on President Nixon's Indochina policy. McCabe was filling in for Phillips at the rally Tuesday morning. Several university administrators, including Dean of Students Roland Patzer, were on hand at the chapel.

—Walter Johnson

Editorial: An Appeal for Reason on the Campus
[May 6, 1970]

Reason has been replaced by emotion on college and university campuses in Vermont and elsewhere because of the organized opposition to the President's war policy and the resultant tragedy at Kent State University. But this is hardly a sudden development. It has been building up for a long time. The Ohio tragedy was the spark that inflamed emotions, engulfing reason, and unless this situation is brought under control—and soon—the nation is going to suffer through repression which may or may not be preceded by civil war.

The radicals are at the heart of the trouble, but by themselves they could not hope to create more than a ripple through the fabric of American society. Their unsuspecting allies are the liberals who may agree with the radicals' grievances but not with their tactics. Yet, as an editorial in the New York Times pointed out last week, "History offers awesome proof that such united fronts destroy the liberals along with the causes they represent." It is clear that a greater disaster can be averted only if campus leaders (students, faculty members, administrators) exert positive and responsible efforts toward the restoration of reason—even if such efforts appear to be the unpopular course at the moment.

Sidney Hook, the eminent philosopher and educator, has written a recently published book "Academic Freedom and Academic Anarchy" in which he underscores the point. "When educators are the victims of violence they should not paralzye themselves or the defense of their institution by invoking pious and irrelevent platitudes about the 'free market of ideas.' Nor should they construe student riots as new and original forms of dialogue. Firmly upholding the principles of academic freedom . . . American educators should at the same time insist on the full acceptance of the responsibilities entailed by these academic rights. For without the sense and discipline of responsibility of the mutuality of respect, academic freedom is indistinguishable from academic anarchy. Where academic anarchy prevails for long, it is followed by academic tyranny or despotism."

Perhaps it is already too late to avert the greater disaster. The crisis has been worsened immersurably by the intellectual perversion and moral cowardice of some outspoken professors and administrators who appear not to realize what they are inviting, or perhaps they just don't care. Professor Shelden Penman of MIT, in a letter to the editor of the New York Times Magazine (April 16), discusses campus politicizing and concludes with this thought. "There is another aspect to the nifty little tactic of the passing of official resolutions on matters of public policy. Not only is this an aborgation of all the tenets of intellectual and academic integrity, it also violates the statutes governing tax exempt institutions. Since tax exemptions are a form of public subsidy, the public has every right to expect that such institutions will forgo political activity. The integrity of an educational institution making political pronouncements designed to affect foreign and domestic policy bothers no one. The principle of the campus being above and outside the law is already widely accepted."

There can be little doubt that the public will not continue to condone campus politicizing, particularly when it turns to radicalization of thoughts and action such as we are witnessing today, and especially in Vermont where citizens revere a long and proud tradition of achievement in the causes of human liberty.

To conclude—There must be a restoration of reason on our college and university campuses, and it should be wrought by the campus leaders most directly involved and concerned. If this does not occur, the public reaction will be swift and uncompromising. Academic freedom will have been slain by academic anarchy. This disaster can be averted, but the hour is late and the prospects are unmistakable.

— Franklin B. Smith

Middlebury Puts Off ROTC Review
[May 7, 1970]

The annual Middlebury College ROTC review has been postponed, President James I. Armstrong announced Wednesday. The review was originally scheduled for this afternoon. The action marked the second day of statewide efforts to reassess the events at Kent State University and the United States military involvement in Southeast Asia. According to presidential assistant T. Richard Miner, the decision at Middlebury was reached in consultation with ROTC officers, college administrators and faculty. Lt. Col. James C. Hefti, professor of military science, said he "concurred with the decision 100 per cent."

At Norwich University, administrators reported academic activities are continuing as scheduled. According to the dean of students, Cmdr. William Beatty, no requests by either students or faculty have been made to eliminate ROTC programs or normal academic instruction. "We feel academics is what the people are here for and it is our obligation to provide them for them," Beatty said.

In what might be considered a harsh irony, Beatty said Norwich University officials have received separate requests from two parties who wished to lower the United States flag to half-staff at the Northfield campus. One student wished to lower the flag in honor of the four Kent State University students who lost their lives Monday. A second party wished to honor Maj. George Hussey, a former member of the Norwich ROTC cadre. He lost his life fighting somewhere in Southeast Asia. The flag remained at full staff, Beatty said, pending the arrival of Maj. Hussey's body in the United States.

At Trinity College, the College Senate, composed of students, faculty and administrators, voted Wednesday afternoon to suspend classes today and Friday. According to Sister Elizabeth Candon, college president, students have always been responsible for their own attendance at classes. But the vote of the College Senate (21-0) now allows faculty members to opt not to conduct classes. Trinity students have joined with St. Michael's and University of Vermont students at a series of rapidly organized seminars, discussions and lectures.

Contradictory reports have been received as to the attendance at these seminars. One student reported a morning session at the UVM Billings Center to be "three-fourths full." Others said more than 400 students were present. Dean Alfred Rollins of the College of Arts and Sciences said no estimate was available of the number of students attending exams. An undetermined number of students has left the UVM campus, not expected to return this semester.

Elsewhere in Vermont, Lt. Gov. Hayes addressed a student gathering at Middlebury College Wednesday night. Middlebury, like most of the state's college campuses, remained calm following the events of earlier this week. "Students here are trying very hard to keep discussion as open as possible," Paul M. Cubeta, dean of Middlebury College faculty, said. "The underlying issue is the war that has brought us to the intensity of feeling we now possess."

About 90 nonstudent members of the Middlebury College community have signed a hard-worded letter to Sens. Aiken and Prouty deploring the "split" caused by the Nixon administration's Asian policy. The letter predicts the tragic pattern of events at Kent State University "will inevitably be repeated if the national leadership pursues its present policy." Refusal of expenditures "which permit this abomination to continue" is also recommended as a last resort, if necessary.

Middlebury, UVM and St. Michael's students have also joined the letter writing campaign to their congressmen. Bennington students plan to charter buses to visit the nation's capital personally, Paul Provost, assistant Vermont Transit general sales manager said.

A group which calls itself the "Committee for New Hampshire and Vermont Canvass" has circulated a petition among residents of both states demanding the "complete and immediate withdrawal of all American forces and military support from Southeast Asia. . . ." The committee is cochaired by Michael J. Ross, a Dartmouth student, and Prof. Charles T. Wood of the Dartmouth history department. There are 2,000 students circulating this petition in the two states, a spokesman for the group said. . . .

Source: *Burlington Free Press*, 5, 6, 7 May 1970. Reprinted with permission of the *Burlington Free Press*.

DOCUMENT 7

"Fragments of a Campaign Diary" (1972)

BERNARD SANDERS

I ran for governor in the recent election. I was the "other" candidate following Salmon and Hackett around the state, the guy from Liberty Union. I got one percent of the vote. Our candidate for attorney general, Peter Diamondstone, did best for us with 3 percent.

This article is not a political article. I do not talk here about the war, or the corporate

evasion of taxation, or the dental care situation in the state, or the monopoly utilities, or the unrepresentative nature of the legislature, or the housing crisis in Vermont, or the grossly inequitable distribution of income in America and Vermont, or the schools which crush the spirit of our children—or about the dozen other issues we raised during the campaign. Nor do I talk here about Liberty Union and my hopes and ideas for its future. What I am doing here is simply recording some events of the campaign, and my thoughts about them, with the hope that they might be of interest to Vermonters who follow the political scene.

I should mention that running for governor of Vermont was one of the most exciting, interesting and informative experiences of my life. So much happened, and I learned so much about so many things, that a hundred pages would barely do justice to the experience. What follows, therefore, is only a very partial and fragmented report on the campaign.

—Drove with Martha (Martha Abbott, Liberty Union Chairperson) up to Orleans for a debate with Salmon before the low income associate up there. Hackett apparently decided not to show up. Not his constituency, I guess. It was a beautiful drive. I hadn't been off the interstate in the night-time for a long while. When we got to the church a young lawyer-politician (sounding just like an old lawyer-politician) was delivering a flowing introduction for Tom who gave one of his better talks of the campaign. As usual, I started my talk by not knowing what I was going to say. I got going well, though, and it was lovely to talk about things which these people instinctively understood. Heads were nodding and there was real rapport as I talked about taxes, corporations and the phone company. I even mentioned that horrible word "socialism"—and nobody in the audience fainted. After the meeting was over people came up to me and told me how the phone company was screwing them, and this and that. One beautiful, toothless old man told me about the socialist meetings they held in Newport during the depression. Newport: Salmon did well and got a good response—but I got a better response. The real differences between us, and the difference between what being liberal and radical is about, became clearer and clearer as the question and answer period went on. Of all the groups that a candidate talks before, I prefer most to speak to low income people. They "know" a lot more than most people because their lives are constantly on the line and they can't escape behind $10,000 a year incomes—as can the good liberals.

—Spoke to the students of St. Anthony's High School in Bennington—and did terribly. It was probably the worst speech I gave during the whole campaign. I drove for 3 hours to get there—(leaving Burlington at 5 a.m.). I got to Bennington in time but got lost getting to the high school. When I finally got there 300 kids were waiting. I threw down my coat, and began talking. Spoke right off the top of my head, didn't put two coherent sentences together, and made very little allowance for the fact that I was speaking before 17 year olds. The talk just never came off. The response I got wasn't bad (the *Bennington Banner* called it "lukewarm"), but it wasn't good. The *Banner* reporter who covered it told me that Salmon had gotten an enthusiastic response before the same audience. I consider talking to young people extremely important—and it bothered me very much that I was unable to convey my feelings to them.

—Spoke before the Vermont Labor Council at their convention on Marble Island. Everyone knew that they were going to endorse Salmon but I very much wanted to go anyway. I really wanted to talk to "the workers." It was a rainy day, and when Martha and I got there we were greeted at the door by two slightly tipsy delegates. It looked like the booze was really flowing. One of the delegates asked me, in a friendly way: "Where is your beard? I thought you had a beard." I've never had a beard in my life but I guess that radicals are supposed to. I said hello to Bill Meyer who had finished speaking a little while before. The lights were on and the t.v. cameras were turning when I gave my talk. (Talking before t.v. cameras is always eerie because you know that they're not going to use your whole talk on the tube. So you think, as you're talking,—are they going to cut this part, or that part, or what?) I spoke about the corporations that own the country, about the regressive nature of our tax system and the things that I usually talked about. (And it turned out that WCAX-TV played back on the news the part about marijuana and abortion). I doubt that I got two votes from the audi-

ence—but they listened. When I started talking everybody there seemed to be mumbling or falling asleep—but they stayed awake and attentive for the talk. Afterwards, a few of the younger delegates came up to us and inquired about Liberty Union and shook hands. As I left I felt that that audience was reachable. They weren't hostile, but it would take a lot of work and a lot of time to get to them.

—Did a radio talk in Brattleboro, did some street campaigning and went through the book binding factory there. The radio show and the street campaigning went well. The factory was depressing. A good half of the workers there were from New Hampshire—and about half the Vermonters there had never heard of Liberty Union. That's always depressing. On the street I got a good response. It was amazing how many people had heard the morning radio show and had liked what I said. This radio show was interesting in that a man had called in and asked; "Did I hear Mr. Sanders say that he was for the legalization of marijuana?" The commentator said; "Yes, he said that." The man said; "Could I ask Mr. Sanders if he has ever smoked marijuana?" Strangely enough, despite all the times that I had talked about the need for legalizing marijuana, that was the first time that question was ever directly asked of me. I said, "Yes, I have smoked marijuana." And that was the end of that.

—Went through a factory in Bennington with endless rows of middle-aged to elderly women sitting behind sewing machines. Horrible. "Excuse me, I'm Bernard Sanders, Liberty Union candidate for governor. Have you ever heard of Liberty Union? Well, if you get a chance I'd appreciate it if you read this." And out goes the leaflet. A very deadly place. Barely made it through. As I left I hear a few women making snickering comments about Dr. [Benjamin] Spock running for president. And I thought everybody liked Dr. Spock. I knew that I wouldn't get one vote from that whole place. . . .

[I] Appeared on "You Can Quote Me" and did horrendously. It was just one of those times that I never got started and was on the defensive throughout. I was kind of in a trance and never really woke up. I can't figure out why, and it was probably the most important half hour of the campaign. Mickey Gallagher gave me a tough time but I should have been able to turn it around on him. But I never did. Charlie Lewis started me off with a bang. His first question was something like: "Mr. Sanders, it seems that the thrust of your campaign is to bring socialism to Vermont. How do you feel about that?" It was downhill and defensiveness from there on out. In a half hour show the momentum is either yours or theirs—and in that half hour it wasn't mine. I felt disgusted with myself when we left the studio—and I didn't handle myself well at all.

—The candidates' forum at Woodstock was a very interesting experience. When I got there I was irritated at having bothered to make the trip as there weren't many more people there than there were candidates. Most of the people were very middle class and League of Women Voter types. I think all the candidates of the 3 parties were in attendance—perhaps for the only time of the campaign. And what happened was that the candidates ended up talking to each other—which was an extraordinary experience. There was no forum or table up front. Just one candidate at a time marching up to the microphone doing his or her thing. (Except for Peter Diamondstone who refused to use the microphone, as did Kim Cheney who felt compelled to do the same.)

What happened that day before almost nobody at all was that morally and in every important way, Liberty Union carried the day. "Proud" is the only word that I can use to describe how I felt because the things that we all were saying were so much more relevant and right than what the others were saying. And I think that *they* even knew it. There weren't 20 voters to convince, there were no reporters there, so it was just a matter of some human beings (who were candidates) talking to other human beings (who were candidates) and we came out well. Peter gave one of the best talks I have ever heard him give. Steve Dunham, a 20 year old student at U.V.M. and our candidate for Secretary of State, raised issues that no candidate for Secretary of State before even knew existed. And Elly Harter, our candidate for Lt. Governor, started off by saying: "I'm not a politican,"—which was obvious and then proceeded to give a fine talk about medical care. When I finished talking Jack Burgess—(I never can figure out Jack Burgess)—said; "Sanders for governor." [Luther "Fred"] Hackett, who was standing near by didn't seem too concerned, though.

What I got out of the Woodstock meeting was a very good feeling about Vermont, and even about Vermont politicians. I have to admit that I like almost (not quite) everybody in that room. Vermont may be one of the few places left in America where people with very strong political differences can still talk to each other like human beings. It was at this Woodstock meeting that I got into the first real conversation (as opposed to debate) that I ever had with Fred Hackett. We had a very friendly chat, and Fred even smiled, which was rare for him. As the campaign wore on, and I debated Hackett and Salmon some 15 or 16 times, I became impressed with Hackett in a certain kind of way. He is a pretty straight-forward, no-nonsense kind of guy who is pretty up front about what he says. He just gets up there and says it. He was a poor speaker in the sense that he had almost no sense at all as to where his audience was at. I don't think that I ever heard him get one round of spontaneous applause during the entire campaign and I am not surprised that he did poorly before high school students.

—Campaigned on Church Street, Burlington. There is no place in the entire state of Vermont that you can hand out more literature and meet more people than at Church and College, Burlington. I met a lot of people who said that they were going to vote for me. I met a lot more, however, who said that they liked what I was saying but that they wouldn't vote for me because they "didn't want to waste their vote" and they wanted to beat Hackett. That was the sad motif I heard a thousand times during the whole campaign. Will they ever learn?

—Early in the campaign the *Free Press* mentioned that I was expected to get between 5 and 10 percent of the vote. An early poll done by students at Johnson State showed me at 12 percent and most of the reporters I spoke to thought that I would get at least 5 percent. As the campaign wore on, though, and as it appeared that Salmon had a chance to win I began to realize that relatively few people who liked what Liberty Union was saying would vote their consciences. In fact the entire last week of my campaign was directed just toward that end—toward telling people that they should vote for what they believed in and not for what they considered to be the lesser of two evils. I guess the appeal didn't work, though. On election day I expected at least 3 percent and was very disappointed with what I got. I was also disappointed that none of us on the state-wide ticket got the 5 percent that we needed to get primary status for the next election.

—The last debate of the campaign took place in Plattsburg, N.Y. It was a taped debate for WPTZ-TV. Plattsburg has got to be the ugliest town in the world and going there, even for just one evening, makes one appreciate Vermont and Burlington all that much more. John [Franco] and I took the ferry across at Grand Isle and, due to wrong information, got to the studio an hour and a half early. We went to Howard Johnson's and split one fish dinner—we had about $3.00 between us. When we got back to the studio Hackett and Salmon were both there—and I found myself in a very strange mood. Completely high and very unnervous for a change. The fact that I knew the two people who were going to be asking the questions (Chuck Butler and Bill Morrissey of U.P.I. and A.P.) made it all that much better. The debate went well and, as I watched it the next evening on t.v., I was surprised to see how much more effective I was when I talked slowly.

—Before the debate I proposed to Fred Hackett that we trade clothing. I suggested that he take off his tie and suit jacket, mess up his hair a bit, and put on my jacket. I would put his tie and suit jacket on. I tried to convince Fred that a great historical moment was at hand—that tens of thousands of people would turn on their t.v. sets and there, right before their uncomprehending eyes, would be a *new* Fred Hackett. Needless to say Fred didn't take my advice—which is probably why he lost the election.

Source: *Chittenden* 4 (December 1972): 37-40. Reprinted with permission of Bernard Sanders.

Document 8

Inaugural Address (1985)

Governor Madeleine Kunin

As I stand here before you—the solemn words of the Oath of Office echoing still in my mind—we know that we have opened another chapter in the proud and independent history of the Green Mountain State. I am the first woman to serve as Governor of Vermont, the third Democrat since the Civil War and the second Governor of European birth.

But I do not stand here alone. I stand with my husband and children, with members of my family who are a source of my strength—and my joy. Their love and support are essential to me. I stand with the memory of members of my family who are no longer with me— my mother, my aunt, my grandmother—the strong women who could never have dreamt I would be in this place on this day, but who, through the courage of their own lives, give me the stamina to stand as tall as they did in their time.

It was my mother, who as a widow, came to America from Switzerland with two small children, aged 6 and 10, in 1940, as war was spreading over Europe. In addition to a limited knowledge of English, she carried with her to these shores a limitless dream of what this country could offer her and her children. And she talked to us about the dream, but it was not until many years later, that I fully understood her. Her dream enabled me to strive, to reach, and to touch some horizons I was certain were beyond my grasp. That dream must continue to beckon to the next generation.

I thank this country, which welcomed me here, greeted by the Statue of Liberty, which, despite layers of scaffolding, continues to send a message of hope, just as it once did for us, and for the generations of Irish, Italians, Polish, French, and Canadians, who came to work in the granite sheds, woolen mills, railroads, farms and factories of Vermont.

My immigrant roots, while more recent than most, are not extraordinary. It is that immigrant spirit of hope which I wish to bring to state government—a spirit which instills in our children the belief that anyone can achieve anything in this country with hard work, an education, and a fair chance. It doesn't matter where you came from. It matters where you are going.

That has been the unique opportunity offered by our country and by our state. And our system of government has been specifically designed to help bring that about. We have not accepted for ourselves the harsh theory of "Survival of the Fittest." Social Darwinism was specifically rejected in the years of this country's evolution when we opted for public education, for public health programs, for social security and unemployment compensation.

But the debate about the proper role of government, which was lively at the time our Constitution was framed, has in fact become more vigorous today. How much are we our brother and sister's keeper? It is a question which we must ask of ourselves, and then, answer through our public policy decisions.

From my personal experience, I believe that because this nation has been generous to me, in providing me with a public education, with an opportunity to achieve my potential, that I have something to give back. We all have something to give back. And what we can give, is the same chance that we were given.

There are many Vermonters who are waiting for that chance. For some, it is a second chance. A second chance to get an education. A second chance to get off welfare. A chance to obtain child care, a chance for job training. We know that for each generation it must be different. In the 60's, it was thought that government could solve any social problem as long as there was money enough to do it. These beliefs must be tempered, re-examined, and in some cases, set aside.

In 1985, we must do it our way. And our way has to be more selective, more creative. We know that for people to be given a second chance in life, they have to fully participate in the process and work for success, instead of merely being on the receiving end of public generosity. And we know that the private sector must also be involved. Government cannot do it alone.

But we also know, just as I did as a child, that what this nation must continue to offer to the next generation, is both hope and opportunity. Without both, we not only deny the next generation a chance to reach its full height and breadth, but we also deny ourselves our own humanity.

As the first woman to take the Oath of Office of Governor of the State of Vermont, I recognize that I was able to raise my right hand before you this afternoon, only because so many women had raised their voices, long before my words were spoken. It was Susan B. Anthony, after all, who told us, "Failure is Impossible."

And if we listen, we can hear the voices of Vermont farm women, who in the pioneer days of this state, worked the soil with rough red hands, alongside the men who cleared the land. I stand here because of the women who worked in the mills in Winooski, who taught in the one-room school houses in Alburg, and who entered this hall of Representatives in Montpelier before me.

Clarina Howard Nichols, the first woman to speak in this Chamber, grew faint from fright when she spoke in favor of a bill which would have given women the right to vote in school district meetings in 1852. It was Edna L. Beard, from Orange, whose portrait hangs outside these doors, who became the first woman to be elected to the House of Representatives in 1921. Peals of laughter rose from the floor when finally a man found the courage to take the seat next to hers.

She was alone. I am not. I, and the 44 women in the House and 4 women in the Senate, stand here in the shadow of Consuelo Northrop Bailey, the only woman to become Speaker of the House, and the first to be elected Lieutenant Governor.

We all paved the way for one another, knowingly and unknowingly....

Source: *Journal of the Senate,* Biennial Session, 1985 (South Burlington, Vt., 1985): 669-671.

DOCUMENT 9

"The Mountains Are For Everyone" (1986)

PRESTON SMITH

There are more than nine thousand square miles of land in Vermont. We have another 331 square miles of water. The state's population, soon to be the least of the fifty states, is approximately 512,000. There is enough land and water in Vermont, it would seem, to accommodate those Vermonters who wish to savor the intrinsic values associated with many outdoor activities. Vermont has a tradition, too, of sharing its natural resources with visitors to our state. Skiing is a significant part of the outdoor life in Vermont. Indeed, the romance and aesthetic beauty of skiing was immortalized decades ago in the song "Moonlight in Vermont." Vermont soon realized that skiing's intrigue could provide a dual benefit to our state: economic opportunity for Vermont and Vermonters and the exhilaration, both physical and mental, associated with skiing. The ski industry is important to Vermont because of the revenue produced for the state, the jobs available for Vermonters and the recreational opportunities which are advantageous to us all.

Today, the future stability of the Vermont ski industry is threatened. . . . No ski area is assured of a long, healthy future. It wasn't so very long ago, after all, that Vermont had twice as many ski areas as it does now.

There has been considerable debate, much of it intensified within the past year, about what the ski industry does or does not contribute to Vermont and at what cost to Vermont's self-perceived image. State government, once anxious to assist businesses and industries that could provide needed revenues and good jobs, has now, through the regulatory process, made it increasingly difficult for some businesses to grow at all. In my opinion, the problem is with those individuals who have decided that their concept of growth limitation is unilaterally correct. They then often disguise their true intent with complex and technical jargon designed to frighten mainstream Vermonters into believing that we no longer live in a state which can accommodate the rights and the needs of all. The current debate over water quality is a good example.

The Wastewater Debate

Vermonters generate more than sixty-six million gallons of wastewater every day. Ninety-five percent of the wastewater is discharged directly into our rivers, streams, and lakes. The effluent is treated by municipal or private treatment plants, generally to a secondary level, before being discharged. . . . There are three common treatment methods.

Primary treatment is the least desirable. Only thirty-five percent of organic matter is removed through primary treatment. Screens catch solid floating and settling organic matter, with the remaining liquid discharged into the receiving body of water. In secondary treatment, the most prevalent treatment in Vermont, additional removal of organic matter (material which has a negative impact on water quality) is achieved through the mixing of waste and bacteria. The "good" bacteria digest the waste until approximately ninety percent of organic matter is removed. The water into which secondarily treated waste is discharged is used for swimming and other recreation and can be consumed by people after being chlorinated and filtered. . . . The third most common method of treatment is tertiary treatment, which provides additional steps of filtration or the addition of chemicals to the secondary process. A greater degree of solids is removed, and phosphates also can be removed through additional

steps. If properly cared for, the waters into which tertiary treated wastewater are discharged can be used as a source of public water supply. Fewer than six million gallons of the sixty-six million gallons of wastewater generated each day in Vermont are treated to a tertiary degree.

Several Vermont communities continue to discharge untreated, raw sewage into streams; and many other communities operate outdated or severely taxed wastewater treatment plants which, with some regularity, allow untreated waste to flow into our public waters. Approximately ninety percent of Vermont's treated wastewater is treated only to a primary or secondary degree.

There is a fourth treatment method which treats wastewater beyond a tertiary degree and does not require a direct discharge into any surface water. This is known as spray irrigation. Wastewater is treated to a sparkling clear state, after which the clear water is sprayed on grass or woodlands. Plants, trees and grasses feed on the remaining nitrates and phosphates (nutrients) as part of their growth cycle. This cycle is complete water reclamation. It is the most environmentally sound wastewater treatment process available today and is used throughout the country. Spray irrigation is recognized by the federal Environmental Protection Agency as the preferred method for treating wastewater. It is more expensive, which is perhaps why most Vermont municipalities do not utilize spray irrigation.

What, then, is all the controversy about in Vermont concerning spray irrigation? Opponents of ski industry expansion declare that the ski industry is a threat to our environment. They charge that the creation of additional human capacity on the mountain or in nearby hotels, motels or lodges will create wastewater and degrade our mountain streams. The fact of the matter is that ski areas, for the most part, have led the way in providing the most sophisticated wastewater treatment programs and have in no way damaged the water quality of the state. Quite simply, I believe that the issue of sewage capacity and sewage treatment is being used as a tool to limit the natural growth of some of our businesses and industries, particularly the ski industry and the second-home industry. A business which cannot obtain state permits for additional sewage capacity cannot expand. A business which cannot expand stagnates and sooner or later faces insurmountable obstacles to regaining the strength and market position it once enjoyed.

There is ample information based on experience to fully calculate the non-impact spray irrigation has had on Vermont waters. Killington is an example with which I am totally familiar. Killington pioneered spray irrigation in 1972. We believe that it is more environmentally sound to apply highly treated effluent to the forest floor, where trees and other plant life will use the nutrients to grow, and leave the remaining water as clean or cleaner than any surface water which it may eventually reach. This treatment method is more expensive than simply running a pipe from a treatment plant to a river or stream, but it is the best method. Since 1972, the state of Vermont, Killington and any environmental group in the state has had ample opportunity to closely monitor the effects of spray irrigation on the ground and surface waters in our spray areas. We have retained professional engineers and water quality consultants to provide us with the most technologically advanced monitoring and reporting systems available. Their work has shown no denigration of any surface or groundwater. . . .

If we are sincerely interested in protecting the quality of Vermont's water while at the same time permitting necessary opportunities for our citizens, then water quality laws should provide for discharges of effluent treated to a quality which is as clear as the receiving body of water. Moreover, these laws should be enforced uniformly throughout Vermont. Instead, philosophical differences now spawn discriminatory enforcement which neither protects water quality nor maintains the economic stability necessary for Vermont's continued vitality. If water quality is the issue, the state and environmental groups would insist that all water treatment plants, public or private, utilize the most technologically advanced systems of wastewater treatment available. We wouldn't have forty-six million gallons of wastewater being discharged daily into Lake Champlain and the St. Lawrence River Basin.

The Issue of Growth

Despite their insistence, the environmentalists who express their concerns about ski area groups are not primarily interested in water quality. What is the[ir] motive, then? . . . Perhaps it is a feeling that ski areas are dominating our Vermont landscape. The fact is,

though, that ski areas, including all trails, parking facilities and other land within ski resorts which will remain undeveloped, comprise less than one percent of the total land mass in Vermont. . . . Killington owns or leases more than 7,500 acres of land. Very little of that acreage has any development on it. Our village, which was planned in 1967 and is currently about one-third complete, will be spread over 400 acres. Within those 400 acres are an 18-hole golf course, ski trails, open areas for parking, a large pond, and acres and acres of open land. The problem then, when looking carefully at the facts, can't be water quality or land-use, because we have been leaders in both areas for nearly three decades.

Another argument often raised is that the companies which operate ski resorts fail to pay their fair share for state and community services. S*K*I Ltd., the company which operates Killington and Mount Snow, last year paid the state of Vermont $3.1 million in land-use fees and taxes. The company retained $2.8 million in profit. Traditionally, ninety-six percent of what is retained is reinvested into our mountains facilities. We also make significant corporate donations to state and local community service groups and organizations like the Rutland Regional Medical Center, volunteer fire agencies and others. Another objection raised by some legislators is that resort industries cut into valuable agricultural land. But what ski resort is located on land which is suitable for farming? And do the problems that plague Vermont farmers result from lack of land, or are they connected to national milk pricing policies and the economic quagmire now threatening our entire national farming industry?

Perhaps the real answer is that objections raised by the most vocal opponents of ski areas have nothing whatsoever to do with any of these issues. Perhaps the objections have more to do with personal likes and dislikes than with environmental considerations or economic contributions. The question of growth and progress raises very real concerns for everyone who lives in and loves Vermont. Development, whether in mountain regions or in urban areas, should be carefully planned and thoughtfully implemented. Singling out the few mountain areas in Vermont which are contributing to their communities and the state is not in the best interest of Vermont or Vermonters.

An overwhelming majority of Vermonters support the ski industry and recognize the economic and recreational contributions our industry makes to Vermont. The percentage of Vermonters who ski is increasing, but the percentage of Vermonters who believe ski area development should continue dwarfs the percentage of our citizens who ski. . . .

We should not fall into the trap set by those who believe travel and recreation are unimportant or undesirable segments of our economy. Among the fifty states, Vermont is the fourth most dependent on travel and recreation. No one is proposing unlimited, careless expansion of existing resorts or the introduction of sprawling new facilities. Vermont's ski industry is interested in remaining competitive with skiing in other states and in maturing just as any business or industry. We must do this in order to provide opportunities for our people and to make significant contributions to the other environment that we in Vermont must monitor so carefully—our economic environment. . . .

There is enough land and enough water for everyone. Applications of existing technology and innovative new technology will permit the continued maturation of our recreation industry and preservation and enhancement of our natural resources. The issue being raised under the guise of "environmentalism" by some people in Vermont has to do with choices. Do we choose to open our mountains, rivers and streams to fisherman, hunters, skiers, snowmobilers? Does the minority decide which activities will be allowed and disallowed on our lands? In a frenzy spawned by misinformation and induced fear, will Vermont fall prey to an elitist attitude or will we look carefully at the facts and make informed, educated decisions?

The mountains are for everyone. In the winter they are available to those who wish to ski, hike, or simply enjoy the outdoors from the perspective of the ridges and peaks. Hikers and skiers, we believe, have the same rights to our woodlands as snowmobilers and hunters. But there are those who would have all public access to all Vermont's mountains removed. They favor a complete wilderness state—no ski lifts, no ski trails, no hunting, no snowmobiling. There are places in Vermont that may be appropriate to retain as natural areas. Indeed, there already are more than 294,000 acres set aside for just such a purpose. But do Vermonters really believe that ski resorts are growing at a rate inappropriate with the wants and needs of all Vermont? Not so many years ago, Vermont attracted nearly as many skiers and skier dollars as Colorado. Today, Vermont shows a skier-day

increase of less than four percent over the last ten years while Colorado has gone on to bury Vermont in the number of skiers it attracts each year. This is not to say that Vermont ski areas want to imitate Colorado in size or scope. It merely points out that the "explosive growth" which is often referred to when discussing Vermont ski areas simply is not accurate. . . .

The issues are sometimes complex. Their complexity is intensified when issues are purposely clouded by misinformation, deliberate misrepresentation or failure to recognize facts. Certainly Vermont can close its borders to our neighbors and those who wish to share our natural resources. The price our children would pay in terms of future opportunities in Vermont would be tragic. Another option is to invite or permit the state to implement land use legislation which imposes the will of a few on every community in Vermont. Or we can decide together how best to serve our natural resources, our people and our communities, so that our mountains, rivers and lakes are not declared off-limits to any Vermonter or to those with whom we have a tradition of sharing.

Preston Smith is President and Chief Executive Officer of Killington, Ltd. Smith initiated development of the Killington Ski Area in 1955. It opened to the public in 1958.

Source: *Vermont Affairs* 1 (Winter 1986): 20-24. Reprinted with permission of Preston Smith and *Vermont Affairs*.

DOCUMENT 10

Bumper Sticker: "Killington: Where the Affluent Meet the Effluent" (c.1985)

and

Cartoon: "Looks Like the Snowmaking Machines Are Clogged Again" (1985)

(depicted on following page)

Sources: Bumper sticker: Vermont Historical Society, Montpelier, Vermont.
Cartoon: Reprinted with permission of Tim Newcomb.

Document 10

DOCUMENT 11

"Strengthen and Improve Efficiency of Land Use Regulations" (1988)

GOVERNOR'S COMMISSION ON VERMONT'S FUTURE

The present state regulatory process for land use in Vermont requires permits from various state agencies and departments, the cornerstone of which is the Land Use Permit required by Act 250.

Locally, municipalities may adopt zoning ordinances, subdivision regulations and capital improvements plans following adoption of a town plan. These actions are enabled in Title 24 Chapter 117 of the Vermont Statutes—popularly called Chapter 117.

While most of the towns and all of the regions have not adopted plans, these documents are usually very general. As a result they often fail to make the essential decisions about where and at what intensity the towns and regions want different types of development to occur.

A consequence of the failure to adopt comprehensive local and regional plans is that basic planning decisions are often left to the regulatory process. Through its evaluation of projects under some 40 criteria and subcriteria, Act 250 reviews whether a proposed development is appropriate in a particular location. For example, the District Environmental Commissions, which administer the Act, maybe are asked to decide whether a gravel pit should be allowed adjacent to a residential neighborhood, a housing project near a deeryard, or a shopping center on agricultural land. The planning process can make these decisions more efficiently. Not only that, it can do so with an eye to the overall goals of the community and the cumulative effect of many projects in a single area; whereas, in general, regulatory programs can evaluate developments only one project at a time, and such case-by-case review draws reactionary and confrontational response.

There are other consequences of the failure to plan effectively. The volunteer District Commission and Environmental Board members become overburdened with reviewing issues that should be decided by the planning process. There are unnecessary redundancies in state and local reviews. Applicants can find little clear guidance for deciding what projects will be ac-

ceptable and where. There is little coordination between the permit programs. Duplication and uncertainty about the outcome of the review process can drive up the cost of projects, including affordable housing projects. Such costs can even discourage potential applicants from going forward with projects that the town and region desire.

The most pressing need, according to those who spoke at the hearings, is to introduce planning into the regulatory process. The Commission has already proposed a new process of land use planning . . . [that] would include the provision of state guidelines and would require comprehensive planning at the state, regional and local levels. The adoption of this planning process would provide the single greatest improvement to the practice of regulation.

Some recommendations should be acted on immediately to improve the effectiveness of regulation:

1. Authorize Greater Control at the Local Level

Towns should be encouraged to exert greater control over local development projects through the adoption of zoning bylaws, subdivision regulations, capital improvement plans and official maps. The General Assembly should expand the authority of the towns in site plan reviews (Chapter 117) to allow consideration of issues beyond traffic and landscaping. For example, the suggestion received through testimony is to allow towns to review criteria modeled after those contained in Act 250, such as drainage, soil erosion and aesthetics. The Legislature should also grant authority to towns to assess impact fees where those towns have adopted a comprehensive capital plan and budget.

2. Evaluate Regulatory Process for Unintentional Barriers and Conflicts

The regulatory process should be evaluated for unintentional barriers to development which may occur as a consequence of a series of strict regulations. For example, the cumulative effect of applying several different regulations, all of which have built in a substantial margin for error, can result in excessive protection which unintentionally inhibits desired development.

3. Mandate Regional Impact Assessment

The Commission recommends the increased participation of the Regional Planning Commission in the Act 250 process by requiring them to provide an assessment of projects which would have inter-town or regional impacts.

4. Strengthen Enforcement

The state needs to strengthen the enforcement of land use and environmental laws. Prosecution should be consistent and should reflect the magnitude of the violation. Currently the state and towns may pursue penalties for violations of land-use regulations only through court action, which can be extremely costly and slow.

The Commission recommends that state and local regulators be empowered to assess administrative civil penalties. The ability to issue the equivalent of a speeding ticket to violators of land-use development law has been used effectively in other states to reduce litigation expenses and provide more consistent, effective enforcement.

The following recommendations, which involve streamlining the regulatory system, would be directed to those communities that have established their own programs to accomplish the objectives of the state planning guidelines. The intent here is to ease the expense and complexity of the regulatory process, and to provide an incentive for adopting the above-mentioned planning system.

5. Provide Streamlined Review of Projects Under Act 250

Where the region and town have adopted plans which conform with the state guidelines, and the town has adopted zoning bylaws and subdivision regulations to implement those plans, state reviews under Act 250 should defer to local decisons, unless the project affects more than one community or impacts on a resource of state or regional importance, such as a river or interstate highway. The District Environmental Commissions would determine early in the application process whether the project has only local impacts. If so, the District Commission's review would be limited to . . . determin[ing] whether the project conforms with the applicable local and regional plans and capital budget.

If the District Commission determines that a project would have intermunicipal impacts or would affect a resource of regional or state significance, the Commission should hold a full evidentiary review on the affected criteria. For example, if a proposed shopping center in one town should substantially increase traffic flows in a neighboring community, the neighboring community would have an opportunity to present evidence on the criteria involving highways and traffic. However, the Commission should not review other criteria where there are only local impacts.

It is important to note that this recommendation for streamlining the Act 250 permit process hinges upon the successful implementation of the recommended local regulatory controls. Unless the towns and regions have in place adequate long-range plans which reflect the state guidelines, and unless the towns have adopted zoning and subdivision regulations, Vermont should continue to rely upon protections afforded by the case-by-case, criterion-by-criterion review under Act 250. With those plans in place, however, much of the existing procedure which causes delay, cost, uncertainty and frustration becomes unnecessary.

6. Encourage Growth in Growth Centers

On a regional level, builders should be encouraged to locate their facilities in designated growth centers—communities identified as suitable for growth because there would be sufficient infrastructure in place, and because they have been identified as such through the planning process. This principle would help promote an orderly rate of growth commensurate with the ability of the town and the area to provide facilities and services.

The designated growth centers should be identified in the regional plan as areas suitable for growth. The designations should take into account infrastructure capacity, population density and existing patterns of growth. Once the local and regional plans have been acknowledged, the state allocation of funds for infrastructure should be targeted to growth centers, and the regulatory process should encourage development to occur in these areas.

To the extent feasible, while maintaining environmental protection, permit approval for projects to be sited in growth centers should be expedited. The state and the regional planning commissions should identify and make recommendations to the Legislature on those aspects of the state's regulatory programs which tend to discourage development in areas identified for growth or which tend to encourage an inefficient allocation of resources. In addition, the technical review at the state level could be eased if each application were handled by a designated permit administrator for each district. The administrator would ensure that permits moved efficiently through the approval process.

7. Restrict Growth in Environmentally Sensitive Areas

On the other hand, once the local and regional plans have been adopted and have identified locations of high environmental value, such as bogs and other wetlands, wilderness areas or necessary wildlife habitat, then access to permits for projects proposed for these areas should be restricted or prevented. The General Assembly should consider extending Act 250 jurisdiction over these areas—including critical wildlife habitats and ecologically fragile areas—in the same manner as Act 250 now reviews all developments on lands above 2,500 feet in elevation.

8. Incentives to Site Unpopular Projects

The Legislature should adopt a system of incentives and a siting process to encourage communities to accept unpopular projects that may have statewide benefits (e.g., hazardous waste facilities). The best approach would be for every region to identify possible locations for these facilities as part of the regional planning process. This option is best suited for projects that are predictable, such as solid waste facilities. However, finding consensus on a site for an unpopular facility will be difficult even with an enhanced planning process. Therefore the Legislature should look at ways to encourage communities to accept these projects.

Source: *Report of the Governor's Commission on Vermont's Future: Guidelines for Growth* (Montpelier: The Commission, 1988), pp. 20-22.

DOCUMENT 12

Poster: Landowners United (1991)

(depicted on following page)

Source: Vermont Historical Society, Montpelier, Vermont.

DOCUMENT 13

"A Petition for Federal Recognition as an American Indian Tribe" (1982)

ABENAKI NATION OF VERMONT

Preface

Long ago, before the English and French and Dutch people brought their dreams and technology, their religions and vices to North America, the Abenaki people dwelled in the forests around Lake Champlain, now the boundary between New York and Vermont. Some families lived at "Mazipskik"—"the place of the flint"—once a name for a village, today, as Missisquoi, the name for a river and a Bay at the northern end of Lake Champlain. For people who hunt and fish, it offered then, as it still does, an inviting habitat. Fish and game abound. Indian corn grew along the shores of the river. Wild rice flourished in the marshes at its mouth.

Corn still grows along the river banks, on vast dairy farms that have taken the place of Abenaki fields and fishing grounds. Wild rice still grows in the marshes, preserved for wild ducks who migrate through Missisquoi every autumn. The descendants of the historic Abenaki people still live around the shores of Missisquoi Bay and Lake Champlain. They too have endured.

It has been almost two centuries since the Indian ancestors of the contemporary Abenakis were driven from their villages by the tide of white settlement in northwestern Vermont. Some fled to Canada. Others stayed. Some who fled returned, joining others that stayed, accommodating themselves to a changed world. This petition contains a history of the Abenaki people of the Lake Champlain valley and Missisquoi Bay, and of individuals and families that maintained themselves in their traditonal home. After years of silent and sometimes painful accommodation, these families are now seeking recognition as an American Indian tribe. The history and genealogy of these families is complex and not all of it can be told here. As Vermont's only endur

NOTICE
This Land is
POSTED

NO TRESPASSING · HUNTING · FISHING · TRAPPING · SNOWMOBILING · CROSS COUNTRY SKIING · ETC.

Due to loss of our Property Rights by Act 200 and the growing bureaucracy in Montpelier, the time has come to "take a stand."

Please Support
"LANDOWNERS UNITED"
P.O. BOX 682, NEWPORT, VERMONT 05855

FIGHT LOSS OF LOCAL CONTROL
Change Your Legislators
REPEAL ACT 200

LANDOWNER _____

LEGISLATOR _____

Document 12

ing Native Americans, it is a story of importance—for the Abenakis, for Vermonters, and for all people concerned about the fate of Native Americans.

A Resolution of the Abenaki Tribal Council, the governing body of the St. Francis/Sokoki Band of the Abenaki Nation of Vermont

WHEREAS, the Abenaki Tribal Council has set the acknowledgment of the St. Francis/Sokoki Band as an American Indian Tribe as a goal of the highest priority, and,

WHEREAS, the Bureau of Indian Affairs has set forth procedures and criteria for acknowledgment . . . and,

WHEREAS, the Abenaki Tribal Council has reviewed and approved the contents of this petition [to be submitted] on behalf of the St. Francis/Sokoki Band. . . .

CERTIFICATION

I, the undersigned Chief of the Abenaki Nation of Vermont, do hereby certify that the Abenaki Tribal Council is composed of 7 members of whom 5 were present at an Abenaki Tribal Council meeting held this 24th day of September 1982; and that the foregoing resolution was duly adopted by the affirmative vote of all members present.

Signed by Leonard Lampman,
Chief, Abenaki Nation of Vermont

An Historical Overview of the Lake Champlain Abenaki

Section 1. *The Western Abenaki Prior to European Settlement: The Homelands of the Western Abenaki*

Until quite recently, relatively little was known about the people who occupied the area from Lake Champlain on the west to the White Mountains on the east, north to the St. Lawrence River Valley, and south along the Connecticut and Merrimack Rivers into areas of southern New England. It was only when Gordon Day began his research on the Western Abenaki twenty-five years ago, that the identity and history of these people began to be clarified. As Day himself has observed:

> The Western Abenaki have always been something of an unknown quantity to histori-

ans and ethnographers. Their interior location prevented encounters with the earliest explorers. The few traders and other travellers who were among them in the 17th century left either very scanty accounts or none at all. Their withdrawals from the southern periphery of their country and the long colonial wars restricted the opportunities of the English to know the Western Abenaki, and English testimony concerning them features (only) battles, treaties and captivities. . . . The best early information on them comes from the French who knew them as converts and allies, but preoccupation with conversion and defense seems to have prevented even those missionaries who knew the Abenaki best from leaving a reasonably comprehensive account of their culture. Moreover, French practice of referring to both Penacooks and Sokokis as Loups, originally their name for the Mahicans, tends to confound the record. As a result, the Western Abenaki have moved through the pages of New England history under the names of their villages, regarded as tribal names, and through the pages of Canadian history under group names of vague denotation.

"Missisquoi" became the name for one of these villages, located at the mouth of the river which bears its name on the northern shores of Lake Champlain. The definite origins of a village at Missisquoi are unknown, though recent archeology in the region has provided evidence of Indian habitation all along the lower Missisquoi River representing the entire prehistoric sequence from Paleo-Indian sites to early contact. The mouth of the river, surrounded by Missisquoi Bay, has always provided a good home for its native inhabitants. Over several centuries, different families of Indians would come to the Bay to harvest its abundant resources. . . .

It is not known exactly how many Indians lived around the Bay and Lake Champlain in the 16th and 17th century. Samuel de Champlain first heard of the Abenaki or "People of the Dawn" from the Iroquois when he travelled up the lake in 1609. The Misseskeek Indians were first mentioned in English records in 1723. . . . But these were "names of vague denotation," representing thousands of people moving about the region in small bands, unsuspecting of the crisis of European colonialism and conquest.

Dr. David S. Kellogg, an early student of the region, was quoted by Vermont historian W.H. Crockett as follows:

> . . . this valley was once quite thickly populated. I know of *at least* forty-five dwelling sites, the greater portion of which I have located and visited. The larger part of these are on or near the lake itself; but there are also many on the rivers and smaller streams and lakes, and some at a distance from any even moderately large body of water.

. . . It is certainly clear that during the historic period the Abenaki continued to live in widely dispersed villages and encampments throughout the region. . . .

Other early historians of Vermont towns confirm the widespread presence of Abenaki encampments in the area. . . . Even the smaller islands in Lake Champlan have been favored locations for the Abenaki. . . .

Again and again, early Vermont historians confirm the widely dispersed presence of Abenakis throughout northwestern Vermont and northwards into Canada along the course of the major rivers. . . .

Research on place-names carried out by Gordon Day among the descendants of Missisquoi families living at Odanak, Quebec, in contemporary times supports the view that the Missisquoi region is indeed the original homeland for many of the Western Abenaki people. Separate names for the village at Missisquoi, the river itself, the bay and the lake, as well as other geographical features attest to a long familiarity with the region. Most significant perhaps, is the Abenaki name given to Rock Dunder which lies in Lake Champlain just west of the city of Burlington. According to Day's informants, the rock was called "Odzihozo," the name of the Abenaki transformer figure which means "he who adds something to himself." After Odzihozo had formed all of the natural features of the Lake Champlain basin—the mountains and rivers and finally the lake itself—he changed himself into a rock in order to enjoy the lake forever. Day argues that:

> By placing their Transformer and other cosmological tales in this region, the St. Francis Abenakis show that they regard it as their original homeland. In particular, by making the formation of Lake Champlain the climax of the Transformer's activities, and by identifying Rock Dunder as the Transformer himself, they give the occupation some antiquity. . . . As argument, I have only that I find it incongruous that a people who can clearly recall historical events which took place in the 17th century would, in the same century, create in a new locale, or move from one locale to another, the principal event of the first age of the earth, and invent or move to this new locale the physical manifestation of the Transformer.

. . . Within this region, blessed with a variety of flora and fauna, the Abenakis could meet all of their basic subsistence needs with a minimum of effort. Accounts of early settlers in the region are filled with references to the natural abundance. . . . Peter Kalm, a Swedish naturalist, visited Lake Champlain during 1749-50 and described Indians fishing and hunting on the lake where he often saw sturgeons "leaping in the air.". . . As late as 1900, accounts of white settlers in the region continue to emphasize the bountiful supply of wildlife, particularly in the areas of Missisquoi Bay with its vast marshlands bordering the lake. George Barney, historian of the town of Swanton, spoke of the wild rice that grew in abundance in the marshes, and of the blueberries that could be harvested by the wagonloads. Russell Hemenway, a contemporary resident of the town of Alburg, described trips that he took as a boy by boat across the Bay from Alburg to Swanton to store up for winter supplies prior to 1920. The duck and Canada geese would be so thick as to form a channel for the boat as it passed, flying up out of the way and settling back down in its wake. He also described muskrat colonies that extended for miles through the marshes filled with lodges too plentiful to number.

Such abundance, scarcely imaginable by local residents today, made it possible for several of the Abenaki families remaining in Vermont to continue a basic subsistence life style well into the twentieth century, including those who had settled into the white villages, and others who were living a more marginal and hidden existence in the most remote areas of a town. John Baker, a resident of Grand Isle town until his death in April, 1982, recounted that as a boy around 1905, he visited with his father a small group of Indians living on Savage Island. These Indians still lived a very traditional style. They dwelled in bark wigwams, wore clothing sewn from animal skins, and spoke an Indian dialect. John Baker left the area around 1910 and did not return until after World War I, at which time he found that these Indians had disappeared. But other stories collected from several people in Swanton indicate that similar groups were still living in the marshes surrounding the Bay as late as the 1930s.

These stories are in sharp conflict with the prevailing view that all of the Abenaki left Vermont around 1800, returning only occasionally for short sojourns .
. . .

While precise population figures will probably never be known for certain, it is clear by now that a number of Abenaki families never left Vermont, and that by 1830, many had begun to reestablish communities in Swanton, St. Albans Bay and Grand Isle which have a documented existence down to the present day. Some families, like the ones witnessed by John Baker on Savage Island in the early years of this century, adapted differently. They maintained a well hidden yet traditional pattern of subsistence, a way of life that continued at least until World War I, largely disappearing only when automobiles and telephone lines penetrated Vermont's backwoods in the years following the war. Other families adopted still a third pattern of accommodation, a more transient mode of existence that took them from town to town, travelling like gypsies (with whom they were often confused), horse trading at county fairs, settling down only briefly and then moving on. Oral histories collected in the past few years have provided evidence of these three modes of adaptation or accommodation to white settlement. All of these families maintained a flexible network of communication and intermarriage, and many have re-emerged in recent years to claim their rightful identity as the Abenaki Nation of Vermont. . . .

The evidence we have gathered to date, suggests that the case of the Missisquoi Abenaki is closely analogous to the patterns of survival that have recently been documented for the Nanticoke, another Algonquian group. . . . [Some] Abenaki families made a decision to stay in their traditional homeland, rather than settle onto a reservation several hundred miles away. This process was facilitated by the need for day laborers in Swanton and surrounding towns, as agriculture and other industries became established in the early decades of the 19th century. It was also made easier by a long history of association and occasional intermarriage with different European families, mostly the French, but also Dutch and English families, or individuals in those families who adapted their frontier lifestyles to Abenaki patterns of subsistence and family life. Abenaki families stayed in Vermont, continued to move about through old hunting territories, settled down on the outskirts of nascent villages, and in other ways slowly accommodated themselves over generations to ever changing circumstances, as first settlements, and then farms, and then industry came to the northwestern corner of Vermont. Through it all, they maintained a sense of their Indian identity, as they found themselves occupying a marginal social and economic position in the dominant society.

They have been sustained, some might say burdened, by a tradition of fear, frustration, and defeat, viewed by others, and eventually themselves, as the very bottom of the social order. It has only been their long and intimate association with the natural resources of the area, their traditional skills, and most importantly their strong sense of family solidarity and loyalty that have enabled them to survive. . . .

Source: "A Petition for Federal Recognition as an American Indian Tribe," submitted to the Bureau of Indian Affairs, United States Government, by the Abenaki Nation of Vermont, October, 1982, pp. ii, iv-v, 1-12; Special Collections, Bailey/Howe Library, University of Vermont.

Document 14

State of Vermont v. Raleigh Elliott, et al. (1993)

Morse, J. Defendants are individuals in a group of thirty-six people who were charged with fishing without a license. . . . The cases arose primarily from an October 18, 1987 "fish-in" demonstration and were consolidated for trial. Before trial, defendants moved to dismiss based on the doctrine of "aboriginal rights." They claimed the doctrine prohibited the prosecution of Native Americans if they were members of a currently viable Indian tribe which had from "time Immemorial" continuously occupied the land where the offenses occurred. According to defendants, because they held "aboriginal title" to the land, they were not subject to state regulation for fishing without a license.

The trial court agreed and dismissed the charges against most of the defendants because they were members of the Missisquoi Tribe, a subpart of the Western Abenaki Tribe whose aboriginal title had not been extinguished. The State took an interlocutory appeal, arguing that the Abenakis (as we shall refer to them for purposes of this opinion) are no longer a tribe, and, even if they are, any aboriginal title to the land was extinguished by governmental action long ago. We agree that aboriginal rights were extinguished and, accordingly, reverse.

"Aboriginal title" gives members of a viable Native American tribe a right of occupancy to lands that is protected against claims by anyone else unless the tribe abandons the lands or the sovereign extinguishes the right . . . .

[The Court, after an extensive analysis of Vermont history, concluded that title] was resolved by the act of Congress admitting Vermont as the fourteenth state. . . . The period preceding Vermont's statehood was a confusing era, and valid questions remain as to the legitimacy of the opposing governing entities. Nevertheless, the tumultuous political context does not preclude a finding of extinguishment. . . . Vermont's admission to the union provided closure to a long period of authority transferred from one body politic to another, giving final, official sanction to the previous events, and eliminating any remaining ambiguity about who had dominion over lands once controlled by the Abenakis. Short of an express statement declaring an intent to extinguish, it is difficult to imagine a demonstration of intent that could be more unequivocal than these cumalative events leading to statehood. We conclude that, by the year 1791, aboriginal rights to the area now known as St. Albans, Highgate and Swanton had been extinguished.

Source: 159 Vt. 102 (1993).

"The Two Faces of Vermont"
NOEL PERRIN

When you cross the bridge from West Lebanon, N.H., to White River Junction, Vermont, practically the first thing you see on the Vermont side is a large green and white sign. This bears two messages, almost equal in prominence. The top one says, "Welcome to Vermont, Last Stand of the Yankees." And underneath it says, "Hartford Chamber of Commerce."

Only Vermont could have a sign like that, I think. Vermont makes a business of last stands. Consider just a few. It is the last stand of teams of horses which drag tanks of maple sap through the frosty snow. It is the last stand for farmers who raise oxen and do the chores by lantern light. Together with New Hampshire and maybe a few places in Ohio, it is the last stand of dirt roads that people really live on, and of covered bridges that really bear traffic. It is the last stand of old-timers who lay up stone walls by hand, of weathered red barns with shingle roofs, of axmen who can cut a cord of stove wood in a morning—of, in short, a whole ancient and very appealing kind of rural life. This life is so appealing, in fact, that people will pay good money to see it being lived, which is where the trouble begins. There's a conflict of interest here.

On the one hand, it's to the interest of everyone in the tourist trade to keep Vermont (their motels, restaurants, chambers of commerce, etc., excepted) as oldfashioned as possible. After all, it's weathered red barns with shingle roofs the tourists want to photograph, not concrete-block barns with sheet aluminum on top. Ideally, from the tourist point of view, there should be a man and two boys inside, milking by hand, not a lot of milking machinery pumping directly into a bulk tank. Out back, someone should be turning a grindstone to sharpen an ax—making a last stand, so to speak, against the chain saw.

On the other hand, the average farmer can hardly wait to modernize. He wants a bulk tank, a couple of arc lights, dry-lot feeding equipment, and a new aluminum roof. Or in a sense he wants these things. Actually, he may like last-stand farming as well as any tourist does, but he can't make a living at it. In my town it's often said that a generation ago a man could raise and educate three children on fifteen cows, and put a little money in the bank, too. Now his son can just barely keep going with forty cows. With fifteen cows, hand-milking was possible, and conceivably even economic; with forty you need all the machinery you can get. But the tourists don't want to hear it clank.

The result of this dilemma is that the public image of Vermont and its private reality seem to be rapidly diverging. My favorite example comes, of course, from the maple-sugar business. Suppose you buy a quart of syrup in the village store in Thetford Center. (This is a good idea: they sell a nice syrup.) It comes in a can with brightly colored pictures on it. These pictures show men carrying sap pails on yokes, sugarhouses with great stacks of logs outside, and all the rest. They are distinctly last-stand pictures.

But suppose you decide to go into the sugaring business for yourself. When you write away for advice, you get a go-modern or private-reality answer. You are told not to use pails at all, much less carry them to the sugarhouse on a yoke. Instead, install a network of plastic pipes. Don't bother to cut any four-foot logs, you're told, even though your hills are covered with trees. Texas oil gives a better-controlled heat. And finally, your instructions say, the right way to market the stuff is to put it in cans that show men carrying sap pails, sugarhouses with great stacks of logs.
. . .

The state is full of this sort of thing. I have seen a storekeeper taking crackers out of plastic-sealed boxes and putting them in the barrel he thinks summer visitors expect him to have. I have driven over a fine old covered bridge, intact and complete from floor to roof, and just as busy with modern traffic as it ever was with wagons. Tourists stop constantly. But whenever one gets out of his car and goes poking around below (it doesn't happen often), he sees that it secretly rests on new steel I-beams, set in concrete. The great wooden trusses up above are just decoration now.

Or take fairs. I've been at a fair where the oxen for the ox-pull were trucked in from fifty miles away. The town was full of oxen. If you didn't happen to notice them arriving in the trucks, you'd have concluded that here was a real last-stand neighborhood. Or you would until the contest began. Then you might have gotten suspicious. What the teams were pulling was more

concrete. Furthermore, when each pair of oxen had made its lunge, a distinctly modern element appeared. This was a large yellow backhoe which would rumble up and give the slab a quick push back to the starting point. The net effect was rather like watching the Dartmouth crew at practice, which I've also done. The college boys are like the imported oxen. They use muscle-power. The crew surges up the river between Vermont and New Hampshire, every man pulling his oar for dear life. The coach is like the backhoe. He skims alongside in a fast motorboat, steering casually with one hand, and shouting orders through a megaphone he holds in the other.

Most of all, though, I see every day the difference between Vermont in photographs, on calendars, in advertisements, and the state as it is actually getting to be. I'm thinking, for example, of roads. Even in California they know what a Vermont road is like. It's a last-stand road. It may be dirt or it may be blacktop, but what matters is that it's narrow and it follows the lay of the land. In most of Vermont, obviously, that means going in curves. The road will curve in so as not to spoil a field, curve out again afterwards, meander up a hill. It has, of course, a stone wall running along each side. Generally a row of big old trees marches beside each wall. Often these are maples, and then the farmer who owns them taps every spring, using buckets.

But what if some Californian gets sick of twelve-lane expressways and moves to Vermont? What if he buys a house on such a road? He hardly gets the place remodeled (exterior unchanged, interior restored to authentic 1820, cellar packed with shiny 1964 machinery) before the town road commissioner comes to see him.

The town's going to resurface the road next summer, the commissioner says. While the crew are at it, they plan to make a few other changes. They're going to take out all the sharp curves, reduce all the steep gradients, and widen the whole road by six feet. Twenty feet, if you count shoulders.

To the Californian's horror, it turns out that this will mean taking all the stone walls on one side, and most of the trees on both sides. It also turns out that the road will no longer follow the lay of the land. In particular, it's going to be raised four feet where it passes his house, and the road commissioner is hoping to use his stone wall for part of the fill. Next year the photographers will have to find some other road to put on their "See Vermont" calendar. But two cars will now be able to pass in midwinter without one stopping and the other slowing down to five miles an hour. And reality and image will be a little further apart.

If the ex-Californian puts up a fight for his stones and his trees, he soon finds that the selectmen and the road commissioner are not wholly against him. They may think he shows his Los Angeles background in wanting to save a stone wall when it's barbed wire you need for keeping cows, but they don't really disapprove. In fact, the road commissioner freely admits to liking last-stand roads himself. He was raised on one. What's on everybody's mind, it turns out, is that the town is not going to get any State Aid unless it widens and straightens the road to state specifications. And, of course, a lot of people in town are tired of having to stop every winter when they see another car coming. But the money is the main thing. The commissioner rather thinks the state itself gets Federal road money on similar conditions. In other words, town and state are under the same pressure all the dairy farmers are: go modern or go broke. That's a strong pressure.

And yet it's not the only one. Opposed to it is the natural cussedness of Vermonters, lots of whom don't want to go modern—or at least to admit that they do. And some would say it's not just cussedness, either. There are deep satisfactions to last-stand life. And, finally, there is that good money the tourists pay.

All this has amounted to almost equal pressure in the two directions, at least until very recently. Probably nearly everyone in Vermont is at least partly on both sides. But most are more on one side than the other. By oversimplifying a little, one can draw up a sort of chart of the battle lines.

Let me start inside the fort. Manning the loopholes, and actually making that last stand of the Yankees, are a hard core of hill farmers, country storekeepers, ox breeders, and so forth. Economically their pressure is small. Most of them earn less money every year. But they aren't about to quit. In my part of the state, a fair number have taken full-time jobs so they can keep farming nights and weekends. These are the kind referred to on the sign in White River Junction.

Allied to them are about half the summer people. (The other half aren't opposed; they're neutral. In fact,

they're mostly too busy water-skiing and playing golf even to have noticed that there *are* farmers in Vermont.) But the first half like coming to a region of old-fashioned farms, and having farmers for neighbors. They may not want to look after cows or build stone walls themselves, but they like to watch other people do it. Meanwhile, the money they pay out for caretaking, barn-painting, and meadow-mowing is what keeps a good many last-stand families going.

Also allied are nearly all of those sometimes called "year-round summer people." Most of them were originally drawn here by last-stand life, and a certain number actually lead it. I know one couple, both with college degrees, whose first action on getting their Vermont farm was to turn off the electricity. They do the chores by lantern light. I know another man, born and bred in Maryland, who has become as good a country plumber and as authentic a rural character as there is in New England.

Finally, there is a scattering of people outside the state who provide economic support in one way or another. Here are the covered-bridge lovers who send money to help a Vermont town keep one. The bridge I mentioned a while back drew contributions from no less than four covered-bridge clubs last year, when the town it's in had to decide whether to repair it or to replace it with a modern highway bridge. Here also are the city people who will spend extra time and money to get old-fashioned cheese, or barnyard eggs, or handmade wooden toys—and in so doing have put a good many country stores in the mail-order business. If you could only get it by mail, some of them would probably buy hill cider that's capable of turning hard, rather than the pasteurized stuff available where they live. If they only had trucks, some of the suburban ones would love to come up and buy half a ton of old-fashioned manure for their gardens. At present the number of such people is small.

Turning to the other side, an equally mixed group is pushing toward modernization. In the center are what I guess to be a majority of all native Vermonters under fifty, starting with the valley farmers who aready have big herds and bulk tanks. They don't want to be the last stand of the Yankees. (After all, look where Custer was after *his* last stand.) They want their sons to be able to go on farming after them—even if the "farm" turns out to be a lot of hydroponic tanks inside a concrete shed, fronting on a twelve-lane expressway.

Nearly everyone concerned with either education or government is also on this side, at least officially. So are all of us who drive to chain supermarkets instead of walking to the village store. And so, with a superb irony, are many Vermonters in the tourist trade, plus the tourists themselves.

The irony is that the tourists don't know they are. They come here to look at last-stand life. They wouldn't cross the road to look at a supermarket or a two-acre concrete shed. Most of them firmly believe they're helping to support old-fashioned Vermont by coming here at all. But though they flock to see the last-stand country—and, if they're here in the spring, to take a free taste of hot maple syrup, or in the fall to do a little free hunting (free as far as the owner of the land is concerned)—inevitably where they spend most of their money is in the hotels, filling stations, and restaurants. Last-standers get only a little directly. They don't get much indirectly, either. Even though the restaurant owner knows that his tourist customers have come to look at last-stand life, and even though he personally hopes it will survive, he's still in business. He mostly buys his eggs at the battery farm, his milk at the big automated dairy, his beef from Kansas City, and so on. His gesture toward last-standism is to make sure his syrup cans have pictures of sap buckets on them.

In the last five years the balance has perceptibly tipped in favor of modernization. Most people agree that the last stand is likely to end in about one more generation. What will happen then? Let me present an admittedly partisan view.

Most of Vermont will look like—well, it will look like central New Jersey with hills. Where there are now fields and meadows, they'll be scrub woods mixed with frequent tree plantations. Every now and then there'll be an automated concrete "farm." Around each lake will be a ranch-style summer resort. The entire state will be linked by superb highways. In more rugged sections, these highways will take most of the valley land there is. (Right now a four-lane highway built to Federal interstate specifications consumes forty acres out of every square mile it goes through, or one-sixteenth of the whole square mile.)

There will, to be sure, be three or four villages left in which last-stand life goes on. Two of these, I guess, will be commercial ventures, and two will be owned by the state. All four will be pure fake. If you drove into one—I'm going to call it Old South Strafford Village—first you'd see a wooden barn with four live cows in it, and a man specially trained to milk them. Then you'd notice a grove of maples next to an old-fashioned sugarhouse. Probably the maples will have to be made of plastic, with electric pumps inside, since the main tourist season begins in June rather than March, and since there's no way to keep a real maple from budding until June. But it will be genuine maple sap that the electric pumps draw up from a refrigerated tank under the sugarhouse.

Beyond the plastic maple grove will be a large woodshed. There for 50 cents you'll be able to watch a man first sharpen his ax on a hand-turned grindstone and then chop up a couple of logs. Every twenty minutes he'll reblunt his ax by smacking it into a block of granite. An expert from Colonial Williamsburg will check his technique twice a day. The crowd of tourists will be huge. And public image and private reality will now be completely separate.

There's only one thing that makes me think this won't happen. I told my vision to a hill farmer I know. "Shucks," he said, "You think I could get hold of some of those logs when the fellow's through with them? My furnace eats wood something awful."

Source: Noel Perrin, "The Two Faces of Vermont," *Vermont Life* 19 (Winter 1964): 31-33. Reprinted with permission of Noel Perrin.

Epilogue

In selecting readings for this volume the editors followed a chronological organization, choosing from material that affected events or captured the spirit of an era. The 1764 King in Council order fixing the boundary between New Hampshire and New York at the Connecticut River is an example of the former. Its enunciation fueled Vermont's subsequent movement for independence. George F. Wells' 1903 report on the status of rural Vermont serves to illustrate how by the turn of the twentieth century urbanization and the displacement of the descendants of Vermont's Anglo-Protestant settlers by a more diverse religious and ethnic population had become a matter of official concern.

After reviewing the selections, it became apparent to the editors that the readings, and presumably the Vermont experience, suggested recurring themes around which the volume might also have been organized. One such theme related to the establishment of Vermont as a Yankee Kingdom, a homogeneous ethnic and religious enclave, and its transformation into a more diverse dominion. The earliest French and English land grants took little note of Indian land titles, claiming either that the land was uninhabited (Champlain's journal) or, as asserted by their Vermont and U.S. government successors, that the original inhabitants had forfeited all claims. The Abenaki never accepted this view and have been unremitting in efforts to reverse what they regard as an injustice. The dominant Anglo-Protestants have not always welcomed those of different ethnic or religious backgrounds. Distrust of immigrants, often labeled "undesirable," recurs in public policy, popular literature, private correspondence, and municipal ordinances. Despite Vermont's well-earned pride in being the first state to prohibit slavery and invoke universal manhood suffrage, and its staunch advocacy of anti-slavery, such incidents as the 1968 Irasburg Affair suggest that Vermonters continue to struggle to eradicate cultural and racial discrimination.

Another recurring reference is the changing role of agriculture as the defining attribute of the state's economy and landscape. The popular identification of the state with the rugged independent farmer eulogized in President Calvin Coolidge's 1928 tribute to "The State I Love" retains tremendous power, but it cannot obscure the historic decline in the numbers of those engaged in farming, the decrease in farm acreage, or other radical changes that agriculture has experienced. By the late nineteenth century the tension between retaining Vermont's pastoral splendor, long appreciated as a marketable asset and magnet for tourists, and industrial development to facilitate greater economic opportunities for the state's often impoverished citizenry, was apparent. Over time various land uses have transformed Vermont's terrain again and again. The cheap land that initially lured speculators in turn attracted the settlers to develop Vermont's storied landscape. By the 1990s, increasingly accessible through a burgeoning interstate highway system, land had become highly valued for housing sites, ski resorts, and shopping malls, and this process threatened to alter the state's environment even more. How to retain a pastoral landscape shaped by dairy farming that no longer serves as a workscape dominated the state's agenda.

In common with other states, Vermont has experienced the growth of state and federal government along with a corresponding decline in local governmental authority. Demography and pre-1965 legislative apportionment ironically quickened this process. With the smallest and poorest towns commanding a legislative majority, the general assembly learned early to vote expenses from the town to the state. By 1902 the practice had become "settled policy." Vermont resembled other states in its drift toward urbanization while its rural population suffered absolute decline. Yet the scale upon which this occurred also distinguished Vermont from its sister states. With a 1999 state population under 600,000, Burlington, its largest city, is the smallest largest city in the nation, and Montpelier is the smallest state capital. Less than 25 percent of all Vermonters live in its eight largest communities, while in other states a majority of the population typically reside in the two or three largest cities. A relatively small population along with unique distribution patterns has helped shape the Vermont ethos. The challenge of the twenty-first century is to sustain Vermont's historic and pastoral environment while sharing the comforts and profits of a global economy.

Bibliography

This basic list is intended as a guide to further materials relating to the primary source texts in this volume. For bibliographies of thousands of additional published sources on Vermont history, readers should consult T. D. Seymour Bassett, *Vermont: A Bibliography of Its History* (Boston, 1981); and the Vermont section of Roger Parks, *New England: Additions to the Six State Bibliographies* (Hanover, N.H.: University Press of New England, 1994) and *Bibliographies of New England, Further Additions to 1994* (Hanover, N.H.: University Press of New England, 1995). The single richest source of published materials is *Vermont History,* which, in various formats, has been published continuously by the Vermont Historical Society since 1846. Perhaps the most frequently consulted reference volume is Esther Munroe Swift, *Vermont Place-names*: *Footprints of History* (1977; reprint, Camden, Me., 1996).

Atlases

Beers, J. B., and Co., *Illustrated Topographical and Historical Atlas of the State of Vermont* (New York: H.W. Burgett & Co., 1876).

Chambers, William, *Atlas of Lake Champlain, 1779-1780* (Bennington, Vt.: Vermont Heritage Press, and Montpelier: Vermont Historical Society, 1984).

Vermont Atlas and Gazetteer (Freeport, Me.: David Delorme & Co., 1987).

Primary Source Collections

Duffy, John, ed. *Ethan Allen and His Kin: Correspondence, 1772-1819.* 2 vols. (Hanover, N.H.: University Press of New England, 1998).

Gillies, Paul S., and D. Gregory Sanford, eds. *Records of the Council of Censors of the State of Vermont* (Montpelier: Secretary of State, 1991).

Graffagnino, J. Kevin, ed. *Ethan and Ira Allen: Collected Works,* 3 vols. (Benson, Vt.: Chalidze Publications, 1992).

Walton, Eliakim P., ed. *Records of the Governor and Council of the State of Vermont.* 8 vols. (Montpelier: J. & J.M. Poland, 1873-1880).

Memoirs, Autobiographies, and Biographies

Aiken, George D. *Speaking From Vermont* (New York: Frederick A. Stokes Co., 1938).

Austin, Aleine. *Matthew Lyon: "New Man" of the Democratic Revolution, 1749-1822* (University Park, Penn.: Pennsylvania State University Press, 1981).

Bailey, Consuelo. *Leaves Before the Wind: The Autobiography of Vermont's Own Daughter* (Burlington, Vt.: G. Little Press, 1976).

Bellesiles, Michael A. *Revolutionary Outlaws: Ethan Allen and the Struggle for Independence on the Early American Frontier* (Charlottesville, Va.: University Press of Virginia, 1993).

Duffus, Robert L. *Williamstown Branch: Impersonal Memories of a Vermont Boyhood* (New York: W.W. Norton, 1958).

Graham, John A. *A Descriptive Sketch of the Present State of Vermont* (London: H. Frey,1797; reprint, Bennington, Vt.: Vermont Heritage Press, 1987).

Jellison, Charles A. *Ethan Allen: Frontier Rebel* (Syracuse, N.Y.: Syracuse University Press, 1969).

Kunin, Madeleine. *Living a Political Life* (New York: Alfred A. Knopf, 1994).

Lowenthal, David. *George Perkins Marsh: Versatile Vermonter* (New York: Columbia University Press, 1958).

Ripley, Thomas E. *A Vermont Boyhood* (New York and London: D. Appleton-Century Co., Inc., 1937).

Rosenblatt, Emil, and Ruth Rosenblatt, eds. *Hard Marching Every Day: The Civil War Letters of Private Wilbur Fisk, 1861-1865* (1983; reprint, Lawrence, Kans.: University Press of Kansas, 1992).

Smallwood, Frank. *Thomas Chittenden: Vermont's First Statesman* (Shelburne, Vt.: New England Press, 1997).

Tanselle, G. Thomas. *Royall Tyler* (Cambridge, Mass.: Harvard University Press, 1967).

Wills, Hazel M. *Bill Wills and Company* (Bennington, Vt., 1953).

General Histories

Allen, Ira. *The Natural and Political History of Vermont* (London: J.W. Myers,1798; reprint, Rutland, Vt.: C.E. Tuttle Co., 1969).

Bruhn, Paul A., comp. *A Celebration of Vermont's Historic Architecture* (Windsor, Vt.: Preservation Trust of Vermont, 1983).

———, comp. *Vermont's Historic Architecture: A Second Celebration* (Windsor, Vt.: Preservation Trust of Vermont, 1985).

Crockett, Walter H. *Vermont, the Green Mountain State.* 5 vols. (New York: The Century History Co., 1921-1923).

Doyle, William. *The Vermont Political Tradition and Those Who Helped Make It* (Barre, Vt., 1984).

Duffy, John J. *Vermont: An Illustrated History* (Northridge, Calif.: Windsor Publications, 1985).

Hall, Benjamin H. *A History of Eastern Vermont* (New York: Appleton, 1858).

Hall, Hiland. *The History of Vermont, From Its Discovery to Its Admission into the Union in 1791* (Albany, N.Y.: J. Munsell, 1868).

Holbrook, Stewart Hall. *The Story of American Railroads* (New York: Crown Publishers, 1947).

Johnson, Charles W. *The Nature of Vermont: Introduction and Guide to a New England Environment* (1980; revised and expanded edition, Hanover, N.H.: University Press of New England, 1998).

Meeks, Harold A. *Time and Change in Vermont: A Human Geography* (Chester, Conn.: Globe Pequot Press, 1986).

Morrissey, Charles T. *Vermont: A Bicentennial History* (New York: W.W. Norton, and Nashville, Tenn.: American Association for State and Local History, 1981).

Sessions, Gene. *Celebrating a Century of Granite Art* (Montpelier: T.W. Wood Art Gallery, 1989).

Stone, Arthur F. *The Vermont of Today, With Its Historic Background, Attractions, and People.* 4 vols. (New York: Lewis Historical Publishing Co., 1929).

Thompson, Charles M. *Independent Vermont* (Boston: Houghton Mifflin, 1942).

Thompson, Zadock. *History of Vermont, Natural, Civil, and Statistical* (Burlington, Vt.: C. Goodrich, 1842).

Williams, Samuel. *The Natural and Civil History of Vermont.* 2 vols. (Walpole, N.H.: 1794; revised edition, Burlington, Vt.: 1809).

Wilson, Harold F. *The Hill Country of Northern New England: Its Social and Economic History, 1790-1930* (New York: Columbia University Press, 1936; reprint, New York: AMS Press Inc., 1967).

Anthologies

Bassett, T. D. Seymour, ed. *Outsiders Inside Vermont* (Brattleboro, Vt.: Stephen Greene Press,1967; reprint, Canaan, N.H.: Phoenix, 1976).

Graff, Nancy P., ed. *Celebrating Vermont: Myths and Realities* (Middlebury, Vt.: Christian A. Johnson Memorial Gallery and Middlebury College, 1991).

Hemenway, A. M., ed. *The Vermont Historical Gazetteer.* 5 vols. (Burlington, Vt., etc.:, 1867-91).

Muller, H. N., III, and Samuel B. Hand, eds. *In a State of Nature: Readings in Vermont History* (Montpelier: Vermont Historical Society, 1982).

Sherman, Michael, ed. *A More Perfect Union: Vermont Becomes a State, 1777-1816* (Montpelier: Vermont Historical Society, 1991).

Versteeg, Jennie E., ed. *Lake Champlain: Reflections on Our Past* (Burlington, Vt.: Center for Research on Vermont, 1987).

Versteeg, Jennie E., and Michael Sherman, eds. *We Vermonters: Perspectives on Our Past* (Montpelier: Vermont Historical Society 1992).

From European Contact to the Early National Period

Calloway, Colin G. *The Western Abenakis of Vermont, 1600-1800: War, Migration, and the Survival of an Indian People* (Norman, Okla.: University of Oklahoma Press, 1990).

Coolidge, Guy Omeron. *The French Occupation of the Champlain Valley from 1609 to 1759* (Montpelier: Vermont Historical Society,1938; 2nd edition, Mamaroneck, N.Y.: Harbor Hill Books, 1989).

Everest, Allen S. *The War of 1812 in the Champlain Valley* (Syracuse, N.Y.: Syracuse University Press, 1981).

Fox, Dixon Ryan. *Yankees and Yorkers* (New York: New York University Press, 1940).

Gilmore, William J. *Reading Becomes a Necessity of Life: Material and Cultural Life in Rural New England, 1780-1815* (Knoxville, Tenn.: University of Tennessee Press, 1989).

Graffagnino, J. Kevin. *The Shaping of Vermont: From the Wilderness to the Centennial, 1749-1877* (Bennington, Vt.: Vermont Heritage Press and the Bennington Museum, 1983).

Haviland, William A., and Marjory W. Power. *The Original Vermonters: Native Inhabitants, Past and Present* (revised edition, Hanover, N.H.: University Press of New England, 1994).

Jones, Matt B. *Vermont in the Making, 1750-1777* (Cambridge, Mass.: Harvard University Press, 1939; reprint, New York: Archon Books, 1968).

Lord, Phillip, Jr. *War Over Walloomscoick: Land Use and Settlement Pattern on the Bennington Battlefield—1777* (Albany, N.Y.: University of the State of New York and New York State Education Department, 1989).

Muller, Charles G. *The Proudest Day, Macdonough on Lake Champlain* (New York: John Day Co., 1960).

Potash, P. Jeffrey. *Vermont's Burned-Over District: Patterns of Community Development and Religious Activity, 1761-1850* (Brooklyn, N.Y.: Carlson Publishing, 1991).

Roth, Randolph A. *The Democratic Dilemma: Religion, Reform, and the Social Order in the Connecticut River Valley of Vermont, 1791-1850* (New York: Cambridge University Press, 1987).

Shalhope, Robert E. *Bennington and the Green Mountain Boys: The Emergence of Liberal Democracy in Vermont, 1760-1850* (Baltimore, Md.: Johns Hopkins University Press, 1996).

Williams, John. *The Battle of Hubbardton: The American Rebels Stem the Tide* (Montpelier: Vermont Division for Historic Preservation, 1988).

Williamson, Chilton. *Vermont in Quandary: 1763-1825* (Montpelier: Vermont Historical Society, 1949).

Woodard, Florence M. *The Town Proprietorship in Vermont: The New England Town Proprietorship in Decline* (New York: Columbia University Press, 1936; reprint, New York: AMS Press, Inc., 1968).

Nineteenth Century

Barron, Hal S. *Those Who Stayed Behind: Rural Society in Nineteenth-Century New England* (New York: Cambridge University Press, 1984).

Bassett, T. D. Seymour. *The Growing Edge: Vermont Villages, 1840-1880* (Montpelier: Vermont Historical Society, 1992).

Benedict, George G. *Vermont in the Civil War*. 2 vols. (Burlington, Vt.: Free Press Association, 1886-1888).

Bonfield, Lynn A., and Mary C. Morrison. *Roxana's Children* (Amherst, Mass.: University of Massachusetts Press, 1995).

Brown, Dona. *Inventing New England* (Washington, D. C.: Smithsonian Institution Press, 1995).

Cate, Weston A., Jr. *Up and Doing: The Vermont Historical Society, 1838-1970* (Montpelier: Vermont Historical Society, 1988).

Coffin, Howard. *Full Duty: Vermonters in the Civil War* (Woodstock, Vt.: Countryman Press, 1993).

Fink, Leon. *Workingmen's Democracy: The Knights of Labor in American Politics* (Urbana, Ill.: University of Illinois Press, 1983).

Graffagnino, J. Kevin. *Vermont in the Victorian Age: Continuity and Change in the Green Mountain State, 1850-1900* (Bennington, Vt.: Vermont Heritage Press, and Shelburne, Vt.: Shelburne Museum, 1985).

Guyette, Elise. *Vermont: A Cultural Patchwork* (Peterborough, N.H., 1986).

Hastings, Scott E., and Geraldine S. Ames. *The Vermont Farm Year in 1890* (Woodstock, Vt.: Billings Farm and Museum, 1983).

Ludlum, David M. *Social Ferment in Vermont, 1790-1850* (New York: Columbia University Press, 1939; reprint, New York: AMS Press, Inc., 1966).

Marshall, Jeffrey, ed. *A War of the People: Vermont Civil War Letters* (Hanover, N. H.: University Press of New England, 1999).

Muller, H. N., III, and John J. Duffy. *An Anxious Democracy, Aspects of the 1830s* (Westport, Conn.: Greenwood Press, 1982).

Pepe, Faith. *Vermont Workers, Vermont Resources, Clay, Wood, Metal, Stone* (Brattleboro, Vt.: Brattleboro Museum and Art Center, 1984).

Rolando, Victor. *200 Years of Soot and Sweat: The History and Archeology of Vermont's Iron, Charcoal, and Lime Industries* (Manchester Center, Vt.: Mountain Publications and the Vermont Archaeological Society, 1992).

Rozwenc, Edwin C. *Agricultural Policies in Vermont: 1860-1945* (Montpelier: Vermont Historical Society, 1981).

Siebert, Wilbur H. *Vermont's Anti-Slavery and Underground Railroad Record* (Columbus, Ohio: The Spahr and Glenn Co., 1937).

Stilwell, Lewis D. *Migration From Vermont* (Montpelier: Vermont Historical Society, 1948; reprint, Montpelier and Rutland, Vt.: Academy Books, 1983).

Wilgus, William J. *The Role of Transportation in the Development of Vermont* (Montpelier: Vermont Historical Society, 1945).

Yale, Allen, Jr. *While the Sun Shines: Making Hay in Vermont, 1789-1900* (Montpelier: Vermont Historical Society, 1991).

Twentieth Century

Anderson, Elin L. *We Americans: A Study of Cleavage in an American City* (Cambridge, Mass.: Harvard University Press, 1937; reprint, New York, 1967).

Bryan, Frank. *Yankee Politics in Rural Vermont* (Hanover, N.H.: University Press of New England, 1974).

Crane, Charles E. *Let Me Show You Vermont* (New York and London: Alfred A. Knopf, 1937).

Cushing, John T., and Arthur F. Stone, eds. *Vermonters in the World War, 1917-1919* (Burlington, Vt.: Free Press Printing Co., 1928).

Flint, Winston Allen. *The Progressive Movement in Vermont* (Washington, D. C.: American Council on Public Affairs, 1941).

Green, Mason A. *Nineteen-Two in Vermont: The Fight for Local Option* (Rutland, Vt.: The Marble City Press, c. 1912).

Hard, Walter R., and Margaret S. Hard. *This is Vermont* (Brattleboro, Vt.: Stephen Daye Press, 1936).

Johnson, Otto T. *Nineteen-Six in Vermont* (No place, 1944).

Judd, Richard M. *The New Deal in Vermont: Its Impact and Aftermath* (New York: Garland Publishing Inc., 1979).

Meeks, Harold A. *Vermont's Land and Resources* (Shelburne, Vt.: New England Press, 1986).

Neill, Maudean. *Fiery Crosses in the Green Mountains: The Story of the Ku Klux Klan in Vermont* (Randolph Center, Vt.: Greenhills Books, 1989).

Nuquist, Andrew E., and Edith W. Nuquist. *Vermont's State Government and Administration: An Historical and Descriptive Study of the Living Past* (Burlington, Vt.: Government Research Center, University of Vermont, 1966).

Resch, Tyler, ed. *The Bob Mitchell Years: Editorials by the Rutland Herald Publisher* (Rutland, Vt.: Rutland Herald, 1994).

Sherman, Joe. *Fast Lane on a Dirt Road: Vermont Transformed, 1945-1990* (Woodstock, Vt.: Countryman Press, 1991).

Sherman, Michael, ed. *The Political Legacy of George D. Aiken: Wise Old Owl of the U. S. Senate* (Montpelier: Vermont Historical Society, and Woodstock, Vt.: Countryman Press, 1995).

——, ed. *Vermont State Government and Administration Since 1965* (Burlington, Vt., 1999).

Vermont Commission on Country Life. *Rural Vermont: A Program for the Future* (Burlington, Vt.: Vermont Commission on Country Life, 1931).

Wrinn, Stephen. *Civil Rights in the Whitest State: Vermont's Perception of Civil Rights* (Lanham, Md.: University Press of America, 1998).

Twentieth Century—Nonprint Sources

AUDIOTAPES

Greenberg, Mark, and Mary Kasamatsu, producers. *Green Mountain Chronicles* (Montpelier, 1988).

VIDEOTAPES (VERMONT EDUCATIONAL TELEVISION)

Fischer, Frederick, producer. *Northern Railroads: Vermont and Her Neighbors* (Colchester, Vt., 1995).

Halstead, Jill, producer. *Land for Learning: Justin Morrill and America's Land Grant Colleges and Universities* (Vermont Public Television, 1997).

Halstead, Jill, producer. *Vermont Memories III: Vanished Images* (Colchester, Vt., 1996).

Moulton, Richard, producer. *Change and Challenge: Vermonters at Work* (Orton Family Foundation, 1998).

Moulton, Richard, producer. *Vermont Memories* (Colchester, Vt., 1994).

Moulton, Richard, and Enzo DiMaio, producers. *Vermont Memories II: Into the '50s* (Colchester, Vt., 1996).

Index

automobile traffic, 271–272, 295, 341, 356. *See also* highways

B

Bailey, Consuelo Northrop, 366
    as speaker of Vermont House of Representatives, 320, 332–333
Bailey, Guy, 269–272
Bailey, H, A., 297–298
Baker, John, 376–377
Baker, Remember, 40, 41–42, 44
    "Bloody Act," response to, 44–46
    New York surveyors, raids against, 39–40
    See also Green Mountain Boys
Baker, Robert, 15
Bancroft, Ernest H., 285, 301–303
bank robberies, 196
banking industry
    concerns about, 136–137
    contributions to state revenues, 296
    strength of during the Depression, 296
Baptist church, 258
Barber, E.D., 149, 157, 159
Barkley, Alben, 326
"Barnburners" (Democratic Party faction), 131, 157–159
Barney, George, 376
Barre
    granite industry, 208, 228–232, 283, 289–291
    population growth, 223, 283
Battle of Bennington, 63–64, 73–74
Battle of Gettysburg, 168, 192–194
Battle of Plattsburgh, 97
    song celebrating, 119–120
Battle of Valcour, 33, 53–55, *54*
Baum, Friedrich, 63–64, 73
Bayley, I., 218
Bayley, Jacob, 64, 74–75, 218
Beal, Shepard, 118–119
Beard, Edna L., 283, 366
Beatty, William, 361
beaver skins, as currency, 10
Bellows Falls, 223
Benedict, George Grenville, 192–194
Bennet, Charles, 118–119
Bennington, 44
    Battle of, 63–64
    charter for, 18–19
    declaration of independence, 50–51
    Green Mountain Boys' defense of, 39–40
    peripneumony epidemic, 116

ratification of U.S. Constitution in, 66
Sanders' campaign in, 363
in 1789, 84
in 1791, 98
settlement of, 6
"Bennington Address" (Coolidge), 295, 299
Bennington College, 285
Bennington County
    forges/iron furnaces, 100
    population changes, 222
"Bennington Mob." *See* Green Mountain Boys
Benson, Egbert, 86
"betterments and improvements" (property rights) law, 79
Bill of Rights (Vermont Constitution), 63
billboards, efforts to ban, 284
Birge, Elijah, 118–119
Birney, James J., 142–144
black Americans. *See* African Americans
"*Black Snake* Affair," 96, 112–113
blankets
    as currency, 14
    need for during Civil War, 190
Blodgett, Calvin, 158
"Bloody Act" (New York province legislature), 32, 43–47, 57
Board of Agriculture, 205–208
boarding houses, 230
boating. *See* recreational opportunities
Bolton Flats strike ("Bolton War"), 130
bonds, railroad, 172-173
bonuses, soldiers'
    during Civil War, 191, 195
    during Korean conflict, 331
    during World War II, 322
books, excerpts from. *See* narratives/memoirs/guides
Boston and Albany Railroad, 170
Boston and Maine railroad, 272
boundaries, border disputes, 6
    between New Hampshire and New York provinces, 19–21, 20–22, 31
    with New York state, 76, 81–83, 86–87
bounties. *See* bonuses
Bowdish, Isaac B., 158
Bowman, H. H., 212
Brackenridge, James, 44. *See also* Green Mountain Boys

Brandon, 85
Brattleboro
    Camp Holbrook, 168, 190
    population growth, 223
    Sanders' campaign in, 363
Brattleboro Reformer articles
    on "Irasburg Affair," 347
Brigham, Elbert, 284, 293–295
Britain. *See* Great Britain
broadsides/flyers/posters
    Act 200 protest, *374*
    anti-license commissioners, arguments for electing, 153–154
    Black Snake affair description, 112–113
    campaign flyer (Fletcher), 277–278
    campaign flyer (Gibson), 326
    Chorographical Map (Romans), *63*
    Civil War recruitment efforts, *188–189*, 195
    Connecticut & Passumpsic Rivers railroad advertisement, *171*
    following St. Albans raid, *198*
    Lake Champlain-Connecticut River canal fundraising poster, 133–135
    Railroad Convention announcement, 145–147
    tourist promotion brochure, 269–272
    Vermont Emigrant Association advertisement, 183
    World War I recruiting poster, *287*
Bromley, Bernice, 283, 286–289
Bromley, Jim, 288
Brooklyn College, 320, 334
Brown, A. L., 183
Brown, Silvanus, 44–46. *See also* Green Mountain Boys
Brown, Stephen S., 157–159
Brown, T. S., 147–149
Brown, W. E., 333
Brownson, Timothy, 76–77
Brush, Crean, 32, 47
budgets. *See* state expenditures
bumper sticker, anti-ski area, *370*
Burchard, Jedediah, 128, 140–142
Burgess, Jack, 364
Burgess, Lyman, 153–154
Burgoyne, John, 63–64, 73
Burlington
    development as lumber market, 170–172
    founding of, 42
    Hawthorne's description of, 129, 144–145

efforts on behalf of women's rights, 166

speech at Woman's Rights Convention, 176–178

Nichols, George W., 166

Nichols, Moses, 73

Nichowizet, Francois, 37

1927 floods, 283–284

Nineteenth Amendment (women's suffrage), 283

Niquette, Russell, 284, 297–298

Nixon, Richard, 360–363

Noble, S. C., 212

North Hero Island, 98

Northrop, Peter Bent Brigham, 332

Norwich University, 361

nostalgia. *See* Anglo-Saxon heritage; rural life and character

Novikoff, Alex, 320–321, 332, 333–335

Noyes, David P., 158

Nutting, Samuel, 15

O

Oakes, James, 354

O'Brien, Bill, 298

O'Brien, Mrs. E. J., 267

Ogden, Abraham, 179

oleomargarine

Grange opposition to sale of, 206

taxing of, 274

Olin, Gideon, 80–81

Onion River Land Company, 32, 41–42

Ontaussoogoe, 13–14

Oppenheim, Bertha, 300

oral histories

Barre granite strike, 283, 289–291

ethnic politics in Winooski (Niquette), 297–298

women in Republican Party politics, 286–289

See also narratives/memoirs/diaries

Orange County

Lake Champlain-Connecticut River canal plan, 133–135

population changes, 222–223

Ormsbee, Ebenezer, 206, 217

Ormsby, Jonathan, 1122

Otter Creek, 23

out-migration (emigration), 139–140, 207

acceleration of, 167, 208, 222–223

capital loss associated with, 209, 210

concerns about, 167, 205, 242

effects on "quality" of Vermont

population, 291

effects on rural life, 259

efforts to organize, 183

"emigration" fever, 167

following Civil War, 209–211

following War of 1812, 127, 131

railroad's effects on, 165

P

Page, Ruth, 355–358

Palmer, Courtland C., 175

Palmer, William A., 128

Parks, Al, 336

Parmalee, Annette W., 242

arguments for women's suffrage, 267–269

letters to opposing women's suffrage, 261–267

Parsons, Eli, 80

passenger train coupons, 173–174

patents (land grants)

between the Connecticut and Hudson Rivers, 6

Hossick/Hoosac, 5–6, 11

Patriote uprising, 129, 147–150. *See also* Canada

Patrons of Husbandry. *see* Grange

Patterson, William, 49, 50

Patzer, Roland, 360

Paul, Bildad, 196

Payne, Elisha, 64, 74–75

Peach, Arthur Wallace, 285, 300, 303–306

Pealtomy, 15–16

pearl ash manufacture, 100

Pease, J. H., 212

Peck Company (Burlington), 170

Peckenowax, Pierre, 37

Peisch, Francis, 333–334

Pelsue, Hosea, 183

Penman, Shelden, 361

Penniman, Jabez, 96, 112

peripneumony epidemic, 97, 115–117

Perkins, Henry F., 291–293

Perkins, Nathan, 65–66, 83–84

Perrault, Louis, 149

Perrin, Noel, 349, 378–381

"personal liberty bill," 167

Peterson, Eugene, 307–308

petitions

by Abenaki, for tribal recognition, 373–377

by New Hampshire title-holders, for New Hampshire jurisdiction, 38–39

by Iroquois Seven Nations, for land claims, 105

Phillips, John, 360

physicians. *See* doctors

Pickett's Charge (Battle of Gettysburg), 168

Pico Mountain, 270

Pierce, Julia Ashley, 267

pine trees, proscriptions against cutting, 18

Pittsford, 100

planning. *See* economic development

Plattsburgh, N.Y., 364–365

battle at, 97, 119–120

poems

call for legal tender act (Rowley), 79–80

response to "Bloody Act" (Rowley), 46–47

"The Whig's Lament" (Saxe), 153

See also songs

police

in Essex Junction, 357

handling of "Irasburg Affair," 354–355

handling of student responses to Kent State, 360

state police, 320

Polier, I., 306

political activism, 205–206, 347–348. *See also* Abolitionists; environmental protection; political parties; prohibition

political cartoons, 119–120

anti-ski area (Newcomb), 348, 369–*370*

Hartford Convention uproar, 97, *121*

Lyon-Griswold fight, 96, *108*

political parties, 95

Anti-Mason Party, 128

Democratic Party of Vermont, 130, 131, 157–159, 166, 207, 220–222, 321, 339–340, 347

Democratic-Republican Party, 95, 96, 103–105

ethnic politics, 284, 297-298

Federalist Party, 95–97, 103–105, 112

factional fights, *108*

following Civil War, 168

Knights of Labor challenge to town politics, 206

Liberty Union Party, 348, 362–364

Republican Party of Vermont, 167, 207, 220-221, 241, 254–256,

response to Kentucky and Virginia
    Resolutions of 1798, 107–110
settlement of 1902 gubernatorial
    election, 242
settlement of 1912 gubernatorial
    election, 243
unwieldiness of, 338
Vermont Highway Department, 284
Vermont, independent
    admission to the Union, 66
    Chipman's arguments for joining
        Union, 87–90
    "Chorographical Map" (Romans),
        63, *72*
    Constitution, 68–71
    declaration of independence and
        petition for statehood, 55–58
    efforts to preserve, 63–64
    efforts to win statehood/join Union,
        63–64, 67–68, 81–83
    establishment of western boundary
        (New York), 86–87
    living conditions in, 83–86
    naming of, 33, 56, 63
    negotiations to rejoin British
        empire, 76–78
    plan for invasion of by U.S. army,
        64
    political power struggles in, 64
    rationale for East Union, 74–75
    U.S. Congress' attempts to adjudi-
        cate land disputes in, 76
    U.S government plans for invasion
        of, 78
Vermont Labor Council, 363
Vermont legislature. See Vermont
    General Assembly
Vermont life. *See* rural life and character
Vermont Marble Company, 205, 241,
    337–338
    strike against, 285, 306–309
    See also Proctor, Redfield
Vermont militia, Third Brigade
    recall of, 97, 117–118
    refusal to return, 97, 118–119
Vermont National Guard, 319
Vermont Planning Act, 359
Vermont Power Authority, 243
Vermont Progressive Republican
    League, 243, 272–274
Vermont Society for the Promotion of
    Temperance, 130
Vermont State Legislature. *See* represen-
    tatives, Vermont General
    Assembly; senators, Vermont
    General Assembly

Vermont Supreme Court
    denial of Abenaki land claims, 349
    rejection of Native American land
        claims, 95
Vermonter, The
    on Green Mountain Parkway, pros
        and cons, 301–306
    on primary election law, 269
Verplank, Gulian, 86
veterans
    bounties for re-enlistment, 195
    political power following World
        War II, 320, 326
Vietnam War, 347, 360–363
Vilas, Levi B., 158, 159
Vindicator, The, 149
Virginia Resolution of 1798,
        legislature's response to, 96,
        107–110

W

wages. *See* salaries/wages
Wallis, Thomas, 13–14
Wallumschack, 44
wampum belts, as currency, 14
Wantastiquet mountain, 270
War Book, The (Vermont State Board of
        Education), 283, 286
War of 1812
    Battle of Plattsburgh, 96–97
    economic development following,
        127
    embargo against trade with Canada,
        114–115
    See also smuggling
War on Poverty, 347
War Powers Act, 331
war savings stamps (World War I), 283,
    286
Wardner, Allen, 145–147
Ware, ___, Dr., 116
Warner, Seth, 73
    defeat by Burgoyne at Huddardton,
        63
    response to "Bloody Act," 44–46
    See also Green Mountain Boys
"warning out of town," 218–219
Washington County, 223
Washington, George, 64
wastewater treatment
    environmental issues, 348
    in ski resort development debate,
        367–368, *370*
water pollution, cleanup efforts, 284,
    357
Waterford, 209

Waterman, Araunah, 133–135
Waterman, Thomas, 118–119
weapons
    defense contracts, 319
    for members of Rutland Light
        Guards, 191
    weaponry industry, 165–166, 168,
        174–176
Weeks, John, 284
Wells, Frederic P., 218–219
Wells, George F., 258–261
Wells, Samuel
    Allen's warning to, 47
    denunciation of Green Mountain
        Boys, 32
Wentworth, Benning
    boundary disputes with New York
        province, 31
    charter for Town of Bennington, 6,
        18–19
    land grants by, 31
    letter to George Clinton, on land
        grants west of the Connecticut
        River, 19–20
    response of New York Council to,
        20–22
West Union, 63–64
western boundary, establishment of, 86
western United States, migration to. *See*
        out-migration
western Vermont
    iron manufacture, 100
    in 1791, 98
    smuggling, 96–97
    See also Green Mountain Boys;
        New Hampshire grants
Westminster massacre, 32–33, 47–50,
    57
Weston, 207, 224
Weston, William, 153–154
Weyler, Valeriano, 246–247
wheat and corn farming
    decline in, 205
    levels of production, 210
    wheat as currency, 11
Wheeler, Adam, 80
Whig Party
    establishment of, 130
    splits within, 131
    tariff protection, 153
    weakening of, 166
White River Falls, navigation of, 25–26
Whittemore, Normal L., 158
Wibecan, Kenneth, 353–354
Wilder, Jonas, 165, 170-174

VERMONT HISTORICAL SOCIETY

The Vermont Historical Society, founded in 1838 by an act of the Vermont state legislature, is an independent membership organization, governed by a board of trustees. According to its 1840 constitution and by-laws, the purpose of the Vermont Historical and Antiquarian Society, the Society's original name, was to "discover, collect, and preserve whatever relates to the material, agricultural, industrial, civil, political, literary, ecclesiastical, and military history of the state of Vermont."

Today, the Society's mission is to collect, preserve, and interpret those things—works of art, artifacts, books, documents, manuscripts, and photographs—that serve to illustrate the history of Vermont and its place within the larger context of American life.

The Vermont Historical Society is the only institution in Vermont that collects artifacts and documents that reflect the entire history of the state, every geographical area, and every chronological period, including the present. Its collections are representative of the domestic life, crafts, trades, occupations, industries, and businesses that have had a significant impact on Vermont's history. In addition, they represent the customs, culture, and material life of all groups who have contributed to the history of the state.

The museum collections are comprised of 20,000+ artifacts of Vermont history from prehistoric times to the present. Some 42,000 catalogued books and serial titles, 1,200 linear feet of manuscripts, 30,000 photographs, 1,000 maps, 8,700 broadsides, and other printed ephemera as well as film and microfilm related to Vermont and regional history and New England genealogy constitute the library's collections.

Due to the extensive nature of its collections, the Society is considered one of Vermont's most comprehensive and important research centers. Each year, thousands of university students, historians, researchers, writers, filmmakers, and genealogists come to examine and study the Society's collections. These artifacts and documents also serve as the basis for the Society's interpretive functions—exhibits, programming, and publications.

To accomplish this mission the Society: operates a museum which creates exhibits and lends and borrows objects for display; sponsors public programs throughout the state of Vermont; provides services, training, and resources for educators, students, and local historical societies; operates a research library; publishes periodicals and books which promote research and the dissemination of information about Vermont history; and collaborates with other educational and cultural institutions and organizations to gather, preserve, and make available to the public resources and information about Vermont's past.

Publications of the Vermont Historical Society

Michael Sherman, Gene Sessions, and P. Jeffrey Potash, *Freedom and Unity: A History of Vermont* (2004)

Deborah P. Clifford, *The Passion of Abby Hemenway: Memory, Spirit, and the Making of History* (2001)

Giro Patalano, *Behind the Iron Horse* (1997)

Esther Munroe Swift, *Vermont Place-Names: Footprints of History*, 2nd. ed. (1996)

David Ludlum, *The Vermont Weather Book*, rev. ed. (1996)

Michael Sherman, ed., *A More Perfect Union: Vermont Becomes a State, 1777-1816* (1991)